THE OBJECT OF ART

THE OBJECT OF ART

THE THEORY OF ILLUSION
IN EIGHTEENTH-CENTURY FRANCE

MARIAN HOBSON

*Fellow of Trinity College,
Cambridge*

CAMBRIDGE UNIVERSITY PRESS

CAMBRIDGE

LONDON   NEW YORK   NEW ROCHELLE

MELBOURNE   SYDNEY

à Michel Jeanneret

Published by the Press Syndicate of the University of Cambridge
The Pitt Building, Trumpington Street, Cambridge CB2 1RP
32 East 57th Street, New York, NY 10022, USA
296 Beaconsfield Parade, Middle Park, Melbourne 3206, Australia

© Cambridge University Press 1982

First published 1982

Printed in Great Britain at The Pitman Press, Bath

Library of Congress catalogue card number: 81–17101

British Library Catloguing in Publication Data
Hobson, Marian
The object of art.—(Cambridge studies in French)
1. France—Civilization—17th–18th centuries
I. Title
944′.03   DC33
ISBN 0 521 24350 5

CONTENTS

GENERAL EDITOR'S PREFACE

This series aims at providing a new forum for the discussion of major critical or scholarly topics within the field of French studies. It differs from most similar-seeming ventures in the degree of freedom which contributing authors are allowed and in the range of subjects covered. For the series is not concerned to promote any single area of academic specialisation or any single theoretical approach. Authors are invited to address themselves to *problems*, and to argue their solutions in whatever terms seem best able to produce an incisive and cogent account of the matter in hand. The search for such terms will sometimes involve the crossing of boundaries between familiar academic disciplines, or the calling of those boundaries into dispute. Most of the studies will be written especially for the series, although from time to time it will also provide new editions of outstanding works which were previously out of print, or originally published in languages other than English or French.

FOREWORD

This book is not a survey of eighteenth-century aesthetics. That has been done, recently and excellently, by J. Chouillet, in *l'Esthétique des Lumières* (1974). Nor, while taking as its subject eighteenth-century theories of illusion, does it aim to present a slice of the history of European man's perception of art. Rather, it attempts to describe a historical change in the way of *conceiving* man's perception of art. That these two histories cannot be identical is evident, though they cannot be separated. For man's perception of art is in the main a praxis: its study must go through psychology, through economics (the art market), anthropology (the place society gives to art), architecture (where pictures are placed, where concerts are heard), etc. But our conception of that perception, in that it is necessarily linguistic, is necessarily, even if unwittingly or unwillingly, theoretical. It embodies – because language embodies – epistemological and cultural assumptions. This is true even of our conception of those arts which are non-linguistic. It is possible to comment on a piece of music by interpreting it, on a drawing by pastiching it; but is not this, even if accompanied by speech, to draw back the work into the orbit of perception, rather than to tie it into (perhaps to tie it up in?) the world of conceptions? This book studies primarily the language of critics, indeed it began as a historical account of one word, 'illusion'. But perception and conception of the perception of art are necessarily intertwined – and the first must be used in the interpretation of the second. To speak baldly, it is best to know what the critics are talking about. The work of art, on the other hand, *calls for* certain kinds of perception, and not others (the term is that of the great art critic Roger de Piles, 'appeler'); it directs us, and changes our conceptions. These in turn, no doubt, change the mode of perception.

I have attempted to exhibit a historical change, mostly within the area of French theories of art in the eighteenth century. This calls for three methodological remarks:

Foreword

This change in conceptions of art is at the same time radical and prepared. The continuous displacement that is culture moves along lines of tension that go back to Antiquity, and it is from within the present situation of these lines of tension that we approach it.

History is not the same as chronology. Certain later writers are, in my perspective, erratic blocks, and illustrate perfectly earlier tendencies. This is unsurprising (there exists in Great Britain in 1980 a Flat Earth Society). That history may proceed by jumps and overlaps does not need defending in general; discussion must centre on the interpretation of individual instances. Out of similar considerations, I have used on occasion two German writers, Lessing and Herder, not for the (considerable) weight of their own merits, but because they illuminate with special clarity tendencies present less sharply in French writers. In the case of Lessing, who is continuing and criticising the work of Diderot, this is conscious.

I haven't – could anyone – exhausted the sources in the most basic sense of locating and reading them. But to have attempted such a method would have suffered from a defect worse even than near-impossibility. It would have assumed its domain and its objects. In history, it is the light thrown on objects which makes them visible. It is then that the objects can reveal that the light is coming from the wrong or right angle.

The debts contracted are many and many are acknowledged in the notes. I have, for example, followed the practice of attributing passages and quotations to the twentieth-century critics who first showed their value and interest, in spite of the fact that in almost all cases I have read the original text.

Here, in this foreword, I have personal debts to acknowledge: to Ralph Leigh, in particular, for what was not just the supervision of my thesis – demanding, sometimes frightening, always friendly – but an education in discrimination and scholarship. Although, as their 'assistante', I was supposed to 'assist' them, Jean Starobinski and George Steiner taught me much by their example as well as by their advice. Without the generosity and patience of Malcolm Bowie, the editor of this series, the manuscript could never have been made ready (as it was, it nearly wasn't). I owe gratitude to Geoff Bennington, for the encouragement and criticism which saw me through bad days; to Simon Harvey who helped check some references; and to Ann and

Martin Wolfe, for great and constant kindness. Most of all I owe to a man who does not prate about women's lib, but practises it: the book is dedicated to him.

INTRODUCTION

I
ILLUSION AND LIKENESS

The illusion of art: this has often been characterised by a scornful twentieth century as a fascination, a passive trance in front of a work which has effaced all trace of its production, which presents itself as directly given or merely there; a branch of the bourgeois drug trade, to lull the consumer from all critical spirit and even all activity, to envelop him and insulate him, to act as a diving bell in which the plunge into unreality may be effected; a smudging over of contradictions, a conjuring up of an idealised harmony (see, for example, Brecht, 1966, pp. 217, 249).* In such terms does the twentieth century reject what was the current eighteenth-century account of the audience's relation to art. Illusion is held now to be the rose colour of unconscious wishes; to give full rein to the spectator's emotional vampirism: 'We willingly overlook [such] contradictions when we are permitted to wallow in the spiritual launderings of Sophocles, in the sacrifices of Racine, in the runnings amok of Shakespeare, in which we try to get hold of the fine and mighty feelings of the principal personages in these stories' (Brecht, 1966, pp. 209–10).[1] Brecht socially and practically condemned the nineteenth century's onanistic use of the theatre, and illusion as its agent: the entering into the souls of others, the taking on of their experiences as if they were real, ensuring that the emotions given play are never directed onto the outside world. His *Verfremdungseffekt* was designed to disrupt it.

What was Marxist in Berlin has become metaphysical in Paris: the *nouvelle critique* has striven to expel or restrict illusion, stigma-

---

* Bibliographical references in the text use the author–date system, except in the case of works by Diderot and Rousseau, which are given in short-title form. Full references will be found in the Bibliography, where a date in square brackets is used to indicate the date at which a book was actually written, if publication was significantly later.

3

tised as part of the 'metaphysics of presence' in Western thought. For the weak consumer of art it is a womb-like version of the search for the unmediated intuitive presence held rightly to be characteristic of some European philosophy. Criticism reflects practice: the *nouveau roman* constantly disturbs the narration to remind us of the medium, preventing an absorption in content by compelling attention to the form.

Such is the present ill repute of illusion. Whereby it is not, clearly, 'unreal' art forms which are accused of effecting this drug-like unreality, not symbolism, not surrealism; but it is rather naturalism, realism, and their progeny, the techniques of railway-kiosk literature, which are supposed to be the mind's morphine. Enemies and friends of illusion alike believe there is a relation between certain types of realism and illusion. Both enemies and friends accept, in one version or another, a proposition like 'the closer art is to nature/truth/reality, the greater will be the illusion', and some sophisticated enemies will wriggle out of this unsatisfactory formula by bidding higher for truth or reality: sentimental art is ultimately unreal, or less real than life-enhancing art (Leavis); bourgeois art is less practical/real because it doesn't produce real effects (Brecht); true art cannot use worn-out techniques (Boulez).

The difficulty we have in separating what seem polar opposites, truth/verisimilitude or reality/illusion, is historically conditioned, and derives from the eighteenth century. 'Illusion' was common currency in eighteenth-century aesthetics, and it was in terms of illusion that the century answered certain general questions about representation. But that specific answer has moulded the cast of those questions as we now ask them, so that any aesthetic available to us now uses 'illusion' explicitly or implicitly in taking up a position on them. To reject illusion in the terms discussed above is then to remain confined within the intellectual purlieus which 'illusion' was used to create, for in general, as Derrida has said,

Prétendre se débarrasser immédiatement des marques antérieures et passer, par décret, d'un geste simple, dans le dehors des oppositions classiques, c'est, outre le risque d'une interminable 'théologie négative', oublier que ces oppositions ne constituaient pas un système *donné*, une sorte de table anhistorique et foncièrement homogène, mais un espace dissymétrique et hiérarchisant, traversé par des forces et travaillé dans sa clôture par le dehors qu'il refoule. (Derrida, 1972a, p. 11)[2]

Thus, in certain modern criticism, one may find that illusion or surrogate concepts are expelled as undesirable aliens from modern writing: but the act of expulsion fails to take into account the dialectic between representation and form, between imaginative tissue and awareness of production. The failure is the more grave in that this dialectic forms the basis of the theory motivating the exclusion. Or, on the other hand, the concept of illusion may be present unacknowledged, at work surreptitiously in theories which are ostensibly moving in a different direction.

Wherein illusion, being thrown out of the door, reenters through the window

The expulsion of illusion has been attempted by Ricardou and Kristeva, among others. In his meaty little book, *Le Nouveau Roman*, Ricardou contrasts a novel's *dimension référentielle* with its *dimension littérale*, the story, to speak crudely, and the text as form, not meaning. *Littéralité*, characteristic of the new novel, is analysed with great care and inventiveness; *dimension référentielle* is not. We gather that this dimension is nearly related, perhaps equivalent, to *fascination*, and possibly to *crédibilité*.[3] It is held to originate in a mistake: 'Demander au récit qu'il fonctionne correctement, c'est exiger de lui qu'il nous donne l'*illusion*, aussi parfaite que possible, de l'entrée de Salomé dans la salle, entière et d'un seul coup [. . .]. Le bon fonctionnement du récit demande une ordonnance littérale telle que le lecteur puisse aisément la mettre en veilleuse et *prendre* Salomé *pour* un être de chair et de sang' which is equated with 'faire croire à l'absence de la dimension littérale' (Ricardou, 1973, pp. 30–1). *Illusion référentielle* and awareness of the text as matter, as *agencement,* are postulated as incompatible: 'En effet, l'attention du lecteur ne peut percevoir l'une qu'au détriment de l'autre, en l'effaçant au moins provisoirement' (Ricardou, 1973, p. 29). No reason is given for this incompatibility; it may be due to the influence of E. H. Gombrich's *Art and Illusion* (see below, pp. 8ff.), but it can clearly be maintained only if the consumer's reaction to the story is as close as possible to a mistake. Ricardou's definition of 'illusion' is in fact a *repoussoir* – if illusion is to be interrupted and expelled vigorously then it must be as ridiculous as possible.[4] He accepts that illusion and literality are, in his definition, inseparable contraries: but the dialectic, the interplay in the excluded middle between false illusion and true text, is never worked out; the conditions of their inseparability are not examined.[5]

In a seminal article Julia Kristeva had earlier proferred a related opposition: 'La productivité dite texte' was opposed to 'la "littérature", le "vraisemblable" ' (*vraisemblance* is the precursor of illusion; see below, pp. 32ff.). The *vraisemblable* is doubly defined: first as 'semantic', where to be *vraisemblable* is to resemble something already there (Ricardou's reference) – the value of Kristeva's account is that she is interested in the process of complying which this assumes; second as 'syntactic' (a covert attack on the first *nouveau roman*, this) which is defined as a reflexive relation holding between the parts and the whole (as such close to probability) in which the sequence of the discourse can be derived from the discourse as a whole. However this latter *vraisemblable* soon threatens to infect all speech: 'Complice de la convention sociale (du principe naturel) et de la structure rhétorique, le vraisemblable serait plus profondément un complice de la parole: tout énoncé grammaticalement correct serait vraisemblable' (Kristeva, 1969, pp. 214–15). In order that *vraisemblable* may remain pejorative, a twin concept, *sens*, must be brought in to take over the productivity of language and text. In Kristeva's argument, it is the adjective *rhétorique* which acts as the razor separating what seems inseparable: 'le vraisemblable est inhérent à la représentation rhétorique et se manifeste dans la rhétorique. Le sens est propre au langage comme représentation' (Kristeva, 1969, p. 215). And this crucial distinction is finally reduced to its chronological position in the linguistic act: the *vraisemblable* 'apparaît obligatoirement à la consommation du texte (par le public qui lit une "œuvre", un "effet")'. So it is the gap between the creative artist and the passive public which jacks up the distinction between *sens* and *vraisemblance*. We have here the heritage of Dada: the consumer is the fall-guy. What is on one level rightly announced as a 'contradiction [qui] constitue toute parole' (p. 209) is, in a gesture close to that of Ricardou, effaced in evaluation.[6]

In these critics, illusion or its precursor *vraisemblance* is established as one term of a dialectical movement, but is then driven out: this causes the argument to implode. In a different type of theory dealing with realism, or more generally with representation, illusion is not hyperbolically defined and expelled; it is not defined at all, but acts as an unacknowledged or semi-acknowledged factor. Thus Philippe Hamon, seeking to redefine the terms of the problem in order to formulate a more valid answer (an attempt which makes his article one of the few useful works on realism available) rejects the question 'comment la littérature copie-t-elle la réalité' in favour of 'comment la littérature nous fait-elle croire qu'elle copie la réalité' (Hamon, 1973, p. 421). The question is ambiguous: does it bear on literature or on our ideas about literature? And

down to this ambiguity it repeats eighteenth-century definitions of illusion: 'L'art consiste donc principalement à paroître historien lors même qu'on imagine, & à tromper agréablement par la liaison & la vraisemblance des faits' (Passe, 1749, p. 104).
Hamon, then, defines realism in terms of the reader's beliefs. But there is an ambiguity in the status he attributes to these beliefs – are they actual? This is clearly an untenable position: we do not, most of us, take even realist art for reality. Or does 'belief' do service for the concept of convention? That is, do we assume literature is aiming to copy reality, and approach any work with this assumption? Even in this hesitation between actual beliefs and convention, Hamon's phrase is true to its eighteenth-century origins.

Roland Barthes, too, in reaction against the rigour and anti-subjectivity of a certain structuralism, reintroduces the reader, his shifts of attention, his vicarious pleasure in the content:

Certains veulent un texte (un art, une peinture) sans ombre, coupé de 'l'idéologie dominante'; mais c'est vouloir un texte sans fécondité, sans productivité, un texte stérile (voyez le mythe de la Femme sans Ombre). Le texte a besoin de son ombre: cette ombre, c'est *un peu* d'idéologie, *un peu* de représentation, *un peu* de sujet: fantômes, poches, traînées, nuages, nécessaires: la subversion doit produire son propre *clair-obscur*. (Barthes, 1973, p. 53)

The matter, the 'ombre', of a text is not 'reality' as for Hamon; it does not cause a mistake; illusion is equated not with presence, but with *fading* of presence. Barthes is switching to the other tradition of the term 'illusion', to art as non-presence, to its ghost-like nature in which the mind dallies in an area between subject and object. The relation of the reader is thus not a mistake, but a voluntary–involuntary seduction. 'Beaucoup de lectures sont perverses, impliquant un clivage. De même que l'enfant sait que sa mère n'a pas de pénis et tout en même temps croit qu'elle en a un (économie dont Freud a montré la rentabilité), de même le lecteur peut dire sans cesse: *"je sais bien que ce ne sont que des mots, mais tout de même* . . . (je m'émeus comme si ces mots énonçaient une réalité)" ' (Barthes, 1973, p. 76).[7] The formulation is again close to the eighteenth-century terms: 'Je me doute bien que les Bergers [dans les Idylles] ne sont pas tels qu'on me les représente et je saurois bien, si je voulois, que ceux qu'on me peind sont imaginaires: mais je ne veux pas sçavoir & je me livre au plaisir qu'ils me font par le plaisir que j'ai à m'y livrer' (Rémond de Saint Mard, 1734, p. 48). This split in the reader, his love of and sadism towards the text, is an oscillation: involvement and consciousness

7

run together and succeed each other in Barthes' brilliant metaphorical play on the erotic zones of the body; and the summing up
is precisely that of illusion, the imaginary non-presence which feels
like presence: 'C'est ce scintillement même qui séduit, ou encore:
la mise en scène d'une apparition–disparition' (Barthes, 1973,
p. 19).

Ricardou and Kristeva reject illusion or its precursor *vraisemblance*; in doing so they mutilate their argument, removing a contradictory factor which should have been investigated, not
suppressed, for as the negative pole in the system they set up, it has
inevitably shaped the structure of that system. Hamon and Barthes
both take for granted the concept of illusion they use. If I have
separated them, it is because this book will in part seek to explore
the conditions of their difference. For Hamon, illusion is a homogeneous experience, for Barthes a series of waves of participation
and retraction from the imaginative tissue of the work.

Art and illusion

Socrates to Theatetus: And if someone thinks mustn't he think
something? – Th: Yes, he must. – Soc. And if he thinks something,
mustn't it be something real? – Th. Apparently. – Soc. And mustn't
someone who is painting be painting something – and someone who is
painting something be painting something real! – Well, tell me what the
object of painting is: the picture of a man (e.g.), or the man that the
picture portrays?   Wittgenstein, *Philosophical Investigations*, § 518

What meaning can be attached to a formulation such as Hamon's:
'Comment la litterature nous fait-elle croire qu'elle copie la réalité?' I have already asked whether it is a question bearing on literature or on our ideas about literature; the problem may be widened
by asking whether it bears on the relation of art to nature, or of
Western man's opinion about this relation, or both? It is one of the
greatnesses of E. H. Gombrich's *Art and Illusion* that it asks such
questions openly and assumes fully the history of 'illusion' which
helped to frame them in the first place. Gombrich constantly relates the natural and cultural history of vision. He shows that if
nature be taken as 'what we really see', we do *not* see retinal
impressions nor a visual field, nor even pure appearance, so that an
art claiming to imitate 'pure vision' is claiming nonsense. But does
this mean that representation in art is merely a style, or a family of
styles, a result of culture? And granted an intention to represent, is
this a bizarre turn taken by Western art since the Greeks? For if the

relation to nature of most Western art is well defined in terms of an intention to transmit information, as Gombrich thinks, then it is a cultural relation but inevitably one latched on to natural conditions. Both physiology and culture, Gombrich shows, determine our interpretation of a configuration of certain lines on a canvas as a representation of an object. We interpret according to what we expect to see. The adaptation of what the eye sees to what it expects to see takes place within a framework of possibilities which is not neutral; it is a scale hierarchised and emotionally alive, where tonality and meaning are acquired through a complex series of contrasting elements. Western perspective is thus correct, 'natural', if vision is monocular and the eye doesn't move – where it is restricted by a peep-hole, say. (But the eye has a natural tendency to move, and if it does not do so, in the end vision fails, as experiments with contact lenses have shown.) I believe Gombrich underestimated the cultural force of these restricting assumptions; they are not 'natural' They may be inevitable simplifications in the development of the geometrisation of space, but as such, they have a history, they are particular developments made by a particular society[8] and imply a particular relation of the individual to the canvas. In fact, the interpenetration of culture and physiology goes very deep if we accept the experiments which seem to show that peoples living in a round culture – Zulus for instance – do not see perspective in quite the same way (Gregory, 1966, pp. 161ff.).

For Gombrich then, perspective has a natural basis: but the projection of a shape from three dimensions to two involves an inherent ambiguity. It can be effected in many different ways, as anamorphoses show, according to the angle of vision and the angle to the canvas of the object to be represented. Our natural and cultural experience makes us expect three-dimensional objects to be seen from certain angles and not from others. However many are the possible geometrical interpretations of what we see, 'we can never see ambiguity', 'we will always see an object at a distance, never an appearance of uncertain meaning' (Gombrich, 1962, p. 219).[9] This is as true of drawings of objects as it is of objects themselves. The trick drawing of the duck which viewed in another way can look like a rabbit, made famous by Wittgenstein, can never be seen as both at the same time. Gombrich holds that the case of the picture is the same: one cannot at the same time see the plane surface of the picture *and* what is represented, the battle horse or scene (Gombrich, 1962, p. 237). It is in this way that the term 'illusion' is justified; it is what happens when we see the something the picture is of. 'The character of that illusion [is that] in certain circumstances we would be unable to *disprove* that a *trompe-l'œil* is "real" – unless, that is, we could apply some movement test either by touching it or by shifting our position' (Gombrich, 1962, p. 233). An eighteenth-century definition again, this time deliberately assumed, though it has the disadvantage of conflicting with other of Gombrich's insights.[10] He is surely right in his account of the development of painting: painters have taught us to interpret cues to shape and depth, in ways related to the functioning of the celebrated visual illusions. But the assimilation of specific visual illusions to the *whole* of painting is as surely excessive. It neglects the problem raised by Theatetus: 'Tell me what the object of painting is, the picture of a man or the man that the picture portrays?' The viewer can see the *picture of a man*, not merely either the man or the dabs of paint. There is a kind of imbrication inherent in all images; we do not ever 'see an appearance'. But what images do – and this is perhaps the source of their power, and of the awe with which they have been regarded – is to make us aware of an *appearance of something*. For an image 'in revealing itself [. . .] also reveals that which it reproduces' (Heidegger, 1962, p. 98), and this process of being given as well as being given as appearance is infinitely relayable. Any image can contain an image: 'From such a reproduction, it is possible to make a new reproduction, e.g., one may photograph a death mask. This second reproduction immediately represents the death mask and thus reveals the "image" (the immediate aspect) of the deceased himself. The photograph of the death mask as the reproduction of a reproduction is itself an image but only because it provides an "image" of the dead, i.e., shows how the dead person appears, or rather, appeared' (Heidegger, 1962, p. 98). The mind can thus oscillate from the image of a thing to the thing the image is of: yet only contemplation of the latter is taken into account by Gombrich, in accordance with his discussion of structures of vision in terms of perception rather than of the imagination.

Seeing the subject of a picture and seeing its surface are both types of perception for Gombrich: but they are mutually exclusive. Husserl accepts this sealing off of illusion, but opposes it not to another perception, but as perception to the work of the imagination. The opposition is not between subject and surface, but between a mistake (a perception) and a seeing an image *of*: 'As long as we *are* tricked, we experience a perfectly good percept: we see a lady and not a waxwork figure that only represents a lady [. . .]. The same matter is at one time matter for a percept and at another

10

time matter for a mere perceptual fiction, but both can evidently not be combined. A percept cannot also fictitiously construct what it perceives and a fiction cannot also perceive what it constructs' (Husserl, 1970, vol. II, p. 609).[11] That the image should refer beyond itself is however essential to Gombrich's own account of Greek art, the crucial turning in Western art. He shows how it was that the onlooker was systematically encouraged to look at art in terms of appearance, as representing, not being. Robert Klein has commented: 'Le réalisme en art est la première conséquence de l'irréalisation corrélative du modèle et de l'œuvre (c'est-à-dire, que l'apparence et l'imaginaire sont psychologiquement du même ordre)' (Klein, 1970, p. 399).[12] Illusion as an aim in art is possible only when the work represents, not when it is.

That the picture could not be simultaneously perceived as plane and as a subject was with Gombrich a psychological incompatibility. For Husserl and also for Sartre it is perception and imagination which are incompatible: the imagination contains within itself the postulating of what is seen as represented, not real. The incompatibility is both logical and ontological. For Gombrich, as in the analysis of realism or the intention of realism by Hamon, what was at stake was the production of the effect of reality; for Sartre, as for Barthes, the work is a kind of phantom. According to Sartre, the 'conscience imageante', the positing of what is seen as represented, is a negation. The work of art is 'posited as unreal' and this positing is an integral part of the imaginative participation the work incites, and not a breaking of the imaginative circuit by reflexion. The image is not immanent in consciousness (and Sartre follows Husserl's critique of Hume here), the mind is not a box with pictures inside it. Images are *objets fantômes*; 'ils semblent se présenter comme une négation de la condition d'*être dans le monde*' (Sartre, 1940, p. 175).[13] What in Gombrich is perceptual inability to see the picture both as object and as image is with Sartre power to make unreal, which finally becomes the definition of imagination and the source of human liberty. 'Nous voyons donc que la conscience, pour produire l'objet en image *Charles VIII*, doit pouvoir nier la réalité du tableau et qu'elle ne saurait nier cette réalité qu'en prenant du recul par rapport à la réalité saisie dans sa totalité' (Sartre, 1940, p. 233). Precisely, to seize reality in its totality and to postulate the work of art as unreal outside that totality, is to negate the world. 'L'acte imaginatif est à la fois *constituant, isolant* et *anéantissant*' (Sartre, 1940, p. 230). The work is thus unreal and real at the same time.[14] Moreover, the subject of the work is real and unreal, this time not in dialectical relation to the world about, but in relation to the *conscience imageante*: the picture, the portrait of Charles VIII, *refers* to something unreal – a man long since dead – and yet we see him: 'C'est lui que nous voyons, non le tableau, et cependant nous le posons comme n'étant pas là: nous l'avons seulement atteint "en image", "par l'intermédiaire" du tableau. On le voit, le rapport que la conscience pose dans l'attitude imageante, entre le portrait et l'original, est proprement magique' (Sartre, 1940, p. 38). For Sartre here, the appearance of the subject is a kind of epiphany: he speaks of 'émanation'; a picture is a 'matière visitée par des images'.

These theories of the nature of our attention to art, to painting or to the novel are thus of two fundamentally different types. For Gombrich and Hamon, there is tension between the surface of the picture or novel and the way in which we read it: but the work is described by them as a *replica*, as a work whose material unreality is ignored in our perception of it. In the second type there is a duality in the very apprehension of the work: a psychological duality for Barthes, an oscillation of consciousness, a kind of seduction by the work, of indulging in the work; an ontological duality for Sartre, where what we see and experience is a *representation*, something real and unreal at the same time, not through any conflict of matter and image, but within the image itself.

Theory of illusion: history of 'illusion'

The first type of theory (Gombrich, Hamon) considers the experience of art to be bipolar: *either* the physical matter *or* the imaginative tissue of the work is present to us at one time. The second type of theory is bimodal: *both* matter *and* tissue may be present simultaneously or nearly so (Barthes' 'fading', a term drawn from Lacan) or the representation itself may be dual (the picture's imaginative reality against its subject's non-presence or non-existence, the picture's non-reality, its image quality, in relation to its actual matter, with Sartre). But both theories conceptualise the image as *appearance*: 'Not a true one, but only like true' (Plato, *Sophist*, 348 b). Gombrich and Klein have already shown how this realisation is a prising loose of appearance from the cult-image: it is only through such a negation that realism is possible. O. Mannoni goes further. It is the contradiction in illusion which makes art as art possible: 'On en viendrait à admettre que, chez l'adulte, les effets de masque et ceux de théâtre sont possibles en partie grâce à la présence des processus qui s'apparentent à ceux de la négation (*Verneinung*);

qu'il faut que ce ne soit pas vrai, que nous sachions que ce n'est pas vrai, afin que les images de l'inconscient soient vraiment libres' (Mannoni, 1969, pp. 165–6). This double-think is here presented as a safety barrier. But another psychoanalyst, D. W. Winnicott, makes of the contradiction more than a semi-conscious mechanism which makes possible contradictory behaviour. The healthy infant develops through a process of illusion and disillusion: illusion that all is one, that it creates magically everything around it; disillusion through gradual weaning and frustration which it learns it can bear. It is this process which develops an area between subject and object which provides relief from the adaptation to reality without being a mere escape (Winnicott, 1974, p. 15). The area is not so much preserved by a double-think as freed from a tension between inner and outer, where without hallucination 'the child puts out a sample of dream potential and lives with this sample in a chosen setting of fragments from external reality' (Winnicott, 1974, p. 60), a paradoxical area which is freed from contradiction and which is the source of creativity. The tension between illusion and negation of illusion is here a tension between magical union with the imagined and external reality. It is, in psychoanalytic terms, constitutive of art. As such it is analogous to a tension within the work of art itself, that between imaginative tissue and material, formal, or conventional factors. Adorno derives the whole development of art from this conflict which in his terms is between *Mimesis* and *Rationalität*: 'The aporia of art caught between regression to literal magic, and the ceding of the mimetic impulse to thinglike rationality, prescribes its whole development' (Adorno, 1973, p. 87). *Mimesis* in art is the remnant of its magical and cult origin: *Rationalität* is represented by 'those elements (construction in modern art, composition in the Renaissance) which are the placeholders of logic and causality in an area which is not that of objective knowledge' (Adorno, 1973, p. 91). Both tendencies end in an impasse: *Rationalität* tends to integrate subjectivity and the imagination, and then to halt the dialectical process by denying them; *Mimesis* tends to lead to mere consumer art and denial of its own truth. The self-negating imaginative space has become in Adorno's aesthetics the central tension embodied by art.

A negation which frees the imagination; a tension within art which dialectically prescribes its development; art as both illusion and resistance to illusion. Such formulations are all derived from Plato,[15] and it was because art was a contradiction that he rejected it. In the *Sophist*, art is one of the many ways in which something may be not real, a type of non-being, part of the technique of which the sophist is master, and yet one which forces the philosopher to admit in some sense the reality of the not-real: 'Not being reduces him who would refute it to such difficulties that when he attempts to refute it he is forced to contradict himself' (*Sophist*, 239 d). This framework which Plato set up is structured by different oppositions, epistemological, moral, ontological: true/false, authentic/ inauthentic, real/unreal, presence/non-presence. The contradiction can be filled in many ways: 'real' and 'unreal' can be attributed to different components in what art is and does[16] as the preceding discussion has shown. At first, in accordance with the technique used to hunt sophistry, the contradiction is denied by dividing the types of imitation into two, the genuine and the ungenuine, the true and the false, *mimetikè eikastikè* and *mimetikè fantastikè* (the same technique is used by Kristeva in her distinction *sens/vraisemblance*). But soon it seems as if the difficulty cannot be driven out in this way; the contradiction is within the very notion of likeness or image – 'what we call a likeness [eikon], though not really existing, really does exist' (*Sophist*, 240 b).

Yet the *Republic* shows that if art is genuine, it is also derived, at a third remove 'from the king and the truth', a pointless reduplication of the real world. If art is ungenuine, false, if it deceives (but it can only deceive children, or the ignorant), it is a sleight of hand, jugglery and witchcraft (*Republic*, 602 d; cf. *Sophist*, 235 a); it plays on a 'weaker faculty which is remote from the intelligence'; it presents as seeming truth what is then revealed to be absent. Plato makes art a victim of a double bind – it is either trivial or dangerous.[17]

Art in the *Republic* is assimilated to deceptive appearance: it imitates *phantasms*, not being as it is but appearance as it appears (598 b). Art plays thus on the relay structure[18] of appearance – the appearance of the appearance, a series which can continue indefinitely. But the deceptive appearance is further analysed, and again in terms of contradiction: 'The same things appear bent and straight to those who view them in water and out, or concave and convex, owing to similar errors of vision about colours, and there is obviously every confusion of this sort in our souls. And so, scene-painting, in its exploitation of this weakness of our nature, falls nothing short of witchcraft, and so do jugglery, and any other such contrivances' (602 c–d). And here the principle of the excluded middle is brought in: 'It is impossible for the same thing at one time to hold contradictory opinions about the same thing' (602 e). The introduction of the law of the excluded middle, $P \vee \bar{P}$, at this precise moment is important: it is to be used to denounce art as appearance which appears true and false. The contradiction proves art's corruption and falsity. Art is more than deceptive, more than a lie; it is both false and true, it contradicts the principle of *tertium non datur*. But this state of affairs, though recognised, is not accepted. $P \vee \bar{P}$ is used to reduce art to a lie; since art is not true, it must be false.[19]

This movement in Plato, from art as true and false, to art as true *or* false and thus false, since it is not true (the better, in other theories of this type, to maintain its 'higher' truthfulness), has constituted the logical framework for reflexion on art for the West. And, as has been shown, the fulcrum on which the notion of the truth or the falsehood of art turns is the concept of likeness.

For Plato a likeness is like, pretends to be like, something it is not. But the act of pretending can be of two types, or lead in two directions (Austin, 1961, pp. 208–9). In that art is an *image of*, a representation, it may *dissimulate*, it may hide or deny its own material reality, by affecting to be mere appearance (cf. Caillois, 1960). Yet art may also *simulate* something that is not there. So that dissimulation points away from the work itself, it is an illusion because it is not what it seems. In simulation, art identifies itself with the appearance of something else. The one hides its own presence, the other by its presence hides the absence of what is simulated. What dissimulates empties itself of reality to fill out something else; but simulation fills itself with a simulated reality and empties what is simulated.[20]

These directions of dissimulation and simulation are controlled by some – only some – of the meanings of 'appearance'. For to 'appear' may mean that what appears shows itself as something it is not, that it merely seems; but this in turn implies that appearance and what appears are *either* true *or* false. Or the appearance can point to something beyond itself – what is indicated but does not show itself.[21] In this case the appearance is true *and* false, false in that it is not what it reveals, true in that it reveals. A relation can be made between these different modes of being like (simulation and dissimulation) and of appearing (seeming and pointing beyond): they are structured by two different theories of truth. The first is the correspondence theory, *adequatio rei et intellectus*; the second, re-velation, uncovering or disclosing of the hidden, *a-letheia*.[22]

S_1	simulation	A_1	seeming
	makes itself like		the work seems (to be)
	something which is		(like) – it is not
	not there		really
	Adequatio		Contrary of *Adequatio*
S_2	dissimulation	A_2	appearing
	hides itself by some		shows itself, and
	diversionary behaviour		points to something
			beyond
	Contrary of *Aletheia*		*Aletheia*

In S_2 and A_2 the relay structure, the pointing beyond, is a reflexion of the definition of truth as *aletheia*; our attention is relayed by the appearance towards what is pointed at. *Adequatio*, on the contrary, seeks a *replica*, a simulation, it excludes what is not truth, it presents the alternatives, T v F, P v P̄. (This was the notion of likeness underpinning the work of Gombrich and Hamon.) But with *aletheia* there is *duplication*; the same thing may be both appearance and the disclosure of what appears. The image is a representation which may be imbricated: it is T & F (the concept of likeness in Sartre and Barthes).

Art as simulation/dissimulation, truth/untruth, appearance/seeming: these oppositions are not a framework, timeless because pertaining to art's essence. On the contrary, they are clearly culturally specific, and largely irrelevant to what is known as primitive art, for instance. As the present discussion has suggested, they turn on the definition of art as *likeness*: they are the workings out of the matrix set up by Plato, perhaps in reaction to the great development of the plastic arts just before his lifetime. But if Western aesthetics has in one sense been a *machine logique*, as Derrida calls it (Derrida, 1972a, p. 213), to work out the consequences of Plato's position, it remains the case that each concept receives different definition at different times. For the machine to have purchase, to be more than a model, it must have historical definition. Clearly, the elements in the matrix discussed above will take on a different interrelation at different historical moments (influenced by, and influencing, social, political and economic factors which are not the field of study of this book). It is in part the working of the machine itself which sets up particular tensions in the aesthetic thought of any one particular period. Such tensions will then mould the development of later ideas on art. Just such a set of tensions is presented by the eighteenth century, when viewed retrospectively, from the point of view of the nineteenth and twentieth centuries.

For in the eighteenth century the definition of 'likeness' is thought of in terms of 'illusion'. This does not merely give a particular shape, a particular set of tensions, to the matrix discussed above. I have already suggested that the use of this particular term to answer a general difficulty about representation has shaped what may be called the problematics of nineteenth- and twentieth-century aesthetics and the proof has already been given, in that it has been shown that 'illusion' or associated concepts are made use of implicitly and even by aestheticians who deny their validity. The importance of this shaping power of 'illusion' is increased when it is realised that the use of 'illusion' in aesthetics is relatively recent. It was novel in the seventeenth century and was used consistently only in the eighteenth. Any exploration of the workings of the *machine logique* of likeness must bear this fact in mind. And the aim of this book is to suggest an explanation of the newness of the term and to explore its significance. The beginnings of the answer must be looked for in the semantic heritage of 'illusion' itself.

II

ILLUSION: OLD WINE, NEW BOTTLES

Plato in the *Republic* treats art as a contradiction, as implying P v P̄, a denial of the principle *tertium non datur*, and thus ontologically false, a deceptive image. In Pliny's famous account of the contest between Zeuxis and Parrhasius, the deception has become merely perceptual.[1] The account is paradigmatic: the stories of the deception of animals infect art criticism from the Renaissance on. Zeuxis deceived birds with his painted grapes, but Parrhasius deceived Zeuxis with a painted curtain. Pliny's story represents a banalisation of the Platonic position: while it serves us up the triumphs of art, it also limits them to a narrow version of *trompe-l'œil*. A mistake about the nature of what is seen is only possible to man for an instant and in regard to furniture. The banalisation is accompanied by an evident change in the status of the artist: the trick is part of a contest, and proves the painter's competence. Art is not a scandalous illustration of the divorce between appearance and essence, but a fascinating play between them.

Pliny's story accounts for the consumer's adherence to art in terms of a mistake. But the mistake itself is the result of a *trick*, a deception, and it is this that is in fact the first meaning of 'illusion'.

Illusion and magic

The sense of Pliny's trick, the inducing of error by appearance, is formalised in the classical Latin meaning of 'illusion'. It is a rhetorical figure, and Quintilian related it to irony and to part of the class of allegory. It is the kind of appearance which hides and reveals (*aletheia*), the meaning of the orator being implicit but disclosed 'either by the delivery, the character of the speaker, or the nature of the subject' (Quintilian, vIII, vi, 54–7).[2] The figure implies an aggressive gap between the appearance of what is being said and the essence of what is actually said.

The aggressivity is sharpened in Patristic writings, where 'illusion' means mockery, derision, the work of the Evil One who gives to the righteous the appearance of failure and ridicule, and who triumphs and scorns. 'We are become a reproach to our neighbours, a scorn and derision (illusio) to them that are round about us', St Jerome makes the Psalmist say (Psalm 79.4). St Augustine even presents the Adversary, the Devil, as created for the mockery of the angels, quoting Job: 'This is the beginning of the creation of God (figmenti Domini), which he made to be a sport to His angels (quod fecit ad inludendum)', which agrees with the Psalm where it is said 'There is that dragon which Thou hast made to be a sport therein (ad inludendum)' (St Augustine, 1973, Book xi, ch. xv).[3]

Illusio comes to mean more than mockery – it is the means whereby the Devil tempts and deceives.[4] Isidore of Seville has a chapter headed 'De nocturnis illusionibus' (Migne, vol. LXXXIII (1850), p. 1163). The illusion is a deceptive appearance which leads into error, and whose nature is then discovered too late. The deception practised is the contrary of *aletheia*: it is irremediable falsehood which is disclosed, not truth, but the structure is still that of *aletheia*, of imbrication, where the image points beyond itself, and thus beguiles. Much has been written, loosely and rigorously, of art's cult and religious origins: but in the Christian heritage art is associated with the Devil's assumption of false appearances – the Council of Constantinople of 754 calls art an invention of men possessed by the Devil, the master of the image which mocks and illudes (de Bruyne, 1946, vol. I, p. 263). For demons illude with *phantasmata* (Plato's term for the appearance of art, *Republic*, 598 b), and these for Patristic writers are both internal states and external apparitions, products of the imagination actually existing outside. 'Illusion' is thus operating in that area of flow and ambiguity between the merely subjective and the intersubjective, between fleeting interior states and exterior incorporeal forms. This marginal area in which demons practise their illusion is the sphere of the *pneuma* both in the early Christian writings and in the complex knot created by the coexistence of late Roman religions, Neoplatonism, and theurgy. The *pneuma*, variously identified with astral body, the soul's envelope, the *corpus subtilis*,[5] whose modern descendant is the mediumistic ectoplasm, was thought to be the substance of visions, of dreams, of the apparitions of the dead, and to be the mode of activity of the demons. Semi-spiritual, semi-material, it was affected by the imagination (the faculty between the senses, which deal with matter, and the soul, which deals with spirit). It was by the working of their own imagination that demons were held to affect their own shapes (and the pregnant woman's imagination was similarly held to affect the foetus (Dodds, 1933, pp. 313ff.)).

The Byzantine writer Psellos is a typical exponent of this theory of the *pneuma*, of the imagination, and of demonic effects: 'Etant souffles (pneūma), les démons se mettent en contact avec notre souffle d'imagination (phantastikòn pneūma). Ils nous suggèrent des mots, mais ils ne se servent pas de la voix réelle. [. . .] C'est de leur substance d'imagination (phantastikè ousiá) que les démons puisent différentes formes, couleurs, et figures et les font passer dans notre souffle d'âme (pneūma tîs psychîs)' (Svoboda, 1927, p. 32). The *pneuma* can thus be affected in two ways: 'Le pneuma fait donc fonction d'un écran sur lequel on peut projeter des images des deux côtés opposés, les objets matériels du monde environnant y projettent les contours de leur forme; d'autre part, chez les démons, les représentations de l'imagination transforment la substance pneumatique d'après les lignes de leur propre figure' (Verbeke, 1945, p. 372). The appearance here mimes both types of truth, *adequatio* and *aletheia*: the *pneuma* by the impression of actual objects simulates the real where it is not (the contrary of *adequatio*), or it dissimulates its demonic origin by pointing beyond (the contrary of *aletheia*). In that it is appearance, its reference to reality is not assumed. The problem for the theurge who produced spiritual effects by material means and who operated 'in the borderland between mind and matter' (Dodds, 1933, p. 319),[6] was to distinguish good from bad spirits; the raiser of spirits might sometimes specify that the god, and not a demon in his shape, should manifest himself (Verbeke, 1945, pp. 378–9). Appearance is 'relayable': any appearance which appears to point to reality may merely point to another appearance. Iamblichus, in dealing with the difference between the manifestation of demons and gods, uses a criterion reminiscent of the Platonic rejection of deceptive art. The dangerous demonic apparitions, the *phantasmata*, 'causes d'erreur et de tromperie qu'ils sont pour les croyants au point d'arracher les contemplateurs à la vraie connaissance des dieux' (Iamblichus, p. 94),[7] are dangerous precisely in that they are derivative copies, not spirits which can cause themselves to be manifest. Any appearance may be epiphany or simulacrum, immediate manifestation of the divinity or derivative action of the *phantasmata*, which illude and mislead. No doubt this is the motivation for the iconoclastic tendencies of the early Church, and of the early Fathers' attitude to the theatre.

It is as if the theatre were a kind of offering of the imaginative aura to the gods; or to the demons. That is the way St Augustine denounces it:

The demons [. . .] have immortality of the body in common with the gods, but passions of the mind in common with men. On which account, say they, it is not to be wondered at that they are delighted with the obscenities of the theatre, and the fictions of the poets, since they are also subject to human passions, from which the gods are far removed [. . .]. Whence we conclude that it was not the gods, who are all good and highly exalted, that Plato deprived of the pleasure of theatric plays, by reprobating and prohibiting the fictions of the poets, but the demons. (St Augustine, Book VIII, ch. xiv; cf. Book IX, ch. vii)[8]

The demons take pleasure in the appearance of passions projected by actors. Theatre is then doubly evil in that it is an appearance which duplicates evil passions and in that this duplication is an offering to devils.

St Bonaventure crystallises the modes of demonic influence: 'The devil can deceive (illudere) our senses either by showing as present what is not, or by showing what is in another manner, or by hiding what is present' (St Bonaventure, 1885, vol. II, p. 228b) – the first 'simulare', the last 'dissimulare'. The logic of appearance controls the modes of the apparition, but the appearance is no longer objective. St Bonaventure rejects the more direct demonic activity in favour of action through the animal spirits, and through the humours. There is a similar movement away from the early Fathers in St Thomas Aquinas: he denies that the demonic *phantasmata* are objective. The Devil does not form an object out of spiritual matter, existing externally, but merely places the same image in the mind's eye of different men (St Thomas Aquinas, P.I.q.114, a.4).[9] In these thirteenth-century saints, the relation between subject and object has altered; the delimitation between outer and inner has hardened, and the middle area where demons' *phantasmata* illuded has been incorporated into the subjectivity.

Well on into the Renaissance, however, the belief in the objective existence and power of the devil's *phantasmata*, 'fantômes', was still held.[10] Erastus testifies to the strength of the belief by his denial that an image can be removed from the head of one man and be imprinted on another: 'No one in their right mind will think that an image fashioned in the spirit of my phantasy can go out of my brains and get into the head of another man' (Walker, 1958, p. 159, n. 6).[11] Similarly, the great Swiss doctor Johannes Wier shows the subjectivising of illusion: in the *Histoires, disputes*

et discours des illusions et impostures des diables, 1579 (Latin edition, 1563), he explains the effects of magic as due to subjective
delusion. The image is misleading, but it is purely internal. And
even an external appearance may be explained not magically but
naturally. Pomponazzi believes he is giving a natural explanation of
the miraculous apparition of a saint when he suggests it may have
occurred through the stamping of the crowd's imaginative effluvia
on the air (Walker, 1958, p. 108). The interstitial area in which the
pneuma and the demons' illusions were effected is being eliminated, as the change in religious concepts shows. The Protestant
Erastus insists that Christian ceremonies are not acts but *representations*: 'For there is no power in ceremonies but that of representing' (Walker, 1958, p. 162, n. 2). Religious services move from
magical operations to representations, from action to substitutions
for action, from epiphany to simulacrum. And this same movement
is that of art: the magicians' artifices become those of the conjur-
ors, and of the theatre decorators.

Magic, machines, perspective

One theory of the Devil's illusions dismissed by Bonaventure was
that the Adversary used a specular medium (natura specularis)
both receptive (susceptiva) and retentive (retentiva) of his imprint.
Thus the explanation of a mirage, simultaneously observed by
many soldiers in Syria, was that the Devil had shown it to them in a
mirror, to illude and betray them. Bonaventure objects that the
soldiers should have seen both vision and mirror (St Bonaventure,
1885, vol. ii, p. 229a). The use of mirrors in magic was a commonplace, precisely because the optical image was thought of as a *phan-
tasma* – something really existing in an odd interstitial space: much
as what is known as a 'real' mirror image is seen projected in space,
not in the mirror. Giambattista Della Porta's work, *Magia naturalis
sive de miraculis rerum naturalium* of 1558, contains an important
section on catoptrics, the optics of reflexion. As his title suggests,
he is concerned to produce visions by natural magic and not by the
forces of demons. The section is a manual for the production of
illusions – for example, the method of projecting images in the air,
much used for ghostly apparitions in nineteenth-century theatre.

Sixteenth- and seventeenth-century scientists used optics *technically*, as part of a project to recreate magical effects by mechanical
means. For example, Salomon de Caux wrote a treatise on perspective published in 1612, which is 'comme un chapitre d'un vaste
traité sur les merveilles du monde où l'harmonie des sons et des

22

figures, le mécanisme de la vision, et les machines hydrauliques sont présentés sur le même plan' (Baltrušaitis, 1969, p. 39). It was he who designed the famous garden at Heidelberg, creating musical grottoes, singing fountains and pneumatically controlled speaking statues (Yates, 1975, p. 114). The young Descartes gleefully seizes on this replacement of the magical by the mechanical:

Il y a une partie dans les Mathématiques que ie nomme la science des miracles, pour ce qu'elle enseigne à se seruir si à propos de l'air et de la lumière, qu'on peut faire voir par son moyen toutes les mesmes illusions, qu'on dit que les Magiciens font paroistre par l'aide des Démons. (Descartes, 1897, vol. i, p. 21)

But if a chain of mechanical causes is to replace magical operation at a distance, a new moment must enter into the wonder. Whereas magical appearance might lead to sickening awareness of deception, here the dispelling of the deception will provoke wonder: 'Vous ayant fait admirer les plus puissantes machines, les plus rares automates, les plus apparentes visions et les plus subtiles impostures, que l'artifice puisse inventer, ie vous en découvrirai les secrets' (Descartes, 1908, vol. x, p. 505).[12] Revelation of appearances no longer causes a recoil from the movement of involvement with them, but the awareness leads, by a kind of reflux, to a quasi-aesthetic appreciation.

The seventeenth-century opera and masque are based on mechanical replacement of magic. The princely fête symbolises royalty's omnipotence by a representation of magic; but it is the very awareness of the perfection of technical means which enhances the aura of the prince. The illusion thus created is not equivalent to a mistake, to perfection of rendering. On the contrary, the fragile evanescent quality of involvement which becomes wonder is essential. In a fête given by Hesselin for Christina of Sweden, everything moved, creating thus a play between illusion and reality. The queen was led into an enchanted domain: 'Tout y était *illusoire*, tout chancelait et tout se transformait. Les murs s'évanouissaient et l'on voyait successivement des salles immenses, des nuages portant une ville en feu, le char de la Renommée, "une enfilade de portes de plusieurs appartemens, dont le premier estoit gardé par deux suisses qu'on croyoit estre seulement représentés et feints" mais qui se détachaient de la muraille et qui dansaient' (Baltrušaitis, 1969, p. 59). What appears real disappears, what seems illusory – the Swiss guards – turns out to be 'real' men, though disguised actors.

Such a fête was action rather than spectacle, but closely related to such *spectacles à machines* as those of Torelli.[13] In both, the spectator is swept along by the speed of the oscillation between apparent and real. But there is a crucial difference in the relation of the spectator to such a fête and his relation to theatrical spectacle. In the first he is spectator and actor; he is included, physically, within the scenic transformations which lead him on from apparent to apparently real to real. In the second, the theatrical spectacle, especially since the development of what Klein has called 'le théâtre illusionniste perspectiviste' – that is, not the imaginary perspectival panorama of Palladio, but the stage with a backdrop – there is an ideal fixed viewing point at the prince's box, and he looks out at a picture frame within which the actor acts. It is as if the proscenium arch were needed to counteract the stage depth, to transform it into image; the spectator, where the incitement to perceptual illusion is strong, is excluded from the stage by the very form of the theatre (Klein, 1970, p. 309). It is perspective, then, that in part accomplishes the elimination of the shadowy borderland between objective and subjective, with the great Renaissance works on optics. Optical illusion relays magical illusion. Defined by the sixteenth- and seventeenth-century dictionaries as 'inane spectrum', its meaning passes from objective to subjective, from something external to the state of mind of the deceived.[14] Such masters as Alberti, Brunelleschi, Kepler and Descartes work to locate the 'inane spectrum' by locating the visual image. *Illusion* thus acquires a subjective meaning – or intersubjective, in so far as it is distinguished from delusion – but in its integration into the mind it brings with it its demonic sense of deceit, of mockery.

It is in works on perspective that the phrase 'deceive the eye' ('L'inganno degl'occhi') makes its appearance.[15] This is not the place to discuss the divergencies among those who developed central perspective, except to say that the notion of deception does not appear early – on the contrary, the very name 'costruzione legittima' suggests the scientific preoccupations of Alberti, Brunelleschi and Leonardo. And even after the principles of central perspective were worked out, the artists' options within them remained remarkably varied – Panofsky, for example, has shown how apparently related intentions in treatment of architectural space in the work of Bernini and Brunelleschi in fact imply radically different attitudes to illusion and to the relation to the spectator (Panofsky, 1919). There is, alas, as yet no systematic history of the development of the treatment of perspective in painting and architecture from the point of view of its implications for illusion and for the spectator.

Central perspective symbolises and perhaps mediates a fundamental sharpening in the relation between subject and object. It is not just a particular method of foreshortening that is at stake. The picture is treated as a window, that is, the picture surface is negated (Panofsky, 1975). The spectator is located at the top of the visual pyramid, and forced to consider the picture space as a continuation of his body space. He is narrowed down to the immobile eye, so that the monocular visual field becomes the outside, all that the spectator can see. The spectator is placed opposite something which is a simulation, an adequation to reality, and this leaves him on the threshold of another space, rather than including him within it.

But perhaps the aim of 'costruzione legittima' does not escape the ambiguity which its name shows that it seeks to avoid. As an intersection in the visual pyramid, the picture represents an appearance placed between the object supposedly represented and the eye: and as such exhibits the recursive nature of all appearance. Is what is seen the appearance of the (supposed) reality? Or the appearance of the appearance-intersection, a question which for the painter is:

Si l'apparence visible présuppose la transformation subjective des impressions, doit-on [. . .] rendre fidèlement les résultats de ce processus – les illusions optiques par exemple – ou doit-on rendre les 'causes' reconstruites par le raisonnement en laissant à l'œil le soin d'opérer sur les éléments ainsi dégagés les mêmes transformations que sur les données sensibles provenant du modèle? (Klein, 1970, p. 272)[16]

As Klein has shown, the two solutions paradoxically reverse themselves. The solution which, aiming at objectivity, does not incorporate subjective vision, thus excluding the spectator, is yet obliged to rely on him for the perception of the work; the solution which includes the spectator in the constructions of the painting excludes him by this very fact from the actual perception (Klein, 1970, pp. 271, 275).

The exclusion of the spectator is taken to an extreme by the painters of anamorphoses (the most famous example of which is the skull in the foreground of Holbein's *The Ambassadors*: here the visual pyramid slants to the side, so that viewed from the middle front the image is incomprehensible). Their chief theoretician was Niceron, and he compares the surprise, felt when the systematically deformed image appearing as a flat surface flicks into shape and depth as soon as the right viewing point is found, to *diabolical illusion* (Niceron, 1652, p. 147):[17] the image dissimulates itself until at a certain point it reveals itself; the consciousness of the picture surface precedes the viewing of it as an image, and as such the anamorphosis is the contrary of *trompe-l'œil*.

The opposite movement, that of the inclusion of the spectator, is developed later at the Farnesina by the Carraci (Panofsky, 1919) but especially by Pozzo at St Ignazio. Here, by a system which directly links *point de distance* and *point de fuite*, the spectator's space and the picture's space are one. He is enclosed in a theatrical space where the foreshortened figures force the onlooker into dialogue (Klein, 1970, pp. 276, 271). Yet this aggressively inspiring decoration is seen in a slighly eccentric way, for one flagstone in the church marks the only spot from which the ceiling is seen in 'correct' foreshortening (and accounts and impressions of what is seen from other points vary widely). So Pozzo's 'panillusionism' sweeps up the spectator at the price of a constant consciousness that what is seen is appearance. The spectator is englobed, physically included, by the *quadratura*, yet this very inclusion is concomitant with awareness of appearance as appearance.

Yves Bonnefoy has shown how this beckoning-on of appearance has spiritual as well as aesthetic meaning: 'En fait les deux expériences, celle de la présence et celle de la désilusion, celle de l'absolu et celle d'un relatif, ont lieu dans un seul instant.' He likens this movement to that of Descartes' hyperbolic doubt: 'Le bien baroque n'est pas le contraire du mal, mais celui du doute. Il faut même que la vie se révèle bien comme un songe pour que, dans l'écroulement des fausses preuves, apparaisse glorieusement la nécessité de la grâce' (Bonnefoy, 1970, p. 179).[18] Cartesian doubt which leads to the *Cogito* appears then as a variant of a journey through appearance towards reality. Such a journey is possible because there exists a point which justifies illusion, or rather which *is* the truth in illusion: the *Cogito*, the flagstone in St Ignazio. And this point is an internalisation of the transcendental spectator (in the case of the *Cogito* (Hobson, 1977a)) or a point supplied by faith (in the case of Baroque art). Consciousness of appearance beckons on to truth;[19] the soul can rise through illusion and disillusion to contact with God. But to be conscious of appearance is to be a spectator of appearance: the soul is at once spectator and actor.[20]

This theme of *desengaño*, of *theatrum mundi*, is embodied in contemporary use of the form of a play within a play. In Rotrou's *Le Véritable Saint Genest*, the hero, oscillating between his part as

Christian martyr and his pagan self, finally causes the two to coincide and, assuming his role, turns it into truth. The real spectator is incorporated into an action which is played out before God:

> Ce monde périssable et sa gloire frivole
> Est une comédie où j'ignorais mon rôle
>
> (Rotrou [1647], vv. 1303–4)

The imbrication of play within play, of appearance into appearance, stabilises into the final reality of God, where play and being coincide.[21]

Yet the form of the play within the play does not necessarily imply a revelation of a higher reality by appearance recognised as illusion and thus as true *and* false. For if no transcendental point or eye justifies, no ultimate reality is beyond. Instead there may be opposition, reality and illusion may be set against one another, and the choice between them may be arbitrary: appearance is true *or* false. Bernini produced a famous sketch in 1637 at Rome, *The Intermezzo of the Two Theatres*. When the curtain rose the audience saw on the stage another audience, part real and part feigned, sitting facing them as if to watch a play. Two braggarts on stage pretend to draw, one the real, one the feigned audience. On falling into conversation they realise that for each the other's audience is illusory. They conclude by drawing a curtain across the stage, and each arranges a performance for his audience only. The comedy played before the real audience was punctuated by laughter from the other side as if the feigned audience were reacting to its own comedy, played on the other side of the curtain (Bernheimer, 1956; Leclerc, 1946). What is seen is thus either true or false. Whereas in the *theatrum mundi* the transcendental spectator was the point from which illusion and reality could be discerned and even harmonised; and for the young Descartes it is the mask which the point of separation of appearance and essence. Bernini gives no such point.[22]

It is with the combination of the structural possibilities of imbrication and reversal that a transition takes place from the play as metaphor for unreality to the play as metaphor for itself: a true *mise en abîme*. In Corneille's *Illusion comique*, a father in search of his son consults a magician: the magician raises apparitions who act out before the father the story of his son, which as it progresses appears to be ending tragically. But the end reveals that the son and his wife have been acting in and not living out a tragedy. As so often with Shakespeare, the shadows raised by magic are compared to actors (*A Midsummer Night's Dream, The Tempest*), a reversal of St Augustine's accusation against actors. The imbrication of the artificial tragedy within the play reverses into the actors' reality, a mirror image of what is behind the play. Magical illusion modulates by this doubling back into aesthetic illusion: we are shown the reality of the appearance and the appearance of reality.

Le passez-muscade: illusion and epistemology

Comment essayer de le saisir, ce qui semble nous échapper ainsi dans la structuration optique de l'espace? C'est toujours ce sur quoi joue l'argumentation traditionnelle. Les philosophes, depuis Alain, le dernier à s'y être montré dans les exercices les plus brillants, en remontant vers Kant, et jusqu' à Platon, s'exercent tous sur la prétendue tromperie de la perception – et en même temps ils se retrouvent tous maîtres de l'exercice, à faire valoir le fait que la perception trouve l'objet là où il est, et que l'apparence du cube faite en parallélogramme est précisément, en raison de la rupture de l'espace qui sous-tend notre perception même, ce qui fait que nous le percevons comme cube. Tout le jeu, le passez-muscade de la dialectique classique autour de la perception, tient à ce qu'elle traite de la vision géométrale, c'est-à-dire de la vision en tant qu'elle se situe dans un espace qui n'est pas dans son essence le visuel. Lacan, *Séminaire XI*, p. 87

In the movement of the Cartesian *Cogito*, absolute doubt, the suspicion that all may be appearance, was powerless against one certainty, that of consciousness: appearance led on to truth. For Pascal, as for Bernini, illusion and reality alternate, reversing one into the other. In the *Pensées*, the fixed point which may stabilise their relationship cannot be won, it can only be given:

De plus, [. . .] personne n'a d'assurance, hors de la foi, s'il veille ou s'il dort, vu que durant le sommeil on croit veiller aussi fermement que nous faisons; on croit voir les espaces, les figures, les mouvements; on sent couler le temps, on le mesure; et enfin on agit de même qu'éveillé; de sorte que, la moitié de la vie se passant en sommeil, par notre propre aveu, où, quoiqu'il nous en paraisse, nous n'avons aucune idée du vrai, tous nos sentiments étant alors des illusions, qui sait si cette autre moitié de la vie où nous pensons veiller n'est pas un autre sommeil un peu différent du premier? (Pascal, 1904, vol. II, pp. 342–3)

Metaphysical illusion takes the form either of imbrication or of alternation: a movement forward towards truth, T & F, or of oscillation, T v F. Descartes' global doubt, that the world and all experience may be *illusion* with the full force of the word's semantic heritage of mockery, is rejected by Gassendi precisely for its dramatisation: 'N' eût-ce pas été une chose plus digne de la candeur d'un philosophe et du zèle de la vérité de dire les choses simplement de bonne foi, et comme elles sont, que non pas comme on vous pourrait objecter, recourir à cette machine, forger ces illusions, rechercher ces détours et ces nouveautés? (Gassendi in Descartes, 1963, vol. II, p. 708.) For Gassendi, our knowledge may be uncertain, but not false.

Descartes' work on optical illusion is in very different vein: in it he carried into the problems of vision the divorce operated by scientists between sense and intellectual knowledge, between the secondary qualities of ordinary experience and the primary qualities which could be expressed mathematically. Descartes explodes the 'formes substantielles' of the scholastic tradition: vision is the result of an interpretation of a language of signs, which represent objects in the outside world the better, the less they resemble them (Descartes, 1963, vol. I, p. 685), as in a picture ellipses represent circles.

The influence of perspective and of its mathematisation is here incalculable: the neglect of a scientific study of aerial perspective, the misprising of colour, which clearly has such strong somatic effects, culminating in the quarrel of the *Poussinistes* and the *Rubénistes* in France towards the end of the century – all bear witness that radiance and effusion are left aside; light is studied as exemplifying the laws of linear projection; and Descartes actually uses the model of the *blind* man and his stick to illustrate this linearity, a paradox brilliantly explored by Merleau-Ponty (1964a, pp. 37ff.). Central perspective had gradually restricted the perceiving subject to a point at the top of the visual pyramid: in 'natural perspective', that is, optics, the point is internalised (as is made explicit in Locke's metaphor of the *camera obscura*, used of the *mind*), and is presented by artificial perspective with a number of precise critical cases in which what could be reconstituted as the retinal image did not correspond with what is seen.

The divorce between what is seen and the process of vision became more and more marked with the work of Malebranche and Berkeley. The object seen is held by Malebranche to be a result of a multiplicity of 'natural judgements'. These are objectively false, but paradoxically not deceptive – they are necessary to our conservation. God causes us to make these natural judgements, for he is the only locus of immediate perception. Descartes' *Malin Génie* has become Malebranche's beneficent occasionalist: 'L'Optique fait voir la différence extrême qui est entre les idées et les objets qu'elles représentent et qu'il n'y a qu'une intelligence infinie qui puisse en un clin d'œil faire une infinité de raisonnements instantanés: tous reglés par la géométrie et les lois de l'union de l'âme et du corps' (Cassirer, 1906, vol. I, p. 606, n. 87, quoting Malebranche).

Epistemological investigation strives to establish what pure visual sensation can be: Berkeley shows, against Malebranche, that what appear to be unconscious inferences, 'natural judgements' – perception of depth, for instance – are in fact other sensations, such as those of eye strain. Tangible and visible objects are heterogeneous – even plane surfaces are not immediate objects of vision. We are tempted to think so by analogy with a picture, where it seems that we see planes which the judgement converts into three-dimensional figures. But planes are no more discernible immediately by sight alone than solids. It is by touch alone that we learn that a plane is flat (Berkeley, 1964, vol. I, p. 235).

Locke describes the general process thus: 'The judgement presently, by an habitual custom, alters the appearances into their causes' (Pastore, 1971, p. 61).[23] The concern in this tradition is with *adequatio*; the visual process must be adequate to what we see. And it is here that the kind of conjuring trick mentioned in the epigraph to this section intervenes. For these theories leave out much – as Merleau-Ponty in particular has shown (Merleau-Ponty, 1972, p. 295). Depth is conceived, for example, to be like width considered in profile (clearly a result of the limiting assumptions first developed by painters and which lead to the homogenisation of space). Depth, hence, cannot be seen, only inferred. Only an omnipresent perception, that is, God, can perceive depth directly. Indeed, the imperceptibility of depth is made explicit by Molyneux in his *Dioptrika Nova* of 1692: 'For *distance* of itself, is not to be perceived; for 'tis a line (or a length) presented to our eye with its end toward us, which must therefore only be a *point*, and that is *invisible*' (Pastore, 1971, p. 68).

Optical illusions, in other words, were studied to refine what was meant by sense-data. The result was that the element-sensation was treated as a basic constituent of reality *and* as scientific construct. It was thus doubly reliable, and the optical error could be located in the judgement: 'Tout ce que nous rapportent nos sens est très vrai en toute manière et l'erreur ne se trouve que dans les faux jugements qui les suivent' (Malebranche, 1965, vol. I, p. 25, n. 7). The epistemological investigation is in fact landing on its feet because the argument from illusion is being used to set up a pair of opposites, 'sense-data' and 'material things'. In between there is the area of illusion, of the judgement which causes us to see a stick 'as' bent, a square tower 'as' round. J. L. Austin has shown how this argument, employed from Plato to A. J. Ayer, is used to 'prove' that we perceive nothing directly except sense-data, and how the concept of 'sense-data' is operating merely as a foil for the concept of 'material things' (Austin, 1964, p. 8).

Illusion is used by this epistemological tradition to establish *a contrario* what is the maximum incorrigible statement (Austin). 'Appearance', what is seen, and the reality of the retinal impression must be separated and their adequation measured.[24] The result for the seventeenth and eighteenth centuries was the pushing of what had been considered intersubjective experiences into subjectivity, to the neglect of the marginal areas of perception – what is seen in the corner of the eye, what is seen when we orientate ourselves.[25] The movement operated by the concept of illusion in the domain of aesthetics repeats this pattern: 'illusion', it will be shown, moves from designating an intersubjective game to applying *either* to a state of mind, a subjective fantasy, *or* to the truth of the work of art seen as a copy, a replica. 'Illusion' thus repeats in aesthetics the double value acquired by 'sense-data' in epistemological theory slightly earlier. The mutually defining opposition set up between material things, which since Locke have been 'moderate-sized specimens of dry goods' (Austin), and sense-data enables a kind of double bind to be made on the mind: what is real is what is perceived – that is, material things – and yet sense-data are (purely or merely) subjective. The effect of the argument from illusion in the eighteenth century is that genuineness and inauthenticity are attributed to the same things. 'Sense-data' are at the same time irremediably subjective and the only means we have of testing empirical statements – the roots of scientific facts. Hume rescues sense-data from this conflict but inevitably it recurs at the level not of elements but of operations.

For Hume uses a rigorous definition of experience from the senses – he refuses to assume operations of combinations of these elementary particles, as in traditional faculty psychology, or indeed in Cartesian and Lockean pyschology. The excitement of his *Treatise of Human Nature*, 1739, hangs on the tension between a deconstruction of common and even philosophical assumptions about the world, and the realisation that these views are necessary to survival. It is the work of philosophy to explain their constitution seriously. It is the 'imagination', our 'propensity to feign', which creates our mental world, our belief in cause and effect, our ideas of substance, of distinct existence, of identity – such views are called 'fictions' or 'illusions'. Hume with such terms insists on their dual nature – such notions are not logically necessary but practically necessary: we need them to survive. So that 'illusion' is not, as with Descartes, opposed to the individual, but is actually *created* by him. The imagination becomes the locus of the mind's creative activity (illusion).[26] With Hume, an epistemological groundwork is given for the modern concept of subjectivity: the difference between 'fiction' and ideas derived from an impression – the difference that is, between unreality and reality – is not embodied in qualitative differences between the mental events themselves. The differentiating criterion is vivacity, which is not necessarily associated with reality.[27] It is possible to argue that a certain definition of belief, first elaborated in aesthetics, is developed by Hume to cover the whole of mental life – but that is another story.[28]

'Illusion', then, in its first sense of mockery, was used of magic and of the Devil's conjurings: it represented some semi-material, semi-spiritual substance, infinitely malleable, present and absent. However, as the interstitial zone was carved up between inner and outer, 'illusions' came to be thought of as subjective, though perhaps also intersubjective, and the objective causes to be analysed. Machines and optical effects were invented, to be part of natural magic, eventually to replace natural magic, and were used thus in the theatre. The effect itself and the surprise it created, whether of itself or by the revelation that it was due to human operation, not to diabolical contrivance, tended in the theatre to take the form of a play within a play (the *Illusion comique*, the masque in *The Tempest*, both plays stage-managed by magicians). But where the play within a play was used to question the notion of reality, the form is not imbrication but alternation: the play is not pointing towards a different reality, it is either real or not, either an illusion or not. The alternation becomes separation in seventeenth-century epistemology: what in modern English philosophy is known as the 'argument from illusion', as it develops, gradually comes to disregard the fascination of illusion to concentrate on its falsity; the concern is to separate in our knowledge what cannot be doubted from the constructs of our minds and customs – the great century of development of the argument coinciding with the century in which 'illusion' was the current account of the consumer's relation to art.

'Illusion' and 'vraisemblance': twins or contraries?

In the seventeenth century, the 'real' is gradually defined in

Locke's way, as material and external: mental life is correlatively drained of a certain sort of reality, becoming internal, 'subjective'. This development will be repeated in the eighteenth century in the domain of aesthetics. But in the seventeenth century, 'illusion' applied to art is first and foremost magical. It is not a subjective state, but the *means* of deceit. D'Aubignac, for example, speaks of the contemporary stage as being 'orné de toiles peintes et d'illusions agréables' (d'Aubignac, 1927, p. 356).[29] It is often used critically. Le Moyne disapproves of Ariosto thus: 'Ajoutez enchantements à enchantements et illusions à illusions comme a fait l'Arioste, ce n'est pas faire un poème, c'est faire une rhapsodie de sortilèges pareille à la *Vie d'Apulée* ou à celle du Dr. Faust' (Le Moyne, *apud* Bray, 1963, p. 236).

Typically, then, 'illusion' is used of stage machinery. But in the accounts of the machinery's effect an important analysis is made:

Il est certain que les ornemens de la Scène font les plus sensibles charmes de cette ingénieuse Magie qui rappelle au Monde les Héros des siècles passés, & qui nous met en vue un nouveau Ciel, une nouvelle Terre, & une infinité de merveilles que *nous croions avoir présentes dans le temps même que nous sommes bien assûrés qu'on nous trompe.* (d'Aubignac, 1927, p. 355)

Here belief and disbelief occur at the same moment; what has been called a bimodal attitude is created by a kind of impelling force. 'Les spectateurs, quoiqu'ils sachent bien que ce ne sont que des terreurs feintes par l'invention du machiniste, ne sauroient néanmoins s'empêcher d'en avoir autant d'épouvante que d'admiration' (Renaudot on the scenic effects of Pierre Corneille's *Andromède*, in Corneille, 1862, vol. v, p. 285). This bimodal experience is clearly linked to opera and opposed, slightingly, to *vraisemblance*:

Or c'est vainement que l'Oreille est flattée & que les Yeux sont charmés, si l'Esprit ne se trouve pas satisfait: mon Ame, d'intelligence avec mon Esprit plus qu'avec mes sens, forme une résistance secrète aux impressions qu'elle peut recevoir, ou pour le moins elle manque d'y prêter un consentement agréable, sans lequel les Objets les plus voluptueux même ne sauroient me donner un grand plaisir. (Saint Evremond, 1709, vol. ii, p. 215)

In this attack on a bimodal experience, in the name of resemblance, the senses are contrasted with the higher faculty of intelligence. Though in other critics the analysis may be reversed and the senses considered absolutely necessary, even so, as in all such attacks, it is the very possibility of a bimodal experience, the T & F, which is denied. There can be no simultaneous showing and pointing beyond to something else – what I called *aletheia* is impossible:

Si le poëte eust renfermé dans sa Tragédie une année entière, un mois, une semaine, comment eust-il pu faire croire aux Spectateurs que des gens qui n'avoient point disparu, avoient passé tout ce long temps [. . .]. Je sais bien que le théâtre est une espèce d'illusion, mais il faut tromper les Spectateurs en telle sorte qu'ils ne s'imaginent pas l'estre encore qu'ils le sachent, il ne faut pas, tandis qu'on les trompe que leur esprit le connoisse; mais seulement quand il y fait réflexion. Or en ces rencontres les yeux ne seroient point deceûs & l'imagination par conséquent ne le pourroit estre, parce qu'on ne la peut decevoir si les sens n'en facilitent les moyens. (d'Aubignac, 1927, pp. 209–10)

Simultaneity, 'illusion' which contains awareness, is here opposed to *vraisemblance*, the successivity necessary for a comparison. For *vraisemblance* measures the match between *vrai* and theatre, it measures the *adequatio*. The experience that d'Aubignac is advocating is bipolar: awareness is to follow, not to accompany, involvement.

'Illusion' is in fact consciously contrasted with the central critical concept of the classical era, that is, *vraisemblance*,[30] magical enchantment with what is plausible, the marvellous with what 'seems true'. The content given to 'seems' is that of rational judgement, based on social consensus. Chapelain defines *vraisemblance* as 'une représentation des choses comme elles doivent avenir, selon que le jugement humain né et élevé au bien les prévoit et les détermine' (Chapelain, 1936, p. 87). As such, *vraisemblance* is opposed to historical truth, *appearing* true, whereas history frequently appears false and must be backed up by reports.

Vraisemblance, what is plausible, becomes after about 1630 closely linked with *bienséance*, what is seemly (the two senses of *devoir*): 'Il [. . .] doit réduire [une matière historique de cette nature] aux termes de la bienséance même aux dépens de la vérité' (Chapelain, 1936, p. 165). The concept has here a rigorously, even oppressively, social significance: 'Synésius a fort bien dit que la Poésie et les autres Arts qui ne sont fondés qu'en imitation, ne suivent pas la vérité, mais l'opinion et le sentiment ordinaire des hommes' (d'Aubignac, 1927, p. 76), and finally: 'Le Vraysemblable est tout ce qui est conforme à l'opinion du public' (Rapin, 1674, p. 53);[31] subjects dealing with regicide, or indeed revolution, are not *bienséant* and are banned (d'Aubignac, 1927, Book 2, ch. 1). The demand for *bienséance*, for *vraisemblance*, is presented as one made by the educated – seeing is *not* believing (Le Bossu, 1675, p. 136).[32] And though in d'Aubignac's case it is defined as precision, sometimes even as a one-to-one correspondence between artefact and model, in effect this adequation is of an idealised, almost abstract nature: 'Une chose [est] véritable ou supposée telle, dont les lieux sont certains, les qualitez naturelles, les actions indubitables, & toutes les circonstances selon l'ordre et la raison' (d'Aubignac, 1927, p. 34); it is adequation to norms, not to reality. D' Aubignac argues against multiplicity of action in the same terms as John Evelyn argues against multiple points of view in perspective: they are confusing.[33] The play's rational organised relation to reality is not magical. It is on the contrary one coolly judged to be adequate:

Je sçay bien que le Poète [. . .] prend le temps, l'allonge et le raccourcit à sa volonté, qu'il choisit le lieu tel que bon lui semble dans tout le monde, & que pour les intrigues, il les invente, selon la force et l'adresse de son imagination. [. . . pourtant . . .] quand on veut approuver ou condamner celles qui paroissent sur nos Théâtres, nous supposons que la chose est véritable, ou du moins qu'elle le doit, ou le peut bien estre, & sur cette supposition nous approuvons toutes les actions & les paroles qui pouvoient estre faites & dites [. . .] parce qu'en ce cas nous croyons que cela s'est véritablement ainsi fait, ou du moins, qu'il se pouvoit et devoit faire ainsi. (d'Aubignac, 1927, pp. 35–6)

Vraisemblance is based on an hypothesis whose consequences must be elaborated.

But this phrase 'je sais bien . . .' illustrates not merely the opposition of *vraisemblance* to 'illusion'; it shows awareness that *vraisemblance* in its etymological sense is an argument that cuts two ways, so that what it covers in 'la doctrine classique' is no more logical than its opposite. This had been the thesis of the pro-Corneille faction during the *querelle du Cid*. They argue that it is no more *vraisemblable* that the happenings of twenty-four hours should be represented in two, than that the happenings of twenty-four days should be – and the author of the *Discours à Cliton* represents the *vraisemblable* as a kind of mutilation, a *sacrificium imaginationis*: 'Je leur dy premièrement, qu'ils veulent passer pour petits esprits, de priver leur entendement de la faculté d'opérer en beaucoup de façons qui lui sont possibles & qui sont ordinaires aux bons Cerveaux, car en voyant représenter une pièce de Théâtre, suppléer le temps, supposer les actions & s'imaginer les lieux sont des Opérations d'Esprit qui de vérité ne peuvent estre bien faites que par les habiles' (*Discours à Cliton*, 1898, p. 267). In the same way, d'Aubignac condemns explanatory prologues as destructive of surprise, and yet maintains that a play previously read can be enjoyed in the theatre.[34] Again, commenting on the stage direction 'la scène est à Argos', he insists that the stage must represent a precise bit of the province, though what happens off-stage can happen anywhere. He makes thus a qualitative distinction between the absent and the present, for the latter fits in with what we see (*adequatio*) – the personage is either absent or present – but does not fit the way we project the seen onto the unseen, the way 'real' smudges into 'imagined' (*aletheia*). In the name of *vraisemblance*, d'Aubignac will only admit 'stances' in a play if the character has had time to go away and compose them; are 'stances', replies Corneille, more or less *vraisemblable*, more or less like prose, when the whole play is in alexandrines anyway (Corneille, 1965, p. 147)?

Corneille shows up the artificiality of *vraisemblance*: the unities frequently work against *vraisemblance*, for instance, but belong to what he calls 'nécessaire' – 'le besoin du poète pour arriver à son but ou pour y faire arriver ses acteurs' (Corneille, 1965, p. 59). Moreover, history itself is frequently *invraisemblable*, but is self-evidently possible – Corneille goes so far as to suggest that there should be 'fictions de théâtre' on the lines of legal fictions – which would release the playwright from the pressures of precision which paradoxically make time and space abstract.

Vraisemblance, then, guarantees nothing about the consumer's subjective state – and this is in mid-seventeenth century referred to by such terms as 'foi', 'créance', 'croyable'. The very term 'apparences' moves from the visual field to mean plausibility – Renaudot, speaking of a play written before the *règle des vingt-quatre heures* was generally observed, says that it was 'bien loin d'imprimer le sujet dans les sens par ses apparences, [ce qui] ôtoit toute créance à une représentation qui ne contentoit les yeux et les oreilles que par la richesse de ses habits et l'harmonie de ses concerts' (Corneille, 1862, vol. v, p. 279).

'Illusion' then is sharply opposed to *vraisemblance*. Writers are conscious of its magical heritage; they use it of scenery, or of the opera, both of which are a kind of reconstruction of magic with natural means. This was La Bruyère's defence of opera: '[La machine] augmente et embellit la fiction, soutient dans les spectateurs cette douce illusion qui est tout le plaisir du théâtre [. . .]. Le propre de ce spectacle est de tenir les esprits, les yeux, et les oreilles dans un égal enchantement' (La Bruyère, 1962, p. 103). The appearance so created *dissimulates* the cardboard which gives rise to the appearance. 'Illusion' is here a variety of *aletheia*, and it is *vraisemblance* which aspires to make the representation *adequate* to what is represented, this 'adequation' being achieved by the approximation of the representandum to something abstract, to a norm.

But *vraisemblance*, though opposed to 'illusion' is not its contrary, since, as I have said, it says nothing of the consumer's state, but speaks only of the work: it does not specify the consumer's experience, it normalises it. As a result, if the hold of art on the consumer is to be considered, a subjective underpinning to *vraisemblance* has to be found: and it is this that the verb 'se tromper', doubtless used first in theories of painting and perspective, is brought in to do. Those theorists, Félibien and Fréart de Chambray (both heavily influenced by Poussin),[35] who were intent on an adequation to a *norm*, barely use the phrase. But 'tromper les yeux' is found frequently in the works of their successor and adversary, the great art critic Roger de Piles, instigator of the quarrel on colour. In accounts of the consumer's experience by Piles, or by those influenced by him, judgement does not oppose illusion, but on the contrary is overcome by it:

On compte parmi les monumens de Rome, la perspective que le Père Mathieu Zacolino, Théatin, a faite à la voûte de l'Eglise de Saint Silvestre à Monte Cavallo. Il a représenté un Dome dans la voûte du chœur de cette Eglise avec un tel artifice, que les yeux les plus fins y sont trompez, sans que le jugement puisse corriger l'erreur des yeux. (Lamy, 1701, p. 194)

The tension between judgement and illusion here set up takes a different pattern in literary theory of the late seventeenth century. The weight in literary vocabulary changes. Instead of rationally assuming the experience of the consumer, as does *vraisemblance*, the fashionable concept 'le je ne sais quoi' expresses ignorance: the phrase explains the attraction of a work as the baffling of judgement. In Bouhours' work, *La Manière de bien penser dans les ouvrages d'esprit*, Philanthe makes an apology for 'tout ce qui est fleuri, tout ce qui brille' where 'le faux en fait souvent toute la grâce' (Bouhours, 1971, p. 13). In fact, in Bouhours' work the two elements of *vrai-semblance* are prised apart. But this is done in order to insert middle terms so that a definition of fiction emerges which is opposed *both* to falsity *and* to truth. A 'système fabuleux' is postulated, where the criterion is inner coherence, not truth: 'Le système fabuleux sauve ce que ces sortes de pensées ont de faux en elles-mesmes & il est permis, il est mesme glorieux à un poète de mentir d'une manière si ingénieuse' (Bouhours, 1971, p. 16). The old observation that the *vrai* was not always *vraisemblable* implied that uncomfortable truth had to be changed into something *vraisemblable* and thus not false. Bouhours' work shows how this

37

rationalising metamorphosis itself changes into a tasteful modulation through falsity to truth: 'Les hyperboles, selon Quintilien, mentent sans tromper et selon Sénèque elles ramènent l'esprit à la vérité par le mensonge' (Bouhours, 1971, p. 31). Art is not amenable to rules – to the educated there will always appear a 'je ne sais quoi' which leads the mind on like a bait. Beauty is alluring, perhaps false: it is defined in terms not of *adequatio* but of *aletheia*. The consumer's experience, the motive for his adherence, is precisely this bafflement, an oscillation caused by the blocking of the judgement.

Dubos

Bouhours exemplifies the development round the turn of the century of what could be called the aesthetics of alluring fiction. For the early eighteenth century, art is an experience which modulates between true and false: it is an oscillation, an interplay between verity and fiction. But after 1750 this will change. In a movement comparable to that discussed in epistemology, where intersubjective areas of experience had been divided into 'hard facts' or subjective sense-impressions, illusion after 1750, as I shall show, is no longer related to an area between art and spectator, but *either* will describe the subjective state of mind of the consumer *or* will be the means whereby the work of art is made adequate to its model, and will thus be the work's truth.

It is as if Abbé Dubos, publishing his *Réflexions critiques sur la poésie et sur la peinture* in 1719, foresaw this development. For his whole aesthetic is designed to relate the work of art and the consumer without recourse to a theory of illusion, and without setting up the work as an object (this is typical of post-1750 aesthetics).

Yet he accepts neither the theories of alluring fiction, nor the explanation of pleasure in poetry as residing in 'difficulté vaincue', which was typical of his contemporaries.[36] Dubos denies the validity of the specialist's judgement in poetry and refuses thus the current definition of pleasure in art as the connoisseur's appreciation of technical matters. His sarcasms about the use of geometrical principles in matters of taste become clichés in the 1730s with Cartaud de la Vilate and Rémond de Saint Mard. He takes art seriously (unlike his contemporaries, La Motte and Fontenelle, whose aesthetics are fundamentally trivial). For him its hold on the consumer derives from its correspondence to a basic human need for emotional stimulus: 'la nécessité d'être occupé pour fuir l'ennui [. . .], l'attrait que les movemens des passions ont pour les hommes' (Dubos, 1719, vol. I, p. 5). This postulation of disquiet in man's nature may be due to Locke's influence – there are, however, similar elements in Pascal's account of man's lack of self-sufficiency.[37] The importance of this need is proved by man's love of spectacle: gladiatorial shows, cock fights, boxing matches and gaming. Pity for the suffering of others is less a movement outwards than a variety of this search for emotional occupation: 'Cette émotion naturelle qui s'excite en nous machinalement, quand nous voyons les dangers & les malheurs des autres hommes, n'a d'autre attrait que celui d'être une passion dont les mouvemens remuent l'âme & la tiennent occupée' (Dubos, 1719, vol. I, p. 11). It is from this that the originality of Dubos' attitude stems: his insistence on art's power to move does not coincide with the concept of 'content', for art's effect, both of matter and means, has been interiorised.[38] The effect of this interiorisation is to combine in one the movements of involvement and distance which constitute two phases of his contemporaries' account of art, and which, as we have seen, were already current in seventeenth-century analyses:

Enfin plus les actions que la Poësie & la Peinture nous dépeignent, auroient fait souffrir en nous l'humanité si nous les avions vuës véritablement, plus les imitations que ces Arts nous en présentent ont de pouvoir sur nous pour nous attacher. Ces actions, dit tout le monde, sont des sujets heureux. Un charme secret nous attache donc sur les imitations que les Peintres & les Poëtes en sçavent faire, dans le temps même que la nature témoigne par un frémissement intérieur qu'elle se soulève contre son propre plaisir. (Dubos, 1719, vol. I, p. 2)

The oscillation is here, but not between faculties, nor between truth and falsehood, as in most earlier and contemporary theory; it is part of the quality of the reaction. The pain and pleasure are seen as a kind of emotion of the second degree. They form a kind of patina over all other emotions. And since pain and pleasure refer emotion to the self, the effect is to inject consciousness of self into all emotional reaction. This will be powerfully developed by later writers and attacked by Kant (see below, p. 277). As a result, in a way that will be typical of much of the century, judgement, emotion and sensation are conflated: emotional activity is accompanied by sensation (the ambiguity in 'sentir'). The manifestations of emotion which induce awareness explain the century's later concern with blushes, tears and faints. For Dubos, 'Les poëmes & les tableaux ne sont de bons ouvrages qu'à proportion qu'ils nous émeuvent & qu'ils nous attachent' (Dubos, 1719, vol. II, p. 305).

Il est en nous un sens destiné pour juger du mérite de ces ouvrages, qui con-

> siste en l'imitation des objets touchants dans la nature. Ce sens est le sens même qui auroit jugé de l'objet que le Peintre, le Poëte ou le Musicien ont imité. [. . .] Lors qu'il s'agit de connaître si l'imitation qu'on nous présente dans un poëme est capable d'exciter la compassion & d'attendrir, le sens destiné pour en juger est le sens même qui auroit été attendri, c'est le sens qui auroit jugé de l'objet imité. [. . .] C'est enfin ce qu'on appelle communément le sentiment. (Dubos, 1719, vol. II, pp. 307–8)[39]

Emotion, sensation and judgement are here conflated. (Dubos balances this conflation with an interesting social account of judgement: individual and perhaps eccentric judgements make up a consensus which is refined by succeeding generations.)[40]

What then is the distinction between art and life? For this account of subjectivity as a kind of necessary instability of the emotions takes no account of the differences in what provokes emotion. Art seems to be like a narcotic: it enables the passions to be exercised without the dangers which attend such exercise in real life. Although Dubos speaks of 'passions artificielles' the distinction he makes is not qualitative but quantitative: the most perfect imitation has not the force and effectiveness which is to be found in the real object.[41] This distinction foreshadows, perhaps influences, Hume's criterion of differentiation between unreality and reality (see above, pp. 31–2). Dubos underpins his position with the old hierarchy of faculties: '[. . .] l'impression faite par l'imitation n'est pas sérieuse, d'autant qu'elle ne va point jusqu' à l'âme, pour laquelle il n'y a point d'illusion dans ces sensations' (Dubos, 1719, vol. I, p. 25). In later editions he substitutes 'raison' for 'âme'. But this is a fragile distinction. It is given substance, and the rejection of illusion as a mistake is made possible, by the spectator function which for Dubos structures the experience of art as it does that of parts of life. The spectator's emotions are not those of the characters he watches, but slightly different: shot through with a kind of muffled self-consciousness, combined perhaps with pleasure at their final safety (here are the beginnings of the aesthetics of torture, to be developed by others before Sade). 'Des personnes d'esprit ont cru que l'illusion fut la première cause du plaisir que nous donnent les spectacles & les tableaux [. . .]. Cette opinion me paroît insoutenable' (Dubos, 1719, vol. I, p. 62). He admits that we can mistake art for reality, occasionally, through naivety or inattention, but goes against his contemporaries when he denies that such mistakes are the source of our pleasure. We know that we are going to see a play; the poster has told us so. We can voluntarily control the extent of our involvement: 'Le Peintre & le

Poëte ne nous affligent qu'autant que nous le voulons, ils ne nous font aimer leurs Héros & leurs Héroïnes qu'autant qu'il nous plaît' (Dubos, 1719, vol. i, p. 28). Dubos does not accept that our feelings are derived from an identification with the characters, because he is concerned to keep a notion of cartharsis: 'Nôtre âme demeure toujours la maîtresse de ces émotions superficielles que les vers & les tableaux excitent en elle' (Dubos, 1719, vol. i, p. 30).[42]

Dubos is the first clearly and expressly to separate illusion as a mistake from other, more mixed forms of the consumer's adherence to art. But if he has expelled illusion as a mistake, he introduces closely related concepts: 'C'est la nature elle-même que la Peinture met sous nos yeux. Si notre esprit n'y est pas trompé, nos sens du moins y sont abusez [. . .]. Il semble même que l'œil ébloui par l'ouvrage d'un grand Peintre croïe quelque fois apercevoir du mouvement dans ses figures' (Dubos, 1719, vol. i, pp. 376–7). In discussing how the same tragedy can be seen twice, Dubos says: 'Nôtre memoire paroît donc suspendue au spectacle' (Dubos, 1719, vol. i, p. 278).[43] Why is it that, illusion having been dismissed, there is this back-door entry, so to speak, of closely related concepts? A possible objection to his account of reality as having greater effect than art is still life painting, where 'Nous donnons plus d'attention à des fruits & à des animaux représentés dans un tableau, que nous n'en donnerions à ces objets mêmes.' He answers this by arguing that we attend merely to the artist's work:

En distinguant l'attention qu'on donne à l'art d'avec celle qu'on donne à l'objet imité, on trouvera toûjours que j'ai raison d'avancer que l'imitation ne fait jamais sur nous plus d'impression que l'objet imité en pourroit faire. Cela est vray même en parlant des tableaux, qui sont prétieux par le mérite seul de l'exécution. L'Art de la Peinture est si difficile, il nous attaque par un sens, dont l'empire sur nôtre âme est si grand, qu'un tableau peut plaire par les seuls charmes de l'exécution, indépendamment de l'objet qu'il représente: mais nôtre attention & nôtre estime sont alors uniquement pour l'art de l'imitateur qui sçait nous plaire même sans nous toucher. Nous admirons le pinceau qui a sçu contrefaire si bien la nature. Nous examinons comment l'Artisan a fait pour tromper nos yeux, au point de leur faire prendre des couleurs couchées sur une superficie pour de véritables fruits. (Dubos, 1719, vol. i, pp. 623–4)

In low genre painting, emotion cannot be held to be transmitted automatically by subject matter, with the result that 'illusion' is used to mediate the transformation of physical qualities into effect on the senses. There is a similar reintroduction of illusion or related

41

concepts in discussing theatre: 'C'est suivant l'exactitude de la vraisemblance que nous nous laissons séduire plus ou moins par l'imitation' (Dubos, 1719, vol. I, p. 176). But why is *vraisemblance* demanded in art and not in nature? Some concept linking the formal qualities of art to its effect on the consumer is needed; and this becomes plain in Dubos' discussion of the highly implausible French opera:

Enfin les sens sont si flatez par le chant des recits, par l'harmonie qui les accompagne [. . .] que l'âme qui se laisse facilement séduire à leur plaisir veut bien estre enchantée par une fixion dont l'illusion est palpable, pour ainsi dire *Ex voluptate fides nascitur*. (Dubos, 1719, vol. I, p. 671)

Where the whole of art's effect is considered in terms of the inter-iorisation of psychological effect, the problem of how this occurs can be ignored. But when such apparently trivial or implausible works as still life painting or French opera are considered, the problem of the nature of our attention to them can no longer be bypassed. Later chapters will confirm the importance of this type of art in the development of concepts of illusion. Dubos has the converse problem to that of Ricardou: the latter, considering the effect in terms of its exteriorisation, needed some account of how a text can be *read at all*. The eighteenth-century writer dispenses with illusion only to fall back on related concepts. If the specific solution of the mistake is rejected, *tromper nos yeux*, *séduire*, are used instead (compare Kristeva's use of *sens* and *vraisemblance* discussed above, p. 6). Dubos' rejection of illusion is no less vigor-ous than Ricardou's. It is no more successful. All this suggests a certain stability in the framework which makes illusion a problem.

'Illusion' and the eighteenth century

'Illusion' as an aesthetic term is new in the eighteenth century, or rather the intensity and statistical frequency of its use are new. Seventeenth-century critics oppose it to *vraisemblance* as opera is opposed to tragedy, for it has magical and subjective connotations incompatible with a rational and social norm. During the eight-eenth century, however, it swallows up *vraisemblance*, so that the latter is held to be a precondition for illusion rather than to be opposed to it. But 'illusion' problematises the nature of our atten-tion to art; it problematises the nature of the appearances of art, where *vraisemblance* assumes them. It forces upon us the question: are we taken in by appearances, or do we lend ourselves to them? And the appearances of what? The eighteenth century answers the questions in terms of involvement and awareness: we are involved in art – sometimes to the point of a mistake – and we are aware of the art. 'Illusion' will either cover the whole experience, the two parts being complementary and the mind oscillating between them (bimodal); or illusion will be applied to only one pole of the experience, which will never be contaminated by an awareness that art is art (bipolar). The century's grapplings with these problems have intrinsic interest.

But this book has a larger thesis. 'Illusion', through its derivation from magic, optics and epistemology, carries into art a change in the concept of likeness in general, from *aletheia* to *adequatio*, from appearing to seeming, from dissimulation to simulation, from appearance to replica. This book seeks to show how the logical structure of 'likeness', the opposition between *aletheia* and *adequatio*, receives particular historical definition from the term 'illusion'; and it is indeed under the aegis of the term that the change in the concept of likeness takes place. As a result, the historical definition of *adequatio* has been irremediably altered by the term 'illusion'. The study of the term may give precision to this historical change, yet the scope of the investigation must be widened to include signs and consequences of this change. The most striking of these is the change in the type of consciousness allowed to the consumer. The retraction of 'illusion' from a containing of awareness to its exclusion both implies and entails a development of a new demarcation between subject and object. Less and less does the consumer apprehend the work dually, as appearance and something behind appearance; he is increasingly reduced to a single, sometimes immobile, point of view. Yet if the spectator is more and more reduced to an internal, even private, view point, the work of art, correlatively, is seen as external, as an object. It 'replicates' its model, it is no longer an intersubjective 'relaying' of appearance, but a copy. These two opposed positionings of the spectator and object are expressed theoretically, as I shall show. But what exactly that theory means within any one art can be established only by looking at artistic practice: different works allow and suggest different relations between subject and object. An examination of the relation between theory and practice is thus central to this book.

The two varieties of relation between consumer and work, *aletheia* and *adequatio*, imply, as I have already suggested, two attitudes to truth: the first that a likeness can be true *and* not true, the second that it must be true *or* false. These two attitudes can once again be related to artistic practice, to the form of the works. In the first, in order to obtain both appearance and what the appearance is of, the form will have to be that of imbrication: both the work as work and the work as 'reality' will have to be included. In the second, the form can be that of reversal. What is presented is *either* real *or* not real; it cannot be both at the same time.

The positioning of spectator and object, and the form are all indicators of the fundamental change in aesthetic concepts in the eighteenth century. 'Illusion' in the earlier part of the century was an intersubjective game. The Kantian separation of categories was not needed, since if intellectually the reality of truth and art were interwoven, for the consumer their practical separation was real enough. But by the end of the century, illusion has hardened: it has become either the designation of a private state of mind, which can be true or false, or the designation of the art object as a copy, true or false to a model. It is this movement which enables the establishment in the nineteenth century of the notion of aesthetic experience as essentially private, as having the same kind of intimate uniqueness as the experience of love or death; but it is also what sets up the modern concept of the art object. What had been a mediate area, a twilight zone between subject and object, is carved up into an experience seen as private and an object which is external. Only the greatest modern thinkers in aesthetics – Kant, Schiller, Hegel – relate these divided areas dialectically. This process was clearly begun before the eighteenth century. 'Illusion', in that it crystallised the movement clearly, perhaps crudely, hastened its completion. The effect, as I shall show, was a revision of the hierarchy of the arts: music, apparently the most subjective, becomes *the* art *par excellence*; correspondingly, increasingly rigorous demands for 'objectivity' were made of other arts, of painting, of the theatre, demands which led both to the movement later called realism and to the invention of the camera.

It is this process that the sequence of the chapters in this book attempts to demonstrate. In such areas as painting and the theatre, the work becomes an 'object': it comes gradually to be thought of as a replica of some preexisting bit of the material or social world. Correspondingly, the relation of the spectator will be reduced to that of the *voyeur*, his experience dependent on his being 'situated' by the play or painting. But in considering the work of the actor and the effect of poetry and music, the experience of art becomes an *internal* replica (in the actor's case), or an experience radically internal, personal and even fantastic.

Part One

ILLUSION AND ART: FROM THE TRUTH OF IMITATION TO THE IMITATION OF TRUTH

I have shown that Baroque perspectival art seems to induce a mistake about the status of what is seen. It is a mistake which, far from effacing the opposition between illusion and truth, by its very momentariness sharpens it: the fragility of the appearance suggests that what is seen can lead on to what is beyond appearance. Appearance does not then coincide with falsity or with truth; it allows us to glimpse something beyond itself – the mechanism I have called *aletheia*. But whether in perspective or in philosophy, the fixed point from which this can occur is always there – the top of the visual pyramid, or the *Cogito*. Yet in the nearly contemporaneous theory of art, in Poussin, Fréart de Chambray and Félibien, neither the word 'illusion' nor what I shall term its satellite concepts have any real place: these critics are all, on the contrary, concerned with adequation, not to the natural, but to an idealised norm.*

Later, with the *coloriste* reaction, and in particular with the work, at the turn of the century, of the great art critic Roger de Piles, a range of concepts close to illusion – its satellites – is used. And after 1740, 'illusion' itself is part of the common furniture of painting theory.

---

* Whereas Vasari, for instance, constantly uses the approach to the natural as a gauge of painting's success. See, among many other passages, the Introduction to the Second Part of the Lives (Vasari, 1890, vol. I, p. 312).

1
ILLUSION AND THE ROCOCO: THE IDEA OF *PAPILLOTAGE*

The language of illusion

Within the purlieus of 'illusion' and its satellite concepts, what I have called the bimodal and the bipolar analyses of art coexist. Yet such satellites as 'tromper les yeux', 'séduire', 'flatter les yeux' in particular contain a reference within themselves to an awareness of art as the artificial. The phrase 'tromper les yeux' used by Roger de Piles in particular, is set implicitly against the notion of 'tromper l'esprit' and thus embodies a distinction between perceptual and cognitive deceit. This distinction serves in fact to resituate the painting as a sensuous appearance between reality and the spectator, rather than abolishing it through concern for the norm (as in Fréart de Chambray or Félibien).

1 Bimodal

In bimodal illusion, involvement and awareness coexist within an experience. It is the satellite terms which tend to be used to express this coexistence. They can do this because, while close in meaning to a mistake, they yet contain within themselves a reference to an awareness of art as artificial. The phrase 'tromper les yeux' embodies a distinction between perceptual and cognitive 'tromperie' which in fact refers to the existence of the painting between spectator and reality. Piles, for instance, writes: 'Les autres Arts ne font que réveiller l'idée des choses absentes, au lieu que la Peinture les supplée entièrement & les rend présentes par son essence qui ne consiste pas seulement à plaire aux yeux mais à les tromper' (Piles, 1708, p. 41), and Coypel: 'Le principal est de tromper' (Coypel, 1721, pp. 155–6). Other terms – 'tromper agréablement', 'séduire', 'flatter', 'imposer', – function likewise in contexts close to that of 'illusion', yet all have a meaning more complex than that of mere mistake. They seem to derive from a fusion operated in the later seventeenth century, within the term 'illusion', of the discoveries in optics and the theories of *amour propre*. Malebranche, for example in *De la recherche de la vérité* (1674), places on a par perceptual illusions and intellectual errors engendered by passion and self-love, and by the errors of the imagination. Though *amour propre* is narcissistic, its self-awareness is not total (hence its use, also, by La Rochefoucauld). The transfer of 'illusion' from morals to aesthetics brings with it the idea that the spectator is an accomplice in his own illusion. Art imposes on him, yet he collaborates in his own deception: 'Ces deux sœurs [la peinture et la sculpture] ont toujours marché sur les mêmes traces, leur but de tout temps, par une parfaite imitation de la nature a été de séduire nos yeux et de les tromper agréablement' (Dézallier d'Argenville, 1745, vol. I, p. i). The sexualised metaphor, 'séduire', reveals, that the capture of the spectator occurs with his complaisance,[1] an ambiguity explored by certain eighteenth-century novels; and this pattern is reiterated, though restricted to the sense of touch, by the metaphor 'flatter'. '[La peinture et la poèsie] excitent en nous une sensation si flatteuse et nous trompent si agréablement que nous croyons voir [. . .] respirer la toile' (Du Perron, 1758, pp. 42–3).[2] The pliability of the spectator corresponds to that of the painting, seen as yielding to all wishes: 'Livré aux illusions d'un art aimable qui se prête à tous ses désirs' (Laugier, 1771, p. 31); 'Peinture enchanteresse, Art séduisant, c'est vous qui trompez nos yeux par cette magie qui nous fait jouir de la présence des objects trop éloignés ou qui ne sont plus: vivez, Peintres charmans, qui vous plaisez à nous rapeller les souvenirs de quelqu'uns de ces momens heureux' (Rouquet, 1755, pp. 30–1).[3] The spectator 'forgets himself', is 'ravished' (Saint Yves, 1748, pp. 83–4)[4] – yet a conditional tense may indicate consciousness on the part of the writer that self-indulgence in vicarious experience may play a role: 'L'illusion est la même pour une mouche qui est peinte sur le fond du Tableau, & qu'on seroit tenté de chasser' (Estève, 1753b, p. xx).[5] Lucretius in *De rerum naturae* had already based the pity felt for a ship in a storm on the spectator's relief at not being directly concerned in the disaster, that is, on what for the eighteenth century was *amour propre*. Critics take this up in a purely aesthetic context, *à propos* of a seascape by Joseph Vernet:

On est effrayé du temps orageux & de la tempête qui y est admirablement dépeinte. L'Illusion se trouve portée si loin, qu'on ne peut s'empêcher de craindre pour les bâtiments qu'on voit en mer. On éprouve des mouvemens de commisération et de pitié à la vue de ce spectacle effrayant dont on partage l'horreur & en effet le tableau, l'image disparoît & la nature reste dans un appareil bien terrible. (*Mercure*, octobre 1757, vol. II, pp. 164–5)

Here the phrase 'ne peut s'empêcher' expresses in antiphrasis the half-aware complicity. Elsewhere a directly reflexive element is introduced: 'L'âme se [complaît] dans la sensation qu'elle éprouve' (Le Blanc, 1747, p. 154). The spectator consents to the deception: 'Nous nous laissons tromper volontairement mais agréablement [. . .] nos yeux et nos esprits y sont si fort attachés que nous voulons nous persuader que les corps peints respirent & que les fictions sont des vérités' (Piles in Meusnier de Querlon, 1753, pp. 76–7).[6] And this aesthetic complicity is described in the hack phrase of the eighteenth century as 'se prêter à l'illusion'.[7]

2 Bipolar

Bipolar illusion insists that the consumer makes a mistake about what he sees, be it only momentarily. This position raises conceptual difficulties which do not arise within the semantic field of the satellite terms, precisely because they incorporate different varieties of awareness. Such is not the case with what may be called 'hard' illusion. A mistake about the nature of what is seen must totally exclude awareness and thus pleasure too. For this reason writers reverse Dubos' psychological schema, where the senses may be deceived but not the reason, and speak of 'une illusion que la raison, pour ainsi dire, ne trouble pas' (Le Blanc, 1747, p. 152). Faced with the undeniable fact that art is enjoyed, it may be described as succeeding illusion (Dézallier d'Argenville, 1745, vol. I, p. iii) or may be distributed to different classes of spectator – awareness to the connoisseur, illusion to the naive (Caylus, 1910, p. 138). Only La Font de Saint Yenne can integrate pleasure into illusion by describing it as of two kinds: immediate enjoyment of the object painted and mediate appreciation of the painted object.[8]

Theorists who think in terms of 'hard' illusion do not merely have trouble with the idea of aesthetic pleasure: they face considerable difficulties in accounting for artistic practice. 'Illusion' as a mistake means that the deceived spectator is unaware of the artist's merits: Liotard (anticipating in reverse Magritte's picture *Le Bon Sens*) recounts an anecdote in which a woman takes a painted bunch of grapes to be real, and to have been framed for a joke. Moreover it is hardly possible to maintain that one whole branch of the plastic arts – that is sculpture – can produce illusion, and sculpture is accordingly decried or pitied for its lack of colour. Yet Caylus points out that coloured statues create no illusion at all (Caylus, 1910, p. 192):[9] what should have destroyed the notion that the spectator's reaction is a mistake, is adduced instead to break up the correlation commonly made between illusion and perfect imitation.

I have separated out features which in eighteenth-century aesthetics coexist and overlap, masking the conceptual difficulties which accompany 'hard' illusion. If I have thus artificially skeined out strands, it is to show more clearly the historical shift which occurs from 'soft' to 'hard', from bimodal to bipolar. Illusion as a mistake, as a homogeneous experience, tends to replace the interplay inherent in the earlier concept. The rest of Part I will show how this is part of a conscious movement, in the art of the time as in its theory: illusion is used as a tool in the replacement of the work of art as representation by the work of art as replica. 'Illusion' in fact comes to mean a kind of naturalism. It certainly did not start that way.

'Soft' illusion and the Rococo

An analysis of the terms of 'soft' illusion would remain abstract unless they could be related to the contemporary art. The illusion which contains consciousness within itself is described by concepts borrowed from the sublime. The spectator is 'surprised', 'struck', 'transported', all terms which, like the related 'séduire', imply a resistance within the spectator which is then overcome by art's force. The sensation of internal resistance being vanquished by an external power is amazement, and is followed by a satisfaction which constitutes a return to rest: 'La Peinture fait paroître au Sens de la Vue les Objets de la Nature avec tant de Perfection, qu'il en est souvent surpris & l'entendement satisfait' (Gautier d'Agoty, 1753, p. 226, quoting the painter Noel Coypel). The movement between surprise and satisfaction when reiterated becomes a 'jeu clos' capable of infinite repetition within dimensions limited by the necessary return to the beginning of the cycle. The mirrors which play such an important part in the interior decoration of the first half of the century are described as provoking just such a movement: 'L'important prestige de plusieurs glaces qui ne font que répéter jusqu'à la satiété les objets qu'on a sous les yeux' (Laugier, 1771, p. 254; cf. Du Perron, 1758, p. 70). As *amour propre* and its illusion fragment the ego, reflect and trap it, so the mirrors fragment and reflect the room, and in the arabesques of the style of the 1730s, the asymmetrical decoration is complemented by the mir-

rors which start ever-new cycles of repetition: 'La symmétrie en est
bannie. La composition & l'élégance des ornements n'ont jamais
rien offert de plus satisfaisant: idées riantes que la magie des glaces
répète encore, & semble multiplier à l'infini.' The actual carved
ribbons and decorative mouldings multiply and yet repeat the same
motif 'dont le plus grand charme est de n'avoir ni commencement
ni fin' (Blondel, 1774, vol. I, pp. 90, 104; cf. Starobinski, 1964, pp.
39–41). With this infinity of facets, the mind is caught for a
moment in the mirror's space but then makes an inevitable return
to rest, and to the mirror's surface.

In the same way, repetition and fragmentation bring the
spectator back to the surface of the painting. For the paintings used
above doors and wall panels may represent a garden, or the open
air and the flight of birds: the illusion is a reference outwards, is
something the wall is not (Le Camus, 1780, pp. 118–19), and inevitably the gaze, penetrating apparently into space beyond, rests
in fact on the surface and is caught within the room's limits. Surface
and depth succeed and interpenetrate; like Charles Bovary's cap,
the trivial becomes infinitely fascinating; art refers away, it
dissimulates its own flatness which it yet finally reveals (this movement is the contrary of *aletheia*). This experience is conceptualised
by a series of terms – 'piquant', 'assaisonné', 'singulier' – which all
combine the notion of the stimulant and the trivial. Such terms
express the love of novelty and of detail which is characteristic of
the taste of the period in the early half of the century; the
preference for porcelain figures, for small bronzes, not massive
marble, shows the interest in the small scale, and the countless
paintings of the elements, or the seasons, express practically the
taste for the cyclic, for the movement outward, and the return to
rest. It seems as if the vocabulary of bimodal illusion can be directly
related to the movement of art called 'goût pittoresque', the great
exponents of which in the 1720s and 1730s were Meissonnier and
Oppenord,[10] and which is thus defined by Coypel: 'Un choix piquant et singulier des effets de la Nature assaisonné de l'esprit et du
goût & soutenu par la raison' (Coypel, 1721, p. 13). The 'piquant'
may in the art object take the form of a striking asymmetry: of a
conflict between material and the use to which it is put, as shown,
for instance, in Meissonnier's silverware for the Duke of Kingston,
crowned with silver lobsters. Or, as in many of Hogarth's
engravings, it may take the form of a constant irritation created by
the complex web of detail to be interpreted,[11] or, on the contrary,
an outrageous novelty and a use of ornament which flouts tradi-

tion, refuses to be a sign, and thus flaunts its own ornamental quality, its own triviality: 'Des ornements qui n'étoient que des ornements, se succédoient les uns aux autres, entremêlés avec des
dragons, des palmettes, des chauve-souris [. . .]' (Blondel, 1774,
vol. I, p. 54). The sun, a metaphor of Louis XIV's radiance, is
replaced by the bat, decorative filigree: again, complexity and
triviality are linked, formal complexity and a refusal of meaning,
or, at any rate, of 'profundity'. Just as the sudden surprise is a
movement outwards and a return to rest, the references refer
finally not outwards to the signified, but to the reality of the sign:
they return to the beginning of the process of interpretation; they
insist on their own lack of meaning.

But this structure of consciousness, called 'piquant' or 'singulier'
in the 'goût pittoresque', is associated with another, slightly
different one. For the filigree of irritation created by formal or
interpretative complexity implies a to-and-fro movement. This
type of intricacy is called by the critics *papillotage*, and the word,
stripped of its pejorative implications, epitomises the art of the first
part of the century. For it expresses both the gaze, the acceptance
of the object seen, and the blink which cuts off the eye from contact
with the world and, in so doing, brings the self back to self. In terms
of colour it forces the eye to move: Caylus, attacking *papillotage*,
says:

Il est difficile de concevoir comment on s'abandonne à des couleurs qui ne
vont point ensemble ou qui détournent l'œil de la figure principale ou de
l'objet dominant, qui l'empêchent d'être conduit sans révolte, sans obstacle [. . .] ces faux réveillans ainsi déplacés sont autant d'instrumens d'un
concert qui en interrompent le bel effet et qui désespèrent l'auditeur.
(Caylus, 1910, pp. 142–3)[12]

The *papillotage* of Rococo painting is quite expressly set up as
the visual version of the techniques of interruption used in narrative by Scarron (and, one might add, by Diderot). Le Camus, for
example, writes:

Toute forme étoit permise; pourvu qu'elle papillotât, on étoit content:
point d'harmonie, point d'accord, point de simétrie [. . .]. Une plante
Chinoise, nom qu'on donnoit à un ornement qu'on ne pouvoit définir, &
dont le hazard seul de la coupe du bois faisoit naître l'idée, rallioit des
moulures & faisoit des milieux: enfin, plus un ornement paroissoit s'écarter de la forme naturelle, plus il sembloit précieux: tels ont été dans la
peinture les égarements où sont tombés les *Vatteau*, les *Callot*, & dans la
Littérature ce genre burlesque qui mit en vogue *Scarron* & ceux qui l'imi-
tèrent. (Le Camus, 1780, p. 53)

Boucher, too, illustrates this lack of relation. His work lacks 'ces analogies fines et déliées qui appelent sur la toile les objets, et qui les y lient par des fils imperceptibles' (Diderot, *Salon de 1765*, p. 76). *Papillotage*, whether of colour or of subject, involves rapid movements of the eye, and rapid changes of reaction: in other words, involves fragmentation of the spectator's attention, a flickering of illusion and awareness. Dandré Bardon gives the following account of a bas-relief by Le Gros:

Des travaux variés & finis, des piquans répandus, des noirs fouillés dans les objets des premiers sites, un Faire sçavamment négligé & presque effacé, des légéretés, des indécisions ménagées avec adresse dans les parties fuyantes, l'embelissement des graces de la vérité. On croit voir l'air rouler autour des corps & tous les corps se mouvoir dans les airs. Quelle magie produit une illusion plus séduisante? N'est-ce pas l'industrie, avec laquelle on expose les différens reliefs, qui prête le mouvement aux objets? Sans doute l'œil attiré successivement sur les divers points présentés par la rondeur des figures *croit voir en elles l'action qu'il se donne pour en parcourir les beautés.* Tel le voyageur du sein d'un navire croit appercevoir les bords de la Mer fuir loin de lui, tandis que c'est lui-même qui s'en éloigne. (Dandré Bardon, 1765, vol. II, pp. 57–8)

Similarly, Coypel speaks earlier of 'indécisions', 'une élégance de forme pour ainsi dire incertaine, ondoyante, et semblable à la flamme' (Coypel, 1721, p. 74). In such cases the flickering of colour, the serpentine line, are linked with an intellectual uncertainty, a development of 'le je ne sais quoi' conceptualised by Piles in 1707, and Richardson in 1715, as 'grâce'.

Such art is bitterly attacked by the new generation of theorists, who start work around 1750, and by Falconet, Grimm and Diderot in particular. The contrasts which break up the spectator's attention forestall any deep impression on him,[13] because they avoid straightforward expression of emotion. Grimm compares Boucher to French opera, where a lover's joy at a *rendez-vous* is expressed by dancers dancing the 'rigaudon'.[14] The same critics use and reuse the anecdote of Fontenelle's question to the sonata – 'Sonate, que me veux-tu?' – not merely of French music, but of French Rococo painting. The painter is not to furnish his painting with figures like a decorator: 'Il faut que ces figures s'y placent d'elles-mêmes, comme dans la nature [. . .] sans quoi je dirai comme Fontenelle à la sonate: "Figure, que me veux-tu?" ' (Diderot, *Essais sur la peinture*, p. 717; cf. *Salon de 1765*, p. 76). Diderot links the fragmented impression created by such an art with the fashionable fragmentation of apartments, and with the taste of the *fermiers-généraux* (Diderot, *Salon de 1767*, pp. 56, 318).

The master of *papillotage* is Boucher, the painter of the *petits-maîtres*. His subjects are conventional or extravagant: 'Quel tapage d'objets disparates', remarks Diderot with disgust. But Boucher, Diderot recognises, is an artist's painter through his technique, for he has gone far in surmounting the 'difficultés de l'art'. The events he paints are for the most part as unreal as his colour. Diderot satirically makes him say: 'Je ne me suis pas soucié d'être vrai. Je peins un événement fabuleux avec un pinceau romanesque' (Diderot, *Salon de 1763*, p. 205; cf. *Salon de 1761*, p. 112). For Diderot, Boucher has turned arbitrariness into a technique. Boucher's talent for apparently capricious changes in colour, in perspective, could be exploited by spectacular opera. He in fact worked regularly as a decorator, and in 1748 he created for the opera *Atys*

une voute d'eau qui jouoit perpétuellement avec les colomnes de l'édifice [. . .]. L'éclat de sa lumière porté dans le fonds, refletant sur les cascades, tandisque le devant de la Décoration entretenu dans un ton plus mate [*sic*] donnoit un beau repos à la vûe: ces colomnes à moitié taillées dans le Roc, ornées de coquillages & d'une prodigieuse variété de plantes marines, formoient un pictoresque admirable. (Baillet de Saint Julien, 1749, p. 50)

But the 'goût pittoresque' is not serious. La Font de Saint Yenne attacks those who find poetry in Boucher's paintings: 'Si cette poësie consiste à rassembler tous les lieux communs des poëtes et des peintres, tel que des Néreides, des Nayades, des Tritons [. . .] attributs qui ne demandent que de la mémoire, j'avoue que le Sr. Boucher est un grand poëte. Mais si la poësie est un feu divin [. . .]' (La Font de Saint Yenne, 1754, pp. 40–1).[15] He reveals how for the new generation of critics 'poetry' is an equivalent of 'subject matter' and, in a precise sense, of 'meaning'. For Boucher's mythologies or pastorals have no meaning beyond the sensations they evoke. Planes slip into each other and decorative use of colour emphasises surface; as in certain works of Rubens, the paintings seem to consist entirely in sensation – but where the Rubens is about sensation, Boucher uses it. Light flickers and reverberates in some of the greatest canvases, in the *Rising and Setting of the Sun*, for instance, where sea and pale flesh whirl in a spiral constructed by the interplay of light and shade – and where the middle is empty, the picture being spun out from the central void. The sweetness derives from Correggio, the master of Boucher, whose smooth scale of colours is enormously admired: 'Charmant [. . .] tendre et suave [. . .] tout y est mœlleux et fondu' (Coypel, 1721, p. 40); but in general his eighteenth-century admirers, like Boucher, heighten the ambiguity of the treatment of subject or sharpen the sense of modulation through steps of the scale. Thus Boucher's sensuality is developed out of Correggio's 'suavity', and Fragonard's 'fouillis' whips up the master's textures into touches of paint which writhe and swirl on the canvas with the energy of his pale lovers rushing to reach the fountain of Love, in the painting of that name.

Hogarth establishes an explicit analogy between riddling complexity and that formal intricacy which is the cause of grace (Hogarth, 1955, p. 41). The discontinuous flickerings of sensation expressed by *papillotage*, transposed in terms of form or composition rather than of brush-work, become a slower serpentine movement in Watteau and later in Hogarth. The analogue of strong contrasts which yet glide one into the other is the rainbow.[16] In Hogarth, the discrete parts, necessary for variety, are thus integrated into a sinuous whole, stimulating the eye to follow it.[17] Hogarth's aesthetics, in the *Analysis of Beauty*, are based on the wavy line, freely drawn, and on the pyramid, a constructed figure. This contrast appears in his pictures, with their sturdy construction which bounds the careful differentiation of facial and gestural expression, the enigmatic complexity of their references, and the sinuous curves (magnificently brought together in, for instance, *Actresses rehearsing in a Barn*). The mind, led on by the contrasting curves, is stopped short by the referential enigma, and is brought back to rest by the planned structure. His work appears to induce movement, not of the eye, but of the mind, between the seen and the sign.

Watteau, earlier, operates differently. His figures turning or moving on different axes create a complex space, a projection of the lines of their gestures (compare Hogarth's notion of space, which is that it is created by a line enclosing volume), but a space often curiously extended into the receding distance: many figures are seen from the back. The dance, used by Hogarth only as an example of his serpentine line, was the central figure for many of Watteau's paintings. In Watteau's *Enseigne de Gersaint* the graceful attitudes thread like a ribbon across the canvas; there is an extraordinary and unemphatic grip on reality – the boy, the dog, the references (a portrait of Louis XIV is being put away by one of the shop boys), the box-stage construction – all seem to prefigure Hogarth. But the differences are here all-important. For Watteau places in the very centre of the painting, which is constructed in two vertical halves (this construction is emphasised by the fact that the painting was later cut in half), an opening backwards, out of the shop darkened by pictures, towards windows and light. Two varieties of space are created: the figures, two triangles on either side, are within a series of frames formed by the street, the shop front, and the door behind. Watteau elaborates his previous contrast between garden statues and living figures. Here the quietly real clients, soberly dressed in blacks and greys, and the shop assistant look at a most magnificent collection of pictures: what might be a Titian portrait on the left, a Rubens *Silenus* on the right, Dutch landscapes, a Settecento *Holy Family* – an unlikely collection for Gersaint, surely, this *summa* of art. This is no trap-like use of the frame form of the picture as in so many Dutch paintings of drinkers or musicians at windows. Instead the relay of frames – street, shop, door at the back – forces us to move between the appearances and the appearance of the appearance, between painted masterpieces and Watteau's figures, the juxtaposition of which surely represents a dying man's claim to his own achievement: *a-letheia*, the not forgetting, the cancelling of oblivion. Watteau is the great master of the incorporation of the awareness of appearance, and the 'relay' of appearance, into the heart of the painting.

Watteau achieves this depth by contrasting 'painted nature' and 'painted paintings'. This contrast is reduced to a pirouette in theorists' writings: 'La Nature seule fait tous les frais de l'illusion' (Dandré Bardon, 1765, vol. II, p. 52); 'Ce fut l'Art qui servit alors de modèle à la Nature' (Batteux, 1746, p. 44). Not merely does the spectator's attention consist of an oscillation between illusion and awareness, the art object forces such an oscillation on the spectator and the very process of creation is described in such terms.

Diderot's demand for adequation

I have already suggested that much of Diderot's Salon criticism, like his dramatic criticism, demands that art escape this trivialising spiral. In his discussion of a painting by Vien he stabilises the succession of contrasts and eliminates *papillotage* explicit:

Et puis, une lumière douce, diffuse sur toute la composition, comme on la voit dans la nature, large, s'affaiblissant ou se fortifiant d'une manière imperceptible. Point de plaques luisantes; point de tâches noires; et avec cela une vérité et une sagesse qui vous attachent secrètement. On est au milieu de la cérémonie; on la voit, et rien ne vous détrompe [. . .]. Les natures ne sont ici ni poétiques ni grandes; c'est la chose même, sans presque aucune exagération. Ce n'est pas la manière de Rubens, ce n'est pas le goût des écoles italiennes, c'est la vérité, qui est de tous les temps et de toutes les contrées. (Diderot, *Salon de 1761*, p. 120) In a diffusion of light which is imperceptible, nature is here both reality and a norm: it is 'la chose même' between the 'poetic' Italian school and the 'low' Flemish. Again and again the *Salons* ask such questions as 'Dites-moi si l'espace que vous découvrez au-delà de ces roches n'est pas la chose qui a fixé cent fois votre attention dans la nature' (Diderot, *Salon de 1763*, p. 225). A series of questions put to Grimm in the article on Greuze of 1765 – which is strongly reminiscent of the *Question aux gens de lettres* at the end of *La Religieuse* – opposes illusion, which induces a mistake in reader or spectator, to beauty which is outside illusion. Yet this casting out of awareness from illusion, in an attempt to escape from the spiral of art and nature, in fact merely brings it back at a different level: 'Rien ne vous détrompe', says Diderot, in the passage quoted above, reintroducing the awareness through the negative.

A similar pattern of escape from and reintegration of awareness takes place with a related concept, that of the 'sublime'. In a letter about the gardens at Marly, the Rococo spiral is not criticised, but apparently cancelled: 'Mais ce passage successif de la nature à l'art, et de l'art à la nature, produit un véritable enchantement. Sortez de ce parterre où la main de l'homme et son intelligence se déployent d'une manière si exquise, et répandez-vous dans les hauteurs. C'est la solitude, le silence, le désert, l'horreur de la Thébaïde. Que cela est sublime' (Diderot, *Correspondance*, vol. IV, p. 163, septembre 1762). Yet the passage to the sublime involves the same resonance, no longer merely within art, but within an experience which contains art. The mind feels its own passivity: 'C'est alors que l'âme s'ouvre au plaisir et frissonne d'horreur. Ces sensations mêlées la tiennent dans une situation tout à fait étrange, c'est le propre du sublime de nous pénétrer d'une manière tout à fait extra-ordinaire' (Diderot, *Correspondance*, vol. IV, p. 196). That the sublime, then, unexpectedly, does not project critic and consumer into unitary feeling, but retains the oscillating structure, explains perhaps how Diderot could denounce *papillotage* and yet write *Jacques le fataliste*. Even within Diderot's art criticism there exists a tension between the theoretical demand for *adequatio*, for the creation of an art object which expels the spectator's awareness, and the actual practice which discriminates, constantly referring the painting to what it is not, and thus revealing the work of art as appearance. The striving towards the unitary, the refusal of oscillation, is undercut by a subjacent binary structure of feeling, and is at its most obvious in the pontifical Diderot, who endeavours to subdue the reader into a certain cast of feeling, when both are aware that something more complicated is at stake. However, the contradiction thus generated and usually left implicit is exemplified and deliberately explored in the article *Vernet*, in the *Salon de 1767*. The article is more than a leisurely disquisition on certain general problems, including aesthetics: for as actual critical practice it reflects in counterpoint the themes it discusses.

The article describes a series of painted landscapes as nature, in terms of an actual set of visits and walks, under the guidance of an abbé. But in the account of what is supposedly real, artistic terms are introduced. Though Vernet is never openly, perhaps never even consciously, considered as a Rococo artist, as a user of *papillotage*, there is an artificiality in his paintings which may have led Diderot constantly to play on the opposition and relation between art and nature. Is the *Vernet* article designed as a piece of bravura,[18] and as a practical joke in the manner of *La Religieuse*? The beginning is rather too quiet in its juxtaposition of artist and natural landscape: 'J'avais écrit le nom de cet artiste en haut de ma page, et j'allais vous entretenir de ses ouvrages, lorsque je suis parti pour une campagne voisine de la mer, et renommée par la beauté de ses sites.' One is aware from the beginning of the subterfuge. The spiral created by describing art in terms of nature and then the supposed nature in terms of art becomes for the reader an oscillation between an imposed naive reading and an imposed examination of that naive reading. Though not a 'mystification' there is mockery in the graduation, in the forced elegance of the steps by which the reader is made to oscillate between natural and artistic terms. His guide in the story asks him whether Vernet could have painted such a site:

Eh bien! dis-je à mon *cicerone*, allez-vous en au Salon et vous verrez qu'une imagination féconde aidée d'une étude profonde de la nature, a inspiré à un de nos artistes précisément ces rochers [. . .]. Et peut-être avec ce gros quartier de roche brute, et le pêcheur assis [. . .]. Vous ne savez pas, l'abbé, combien vous êtes un mauvais plaisant. (*Salon de 1767*, p. 130)

Mockery is also there in the threatened storm, so suitable to Vernet's seascapes, but which remains entirely conditional, entirely literary.[19] The threatened storm is described as 'poetic'. Does this imply then that the smooth passage Diderot and his guide experience is real? But the whole is an imagined incident, a story told *à propos* of an actually existing piece of paint. This resonance between different relations to the real, complicated by the difference between painting and literature, could be described by going back to the ancient meaning of 'illusion', which, as we have seen, was a rhetorical figure meaning a mocking, a making sport of. Yet the article is more than a marvellously complex and graceful structure, a game of hide-and-seek with the reader, more than a pretext for the elaboration of a series of brilliant ideas: language and the problem of its acquisition, the relation between body and brain, the instability of public opinion, the question of how to act justly in a corrupt society, the relation of morality and the individual.[20] It seems as if the article goes beyond the game with the reader, in order to burrow down to a philosophical significance which could be given to that game, to the meaning which can be given to textual practice. For the reader is made aware of his own puppet-like oscillation, and thus of the writer's freedom to impose what reactions he will. The reader's awareness in fact counterpoints the thematic treatment within the article, for this goes on to explore the relation between nature and art in terms of the opposition between necessity and freedom. The Diderot of the article describes nature as art, and the emphasised arbitrariness of the description implies the necessity of a painting, a necessity which is both formal – for art limits and selects – and causal – for the painting is created by one man. But the situation within the article is the reverse of what is really going on; what Diderot is really doing is describing a painting in terms of nature, which in turn is described as art. And this art is immediately reintegrated into nature; its necessity is neither more nor less than the necessity of the whole world. The dust storm which he and his guide are caught in, for instance, is every bit as necessary as a work of art. In this perspective, beauty is not necessity but rarity, and pride in creativity is possibly as ridiculous as pride in nature's works: both are equally necessary.

So much for the 'premier acte'. In the following conversations, eddying circles of necessity are created. Diderot and the abbé discuss the savages who take a ship's figurehead to be real, and the child who reacts vividly to every word of poem or story: these are then the victims of illusion, the victims of the artist. But the artist's trick which removes their freedom in fact cancels the Rococo spiral, the oscillation between illusion and awareness. By a reversal, the gullibility of the savage or the child becomes freedom: they have contact with immediate feeling, with natural reactions. These are unavailable to civilised man, who is bound to the city by his pleasures and his occupations (for even in the country he knows only the pleasures of society) and who proceeds to acquire landscapes and seascapes such as Vernet's, which, placed within a sumptuous frame, allow him at least a vicarious contact with spontaneous feeling – he can play the role of natural man through art. Consciousness inevitably accompanies any violent emotion in civilised man, and this is precisely what makes art possible, particularly tragic art, described as awareness of one's own safety when confronted with the (painted) peril of others.

The freedom of immediate feeling is thwarted by society, says Diderot: the genius' freedom is curbed or he is destroyed. Yet, again by the process of reversal which Diderot makes use of, freedom occurs within the deepest submission to mediocrity or mechanical reaction. Morality itself may be an arbitrary force, Diderot suggests: the laws of a being's nature are necessary, dependent on its organisation and thus ultimately on its classification in regard to other beings. (Freedom in regard to conventional morality may thus coincide with a necessary compliance to moral laws of a more fundamental kind.) Beyond the domain of society, a more far-reaching constraint on the imagination and on self-expression is exercised by the intellect, whether in the form of rough and comfortable common sense, or by reason in the form of the 'esprit philosophique'. For this is the domain of the deepest constraint, that of language which moulds reason and indeed thought itself. If thought is to be possible at all, words must be signs: yet this is precisely what cuts out immediacy of feeling, for words are a form of representation. But this abolition of a primary freedom of expression, says Diderot, renders possible a secondary creativity: the accents of the voice, like facial gestures, are unique: they allow individuality of expression, though they necessarily betray.

Art then is separate from nature, and part of nature: civilised man has escaped from her but is yet subject to her. What appears at first a trivial oscillation in the *Vernet* article is developed as a structure imbued with philosophical meaning and widened to its utmost. For the very division and reunion of the waves repeat it, and so construct man's haphazard destiny:

Je me trouvai entre des arbres et des rochers, lieu sacré par son silence et son obscurité. Je m'arrêtai là et je m'assis. J'avais à ma droite un phare qui s'élevait du sommet des rochers; il allait se perdre dans la nue et la mer en mugissant venait se briser à ses pieds. Au loin, des pêcheurs et des gens de mer étaient diversement occupés. Toute l'étendue des eaux agitées s'ouvrait devant moi; elle était couverte de bâtiments dispersés. J'en voyais s'élever au-dessus des vagues tandis que d'autres se perdaient au-dessous; chacun à l'aide de ses voiles et de sa manœuvre suivant des routes contraires quoique poussé par un même vent: image de l'homme et du bonheur, du philosophe et de la vérité. (Diderot, *Salon de 1767*, p. 146)

Art in this article refers to nature, to what is beyond itself, and of which it is yet a part. This is the structure I defined as *aletheia*. The contrary, *dissimulatio*, is explored in Diderot's adaptation of Plato's allegory of the cave in the *Salon de 1765*. This adaptation forms part of his discussion of Fragonard's *Corrésus et Callirhoé* (now in the Louvre). He recounts the painting as part of a dream, in which he and the rest of mankind imprisoned in a cave watch a magic lantern show projected by kings, priests, and politicians. For these 'artisans d'illusions' have with their puppets 'de quoi fournir à la représentation de toutes les scènes comiques, tragiques et burlesques de la vie [. . .] si naturelles, si vraies, que nous les prenions pour réelles et [. . .] tantôt nous en riions à gorge déployée, tantôt nous en pleurions à chaudes larmes' (Diderot, *Salon de 1765*, p. 189). In Platonic terms, art is twice separated from reality because it imitates the world, which is itself imitation. But in Diderot's dream, it is not shadows of reality seen in a cave, but shadows of mere puppets, a mystification. The Platonic hierarchy has been doubled back: all is dissimulation, of which art is only one kind. The very notion of the real is lost, because the reality attained by the philosopher is merely awareness of a trick. Painting (here the shadows, a Platonic word) is not different in nature from what is painted (the puppets); it is the contrary of *aletheia*. Fragonard's work is merely a 'grande machine' referring to the non-existent.

Diderot's critical practice then, in its constant play between art and nature, represents *papillotage*, however much his critical pronouncements may decry it. Yet his critical position was characteristic of the latter half of the century. The whole notion of the relation between art object and nature is changing from that of reference to that of replica.

2

ART AND REPLICA: THE
IMITATION OF TRUTH

Though critical vocabulary may waver, the bimodal account of illusion, 'soft' illusion, and the 'goût pittoresque' of artistic practice is under attack from about mid-century. A radically different account of illusion strives to exclude, not to include, consciousness: 'Que se propose la peinture? Sinon de nous donner une représentation de la chose assez vraisemblable pour que l'esprit se prenne au piège dans l'illusion et croie voir la réalité même' (Laugier, 1771, p. 84). The exclusion of awareness, it has been shown, reverses the earlier schema where the senses, but not the reason, might be deceived, and speaks of 'Une illusion que la raison, pour ainsi dire, ne trouble pas' (Le Blanc, 1747, p. 152).[1] The exclusion of awareness, the insistence on what I have called 'hard' illusion, is typical after 1750 of the *littérateurs* interested in painting – La Font de Saint Yenne, Le Blanc, Diderot. I have already suggested when considering their remarks on sculpture (see above, pp. 49–50) that their attitude is not without its difficulties. In particular, the timelessness of paintings makes it difficult to interpret them as replicas of a mobile world. Le Blanc is reduced to praising Poussin's *Death of Germanicus* because the figures could be supposed to have sat still for the time the spectator looks at the picture! (Le Blanc, 1747, pp. 149–50) For La Font de Saint Yenne, the choice of the right moment is crucial to the painter 'pour lutter avec l'immobilité de ses figures qui gardent toujours leurs mêmes positions & qui sont comme autant de statues collées sur la toile & que l'œil même ne sauroit fixer longtemps sans que l'illusion à laquelle il s'efforce de se prêter ne disparoisse' (La Font de Saint Yenne, 1754, p. 19). Such accounts of illusion lead to an impasse and Rousseau the revealer of paradoxes, or rather his 'spectre exsangue', the René of the *Histoire de Madame de Montbrillant*, points this out:

Il disait que la peinture, les tapisseries etc. étant un art d'imitation, il lui semblait absurde de mettre des personnages en tapisserie dont les pieds

Art and replica

pesaient sur les lambris: A la bonne heure, dit-il, quelques petites figurines dans le lointain d'un paysage, la perspective étant bien observée, peuvent m'entraîner et me faire illusion. Quoi, lui-dis-je, vous ne pardonnerez pas même à Poussin d'avoir placé le déluge universel dans l'espace de quatre pieds . . .! (Madame d'Epinay, 1951, vol. II, p. 403)

Cochin and illusion

Perhaps because of their 'hard' interpretation of illusion, the *littérateurs* demand stillness and dignity in the painted figure's attitudes. They were certainly having an effect on the style of painting, whether through their powers of patronage or through their writings (see Locquin, 1912). As a result, their attempt to take illusion seriously probably counted for something in the painter's attempts to achieve a more statuesque effect (powered also by the archaeological discoveries at Pompeii and Herculaneum). It is the obvious inadequacy of the concept of illusion as a mistake which provokes the engraver Charles Cochin. Allied with the Marquis de Marigny (the brother of Madame de Pompadour, and instrumental in promoting the new style), friend of the *philosophes* (he engraved the frontispiece of the *Encyclopédie*), all of whom resist *papillotage*, Cochin's work as an engraver is nevertheless Rococo, and his theory will attack the *Société d'Amateurs* in particular, and the *littérateurs* in general, for the unsatisfactory theories of illusion they proclaim.[2] His resistance to such theories shows the more clearly which way the wind is blowing.

Cochin's early writings, produced after the journey to Italy he undertook with 'Poisson-Mécène' (the future Marquis de Marigny), the Abbé Le Blanc (another of Madame de Pompadour's protégés) and the architect Soufflot, use 'illusion' seriously as a critical term.[3] Yet illusion is not always attainable: 'Quoique la peinture, dans ces grands objets, ne puisse pas atteindre à un degré d'illusion capable de tromper les hommes, ce doit toujours être son but & le peintre ne doit rien faire volontairement qui détruise l'erreur, puisqu'il tâche de l'exciter dans tout le reste par le dessein & la couleur' (Cochin, 1758, p. 150). It is this paradox that he works out in the article *De l'Illusion*,[4] a paradox rendered more scandalous by the ambivalent relation which operates between a painting's power of illusion, about which there is little room for disagreement, and the consensus as to aesthetic value – for various Dutch *bambochades* may possess more power of illusion than a Raphael.[5] He redefines illusion, not as an absolute mistake, but, within a diluted Berkleyan epistemology, as 'la nécessité

63

d'employer le toucher pour s'assurer de la vérité' (Cochin, 1757–71, vol. II, p. 45).[6] Even this restricted illusion, he says, can only take place in certain circumstances, where the object painted has little relief. Engendered by technical tricks, such illusion occurs under special constraints and is of limited duration: the frame of expectation must be right, and the attention given cursory.[7]

We learn from experience to interpret visual cues which indicate distance: shadows in a painting play on this and invite us to interpret them as shape. But this can only partially destroy our perception of the painting's surface, which is reflecting light with a force relative to its real distance. A painting thus gives us contradictory information: 'Tout espoir d'illusion, prise à la rigueur, est refusé à la peinture, lorsqu'elle entreprend des sujets un peu trop compliqués quant aux saillies inégales & aux distances qu'elle ose supposer entre les objets' (Cochin, 1757–71, vol. II, pp. 49–50). 'On ne peut être trompé au point de ne pas voir que ce n'est qu'un tableau' (Cochin, 1757–71, vol. II, p. 54).[8]

Illusion is then redefined: 'Un second degré d'illusion improprement dite [. . .] c'est que le tableau puisse rappeler si bien le vrai [. . .] que l'image fasse le même plaisir que si l'on voyait la nature même' (Cochin, 1757–71, vol. II, p. 55). This is a defective redefinition since it assumes that the pleasure from a painted object is the same as from the object; but perhaps deliberately defective. The redefined account of the state of mind, 'illusion', is not merely related to but identified with the kind of picture likely to be associated with it: 'C'est que le tableau puisse rappeler si bien le vrai' slips into 'C'est cette *vérité d'imitation* dont la peinture est susceptible.' For having demolished 'hard' illusion as a criterion of value, Cochin needs both to create a criterion of relation to reality, 'vérité d'imitation', to take over the function of 'hard' illusion, and yet to be able to reject it as accounting for art. 'Vérité d'imitation' exhausts the experience of a painting, for it only accounts for the first glance and it fails to explain the difference in reaction between a connoisseur and a man without technical knowledge (Cochin, 1757–71, vol. II, p. 56). And with intentional wish to shock, he points out that 'vérité d'imitation' and commonly associated valuations of paintings conflict: 'Ceux du divin Raphael en sont souvent très éloignés.' Michaelangelo's *Last Judgement* is 'unnatural' and even displeasing: 'Sa beauté consiste dans la force d'une imagination grande, fière, qui présente à nos yeux des objets surhumains sous l'aspect le plus

Art and replica

imposant, dans un caractère de dessin chargé & articulé avec
excès'; it is the lesser painters, Guido Reni or Piero da Cortona,
who may create more illusion (Cochin, 1757–71, vol. II, p. 59).
For Cochin, 'art' is the quality which distinguishes the great painter; he defines it as: 'Sorte de poésie par laquelle le génie se rend
maître de la nature, pour l'assujettir à produire toutes les beautés
dont l'art peut être susceptible.' Thus a great colourist, for
instance, may eliminate certain qualities of light to augment harmony. And with Boucher perhaps in mind, whose colour by such
methods became totally artificial, Cochin claims that the pleasure
created compensates for the lack of the appearance of *vérité*
(Cochin, 1757–71, vol. II, p. 65). Cochin is in fact defending a painter's technique as a value; 'faire' is what distinguishes Chardin's
still lifes from Oudry's: 'L'illusion étoit égale dans les deux tableaux [. . .]. Quelle en étoit la différence sinon ce faire qu'on peut
appeler magique, spirituel, plein de feu, & cet art inimitable?'
(Cochin, 1757–71, vol. II, p. 73).[9] Cochin appropriates Voltaire's
comparison between Pradon and Racine's *Phèdre*, where the feelings expressed may be the same, 'mais quelle différence dans la
manière de les exprimer' (Cochin, 1757–71, vol. II, p. 72).[10] Having
thus approached, through the notion of 'faire', values such as vision
and imagination which abolish a distinction between form and content, Cochin returns through the polemical use of a dubious
analogy to the intellectual assumptions of the very contemporaries
he is criticising. But he has to do this in order to resolve the paradox
which was his starting point, to reintegrate 'illusion' into an account
of art: 'illusion' has heuristic not aesthetic value.

Concluons donc que ce vrai qui semble tendre à faire illusion, est la
première qualité essentielle; que les connoisseurs & le public sont en droit
de l'exiger, que tout ouvrage qui s'en éloigne trop, est très-répréhensible,
quelques beautés qu'il ait d'ailleurs: que cependant non seulement ce n'est
pas la seule beauté de l'art, mais que ce n'est pas même celle qui sert le plus
à distinguer l'excellent artiste d'avec le médiocre; que ce n'est point celle
enfin qui constitue le sublime de l'art. (Cochin, 1757–71, vol. II, p. 74)

The significance of Cochin's article has an art-historical as well as
a conceptual dimension. He criticises the Rococo, in 'Supplication
aux orfèvres' (Cochin, 1757–71, vol. I) but does not align himself
totally with its opponents. He is also the critical annotator of
Laugier's *Manière de bien juger les ouvrages de peinture*, 1771, a
book which opposes Rococo aesthetics in that it consistently
applies as a criterion the extreme form of illusion, the mistake.
Cochin's article on 'illusion', interpreted in relation to his own

career, suggests that there is some change within the concept. Illusion is hardening into a mistake and is succeeding a more flexible concept. This less rigid concept of illusion is correlated with an art he attacked and yet of which he was an exponent. His comments on the neoclassicising *littérateur*, Laugier, are those of the artist who realises that the latter's whole theory is explicitly designed to exclude the possibility of aesthetic judgement being made, witness Laugier's assertion 'Les oiseaux qui vinrent bequester les raisins de Zeuxis décidèrent plus sûrement la beauté de l'ouvrage que n'aurait pu le faire un de ces savans en dissertant fort au long sur les lumières, les ombres et les reflets' (Laugier, 1771, pp. 12–13). Falconet's attitude in his controversy with another *littérateur*, Diderot, bears an ambiguity similar to Cochin's relation to Laugier. Like the connoisseur Richardson before him, he dismisses stories of illusion as indications of a painting's value. Yet in his anxiety to score debating points, unlike Cochin, he uses the concept as a criterion, and reveals how far 'illusion' has contracted and awareness has been excised. Pliny's account of the statue of the seated Jupiter 'dont la tête touchait presque aux voûtes était une *sottise*, mais une grosse sottise; parce que s'il se fût levé, il aurait crevé le voûte ou se serait cassé la tête', a criticism which relies on the notion of illusion as a mistake. Likewise, he uses a phrase which earlier had implied a willing complicity on the part of the spectator to criticise the statue: 'Cette tête *faisait trembler le méchant*, mais ce n'est qu'à condition que le méchant se prêtait à l'illusion.' There must be no integration of awareness. It is left to Diderot to define the statue not by elaborating the notion of consent, but by stressing the immediate if momentary effect of illusion: 'Le point important, c'est que tandis qu'il y est, il frappe, il épouvante, il effraye' (*Diderot et Falconet*, 1958, pp. 112, 215).[11]

Cochin attacks both the extravagance of Rococo practice, and the imbecilities of the theorists of 'hard' illusion. He is concerned, over Chardin's case, for example, with asserting painterly values of technique, of 'faire', against the sole criterion of 'illusion'. The demolition of the notion of illusion comes, as is to be expected, at a critical point both in the practice of artists and in the theorising of theoreticians: values are changing towards a severer art and the concept of illusion is being restricted into the mistake. Cochin is in a Janus position. He attacks the excesses of the Rococo *ornemanistes*, yet he takes to its logical extreme the *littérateur*'s concept of 'hard' illusion, in order to show up its inadequacy. And this in the name of 'faire', of a properly artistic value. Diderot on the contrary had criticised the Rococo in the name of illusion; but, like Cochin, he accepts neither the *littérateur*'s theory of painting, nor 'hard' illusion. He endorses the latter neither in critical practice (for he uses the structure of *papillotage* in the great *Vernet* article) nor totally in theory. For he too recognises the value of 'faire'. Cochin and Diderot are almost alone in this among critics. For illusion is contracting into a mistake, awareness is being excised, and with it the appreciation of technique.

Illusion and the low genres: 'faire'

After about 1750, *aletheia* is being abandoned for *adequatio*. Subjects with which ceilings were decorated, and which earlier were justified in terms of illusion, are now attacked as incapable of being adequately represented in paint – attacked for *lack* of illusion. Dubos had already suggested that the ceiling of Il Gesù was not as successful as had been claimed (Dubos, 1719, vol. I, pp. 386–7).[12] Critics in mid-century tend to subject 'plafonniers' to the strict rule of *vraisemblance* – the only subjects to be used on ceilings are those which could not take place on earth. For painted ceilings have the same effect as the mirror in interior decoration: both suggest space where there is none. 'L'usage de peindre les Plafonds est un abus semblable à celui de mettre les Glaces sur les cheminées; les Plafonds peints et les Glaces représentent des vuides où doivent être des pleins & font une fausse illusion' (Du Perron, 1758, p. 70). Cochin indeed uses the notion of 'illusion' to *criticise* illusionistic devices.[13] Such *décor* gives false appearances: 'L'on ne sera plus alors tenté d'abandonner cette décoration naturelle, satisfaisante, pour y substituer [. . .] l'apparence d'une construction imaginaire qui, n'étant pas la construction réelle de l'édifice, donne de celle-ci une idée fausse' (Kaufmann, 1968, p. 211).

Yet, as much as mirrors, the low genres, landscape and still life are connected with Rococo taste. Laugier satirises such taste for dismissing the grand style of Italian masterpieces 'qui se ressentent du triste genre d'Homère et de Virgile, pour le remplacer par les aimables bambochades des Pays Bas [i.e. genre painting and still life] beaucoup plus analogues à l'amour délicat que l'on a eu pour les pantins, les bouffons & les cabriolets' (Laugier, 1771, p. 197; cf. Cochin, 1757–71, vol. I, p. 139, which attacks the taste of amateurs). But, unlike illusionistic *décor* with its pretensions to seriousness, such low genres, even when accused of frivolity, are all, in the 1750s and 1760s, praised in terms of illusion. Oudry's animals, the portraits of Tocqué, La Tour and Perronneau, Bachelier's flowers, Roland de La Porte's painted bas-reliefs: all are held by mediocre journalists as well as by serious critics to provoke illusion (Diderot, *Salon de 1761*, pp. 135–6, among many other instances in his work). 'Illusion' has become a fashionable word of praise, as the coyness of a comment from Diderot's *Salon de 1771* suggests: 'L'illusion y est de la plus grande force et j'ai vu plus d'une personne y être trompée. Il me semble qu'on pourrait dire de M. Chardin et de M. de Bouffon que la nature les a mis dans sa confidence' (Diderot, *Salon de 1771*, p. 178; the comment is undoubtedly not by Diderot, but is taken from a brochure which he pillaged).

'Illusion', then, dismisses a high genre and praises low ones. The reason for this is as follows. In the eighteenth century, landscapes, still lifes and portraits were held inferior to paintings of historical, religious and mythological subjects. Since painters of low genre could not teach in the Academy, this entailed a financial loss as well as one of standing, and explains Greuze's production of a historical subject for his *morceau de réception*.[14] And yet this hierarchy is in flagrant contradiction of the twentieth-century location of value in eighteenth-century art – it is the portrait, the still life, the furniture which are admired, just as it is the novel and the *conte* which survive, rather than the two hundred or more 'classical' tragedies produced at the Comédie française between 1715 and 1789. In fact, the movement of taste from 1750 tended to make the hierarchy of genres and the real location of artistic value coincide (Locquin, 1912). 'Illusion', then, serves even sensitive critics as a word recognising the location of value, in spite of the hierarchy of genres: 'Il faut sçavoir faire quelque chose de plus que copier servilement la Nature, *ce qui est déjà beaucoup*', Dubos had said, adding the italicised words in later editions. But he had argued:

Ces peintres flegmatiques ont donc eu la persévérance de chercher par un nombre infini de tentatives, souvent réitérées sans fruit, les teintes, les demy-teintes, enfin toutes les diminutions de couleur nécessaires pour dégrader la couleur des objets, & ils sont ainsi parvenus à peindre la lumière même [. . .]. Sans invention dans leurs expressions: incapables de s'élever au-dessus de la nature qu'ils avoient devant les yeux, ils n'ont peint que des passions basses ou bien une nature ignoble. (Dubos, 1719, vol. II, p. 65)

And this tension continues as the century goes on:

J'admirerai toutes les imitations de la nature portées à un certain degré d'habileté & d'illusion [. . .], la représentation des actions humaines les plus simples & les plus familières [. . .] scènes pastorales, festes champêtres, foires, noces de village, enfin jusqu'aux cuisines, aux tavernes, aux écuries, sujets favoris & ignobles des Flamands, uniquement recherchés pour y admirer une séduisante imitation, une fraîcheur & une fonte merveilleuse de couleurs, une suavité de pinceau & c. Tous ces objets présentés à nos yeux avec l'artifice & la magie pittoresque doivent nécessairement amuser nos regards & avoir place dans nos cabinets. Mais il n'en est pas de même des tableaux d'Histoire. [. . .] la Peinture, outre l'amusement du plaisir & de l'illusion, doit être encore une école de mœurs . . . (La Font de Saint Yenne, 1754, pp. 74–5)

'Illusion' thus expresses a notion of compensation: where subjects are negligible, it is the work's power of illusion which is praised. Diderot, like La Font de Saint Yenne, while using 'illusion' in much of his art criticism as a quick word of praise, emphasises the mere facility of such technical prowess. 'Illusion' might be held to supply a subterranean aesthetic for an art which the official code of values could not easily accommodate. I have shown, on the contrary, that 'illusion' is often used by the eighteenth century to criticise illusionism in painting. The painted sculpture or bas-relief, as practised by Chardin and Roland de La Porte, could be considered as a piece detached from such an illusionistic ensemble as the Villa Borghese at Rome, where statues, painted statues, and bas-reliefs are intermingled. But the very possibility of detachment marks the difference: illusionism refers away, it is an image of something absent, or whose presence is intimated only. But with the *trompe l'œil* of low genres there is no other-worldly transcendence: reality has been claimed by this world. Painting, far from wishing to create the consciousness of a gap between art and reality, strives to close it.

'Illusion' used of low genres expresses the transparency of such paintings: 'C'est la chose même.' But such transparency omits the spectator, since the painting and visual image of the object are identified. It is for this reason that the new critical movement frowns on references to the spectator, or self-references. Nothing is to be supposed outside the canvas itself: 'La toile renferme tout l'espace et il n'y a personne au-delà.' The analogy with the new theatrical theories is striking (cf. *Pensées détachées sur la peinture*, p. 792)[15] and Diderot, like many theatrical critics, used in his art criticism the criterion of an actual mistake as proof of emotional effect (*Salon de 1763*, p. 233).[16]

There is to be no complicity with the spectator; the picture is to be alone in the world (cf. some paintings of Magritte, for example, where a painting on an easel stands in the midst of the scene painted). The excision of the spectator is reflected in painters' practice

by a change in the dominant plane of late eighteenth-century painting: the hardness and stillness of the bas-relief becomes a model;
the picture space no longer recedes away from the spectator, invi-
ting him to follow, but like a frieze unrolls before him. Greuze, for
example, plans his later pictures, *Le Fils prodigue* and *Severus et
Caracalla* horizontally, and the effect is still more evident in the
work of David. Critics demand stillness, not 'tapage' and strength,
an 'art sévère', not 'petites mines [. . .] manière, afféterie'
(Diderot, *Salon de 1765*, p. 76, on Boucher). They complain again
and again that the art of the century is far removed from the maj-
estic simplicity and noble pathos typical of Raphael and Poussin,
and in general from the taste for classical art (see, for instance,
Saint Yves, 1748, pp. 24–5). Such statements undoubtedly hasten
the Pompeian style of interior decoration, which now seems only
faintly distinct from the Rococo. They also hasten the use of a
symbolism which, as in the great *Marat* by David, refers inwards to
the event, not outwards to the spectator: the coffin-like bath, the
tomb-stone-like box beside it.

The most striking intellectual position taken up by the advocates
of the new style is the separation they make between matter and
treatment, and which they are able to make thanks to 'illusion'.
'Illusion' used of low genres was the value of the artist's work in
creating a transparent view of the valueless object. But if the view
is transparent, it must tend to annul its own process of production,
the very 'faire' which brought it into being. 'Faire' does not mediate
between the subject of the picture and the spectator, but strives to
cancel itself. 'Illusion' when it means this transparency of art,
serves indeed as part of the *littérateurs*' attack on Rococo artists –
occurring in particular after the resumption, in 1745, of regular
exhibitions of paintings in the Salons. 'Illusion' ensures that amateurs, and not merely the artists or connoisseurs, are competent to
judge: 'Celui qui opère en vous une aussi puissante illusion est un
grand peintre. Mais puisque vous l'éprouviez vous vous y con-
noissez autant qu'il est nécessaire' – connoisseurs are unnecessary,
'illusion' is enough (Le Blanc, 1747, pp. 124–5; cf. Diderot, *Pensées
détachées sur la peinture*, p. 765; and Laugier, 1771, p. 2).

What for the artist is 'faire', for the *littérateur* is 'mécanique': it
may compensate for low subjects in Flemish painting;[17] but even
this role is denied by such a critic as Laugier: 'Son tableau parfaitement bien inventé quand même il serait médiocrement peint, réussira beaucoup mieux que s'il était du pinceau le plus excellent
avec une invention médiocre' (Laugier, 1771, p. 110). 'Faire' or

'méchanique' is opposed to 'idéal', and behind this opposition lurks the earlier one between *Rubénistes* and *Poussinistes*, which had informed the Academy quarrel of the late seventeenth century, where colour was opposed to 'dessein', often punningly interpreted as purpose, meaning. Those who defend colour in the eighteenth century, Desportes and Blanchard, do so in terms of illusion, as their seventeenth-century predecessors had done so in terms of *trompe l'œil*. Even Diderot, who acquires not merely knowledge of the difficulty of an artist's technique but the ability to describe it, is often content with a slick distinction between poetry and paint (e.g. *Salon de 1763*, p. 226).[18] And though when he is in front of an actual picture, he sometimes goes beyond this, in much of the *Salons* criticism his attitude is 'Ôtez à Teniers son faire, et qu'est-ce que Teniers! Il y a tel genre de littérature et tel genre de peinture où la couleur fait le principal mérite' (Diderot, *Salon de 1767*, p. 208). Technical effects are for Diderot a sacrifice to considerations other than those of expression of the subject of the painting: 'Touche-moi, étonne-moi, déchire-moi; fais-moi tressaillir, pleurer, frémir, m'indigner d'abord: tu recréeras mes yeux après si tu peux' (Diderot, *Essais sur la peinture*, p. 714).[19] With the depreciation of technique, with 'illusion' as transparency, the concept of imitation retracts from its earlier, wider sense, till it comes to guarantee meaning, and finally reference, or subject matter. It is the subject matter which ensures that the painting means something, that a painting is a 'simulatio', its reference blocked by its model. And since properly artistic concerns tend to be eliminated, the notion of subject matter itself becomes narrower. Caylus, no mean critic and moreover a friend of Watteau, can maintain that the latter's paintings 'n'ont aucun objet' (Caylus, 1910, p. 18), and this is an aesthetic, not a moral judgement. Subjects are explicitly thought of as objects of reference, as discrete elements in the world or in experience (perhaps because of the threatened continuity between spectator and world created by the neglect of art's mediating technique). Repertories of subjects are compiled by helpful *littérateurs*;[20] as in the theory of the theatre, complaints are made that there are no new subjects (La Font de Saint Yenne, 1747, pp. 6–7). Whether Diderot is in a natural landscape or in front of a painted one, when contemplating the beauty of the stream, of the trees, the *philosophe* imagines the ships' masts that the trees will become, the metal that the mountains hide, the mill wheel the streams will turn (Diderot, *Essais sur la peinture*, p. 737).[21] Likewise the later development of both H. Robert and Loutherbourg in their painting is away from their first idealised style and towards an industrialised landscape.

It was a commonplace in the eighteenth century that a painting was immediately comprehensible: 'La Peinture produit sur nos sens les mêmes impressions que les objets naturels '(*Réflexions sur la musique*, 1754, p. 7). The concept of a painting as a mediation between subject and object is disappearing, the paint surface is now to be a replica. Correspondingly, the conception of the subject of a painting is contracting into the anecdote, which can be circumscribed and listed in repertories. But how can it be transmitted? For Dubos, 'La Peinture emploie des signes naturels dont l'énergie ne dépend pas de l'éducation. Ils tirent leur force du rapport que la Nature elle-même a pris soin de mettre entre les objets extérieurs & nos organes, afin de procurer notre conservation' (Dubos, 1719, vol. I, p. 378). The relation with contemporary epistemology is clear: for Berkeley sense impressions are signs, but signs instituted by nature and hence immediate. The paint surface is abolished in that it is equivalent to retinal impression. But how can subject matter attain the same immediacy? 'Afin que les mouvements de la sensibilité deviennent palpables et visibles, il faut les prendre dans leurs effets sur les organes' (Estève, 1753a, vol. II, p. 91). The listing of subjects in repertories is continued at the level of gesture, of expression, of the characteristics of social function; the study of deaf mutes is even advocated by Coypel (1721, p. 162).

As subjects are held to be individually identifiable, and thus to be listable, so are signs of character or social role. The extreme incarnation of such a theory is caricature. It is not by accident that the century sees a great flowering of the genre, nor that the great art critic Winckelmann should react against this in favour of a more noble and general style, nor that this reaction should take the form of a denial of painting's capacity for particularised expression:

A cet égard, nos Artistes se trouvent comme dans un pays désert. Les langues des Sauvages qui n'ont point de termes pour exprimer les idées de reconnaissance, de durée, d'espace ne sont pas plus dépourvues de signes pour rendre les conceptions abstraites que l'est notre peinture moderne. (Winckelmann in *Journal étranger*, 1756, p. 149)

The low genres are of less value; yet again and again writers lament that high genre painting is technically less exact and less historical in the sense defined by contemporary poetics, namely, that of making accurate reference to a real event, than the low genres. The term *peinture d'histoire* and all that it implies of awareness of historical period acquires full force with such critics.[22]

Costumes, even faces, are to be copied from medals and from classical portraits. Cochin in his annotations to Laugier maliciously opposes this idea to that of decorum:

Il y a fort peu de héros dont la physionomie réponde au portrait que l'histoire nous trace de leur caractère [. . .]. C'est pour cela que de tous les tableaux représentant les saints, les plus ingrats à traiter sont ceux où doit être Saint Vincent de Paul dont malheureusement on nous a soigneusement conservé la ressemblance. (Cochin in Laugier, 1771, p. 93)

He both criticises the artistic value of such accuracy, and doubts whether methodologically it is possible. Critics explicitly relate their attitude to the attempts to reform 'costume' in the theatre at the same time (Saint Yves, 1748, p. 169; Richardson, 1728, vol. I, p. 4); and both brochures on the Salons, and Diderot in his Salon criticism, note faults in historical accuracy (Diderot, *Salon de 1767*, p. 86; *Salon de 1763*, p. 215). Laugier, with his usual care to exclude aesthetic judgements, says of such criteria: 'Ces objets seront pour vous la matière d'une critique qui décidera du génie du peintre' (Laugier, 1771, p. 97).

Though decried, the low genres mediate, through the notion of illusion, ideas crucial to the development of imitation as a replica, of adequation to an actually existing object in the material world. It is through the low genres that the idea of detached historical accuracy, of fidelity to place, face and costume, is constituted. It is also through the low genres that the idea of illusion as self-cancelling, of the painting as a transparent window on to reality, is mediated. Paradoxically, low-genre painters are praised for their illusion, for the technical competence which makes technique invisible: 'Rien ne vous détrompe.' But can the lowness of the genres be refused, yet their technique retained? At various moments in the *Paradoxe sur le comédien* as well as in the *Salons*, Diderot uses the excesses of the high and low genres in a pincer movement to define something which might be in between, and be 'real'. The right painting should be neither Flemish nor Italian in style, neither banal nor *outré*, neither base nor idealised. Here, as in the theatre, Diderot requires a middle genre, and as in theatre,[23] that demand helps define the notion of reality to which it should apply:

Je prétens que c'est dans cet intervalle du troisième rang, du rang de portraitiste de la plus belle nature subsistante soit en tout soit en partie que sont renfermées toutes les manières possibles de faire avec éloge et succès, toutes les nuances imperceptibles du bien, du mieux, et de l'excellent. Je prétens que tout ce qui est au-dessus est chimérique et que tout ce qui est au-dessous est pauvre, mesquin, vicieux. Je prétens que sans recourir aux

notions que je viens d'établir, on prononcera éternellement les mots d'exagération, de pauvre nature, de nature mesquine, sans en avoir d'idées nettes. (*Salon de 1767*, p. 63)

Other critics too show an awareness of the need to find a middle ground, if only through their contrasting of the 'ideal' and the 'low'. If the 'low' dismisses itself, the 'ideal' is increasingly recognised to be artistically dangerous in that its embellishment of nature may be merely a justification for the artist's *pratique*. Reynolds describes his coming upon Boucher in his studio constructing large scale canvases out of his head and censures him for it (Reynolds, 1887, p. 209). Diderot maintains that a portrait is distinguishable from a head painted 'de pratique' (Diderot. *Salon de 1767*, p. 168, on a portrait by La Tour). And Reynolds and Diderot denounce a mixing of the ideal and the real in painting (Diderot, *Salon de 1781*; Reynolds, 1887, p. 240, on a painting by Wilson). Lacombe, like Diderot, shows clearly that an unsatisfactory mediate genre is being sought, a portrait-like reproduction of unreal or remote events and figures – a wish that will lead directly to M.G.M.'s Ancient Rome.

On peut distinguer plusieurs sortes de vrai: Le vrai simple qui est une copie fidelle des objets qu'on a sous les yeux; c'est celui qu'on recommande ici; le vrai idéal qui vient de la pratique & qui a sa source dans l'imagination: il est toujours défectueux, toujours froid; on voudrait le voir moins employé. Enfin le vrai composé est cet ensemble de diverses perfections qui ne se trouvent jamais réunies dans un seul modèle mais qui se tient de plusieurs. (Lacombe, 1753, p. 18; cf. Piles, 1708, pp. 31–4)

Here, the real has been defined as 'les objets qu'on a sous les yeux' – a radical limitation; yet the 'vrai idéal' is criticised. What critics ask for is a portrait of great events. The notion of a work of art as a replica of material objects and persons has been constituted. Such an attitude will have profound consequences for the concept of the work of art. As a replica, a copy, it is true *or* false but it is an *object*. Correspondingly the state of mind in which it is perceived is private and subjective.

The replica and manner

These correlative definitions of illusion and reality tend to lead painters to attempt a replica of the real which is neither 'ideal' and conventional, nor restricted to a still life. But if they are successful, then their technique must be transparent and the painter's manner becomes a scandal: 'La nature n'a point de manière' (Dézallier d'Argenville, 1745, p. xx).[24] For in this century nature transcends

the artist and art, as once the transcendental did nature; art replaces religious institutions as mediator between man and nature,
and painter's styles 'which are known to differ so much from one
another and all of them from nature' are thus 'so many strong
proofs of their inviolable attachment to falsehood converted into
established truth in their own eyes by self-opinion' (Hogarth, 1955,
p. 25). In that manner disrupts the transparency of the relation
between replica and model, between art and nature, it is false: 'Il
n'y aurait pas de manière ni dans le dessin, ni dans la couleur si l'on
imitait scrupuleusement la nature' (Diderot, *Essais sur la peinture*,
p. 673). But these are habits not merely at the level of execution,
they influence the very way nature is seen: 'Ils voient la Nature non
pas comme elle est en effet, mais comme ils sont accoûtumés de la
peindre et de la colorier' (Piles, 1708, pp. 262–3). Manner for critics
and especially for Diderot, is a trick, a 'protocole' as he calls it. But
'L'imitation seule ne produit que des glaces' (Caylus, 1910, p. 185).
Technique is clearly what marks a painter most, and what the connoisseur is trained to detect (and even paid for doing so, if he is able
to distinguish different 'hands'). 'Illusion' as a transparent window
on to a replica cannot give an account of the facts – it cannot
explain manner, nor, worse, technique. It is powerless to do so
either in its negative manifestations – as a box of tricks – or in its
positive ones as the 'faire' which induces a mistake in the spectator.

To solve this dilemma, various methods of founding technique in
nature are evolved. How, for instance, out of the continuous space
of the mirror, or of the painting's surface, seen as transparent, can a
discrete subject be presented? This is a technical problem, parallel
to that of the subject matter, which I mentioned earlier: critics
attempt to construct a repertory of lines and colours, just as they
classify subjects. Hogarth speaks of an 'alphabet and grammar' of
lines which the artist can use. But their status is ambiguous. They
appear to exist in nature and to be discoverable. They are also said
by him to be a mnemonic, a convenient method of transcription on
to the paper of what is seen, which implies that they are conventional. (This is a particular version of a general eighteenth-century
scientific problem: is classification natural, or a problem of human
agreement?) For colour, artists were in the habit of using not an
'alphabet' but the 'rainbow' as their basis. The 'rainbow' was a
gradation of the tones which break up the colour continuum, yet
was often in fact used as a rule which gave the order of colours to be
employed (cf. Diderot, *Essais sur la peinture*). Or again, an analogy
with musical construction is urged: 'Le plaisir que nous donne la

Peinture, considérée comme un Art muet ressemble à celui que nous donne la Musique, ses belles Formes, ses Couleurs, & leur Arrangement agréable sont aux yeux ce que les Tons & leur Harmonie sont aux Oreilles' (Richardson, 1728, vol. I, p. 4); 'Le premier Ton d'un Tableau est arbitraire mais il décide de tous les autres, comme le ton du premier violon d'un concert règle le ton de toutes les voix [. . .]. Cette première nuance est dépendante de toutes celles qui l'environnent; elle n'a d'autre valeur que celle que lui prêtent les contrastes qu'on lui oppose' (Dandré Bardon, 1765, vol. I, pp. 174–5).

Early in the century, le père Castel had attempted to found the relation between colours and sounds on nature. His 'clavecin oculaire', the object of his contemporaries' fascinated mockery, is frequently interpreted as an earlier incarnation of nineteenth-century theories of synaesthesia: contemporaries, however, took what is a directly opposed view. Many understood his work to be an extreme version of the epistemological theories which consider that all senses give the same information.[25] But he is a follower of Descartes, and his commentary on the 'clavecin oculaire' tends to prove that, just as there is an innate structure in the mind, so there is an inherent structure in colours, comparable with that in sound. Following Newton's *Opticks* (1704) and Rameau's *Traité de l'harmonie* (1722), he is less concerned with analogies between sound and colour than with constructing a graduated scale out of the continuum of colour, with taking the notion of colour harmony seriously: 'L'harmonie n'a jamais été après tout que nombre, mesure, rapport' (Castel, 1735, p. 1451). After experiments, Newton's rainbow gives the colours of the octave, and blue is fixed on as the tonic which generates the other colours:[26] red the fifth, yellow the major third. To the notes of the chromatic scale are made to correspond twelve colours, and the continuous natural colour transformation is limited by a kind of lower bound (Castel, 1735, pp. 1462–3). Black and white are the union of all colours – this represents a conscious attempt to unite dyers' practice and Newton's theory. He hopes to provide a *basse fondamentale* for painters as Rameau had done for music, and at the end of his series of articles he suggests not merely that a notation for the dance should be sought, such as had already been put forward by Feuillet, but that a similar *basse fondamentale*, or basic system of relations, could be found for painters (Castel, 1735, pp. 2742ff.). The ridicule poured on the 'clavecin oculaire' by his contemporaries shows that Castel's attempt to give a scientific basis to colour harmony was unsuccessful and unacceptable. The problem of the status of technique, and of the artist's manner, remained entire.

Le cas Chardin

It is the great genre and still-life painter Chardin who for the eighteenth century embodies the problem of the value of subject matter and its correlative problem, the nature of technique. Universally praised for his 'faire', the painter of such 'low' subjects as *La Raie écorchée,* he is the focus of praise and blame, for it is he who threatens most directly the link between subject matter and value. The more sensitive the critic, the more critical is the problem of Chardin's *œuvre.* La Font de Saint Yenne evolves from condemnation to a much warmer approval, not merely of Chardin's extraordinary technique in the handling of light and colour, but of his vision as well: 'Il est certain qu'il joint au talent particulier de voir dans la nature des naïvetés & des finesses qu'elle cache aux autres, celui de les rendre avec une vérité d'illusion qui paroît toujours neuve & qui attache indépendammant de la médiocrité du sujet' (La Font de Saint Yenne, 1754, p. 124). The paint surface, then, is not transparent but mediates between the natural object and the visual image. Lacombe in a remarkable passage anticipates, or was pillaged by, Diderot:

Rien n'est en effet plus difficile que de rendre le naturel avec cette vérité piquante qui en fait tout le mérite & l'agrément [. . .]. C'est un travail qui ne produit tout son effet qu'à une certaine distance, de près, le tableau n'offre qu'une sorte de vapeur qui semble envelopper tous les objets [. . .]. Cette pratique est séduisante, mais elle demande surement beaucoup de patience & de tems. (Lacombe, 1753, pp. 23–4; cf. Diderot, *Salon de 1763,* p. 223)

but it is with Diderot that the problem posed by Chardin precipitates an aesthetic mutation. He uses the language of illusion to describe the work, playing on the epistemological crux of the time, the relation between touch and sight: 'Vous prendriez les bouteilles par le goulet, si vous aviez soif; les pesches et les raisins éveillent l'appetit et appellent la main' (*Salon de 1759,* p. 66),' C'est la nature même; les objets sont hors de la toile et d'une vérité à tromper les yeux' (*Salon de 1763,* p. 222). Yet it remains the case that 'Si le sublime du technique n'y était pas, l'idéal de Chardin seroit misérable' (Diderot, *Salon de 1765,* p. 108). It is Chardin's work and conversation which force Diderot to recognise this necessity of technique – to recognise that art is mediation and not transparency. It may well be Chardin who provokes the revaluation of technique which leads Diderot to the crisis expressed in the *Paradoxe sur le comédien* (cf. Hobson, 1973), where technique is both necessary and scandalous. The implications of Diderot's treatment of Chardin's work are contradictory. Chardin has no art, 'c'est la nature même'; Chardin is all art: 'Il n'a point de manière; je me trompe, il a la sienne. Mais puisqu'il a une manière, sienne, il devroit être faux dans quelques circonstances, et il ne l'est jamais' (Diderot, *Salon de 1765*, p. 114).

If Diderot is thus ambivalent in his attitude to Chardin it is because he fears technique: 'Je crains bien que les peintres pusillanimes ne soient partis de là pour restreindre pauvrement les limites de l'art, et se faire un petit technique facile et borné, ce que nous appelons entre nous un protocole' (Diderot, *Essais sur la peinture*, p. 678). And yet as he becomes close to artists, he takes up and works on Piles' definition: 'La Peinture est une superficie plate qu'il faut anéantir en trompant les yeux et en ne laissant rien d'équivoque' (Piles, 1707, p. 36).[27] Diderot learns that a given colour is not absolute, but derives its value from other colours in the painting;[28] he takes up the metaphor of harmony to develop it into the musical notion of preparing and resolving discord: 'Quel travail que celui d'introduire entre une infinité de chocs fiers et vigoureux une harmonie générale qui les lie et qui sauve l'ouvrage de la petitesse de forme. Quelle multitude de dissonances visuelles à préparer et à adoucir' (Diderot, *Salon de 1763*, p. 226). Just as harmony is derived from a set of natural relations between sounds, so the painter's technique, he suggests, may itself even be based on a natural structure. 'Je n'ai garde de renverser dans l'art l'ordre de l'arc en ciel. L'arc en ciel est en peinture ce que la basse fondamentale est en musique' (Diderot, *Essais sur la peinture*, p. 678). And this natural structure in colour corresponds to our visual experience:

L'habitude perpétuelle de regarder les objets éloignés, d'en mesurer l'intervalle par la vue, a établi dans notre organe une échelle enharmonique de tons, de semi-tons, de quarts de tons, tout autrement étendue et tout aussi rigoureuse que celle de la musique pour l'oreille, et l'on peint faux pour l'œil, comme l'on chante faux pour l'oreille. (Diderot, *Pensées détachées sur la peinture*, p. 806)

Techniques, whether based on nature or on convention, are necessary and inevitable. But the conception of imitation as replica thus becomes unacceptable. This is the thrust of the preface to the *Salon de 1767* where there is a *reductio ad absurdum* of the notion of imitation. There, the painter, even the portrait painter, who believes he imitates nature is a fool. A portrait is commonly supposed to be an exact imitation of the sitter, but, says Diderot, the portrait of a hand, of a finger, of a nail, is an infinitely receding aim which can never be attained. A great painter is in fact not engaged in replication at all, but in elaborating an ideal beauty, 'la ligne de beauté' (*Salon de 1767*, p. 61). This line is approached slowly through a process which consists of setting upper and lower bounds (cf. the passage quoted on pp. 73–4): the painter is to be neither *outré* nor conventional, neither *guindé* nor *bas*. The area thus defined is a 'limite qui sépare le beau réel du beau idéal, limite sur laquelle se jouent les différentes écoles' (Diderot, *Paradoxe sur le comédien*, pp. 340–1). Chardin's art is redefined in terms of Diderot's interpretation of Plato in the preface to the *Salon de 1767*, where art is at one remove from truth:

Chardin est entre la nature et l'art: il relègue les autres imitateurs au troisième rang. Il n'y a rien en lui qui sente la palette. C'est une harmonie au delà de laquelle on n'en songe pas à désirer; elle serpente imperceptiblement dans sa composition sous chaque partie de l'étendue de sa toile; c'est comme les théologiens disent de l'esprit, sensible dans le tout et secret en chaque point. (*Salon de 1769*, p. 83)

Yet if even Chardin is between nature and art, art can only lag: and it is perhaps for this reason that Diderot in his critical theory, as in his critical practice in the *Vernet* article discussed earlier, plays with the return of art to nature.

Le meilleur tableau, le plus harmonieux n'est [. . .] qu'un tissu de faussetés qui se couvrent les unes les autres. Il y a des objets qui gagnent, d'autres qui perdent, et la grande magie consiste à approcher tout près de la nature et à faire que tout perde ou gagne proportionnellement; mais alors ce n'est plus la scène réelle et vraie qu'on voit, *ce n'en est pour ainsi dire que la traduction*. (Diderot, *Salon de 1763*, p. 217)

But the return of art to nature is really a circle: the painting remains a mediation, a translation, a series of *à peu près* which substitute themselves for nature rather than replicate it. In such a theory, which goes back to Roger de Piles, the painting does not give the same impression as the actual object: '[Il] les supplée entièrement' (Piles, 1708, p. 41), it is a substitute which does not cause a mistake but which stands in *lieu* of its object.

Diderot in fact swings between two attitudes to Chardin and to art in general. Chardin's work is 'la nature même'; it is also 'un tissu de faussetés'. Diderot's work on Chardin has finally brought out into the open the central problem in the relation between 'illusion', 'faire' and the low genres. For if in seeing a painting the spectator has an illusion, then the art is transparent – he does not perceive it, but only the object the painting is of. But if, in the low genres, the 'illusion' is a source of admiration, then it is equivalent to 'faire' which is *not* totally self-cancelling; art is therefore not transparent.

But the two patterns of judgement in terms of which Diderot confronts Chardin, like the dual attitude towards illusion in later eighteenth-century critical usage, are versions of what I have called *adequatio* and *aletheia*. In the first, art is transparent and the painting is a true/false replica of the original (TVF). In the second, truth to nature is mediated by art which is not nature: 'la vérité de l'illusion' in La Font de Saint Yenne's phrase, above, p. 77, so that art is true *and* false (T & F). Diderot's aesthetics, in painting as in other arts, is both given energy and bounded by a movement between these two.

The movement of painting theory, as of painting practice, in the century can be comprehended as a restriction of the notion of illusion: from a combination of consciousness and involvement, a *papillotage*, it is reduced to an involvement which excludes reference outside the painting, which seeks to make copy and model coincide, and which constitutes the notion of replica.

Part Two

ILLUSION AND FORM IN THE NOVEL

Painting theory and painting itself during the eighteenth century move from *aletheia* to *adequatio*. By the end of the century, a particular concept of representation has emerged: a painting is to replicate, even if its model is imaginary. However, in the theories of the novel, as in novelists' practice, there is no comparable chronological development. Some of the greatest novels written towards the end of the century – *Jacques le fataliste* (1778–80), *Faublas* (1787), for example – can certainly not be seen as attempts to realise a model. The novel, unlike painting, theatre, poetry or music, resists this kind of historical treatment.

Yet, it might be argued, there are two aspects of eighteenth-century novels which clearly concern replication, and which can be treated chronologically. The first is the concern with authenticity, the apparent passing off of novels as genuine memoirs or collections of letters; the second, 'an increasingly accurate representation of life'; 'a fidelity to human experience'; technical progress whereby 'successive writers discover and learn to exploit effective ways of portraying real life'. (Mylne, 1965, p. 2; cf. Stewart, 1969, p. 5). I hope to show that this interpretation of features in certain eighteenth-century French novels as *adequatio* is over-simple. (Moreover, it is based, as I shall show, on a phenomenology of the consumption of art far grosser than that of the eighteenth century itself.)

In regard to 'authenticity'

Even the 'faux mémoire' seeks less to simulate, to replicate, than to dissimulate. It is possible to simulate only what is clearly identifiable. But 'history' is *not* clearly identifiable in the eighteenth century. The novel is in fact a transgressive genre and is felt to be such. It operates in the space between romance and history: one could argue that it defines this pair for the succeeding period by its very movement between them. At the beginning of the century, for

81

reasons which will be explored, it poses the objective version of the poet's problem. Of the poet it is asked, 'What is he saying, by what right does he say what he does?' But the problem the novelist must face is: 'What is the status of what is offered in a novel?' – is it historical? and if it is not historical, is it untrue? – that is, false? (One could argue that the novel succeeds theatre, and precedes the film, as the art form felt to embody illusive appearance in its most dangerous and perhaps subversive form.)

In regard to reality

Much nineteenth-century art, preceded by eighteenth-century definitions and practice, seeks to make likeness a 'seeming like': that is, to block off the apparition-like nature of appearance. As I have shown, this eighteenth-century reaction against *papillotage* in painting sought to contain the appearing within itself, to make of it a *replica* of something really existing (either externally, or, as sincere feeling, internally).

But for the novel, things are not so easy. The 'real' is less plausibly restricted to 'moderate-sized specimens of dry goods' than in painting. It is only definable when contrasted with 'the specific way in which it might be, or might have been, *not* real' (Austin, 1964, p. 70). Now this was actually recognised, even by those novels claiming to be authentic. For in purporting to be genuine, they deny that they are novels. But the reflexive nature of their definition of the 'real', made by reference to the novel as unreal, destabilises the adequation they seek to establish between text and reality. This still defines itself as appearance, because it refers to what it is not. It is only when the novel is claimed theoretically as fiction ('fiction is truer than truth') or when fiction as illusion is thematised, that some kind of stability is found. One may wonder why it is the novel, of all art forms, which allows the 'unreal' to define the real, and thus to reveal that even *adequatio* is only a form of likeness ('not the truth but only like the truth', as Plato says). It may be that the possibility of truth or falsehood is inscribed in every specimen of written language, and thus in literary work, in a way that is less obvious than in the theatre or in painting. In addition, in more recent times, we have tried to neutralise this possibility of truth/falsehood by sending the novel to a critical vacuum, where we claim that the question true/false is naive (but, according to certain critics, not if true happens to mean 'life-enhancing', part of a praxis, or whatever).

If the novel resists chronological treatment in terms of *aletheia* and *adequatio*, it can be treated formally by adopting the attitudes to truth behind these concepts. For the form of the eighteenth-century novel can be considered to be governed by the two relations which it is possible to establish between real and unreal. In the first, the unreal defined as a novel is expelled (or, parasitically, the real defined as history is excluded). This type of novel may seem to claim *adequatio* (or its contrary) but in regard to something else held to be not real (or real). As such, it resembles the interlude by Bernini, or Pascal's account of dreams (see above, pp. 27 and 28). In the second form, the disjunction real/unreal is made within the novel (usually as a tale within a tale), so that the novel is both true *and* false, real and unreal, and contains both the fictional reality and the fictional appearance – this being the structure of *aletheia*. It is these two models of the novel form that I shall use in what follows.

3

THE EXCLUSION OF THE FALSE

Illusion and 'realism'

Any attempt to relate critical theory and novelistic practice must face the great disparity which exists between them in the eighteenth century. Until the 1760s, with Diderot's *Eloge de Richardson*, and Rousseau's prefaces to *La Nouvelle Héloïse*, treatises on the novel merely remain denunciatory or highly critical of the genre (with the exception of the articles of Passe, Desmolets, and the scurrilous work of Lenglet Dufresnoy). Reviews and discussions in journals are much more interesting; but their use by the modern scholar can be only fragmentary at best, and again much of the criticism is in the form of attack. It is in terms of the attacks the novel underwent that Georges May has attempted to explain its development; it was criticised as both *invraisemblable* and immoral, in a way reminiscent of the seventeenth century's attacks on the theatre (May, 1963). The paucity of criticism is certainly due to the widely held view that the novel was an upstart genre without literary pedigree (comparable in this respect, as in others, to the *comédie bourgeoise*).[1] Aesthetically transgressive, the novel is criticised for cutting across traditional genre classification; socially transgressive, it was blamed for moral decadence, and its popularity attributed to the weakness of female readers' minds (see Desfontaines, 1757, vol. I, p. 223; Granet, 1739, vol. IX, p. 49). Marmontel, much later and far more interestingly, suggests that its development and success were in fact due to the degeneration of poetry and the extreme difficulty of French prosody (Marmontel, 1819–20, vol. III, p. 568). Can this social and aesthetic transgressiveness be held as evidence for a movement towards 'realism'? *Do* 'successive writers discover and learn to exploit effective ways of portraying real life'? I have already suggested that an uncritical use of 'real' to construct a teleological history of the novel is inadequate. A historian of the English novel, Ian Watt (1963) uses apparently similar concepts, 'fidelity to human experience', 'a transcription of real life'. However, he gives body to these definitions by offering the criterion that the individual should be treated seriously as an individual. Watt has shown all that the notion of an 'individual', as constrained and identified by space and time, owes to Locke. Whereas Baroque theories of the world as illusion located reality elsewhere, in Lockean theory the reality *is* the appearance: appearance makes us believe it is reality and *it is*, in the sense that we don't go beyond it. (One or two carefully explored hitches – the bent stick in the water, for instance – are included in this account.) In the same way, perhaps, realist novels of the nineteenth century block away any attempt to interpret them as other than *adequate* to 'reality' conceived in material, precisely located spatio-temporal terms. This notion of the individual is part of a comparatively recent ideology, and one that was in the process of constitution during the eighteenth century. Treating it as *the* criterion relevant to the history of the eighteenth-century novel does not merely cause one to lose sight of other, equally important processes; it tends to erase the fact that the criterion may even be anachronistic. For although it is evidently true that eighteenth-century writers were seriously and not merely scurrilously concerned with the habits of those social classes whose activities had hitherto reached the field of 'literature' (or indeed of the written word, other than police archives) only by way of satire, 'realism' is not a term used by eighteenth-century criticism. Indeed, modern critics, impatient to find traces of the substance 'realism' in eighteenth-century theory and practice, have not always appreciated how *unreal* descriptions of low life were felt to be. For at the level of the teller of the story, there was no motive for their having been written at all:

L'Auteur qui la descrit est poussé à le faire, par une raison principale, soit par la singularité des avantures dont elle est remplie, soit par la sévérité de sa conduite & l'exactitude de ses actions qu'il descrit en les admirant lui-même, & en les donnant pour examples de vertus à la postérité, ou pour s'attirer la protection et la récompense des successeurs de celui de qui il descrit la vie. (*La Coquette punie*, 1740, p. 3)

In other words, the eighteenth century was concerned not merely with the tale, but with the circumstances of its telling; if these were not plausible, not felt to be real, then the tale was not either.

A remark such as that just quoted brings us back to Georges May's account of the eighteenth-century novel as navigating between charges of lowness, and thus immorality, and *invraisemblance*; but here it is low life itself which, while 'existing', is not plausibly to be written about, since the text cannot plausibly be passed off as genuine memoirs. Surely here, if 'illusion' and realism cannot be correlated unequivocally, 'illusion' and 'authenticity' can?

Illusion and authenticity

There was from about 1670 onwards what Tieje in a fundamental article has called 'a peculiar phase' in the development of the French novel (Tieje, 1913). This was the publication of a spate of 'faux mémoires' claiming authenticity: collections of letters purporting to be real; imaginary voyages backed up with 'sources'. This phase has been explored in depth: by Tieje, the oldest and least acknowledged critic (1912, 1916); by Mylne (1965); and by Stewart (1969). The explanation of the last two critics is in terms of illusion as a mistake. The authors supposedly wish their works to be taken for genuine, for this was the ultimate test of their plausibility. The phase is said to be part of the growing pains of the novel, the necessary technical experiment to render possible the omniscient narrator, and to examine what the assumptions underlying the narrator's position must be for the narrative to be plausible.

It is true that these 'faux mémoires' were attacked in the eighteenth century as inducing actual mistakes. Critics complain, for instance, that future generations will be unable to distinguish history from fiction:

Quant à ceux-ci [les romans] plût-à-Dieu que nous n'y lussions que des noms inventés, nous ne serions pas dans le cas de craindre que la postérité ne prît des recueils de fables pour des fragmens précieux de notre Histoire. Pour moi, je suis persuadé que cela arrivera un jour. La vraisemblance des aventures, le rapport de certaines circonstances, imaginées avec les traits les plus connus de l'Histoire générale, un mélange adroit et continuel du mensonge avec la vérité tout cela contribuera à faire tomber dans l'erreur ceux qui dans quelques siècles voudront écrire ce qui s'est passé de notre tems. Il en sera infailliblement qui regarderont alors comme un trésor inestimable d'anecdotes quelques-uns de ces prétendus *Mémoires* donnés sous des noms célèbres par Gatien de Courtilz. (*Bibliothèque françoise*, 1741, vol. xxxiii, pp. 355–6)

Such fears were not vain: Courtilz de Sandras' novel, *Les mémoires d'Artagnan*, like the *Lettres d'une religieuse portuguaise* (Guilleragues, 1962) have been taken as authentic. It is clear from major bibliographies that works called 'lettres' and 'mémoires' cannot always be said definitely to be either authentic or fictional (Jones, 1939; Martin, Mylne and Frautschi, 1977). Swift (or Steele?), writing as Sir Isaac Bickerstaff, asserts roundly 'The word memoir is French for a novel' (Stewart, 1969, p. 235). The problem is complicated by the status of history at the time: defenders of the novel frequently point out that historians elaborate on their material, inserting motives, putting speeches into personnages' mouths (Baculard d'Arnaud, 1782, vol. I, pp. vi-vii).[2] Thus Bayle, whose effort was so greatly directed to the criticism of historical sources, complains that novels are rendering impossible the only method of establishing historical truth – the cross-checking of texts – and, perhaps prophetically, adds: 'Je crois qu'enfin on contraindra les Puissances à donner ordre que ces nouveaux Romanistes ayent à opter: qu'ils fassent, ou des Histoires toutes pures ou des Romans tout purs' (in May, 1955, p. 160). The difficulty was compounded by the novel's chameleon-like absorption of historical techniques. Swift criticises the status of the manuscript in *Gulliver's Travels*; the *Histoire des Sevarambes* claims to insert the transcription of a manuscript. Prévost establishes a pedigree for his 'editor' throughout his great novels – the success of the *Homme de qualité* is said to have led Cleveland's son and the heirs of the Doyen de Killerine to ask his help in preparation of the manuscript.[3] But the question of the relation of the editor to his text is raised by his work on a genuine history: Prévost actually says of the *Mémoires de M. de Thou*, which he was editing: 'On pourrait juger par cette Préface de Rigault, qu'il seroit l'auteur des Mémoires de la vie de M. de Thou. Cependant l'opinion commune, jointe à la vraisemblance, est que ces Mémoires ont été écrits par M. de Thou même, quoiqu'ils paroissent écrits par un de ses amis.' He criticises Thou's oblique self-praise in a way that recalls critical attacks on the novelist for disguising his presence in novels: 'De Thou pouvoit y parler avec dignité en tierce personne, comme a fait César dans ses Commentaires: mais il devoit, ce me semble, s'abstenir de faire illusion à son lecteur en prenant trop le ton d'un autre écrivain que lui, comme il fait souvent. Ç'a été sans doute pour augmenter cette illusion & pour se déguiser davantage qu'il s'est donné souvent des louanges dans ses Mémoires' (Prévost, *Histoire universelle*, 1734, p. xxv).

The novel considered in terms of 'realism' moves between the low and the implausible. In terms of 'authenticity', that movement is between Romance and history. But is the space between these two made continuous by the 'faux mémoires' imitation of historical method? Are writers seeking to erase awareness that what we read is a novel? The first objection to such an interpretation is that such

techniques have ancient roots: 'Authors' declarations of veracity date back to the Greek novel and are found in abundance during the *régime* of the chivalrous romance and the Italian *novella*, but it is chiefly during the seventeenth century that three motives governing this veracity are widely proclaimed: the wickedness of lying, the utility or verified narrative and the pleasure truth affords a reader' (Tieje, 1912, p. 415). It is significant that in the later eighteenth century, where the novel's right to existence has been established, these motives are reversed: it is fiction that is useful. The problem is thus not the techniques by themselves, but their intensified use after 1670: 'None of the works appear with the startling embroideries which adorn the preface and first chapters after 1670' (Tieje, 1912, p. 415). The second objection is that such novels as those of Madame de La Fayette and Saint-Réal show little sign of technical difficulties ill-surmounted, and none at all in the constitution of an omniscient narrator, and that these works are prior to the 'faux mémoires' vogue. The teleological explanation, according to which the novel is supposedly refining its techniques of plausibility, hardly survives such an objection. Perhaps the spate of 'faux mémoires' should rather, Henri Coulet has suggested (Coulet, 1967), be related to the 'crisis in consciousness', to use Paul Hazard's phrase (Hazard, 1935), which seems to have taken place at the end of the seventeenth century: that is, the profound shift in Western apprehension of experience and uncertainty about how that experience should be analysed. This relation cannot be further elaborated here. What seems evident, and to be relevant evidence for the development of the novel, is that the concept of 'truth', and that of 'reality' too, change radically – truth comes in fact to mean historical truth. History and Romance are consciously separated and it is between these two that the novel moves. Their mutual definition is expressed in the work of Lenglet.

Lenglet Dufresnoy's work, *De l'usage des romans*, a defence of the novel, was written in 1734 under the pseudonym of Gordon de Percel. In the very next year he wrote, under his own name, an attack on his own book, entitled *L'Histoire justifiée contre les romans*. Modern critics have taken the defence of the novel entirely seriously (see Sgard and Oudart, 1978). But *De l'usage des romans* has to be read in the light of its spoof title page, and its companion volume, so to speak. It deals with the romance rather than the novel, repeats the old theory of the novel as an epic in prose, and treats the shorter *nouvelles* in vogue as merely amputated parts of a romance. The defence of the novel assumes its

fictionality: 'En commençant à le lire, je sçai que tout en est faux; on me le dit & je me le persuade; tant mieux s'il y a du vrai, c'est autant de profit dès qu'on me le fera connoître', or again, 'je sçai que tout est faux dans le avantures qu'ils me racontent mais on me les donne pour telles; & cependant tout y est si vraisemblable que je voudrais que tout en fût vrai' (Lenglet, 1734, pp. 59. 62). He attacks history – the novel is more truthful in that it shows the power of women in politics. The sincerity of such a defence of the novel may be doubted, especially when *L'Histoire des favorites* is recommended reading for young girls. But *l'Histoire justifée contre les romans,* and its defence of history, is equally suspect. It insists on the satisfaction procured by 'la verité & la certitude des faits' (Lenglet, 1735, p. 33), yet attacks the historian Varillas[4] for inaccuracy: his work is suitable material . . . for a novel. In spite of Lenglet's serious bibliographical interest in the novel, the justification of the novel cannot be read naively. Not merely do the two theoretical works oppose each other, but within each text the novel and history are contrasted. In fact, the texts work the space between Romance and history by playing one off against the other, by defining each against the other. Lenglet had himself put this into practise; the *Bibliothèque universelle des romans* calls Lenglet's novel, *La Catanoise* (1731) 'un mélange indigeste d'histoire et de fiction'. The theoretical disreputableness of Lenglet – 'Ainsi M** par un privilège qui lui est particulier, trouve le moyen de penser indifféremment le pour et le contre' (*Journal de Trévoux,* avril 1734, p. 678), said, it should be noted, *before* the publication of *L'Histoire justifiée* – reflects, as we shall see, the plying of the novel between the two modes: 'real' history is defined against 'unreal' novel, or the 'real' novel against deformed history.[5] Lenglet's theoretical work defines 'real' by reference to the 'unreal'; his two opposing treatises on history and Romance each embody the opposition within themselves. This double embodiment can be related to novel theory and novel practice, as we shall see.

The novel and history: the double bind

Bayle's insistent concern for a clear distinction between history and Romance shows that actual practice tended to ignore such a distinction. As a result, the theory or theories of the novel in the early part of the century worked to make a demarcation between the novel and history. Moreover, 'truth', in an important epistemological change, seems to become historical truth: 'Un récit qui ne contient rien que de vrai est une *Histoire*; un tissu de fiction est une *Fable*; le mélange de la Fable et de l'Histoire fait le Roman' (Desmolets, 1739, p. 193).

Whether or not what is presented is *plausible*, it is presented by novelists as authentic. The techniques are in fact, I have suggested, borrowed from history. But it is the parasitic nature of these techniques which creates Bayle's problem. Earlier, critics would defend the novel from such criticism by insisting on an asymptotic relation to historical truth – fiction is necessary in the novel, for this is what distinguishes the genre from truth:

Si nous consentons d'être trompés, nous voulons que ce soit avec art [. . .]. Mais lorsque nous voyons qu'un Auteur a puisé dans le sein de la nature tout ce qui est de son invention ou que du moins il l'a rendu conforme aux idées reçues, quand nous sentons la vérité des portraits, & des caractères qu'il trace, quand tous ces événements nous paroissent liés & enchaînés les uns aux autres, alors loin d'être en garde contre l'illusion nous nous persuadons presque qu'il n'y a rien de feint dans ce que nous lisons: l'art consiste donc principalement à paroître historien lors même qu'on imagine & à tromper agréablement par la liaison & la vraisemblance des faits. (Passe, 1749, p. 104)

(This is a specific version of the general problem of the replica: if an art object replaces its model, then is it not as good as its model, and therefore not an imitation?) The novel must remain a parasite, not turn into the host. Illusion which contains awareness is used to prevent the total absorption of the novel into history: 'Il en est [. . .] comme de l'opéra: quand on y va, on ne s'attend point à un spectacle naturel' (Passe, 1749, p. 105). Or fiction is equated with art: pleasure-creating, but also pleasure-destroying if it reveals itself.[6] The asymptotic relation to history is ensured by the dual analysis of illusion: it is 'une espèce de bonne foy sur laquelle on se repose' (Bridard de La Garde, 1740, p. 34); and it is also based on connivance, on awareness that the fiction is not truth. 'Quelque fausseté qu'on sache qu'il y ait dans un Roman, le titre commence d'engager à le lire et l'on n'en a pas plutôt vu le commencement qu'on devient curieux de voir la fin. Les intrigues suspendent agréablement l'esprit du Lecteur' (*La Coquette punie*, 1740, p. 3). It is like watching a game, or a ship in a storm, but yet again, pleasure is possible only if the reader 'se figure que toutes ces fictions sont autant de vérités' (*La Coquette punie*, 1740, p. 2). 'Illusion' here prises apart Romance and history: yet illusion can be created only by truth. The novel is caught in a double bind: it must approach historical truth, yet must not be historical truth.[7]

Prévost's work illustrates this double bind. With his Jesuit and

Benedictine training and his imaginative energy, he writes works which exhibit every step of the scale from fiction to history: his fusion of the two is the 'histoire particulière', fictionalised biographies of *Marguerite d'Anjou*, or *Guillaume le Conquérant*, which admit the grandeur of history yet contain details which might appear puerile, though they achieve, he says, 'L'Agrément des Mémoires les plus circonstanciés' (Prévost, *Marguerite d'Anjou*, 1740, vol. I, p. xi). Objective truth and subjective illusion are harmonised; the moral and complaisant softness of such a novel immediately produces condemnation from critics who 'ne font jamais grâce à de séduisans mensonges travestis sous la livrée de la vérité, que quelques-uns d'entre eux appellent des brochures romanesques appliquées sur une trame historique' (Bridard de La Garde, 1740, p. 31). Prévost's work provokes the ironic remark from Desfontaines: 'L'auteur n'a point eu dessein de faire illusion. Il écrit son histoire comme un roman, afin que personne n'y fût trompé' (*Observations sur les écrits modernes*, vol. XXVIII, 1742, pp. 284–5).

But this criticism of novels for going too close to history ('séduisans mensonges travestis sous la livrée de la vérité'), and of history for being too close to a novel, is only one version of the plying between history and Romance discussed theoretically *à propos* of Lenglet. For novelists may be criticised if they do not present their work as 'real' history, thus destroying illusion: 'Le plus grand défaut des Romans ordinaires, de ceux qu'on a la bonté de lire, est de paroître trop Romans; jusques-là que leurs Auteurs font souvent la sottise d'en avertir les Lecteurs à la tête de l'Ouvrage. Quelle illusion prétendent-ils faire après cela?' (Desfontaines, 1757, vol. I, p. 220). Or, on the contrary, novelists may prefer to write a 'real' novel rather than deformed history, where the hero is a well-known historical figure; the admission that the work is a novel may be necessary in order to avoid its rejection as a false memoir (rather than as a novel). Madame de La Fayette and Edmé Boursault thus admit openly in two of their prefaces that their work is a novel. They need to do this precisely because the hero is an historical figure, and the name of the Princesse de Montpensier is so famous that the author must say that the work

N'est tiré[e] d'Aucun Manuscrit qui nous soit demeuré du temps des personnages dont elle parle. L'Auteur ayant voulu pour son divertissement escrire des avantures inventées à plaisir, a jugé plus à propos de prendre des noms connus dans nos Histoires, *que de se servir de ceux que l'on trouve dans les Romas* [sic] croiant bien que la réputation de Madame de Monpensier ne seroit pas blessée par un récit effectivement fabuleux. (La Fayette, 1674, p. iii)[8]

Here the admission that the work is a novel is played off against other novels: admitted fiction is more true than disguised fiction.

If critics encouraged the novel's parasitising of historical techniques while insisting that the two genres must be separate, for writers this became a problem. The very success of art is self-cancelling: 'Les romanciers se sont mis l'esprit à la torture pour inventer quelque circonstance capable de persuader que l'ouvrage qu'ils s'étaient bien donné de la peine à faire n'était pas d'eux' (Béliard, in Mornet, 1925, vol. I, p. 40).[9] Yet it is the very shifting nature of the parasitising that is exploited both by critics and by writers. It is not any one set of techniques which can be used, but their reversible significance which is exploited. The notion of *vraisemblance* provides scope for a typically reversible argument, as has already been pointed out (above, p. 35). Does the lack of precise place names in an (imaginary) voyage prove its fictional quality, or rather the authentic status of the narrative, because the captain does not wish to reveal the sources of his wealth? 'Mais on peut regarder cette suppression même si elle est volontaire, dans un lieu où l'on est porté à la regretter, comme un caractère de bonne foi pour le reste de l'ouvrage, puisque avec *moins de respect pour la vérité il aurait été facile de remplir ce vide par des suppositions imaginaires*' (Prévost, quoted by Stewart, 1969, p. 276). What is *invraisemblance* in a fiction is *vrai* in reality and thus, by conversion, becomes *vraisemblance* in fiction. Where in the seventeenth-century theory there was a stable divorce between true and seeming true, with the seeming true, *vraisemblance,* being adequate to a norm (see above, pp. 34ff), here there is a parasitic relation. If truth as the *vraisemblable* is what is left after the truth which is surprising has been excised, then even the most unlikely narrative can define its reality by reference to the more unlikely it has omitted. Thus, Lambert's 'dame de qualité', the supposed author of memoirs not striking for their plausibility, states: 'J'ai souvent sacrifié la Vérité à la Vraisemblance, je veux dire, que je n'ai retranché bien des Faits très-réels & très véritables que parce qu'ils pourroient paroître peu vraisemblables' (Lambert, 1741, *préface*). For the exception may be *invraisemblable*: 'Pour peu qu'on réfléchisse, il est aisé de convenir que je n'ai aucune raison pour en imposer au Public. Si j'eusse désiré faire un roman, je ne m'en serais pas tenu à des récits si simples & à des faits si ordinaires, j'aurais écrit en romancier, ainsi que je l'ai fait dans d'autres ouvrages que je n'ai mis sur le compte de personne' (Doppet, 1789, pp. vii–ix). Or the surprising nature of the events may be precisely what causes them to be recounted, and guarantees the authenticity of the act of writing: 'Si l'on trouve dans cette histoire quelques aventures surprenantes, on doit se souvenir que c'est ce qui les rend dignes d'être communiquées au Public. Des événements communs intéressent trop peu pour mériter d'être écrits' (Prévost, *Homme de qualité*, 1731, p. 2).[10] Or, alternatively, the surprising is necessary for a good novel, but stamps it inevitably as fictional:

Si dans l'histoire de chaque personne en particulier on pouvoit trouver assez d'actions héroïques admirables & surprenantes pour en former un livre intéressant, on ne seroit pas obligé d'emprunter de la Fable des sujets étrangers pour composer des Romans; mais il y a si peu de gens de la vie desquels on puisse trouver une histoire admirable & vraie tout à la fois, qu'on ne peut se dispenser de donner au public des histoires assez bien imaginées pour qu'elles ayent apparence de vérité. (*La Coquette punie*, 1740, p. 3)

Verisimilitude, then, like history, puts the novel in a double bind. Is it more or less *vraisemblable* to admit that a novel is a novel? Or to describe extraordinary events? Is it better to 'extend' history by relating fictional events in the lives of well-known people, or to create a substitute for it, by inserting fictional lives into an historical background? My point is that many eighteenth-century novels exploit this double bind, not so much causing us to make a mistake about the status of what is being read (illusion as *adequatio*), as inducing doubt: perhaps it isn't a novel? perhaps it is more than a novel? (illusion as *aletheia*). The novels exploit the gap opening between Romance and history not by occupying and colonising it so much as by moving between these poles: they do this by virtue of a feature of language, difficult though not impossible to reproduce in painting (compare Magritte's pictures seen through a painted window). In any utterance there is an implicit or explicit statement maker as well as a statement. The question of truth and falsehood can thus be applied to an implicit or explicit utterance about the statement maker as well as to the statement. As a result sets of truth values can be assigned not merely to the novel-as-statement, but to statements about the novel, or about the statement maker ('meta-statements') (see table on p. 95).

It is Diderot's *Jacques le fataliste* which exploits this transference of truth value with most virtuosity. But even in those forms which appear to exclude the unreal, by virtue of the statement maker's claim to speak authentically, the very act of exclusion reintroduces

Fact	Statement	Statement about the statement or about the statement maker	
Yes	T (i.e. not a novel)	'it is not a novel' 'he speaks of what he knows'	T
		'it is a novel' 'he is inventing'	F
No	F (i.e. is a novel)	'it is not a novel' 'it really happened' 'he is not inventing'	F
		'it is a novel' 'he is making it up'	T

doubt, or awareness of the possibility of fiction. This appears true of the 'faux mémoires', as I shall now show.

Illusion and 'faux mémoires'

To make a novel so similar to the form of memoirs that it is taken to be authentic would seem to be a putting into practice of, or at least the practical counterpart of, the idea of illusion as a mistake. But is it? Writers certainly make a living out of the 'fait divers'. Baculard d'Arnaud's *Les Époux malheureux*, and Mouhy's *Anne-Marie de Moras* exploit well-known court cases. Yet this is not a passing off as fiction but the romancing of history. The great writer conducts this on a psychological level. When Prévost uses the story of Mademoiselle d'Aissé in *Histoire d'une Grecque moderne*, it is the reader, not the narrator, who must decide what is true: 'Je dois m'en fier à des apparences dont j'abandonne le jugement à mes lecteurs' (Prévost, *Histoire d'une Grecque moderne*, 1965, pp. 4–5). In this novel, the narrator's position does not authenticate – on the contrary, it is avowedly partial, perhaps false. As a result, the narrator's own judgement is inhibited: 'Une passion violente ne fera-t-elle point changer de nature tout ce qui va passer par mes yeux ou par mes mains [. . .]? Voilà les raisons qui doivent tenir un Lecteur en garde. Mais s'il est éclairé, il jugera tout d'un coup qu'en les déclarant avec cette franchise, j'étois sûr d'en effacer bientôt l'impression par un autre aveu' (Prévost, *Histoire d'une Grecque moderne*, 1965, p. 3). The great writer, then, turns appearance of reality into appearance of appearance.

Many of these attempts to authenticate are not as simple as they look. Even Courtilz's case, quoted as dangerous by Bayle, is not clear-cut. Henri Coulet has rightly doubted whether his novels –

95

held by Mylne and others as pure examples of the passing off of 'faux mémoires' as real – deceived anybody (Coulet, 1967, vol. I, p. 213). It is true that the prefaces of his works produce evidence for their genuineness: appeals to those who have known the supposed author; explanations of why he wished to write the memoirs (Courtilz de Sandras, 1687, *préface*). Yet the prefaces all contain curious turns of phrase, significantly omitted by Mylne. In one, the editor says of part of the memoirs: 'Si M. le C.D.R. se montre ainsi sincère dans un récit *qui ressemble si fort à un conte fait à plaisir* combien à plus forte raison devons-nous ajoûter foi aux choses qu'il raporte d'ailleurs';[11] and in another series of memoirs:

Il paroît de temps en temps des Livres, où l'esprit a travaillé avec tant de succès que le public reçoit comme des vérités ce qui n'est souvent qu'une fable. J'en connois quelques-uns de cette espèce où les choses sont rapportées avec tant de vrai-semblance que l'on demeure partagé *entre les apparences trompeuses & la connoissance que l'on a de la vérité.* (Courtilz de Sandras, 1701, *préface*)

(The latter comments are followed by a statement that doubters need only consult certain nobles, who know the truth of what is recounted.) Here, the 'apparances trompeuses' are those of novels: 'vérité' is used of history. The statement appears designed to assert truth by excluding appearances of truth, by setting them to the account of the novel. It seems to incorporate the distinction appearance/truth in order the better to expel appearance, and awareness of appearance, from the memoirs. But of course it also does the opposite: it enables the reader to reverse the incorporation and to apply the remark to the novel's own technique. Courtilz asserts the truth of his work by assurances that it is not a novel. This surely does not so much assure us of its authenticity as make us wonder how much is fiction? Courtilz is sowing doubt rather than certainty.[12] Rather than make the text adequate to some external model, this exclusion of the 'false' novel and consequent definition of true 'history' in fact causes us to wonder about the status of what we are reading.[13] Similar statements are made by writers of imaginary voyages. Thus Vairasse d'Alais in the *Histoire des Sevarambes* contrasts the truth of this work with the fictional republic of Plato, Bacon's *New Atlantis,* and More's *Utopia* (Vairasse d'Alais, 1702, *préface*). Or the definition of real and unreal by their opposition may even be formalised: statements about historical reality may be made in the body of the novel, while the preface discusses the events as a novel. Thus in Eustache Le Noble's *Ildegerte, reine de Norwège* (1694), the introductory passages insist on the historical truth of what is recounted, yet the *Au Lecteur* had discussed the way in which French taste in the novel had changed.

That novels were read as possibly historical, and history as possible Romance, becomes evident when the cases of Diderot and Doppet are considered. Diderot and Grimm doctored Madame d'Epinay's *autobiographie romancée* so that, with the manipulations of later editors, it was until fairly recently taken as a set of totally genuine, if dubiously truthful, memoirs (d'Epinay, 1951). But what was the purpose of the doctoring? They did not insert names: the (possible) readers were to be led to fill in the references. And they intended this work by the reader to blacken Rousseau. The pair were actually exploiting the *public's use of the novel*, not a crude faith in the veracity of memoirs. The public were to read behind the fictional lines to the (false) history. Slightly later, Doppet makes a whole career from the reading of memoirs as fiction and fiction as memoirs. His novel *Les Mémoires de Madame de Warens* attacks Rousseau's *Confessions* as a defamatory novel. In imitating the traditional remarks about the veracity of what is told, he is not merely reversing autobiographical truth and fiction; he is exploiting the reading of novels as 'true' memoirs and of 'faux mémoires' as novels.

En comparant ce qu'on a vu dans les Confessions, avec les Mémoires qu'on va lire, peut-être les croîra-t-on supposés? Rousseau avec un air de candeur dont personne n'a su se masquer mieux que lui, a fasciné tous les yeux, a séduit tous les esprits, on s'est accoutumé à l'envisager comme un homme extraordinaire qui s'est élevé au dessus de tout & pour qui rien ne fut sacré; on lui a pardonné ses écarts en faveur des lumières qu'il a répandues sur la surface du globe; tous nos lecteurs sont prévenus; aussi croirions-nous que ce seroit perdre beaucoup de tems, que de faire une longue dissertation pour appuyer l'authenticité des titres que nous allons mettre au jour, peut-être même les affoibliroit-on en travaillant à les étayer par tous les moyens que la vérité unie à la saine logique peuvent suggérer. (Doppet, 1786, pp. xiv–xv)

Rather than a negation of Rousseau's memoirs we have a parasitic use of them, a confrontation of truth with a new truth, defended further in the preface to *Vintzenried*, a picaresque novel about a young and authentic wastrel who ends up as one of Madame de Warens' protégés. Doppet's gaining of plausibility by turning the *Confessions* into a novel is typical of the 'faux mémoires'. The force is less that of a practical joke than that of a deliberate parasitic use of memoirs, a deliberate exploitation of the need to define the real by defining the unreal. Furthermore, far from being read as pieces of reality or even as a 'fictional world resembling the real one so closely that the reader does not notice the difference' (Stewart, 1969, p. 5), such novels were read in a highly sophisticated way, the reader passing from historical truth to levels of imitated history in much the same way as Doppet makes the *Confessions* engender a series of novels. The interplay between feigned authenticity and admitted deceit has here become complicated. To exclude appearances of appearance is to exclude the novel, and thus to expel awareness; but this possibility of deceit which by its extension makes the written novel declared to be 'authentic', has then the appearance of truth. But the excluded novel is presented as appearance of appearance of truth. Awareness of the novel is thus brought back.[14]

To sum up, even apparently clear-cut cases of 'faux mémoires' define themselves by defining what they are not: they are not novels. In saying this, in affirming their historical nature, they are rejecting the Romances. But in so doing they cast doubt on their own status. Are they truer than a novel? Or has a fictional light been shed on an episode in history?

Diderot's 'La Religieuse'

Diderot's *La Religieuse*, and indeed the short story, *Les Deux Amis de Bourbonne*, would appear to be a specially powerful counterexample to the thesis I am developing. They both began, it seems, in the passing off of a text as reality, as practical jokes. Diderot seems to have developed the tradition of *la burla*,[15] the practical joke played within a close circle on one of its members. 'Illusion' here is an actual mistake but also regains its older sense of 'mocking'. Grimm, in his account of the genesis of *La Religieuse*, published in the *Correspondance littéraire* in 1770, speaks of the novel as fragmentary: it was, he says, written as a by-product of the letters which were concocted by the circle around Madame d'Epinay, and which were designed to tempt a friend, the Marquis de Croismare, back to Paris. The letters purported to be from a nun who, having applied to have her vows annulled and having lost her lawsuit, describes her plight and begs the Marquis for help. This nun really existed, as Georges May has shown (May, 1954). Yet Grimm's account of the practical joke is not convincing, as Vivienne Mylne has rightly pointed out (Mylne, 1962): why have the nun appear anxious to leave Paris and beg for a place in the Marquis' country house, if the aim is to get him back to Paris? Moreover, Diderot clearly thought, at least momentarily, that the

Marquis' letters of reply were forged, and that he was himself the victim of the joke (Diderot, *Correspondance*, vol. III, p. 18, letter about 10 February 1760). Whoever was the object of the *illusio*, whether the Marquis or Diderot, the game did not stop there. Grimm published the bogus letters of the nun and the apparently 'real' letters of the Marquis in the *Correspondance littéraire*. (The text of the novel itself was only distributed in the *Correspondance littéraire* in 1780–2.) Diderot, when he came to revise his novel, also revised Grimm's account of the practical joke, now known as the *Préface-annexe*, and clearly intended the two to be published together. What did he mean by this? Is the novel intended to extort sympathy from the reader, just as the letters were intended to get the Marquis to act on behalf of a nun who existed only hypothetically, in Diderot's letters? And is the *Préface-annexe* intended to reveal that the sympathy, passive and active, has been gained by a trick?[16] By putting *Préface-annexe* and novel together, Diderot shows he intended disclosure, indeed that the revelation is essential: the practical joke which is so perfect that it remains unknown is the most imperfect. The themes of the *Vernet* article in the *Salon de 1767* are put into practice; the reader must be forced to recognise his own mistake in order to recognise the novel's power: he must be *seduced*, to use the vocabulary of illusion, but there must be a making conscious of this illusion. (That the temporality of this is complex is recognised by the title under which it is now known, *Préface-annexe*, as it was in the manuscript, where it is called *Préface du précédent ouvrage* (Dieckmann, 1952).)

If in Diderot's case 'illusion' is a problem of gaining power over the reader, it is also an aesthetic problem, as the annexe in the *Préface-annexe* – the *Question aux gens de lettres* – shows:

M. Diderot, après avoir passé des matinées à composer des lettres bien écrites, bien pensées, bien pathétiques, bien romanesques, employait des journées à les gâter en supprimant, sur les conseils de sa femme et de ses associés en scélératesse, tout ce qu'elles avaient de saillant, d'exagéré, de contraire à l'extrême simplicité et à la dernière vraisemblance; en sorte que si l'on eût ramassé dans la rue les premières, on eût dit: 'Cela est beau, fort beau . . .' et que si l'on eût ramassé les dernières on eût dit: 'cela est bien vrai'. Quelles sont les bonnes? sont-ce celles qui auraient peut-être obtenu l'admiration? Ou celles qui devaient certainement produire l'illusion? (*Diderot*, 1963, p. 207)

But the process of 'illusion', the process of getting the reader to accept for reality what is only a sham, does not stop here. Diderot's revelation of the mystification by seeming to wish to place the

99

Préface-annexe alongside the novel is itself a trick, a mystification. The *Préface-annexe* recounts how a Monsieur d'Allainville found Diderot in tears at his writing desk during the composition of the novel and on enquiry was told: 'Je me désole d'un conte que je me fais' (1963, p. 181). The incident was used for many years by critics as evidence of Diderot's sentimentality. It was left to the discovery of a manuscript and to textual scholarship to show that Diderot actually inserted the incident into Grimm's text (Dieckmann, 1952). The revelation of the mystification only mystifies further. This comes about by a use of *dédoublement.*[17] The reader is presented not only with the ludicrous figure of Diderot *dédoublé* – 'Je me désole d'un conte que je me fais' – but also with a possible account of his own mode of feeling when reading the novel itself. Yet Diderot is not ludicrous because he is not *dédoublé*; he is not even there at all, since, on the contrary, he is exerting power over Grimm at a distance by making Grimm speak with his mouth, and power over the reader by the trick. Reality and appearance are not clearly distinguished, feeling is here provoked and not spontaneous, derived from reflexive exhibition – he is saddened by a story he is telling himself – or from a trick. But the revelation of the trick is yet a further manœuvre, and does not engender truth. For truth is *not* identical with openness and frankness. In the novels of the early part of the century the assertions of truth, of openness, of the absence of deceit, engendered a feeling of falseness; in *La Religieuse*, the disclosure of the unreal does not result in truth, but, because the disclosure is not itself untrue, plunges us further into doubt.

There is a similar movement within the body of the novel. The heavy rhetoric of Suzanne the nun resembles to an almost confusing degree the eloquent letters rejected by the *Question aux gens de lettres* just quoted (Ellrich, 1961), though it is also true that the novel is not well-written in the conventional eighteenth-century sense. The strong-arm tactics of such rhetoric are underlined by the famous *bévues* – the letter from the nun's mother which proclaims that it was sent the day before it was written; the 'forgetting' that the friendly Sœur Ursule was to die; the professed ignorance of the intentions of the lesbian Mother Superior, though at the time Suzanne is supposedly writing she has listened at the confessional and is fully enlightened. These have sometimes been explained by a composition in stages, or a formal conflict between journal form, in which the narration is roughly contemporary with the events narrated, and the retrospective memoir form (May 1954). The first hypothesis can be eliminated: the manuscript published by Jean

Parrish shows similar 'errors' (*Diderot–Parrish*, 1963). The second hypothesis had been taken to imply that

Diderot n'est pas un auteur assez détaché pour raconter une histoire déjà faite. Il s'identifie à chaque instant du devenir de son personnage, et il prend chaque fois à son compte ses ignorances et ses illusions provisoires, sans songer qu'elles sont incompatibles avec les découvertes futures déjà faites pourtant au moment où le récit est sensé être écrit. (Mauzi, in Diderot, *O.C.*, vol. IV, p. ix)

The second hypothesis conflicts with the state of awareness of *illusio* that the *Préface-annexe* induces in the reader – the 'real' genesis of the novel turned out to be immersed in disquieting fiction, and worse, the hypothesis fails to explain the disquieting feeling in the reader that Suzanne is posturing for the pity and admiration of the Marquis, an awareness that the 'errors' can only reinforce. The reader is conscious of Suzanne's striving for effect, but so is she: like the actor in the *Paradoxe*, she herself watches her effect on others: 'Je ne sais pas ce qui se passait dans l'âme des spectateurs, mais ils voyaient une jeune victime qu'on portoit à l'autel.' By saying 'je ne sais' she leaves a freedom of reaction to the audience, and to the reader, she emphasises her moral absence from her forced vow (Lewinter, 1976), but it is an illusory freedom since the effect is in fact described. In the description of her recovery from a faint she describes herself as if from outside (Ellrich, 1961). She is both meek in her description of herself and violent in her actions. The whole tenour of the writing is calculated to make others sympathise and to persuade them to action. Thus it mirrors directly her experience as described within the novel. For she herself is compelled to do something, whether by deceit (the first convent) by a change of will (Madame de Moni, the spiritual Superior), by being crushed into submission (Sœur Christine, the sadistic Superior) and by seduction (the lesbian). This theme is embodied in the form: both the search for power, through the plea for sympathy, and the awareness of her effect on others, derive from her being alienated from her liberty.

The whole work, novel and *Préface-annexe*, uses the principle of internal formal reflection. Suzanne's subjection to power reflects the reader's subjection to her rhetoric. Her alienation from herself is an alienation from her liberty and at the same time a preservation of it: were she at one with herself, she would not have survived. But this serves to catch the reader, who sympathises (comes under the novel's power) and rejects such distorted sympathy (keeps his freedom). Each mirrored relation in fact obscures the relation

101

between fiction and fictional truth: the reader slips between them. Such a structure explains the curious contradictory corrections: 'La tristesse la plus naturelle' (*Diderot–Parrish*, 1963, p. 61) becomes 'la tristesse la mieux étudiée (*Diderot*, 1963, p. 6); 'physiquement aliéné' replaces 'moralement' (*Diderot–Parrish*, 1963, p. 86 and *Diderot*, 1963, p. 35); the jumps in the quality of experienced time: 'On avait fait des dots considérables à mes sœurs; je me promettais un sort égal au leur, et ma tête s'était remplie de projets séduisants, *lorsqu'*on me fit demander au parloir' (*Diderot*, 1963, p. 5); the jumps in characterisation: the mother's confessor 'avait de l'humanité: il était entré tard en religion' and yet plays an odious role; Dom Morel protects Suzanne's chastity only to attack it. Suzanne's 'palier de conscience' is also a 'piège à consciences'. Diderot is at the same time present and absent in Suzanne, and she is present in the nun's body, for she is imprisoned in the convent, as she is absent in the nun's spirit, for she is imprisoned against her will; and the absence and presence is again reflected in the planting of the sentence in the *Préface-annexe*: 'Je me désole d'un conte que je me fais.' This is not a reporting of emotion: Diderot uses the line to trap us, he is absent where he appears to be present (*dissimulatio*).

The novel appears to induce illusion, it appears to be determined to tear-jerk, yet to do this by strong-arm tactics. As in the *Vernet* article in the *Salon de 1767*, the relation between reader and writer is conceived of in terms of *power*: and for this power to be seen it must be revealed. Hence the practical joke. But the novel deepens the structure of power and submission by implicitly comparing Suzanne's alienation to the reader's. As in the *Vernet* article we have here a use of reference outwards, of *papillotage* rather than of *adequatio*, of conformity to a model. The facetious frame sharpens the awareness of the scurrility in the exercise of power far more than any ponderous treatment would have done.

Parody, the contradictory of authenticity

So far I have argued that even the 'faux mémoires' are claiming authenticity not so much by adequation to the model of true memoirs, as by the assertion that they are not novels. They are parasitic on the techniques of history; by excluding the false, they define themselves in relation to Romance. Thereby, rather than being read 'straight' by a naive eighteenth-century reader, they were read as playing between truth and falsehood. In sophisticated versions, in Diderot's *La Religieuse*, for instance, the play between the poles of history and Romance becomes a play between planes of narration, between the fictionalised 'real' events of the *Préface-annexe* and the fictionalised fiction (the heavy rhetoric) of the main novel. A whole set of novels appears to contradict the principle of the 'faux mémoires'. If the novel claiming authenticity made 'sideglances' towards the fiction it asserted it was not, other novels claim nothing but facetiousness: 'Je donne une histoire au public qui ressemble assez à la mienne, sans l'être entièrement. Je prendrai sur mon compte quelques aventures arrivées à des personnes de ma connaissance. Je mentirai un peu [. . .], parce que naturellement j'aime à mentir' (Stewart, 1969, p. 306, quoting the preface to *L'Amour apostat,* 1739, probably by Delmas). This is to include the false and exclude the true, to insist on the reader's awareness that what he is reading is a novel. It leaves us in doubt as to whether there is a reality which acts as a backstop or *whether there is not.* Novels of this type may go further and become the mirror image of the 'faux mémoires': they ogle the real as the 'faux mémoires' did the fictional. 'Je ne suis qu'un pauvre libraire, et je ne sais guère bien ce qui en est; mais le public peut acheter mon livre comme roman, s'il ne juge pas a propos de l'acheter comme histoire' (Montesquieu, 1949, vol. I, p. 416), says the bookseller at the beginning of Montesquieu's *Histoire véritable,* in which the terms of the title take on a meaning entirely opposed to their usual one. For the 'veritable history' is built on outrageous assumptions: an oriental sponger recounts the story of his transmigration from fly to *maltôtier* to prude to doctor, and through the Alexandrian domain from Greece to Bactria to India. The multiplication of the *mémoire* principle and the arbitrariness of his metamorphoses speed up the discontinuity. There is no tension of gradual ascent or descent, only constant change which gives the work a structure related to *papillotage,* to the flickering of illusion. There is moreover a second-degree oscillation between the usual expectations one has of a novel and the events recounted, which are, to some degree, the inverse of these expectations. In this admirable *conte,* left unpublished, the aesthetic intention is reflected in the satire. The speed and the kaleidoscopic experiences make the 'hero' merely a succession of individuals: 'Je pourrais me comparer, dans toutes mes vies, à ces insectes qui semblent naître et mourir plusieurs fois, quoiqu'ils ne fassent que se dépouille successivement de leurs enveloppes' (Montesquieu, 1949, vol. I, pp. 443). Yet because he is composed out of these successive cycles (the atomism of the empirical concept of experience is conveyed by the metaphor of the unit of a life), he lacks a basis to this personality which is both continuous and individual, and is thus a total generality: 'je ne me regarde pas comme un individu' (Montesquieu, 1949, p. 423). The assertion that this is a 'histoire véritable' seems by its very absurdity and frivolity to bring into relief the reality of man's moral nature – his identity is merely an assemblage of different events. Fictional parody presents itself as not what it seems, as less than what it seems; but that is the very structure of the 'hero's' experience. The very same structure appears *in nucleo* in a phrase from *Le Temple de Gnide*, another 'roman de jeunesse' by Montesquieu, 'Les faveurs n'y ont que leur réalité propre' (Montesquieu, 1949, vol. I, p. 401). This is apparently a criticism of the crude sexual realism of the Sybarites, for whom the secondary qualities of experience are assimilated to the primary. In fact, however, the phrase undoes itself, the circumlocution 'les faveurs' suggesting a realism which the Sybarites only confirm. Both novels operate a contrast between fictional parody, left to the reader to negate, and the realities, moral and sexual, which are implied to be the reality.[18] In the same way, Montesquieu's denials of authorship are not what they seem: they were meant to be disbelieved. 'On dira vainement que ce n'est là qu'une plaisanterie, que l'auteur tout en affirmant, ne vouloit persuader personne, qu'il n'a persuadé personne en effet, et que le public n'a pas douté un moment qu'il ne fût lui-même l'auteur de l'ouvrage prétendu Grec dont il se donnoit pour le traducteur' (Rousseau, *O.C.*, vol. I, p. 1030).

The parodies demand a complicated flickering interpretation, because this must be made *a contrario*. In that sense they mirror and reverse the techniques of authenticity. The 'faux mémoires' often ogled the fictional by their affirmation that they were not novels. If the contradicting effect of the exclusion of the novel by a novel is not admitted (as it is not by Mylne or by Stewart), then satirical prefaces cannot be accounted for. What is worse, neither can the satire. But satiric allegory or facetious novel bulks large in eighteenth-century production, as consultation of such periodical collections of novels as the *Bibliothéque choisie et amusante* (1745) shows. Much of the satire is in fact an extension of facetious techniques.

Néel's *Voyage de Saint-Cloud*[19] may be satiric of Richardson-like detail: today it reads like an eighteenth-century *Molloy*. Other authors like Bricaire de la Dixmérie write transparent historical allegories, and innocuous political ones (*L'Isle taciturne et l'isle enjouée* (1759), *La Sibyle gauloise* (1779)). Others again write what are allegories but where typically the ogling exclusion of fiction covers the ogling exclusion of reality:

Je ne sçai en quoi consiste l'allégorie que l'Auteur annonce; on ne sçauroit douter que dans son origine cette Histoire n'en renfermât une très marquée. L'Auteur étoit trop honnête homme pour tromper le Public, comme font tous les jours ces Faiseurs de Contes de Fées, qui sont si jolis, si pleins d'esprit, & qui font tant d'honneur au goût de notre siècle, lesquels pour hâter le débit de leurs charmantes Brochures, y promettent une allégorie qu'ils savent bien n'y avoir pas mise: Dom Anrel Enime n'étoit pas capable de jouer un pareil tour à ses Lecteurs, & c'est grand dommage que sa mort nous ait empêché d'apprendre quelle étoit l'allégorie de son Livre: peut-être en renferme-t-il une pour notre tems & nos mœurs: je laisse au Lecteur plus clairvoyant que moi à la deviner. (La Solle, 1740, *préface*)

The existence of a backstop to the game of interpretation, that is, the appearance of a fixed reality behind the allegory, is no sooner suggested than erased: the novel is firmly locked into fiction, but a fiction which brings us back to surface triviality.

The allegory which hides and reveals is compared to a veil: 'gaze légère, gaze infidèle qui ne voile rien et qui ne sert qu'à irriter la curiosité et les passions' (Bérard de la Bérardière, 1776, p. 386). The *papillotage* inherent in such an aesthetic is evident from the term 'irriter'. The reader's awareness is to be excited as his attention moves between what discloses and what is disclosed. What is supposedly meant to hide, in fact reveals all the more clearly (*gaze*); we return to what we first saw.[20]

Interpretation 'à clé' and the proscription of the novel

The 'faux mémoires' novel, by claiming to be true, by excluding the novel, nudged the reader into searching for the false. Parodies and allegories, on the other hand, admitting their falsity, seem to encourage the reader to search for truth. The use of *à clé* allusion within a novel, the letting the veil slip, does not perhaps go further back in France than such works as the *Histoire amoureuse des Gaules* (1660). Many novels acquired – one might say, sought to acquire – the reputation of being *romans à clé*, from Duclos' *Confessions du Comte de****, to Laclos' *Les Liaisons dangereuses* (or even to Stendhal's *Le Rouge et le noir*). But in the case of certain classes of novels, it can be shown that the reputation is merited, and that they did use such references, often in a systematic way; this is especially true of revolutionary *contes* and pamphlets (Cook, 1982).

Since Georges May's *Le Dilemme du roman au dix-huitième*

siècle (1963)[21] it has seemed that the novel was at one point in the 1730s as good as proscribed, and that only carefully filtered or powerfully patronised works were being published. (The numbers of novels published with *privilège* or *permission tacite* declines sharply for a while after 1737.) The attacks on the novel which May discusses, showing how heavily it was criticised for lack of *vraisemblance*, for immorality or for both, should be related, as it was by contemporary commentators, to the second round of the *Querelle des Anciens et des Modernes* which reaches its height in the 1730s. Novels are seen as a commercial stop-gap rendered necessary by the decline in 'literature': 'Les Romans font survivre les Libraires à la mort des Lettres. Nos Muses modernes sont de jeunes filles, qu'une sévère éducation, une austère captivité ont rendues très libertines' (Desfontaines, 1757, vol. I, p. 223). Lenglet, on the other hand, in *De l'usage des romans*, in line with his semi-facetious defence of the novel as epic, laments that novels are not written in dead languages: 'Hé, que nos beaux Romans ne sont-ils en Vers Grecs ou Latins, on les regarderoit comme les oracles de la belle littérature. C'est là qu'on croit puiser les caractères du Héroisme [. . .] mais ils ont le malheur d'être en françois' (Lenglet Dufresnoy, 1734, p. 51; a clear reference to the *Querelle*).

The novel, then, is attacked for being a dangerous upstart: it appears to be Daguesseau who, having recovered the post of Garde des Sceaux in 1737, puts into practice the talk of proscription, the high point of the attacks being the famous discourse of le père Porée in 1736 (cf. May, 1963). [22] It should be noted however that two writers earlier than 1736 speak of attempts to proscribe novels. Lenglet, in 1734, locates the origin of these attacks, saying they stem from both Jansenists and Jesuits:

Il est surprenant de voir avec quelle vivacité on s'est déchaîné contre les Romans; il semble que la plûpart des hommes se soient entendus pour les décrier. Cependant ils n'en sont pas moins lus, toutes ces déclamations leur servent de relief. Il faut qu'on y trouve bien de l'agrément puisqu'on a fait tout ce qu'on a pû pour les interdire. (Lenglet, 1734, pp. 2–3)

And Bruzen de la Martinière, in an even earlier bibliographical work dating from 1731, pleads: 'Voilà ceux pour qui je demanderois grâce, si on vouloit envelopper tous les Romans dans une proscription générale' (Bruzen de la Martinière, 1756, p. 267).

This episode in the history of the French novel is far from being clear. It must surely however be studied in connection with the type of interest the police took in the book trade. The 'fichier d'Hémery', unfortunately only constituted in 1741, frequently mentions 'auteur travaillant pour la police'. Hacks and journalists who operated the *bureaux de nouvelles*, the distributors of manuscript journals, formed a complex system of police spies often working for different officials and against each other. Typical of this world is Mouhy, 'mouche [police spy] de M. Berryer' as he is called in the 'fichier d'Hémery'. Mouhy, a *nouvelliste*, wrote for the police a regular diary of what he heard or overheard in cafés: it is known as the 'Journal de Poussot'. But he also *published* journals, and the spying activities fade into the scurrilous gossip column, in his as in other cases. He was incarcerated several times. There is a close relation between a novel like *La Mouche* (the name alone is significant), a satire like *Anecdotes pour servir à l'histoire secrète des ébugares* [=*bougres*], which has been attributed to him, and his police work: 'Il s'était avisé que les romans à clé étaient fort goûtés du public et comme ses relations autant que ses goûts lui ouvraient chaque jour les portes les mieux fermées, il battait monnaie avec les anecdotes qu'il récoltait chemin faisant' (d'Estrée, 1897, p. 197).[23]

The 'fichier d'Hémery' reveals clearly that one of the principal reasons for an author being 'incommodé' or imprisoned in Vincennes or the Bastille was his having written something offensive to someone in power. It is hard to ascribe the difficulties the authorities made for the publishing of novels merely to moral or aesthetic concerns. I wish to reinforce the suggestion, made fifty years ago by F. C. Green, that the reason for the near-proscription of the novel was the allusions to contemporary events that certain novels contained. Contemporary criticisms of the novel, as I shall show, frequently comment obliquely on the allusions they contain, and this is true not only of parodies but of 'straight' novels. The catalyst for the (hypothetical) proscription may have been Quesnel's *Almanach du diable*. The search for its author certainly fills the police papers for 1737.[24] Drujon describes this rare book as 'rempli de faits, d'anecdotes méchantes et de traits satiriques sur plusieurs personnages de la Cour, sur les prélats et les beaux esprits, [il] fit beaucoup de bruit: la police le recherca et fit détruire tous les exemplaires qu'elle put saisir; plusieurs libraires furent inquiétés' (Drujon, 1885, vol. I, p. 25a). Quesnel hanged himself in the Bastille. This particularly virulent pamphlet caused the largest stir. But when *Les Princesses malabares ou le célibat philosophique* (1734) – variously attributed to Lenglet or to Louis-Pierre de Longue, a member of the Conti household – was ordered to be burnt by Parlement on 31 December 1734,[25] it had already shaken the police by its combination of impiety and satire. It seems clear that readers were practised in the decoding of references and that authors relied on this. But the references do not, I think, operate as a backstop which, as 'real', finally authorises the fiction. Rather, they are fleeting glimpses inducing the reader to navigate between history and Romance. Just as 'authentic' novels, as well as parodies, ogle what they are not, provoking doubt in the reader, so many of these topical references are not systematic, but are incitements to deciphering, incitements which may be illusory but which sustain the flickering consciousness typical of *papillotage*.

Crébillon *fils* and Mouhy are two writers who used or were interpreted as using *à clé* references. There is no doubt that Crébillon *fils* played with allusions in *L'Ecumoire, ou Tanzai et Néadarné*, combining political references and *à clé* allusions: 'Indépendamment de l'*Ecumoire* où on a reconnu la Constitution, on a voulu y trouver les portraits de toute la Cour.'[26] Crébillon was actually imprisoned in Vincennes for writing it. That there *are* allusions is perhaps unsurprising in what seems even to a twentieth-century reader like a parodistic fairy tale. More interesting is that Crébillon's greatest novel, *Les Egarements du cœur et de l'esprit* (1736–8), was so interpreted, and by people who were in a position to know. In the very same article in the *Bibliothèque françoise* which speaks of the proscription, and which is quoted by May, it has escaped attention that the author prophesies that Crébillon *fils* will not finish the *Egarements* because of the public's finding, rightly, that it contained allusions. The author also points out that this is inevitable: 'on a mis les Romans sur le pied de la Comédie, [qu']on les a rendu le tableau de la vie humaine'[27] – given, that is, precisely the contemporary pattern of reading.

The earlier novel, *Tanzai*, is an oriental fairy story. The game of relaying references is suggested by the parody of relaying sources (see above, pp. 14 and 310, n.18). It is supposedly derived from a series of translations from Chechian to Japanese to Chinese to Dutch to Latin to Italian to French. The story itself mixes sex and politics (the two uses of the veil, a physical and a metaphorical cover). The prince Tanzai can avoid punishment for having fallen in love against the command of a fairy only by forcing a huge strainer (the *Constitution*) down the throat of the High Priest. When this fails he is punished by having the strainer hung where the penis should be; the only remedy is for him to sleep with the fairy Concombre and for his wife, Néadarné, to sleep with Jonquille. The grotesque symbol, the 'écumoire', the erotic themes, are in sharp contrast with the political references, and this kind of gap may usefully be related to the *papillotage* of contemporary art. At the narrative level, the same kind of play is used: the 'illusion' of the fairy story is made patent, and, while teasing the reader with its detail (some of it delightful), hints at the reality, sexual and political behind it – a contrast which the chapter headings underline: 'Qu'il faut bien se garder de passer tout impatientant qu'il est.' At the thematic level there is again a similar discrepancy, in that the illusions of the princess Néadarné about the motives for her seduction by the fairy are made clear. She is unable to recognise her own desire, but is forced to do so, her mind vibrant with emotion and half-truths.

In Crébillon's *Tanzai* 'references' placed within a studiedly artificial setting 'irritated' the reader; such settings were 'un léger voile qui ne fait qu'irriter l'attention et la curiosité' (Desmolets, 1739, p. 195). Just as the sexual references titillate, so the game of the reader's connivance is alternately exploited and revealed. If the play in this gap between 'real' references and far-fetched story is exploited at the thematic and narrative levels in *Tanzai*, in others of Crébillon's novels the complicity of the reader which such play requires is further used, for he is made to acquiesce in the cynical unmasking of illusion as illusion. The contrast with Marivaux is absolute: whereas the latter presents the apparently trivial, that is, the instincts at work behind everyday events, with seriousness and depth, Crébillon's work unmasks triviality as triviality. Appearance and reality are separated in analysis only to be made to coincide in such a phrase as: 'De simples mines, devenues un sujet de spéculation *et traitées sérieusement et avec autant de profondeur que pourroient l'être des faits de la plus grande importance*; une analyse exacte jusqu'au ridicule du cœur, des caprices et des petits motifs d'une femme' (Crébillon, *Les Heureux Orphelins*, 1772, vol. v, p. 289). The reality behind the 'mine' is shown to be a contemptible surface. The relationship to Boucher seems clear. The references to a contemporary reality, like the painter's 'reflet', while giving a flickering impression of constant movement towards somewhere else, in fact mean that the illusion is the reality both on the moral and on the aesthetic levels.[28]

A movement as if from the novel's surface, from 'references' to the thematisation of illusion and back to surface, to the showing up of illusions as only illusions, is created by the relay structure in the narration of the unfinished *Les Egarements du cœur et de l'esprit*. The narrator, Meilcour, looks back on his youth and satirises the society around him. In the corrosive drive against illusion the satiric 'je' must also be satirised – not through the complex layers of irony as in Marivaux's *Paysan parvenu*, but through a relayed narrator, the rake Versac, who takes over from Meilcour, as an experienced older man talking to a younger man. He becomes the bearer of satire: 'Les gens du bon ton laissent au vulgaire et le soin de penser, et la crainte de penser faux' (Crébillon, *Les Egarements,* 1772, vol. I, p. 300), but is also satirised – see for example his vulgar attempts to please Hortense. Satirised and satiriser: 'Je ne suis pas le seul qui ait senti que, pour ne point passer pour ridicule, il faut le devenir ou le paraître du moins' (Crébillon, *Les Egarements,* 1772, vol. I, p. 304); 'Ce n'est qu'en paraissant se livrer soi-même à l'impertinence, qu'il n'échappe rien de celle d'autrui' (Crébillon, *Les Egarements*, 1772, vol. I, p. 286). In this vertiginous separation of *conscience de soi* and social appearance, Versac has no place from which to operate: he has no depth or truth, only awareness of illusion. His foolish appearance is his reality; the relaying of narrative position leads not to depth but back to the surface.

The *à clé* or allegorical disowning of its own seriousness, exploited in *Tanzaï* (as in Diderot's *Les Bijoux indiscrets* and many other oriental fairy stories) has here been turned into something deeper, and more elusive.

'Fiction is truer than history': the theory of the later eighteenth-century novel

The *à clé* novel alludes to reality through false and facetious names and contrived situations; the 'faux mémoires' narrate false events under real names, but both, I have argued, use the oscillation which is the underlying structure of illusion for their effect. The reference to the real appears in one case to validate the effect, in the other to undercut it; but the undercutting makes real: 'This is a novel', being true, seems to shed truth on the content. But to back up a novel by claiming that it is real, in that it excludes falsehood, seems to suggest untruth: 'This is not a novel', being false, contaminates the content with falsehood.

In the later part of the century, the admission of fiction as fiction is taken to imply higher truth by some defenders of the novel. What in Gachet d'Artigny had been a satirical résumé of Lenglet Dufresnoy's argument in *De l'usage des romans*: 'Dans l'Histoire, je trouve mille faits faux que l'on me donne comme vrais; je trouve mille faits vrais dans le Roman sous le voile de la Fable' (Gachet d'Artigny, 1739, p. 81),[29] becomes a serious defence of the novel in the last third of the century. 'Le romancier [. . .] tandis qu'il paroît livré tout entier à l'imagination trace des tableaux plus voisins de la vérité que ces fictions honorées du nom d'histoire' (Mercier, 1784, vol. II, p. 328). This assumption of fiction accompanies the higher estimation of the novel typical of the latter part of the century. The collections of novels, of imaginary voyages, undertaken after 1760 point to the same change in common opinion of the novel: 'Mais cette même lecture, dirigée par la Philosophie & embrassant la généralité des fictions, devient l'étude la plus sûre & la plus suivie de l'Histoire la plus secrette & la plus fidèle par les faits qu'elle rassemble & les mystères qu'elle dévoile' (*Prospectus à la Bibliothèque universelle des romans*, 1775, p. 6).[30] An article in the *Esprit des journaux* defines this relation as being that of 'vérité philosophique': 'Les rapports du roman à l'histoire sont aisés à assigner quand on prend la vérité philosophique pour caractère distinctif des deux genres. Le roman est vrai, l'histoire est problématique. Dans le roman la cause de tous les événemens se trouve assignée, la marche est philosophique' (*L'Esprit des journaux*, janvier 1794, pp. 178–9).[31]

Fiction may be truer than history because 'truer' morally: more comforting in adversity, the epitome of the useful lie (such is the opinion of Marmontel, Dorat and, with modifications, Rétif). Fiction is more real than reality – this is the brandished manifesto of one of the two great eighteenth-century discussions of the novel in French, Diderot's *Eloge de Richardson* (the other is Rousseau's preface to *La Nouvelle Héloïse*): 'L'histoire est un mauvais roman: le roman, comme tu l'as fait, est une bonne histoire' (*Eloge de Richardson*, p. 40). His obituary of Richardson starts with a conventional defence of the novel, often used by Prévost: a novel is 'une morale mise en action'. There follows a crescendo of identification with the good characters, of dissociation from the bad, till he makes of the novel a private theatre. The reader enjoys his overview, and uses it to manipulate the opposing forces, laid down by the plot. His reaction is no longer mere identification but is a judgement in which one is implicated in spite of oneself: 'On prend, malgré qu'on en ait, un rôle dans tes ouvrages.' Like children at the theatre, 'Combien de fois ne me suis-je pas surpris [. . .] criant "Ne le croyez pas, il vous trompe" ' – the classical proof of illusion has been transposed into the novel. Typically, Diderot casts his account in terms of power. This apparent invasion of the novel is in fact the contrary: the novel has invaded the reader. In Richardson's novels: 'Le monde où nous vivons est le lieu de la scène; le fond de son drame est vrai; ses personnages ont toute la réalité possible; ses

111

caractères sont pris du milieu de la société' (Diderot, *Eloge de Richardson*, pp. 30–1). The truth of the novels ensures that the reader has the sensation of his own recalcitrant soul being bent to compliance. Employed actively in Diderot's own novels, the enjoyment of the *prise de force* of fiction is here passive; the comparison with a conversion is tacitly made. Diderot says that it is the multitude of details which overcomes resistance – the dam breaks and feeling overflows: 'C'est alors qu'affaissé de douleur ou transporté de joie, vous n'aurez plus la force de retenir vos larmes prêtes à couler, et de vous dire à vous même: *Mais peut-être que cela n'est pas vrai*' (*Eloge de Richardson*, p. 35). The model of such feelings is onanistic; Richardson writes for the man who takes pleasure in solitary effusion, 'Qui aime à habiter l'ombre d'une retraite et à s'attendrir utilement dans le silence' (p. 34). The surrogate experiences that the novel provokes are not disinterested. They are combined with a congratulatory return to the self: 'Combien j'étais bon! combien j'étais juste! que j'étais satisfait de moi! J'étais, au sortir de ta lecture, ce qu'est un homme à la fin d'une journée qu'il a employée à faire le bien' (*Eloge de Richardson*, p. 30). In the experience of 'bons sentiments' with which the novel overwhelms the reader, actual duty may be submerged: 'Gardez-vous bien d'ouvrir ses ouvrages enchanteurs, lorsque vous aurez quelques devoirs à remplir.' The reaction to this surrogate experience becomes a touchstone for man's true nature. The power of the invasion, of the 'envoûtement' is thus explored: the moral book whose moral effect is to take over the personality so that moral duties are left undone . . . This ambiguity arises precisely because the reader's reaction is not one of identification but is the assuming of a role in relation to the characters of the book, a role of interference which the novel has provided: 'On se mêle à la conversation, on approuve, on blâme, on admire, on s'irrite, on s'indigne' (*Eloge de Richardson*, p. 30). The reader feels he has acquired experience: in fact he has been taken in charge by the illusion, an illusion which has re-acquired much of its older moral meaning. The novel has been radically internalised, yet the role-playing, the lack of a central source of authenticity, means that what is subjectivised is also illusion – a filling out with imaginary substance, as in neoplatonic theory (see pp. 19ff., above), but now wholly interior. The novel is truer than history, for its imaginary scope is wider (*Eloge de Richardson*, p. 40).

Other theories of this ilk do not play with ambiguities in this way, but are merely subject to them. Marmontel, for instance, claims that Xenophon's *Cyropaedia* is a novel. The work is true because exemplary:

> Je concluerais que rien de tout cela ne lui fut transmis par les Perses; mais qu'ayant pour base le grand caractère de Cyrus, ses expéditions, ses conquêtes, il lui a fait penser, dire, et faire tout ce qu'il a jugé propre à servir d'exemple et de leçon. (Marmontel, 1819–20, vol. III, p. 590)

And this is reflected in Marmontel's history of the novel. He does not derive the novel from history: the first narrative form existed before the epic, and the present novel by an inverse procedure is derived from it, from 'la poésie dégénérée'.[32]

The novel written in this perspective set out deliberately to provide escapist illusion: 'Une sorte de roman bien cher au philosophe, c'est celui qui offre en idée le plan de félicité publique & nationale, [un] rêve consolateur' (Mercier, 1784, vol. II, pp. 331–2). Mercier's own publicly orientated *An 2440* sets out to do this. Marmontel is the most voluble exponent of such a theory: the practice his theory is designed to support will be examined later. History or novel solicits a reaction not to what is but to what may be. The old definition of *vraisemblance* becomes the hinge for a very different theory: 'La persuasion ne tient pas exclusivement à la certitude; elle tient au besoin de croire, et l'homme sait qu'il a besoin de croire ce qu'il lui est bon de pratiquer' (Marmontel, 1819–20, vol. III, p. 595). The good and the true are distinct and separate, as Dortous de Mairan explains to the young philosopher in the short story *Le petit voyage*:

> L'Homme est de glace aux vérités
> Il est de feu pour le mensonge
>
> a dit La Fontaine. J'ose penser différemment: car si la vérité nous touche d'aussi près et aussi sérieusement que le mensonge, nous l'aimons, nous la saisissons, aussi avidemment et plus avidemment encore. Mais si elle nous est étrangère, elle nous est indifférente, et si elle nous est odieuse et nuisible, nous avons droit de lui préférer l'illusion qui nous console, la fiction qui nous instruit, le mensonge qui nous encourage d'être justes . . .
> (Marmontel, 1819–20, vol. III, p. 596)

The theory which holds that the consoling fiction has a good effect justifies the momentariness of the aesthetic illusion. The fiction disappears with our illusion; the consolation is left like a residue:

> Si pour son plaisir il se livre un moment aux illusions de la feinte, n'a-t-il pas toujours en lui-même le sentiment secret qui l'avertit que les songes qu'on lui fait faire n'ont aucune réalité? Sans doute, il l'a, ce sentiment confus; et quand vient la réflexion, toute illusion est détruite. Que lui reste-t-il donc de cet enchantement? Ce qui lui reste, est une vérité in-

destructible, inaltérable, qui se fixe dans l'âme comme au fond d'un creuset, quand tout le reste est dissipé; et c'est en elle que consiste la moralité poétique, la moralité du roman. (Marmontel, 1819–20, vol. III, pp. 594–5)

Illusion is, then, merely a momentary escape, allowing entry to a morality which does not correspond to any experience available through the imagination, but which supposedly satisfies the impulses which motivated the escape, the 'besoin de croire', the need to wear rose-coloured spectacles. The morality *is* the truth of the escape. Appearance and essence coincide – both are illusions.

It is not surprising, then, that the morality of the *Contes moraux* is doubtful. It is what a certain society wishes to hear. Marmontel's *Soliman II*, for instance, recounts how a sultan attempts to fulfil his plan: 'C'est à des cœurs nourris dans le sein de la liberté qu'il serait doux de faire aimer l'esclavage.' But a French slave enslaves him: a sense of political and personal liberty is confused deliberately here with the impudence of a born prostitute. The 'petite cause' is found for the 'grans événemens' (Marmontel, 1819–20, vol. II, p. 17), thereby confirming what the cynical have always wished to believe of both love and history. In the same paradoxical vein, Socrates proves to Alcibiades in *Alcibiades ou le moi* that his wish to be loved for himself is *philosophically* wrong – not just against the way of the world. His talents, rank, youth, beauty are the embroidery: 'Le *moi* qui réunit ces agrémens n'est en vous que le canevas de la tapisserie; la broderie en fait le prix' (Marmontel, 1819–20, vol. II, p. 16). The tales, then, are falsely moral; they are also falsely naive. The 'simple' and 'familiar' events, which in his preface Marmontel proclaims himself to be using, are in fact the height of convention. 'La Bergère des Alpes' is a *marquise* in disguise; the shepherd who woos her is the son of an Italian noble, the sounds she takes for birdsong are his airs on the hautbois, learnt from the lessons of a famous player, Besuzzi, for 'les gardiens de troupeaux errans sur ces collines ne lui avaient jamais fait entendre que les sons des trompes rustiques' (Marmontel, 1819–20, vol. II, p. 136). But, swelling the moral wind which was already blowing, the moralities of the *Nouveaux Contes moraux* (1790–3) will no longer be dubious: they display openly this time the full and dangerous equivalence between what is good for the reader to hear and what he wants: between private escapism and public judgement about what should be heard. *Bélisaire* is the masterpiece of this equivalence, embodying even the gap between public opinion and government in the contrast between the treatment of Bélisaire by his emperor and the heroisation by *le peuple* who listen to his lessons. All of which leads to such massive and reactionary platitudes that only the Sorbonne constituted as it was in 1767 could take offence (Renwick, 1967).[33]

Rétif de la Bretonne and Sade are the continuators of this stance, although aesthetically they overshadow their predecessors. Rétif writes incessantly of his own life, of the women he has possessed and lost or possessed and found – yet the constant fictional reworking, in its very obsessive quality, makes the books real. Sade is deliberately *romanesque*: the different figures of debauchery, men and women, however similar, must take on within the novels a difference. They represent incessant novelty, not reappearance of the same. The acts of copulation and cruelty are the same in different décors, with incessantly different objects – from this derives the *invraisemblance* and the horror, and that deliberate refusal of situations which would have constrained the heroes, be it even by the constraint that links torturer and victim if their relationship is prolonged, which is central, as Blanchot has shown, to the Sadian machine (Blanchot, 1967, pp. 46–7).

Like Marmontel, Sade proclaims the moral effect of virtue *not* triumphant. As with Marmontel, what is and what is desired are presented as one. *Les Idées sur les romans* announces the *romanesque* intention: 'L'Ouvrage doit nous faire voir l'homme, non pas seulement ce qu'il est, ou ce qu'il se montre, c'est le devoir de l'historien, mais tel qu'il peut être, tel que doivent le rendre les modifications du vice, et toutes les secousses des passions' (Sade, 1966–7, vol. x, p. 12). And one traditional defence of the *romanesque*, that it paints man as he could be, takes on a deeper meaning when it comes from the pen of the author of *Les Cent Vingt Jours de Sodome et Gomorrhe*:

La nature, plus bizarre que les moralistes ne nous la peignent, s'échappe à tout instant des digues que la politique de ceux-ci voudroit lui prescrire; uniforme dans ses plans, irrégulière dans ses effets, son sein toujours agité ressemble au foyer d'un volcan, d'où s'élancent tour à tour ou des pierres précieuses servant au luxe des hommes ou des globes de feu qui les anéantissent. (Sade, 1966–7, vol. x, p. 19)

The release of energy, a literature of hidden possibilities, is given an historical analogy by Sade, when he speaks of the Gothic novel: it is an attempt to outdo history, to outstrip the speed and terrible nature of Revolutionary events. The celebration of natural or historical energy is countermanded by the epigraph taken from Young:

Tu me demandes pourquoi je m'obstine à n'offrir à tes yeux que des idées de mort. Sache que cette pensée est un levier puissant qui soulève l'homme de la poussière et le redresse sur lui-même; elle comble l'effroyable profondeur de l'abîme infernal, et nous fait descendre au tombeau par une pente plus douce. (Sade, 1966–7, vol. x, p. 1)

Here, in spite of the feebleness of the gentle slope, it is not history but 'l'effroyable profondeur de l'abîme infernal' which calls forth the destructive fury of the novels.

Tempting as such a direct application of the *Idées sur les romans* to his own novels is, it overlooks Sade's account of the derivation of the novel. The novel is generated from the original lie, religion: 'A peine les hommes eurent-il *soupçonné* des êtres immortels, qu'ils les firent agir et parler; dès lors, voilà des métamorphoses, des fables, des paraboles, des romans, en un mot, voilà des ouvrages de fiction, dès que la fiction s'empare de l'esprit des hommes' (Sade, 1966–7, vol. x, p. 4). The novel is the irredeemably fictional: in the beginning it was an instrument of religion, that is, of an institution whose motive is 'La crainte, l'espérance, et le dérèglement d'esprit'. The novel – originally a mystification, the tool of an illusion then (for the stories of heroes, and thus the semi-historical legend, come afterwards) – is a result of the weakness of man: 'Partout il faut qu'il *prie*, partout il faut qu'il *aime*' (Sade, 1966–7, vol. x, p. 5). It is thus product and servant of man's illusions. Such a short circuit, where man is both victim and conniving creator of fictions, makes possible the aggressiveness of the Sadian novel; like the characters themselves it intends to seduce and 'aggress' at the same time. The novel as genre derives from the original lie; likewise in the novels themselves there is no opposition between the *romanesque* and reality, no tension between the desired and the real. Instead, there is a Sisyphean striving to continue the original fiction. Juliette, the greatest heroine, rushes round Europe from crime to coincidence to crime; from brigand to minister to pope to pimp. The horror of the events, so much stronger than that of the Gothic novel, makes the reader react: but the puppetry, the annihilation one by one of victims whose lack of relation to the executioner is postulated from the beginning, the mechanical inventiveness of the crimes, undercuts the horror and increases it. The illusion is primary but it is also illusion.

Rousseau, illusion, imagination

Rousseau's embarrassment about having written a novel is increased by the contemporary novel's uncertain position. He writes two prefaces to *La Nouvelle Héloïse*, and in the second one sets up a censor, N., to pre-empt actual criticism. N., though taken with the novel's plot, is yet critical. He accepts the reality of Julie's fall for didactic reasons: 'Si votre Héloïse eût été toujours sage, elle instruirait beaucoup moins' (Rousseau, *O.C.*, vol. II, p. 26). (This is exactly the view of Marmontel, when he amends the plot of *La Princesse de Clèves* – it would have been much more moral if the Princesse had succumbed to Nemours' attentions.) Yet N. constantly criticises the characters as 'romanesque'. Above all, he badgers R. to tell him whether the novel is true, whether the letters are genuine. Rousseau turns the tables on his criticism of the novel as *romanesque*; yes, it is *romanesque*, for fiction is truer than truth. Thus far, we seem to be on familiar ground. But this fiction happens to be true: the lovers escape into an illusion which actually exists, says R.:

Ils se refusent aux vérités décourageantes: ne trouvant nulle part ce qu'ils sentent, ils se replient sur eux-mêmes; il se détache du reste de l'Univers; et créant entre eux un petit monde différent du nôtre, ils y forment un spectacle véritablement nouveau. (Rousseau, *O.C.*, vol. II, pp. 16–17)

This fiction is truer than truth, because it is lived. There are other elements of the conventional attitude to illusion around 1760, and they are all used in the same way, to cut the ground from under poor N. (whose very constitution as censor is reminiscent of Diderot's use of such fall guys as the abbé in the *Vernet* article in the *Salon de 1767*). There is, for example, in the preface, a mystification as to whether the letters are genuine or not; as to whether the 'topographie grossièrement altérée' is a result of the ignorant invention by the 'editor', or of an attempt to cover up and disguise the authors of the letters. Another echo both of Diderot, and of contemporary discussions is the opposition between letters which are 'well written' and those which are 'true' and not necessarily exemplary in style (this opposition is found, for instance, in the *Question aux gens de lettres,* at the end of *La Religieuse*). But, as always with Rousseau, the difference from Diderot in the handling of such an opposition is striking. For Diderot, the terms of the contrast are 'saillant, exagéré' set against 'extrême simplicité', 'dernière vraisemblance'. For Rousseau, 'agitation passagère et sèche', 'un bel esprit qui veut briller' contrast with 'lâche, diffuse, toute en longueurs, en désordre, en répétitions'. Rousseau continues his account:

Son cœur, plein d'un sentiment qui déborde, redit toujours la même chose, et n'a jamais achevé de dire; comme une source vive qui coule sans cesse et ne s'épuise jamais. Rien de saillant, rien de remarquable; on ne retient ni mots, ni tours, ni phrases; on n'admire rien, l'on n'est frappé de rien. Cependant on se sent l'âme attendrie; on se sent ému sans savoir pourquoi. Si la force du sentiment ne nous frappe pas, sa vérité nous touche, et c'est ainsi que le cœur sait parler au cœur. (Rousseau, *O.C.,* vol. II, p. 15)

Diderot in the *Préface-annexe* sets up the letters as a mystification – the admirer finds the letters, picks them up, and says 'Cela est beau', 'cela est bien vrai'. In Rousseau the letters fade from awareness, and there is only emotion, communicated not through eloquence but through a process of attrition. The freshness of feeling is genuine, 'une lettre que l'amour a réellement dictée', whereas in Diderot it is a mimetic letter which aims to catch the unwary.

The stooge, N., in line with the tradition of 'faux mémoires' and false collections of letters, seeks to know whether they are real or fictional. He appears to catch R. out: a portrait is valuable through its resemblance, even if few people are interested because few people know the original. A 'tableau d'imagination' pleases everyone but must be governed by a human norm, and R. draws the conclusion: 'Si ces Lettres sont des Portraits, ils n'intéressent point: si ce sont des Tableaux, ils imitent mal' (Rousseau, *O.C.*, vol. II, p. 11). But it is in fact the censor who is caught: he is making diametrically opposed judgements about what are the *same letters*. The question of their authenticity masks what is an incompatible criticism of them. R. riposts with a plea which Sade will take up. The norm in art as in morality restricts what human possibilities may create:

Savez-vous jusqu'où les Hommes diffèrent les uns des autres? Combien les caractères sont opposés? Combien les mœurs, les préjugés varient selon les temps, les lieux, les âges? Qui est-ce qui ose assigner des bornes précises à la nature et dire: Voilà jusqu'où l'Homme peut aller, et pas au delà? (Rousseau, *O.C.*, vol. II, p. 12)

And yet, while urging the limitless nature of man, he admits that the events are unremarkable: 'Tout est prévu long temps d'avance; tout arrive comme il est prévu. Est-ce la peine de tenir registre de ce que chacun peut voir tous les jours dans sa maison, ou dans celle de son voisin?' (Rousseau, *O.C.*, vol. II, p. 13). This, as has been seen, is a statement of the predicament of the eighteenth-century French novel. Just as Rousseau assumed that 'fiction is truer than truth', in order to be able to thematise it as an escape, so he assumes the novel's navigation between the *romanesque* and history.

118

N. is right. The novel is at the same time ideal escapist illusion and real, a series of domestic events. But ideal for whom? In Marmontelian illusion the moral is at the same time consoling and deceptive: life may not be rose-coloured, but it ought to be. The genesis, personal and literary, of *La Nouvelle Héloïse* might have led to the same sort of escapism. Some parts of the novel still bear traces of this; yet as a whole it goes beyond. This attitude of search for escape, instead of being carefully restricted to the consumption of the reader, is thematised in the novel. The heroes, Julie and Saint-Preux, desire a life which is ideal in intensity, and yet must face the real, which is impenetrable to desire. Jean Starobinski has shown what the novel owes to the pastoral tradition in this respect, but also how this 'romanesque', this search for an ideal, is revalued by being replaced in the real or on the margin of the real. For a Parisian, Switzerland is both exotic and actual (Starobinski, 1971b). Illusion here becomes the very theme of the novel – illusion as the generous movement of the imagination, its attempt to seize the real, its demand that reality measure up to human possibilities of feeling and experience. What in Marmontel is trivial manipulation of the reader becomes here the means whereby the reader can live the fictional events, with the character, but without the dangers inherent in vicarious experiences which pass like an illusion. The struggle to face reality is lived out at its noblest: the imagination is what fills experience with value, what can fix time by crystallising in the memory, but also what reveals life as unsatisfactory. In the words of Julie's devastating letter:

En effet, l'homme avide et borné, fait pour tout vouloir et peu obtenir, a reçu du ciel une force consolante qui rapproche de lui tout ce qu'il désire, qui le soumet à son imagination, qui le lui rend présent et sensible, qui le lui livre en quelque sorte, et pour lui rendre cette imaginaire propriété plus douce, la modifie au gré de sa passion. Mais tout ce prestige disparoit devant l'objet même; rien n'embellit plus cet objet aux yeux du possesseur: on ne se figure point ce qu'on voit; l'imagination ne pare plus rien de ce qu'on possède, l'illusion cesse où commence la jouissance. Le pays des chimères est en ce monde le seul digne d'être habité, et tel est le néant des choses humaines, qu'hors l'Être existant par lui-même, il n'y a rien de beau que ce qui n'est pas. (Rousseau, *O.C.*, vol. II, p. 693)

La Nouvelle Héloïse turns into a theme the eighteenth-century novel's own development, its plying between the real and the imagined. For the imagination is doubly valued in the novel: the source of human striving, it is also the source of failure to live fully, because it provides surrogate experience. In Julie's letter, the imagination both confers value and empties of value – a terrible synthesis. Only what has been deeply lived by the imagination is worth having: but the imagination can only operate on what is not present, what cannot be possessed. And this pattern of desire and dissatisfaction is aesthetic as well as moral: 'Il n'y a rien de beau que ce qui n'est pas.' The reader lives the longing for such an ideal, yet the wearying length of the novel mimics the trivial, the humdrum, which disciplines the idealisation for the characters. In this, which could be said to be the only tragedy written in eighteenth-century France, the illusions of the imagination have been revalued. The mirrors which bound illusion are lifted, and it becomes the imagination, creative of good or of evil.

The *romanesque* and the real are miraculously fused in *La Nouvelle Héloïse* in a deep and disconcerting statement about the limits of man, these limits being tested continually by his desire. The spiritual dimension given to the *romanesque* by making it part of his search for the ideal, enables it to probe the real. The movement away from the centre, so typical of *papillotage*, is *papillotage* no longer; the *romanesque* now represents both escapism and the search for the ideal; it has been thematised as problems of human weakness and striving.

4

THE INCLUSION OF THE FALSE: THE NOVEL WITHIN THE NOVEL

I have shown thus far that the 'faux mémoires' claimed to be 'real', not a novel. They appear to try to create an illusion in the reader in the most literal sense, to make him make a mistake. But in expelling the unreal, this form also defines it – as a novel – and this definition introduces a kind of ogling of the novel, a mild *papillotage*, a hint that the reader is being tricked. Their mirror image, the parody, the facetious novel, claims nothing more than to be a novel. It thus appears to eschew illusion, expelling the real, which it nevertheless defines through references or allegorical allusions, and which it constantly brings before the reader's mind; this is a process close, structurally, to the *papillotage* of the plastic arts discussed in Part I. A third type of novel claims at the same time to be a novel and to be authentic – in the case of Marmontel the claim is based on a dubious identification of what is and what one wants, whereas in Sade the lie takes over entirely to generate the novel. In Rousseau's *La Nouvelle Héloïse*, however, the aesthetic problem of *adequatio* is transferred to a metaphysical level: it is less a wish-fulfilment than a statement of discrepancy – what is, is not what is desired. In this way the work, the novel, acquires a subjective truth even when illusory: the making private of the experience of art is complete.

In Rousseau's novel then, illusion is made into a higher truth: aesthetic concerns of credibility (are the characters taken from reality or not?) fuse into metaphysical questioning (is what they undergo real or unreal? what is the effect of the imagination on experience?). Thematisation achieves here what *Don Quixote* much earlier had obtained by different formal means. In Cervantes' novel, the imbrication of tales with the novel forces us to move between different realities – idyllic or banal. This structure is reinforced at the level of the plot by the effect romances have had on Don Quixote's brains: apparently addled, he constitutes himself knight-errant, and seems to take inns for castles and whores for maidens. Reality seems to be contrasted with what Don Quixote thinks is real, based on books of *chevalerie*, which, as in Courtilz de Sandras, represent the unreal. But the novel is more complicated than this. Not merely is Don Quixote attempting to make two worlds coincide which constantly slip apart – he knows, for instance, that the real Aeneas was not as pious as is said, nor the ladies as chaste. The unreal represented by the romances *should* be real. Don Quixote does not merely make mistakes, he attempts to right wrongs, as did knights of old. We move constantly between different levels of appearance, of illusion, which are defined only by contrast with a level perceived as 'more' or 'less' 'real'. Likewise, the aesthetically 'real' is defined against various levels of textual transmission (the work is by a Moor, Sidi Hamete Benengeli, translated into Spanish) but the most immediate level, the experiences of Quixote, is also the farthest removed, in terms of the text's 'history', since what we read is supposedly a commentary on a near extempore translation by a Moor, picked up in the Alcazar at Toledo. Aesthetic and metaphysical illusion are fused – the world is a set of novels, and the set of novels is a world, after the manner of the great *theatrum mundi*.

Don Quixote was one of the two great crucial influences on the eighteenth-century tale within a tale. The other was Cervantes' imitator, Scarron. In the *Roman comique*, Scarron picks up only the playing off of styles one against the other and the theme of the 'burla', the practical joke. The inserted tales contrast not appearance and reality, but styles, and the *vraisemblance* of the action is inversely proportional to the seriousness of the style. A series of stories are told about, and by, a company of itinerant actors. The stories about the actors can be considered to be the first style function. They are 'low'; the 'burla' or practical jokes are related in burlesque style, allowing interruptions by the narrator and such facetious titles as 'Qui contient ce que vous verrez si vous prenez la peine de le lire' which will have a constant heritage in the eighteenth century. The secondary narrative level, the story of the main actors in the troupe, is quite different. The burlesque events are gone; the social level is neither high nor low; the stories are of disguises and recognitions. The highest stylistic level, the hispanomauresque stories, are again of feintes, mistakes, surprises. But here, it is remarkable that two stories are taken over by the author, for though the stories are in fact those of the character, the author replaces their words with his. In the other two he allows them to recount. One character, Inezilla, thus has her words replaced on one occasion and left on the other. In this game between style and plot, the chiasmus operated between them has a fixing effect. It preserves the hierarchy of genres, while allowing a play on the relation between them. And the narrator figure is necessary to this effect, removing what otherwise might have been disquieting in this placing of *romanesque* and 'reality' in the same neighbourhood. The 'author' here authorises.

Marivaux

In his early work, Marivaux develops both the parody and the travesty found in Scarron's *Roman comique* and the contrast between the imaginary and the real derived from *Don Quixote*. These two strands, which are, by and large, separated in Marivaux's early work, are brought together in *La Vie de Marianne* (of the *Paysan parvenu*, which is more unfinished than *Marianne*, it is harder to say the same, though a case could be made), to give a novel of incomparable psychological depth.

The early novels use both the forms discussed in the previous chapter: some include the not true, others exclude the false. Either they include the *romanesque* by systematising the tale within a tale; or exclude it by travestying it (a development of the parody form discussed earlier). In his first novel, *Les Effets surprenants de la sympathie* (1713), which uses the tale within a tale, the form is used to create surprise. The novel embeds *romanesque* stories to the sixth function (a man meets a man who tells a story in which he meets a man who tells a story . . .) creating a virtuoso filigree of reported narration, held together by a strict pattern of reversal and repetition in the incidents themselves, which makes the novel like an echo chamber. The constant changes of fortune related in the *Effets surprenants* are mirrored by the changes in narrative level, as one narrator takes over in relay from another. The relation to *papillotage* in painting seems clear: the 'piquant', that is, the renewed effect of novelty, is both thematic and formal. In the preface to a burlesque early work, the *Homère travesti*, Marivaux sketches what could be called an aesthetics of surprise:

Ainsi, toutes charmantes que sont les aventures des Héros d'Homère [. . .] elles ne piqueront plus notre esprit de ce premier trait de plaisir que portent en lui des aventures qu'on ne prévoyait en aucune façon, et qui naissent les unes des autres d'une manière d'autant plus surprenante, qu'elle est toujours nouvelle. (Marivaux, 1972, p. 966)

The burlesque, in this apologia, replaces surprises in the plot by surprise at the mixture of styles.

The latter technique is developed in the *Télémaque travesti* (c. 1715, published 1736). Here the *romanesque* is excluded, for it is in the text of Fénelon's *Télémaque*, which is travestied not merely in the plot (the search for the father) but also line by line.[1] The surprise and reversal are here in the burlesque application of low language to a high-flown plot. Yet the term of the contrast, the rose-coloured classicising of *Télémaque* itself, is missing, and we read a novel extraordinary for its richness and harshness of tone. Yet if the model is outside and, in a pattern now familiar, the reference is relayed, on the other hand the *political* references, which Fénelon had relegated outside his novel by the mildest of allusions, are integrated fully by Marivaux. But there is more. The *travesti* is not merely stylistic: it must be related to the *Modernes'* attack on the sublime as a ridiculous living-up to a code. In the sublime mode, the heroes present an 'important et brillant aspect' but their virtues 'ne sont à vrai dire que des vices sacrifiés à l'orgueil de n'avoir que des passions estimables' (Marivaux, 1972, p. 718). The debunking implication of the burlesque exercise as practised by Scarron is toned down (in that the excluded object of the *travesti*, *Télémaque*, or at least its author, seems to have been admired by Marivaux), but the search for origins and the living-up to a code are laughed at. It is this which, when given a more precisely located social context in *Marianne* and the *Paysan parvenu*, will be used in an entirely original way. Through a softening of the burlesque practices, and in particular through their thematisation, Marivaux will probe the relation between illusion and reality, between what the characters are and their striving within themselves. In the *Télémaque travesti*, however, the implied reality is that of Marivaux's novel, while the implied illusion – higher and nobler, but unreal – that of the excluded novel which is travestied.[2]

The apparently incompatible burlesque and *romanesque* traditions are in fact superimposed in *Marianne*. The incomparable psychological depth is obtained by internalising the problem of what status is to be accorded to imaginative experience. What for us is the extraordinary 'realism' of the novel derives no doubt from our partial blindness to Marivaux's superimposition of high and low styles, the final product of the burlesque, where the burlesque and its target are brought together. Within both plot and style, then, there is oscillation. This becomes obvious in the reaction of Marivaux's contemporaries: for them this style 'flickered', moved rapidly between high and low registers; the 'style néologique' which they particularly associated with him is related by them in its cultivation of controlled surprise to Scarron's burlesque,[3] and is also linked in their minds to the *papillotage* which characterised the style of the *fermiers-généraux* (cf. Le Camus, 1780, pp. 52–3, cited above, p. 52). The 'base' adventures – the underwear bought for her by the *faux dévot* Climal, the famous quarrel between the draper Madame Dufour and the coachman – are related to the debunking adventures of the burlesque. So are the interventions by the 'author', the Scarron technique of the self-conscious narrator, but these are now made by the older version of the young heroine; that is to say, they are fully integrated into the texture of the novel, and reinforce rather than radically change the effect. For it is the old lady, not the 'author', who comments ironically on her younger self.

The conventional trajectory of the *romanesque* heroine, where she lives up to a code, is also a becoming of what she is.[4] Her adventure is the awakening of the young mind, constantly surprised by what it sees. Thus are the early techniques deepened. The tale within a tale, the other method of integrating the unreal within the novel, is used to counterpoint thematically Marianne's adventures against the usually neglected story of the nun Tervire. Tervire's adventures mirror and reverse Marianne's: in both the itinerary is clear – social ascent, the retiring into a convent – and the shifts and surprises (Marianne is jilted, so is Tervire) work within this frame. Tervire, like Marianne, refuses a marriage (but because the future husband had credulously believed ill of her, whereas with Marianne the would-be suitor had believed well of her, though again only on report); she helps her own mother, without knowing, whereas Marianne is helped by the woman who is to stand instead of her mother. In Marianne's case, however, the relation between reality and expectation looks forward, while in Tervire's it looks backward (again the combination of surprise and reversal). Marianne awakens to existence, while for Tervire the conditions of life deaden: 'les tristesses retirées dans le fond de l'âme la flétrissent' (Marivaux, 1957, pp. 446–7). In both cases, the natural spontaneous feeling evolves along a path felt to be predestined. This sense of knowing what curve the story will take is obtained by use of the *romanesque* framework. But though the evolution of the heroine's destiny seems certain, the adverse circumstances, treated once in soft though 'real' vein (Marianne), once in a harsh and more novelish one (Tervire), render the spontaneous feeling more fragile as it evolves along the set path.

Illusion and the novel

The novel as unreal has been fully internalised: it provides a sense of destiny, and the scope of the imaginative play within which Marianne can evolve. But the imbricated *romanesque* novel, Tervire's tale, makes 'real' in contrast Marianne's experience, her *romanesque* strivings against her plebeian background. This double use of the form of the tale within a tale, one direct, one as the older narrator's commentary, creates an illusion which incorporates consciousness, which moves between narrative levels, playing one against the other. But this structure can only shape horizontally, can create a succession of events, but not an end which is more than a coming to a standstill. Perhaps this is one – only one – of the reasons why *Marianne* and the *Paysan parvenu* are unfinished.

Faublas

The tale within a tale is also used as a heavier toned counterpoint in the *Amours du Chevalier Faublas*. Into the Parisian episodes is interpolated a story set in Poland, with all the attributes of the *romanesque* – burning castles, brigands, politics. Like the Tervire story, in relation to Marianne's, the Polish story of Faublas' father-in-law, Lovzinski, resembles that of the hero himself, but in another key. But the change of key is all important. For the story of Faublas is that of the adventures of an immeasurably young Cherubino-like figure, who moves through Paris and in and out of beds, pursuing his true love Sophie, and chased by jealous husbands or jealous lovers. His female disguises enable both escape and reaction in a world of changing façades. He is 'une créature amphibie' in a world of name changes: 'les uns te baptisent Faublas et te soutiennent beau garçon; les autres vous nomment du Portail et jurent que vous êtes très jolie fille' (Louvet, 1966, p. 89). He lives in a world of masks:

Mes yeux furent d'abord agréablement flattés de la nouveauté du spectacle. Les habits élégans, les riches parures, la singularité des costumes grotesques, la laideur même des travestissements baroques, la bizarre représentation de tous ces visages cartonnés et peints, le mélange des couleurs, le murmure de cent voix confondues, la multitude des objets, leur mouvement perpétuel, qui variait sans cesse le tableau en l'animant, tout se réunit pour surprendre mon attention bientôt lassée. (Louvet, 1966, p. 84).

There are fainting fits, resurrections, disguises: 'C'est ici la salle de bal, on n'y danse pas, mais on se déguise; vous prenez cela pour une armoire? c'est une porte de communication' (Louvet, 1966, p. 116). Disguises are taken for granted:

Une femme de qualité [. . .] se déguise en suivante, montre ses appas sur la bure, et reçoit les vigoureux embrassements d'un rustre grossier, déguisé en prélat, ou d'un gros prélat, si naturellement travesti qu'on le prend pour un rustre: ainsi l'on se rend mutuellement service; et comme personne ne se reconnaît, on n'a d'obligation à personne. (Louvet, 1966, p. 116).

It is a world of overhearing and spying: Paris is the realm of uncertainty, of feintes and disguises (the novel is dedicated to 'mes sosies').

Here Faublas does not represent a threat, but is merely one who profits from *la nuit et le moment*, whose attractiveness is such that it excuses him from the charge of seduction. The disguises occur against the directionless and yet active world of Paris: 'Toujours poursuivi par les huées dérisoires d'une folle jeunesse, toujours porté par les flots tumultueux de la foule empressée' (Louvet, 1966, p. 91). The uncertainty is continued and increased by the parallel between his own and his father's philandering adventures. The result is that it is the contemporary Parisian episodes which are fleeting, evanescent, unreal; the Polish ones which in their romanesque extremity represent reality in the novel, just as Sophie, a Pole, is Faublas' real love (see Crouzet in Louvet, 1966). (Compare the way Montesquieu uses the highly coloured plot of harem jealousy to give coherence and depth to the Parisian satire in the *Lettres persanes*.)

In *Faublas*, the tale within a tale incorporates the *romanesque*, which by a chiasmus shows up the real Paris as wanting, as unreal. The aesthetics of the novel which were to characterise the later part of the century – 'fiction is truer than history' – are given body here by the form of the tale within a tale. Not surprisingly the solution of the plot is in madness: Faublas must move from unreal reality into insanity before the reality of feeling can be his.

'Jacques le fataliste' and illusion

Part II has been structured round two relations to the *romanesque*. One excludes the novel and claims authenticity (or, by parodistic inversion, excludes only reality and claims only falsity). The other includes it, resituating the distinction between reality and fiction within the novel. These structures correspond to 'hard' illusion and 'soft' or oscillating illusion as defined in the chapters on painting. Yet the novels which claimed authenticity induced doubt about their status by their very insistence that they were not novels. And, conversely, this is parried by a change in theory, later in the century. The implicit attitude to truth of the allegory and parody is now made explicit and defended highly seriously: critics assert that fiction is 'truer' than history, claiming authenticity but not historical truth. Rousseau's *La Nouvelle Héloïse*, by thematising this claim to the 'truth' of the imagination, stabilises the novel's relation to authenticity by radically subjectivising it. Correspondingly, the novel which inserted 'unreality' in the form of a tale told, a novel read, could use these both to burlesque the novel and to play with the problem of what reality is. One must ask, however, how it is that an inserted tale can raise this question. How does the structure of imbrication work so that the framing tale and the tale inserted play against each other? (The effect is not automatic, as may be seen from the story of Milord Edward Bomston, in *La Nouvelle Héloïse*, for instance.)

The highest virtuosity in the use of the tale within a tale in eighteenth-century France is found in Diderot's *Jacques le fataliste*, and this novel provides a series of answers, exemplary in their subtlety and inventiveness, to these questions. For *Jacques* discusses what is assumed in the reading of a novel – what is 'illusion' – almost before the omniscient and nearly invisible narrator, dear to critics, is supposed to have been established. This in itself suggests that something is wrong with their view of the novel at this period; that if the conditions of fiction could be satirised, they were recognised; and that what are called infelicities or *invraisemblances* in eighteenth-century novels by critics who take the developmentalist line are in fact something else.[5]

Now *Jacques*, a complex collection of tales, fully exploits the burlesque possibilities of the tale within the tale. Jacques' telling his love stories as he ambles through the countryside on a journey with his master sets up echoes and counter-echoes: the country ribaldry of Jacques' youth contrasting with Madame de la Pommeraye's revenge for her spurned love; the bawdy fable of the Gaine and the Coutelet following immediately on the self-quoted beautiful lament on human unfaithfulness.[6] But the presence of an 'auteur' who talks to a reader (thus duplicating the structure of the journey where Jacques talks to his master) allows for more complex burlesque effects: the novel parodies other novels by emphasising their absence, for the 'auteur' dangles in front of the reader what *Jacques* might have been: 'J'aurais pu [. . .] mais cela aurait pué le *Cleveland* à infecter.' His work appears both like other novels and better than other novels; the 'auteur' forces certain stories down the 'lecteur''s throat, yet refuses others – for example, one never finds out who the band of armed men one takes for the brigands out for revenge on Jacques are:

Vous allez croire que cette petite armée tombera sur Jacques et son maître, qu'il y aura une action sanglante, des coups de bâton donnés [. . .] et il ne tiendrait qu'à moi que tout cela n'arrivât . . . mais adieu la vérité de l'histoire, adieu le récit des amours de Jacques. Nos deux voyageurs n'étaient point suivis; j'ignore ce qui se passa dans l'auberge après leur départ. (Diderot, *Jacques le fataliste*, p. 18)

The novel satirises explicitly the portrait, the allegory, the long-winded consolation. There is a complicated pattern of self-quotation and discussion of other works: Goldoni's *Bourru bienfaisant* is rewritten, Rabelais is continued (p. 298), there is a passage which may, it is proclaimed, have been plagiarised from *Tristram Shandy* (*Jacques le fataliste*, p. 375). The question of stylisation is brought up through a comparison with Molière:

Lorsque j'entendis l'hôte s'écrier de sa femme, 'Que diable faisait-elle à sa porte', je me rappellai l'Harpagon de Molière, lorsqu'il dit de son fils: *Qu'allait-il faire dans cette galère?* et je conçus qu'il ne s'agissait pas seulement d'être vrai, mais qu'il fallait être plaisant, et que c'était la raison pour laquelle on dirait à jamais: *Qu'allait-il faire dans cette galère?* et que le mot de mon paysan 'Que faisait-elle à sa porte?' ne passerait pas en proverbe. (*Jacques le fataliste*, p. 21)

It is clear that the novel is not merely using burlesque techniques but is also posing the question of *what is real* – not metaphysically but aesthetically real. 'Dire la chose comme elle s'est passée' is next to impossible. The form of a tale within a tale is coupled with a constant denial that *Jacques* is a novel – 'Ceci n'est pas un conte' – and an equally constant, and incompatible, reminder that what we are reading is a novel. This discussion is more disruptive, goes farther, than what can always pass for the 'Life and opinions of Tristram Shandy'. After the *nouveau roman* the constant interruptions are unlikely to astound and irritate as they did until fairly recently. The play between the denial and the affirmation that what we are reading is a novel constructs a double bind analogous to that of *vraisemblance*, but in terms of illusion: is the breaking of illusion more or less likely to increase it, is 'ceci n'est pas un roman, lecteur' an admission or an admonition? If it is not a novel, is it true? Interpreting this structure in terms of the century's aesthetics we seem to have before us, put into practice, the oscillating theory of illusion. Fictional material is allowed to coalesce, only to be interrupted. It is as if we are to watch ourselves under the illusion, or rather, since for Diderot's psychology immediate introspection is impossible, to turn back and watch the illusion disappear.

It may seem as if much of this watching of illusion, this investigation of the conditions of the novel, is done through the figure of the 'auteur'. A number of factors might be thought to support this view. For instance the question of how the author knows what he does is raised. The 'auteur' claims at one point that he cannot continue the story without Jacques; the relation between author and reader's time and the character's time is brought out: 'Au moment où nous en parlons il s'écriait douleureusement [. . .]' (*Jacques le fataliste*, p. 34); the relation of the novel to the audience's reaction is also questioned – is this reaction to be sceptical like the master's about the prostitute's motives for honesty in the story of Madame de la Pommeraye, or enthusiastic like the master's generous anger at Jacques' fate after his good deed? (*Jacques le fataliste*, pp. 107–8). A defence of obscenity is taken from Montaigne and the plagiarism admitted. The 'auteur' harasses the reader, threatening to digress or to omit, proclaiming his independence or asking the reader what he wants:

Lecteur, si je faisais ici une pause, et que je reprisse l'histoire de l'homme à une seule chemise parce qu'il n'avait qu'un corps à la fois, je voudrais bien savoir ce que vous en penseriez? Que je me suis fourré dans un [*sic*] impasse, à la Voltaire, ou, vulgairement, dans un cul de sac, d'où je ne sais comment sortir, et que je me jette dans un conte fait à plaisir pour gagner du temps et chercher quelque moyen de sortir de celui que j'ai commencé. Eh bien, Lecteur, vous vous abusez de tout point. (*Jacques le fataliste,* pp. 110–11)

(As in so many other of Diderot's writings, the 'auteur' here pre-empts the dialogue: putting words into the mouth of the puppet 'lecteur', and, as we shall see, emptying the real reader of his reality.) But this discussion of the novel form, this self-commentary, is made possible by a radicalisation of both the familiar tale-within-a-tale format and the self-consciousness familiar in the burlesque. For the burlesque author becomes one more tale, the structure is that of a complex series of frames. The author-figure recounts to the reader-figure the story of Jacques' and his master's journey. Jacques, to while away the time, relates – in jumbled order – his love affairs, and later so does the master. They also meet characters who tell stories. The functions are thus three and the structure of *Jacques* can be plotted as on page 131.[7]

The structure is a virtuoso treatment of the old *romanesque* form. Jacques tells his own tale, as does the master: but the other major tales, those of Madame de la Pommeraye and of le père Hudson, are not told by the protagonists themselves but about the protagonists, the Marquis des Arcis and his servant Richard. Arcis is thus both told-about and a teller, though he does not tell his own tale but someone else's. The first variation on the traditional use of the tale within a tale is that Diderot's construction is not that of Chinese boxes, each tale enclosed within another. The insertions in fact overlap. The second variation is the complex use of interruptions between f, f^i and f^ii. This compels the reader to read by moving rapidly from one story to another and back again (*papillotage*). He can barely 'get into' one before another crosses his path. But this complex structure of interpolation and insertion, while not allowing an uninterrupted vertical movement 'in', does force a movement inwards in stepwise fashion from the outer relation of author and reader to the journey of Jacques, through and 'down' to the highly coloured and relatively unbroken fiction of the story of Madame de la Pommeraye.

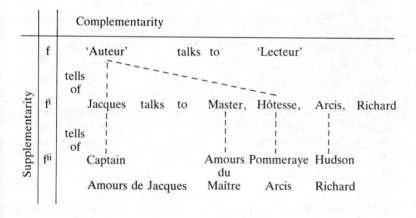

Though the levels of narration, f, f^i, are symmetrical, as I have mentioned, the 'auteur' and Jacques both have the upper hand, the freedom to speak or to refuse to speak, to harry the 'lecteur' or the master: 'Ecoutez, n'écoutez pas, je parlerai tout seul.' They are complementary to their listeners – the 'auteur' does need a listener, just as Jacques and his master are interdependent. The power relation between them – Jacques is socially dependent on his master but manages on occasion to manipulate him like a puppet, just the same – is a mirror of the power the 'auteur'

exercises over the 'lecteur' by refusing to satisfy the usual conventions of a novel. For *Jacques* exploits fully the domination that comes from upsetting our expectations, and it is this that supplies the link with the theme of fatalism in the novel. Jacques believes that his life is pre-determined, but upsets expectations of what behaviour should result from this belief by acting like a free man. Reciprocally, the master believes in free will and acts like an automaton. In turn, this mirrors one aspect of the novel's commentary on itself. Jacques believes his life is pre-determined, and indeed it is, by the 'auteur', who yet treats him as though he had an autonomous existence. Jacques conceives of his fate as 'le grand rouleau' and 'ce qui est écrit là-haut', an evident metaphor for the author's intentions, for the fate the author will wish on him, and thus for the complete book, which exists on one plane (it is printed and bound) but not yet in terms of Jacques' life or of our reading of it; and these intentions, like events in Jacques' life, have every appearance of the perfectly arbitrary. The horse which leads Jacques to any and every gibbet he passes may be an omen of impending doom, as the master presages – despite his belief in free will – but it is the hangman's horse and is merely following the stages of its habitual journey. Yet Jacques does seem to be going to end badly: he lands in prison, but is rescued in unlikely though traditionally *romanesque* fashion by brigands. Determinism and mere chance meet here – 'Chaque balle a son billet' – but since the trajectory of events in the novel, as of bullets, is largely unpredictable, and can only be established *ex post facto*, complete determinism looks like absolute chance. What is the most uniform – determined, that is – is also the most dispersed, apparently occasioned merely by hazard. And on the level of the commentary on the novel, the theme of fatalism becomes that of authorial power – even where the author disclaims responsibility for the story he is telling. *Jacques*, in fact, goes beyond the usual resources of the parodistic tale as developed by Scarron and by Diderot himself in *Les Bijoux indiscrets* (1748). For the 'author' is absent from where we expect to find him – he can deny he was there, or assert that he was plagiarising Montaigne or imitating Molière. The introduction of the 'reader' makes more subtle the technique developed in the *Vernet* article and in *La Religieuse*. The 'reader' is also developed beyond the parodistic part assigned to him by previous writers, for his role is complementary to that of the author. The introduction of the reader-listener is not merely one more step in the illusion game.

Lorsqu' on fait un conte, c'est à quelqu'un qui l'écoute; et pour peu que le conte dure, il est rare que le conteur ne soit interrompu quelquefois par son auditeur. Voilà pourquoi j'ai introduit dans le récit qu'on va lire et qui n'est pas un conte ou qui est un mauvais conte, si vous vous en doutez, un personnage qui *fasse à peu près le rôle du lecteur*. (Diderot, *Contes*, p. 124)

The real reader, in a similar but not identical situation to the 'lecteur', is manoeuvred into a lack of authenticity where his power of reply is preempted, he is forced to be absent.

A letter of Diderot's enables my analysis to be pushed farther:

Ah mon amie, quelle différence entre lire l'histoire et entendre l'homme! Les choses intéressent bien autrement. D'où vient cet intérêt? Est-ce du rôle de celui qui raconte ou du rôle de celui qui écoute? Serait-ce que nous serions flattés de la préférence du sort qui nous adresse à celui à qui tant de choses extraordinaires sont arrivées, et de l'avantage que nous aurons sur les autres par le degré de certitude que nous acquérons, et par celui que nous serons en droit d'exiger lorsque nous redirons à notre tour ce que nous aurons entendu? On est bien fier, quand on raconte, de pouvoir ajouter: Celui à qui cela est arrivé, je l'ai vu; c'est de lui-même que je tiens la chose. Il n'y a qu'un cran au-dessus de celui-là: ce serait de pouvoir dire: J'ai vu la chose arriver, et j'y étais. Encore ne sçais-je s'il ne vaut pas mieux quelquefois appuyer son récit de l'autorité immédiate d'un personnage important que de son propre témoignage; et si un homme n'est pas plus croyable quand il dit: je tiens la chose du maréchal de Turenne ou du maréchal de Saxe, que s'il disait: je l'ai vue. Quoiqu'il puisse aussi facilement mentir sur un de ces points que sur l'autre, il me semble que du moins il nous trouve plus disposés à recevoir pour vrai un de ces mensonges que l'autre. Dans le premier cas, il faut qu'il y ait deux menteurs, et il n'en faut qu'un dans le second: et entre les deux menteurs, il y a un personnage bien important. (Diderot, *Correspondance*, vol. III, pp. 229–30; letter to Sophie Volland of November 1760)

This letter makes exactly the slippage discussed much earlier in this chapter: the truth value which resides in the reliability of the teller of the anecdote is conflated with the truth of the anecdote itself. How does this happen? It seems as if the teller, who interposes between the hearer and the eye-witness account, is elided. And this is possible because there is relayed narration ('I heard it from a man who saw X take place'). Diderot, as has been pointed out, constructs something more complicated in *Jacques*. Here there is not only relayed narration (f, f^i, f^{ii}); there is also however at both f and f^i a relation of necessary complementarity. The author and the reader are interdependent; so are Jacques and his master. Because the reader, like the master, is forced to play 'plus ou moins le rôle du lecteur', he listens, and like the 'lecteur' he forgets at which degree of narrative function the story is situated – an erosion of the awareness of degrees of narrative function takes place, and this is how the reader moves into the story. We have, in other words, an analysis of the process of illusion. Yet any reader of *Jacques*, and Jacques himself, knows that stories are broken off at the crucial, or at any arbitrary point (the important near-exceptions, occurring near the *centre of the book*, are the stories of Madame de la Pommeraye, and le père Hudson). The structure of insertion of dialogue is deliberately manipulated so as to bring the insertions to our attention. How can these two structures, the *elision* of the teller, and the *insertions* called to our attention, be related? It seems as if the relation of complementarity, Jacques and his master, 'auteur' and 'lecteur', is set beside a relation of supplementarity, which operates between f, f^i, and f^{ii}. If, in reading the novel, one follows the tale Jacques tells, one momentarily makes absent, annihilates, the tale at the level of the journey. One replaces, substitutes for, Jacques and his master on the journey, and all attention is turned to the story told (this type of substitution is thus radically different from what is familiarly termed identification: for to identify with Jacques making the journey would be to hold in mind the details of that journey). What is substituted for is absent: to retrieve it the substitution must be broken. Does this mean that in the moment of breaking the substitution, all narrative levels – from 'auteur' – 'lecteur', through Jacques and his master, to the story told – can be held in mind? No: they represent vertical absences, towards which attention is orientated, but which are not actually in the field of attention. For this field is simultaneous; it operates at the level of complementarity, so that the reader's mind is turned to the *presence* of the partner in the horizontal dialogue. Within a system, such as a novel, 'absent' can represent what is not in the system at all, or what is not in the field of perception, though it is in the system, and can be made to appear: it is the latter that provides the relation of supplementarity, thematised in the novel by what is 'écrit là-haut' – the structured possibilities made available by the unfolding of the novel.

The structure of *Jacques*, that of complementarity and supplementarity, is constantly suggested within the novel by the treatment of fatalism. I have already suggested that authorial power and Jacques' belief that he is fated are linked – the obvious bridge being the metaphors which Jacques uses to express his belief: 'le grand rouleau' and 'tout est écrit là-haut'. The complementarity of Jacques and his master is emphasised in their attitudes to fatalism by their being called 'theologians' eternally shadow-boxing on the problem of whether man is determined. But the structure of supplementarity is also present: 'Jacques suivait son maître comme vous le vôtre; son maître suivait le sien comme Jacques le suivait' (*Jacques le fataliste*, p. 63). Each man has a master, but the multiplicity of masters makes of each man both servant and master, both contradicting and confirming the relation, which is that of 'and/or'. This relation is exhibited very funnily and neatly in many of the novel's incidents. Thus Jacques, when he has retrieved his master's watch, is pursued by the peasants rounded up by the pedlar; he walks his horse away, on the grounds that if he is fated to be caught, he will be, and that haste is of no use. But this is interpreted by the peasants as proof of his innocence, for they attribute free will to him, and assume that he would hurry if he could and needed to. The same relation is illustrated by the series of stories about the compulsion to duel: Jacques' captain and his friend cannot stop duelling; the same story is told of a Monsieur de Guerchy, and his opponent, and finally of Desglands, a friend of the master. The relation of 'and/or' is one of relaying and contradiction: that is, of supplementarity and complementarity. It is through the workings of this structure which is at once complementary and supplementary that *Jacques* can so constantly interrupt any narrative line and yet hold our attention. We are interrupted (complementarity) and in this we attend to the supplementary narrative level offered. The structure of complementarity and supplementarity can also be related to the theme of fatalism. For if the 'auteur' and the 'lecteur', like Jacques and his master, seem to be necessarily complementary, the slipping into one of the supplementary levels of narration suggests the arbitrary, the random.

In its treatment of fatalism, *Jacques* plays on the opposition of truth and falsehood. The 'auteur' constantly asserts 'ceci n'est pas un conte' and yet with specious anxiety discusses the nature of 'truth' in fiction, thus destroying the affirmation of truth. Diderot takes care to remain within this opposition of truth and illusion, truth and lie, where other writers have moved outside it. For truth and 'truth' enable Diderot to play with freedom and necessity in the novel. Truth is what happened, what is, or was, necessary, while 'truth' is what the 'auteur' invents – in eighteenth-century terms 'un conte fait à plaisir' – what is arbitrary, because contingent.

Jacques, then, is a virtuoso exploration of illusion, an exploration which is done through the structure, and which forces the reader to go through an itinerary in relation to that structure. Based on a pattern of complementarity and supplementarity,

Jacques is formed from 'les mots de l'absence' (Lewinter, 1976), for the supplement excludes what is substituted for. *Jacques* is an admirable and profound illustration of Diderot's concern with our inability to think more than one idea at any time – the supplement breaks the substitution – and with the necessity of our keeping a structured field of possibilities just outside the zone of attention (see Hobson, 1977a).

The novel, then, like painting during the eighteenth century, exhibits two different concepts of representation which can be labelled *adequatio* and *aletheia*. Unlike painting, however, and unlike the other arts, the novel cannot be said to display a development from *aletheia* to *adequatio*. At the very most, looking at the matter in chronological terms, it is true to speak of a gradual adequation to fiction, for the later theory of the novel tends to insist that fiction is truer than fact.

Instead the novel exploits the formal possibilities made available by the logical fact that 'real' and 'unreal' are mutually defining. In the first possibility, the 'real' is defined as that which is not a novel, or, *vice versa*, the novel is defined as that which is not real – what we read is *either* true *or* false. This corresponds more or less to representation conceived as *adequatio*, or its contrary. In the second, what we read is more or less true in relation to some element included within the novel, usually as an inserted tale. Here the novel contains appearance and something against which it appears as appearance (and not as reality). This corresponds to *aletheia*.

The greatest novels of these two types show interesting features in common: Rousseau and Marivaux take as themes the assumptions about reality and illusion implicit in their aesthetics. For Rousseau, fiction is truer than truth – and the relation to illusion, to imaginative experience, is the thread running throughout the book. Marivaux, in *Marianne*, uses the burlesque possibilities of the tale within a tale, but softens and subjectivises the clash between the low life 'reality' and the pretensions and aspirations (*romanesque*) by turning this opposition into a theme.

The fact remains that the novel is a transgressive genre: even where it appears to exclude the false, to present only the true, it shows that even *adequatio* is based on appearance: although *adequatio* would replicate a model, substituting itself for it, it still relays appearance. The most vertiginous exploration of the relaying which is inscribed in all appearance is *Jacques le fataliste*. *Jacques* on one level claims authenticity, like the 'faux mémoires':

'ceci n'est pas un conte'. But the claim is inserted into a complex structure of relaying narrators, of tales within tales, so that it seems both true and untrue. The *adequatio* is set in a relativising context, and we have appearance, and the 'truth' of appearance, defined by the different narrative levels – *aletheia*.

Part Three

ILLUSION AND THE THEATRE: PLAYS, SPECTATORS AND ACTORS

The eighteenth century held drama in the highest esteem. In the early part of the century, at least, a tragedy was a social pass-key, and every young man of literary bent, even such a subtle anti-traditionalist as Marivaux, tried his hand at one. Later, it was said of Diderot that he wrote his *drames* to attempt to gain entry to the Academy (Wilson, 1972, p. 264). The crises and feuds in the theatre and opera occupied the public more than the Seven Years War; Rousseau maintained that the *Querelle des Bouffons* at the Opéra stopped a political crisis, and it was said that the theatre was never so successful as just before the Revolution. But none of the tragedies acted at the Comédie française between 1715 and 1789 – and there were nearly two hundred (Fabre, 1958, p. 809) – and none of the *drames* published in increasing numbers in the latter half of that period survives as more than literary history. In the century in which theatres were first constructed for theatrical purposes (Lawrenson, 1957, p. 182),* in which queens and royal mistresses acted, in which everyone from the king to courtesans to a provincial *procureur* had a private theatre (Bapst, 1893, pp. 420–38), the theatre was above all a social activity. The audience watches itself as much as the actors, and designers of opera houses overtly include the females of the audience within the spectacle: 'Personne ne va au spectacle pour le plaisir du spectacle, mais pour voir l'assemblée, pour en être vu' (Rousseau, *O.C.*, vol. ii, p. 254). But as the century moves on, the social 'being seen' of eighteenth-century theatre becomes, as I shall show, a 'being seen to be affected by the spectacle'. The play is no longer offered to the prince's box, the viewpoint for the *décor*'s perspective, and in turn the cynosure of the rest of the audience. Instead there is a multiplicity of viewpoints, and a complex pattern of ricochetting glances,

---

* Soufflot's *Grand théâtre* at Lyon, 1754, was the first.

139

communicating the external symptoms of the feeling created by the spectacle. This communication, as Rousseau was to point out in the *Lettre à d'Alembert*, is not a confusion of individual feelings in one enthusiasm, however much Diderot in his early theatre, or Rousseau himself in his accounts of the *fêtes* in Geneva, might have wished it to be so. Instead, it is an interplay between self-consciousnesses. The glance looks outwards at others, but through others' reactions learns of its own. The self-consciousness is thus individualised. If by technical means it is then isolated at the apex of the visual pyramid, the spectator becomes a *voyeur*. He looks out on to a stage which will increasingly present itself as replica, and seek to lock the spectator into his illusion–mistake. The audience's experience becomes private and its enjoyment private also, reflected within the self, self-conscious. If the spectator is a voyeuristic onlooker, there is space between him and the stage happenings, but no mediation. As a result, he must 'identify' with the actor, take on his feelings. And the actor, in his turn, 'identifies' with the character he portrays.

Part III, the centre of this book, shows most clearly a marked movement in the relation of audience to play, but one that throws light on general changes in the relation between consumer and work of art. The spectator's relation changes because the object of his view changes. Theatre and its theory move from an interest in spectacle, or a deliberate exploitation of its own unreality, to a concept of the play as a copy whose techniques of *décor* and of construction must provoke illusion in the form of a mistake in the spectator. As in painting theory, there is a development from *aletheia* to *adequatio*. But in that the spectator's participation moves from the interpersonal to the private, in that his experience must be unmediated, transparent, he will take on, as I have indicated, the feelings of the actor.

5

PLAYS

Illusion and spectacle

It is through its connection with magic that 'illusion' is first used as a term in aesthetics, and it is through opera that the transition came about. Seventeenth- and even eighteenth-century French opera uses primarily magical and mythological subjects where spectacular effect is all-important. The French in fact prolong this stage in the development of opera when the Italians have already abandoned it (L. Riccoboni, 1738b; Nagler, 1957, p. 128) and *décor* plays a controlling part in much eighteenth-century grand opera. The machines may be invented before the plot (Leclerc, 1953), or, in the case of a librettist like Cahusac, working around mid-century, at the same time: of his work on Rameau's *Nais* it was said:

Les Titans entassent montagnes sur montagnes; une machine élève les géants et les montagnes à la fois, en sorte que l'illusion est poussée au point de croire que ce sont les fils de la terre qui grimpent sur les rochers qu'ils mettent les uns sur les autres et qui les font monter jusqu'au ciel d'où ils attaquent les dieux. (Nagler, 1957, p. 132, quoting Collé, *Journal*, vol. I, p. 70)

'Illusion' applied thus to opera is merely one in a range of terms, all of magical origin – 'L'illusion, les prestiges, l'enchantement' (Charpentier, 1768, vol. I, p. 93; cf. Patte, 1782, p. 191) – used to describe the splendour of opera as a fusion of the arts of *décor*, lighting, and machinery. 'Illusion' is thus a product of the 'merveilleux', and the mythological or supernatural plot is reduced to a mere framework for the effects of machines and light, whose purest expression is the series of spectacles produced by Servandoni in the 1740s and 1750s at the Tuileries. These consisted only of music, mime, and scene effects.[1] The content given here to 'illusion' is surprise, bedazzlement, a sort of rape leaving no time for reflection (*Encyclopédie*, article *Décoration*; Maillet Duclairon, 1751, p. 22).

Movement and scene transformations are thus essential to the continuation of the effect of surprise:

Un poète qui a une heureuse invention jointe à une connoissance profonde

141

de cette partie [décor] trouvera mille moyens fréquens d'embellir son spectacle, d'occuper les yeux du spectateur, de préparer l'illusion. Ainsi à la belle architecture d'un palais magnifique ou d'une place superbe, il fera succéder des déserts arides, des rochers escarpés, des antres redoutables. Le spectateur effrayé sera alors agréablement surpris de voir une perspective riante coupée par des paysages agréables prendre la place de ces objets terribles. De là en observant les gradations il lui présentera une mer agitée, un horizon enflammé d'éclairs, un ciel chargé de nuages, des arbres arrachés par la fureur des vents. Il le distraira ensuite de ce spectacle par celui d'un temple auguste: toutes les parties de la belle architecture des anciens rassemblées dans cet édifice, formeront un ensemble majestueux & des jardins embellis par la nature, l'art & le goût, termineront d'une manière satisfaisante une représentation dans laquelle on n'aura rien négligé pour faire naître & pour entretenir l'illusion. (*Encylopédie*, article *Décoration*)

The spectator must, so to say, run the gauntlet of his emotions; there is something essentially passive in such a conception, for he must be subject to a continuity of surprise, constituted out of a succession of different emotions. To provoke this, a subject must be chosen 'qui promet le plus de variété, qui fournit les contrastes les plus marqués, qui occasionne de rapides passages des ténèbres à la lumière, de l'épouvante au plaisir, du terrible au gracieux, surprises qui font les situations d'un Spectacle muet' (Servandoni, 1740, p. 7).[2] The rapid oscillation between extremes of emotion is a fundamental of the period's aesthetic of *papillotage*. (What is described here is a version, speeded up, and between poles which are farther apart, of the effect of the new dramatic genre of the 1730s, the *comédie larmoyante*, the comedy which is watched with tears in the eyes.)[3] The continuity of illusion, of the magically befuddled mind, is created by an oscillating series of discrete elements, which are in this case *décors* largely stereotyped already by the mid-seventeenth century: 'Les mêmes descentes de divinités, les mêmes enlèvements au ciel, les mêmes palais, forêts enchantées, paysages marins' (Leclerc, 1953, p. 263).[4]

'Illusion' operates then in this context as the aesthetics of spectacle, an aesthetics of sumptuosity and extravagance,[5] a vastness of effect which is nevertheless mobile, not static: 'un sujet vaste également susceptible de l'illusion qu'on peut emprunter du merveilleux, & des grâces que fournit la variété' (Servandoni, 1742, p. 7). And conversely, the achievements of the stage designer can be used to elucidate the concept. Thus the idea of distributing irregularly the chassis carrying the scenery attributed to the Bibiena family (Leclerc, 1953, p. 273), and brought to France by Servandoni, made possible a far greater variety in the setting out of

the *décor*. The introduction of several vanishing points created a
sense of expansion in the spectator precisely because he could not
make them coincide.[6] Servandoni in particular was adept at making
the *décor* appear vast: he used, for example, in the foreground
enormous bases of columns, leaving them incomplete so that the
eye was led up into unimaginable heights; he varied the horizontal
and vertical space between the elements of the *décor* at the same
time as the dimensions of the elements themselves. Overall, he
profoundly altered the relationship of the spectator to the stage.
For in designs dating from the end of the seventeenth century –
those of Bérain, for instance – the stage was an independent picture
within which the actor moved, having its own perspective, leading
the eye to a single point at the back of the stage. Servandoni inverts
the visual pyramid, so that the eye is led outwards (Bjurström,
1959, pp. 155–6). The audience is thus at the same time contained
within, because dwarfed by, the vastness of the architecture, and
yet brought outward through imaginary space; an intimate and yet
expansive relationship is established.[7] The impression of participation in a superreality is reinforced by Servandoni's subjects: his
landscapes are imaginary, 'horrid', his architecture fantastical.

It seems, then, that the psychological analysis of 'illusion', in
which reason is opposed to the delights of the senses, applied particularly to opera and to spectacle; conversely, the magnificence of
the opera is needed to bemuse the spectator into neglecting the
fundamental lack of *vraisemblance*. 'Plus toutes les espèces de
vraisemblance y sont négligées, plus nous avons besoin que la
séduction de nos sens ne nous permette pas d'y faire usage de notre
raison' (Rémond de Sainte Albine, 1747, p. 187).[8] It might seem
then that the overpowering of reason by the 'illusion of the senses'
is the aesthetic of spectacular opera. But this is to neglect the force
of words like 'séduction' (see above, p. 48). The very idea of
seduction, of overpowering, implies resistance. Hence, in many
critics, 'illusion' implies its opposite, awareness not merely as a
succeeding state of mind, but as a ground on which the illusion is
superimposed. It is impossible for those critics to speak of 'illusion'
without speaking of its unreality, as the language of spectacular
opera ('prestige', 'charme', and so forth) shows. Phrases which
appear at first a compliment to the strength of the illusion in fact
incorporate in half-realised form the dual nature of this type of
illusion: surprise or rapture are accompanied rather than succeeded
by their opposite – awareness of the artifice: 'Les Machines sont les
effets de la magie & du merveilleux; & l'on a souvent besoin de se

rappeller la construction du Théâtre, & que tout ce que l'on voit est porté par des poutres, des cordages, des fers & des contrepoids, pour se défendre de l'illusion de nos sens, qui nous persuade que ce que nous voyons est véritable' (L. Riccoboni, 1738a, p. 44; cf. Cahusac, 1754, vol. III, p. 66).[9] In such critics, theatrical illusion is the Malebranchian 'illusion de nos sens' made sensible, momentarily apprehensible. To be aware of the appearance is almost simultaneously to be aware of what is seen *as* appearance.

But the very use of improved modes of *décor* for opera and spectacle generates a contradiction. For the improvements in methods of staging discussed above suggest that the idea of the relation between reality and the stage is also changing. The methods are interpreted by the group of opponents of French opera, by Rousseau, and by Grimm *à propos* of Servandoni, as an attempt to create a *replica* of what is purely imaginary or fantastical.

Le merveilleux n'est pas fait pour être représenté [. . .]. Le merveilleux n'appartient de droit qu'au poëte épique qui peint sans couleur, non pas pour nos yeux mais pour notre imagination. Le poëte dramatique et le peintre ne doivent me représenter que des objets dont le modèle existe dans la nature [. . .] dès qu'on me mettra sous les yeux ce qu'il est impossible de représenter, le charme cessera et l'illusion sera détruite. (*Correspondance littéraire*, vol. II, p. 345, avril 1754)[10]

Such spectacles are a mistake of genre, a misguided attempt to stage the epic. For this new generation of critics – Rousseau, Grimm, Diderot, Lessing – theatrical reality must not obtrude. The parallel with the attitude of the first three to painting is evident. Nothing must refer away from the subject, from what is seen: there must be no awareness that what is seen is appearance, no flickering between the reality of the theatre and the subject which is represented. They castigate such spectacle by taking literally the dual analysis of illusion: it satisfies neither feeling nor reason.[11] Awareness of the artifice destroys illusion for such critics, rather than enhancing it: 'Lorsqu'on voit descendre une Divinité [. . .] le prestige commence, mais à peine le char a-t-il percé le plafond que les cordes se montrent & l'illusion se dissipe' (Patte, 1782, p. 189). The unsatisfactory techniques of representation symbolised since La Fontaine by the scene-changer's whistle (Nagler, 1957, p. 129)[12] reinforce the rejection of the representation of the magical. But it seems likely that there is a further, more important, factor. The improvements in staging are powered by a conception of reality which must undercut the very basis of the genre in which they are made. The very notion of reality which could produce Favart's snake as a stage property (Nagler, 1957, p. 135) could not accept the mythological and magical content of opera (Cochin, 1781, p. 61).[13] It is therefore 'illusion' as an involvement in art unalloyed by consciousness which is used to criticise spectacular opera – the meaning of 'illusion' is shifting from that of enchantment as if by magic to that of the mistake. The notion of likeness in the theatre is in fact shifting from representation to replica. 'Illusion' now implies not seduction but belief, well founded or not. And this notion of belief probably spread from aesthetics to epistemology, as has already been suggested of Humean belief (see above, p. 32).

This is pointed out by a curious phrase in Maillet Duclairon's account of the poverty of opera's *décor*: 'Notre imagination ne supplée pas assez pour grandir les objets et nous croyons simplement voir des desseins de cartes' (Maillet Duclairon, 1751, p. 24). The 'croire voir' usually applied to what is perceived in the art and which can be taken to indicate the unreality of what is seen (landscapes on flat expanses of canvas, for instance) must here refer to an extra cog in the perceptual process: we do not see objects directly, but an element of 'belief' enters irrevocably into perception.

The improvements in staging, an object of social pride as well as of aesthetic concern, are usually justified in terms of an illusion which excises awareness. Some techniques are merely a perfecting of those already in existence – the advocacy of perspective in *décor*, for instance, is taken to ridiculous lengths by Noverre, who maintains that the use of dancers of graded sizes can give an effect of distance (Noverre, 1760, pp. 104–5). The discussions about the optimal shape of the stage, vigorous in the latter half of the century, are conducted in terms of illusion. In particular, Patte, quoting Algarotti, criticises a stage which advances too far into the audience as separating actors and *décor* and thus destroying illusion (Patte, 1782, pp. 22, 132). Yet the relation he wishes to create is not that of fusion: he insists on the necessity of the actor's being cut off from the audience, a continuation of their space, but separate from it. Such a relation had in fact been obtained by a reform of 1759, after which spectators no longer sat on the stage of the Comédie française (Préville, 1823, p. 115; Patte, 1782, p. 177). Spectator and scene are now separated completely – so that the distance between them is negated, made as if it did not exist.

This movement in the relation of audience and stage does not have the effect of expelling spectacle. On the contrary, opera influences the stage and spectacular effects are carried into tragedy. Successive *décors* in productions of Voltaire's *Sémiramis* confirm visually the disintegration of the role of unity of place (Bjurström, 1956) and the new production of *Mérope* in 1763 finally settles this. Events which had occurred off-stage are brought on (Lanson, 1920, pp. 134–6): thus the funeral pyre of the *Veuve de Malabar*, missing in 1770, appears in 1780. The use of spectacular effects, however, confirms the new relation between audience and theatre. It is designed to bring back on to the stage what earlier had happened off, not to open a gap between appearances and what is seen, but to make them consistent. Corneille's seventeenth-century *Horace* had chased his sister behind scenes to kill her. Lekain in 1756 dared to emerge from a tomb, his hands bathed in red paint. Vaucanson constructs a mechanical scorpion for Marmontel's *Cléopâtre*. But the satisfaction with such improvements expressed in terms of illusion reaches its height in regard to stage costume (Dorat, 1766, p. 23).[14] The actress Clairon, in the vanguard both of stage-effects and of philosophy, is lauded for her courage in appearing on the stage without 'paniers' as Idamé in Voltaire's *Orphelin de la Chine* (though Madame Favart of the *Opéra comique* had done so some years earlier). For the role of Roxane in *Bajazet*, she borrows the harem costume that the same Madame Favart had procured from Istanbul. Yet the search for exactitude in costume is countered by other concerns. The clothes given by Madame de Pompadour for a performance of Crébillon's *Catalina* in 1746 are indeed togas and not the usual stylised Louis XIV costumes with bits of armour and 'brodequins à l'antique', but they are magnificent togas garnished with silver, purple and diamonds (Bapst, 1893, p. 466). La Guimard danced in ballets in peasant costume, but that of a Boucher peasant. Do such lapses represent the limits of contemporary taste? Or the limits of contemporary comprehension of the past? They are perhaps a kind of *papillotage*: the details refer to what is, by social agreement, thought to represent reality, controlled by conventional agreement, based on what is accepted in Paris as courtly and at court as peasant-like. However, in general, as *décors* and costumes change, the details do not *refer* – they *simulate*. As such they are held not to be conventional. This is proved by the criticism of the older generation, who complain that such 'grotesque' effects run against agreed convention and thus call *attention* to the stage, by bringing in awareness where it is not wanted, by breaking a certain sort of illusion. Voltaire finds that his emulators in tragedy as in philosophy have gone too far: 'Un tombeau, une

146

chambre tendue de noir, une potence, une échelle, des personnages qui se battent sur la scène, des corps morts qu'on enlève, tout cela est fort bon à montrer sur le Pont-Neuf' (Lekain, 1825, p. 258, letter from Voltaire, 16 décembre 1760). The importing of such details is experienced as a breaking down of the barriers between genres and thus as burlesque – and it is not by accident that the most thorough-going experiments in stage *décor* and costume went on at the *Opéra comique*. Electre, says Marmontel, in the *Encyclopédie* article *Décoration théâtrale*, should drag real chains. Such devices of the 'real elephants' variety of course reach their climax in the nineteenth century, with, say, *Aida*. But such a replica is every bit as imaginary and conventional as a Racinian production with 'brodequins à l'antique'. What the younger generation sees as a copy the older generation sees as burlesque and atomised signs. It is unsurprising that it is an exponent of the spectacular who alone investigates the value of such 'real' items, and brings out the submerged rationale behind their use. Servandoni inverts Torelli's and Vigarani's practice of placing painted figures in stage crowds:

Toutes les principales Divinités, avec leur suite, & tous les Dieux secondaires formeront un concours de plus de deux mille Figures de relief, parmi lesquelles il y en aura plusieurs naturelles; & ce mélange ingénieux communiquera, pour ainsi dire, la vie à tout ce grand Spectacle. (Servandoni, 1739, pp. 9–10)

The real on the stage is not a replica, but a sign, contaminating the non-real, so that the mind will oscillate between them.[15] However, Servandoni's view will be passed over – and writers, as well as creators of theatrical scenery, will increasingly strive for coincidence between copy and model.

Illusion and plays

'Illusion' thus expressed the magical effect of spectacular opera: an effect compounded from a series of rapidly changing sense impressions, of *ravissement*, of surprise; but an effect which incorporated as an essential the awareness of the spectacle's unreality. Increasingly, however, the same term was used to criticise spectacular theatre: not merely was the awareness to be denied, it was to be excluded from the spectator's experience, so that a fundamentally different type of impression was to be created, one not of rapid oscillation between awareness and involvement but of absorption into the theatrical performance. 'Illusion' has then contracted, and awareness is to be excluded. As in the theory of art, what creates awareness is excised, and the corresponding concept of truth is changing from *aletheia* to *adequatio*.

Although reduction in the scope of 'illusion' is at its clearest in the discussion of the development of *décor*, fashions in stage decoration cannot be divorced from the subjects of plays and their treatment. An attempt to create with the *décor* a stage replica of the play's content is intimately dependent on notions of reality, for one can construct a replica only of something already in existence, which thus becomes the definition of the real. Although to read the notion of 'realism' into eighteenth-century art and aesthetics is to commit a serious anachronism, there is no doubt that theatrical taste in the century developed a concern with material and social reality. Is then 'illusion' as a mistake, unalloyed by consciousness of art, an attempt to conceptualise this development? – an apparently paradoxical evolution in that a cruder concept, 'illusion', is applied to a later form of relation between art and reality? Yet the paradox is removed if the movement in question is defined as a collapse of the notion of genre (Auerbach, 1953) or of the agreement about conventions in art forms (Tocqueville, 1951). For in that case, if agreement about what type of consciousness is to be incorporated into the consumer's experience is lacking, then the attempt to excise it from that experience is comprehensible and perhaps inevitable. And in eighteenth-century aesthetic discussion, as I shall show, the question of artistic convention is bound up with the role of consciousness in illusion.

The excision of consciousness

The Thespis of legend developed monologues from narrative, and dialogues from monologues. For Brumoy, this development is one from imitation into a form of verity:

Ce seroit en quelque sorte une action véritable. Du moins, les spectateurs plus agréablement trompés verroient en effet, ce qu'ils ne font qu'entendre & supposer, quand un seul & même Acteur fait l'un après l'autre le double rôle d'Agamemnon, & d'Achille. Les yeux & l'esprit séduits par cette peinture croiroient voir la chose même. (Brumoy, 1730, vol. I, p. lxv; Méhégan, 1755, p. 30; Lacombe, 1758, p. 102)

The force of the concept of drama as a replica appears from a distinction made by Rémond de Sainte Albine between paintings' 'représenter' and the theatre's 'reproduire'. The theatre is the more perfect form of art, he maintains, because the consumer need not supplement with his imagination the lack of force which typifies the other imitative arts: 'Le peintre ne peut que nous représenter les événements. Le Comédien en quelque sorte les reproduit' – an idea contrasting sharply with the medieval and Renaissance notion of actors as shadows (Rémond de Sainte Albine, 1747, pp. 14–15). The consumer, in other words, need not interpret what he sees. When drama is thought of as replica, illusion can function as a criterion: that an actual mistake is made is evidence that the replica is complete, or negatively, if illusion does not occur, the play is defective (Servandoni d'Hannetaire, 1774, p. 248; Marmontel, *Encyclopédie*, article *Déclamation théâtrale*). Thus Louis Ricoboni uses the concept tentatively, to criticise the pompous French style of declamation from the stand point of the *Commedia dell'Arte*:

Le grand point sur la Scène [. . .] est de faire illusion aux Spectateurs, & de leur persuader, autant qu'on le peut, que la Tragédie n'est point une Fiction, mais que ce sont les mêmes Héros qui agissent et qui parlent, & non pas les Comédiens qui les représentent. La Déclamation Tragique opère tout le contraire: les premiers mots qu'on entend font évidemment sentir que tout est fiction & les Acteurs parlent avec des tons si extra-ordinaires & si éloignés de la vérité qu'on ne peut pas s'y méprendre. (L. Riccoboni, 1738b, pp. 34–5)

Riccoboni demands a diction which gives the illusion not merely of reality, but of fluidity of thought, of spontaneity (L. Riccoboni, 1738b, pp. 31–2).

Has 'illusion' then merely replaced *vraisemblance*, being used in a similar way as a critical term? It certainly acquires much of *vraisemblance*'s two-way force in argument (see above, pp. 35, 94), is illusion more or less likely to occur if the scene changes? or should a setting be chosen where all the play's events could have plausibly taken place – in practice, a street corner or an entrance to a palace?[16] Unity of action and unity of time are also justified.[17] A historical basis may be necessary for illusion, or, as in Diderot's opinion, it may destroy illusion: 'Je ne blame pas qu'on cherche son dénouement dans l'histoire. Alors il est impossible qu'il soit faux; mais il ne faut pas que le spectateur s'aperçoive de cet emprunt. Il se rappelle le trait historique et il n'est plus étonné' (Diderot, *Correspondence*, vol. III, p. 21, 23 ou 25 février 1760). Again, speed in the plot may be accounted for thus: 'l'Ame attentive à ce qui se passe n'a pas le tems, s'il m'est permis de parler de la sorte, de réfléchir sur la tromperie qu'on lui fait' (Nougaret, 1769, vol. I, p. 188).

Yet 'illusion' does not so much replace *vraisemblance* as overtake it. For far from representing a social agreement between audience and author as to what is plausible, it implies in fact an obliteration of that *doxa*. This is made clear (inadvertently) by Mirzoza, the heroine of Diderot's *Les Bijoux indiscrets*. Uninterrupted illusion guarantees the perfection of the spectacle: 'La perfection d'un spectacle consiste dans l'imitation si exacte d'une action, que le spectateur, trompé sans interruption, s'imagine assister à l'action même' (Diderot, *O.C.*, vol. I, p. 634). Yet her illustration of this definition unintentionally reveals that there are many reasons besides the replica's perfection why it might be taken for reality. She is obliged to suppose, for such illusion to take place, someone totally new to the country, 'un nouveau débarqué d'Angote, qui n'ait jamais entendu parler de spectacle'. If the illusion is not to be interrupted, the whole social activity that the theatre is must not merely be ignored, it must be unknown. In Mirzoza's account the relation between illusion and awareness is successive, alternating, and, for awareness to be excised, it must never have developed in the first place.

Such views give way to something more practical in Diderot's later *Discours sur la poésie dramatique*. Social agreement about the theatre is defined as 'voluntary' illusion, and since the required ignorance of a 'nouveau débarqué d'Angote' is impossible, an equivalent is obtained by thinking of the audience as forced to make a mistake, that is, as having erased social agreement: 'L'illusion n'est pas volontaire. Celui qui dirait: je veux me faire illusion, ressemblerait à celui qui dirait: J'ai une expérience des choses de la vie à laquelle je ne ferai aucune attention' (Diderot, *Discours*, p. 215). An error is certainly not voluntary in any simple sense. But can the consumer's experience of drama be equated thus with a mistake? Again, as with Mirzoza, Diderot is obliged to formulate the notion in ways which reveal its inadequacy. He rejects voluntary error, which he defines as a decision to reject past experience – 'une expérience des choses à laquelle je ne ferai aucune attention'. This cannot be done, clearly. But Diderot's argument here bears an important implication. If voluntary error is impossible, then attention is paid by the consumer to his past experience in involuntary illusion: that is, he conducts a constant mental comparison which should preclude the description of his state of mind as *passive* error. Yet passive and involuntary error is what Diderot requires of the spectator. He represents it metaphorically as a constant placed on one side of an equation, the other side of which is composed of positive and negative terms: 'Les termes positifs représentent les circonstances communes, et les négatifs les circonstances extraordinaires. Il faut qu'elles se rachètent les unes par les autres' (Diderot, *Discours,* p. 215). The extent of Diderot's reduction of the semantic field of illusion is here apparent, in that unalloyed illusion has been shorn even of the connotation of involvement, which implied a movement of the imagination towards the stage happenings. Instead, the consumer has been separated from the stage, for the mistake is *imposed* on him: 'Le poète se joue de la raison et de l'expérience de l'homme instruit, comme une gouvernante se joue de l'imbécillité d'un enfant. Un bon poème est un conte digne d'être fait à des hommes sérieux' (Diderot, *Discours,* p. 215).

However, 'illusion' reduced to mean 'involuntary error' functions as more than a tool to criticise certain contemporary theatrical forms, in a way that the vocabulary of such criticism itself reveals. It is said, for example, of Marivaux:

Il avait un art merveilleux pour rapprocher ses temps, en faisant, pour ainsi dire, passer le cœur par tous les différents mouvements en deux ou trois scènes, qu'il n'auroit dû éprouver qu'en deux ou trois ans. Ce n'est pas un genre de comédie vrai et dans la nature; il faut trop se prêter à l'illusion. (Collé, 1868, vol. II, p. 289)

La Place, the translator of Shakespeare, claims that the English, 'naturellement mélancholiques, sont moins disposés que d'autres à se prêter à l'illusion. La constante étude du vrai rend souvent le cœur indocile & rebelle à la vraisemblance' (La Place, 1746, vol. I, p. xxxix). There is here a refusal of bimodal illusion ('se prêter à l'illusion'), of any movement of the spectator outwards towards appearance which implies a return to self ('se prêter'), and which thus brings with it awareness. This is one of the signs that for the later part of the century, *vraisemblance* is not enough to account for art's relation to reality: 'vérité' is demanded instead,[18] and one has no need to lend oneself to 'vérité', for it imposes itself. Theorists are increasingly prepared to use 'vérité' to formulate aesthetic demands: 'Cette simplicité dans le tissu de l'intrigue, ce naturel dans le dialogue, cette vérité dans le sentiment, cet art de cacher l'art même dans l'enchaînement des situations, d'où résulte l'illusion théâtrale' (Marmontel, 1763, vol. II, p. 377). In the traditional hierarchy art is the repository of illusion, expressed for instance in the speech written by Voltaire on the death of the actress Lecouvreur. Here an actor implies that his art is produced by illusion, and begs forgiveness for the actors stepping forward and speaking 'devant vous [. . .] dépouillés des ornemens et de l'illusion qui nous soutiennent' (quoted by d'Allainval, 1822, p. 252). But the new relation between art and reality is quite different. Truth is now a tool to produce illusion as an end. Consequently the traditional moral hierarchy is inverted and truth serves to define illusion: 'La perfection que nous désirons le plus dans la Représentation est ce qu'au Théâtre on nomme Vérité. On y entend par ce mot le concours des apparences qui peuvent servir à tromper les spectateurs' (Rémond de Sainte Albine, 1747, p. 135).[19] Truth created illusion, itself an appearance of truth: is such an account merely intellectual coquetry on the part of the theorist? The oscillation between involvement and awareness which constituted the consumer's experience for a certain type of theory is reproduced here in a different form. Those theorists who insist on involuntary illusion transfer the awareness from within the consumer's state of mind to implant it in the art object in the guise of 'truth'. Correspondingly, the consumer's reaction becomes a private phantom. The play is adequate to what it represents, and substitutes itself for it. But as long as reference inherent in representation cannot be entirely excised, the contrast between the state of mind, 'illusion', and the truth of the play cannot end here. For the 'vérité' which produces illusion is stage truth, and it is by reference to the real that it acquires the force necessary to create illusion, the impression of truth: 'Je tâche [. . .] de m'approcher de la vérité pour faire plus d'illusion' (Favart, 1808, vol. i, p. 20, quoting Garrick); and Noverre expands this: 'Cette sorte de vérité séduisante [. . .] dérobe l'illusion au Spectateur' (Noverre, 1760, p. 18). 'Vérité' here acts the part of illusion: it seduces, it covers what is false, inverting the traditional roles assigned to truth and illusion. So what is real is the product of the artist's invention: 'Plus il persuade qu'il ne feint pas, & plus il excelle dans l'art de feindre' (Marmontel, 1763, vol. i, p. 322).[20]

The spiralling assignment of truth and illusion, whereby the audience is deceived with truth, but this truth is itself only an appearance of truth, still has the structure of *papillotage*, of *aletheia*. Although the play is 'vrai' it still refers outside itself. A large part of Diderot's two manifestoes on the theatre, the *Entretiens sur le 'Fils naturel'*, and the *Discours sur la poésie dramatique*, is an attempt to excise this referring outwards. In the *Discours* he seriously, indeed pompously, compares art to a relation of power and dependence (nurse and child) which is abused ('se jouer', 'imbécillité'). The combination of pomposity and scurrility is typical of the *Discours*, with its public pretensions to being a serious treatise and its coquettish private references. Yet the oscillation between truth and illusion is not eliminated to the profit of 'truth'. For if Diderot no longer locates the oscillation in the art object, as with the Rococo spiral traced above, he still places a comparable ambivalence at the heart of the relation between artist and consumer. The falsity of art is not located so much in the art work, as in the imbalance of the relation between spectator and author. The artist, the playwright, tricks the consumer. As in his art theory, Diderot rejects the spiral of *papillotage* but reconstitutes it at a different level.

For the Diderot of the *Discours sur la poésie dramatique*, the work of art is composed of particles: 'Des mensonges mêlés à des vérités avec tant d'art qu'il [spectateur] n'éprouve aucune répugnance à les recevoir.' Individual facts are juxtaposed with individual fictions and mere juxtaposition becomes contamination in the mind of the spectator: 'Les choses qu'il invente reçoivent de la vraisemblance par celles qui lui sont données.' In this way disparate atoms of truth and falsehood combine into illusion in the consumer's reaction. The poet's art is a judicious arrangement of these particles, creating a consistency in the work itself: 'Le poète veut, lui, qu'il règne dans toute la texture de son ouvrage une liaison apparente et sensible' (Diderot, *Discours*, p. 214). Although he adopts 'L'ordre de la nature [. . .] lorsqu'elle se plaît à combiner des incidents extraordinaires' (Diderot, *Discours*, p. 217), he can relate these particles on analogy with the relations existing in the world. To draw attention to those relations eliminates surprise and thus implausibility while retaining the extraordinary nature of the events. It is thus not contradictory for Diderot, while claiming that the poet tricks the consumer, to assert: 'Tout doit être clair pour le spectateur. Confident de chaque personnage, instruit de ce qui s'est passé et de ce qui se passe, il y a cent moments où l'on n'a rien de mieux à faire que de lui déclarer nettement ce qui se passera' (Diderot, *Discours*, p. 227). The elimination of oscillation in the spectator, caused by surprise within the *course* of the play, is an essential part of Diderot's reaction against the contemporary theatre, and is on a par with his refusal of 'contrasts' in characters, of 'coups de théâtre' in plots and of *papillotage* in painting. But for all his insistence on coherence, his atomistic conception of the art object as a juxtaposition of separate truths and falsehoods means that he retains the scurrilous notion of a trick played on the audience. ('Illusion' returns to its earlier meaning: *illusio*, a mocking.)

Rousseau, whose aesthetic is closely related to Diderot's, does not delight in this ambivalence. It is not the relation between artist and consumer, but the art object itself which is false. From this he can derive two opposed attitudes. For the Rousseau of the *Imitation théâtrale* and the *Lettre à d'Alembert*, contemporary theatre is false, its motto being 'Qu'importe la vérité d'imitation, pourvu que l'illusion y soit?' (Rousseau, *Lettre à d'Alembert*, p. 82); he thus divorced what contemporaries were attempting to link. Moreover, by the very nature of theatre, 'vérité d'imitation' cannot be attained. Yet in *La Nouvelle Héloïse*, when suggesting an aesthetic by which the contemporary theatre can be judged, Saint-Preux states: 'Le Français ne cherche point sur la scène le naturel et l'illusion' (Rousseau, *O.C.*, vol. II, p. 254). There is no conflict between 'naturel' and 'illusion'. If Saint-Preux's criticisms can be laid at his author's door, Rousseau has two attitudes to art. Some art can be 'truer' (le naturel et l'illusion'); there can be 'adequation' between art object and what it represents. On the other hand, that truth is made ontologically unobtainable by the very structure of representation and substitution which the theatre as a social institution requires.

Lessing's work is instructive in this respect, because he understood so clearly the dilemma in which Rousseau and Diderot were placed. He takes from both and resolves the conflict. Like Rousseau, he speaks of 'le vrai chemin de la nature & de l'illusion' (Lessing, 1785, vol. II, p. 143). Nature, truth, and illusion are dialectically matched, and finally resolved into an idealising conception of art's truth. The poet does not use historical truth simply because it happened, for that is merely external plausibility. Lessing interiorises the consistency demanded: he speaks of 'inner plausibility' (*Wahrscheinlichkeit*). Art may be opposed to historical truth, but it is not on that account false: it has a higher kind of truth.

The content of 'vérité'

Conceptually, then, illusion which excludes awareness does not merely put into relief all that is wrong with certain art forms (those that fail to provoke it). It is seen as the result of the play's 'truth'. But what content can be given to this demand for 'vérité'? That writers are prepared to use the term suggests a change in the way the relation between art and reality is conceived of; but such a change is hard to distinguish, on the evidence of discussions of art, from a shift in the notion of what is real. It seems likely in fact that both types of change were occurring.[21] It is significant that Tocqueville puts the two together in his comment on the rise of the *drame* within a democracy: 'Ils aiment à retrouver sur la scène le mélange confus de conditions, de sentiments et d'idées qu'ils rencontrent sous leurs yeux; le théâtre devient plus frappant, plus vulgaire et plus vrai' (Tocqueville, 1951, p. 86). Again, Grimm's attack on Servandoni's spectacles for seeking to represent what cannot be visually represented (see above, p. 144) may appear to be an example of the growing eighteenth-century awareness of the distinctness of the arts – an awareness usually associated in particular with Diderot, and with Lessing's *Laocoon*.

Yet the distinction Grimm makes between epic and drama is in fact based on the assumption that a play, and indeed a painting, are replicas, and can thus refer only to what has or has had some form of material existence. As a result, 'vérité' tends to acquire the meaning of accuracy of duplication of material existence, but may thus imply a participation through the imagination in events of other times and other countries: 'La vérité dans les habits comme dans les décorations augmente l'illusion théâtrale, transporte le spectateur au siècle et au pays où vivaient les personnages représentés' (Talma, in Lekain, 1825, p. xvi, c.f. Noverre, 1760, pp. 18–19). Or again:

L'essentiel est de faire en sorte que le spectateur se croie véritablement transporté dans les tems & dans les lieux où se passe l'action, que tout les lui rappelle sans cesse, les retrace à son imagination, comme si la chose étoit réelle, qu'il y remarque les habillemens, les armes, le goût des peuples, les différens costumes. (Patte, 1782, p. 188)

A carefully reconstructed replica of historical and geographical circumstances will induce illusion. Illusion will place the spectator back in past times or different countries. Lekain can thus argue that the theatre re-enacts history:

Il n'est personne qui ne convienne que la représentation théâtrale ne soit le tableau mouvant des événemens que l'histoire nous peint souvent, avec tant de langueur et si peu d'intérêt. Il est donc absolument nécessaire que le Théâtre s'occupe à donner une nouvelle vie à ces fameux personnages de l'antiquité, si célèbres par le mélange de leurs vertus et de leurs vices. Qui peut en donner une idée plus frappante que les talens d'un acteur, secondé de tout ce que l'illusion peut offrir de plus vrai et de plus majestueux? (Lekain, 1825, p. 148)

Such a conception of the theatre is possible only where notions of historical difference and geographical originality have already been acquired,[22] and are considered to constitute 'vérité'; where reality is a point defined by the axes of time and space, a definition far removed from seventeenth-century conceptions. Patte's criticism of fantastic *décor* reveals the trend towards a material conception of reality, correlated with a movement from the magical to the perceptual connotations of illusion:

Il faut éviter surtout que les décorations paraissent des espèces de labyrinthes d'architecture ou des amas de colonnes distribuées au hasard sans aucune vraisemblance de solidité & dont les plans soient fantastiques: car ce seroit agir contre le but qu'on se proposeroit; toujours l'illusion doit avoir pour base l'apparence de la réalité. (Patte, 1782, p. 189)[23]

Not merely has the concept of what is real changed: the concept of art's relation to reality has altered. Louis Riccoboni, writing to Muratori, explains the originality of Nivelle de La Chaussée thus:

Elle [la comédie] avoit toujours représenté les incidens domestiques des Bourgeois, des gens aisés, & quelquefois même des Artisans: le Théâtre ancien, tant Grec que Latin, ne nous fournit plus d'autres modeles que ceux de cette nature, que les modernes ont imités: il y a cependant dans la société une espèce de personnes qui sont exclues d'une action comique; on croit les Gentilshommes & les Seigneurs d'une haute naissance trop élevés pour entrer dans les situations domestiques, qui ont toujours été le partage & l'objet de la Comédie; ils ne peuvent pas non plus agir dans le tragique [. . .]. Ce sont ces mêmes personnes qui occupent, si l'on peut se servir de ce terme, *une espèce de niche isolée, & un certain milieu entre le rang élevé de la Tragédie & le populaire de la Comédie*. (L. Riccoboni, in La Chaussée, 1762, vol. v, pp. 198–200)

The interest of this passage lies not in the accuracy of its account of La Chaussée but in the idea that art maps society. For earlier drama *took as its subject* kings or artisans, and was thus founded upon a totally different relation between art and reality: because it did not contain the notion of art *covering* society, it had no need to formulate a demand that the coverage should be complete.[24]

Is 'illusion' a proto-'realism'?

The change in the concept of 'reality' which gave it a more material, socio-historical content, and the change in the conception of the relation between art and reality may both seem to make possible a more 'realistic' art in the loose sense of that term. Diderot's theory that drama, having exhausted 'caractères' should turn to 'conditions', seems to exemplify a demand that men in their social functions should be represented on the stage. Yet it was not in the 'straight' theatre but at the *Opéra comique* that 'conditions' were first used as theatrical material. Grimm complains that soon all the *métiers* will have been put on the stage (Grimm, *Correspondance littéraire*, vol. VI, p. 175, 1 janvier 1765).[25] Such subject matter was thought of as 'low' by many critics, and this no doubt constituted part of the attraction of the *Opéra comique*, a less thorough going version of the *genre poissard*, the playlets in argot acted at the fairs. It is in a critic of the *Opéra comique* that evidence of subterranean links between illusion and low subjects is found. Nougaret's *Art du théâtre*, although it has been taken seriously,[26] is a satirical attack on the Opéra comique for its treatment of low subjects. In this attack he uses the state of mind of the spectator, the mistake, as evidence for the perfections of the imitation which creates that state, and links this constantly with the low subject of the imitation:

Représente-t – il [le poète] une action villageoise, on croit voir agir les vrais habitants de la campagne; l'âme trompée par les charmes de l'illusion, éprouve alors le même sentiment dont elle est pénétrée, quand nos oreilles sont frappées du son rustique des chalumeaux [. . .] enfin, jamais Spectacle ne copia si bien la Nature. (Nougaret, 1769, vol. i, p. 133)

But this simple correlation of low subject and illusion as a mistake is made problematic precisely because Nougaret is discussing the *Opéra comique*. It is as if the sophistication of the artistic medium, opera, offset the low subjects for the eighteenth-century audience: as with the popularity of the *parades* at the fairs, a titillating enjoyment of the socially unseemly is made possible by the highly stylised form in which it is presented. Once again the consumer's oscillation between involvement and distance appears to have been separated out – involvement remaining as the state of mind, but set against the distance created through the stylisation of the medium. Nougaret, however, is not concerned with this particular paradox, but only with one of its elements, the trivial subject. This he satirises by taking the idea of imitation to its farthest extremes: he tells, for example, the story of a king who, invited to listen to the imitation of a nightingale, replied that he had often heard a real one. He does this to bring out one set of incoherences in the crude correlation between imitation and illusion in art and then uses these to undermine any recommendation of the use of an 'ordinary' subject – for, Nougaret says, one would not enjoy a real shoe-maker's song, and they sing better at the *Opéra* (Nougaret, 1769, vol. i, p. 138). To sum up: he makes use of a crude correlation between imitation and illusion to satirise the triviality of the *Opéra comique's* subjects.[27] And in general his satiric procedure is to turn what he appears to assume is the opera's aesthetic against itself. But parodistically this also shows up the inadequacy of 'illusion' as an account of audience reaction. Satirically – and he is satirising Marmontel as well as the *Opéra comique* – he casts around for other justifications of the opera's activities, and actually arrives at the chapter heading: 'Les poètes de l'Opéra Bouffon comparés aux Auteurs naturalistes'. They must imitate the Abbé Pluche, author of the *Spectacle de la nature*, or the scientists studying and classifying insects and animals, and make a catalogue of artisans: 'Faites-nous passer en revue les derniers artisans de nos Villes' (Nougaret, 1769, vol. ɪ, p. 148).[28] He even goes as far as to insist: 'Les Poètes du nouveau Théâtre devroient habiter avec leurs personnages. En effet, comment est-il possible de sçavoir les sentimens, les façons de parler, d'une foule de gens que l'on ne fréquente jamais?' (Nougaret, 1769, vol. ɪ, p. 152).[29]

In fact Nougaret's obvious scurrility (he takes pleasure in expounding risqué subjects in order to condemn their use in opera) is paralleled by another scurrilous ambiguity. In satirizing the *opéra bouffon* by turning against it the aesthetic of imitation and illusion, which is its justification, he is showing the feebleness of that aesthetic: this should in turn destroy the grounds of his satire. But does he realise this? The oscillation between awareness and illusion can, I have suggested, be translated on a formal level into an oscillation between seriousness and parody. These poles nearly coincide, or rather they are nearly indistinguishable, in Nougaret. His book is a satire, but only just recognisable as such. Can it be that, just as 'realism' as a group of literary techniques appears to have developed out of satire, so the theory of realism developed out of parody? Whatever may be the case, it is clear that the satirical drawing out of the consequences of illusion as applied to low subjects may be taken as an indication that the two ideas were linked in critics' minds, however unjustifiably.

Nougaret's parody relied on assumptions about what is suitable material for art. As has been shown, his use of 'imitation' to parody the low subjects of the *Opéra comique* in fact shows up inadequacies in a certain concept of 'imitation' and 'illusion' as aesthetic criteria, though it is not clear whether such was his intention. Yet a link between 'illusion' and low subjects does exist in the minds of mid-century critics. This can be shown *per contra* by the function they assign to 'voluntary' illusion. If illusion is voluntary, if, that is, it is possible for it to remain incomplete, then the distressing can be avoided. The imitation of the old and ugly should not go as far as coincidence, not so far as to provoke a mistake. Such would appear to be the meaning behind the inane and long-running discussion as to whether an older or a younger actress should play an old woman.[30]

These assumptions, connected with voluntary illusion as opposed to the idea of the mistake, are embodied in the concept of *belle nature*. It is in the name of *belle nature* that critics insist that art should not shock, that illusion should remain voluntary, that it should not go so far as to be a mistake (Rémond de Sainte Albine, 1747, pp. 126–7; Sticotti, 1769, pp. 53, 56, 74). Developed in the later seventeenth century, and perhaps revealing already a questioning of the status of art, *belle nature* is an ambiguous notion. It always implies a distinction between nature and the art object, and this is no doubt the generating force for Batteux's use of it in *Les Beaux Arts réduits à un même principe* of 1746, which insists on the artificiality of art. The distinction may be related to either of the two words composing the concept. Thus the artist may be considered to imitate, or to collect together, beauty already inhering in natural objects. Or he may embellish nature, conferring on it beauty by his art (Batteux manages both: Batteux, 1746, pp. 24–5, 27). But even with *belle nature* the oscillatory structure of the mid-century aesthetic is revealed. Art is 'pour ainsi dire plus naturel que la nature même', a transmutation not of nature into art but of art into nature: 'C'est ici que les extrémités se touchent: l'art porté à son comble devient nature et la nature négligée ressemble trop souvent à l'affectation' (Sticotti, 1769, p. 10). Here another spiral is created, not this time moving between truth and illusion, but between art and nature.[31]

In general, however, *belle nature*, although treated as if it covers a wide variety of styles and achievements in art, represents in fact a radical diminution of art's power and scope.[32] It is as if the formulation of the concept were a result of a greater consciousness of the nature of French art, provoked by a better knowledge of the art of other nations. Within the realm of the theatre it schematises for critics one particular French tradition, that of Racine and his followers: avoidance of violent spectacle, a plot so dependent on love as to verge onto 'galanterie' (hardly a description of Racine which would satisfy the twentieth century). Such a restricted application of *belle nature* creates a sharpened awareness of the art which it cannot describe: 'L'imitation exacte de la nature commune', to use a phrase of Sainte Albine's, which likewise brings together two concepts within the same expression (Rémond de Sainte Albine, 1747, p. 216). For Sainte Albine, 'imitation exacte', a portrait even of a hero, may offend, and 'nature commune' may be insipid or even disquieting ('Je me garde bien de penser qu'il faille avilir notre scène par la peinture des mœurs de la vile canaille' says Cailhava (1772, vol. II, p. 313)). Moreover, exact imitation is held to require little art (Clairon, an vii, p. 262). 'Imitation embellie' is then 'le nœud secret qui unit l'art à la nature' (Brumoy, 1730, vol. I, p. lxxxi). Because *belle nature* receives definition from its opposition to 'imitation exacte' and 'nature commune' it oscillates between merely revealing snobbery, whether social or moral, and representing an embryonic concept of stylisation. This ambiguity is especially apparent with the writers who have a strong sense of typification. Thus of the 'bas Comique', which might be taken as painting 'les mœurs de la vile canaille', Sainte Albine writes:

Chaque objet est susceptible d'une espèce de perfection & sur la scène il importe de n'en présenter aucun qui ne soit aussi parfait qu'il peut l'être. Que votre personnage ressemble aux personnes de sa condition, mais qu'il leur ressemble en beau. Colette au théâtre n'est pas la même que dans son Village. Il doit y avoir entre ses manières & celles de ses pareilles la même différence qui est entre ses habits & ceux d'une Paisanne ordinaire. (Rémond de Sainte Albine, 1747, p. 305)

The actor of the 'bas Comique' is not to use the grotesquely parodying effect of the farces (F. Riccoboni, 1750, pp. 66–7).

There is no conceptual reason why *belle nature* should not produce illusion in the consumer. Theorists, however, do not consider that it creates a mistake, perhaps because it is associated with certain types of art only. For *belle nature*, whether as a form of snobbery about choice of material or as a more properly aesthetic concept relating to the artist's treatment of that material, represents a demand for a prettification of the grimmer parts of life, for the avoidance of the distressing. *Belle nature* comes to mean 'beau' and nothing more. What the two terms of the phrase link is split up, and an exaggerating or prettifying art is contrasted with an insipid or ugly reality, which may in turn be thought to be represented in a different, 'low' type of art. For innovating eighteenth-century critics, these poles are presented by Racine and Molière, and they strive to reject both, to create a 'genre intermédiaire'.

Thus Diderot's proposals for the reform of the theatre arise directly from a critical attitude to Racine. Racine uses epic rather than dramatic material, and must therefore remove much action from the stage and cast it in the form of *récit* – for no actor can show Calchas before the sacrifice of Eriphile. But *récit* is inevitably less theatrically effective than action. Moreover, 'dans l'épopée, les hommes poétiques deviennent un peu plus grands que les hommes vrais' (Diderot, *Entretiens sur le 'Fils naturel'*, p. 151), and the implication is that Racine's use of epic material has resulted in exaggeration. Still more, verse contaminates even the Ancient theatre:

Plays

Quoi qu'il en soit, que la poésie ait fait naître la déclamation théâtrale; que la nécessité de cette déclamation ait introduit, ait soutenu sur la scène la poésie et son emphase; que ce système, formé peu à peu ait duré par la convenance de ses parties, il est certain que tout ce que l'action dramatique a d'énorme se produit et disparaît en méme temps. (Diderot, *Entretiens sur le 'Fils naturel'*, p. 123)

Such a criticism of Racine was not new: Louis Riccoboni had already commented on tragedies where people 'nous paroissent organisées et penser autrement que le commun des hommes, & que nous n'oserions jamais imiter, parce que nous les croyons fabuleuses ou surnaturelles' (L. Riccoboni, in La Chaussée, 1762, vol. v, p. 212). In fact, Diderot's, Grimm's and Rousseau's criticisms of the theatre are related, and spring undoubtedly from conversations between them. The Rousseau of the *Lettre à d'Alembert* condemns the theatre to insipidity or to exaggeration. Tragedy 'nous présente des êtres si gigantesques, si boursouflés, si chimériques, que l'exemple de leurs vices n'est guère plus contagieux que celui de leur vertu n'est utile' (Rousseau, *Lettre à d'Alembert*, p. 92).[33] But comedy trivialises men, so that the theatre is balanced between 'le défaut et l'excès', between idealising and satiric exaggeration. 'C'est une erreur, disait le grave Muralt, d'espérer qu'on y montre fidèlement les véritables rapports des choses: car en général le poète ne peut qu'altérer ces rapports, pour les accommoder au goût du peuple' (Rousseau, *Lettre à d'Alembert*, p. 81). And, cruelly, Rousseau denounces the efforts of those poets – the foremost of whom was Diderot – who had attempted to escape from this Scylla and Charybdis, as merely resulting in boring plays: 'Autant vaudrait aller au sermon' (Rousseau, *Lettre à d'Alembert*, p. 112).[34]

For Diderot, Terence had suggested ways of escape: a form of drama might be created which would avoid the exaggeration and triviality which are left to contemporary tragedy and comedy. And instead of over-exploited 'caractères' and the misfortunes of kings, 'conditions' are to form the subject matter of the intermediate genres. 'Conditions' have been interpreted as meaning social problems, a step towards the enlargement of the theatre's scope. There is no doubt that Diderot does suggest the replacement of psychological subjects by social ones, but the 'conditions' he proposes that the theatre should represent are the opposite of a particular social reality. They reveal instead a new typification of experience: 'L'homme de lettres, le philosophe, le commerçant, le juge, l'avocat, le politique, le citoyen, le magistrat, le financier, le grand seigneur, l'intendant. Ajoutez à cela toutes les relations: le père de

161

famille, l'époux, la sœur, le frère' (Diderot, *Entretiens sur le 'Fils naturel'*, p. 154). Just as the polarisation of comedy and tragedy gives rise to the middle term, the 'genre sérieux', so the association of *belle nature* with an emasculating embellishment opposed to grim reality implies a norm: and it is this norm to which the word 'conditions' gives expression. For the Diderot of the *Entretiens sur le 'Fils naturel'*, the norm is not a middling social reality merely transposed on to the stage, but is compared to the nude in sculpture:

C'est dans le genre sérieux que doit s'exercer d'abord tout homme de lettres qui se sent du talent pour la scène. On apprend à un jeune élève qu'on destine à la peinture, à dessiner le nu. Quand cette partie fondamentale de l'art lui est familière, il peut choisir un sujet. Qu'il le prenne ou dans les conditions communes, ou dans un rang élevé, qu'il drape ses figures à son gré, mais qu'on ressente toujours le nu sous la draperie; que celui qui aura fait une longue étude de l'homme dans l'exercice du genre sérieux, chausse, selon son génie, le cothurne ou le soc; qu'il jette sur les épaules de son personnage un manteau royal ou une robe de palais, mais que l'homme ne disparaisse jamais sous le vêtement. (Diderot, *Entretiens sur le 'Fils naturel'*, pp. 137–8)

The 'genre sérieux' presents a kind of basic humanity to which a style – comedy or tragedy – may be attached. This is in no sense 'realism': the 'here and now' of the individual in an individual situation is explicitly denied (Diderot, *O.C.*, vol. III, p. 678).

It is this conception of the norm being that of a fundamental humanity which underpins Diderot's refusal to operate a concept of aesthetic level, a refusal which often appears wrongheaded and even sentimental: 'Si vous avez vu expirer un père au milieu de ses enfants, telle fut enfin la fin de Socrate au milieu des philosophes qui l'environnaient' (Diderot, *Discours*, p. 273). Or again, speaking of a peasant woman, he writes: 'Croyez-vous qu'une femme d'un autre rang aurait été plus pathétique? Non. La même situation lui eût inspiré le même discours. Son âme eût été celle du moment, et ce qu'il faut que l'artiste trouve, c'est ce que tout le monde dirait en pareil cas'; or, 'Si la mère d'Iphigénie se montrait un moment reine d'Argos et femme du général des Grecs, elle ne me paraîtrait que la dernière des créatures. La véritable dignité, celle qui me frappe, qui me renverse, c'est le tableau de l'amour maternel dans toute sa vérité.' (Diderot, *Entretiens sur le 'Fils naturel'*, pp. 99, 91). This effect is nicely parodied by Marchand, whose 'vidangeur sensible' kills his son:

Peut-être quelques personnes blâmeroient-elles le sacrifice auquel il se résout; mais elles ne pourront en même tems s'empêcher d'admirer son stoïcisme, excusé en quelque sorte, par le motif et par les circonstances où se trouve ce père infortuné. Brutus et Caton, dans le même cas, auroient pris le même parti. (Marchand, 1880, p. 24)

A more full-blooded search for the norm maintains that it is the common people, least affected by convention, who combine vigour and nature; they are 'vrais modèles de la forte expression' (F. Riccoboni, 1750, p. 43). This belief was confirmed for Talma by the Revolution:

Les grands mouvements de l'âme élèvent l'homme à une nature idéale, dans quelque rang que le sort l'ait placé. La révolution, qui a mis tant de passions en jeu, n'a-t-elle pas eu des orateurs populaires qui ont étonné par des traits sublimes d'une éloquence non recherchée? (Talma, in Lekain, 1825, p. xxviii)

Diderot, however, remains the victim of a divided purpose. The norm, common humanity, is to make experience meaningful by stripping it of accident, by generalising it. With the concept of 'conditions', like that of 'relations', from which he does not distinguish it, he strives to get at the basic pattern of human relations. But at other times the movement is reversed and he appears to wish to pump epic feeling into the everyday, with the inevitable descent into inflated banality.

Lessing, who understood so well Diderot's aesthetic dilemma, points out what is wrong. His criticism is directed at Diderot's belief, shared by Richard Hurd, that tragic characters are less universal and more individual than comic ones. Lessing points out that this belief is based on an unconscious use of 'universalité' in two senses:

Dans le premier sens, un caractère général est celui dans lequel se trouve réuni ce qu'on a remarqué dans plusieurs ou dans tous les individus; en un mot, un caractère chargé. C'est plutôt l'idée personnifiée d'un caractère qu'un personnage caractérisé. Dans l'autre sens un caractère général est celui dans lequel ce qu'on a observé dans plusieurs ou dans tous les individus, est reglé sur un certain milieu pris dans une moyenne proportion. Cela s'appelle en un mot, un caractère ordinaire, non pas en tant que le caractère même est ordinaire mais seulement en tant que le degré et la mesure en sont ordinaires. (Lessing, 1785, vol. II, p. 201)

The criticism applies equally to Diderot's concept of the norm and explains the impression of exaggerated ordinariness, which is conveyed by such remarks as the one quoted above about Iphigénie's mother. The norm in Diderot's thought is then a moral as well as an aesthetic concept. Used in the 'genre sérieux' it was designed to eliminate the contemporary defect of polarised characters, 'les contrastes'. Thus, in discussing Terence's *Adelphi*, Diderot complained of the absence of a norm: 'On finit sans savoir pour qui l'on est. On désirerait presque un troisième père qui tînt le milieu entre ces deux personnages et qui en fît connoître le vice' (Diderot, *Discours*, p. 238). Lessing shows that the norm is interiorised so that the audience does not need a third father to be present. Moreover, if the norm is actually represented on stage, it is likely to result, says Lessing, in the unreal: 'Les Pièces qui représenteront le vrai père, seront chacune plus hors de Nature, mais encore toutes ensemble plus uniformes que celles qui représentent des Pères de différente opinion' (Lessing, 1785, vol. II, p. 150).

Yet Lessing's very formulation of the problem derives from Diderot. If tragedy is exaggerated, conventional comedy is trivialising. He sharpens the polarisation in a way similar to that of Diderot in the *Essais sur la peinture* and the *Paradoxe sur le comédien*. If 'imitation of nature' is taken literally, then the consequence is the following: 'Le plus artificiel [art] dans ce sens est ici le plus mauvais; le plus hasardé le meilleur' (Lessing, 1785, vol. I, p. 143). The two sides of the argument about imitation – 'copier fidèlement la nature' and 'l'embellir' – are often correlated with two types of drama, 'gothic' and Greek. The partisans of the former explain the existence of pleasure even in an art which expresses the distressing by saying that it is imitation which pleases, not the particular nature imitated. Others regard *belle nature* as a chimaera: 'Une nature qui veut être plus belle que nature, n'est par cela même plus nature' (Lessing, 1785, vol. I, p. 144). For Lessing, to be 'admirateur de la nature commune & journalière' does not imply acceptance of mixed genres; to refuse as monstrous what had pretentions to being more beautiful than nature does not imply rejection of the Greek theatre. And earlier La Place had discussed the same opposition:

Ainsi cette vérité Théâtrale que j'appelle *Vérité de sentiment* n'est ni une vérité réelle qui présente les faits & les personnages tels qu'ils ont été, ni même une vraisemblance qui les montre tels qu'ils ont pû être: mais un tableau qui les représente tels qu'il faut qu'ils soient, dans le moment où il [*sic*] sont présentés, pour faire impression sur le spectateur dans la situation actuelle où il les voit. (La Place, 1746, vol. I, p. lv)

Here the terms 'vérité de sentiment', 'vérité réelle' and 'vraisemblance' are one way in which the norm subjectively resolves the conflict between real and ideal, or between insipid and exaggerated. Lessing's solution of the dilemma is likewise subjective, but prefigures the aesthetics of Goethe and Schiller: literal imitation of nature only copies phenomena, it fails to incorporate the quality either of our sensations or of our faculties. For the mind assailed by flux of sensations is obliged to abstract from this, otherwise consciousness would be impossible:

La destination de l'art est, de nous épargner cette abstraction dans l'empire du beau & de nous faciliter l'application de notre attention. Tout ce que nous séparons en pensée dans la nature des objets ou dans la liaison de divers objets, soit à l'égard du temps ou de l'espace; tout ce que nous désirons de pouvoir séparer; l'art le sépare en effet, & nous donne l'objet, ou la liaison de divers objets, aussi pure & aussi conséquente que le sentiment à produire le permet. (Lessing, 1785, vol. I, pp. 145–6)

To sum up: Nougaret's parody supplies evidence of a relation existing between low subjects and 'illusion'. But there is a further connection, apparently opposed to this: one linking the expression of common humanity as a norm and 'illusion'. This relation of norm and 'illusion' is central to Diderot's projects for the reform of the theatre.[35]

Voluntary illusion and convention

'Illusion' often appears in the writings of theorists to be an evaluation of dramatic technique: 'le public [. . .] n'a pas besoin de la moindre complaisance pour se prêter à l'illusion' (Cailhava, 1772, vol. II, pp. 190–1). Those plays are best in which one least has to turn a blind eye to their lack of congruence with reality. Cailhava, like the earlier writer Charpentier (1768), has a chapter headed 'De l'illusion théâtrale'. Charpentier actually defines illusion as an accumulation of dramatic techniques:

L'illusion théâtrale est, dans ce qui appartient à la Scène, un assemblage de circonstances, une suite de rapports qui fait prendre l'image pour la vérité. C'est une douce violence que le Théâtre fait au Spectateur pour l'intéresser à l'action & lui cacher la source de ses plaisirs. (Charpentier, 1768, vol. I, p. 64)

There are features in this account which suggest that 'illusion' may have a more complex function than that of recommending dramatic techniques. Like Diderot, later writers – Nougaret, Cailhava, Charpentier – use 'illusion' to suggest that, for example, the actor should not address the audience or reply to it. But unlike Diderot, they show a curious imbalance between often long discussions of illusion and the trifling recommendations which the discussions are used to support. Has then such writers' treatment of 'illusion' more

Illusion and the theatre

than modish significance, a pedantically elaborate obedience to fashion?

For these writers, the audience's illusion is fragile: 'L'Oubli le plus léger suffit pour détruire toute illusion; [. . .] une petite circonstance omise ou mal présentée décèle le mensonge', warns Diderot (*Discours*, p. 233). The audience's adhesion is a product of effort underscored by a willingness to seize on whatever breaks the illusion:

D'ailleurs, après que je me suis efforcé d'imaginer que je suis véritablement dans une salle, ou tel autre endroit où se passe la Scène, n'est-ce pas abuser de ma bonne volonté & me mettre dans le cas de perdre à la fin toute l'illusion que je serais charmé de ressentir, que de me contraindre à recommencer à tout moment le même ouvrage? (Nougaret, 1769, vol. ɪ, pp. 216–7)

Charpentier goes further, and seems first to insist that the theatre has, in his century, become a frivolous activity: 'Cette illusion est d'autant moins facile à produire sur les Théâtres modernes, qu'ils sont peu propres à en imposer & que l'on ne s'y rend guère que comme à un jeu auquel on sait qu'on ne prendra nulle part.' The spectator has to be forced, against his own better knowledge, to believe in the reality of what he sees: 'Forcer le spectateur, qui sait qu'il va voir une fiction, à croire que c'est une action véritable.' And Charpentier goes further, defining the spectator's knowledge, which impedes illusion as acceptance of the play as a social activity. 'J'arrive à la Comédie comme dans un appartement d'ami; il faut détruire cette idée: il faut me transporter dans le palais d'Auguste, dans le Serail, dans le Temple' (Charpentier, 1768, vol. ɪ, pp. 54, 71). This account of the audience's involvement is the justification for a series of commonplace instructions about *décor* and costumes: there should be new scenery for a new play, for example.[36] Such an imbalance between the analysis of illusion and practical recommendation suggests that Charpentier is obscurely dealing with a totally different question. What question this might have been is indicated by his going further than Nougaret and Diderot in his account of the audience's suspicions: 'La prévention où est le spectateur contr'eux [the actors]' (Charpentier, 1768, vol. ɪ, p. 71). But this 'prévention' turns out to be the whole framework of the theatre as a social activity. He returns several times in his argument to an insistence on the fragility of illusion, justified by a familiar account of the audience's preparedness to be disturbed:

C'est un édifice de cartes qui tombe au moindre souffle. Nous savons que les représentations théâtrales nous trompent; nous nous plaisons à en être

166

trompés. Mais pour peu qu'on nous fait sentir notre erreur nous voyons le plaisir s'enfuir avec elle. (Charpentier, 1768, vol. I, p. 74)

Illusion must then be uninterrupted during the performance, but it is superimposed on a basis of awareness – not that the *décor* is *décor*, or that the actors are actors in any trivial sense, but an awareness of the whole social convention which is art. Why then does Charpentier demand that this awareness should be destroyed? His discussion is better interpreted on a theoretical level than on a practical one, for he seems to be struggling with several inadequately grasped problems which he conflates: art is a social activity (and this is perhaps more obviously and trivially true of the eighteenth century than of the theatre of other centuries); the theatre is an activity non-continuous with life; it is based on convention, that is, on tacit agreement between artist and audience as to the ways in which life may be rendered, although it is by changes within the framework of convention that artists have gained approval and appear to have got nearer 'reality'. Hence, for Charpentier, it may appear that a playwright must make his effect (illusion) *in spite of* convention – he speaks, after all, of 'forcing' the spectators to believe in the play's reality. The question then becomes the relation between innovation and convention: Charpentier suggests a dynamic relation in that the familiar loses power to produce illusion (Charpentier, 1768, vol. I, p. 76); Servandoni d'Hannetaire affirms that the new has automatically more power of illusion (Servandoni d'Hannetaire, 1774, p. 133); and Cahusac, without using the word 'illusion', suggests that artistic change has significance which is not intrinsic but which derives from the framework against which it is made, or within which it represents a change (Cahusac, 1754, vol. I, pp. xxii–xxiii).

'Illusion', 'drame', tragedy

I have shown so far that Charpentier's account of an illusion which is not interrupted by consciousness, but which is yet voluntary in some sense, is a theoretical grappling with the idea of artistic convention and the way in which innovation must be accommodated within it. But innovation is, in practice, a rejection of traditional tragedy and comedy. Statements such as 'Je pourrais alléguer que le spectateur va à la comédie dans le dessein de se prêter aux *aparte* ainsi qu'aux différentes illusions qu'il est obligé de se faire pour sa propre satisfaction: comme de prendre une toile pour une ville' (Cailhava, 1772, vol. I, p. 447) become a defence of convention

against innovation, acquiring a precise, indeed prescriptive, meaning, given the sharpened antagonism of the artistic tendencies in the second half of the century. In the case cited, Cailhava is justifying the aside, one part of the traditional comic techniques which were coming under attack. Beaumarchais makes clear that, on the contrary, the aim of the 'genre sérieux' is 'de transporter si loin des coulisses & de faire si bien disparaître à mes yeux tout le badinage d'Acteurs, l'appareil théâtral, que leur souvenir *ne puisse pas m'atteindre une seule fois dans tout le cours de son Drame*' (Beaumarchais, 1964, p. 16), though the consciousness he maintains he is excluding creeps back in the parodistic underlining, typical of Beaumarchais, of 'badinage'.

It seems as if rejection of voluntary illusion, to use Diderot's phrase, or bimodal illusion, is tied to the *drame* and as if acceptance of it amounts to a defence of conventional forms. Marmontel roundly contradicts Diderot's 'l'illusion n'est pas volontaire', and this contradiction must bear the same interpretation. He makes a soundly based conceptual distinction between the frame of mind in which one goes to the theatre (voluntary illusion) and intrusions of awareness during the theatrical experience: 'Le spectateur veut bien qu'on le trompe mais il ne veut pas s'en apercevoir' (Marmontel, 1763, vol. II, pp. 11–12).[37] Like Nougaret, he exhibits the nonsense of the crude illusion–imitation paradigm when taken to extremes, using the designer of scenery as an analogue of the playwright: 'Sans doute le décorateur, qui pour représenter sur le théâtre une cascade employeroit de l'eau, renonceroit à la gloire du Peintre, au mérite de l'illusion; & l'on auroit raison de dire, ce n'est plus la ressemblance, c'est la réalité, ce n'est plus l'art c'est la nature.' Yet the estimate of the poet's worth with which he concludes – 'plus il persuade qu'il ne feint pas & plus il excelle dans l'art de feindre' (Marmontel, 1763, vol. I, p. 322) – is the paradoxical equivalent of the definition of an art which is more natural than nature. Marmontel has here removed the oscillation between awareness and involvement from the spectator's consciousness to the critic–spectator's account of art, and this corresponds to his attitude towards the emerging *drame*: flirtatious rejection. Later, however, he specifically brings together awareness of the actor's art and involvement in the play:

On a beau avoir l'imagination préoccupée, les yeux avertissent qu'on est à Paris, tandis que la scène est à Rome & la preuve qu'on n'oublie jamais l'acteur dans le personnage qu'il représente, c'est que dans l'instant même où l'on est le plus ému, on s'écrie, *Ah! que c'est bien joué*: on sait donc que ce

n'est qu'un jeu, on n'applaudiroit point Auguste, c'est donc Brizard qu'on applaudit. (Article *Illusion*, in the *Supplément à l'Encyclopédie*, 1777)

Elsewhere, Marmontel describes the spectator's attitude to the spectacle as composed of warring principles: involvement associated with feeling, and awareness which is related to the intelligence.

On porte à nos spectacles deux principes opposés, le sentiment qui veut être ému, & l'esprit qui ne veut pas qu'on le trompe. La prétention à juger de tout fait qu'on ne jouit de rien. On veut en même tems prévoir les situations & s'en pénétrer, combiner d'après l'auteur & s'attendrir avec le peuple; être dans l'illusion & n'être pas; [. . .] chacun des connaisseurs est comme double & son cœur a dans son esprit un incommode voisin. (*Encyclopédie*, article *Dénouement*)

In what way is the social structuring which Marmontel apparently applies to illusion to be understood? In terms of the century's practice it is as if the warring principles have split: the *drame* might be taken to be designated by 's'attendrir avec le peuple', eighteenth-century tragedy by 'prévoir les situations', 'combiner d'après l'auteur'. Rousseau suggests that contemporary tragedy does not aim at illusion at all ('Le François ne cherche point sur la scène le naturel et l'illusion, et n'y veut que de l'esprit et des pensées'), so that in comparison with the tolerance given to opera, 'Il semble que les esprits se roidissent contre une illusion raisonnable, et ne s'y prêtent qu'autant qu'elle est absurde et grossière' (Rousseau, *O.C.*, vol. ii, 'p. 281). Such evidence suggests that the attitude of the spectator, when at French tragedy, tended to exclude involvement. Mangogul, in *Les Bijoux indiscrets*, turns to his magic ring during a performance 'pour se sauver du ridicule qu'il y avait à écouter les endroits touchants' (Diderot, *O.C.*, vol. i, p. 626). To the questions 'What is wrong with a spectator's reaction shot through with consciousness? Why should awareness or reflexion be excluded?' such comments appear to give a simple answer: the spectator cannot become emotionally involved, for illusion is destroyed, not balanced, by reflection, and the dreamer is awoken from the dream.[38] Thus Lessing says: 'Le Poëte tragique doit éviter tout ce qui peut faire penser au Spectateur que ce qu'il voit n'est qu'illusion; car aussitôt qu'on l'y fait songer, elle s'évanouit' (Lessing, 1785, vol. i, p. 205). But in fact less limited, more properly aesthetic reasons are suggested. *Les Bijoux indiscrets* produces one: to Mirzoza's criticism of the theatre, namely that it is impossible to pass off a theatrical performance as reality, Sélim objects that illusion is voluntary:

On se rend au spectacle avec la persuasion que c'est l'imitation d'un événement et non l'événement même qu'on verra. Et cette persuasion, reprit Mirzoza, doit-elle empêcher qu'on n'y représente l'événement de la manière la plus naturelle?' (Diderot, *O.C.*, vol. I, p. 637)

The awareness of the necessity of convention is left then to be used as an argument to impede artistic innovation – here, a movement towards the 'natural'. Hence, therefore, Diderot's emphatic 'L'Illusion n'est pas volontaire'; hence the support given by partisans of grand opera or of classical comedy, like Cailhava, to an analysis of illusion which includes consciousness, whether thought of as alternating with involvement or underlying it as voluntary illusion.

Beyond the need to safeguard innovation, which appears difficult to defend if convention is recognised, a further problem appears. Conventions are necessary to art, yet they make it 'unnatural', for once a separation from nature is admitted, and art becomes arbitrary, there is apparently no limit to how unnatural art may be. Diderot, who had met a related problem in the paintings of Chardin, where technique, and thus what made art art and not nature, was all important, will struggle with the question of convention in the *Paradoxe sur le comédien* (see Hobson, 1973). What is a dilemma in Diderot becomes, typically, a simple rejection of convention in the name of the natural for Beaumarchais:

On fait faire à l'esprit humain autant de pas qu'on veut vers le merveilleux dès qu'on lui a fait une fois franchir les barrières du naturel; les sujets n'ayant plus alors qu'une vérité poétique et de convention, il s'accommode aisément de tout. (Beaumarchais, 1964, p. 15)

But deeper meaning can be given both to Rousseau's statement that tragedy does not intend illusion, and to the rejection of convention, when the nature of contemporary tragedies is considered. In general they were in no sense replicas of life, nor had they any direct relation to actual events. Nor were they, however, a mere collection of conventions. In many cases tragedies were a kind of semaphore, whose force derived from rearrangement of distinct and commonplace elements. Nor did they, as it were, contain their own meaning; witness their lack of action, so that events were recounted, and emotions were transcribed, by language rather than be being enacted (Voltaire being a partial exception, as Rousseau points out). But since the conventions of French tragedy excluded overt reference to recent and present events, a whole system of oblique references had to be established. Voltaire, for example, complains that Otway's *Venice Preserved* had to be set in the abstraction that was ancient Rome for the Comédie française when adapted by La Fosse (Voltaire, Kehl, vol. i, p. 347). Blin de Sain-more rewrote Lillo's *London Merchant* as a tragedy (Gaiffe, 1910, p. 101);[39] even French history was disguised, the *Lagus Roi d'Egypte* attributed to the Marquis du Terrail being a resetting of the story of Louis le débonnaire (Myers, 1962, p. 62). Voltaire himself 'met en tragédie ce qui, pour d'autres, ferait un article de journal' (Lanson, 1920, p. 118). To interpret this state of affairs as if the audience were merely victims of the stranglehold of convention upon tragedy is inadequate. It seems rather as if a large part of the point of tragedy lay precisely in the decipherment of such a system of references. It is as if the audience's pleasure were derived from the very way in which behind the immediate meaning of a given episode there lay a reference to something else – that is, *dissimulatio*. Covert attacks on religion and clerics are disguised as attacks on Muslim fanaticism or put into the mouth of Iphigénie (in *Iphigénie en Tauride*, when it seems she will have to sacrifice Oreste). Just how many conventional tragedies and indeed comedies were read as having overt political meaning can be shown by the list of plays held up by the censor which the great actor Lekain drew up in his plea for a freer stage.[40]

The tragedies are in many cases pretexts: their overt subject is a sign for a different, more subversive content (there is a clear similarity to the *à clé* novel). Such, too, is the technique of certain contemporary comedies, of Beaumarchais for instance, where, as if by an inverse process, a remote and stylised structure is not loaded with metaphorical reference, but clear contemporary reference is disguised in a Spanish setting (Beaumarchais, 1964, p. 239).[41]

The audience's pleasure derives, then, from awareness and decipherment of a system of allusions: conventions are enjoyed for their own sake, and the plot's meaning is a mere basis, trivialised and unimportant. The same trivialisation is apparent if the emotions generated by the tragedy of the time are considered. And just as the *dissimulatio*, the uncovering of a dissimulating code, implied an oscillation between sign and reference, so an oscillation is apparent in the emotional structure of the plays. In the opera of the period, well-used and almost standardised incidents are put together to create surprise: 'Toujours des conspirations, des conjurations, des Rois légitimes détrônés et souvent assassinés, des tyrans, des usurpateurs, des prisons, des meurtres, des jeux de poignard' (Myers, 1962, p. 121). Crébillon *père* and Voltaire base their plots on concealed relationships, patent or declared to the audience. These power a swing between catastrophe and safety which is as mechanically controlled as a pendulum, and create a density of events which is correctly diagnosed by contemporary critics to be a product of the novel's influence (see Myers, 1962, p. 72). The heroine of a comedy complains that tragedy is merely:

Un tintamarre d'incidens impossibles, des reconnaissances que l'on devine, des Princesses qui se passionnent si vertueusement pour des Héros que l'on poignarde quand on n'en sait plus que faire, un assemblage de maximes que tout le monde sait et que personne ne croit, des injures contre les grands & par-ci par-là, quelques imprécations. (Poinsinet, 1765, scène iii)[42]

Lessing's remarkable comparison of Voltaire's *Mérope* and the play by Maffei from which it was derived brings out clearly the reduction of tragic fear to surprise in contemporary tragedy. He points out how Voltaire's play uses the structure of reversal typical of eighteenth-century practice, to hold back the fear until the moment when it can be sharply metamorphosed into relief (Lessing, 1785, vol. I, pp. 236–8).[43] The oscillation in the spectator's mind created by his decoding the allusions of French tragedy, and the oscillation in his emotional attention, deliberately stimulated by the combination of surprise and predictability in the plot, are completed by the consistent awareness of the poet's hand, of the actor's technique. The scintillation of wit is contrasted with the coherence of genius:

L'Esprit [. . .] ne cherche que des ressemblances & dissemblances [. . .] ne s'amuse qu'à des événemens qui n'ont rien de commun entr'eux que d'être arrivés en même temps. Lier les événemens ensemble, nouer & embrouiller leur fil, de manière que nous perdions à tous momens l'un par l'autre: voilà ce que l'esprit sait faire, & pas davantage. Croisant continuellement de tels fils de différentes couleurs, il fait naître une contexture qui est dans l'art poétique ce que l'ouvrier en soie appelle dans le sien 'changeant', une étoffe dont on ne saurait dire si elle est bleue ou rouge, verte ou jaune. (Lessing, 1785, vol. I, p. 153)

In this analysis the metaphor of shot silk has the same function as *papillotage* in Diderot's dramatic and art criticism. In *Les Bijoux indiscrets*, Mirzoza had already insisted of contemporary tragedy: 'L'emphase, l'esprit et le papillotage qui y règnent sont à mille lieues de la nature' (Diderot, *O.C.*, vol. I, p. 635). Both Diderot and Lessing react against French tragedy, and both insist on coherence, on consistency and on solidity in art (Diderot, *O.C.*, vol. I, p. 636),[44] on the elimination of surprise, 'emphase' and 'esprit', all of which provoke a constant awareness of art. Well-turned verses, *sententiae*, Polonius-like moral truths – and their contraries, epigrammatic expressions of evil – are attacked not merely because they are 'unnatural' but because they give the author away at every moment (*Correspondance littéraire*, vol. III, p. 483, mars 1758).[45] Such mannerisms, typical of Corneille, are denounced by Mirzoza: 'C'est en vain que l'auteur cherche à se dérober: mes yeux percent, et je l'aperçois sans cesse derrière ses personnages. Cinna, Sertorius, Maxime, Emilie, sont à tout moment les sarbacanes de Corneille' (Diderot, *O.C.*, vol. I, p. 635). And Saint-Preux in *La Nouvelle Héloïse* says similarly:

Racine et Corneille avec tout leur génie ne sont eux-mêmes que des parleurs [. . .]. Communément tout se passe en beaux dialogues bien agencés, bien ronflans, où l'on voit d'abord que le premier soin de chaque interlocuteur est toujours celui de briller [. . .], une Sentence leur coûte moins qu'un sentiment [. . .]. Il y a encore une certaine dignité maniérée dans le geste et dans le propos, qui ne permet jamais à la passion de parler exactement son langage, ni à l'auteur [misprint for acteur?] de revêtir son personnage et de se transporter au lieu de la scène, mais le tient toujours enchaîné sur le théâtre et sous les yeux des Spectateurs. (Rousseau, *O.C.*, vol. II, p. 253)[46]

These criticisms are taken up again by Diderot in the *Paradoxe*, and are frequently made by Grimm: 'C'est le poète qui est en spectacle, et non pas la chose représentée' (Grimm, quoted by Gaiffe, 1910, p. 19).

Thus Lessing's profound attack on Voltaire's use of the ghost in *Sémiramis* shows that the ghost is not there for its own sake, but as a sign of the poet's aesthetic daring, a daring which he is too cowardly to pursue too far (Lessing, 1785, vol. I, p. 40). The extent to which Lessing diverges from the *papillotage* typical of French tragedy, where consciousness is deliberately inserted into enthusiasm, is revealed by a note appended by his first French translator. Lessing had criticised Voltaire's appearing on stage to receive the audience's applause after *Mérope*: 'Le vrai chef d'œuvre nous remplit si entièrement par lui-même que nous ne le considérons pas comme produit d'un individu mais comme de la nature même'; to which the translator replied that the sort of mutual congratulation between public and poet, 'ces démonstrations de reconnaissance et d'amitié entre le Public et le Poète' are part of enthusiasm (Lessing, 1785, vol. I, pp. 171–2, 'remarque du Traducteur').

Such criticism had been made earlier. Maffei's letter to Voltaire on *Mérope* criticised the French style of theatrical representation on these grounds: the Comédie française was like an audience chamber; the presence of the audience on the stage dissipated all illusion, 'd'où l'illusion, qui est le premier plaisir de la représentation, s'évanouit'; in other words, on grounds of a rigid formal quality, with a constant awareness of the physical theatre. As to dramatic style, the use of rhymed verse has the same effect. The poet may speak in his own voice in lyric or epic poetry:

Mais comment pourrait-elle [rime] convenir à la Tragédie, où le Poete ne parle jamais, & où se doivent imiter & représenter les discours naturels des hommes? Cependant, la douleur, le dédain & les autres passions ne s'exhalent point en paroles étudiées; & la rime montre la réflexion, découvre l'étude, fait connoître trop visiblement que le Poete parle, & non un furieux ou un affligé. (Maffei in Lessing, vol. I, pp. 266, 297)

Rhyme, for Maffei, thus represents a materialisation of aesthetic pleasure, almost a forcing of awareness on the reader.

For proponents of a new theatre, this constant consciousness in the audience must be eliminated. Lessing, reacting against a tradition central to sixteenth- and seventeenth-century drama, wishes to cut out even metaphorical reference to the theatre: 'Ces seules paroles, *fables, théâtre*, sont déjà si désavantageuses, qu'ils [*sic*] nous remettent justement dans le chemin dont elles devoient nous écarter' (Lessing, 1785, vol. I, p. 205). Conventions are to be banished: 'Les Timantes, les Orontes, les Mondors, les Lisimons' must disappear, says Grimm, although Lisimond is a character in his friend Diderot's play, *Le Fils naturel* (*Correspondance littéraire*, vol. VIII, p. 244, 15 janvier 1769). Lessing quotes Schlegel: 'Quand les personnages arrivent dans la salle ou le jardin, seulement pour paraître sur le Théâtre, l'Auteur de la Tragédie auroit mieux fait, au lieu d'écrire: "La Scène est dans la salle de la maison de Climène" de dire "La Scène est sur le Théâtre"' (Lessing, 1785, vol. I, p. 216). Contemporary tragedy emptied its plots of natural meaning to re-create, by a system of allusions, a meaning exterior to the play – *dissimulatio*. No wonder Rousseau, with his ethic of personal autonomy, dislikes such an art. In reaction to such theatre, the meaning of the *drame* was to be concentrated within the play, so that the play does not *refer* to experience, but is a replica of it. This is the explanation for the superficially surprising fact that the *philosophe*, Grimm, criticises the philosophic content of contemporary tragedy.[47] Apparent failures of aesthetic understanding in Lessing can also be explained in this way. He refuses any interpretation of incidents in a play which involves treating them as signs rather than as having intrinsic meaning; to Dubos' comment that the death of Narcisse in *Britannicus* passes almost unperceived, he replies that for that reason it should have been cut out.[48]

How was it, then, that the conventionalised tragedy held the stage? How did the audience approach it? It is clear from the reaction of Lessing's translator that the participation of the spectators was not merely intellectual and self-conscious. But I shall argue that the counterbalancing involvement, the *élévation* and *force*, is permeated with self-consciousness, indeed with self-congratulation. The principal pleasure seems to have been one of playing an elaborate game: on the first night of the *Ecossaise* (Fréron, *Année littéraire*, 1760, vol. v, p. 209), or of the *Mariage de Figaro*, enthusiasm is given to the actor, to the author, to the literary–political implications of the performance, as well as to the play itself. Within the game, the actor's words are constantly applied to himself; a tradition of witty repartee is established. 'Es-tu content, Coucy?' asks a character in *Adelaïde de du Guesclin*: 'Couci-Couça' answers the *parterre* (Voltaire, Kehl, vol. ii, p. 135). There is an evident parallel with the self-conscious novel. It is almost as if the audience enjoyed watching a way being cleared through the spectators on the stage for Ninias' ghost in *Sémiramis*, or watching 'Mithridate expirer au milieu des gens de notre connaissance [. . .], Camille tomber morte entre les bras d'auteurs comiques connus, Marivaux, ou de Saint-Foix' (Bapst, 1893, p. 443, quoting Collé).

Pleasure in French tragedy is an oscillation, indeed an enjoyment of the discrepancy, between the appearance and what lies behind, between the conventions, between the transparent allusions and what is alluded to – this is the structure of *dissimulatio*.[49] The *drame* is defined in opposition to this structure, as the contrary of tragedy; the actor is to be excluded: 'Il n'y a point d'acteurs dans le salon de Vanderk, il faut que le public les perde de vue' (Préville, 1823, p. 174); so is the author: 'La moindre affectation détruit l'illusion. Il ne faut pas que le Poète paraisse, lorsqu'il ne doit montrer que ses personnages' (Lacombe, 1758, p. 126). But to this literary–polemical definition is added a notion of the real which has political overtones:[50] 'Il y a dans cette grande ville cinq ou six cent milles âmes dont il n'est jamais question sur la scène' (Rousseau, *O.C.*, vol. ii, p. 252). The two notions – of a reality which is a middling social one (characterised in phrases like 'le cours ordinaire des choses' (Mercier, quoted by Gaiffe, 1910, pp. 454–5)), and of the theatre as representation ('une Pièce Dramatique est une représentation de la vie' (Landois, 1742, p. 14)) – combine to describe and justify the *drame*. Louis Riccoboni claimed early on of the *comédie larmoyante* that it would have more moral effect than tragedy because it dealt with events close to the audience

(L. Riccoboni, 1738b) and such an assertion may take on an almost
political significance[51] though it is of course made quite as much
about conventional comedy: Cailhava and Fenouillot de Falbaire
both maintain of failed plays, the former's a *comédie en règle*, the
latter's a *comédie sérieuse*, that they failed because, being too
moral, in effect they upset the theatre-going public.[52] A series of
innovations is justified by its relation to the real: verses are not
appropriate for the expression of passion, and are moreover too
closely related to the taste of the court (Beaumarchais, 1964, pp.
14–16); real names are used. Techniques are transferred from the
novel, testifying to that genre's greater adaptation to developments in eighteenth-century taste. Details of dress, manner, and
mode of living are connected with illusion and with an intimate
rather than a lucid knowledge of character:

Je me suis proposé d'en présenter un tableau simple, naturel & tout à fait
vrai [d'une famille bourgeoise tombée dans l'infortune]. Je me suis dit: Je
commencerai par peindre l'intérieur de la maison de mon Fabricant, je
tâcherai de faire aimer ceux qui l'habitent; & quand j'aurai bien familiarisé
mon spectateur avec tous mes personnages, qu'il aura pour ainsi dire vécu
avec eux dans l'intimité domestique je lui montrerai le désastre de cette
même maison, & il en sera plus vivement affecté. Voilà pourquoi j'ai mis
beaucoup de détails dans les deux premiers actes. (Fenouillot de Falbaire,
1771, pp. viii–ix)[53]

Beaumarchais wrote a trilogy, two conventional comedies and a
drame, and intended to create a tetralogy by adding *La Vengeance
de Bégearss ou le mariage de Léon*, thus transposing the novel's
instalment technique to the stage. He attempts to create a past for
the characters, to make their reality extend beyond the dimensions
of the play. In spite of the *imbroglio* form of the first two, he
certainly intended to create the impression that his characters had a
continuous existence. This has been prefigured in his first work,
Eugénie, also a *drame*, by his elaborate attention to temporal continuity within the play:

L'action théâtrale ne reposant jamais, j'ai pensé qu'on pourrait essayer de
lier un Acte à celui qui le suit par une action pantomime qui soutiendrait,
sans la fatiguer, l'attention des spectateurs, et indiquerait ce qui se passe
derrière la Scène pendant l'Entr'acte. Je l'ai désignée entre chaque Acte.
Tout ce qui tend à donner de la vérité est précieux dans un Drame sérieux
et l'illusion tient plus aux petites choses qu'aux grandes. (Beaumarchais,
1964, p. 37)

Illusion is here associated not merely with non-interruption, but
with impressions of temporal density, and this is given new force by

a new definition of what is real and a new conception of the relation between art and reality.

As has been shown, the older theatrical forms – conventional tragedy, opera – on the contrary, deliberately interrupt the consumer and produce an intermittent illusion where the consumer oscillates between the involvement of enthusiasm, of magical rapture, and awareness of unreality, artifice, and convention. But what of the ludicrous implausibility of the plots of many *drames* – that of *Le Fabricant de Londres*, for example, where manufacturer and aristocrat coincide in their suicide attempts on the Thames embankment? Rather than a calculated interruption, this is a failure to solve the problem of the norm, discussed earlier. Meaning is pumped into events until they swell into melodrama.

Yet the work of Beaumarchais suggests that this simple correlation of a given type of illusion with a given dramatic form – uninterrupted illusion with *drame*, illusion which includes awareness with tragedy – is insufficient to explain theatrical practice. For the third part of his series, *La Mère coupable*, is far from being a minor deviation towards the *drame*, something in the line of Mercier's *Brouette du vinaigrier*, but is a melodrama with blackmail, tears and treachery. This was not merely opportunism on Beaumarchais' part – his first play, *Eugénie*, as I have said, was also a *drame*. What does this binding together of highly conventional comedy and *drame* in the same series of plays concerning the same characters signify? There is a further complication, this time within the plays themselves. Beaumarchais had to excise from *Eugénie* elements which were too comic; *per contra*, the Comédie française cut severely Marceline's speech on the subjection of women from the *Mariage de Figaro*, because it was felt to be too serious. Can this juxtaposition within the same plays of disparate comic and serious elements be explained by lack of sureness of touch, a consequence of the collapse of artistic conventions which structure the relation considered to obtain between art and reality?[54] This artistic uncertainty might be related to Tocqueville's statement that it was felt that art was divorced from life, that it was no longer 'vrai'.

Such an explanation is undoubtedly correct, but does not go far enough. The bringing together of what to the twentieth century are aesthetic incompatibles, of flippancy and seriousness, is found in great and poor work alike – even within one work by Beaumarchais, as has been mentioned, and within the scope of his works. But this slipping from gravity into cynicism is not a result of lack of aesthetic consciousness; on the contrary, it is a result, as in

Diderot's *La Religieuse*, of hyper-consciousness. In great works, this is exploited: for example, in the *Mariage de Figaro*, Figaro's monologue in Act v recounts in miniature his biography, spread over the two comedies of which he is hero: from surgeon to barber, journalist and finally intriguer. His self-questioning as to who he really is brings out the existential meaning of the *imbroglio* form: 'Pourquoi ces choses et non pas d'autres? Qui les a fixées sur ma tête?' What is the relation between personality and events of the life which appear to define it and yet do not? This monologue has an existential significance. But it also has an aesthetic one, for it comments on the form of the play, and in particular, on the form of the scene which follows, and in which the jilted husbands or lovers (as they think), pull out of the garden pavilions someone else's wife or mistress. The monologue widens and deepens the play by commenting on the *imbroglio* form, and on its seemingly arbitrary construction.

There is then a balanced suggestion of significance behind the highly conventional form of the comedy, but Beaumarchais elsewhere unfortunately reverses the balance. A serious subject, in the opera *Tarare*, is undermined by suggestion of the comic. For the prologue attempts to give cosmic dimensions to this tale of the justification of the righteous and simple man who finally triumphs over the despotic king he serves, not by open rebellion, but by popular acclamation. Yet it is as if Beaumarchais wished to underline the difficulty of giving deep meaning to the ordinary, by his plot – a pure Arabian Nights affair of smuggling in and out of the harem – and by the hero's name – echoing throughout the play. The self-consciousness, which in *Figaro* was purely aesthetic, in *Tarare* has become parodistic. In this way, *Tarare*, though an opera, is closely related to many *drames*, for one cannot always decide whether they are conscious or unwitting parodies.

Moreover, it is in the preface to a parody, *Le Vidangeur sensible* by Marchand (in collaboration with Nougaret, the author of the parodistic *De l'art du théâtre en général*), that there appears the clearest statement of the *drame's* aim. Lessing indeed brings out this ambivalence *à propos* of Diderot's first manifesto on the theatre, in *Les Bijoux indiscrets*: 'Mais il s'en expliqua [about the new form of theatre he was proposing] alors dans un livre où le ton de persiflage domine si fort, que ce qu'il contient de raisonnable ne paroît à la plupart des Lecteurs que badinage et moquerie' (Lessing, 1785, vol. ii, pp. 134–5). The near-incompatibility of tone and matter that Lessing complains about in Diderot's novel can be seen

within the theatre itself. Whereas some eighteenth-century tragedies were so pared down to the base of convention that they are
their own parodies[55] and consciousness is part of them, in some
drames consciousness, often provoked by aesthetic *maladresse*,
succeeds belief and involvement, so that cynicism and sentimentality are juxtaposed. It is in Mozart and Da Ponte's *Don
Giovanni* that this trait of eighteenth-century sensibility goes
deepest: depths of hell are behind the *décor* of an *opera buffa*. In
this opera, the hero's refusal of tragedy, like the century's turning
of tragedy into something trivial, has tragic dimensions.

Conventional tragedy refers away from what it is: it ogles a
meaning which is not within it; like certain scurrilous novels it is
often *à clé*; it accepts theatrical convention and sharpens it to an
extreme of artificiality; its defenders use the theory of voluntary
illusion. The reform of drama, on the contrary, tries to make
meaning and play coincide: signs are to be eliminated in favour of
the thing signified. But this reform in fact postulates an entirely
different relation between theatre and audience.

6

SPECTATORS

Towards the spectator-voyeur: illusion and the audience

So far, I have considered analyses of illusion in relation to the art object, a relation established by theorists, but one which was complemented or contradicted by dramatic practice. The fundamental division in accounts of illusion – illusion which excludes versus illusion which includes awareness – was related by theorists to opera, tragedy, and *drame*:

Nos Tragédies destinées à être mises en Musique diffèrent essentiellement de celles qui doivent être déclamées. On cherche ici à faire plus illusion aux sens qu'à l'esprit, & l'on veut plutôt produire un spectacle enchanteur qu'une action où la vraisemblance soit exactement observée. (Lacombe, 1758, p. 144)[1]

Lacombe here appears to make a distinction between perceptual and cognitive illusion, correlating the former with opera and the latter with tragedy. Yet the cognitive illusion is in practice constantly disturbed by the audience because the spectators inject awareness. Saint-Preux comments on the perversity of this attitude in a passage already quoted: 'Il semble que les esprits se roidissent contre une illusion raisonnable, et ne s'y prêtent qu'autant qu'elle est absurde et grossière' (Rousseau, *O.C.*, vol. II, pp. 281–2). Where awareness is not guaranteed by the convention, as in opera, it is inserted as a kind of sabotage. But what is the nature of the resulting illusion, of involvement which is constantly thwarted? The question is answered by Marmontel, in a passage which, incidentally, contains a semantic switch illustrating the near identity of *vraisemblance* and *illusion* at this time: 'Il est deux espèces de vraisemblance, l'une de réflexion et de raisonnement, l'autre de sentiment et d'illusion' (Marmontel, *Encyclopédie*, article *Dénouement*). The illusion, which is opposed to awareness, may be perceptual or emotional, and when analysed further takes three forms: identification with the hero; later in the century, an awareness by the spectator of his own sensibility refracted through his view of others' emotion; and finally, especially marked in Diderot's theory, an internalisation of this awareness to make of the spectator a kind of voyeur.

Illusion as identification

'Nous n'y sommes affectés qu'autant que l'illusion nous séduit' (Maillet Duclairon, 1751, p. 3). Illusion is necessary for the emotional effect the century considers so important. This illusion may be defined as a mistake,[2] yet the metaphor 'séduire' at once suggests half-aware connivance and sensual rather than spiritual pleasure. Theorists are indeed seduced: they do not see that illusion fails to account for aesthetic judgement and, worse, for aesthetic pleasure. For Dubos had pointed out that the very fact that one can see a play twice disposes of the thesis that the audience makes a mistake during the play. Later theorists are not concerned with logical analysis, but are taken up with the intensity of the audience's involvement, which shuts out anything more than the actual scene before their eyes, or which prevents reflection.[3] Unlike Dubos, mid-century writers describe the illusion itself as pleasurable: pleasure is not derived merely from the theatrical proceedings (for clearly tragic action is not pleasurable in any ordinary way) but from the process of being present at the proceedings. Maillet Duclairon uses a dubious metaphor to describe this: 'Le Théâtre est le temple de l'illusion, on n'y va même que pour en éprouver tous les charmes' (Maillet Duclairon, 1751, p. 5). Conceptual confusion is the price paid for the flirtatious oscillation between mistake and awareness, and is the cost of critics' conniving account of the pleasures of illusion. They accept Dubos' position that man needs constant stimulus for his emotions, yet few accept his view that it is the non-reality of stage events which cuts out the violence in the emotions aroused. Instead, emotions are weaker because they are purer: 'Les émotions sont plus faibles et ne vont pas jusqu'à la douleur [. . .] parce qu'elles sont pures et sans mélange d'inquiétude pour nous-mêmes' (Rousseau, *Lettre à d'Alembert*, pp. 78–9).[4] But when this 'purity' is analysed, its paradoxical nature is brought to light – it is *amour propre* that is at work. Lucretius is often invoked: 'Il est doux de voir des maux qui nous sont étrangers' (Brumoy, 1730, vol. I, p. lxviii).[5] Such pleasure constitutes a reflexive element: the emotion at the spectacle is underscored for the spectator with pleasure which is necessarily referred to the self. For these writers, there can be no such category as 'aesthetic': the awareness is not of the object itself, whether as nature or as art (real or unreal, in Dubos' terms), but merely of emotional activity, within the subject, and pleasure derived from the safety of such activity. Emotion and pleasure may permeate each other, and reflexion and emotion may thus be simultaneous. Indeed, in much eighteenth-century thought, experience of emotion is not merely experience of affects, but also of accompanying sensations of pain or pleasure. Stimulation of the emotions may be pleasurable in itself: a reflexive element is thus built into even supposedly painful feeling like hate: 'Il y a néanmoins une sorte de douceur qui tempère leur amertume. L'âme s'y complaît comme dans les mouvements qui conviennent le mieux à sa situation présente et qui ont pour objet d'anéantir ce qui la menace' (Levesque de Pouilly, 1747, p. 50). The expense of painful feeling is not then merely relief; the relief actually becomes conscious pleasure and is transposed back into the experience itself. This bourgeoisification of cartharsis incorporates an aesthetic element into the moral experience itself. Here, as in theories of perception, a series of cogs have been inserted which make the experience private. They mitigate the awareness of its unreality, which has been transformed into the relation of spectator and spectacle. In the aesthetic as in the moral theory of the time, pity is identification with another's sufferings; it is automatic and epidemic. 'Il suffit de voir ou d'entendre une personne sincèrement et justement affligée pour s'attrister avec elle' (Rémond de Sainte Albine, 1747, p. 93). But the 's'identifier' made so much of by theorists is not the movement out to the other, but a simulation, a creation of a replica of the feelings within oneself – and its distinction from real suffering is created by the constitution of the self as spectator, of others or of oneself. Experience at a tragedy is not cathartic, but sado-masochistic.

The audience, however, identifies not merely with suffering but with greatness. Rémond de Sainte Albine reminds the actor: 'Lorsqu'en représentant un grand homme, vous êtes rempli de cette chaleur céleste dont il fut animé, vous la faites passer dans les âmes les plus communes' (thus far we have a rehearsal of ideas at least as old as the Institutio *Oratoria* of Quintilian). But: 'Vous transformez un cœur foible en un cœur magnanime & vos auditeurs due moins pour le moment deviennent autant de Héros' (Rémond de Sainte Albine, 1747, p. 89). The movement of generous expansion associated with Cornelian heroism has been transferred in dubious fashion from agent to audience:

Qu'est-ce qu'une Tragédie [. . .]? Une ressource à l'avidité de notre âme, un moyen heureux de la sauver pour un temps de sa petitesse ordinaire, en la transportant dans des émotions qui la rendent à son orgueil & à son activité [. . .] pensez-vous qu'on ait eu raison d'avancer qu'elle cherchait à s'éviter dans l'illusion? Je crois pour moi qu'elle ne veut que s'y retrouver. (Granet, 1738, vol. v, pp. 245–6)[6]

The theory of identification with the great, developed by insistence on Cornelian rather than Racinian practice, pays a tribute of sympathy to their suffering and leads the spectator to pleasurable sensations of his own force of soul:

[L'âme s'élève] pour ainsi dire au-dessus d'elle-même par un essor agréable, auquel elle se livre toujours avec délices. Qu'on l'interroge alors sur sa nature, cette âme, lorsqu'elle est plongée dans ce ravissement qui la saisit sans trouble, & la pénètre sans confusion: ne répondrait-elle pas que ce sentiment généreux & magnanime qu'elle éprouve est un témoignage aussi certain que délicieux de sa supériorité sur tout ce qui l'environne dans l'univers & que lui seul démontre le caractère inéffaçable de son élévation naturelle? (Seran de La Tour, 1762, p. 91)[7]

Or, 'On se place dans la classe des âmes généreuses, en accordant à d'illustres infortunés la compassion qui leur est dûe' (Rémond de Sainte Albine, 1747, p. 96). Such pleasure is derived from self-congratulation: 'Dans la Tragédie, nous soupirons, nous aimons nos larmes & celui qui les fait répandre; ce sentiment nous rend estimables à nos propres yeux' (Sticotti, 1769, p. 57). Pity disintegrates into benevolence and self-esteem.

The soul realises its 'élévation naturelle' through identification with greatness or through pitying human suffering: this emotion at a play is shot through with self-awareness. The identification is only with what is good: 'La commisération qui nous substitue toujours à la place du malheureux et jamais du méchant, agitera mon âme. Ce ne sera pas sur le sein d'Irène, c'est sur le mien que je verrai le poignard suspendu et vacillant' (Diderot, *Entretiens sur le 'Fils naturel'*, p. 150). It is in this way the plays can be said to have moral effect:

Lorsque je vois la vertu persécutée, victime de la méchanceté mais toujours belle, toujours glorieuse, et préférable à tout, même au sein du malheur, l'effet du Drame n'est point équivoque [. . .] et alors si je ne suis pas heureux moi-même, si la basse envie fait ses efforts pour me noircir, [. . .] combien je me plais à ce genre de spectacle et quel beau sens moral je puis en tirer. (Beaumarchais, 1964, p. 12)

At its most innocuous, this form of identification brings out, by its use of such terms as 'intérêt' and 'flatter', the confusion between emotion and *amour propre*:

Elle [la belle nature] doit nous flatter du côté de l'esprit, en nous offrant des objets parfaits en eux-mêmes qui étendent & perfectionnent nos idées; c'est le beau. Elle doit flatter notre cœur en nous montrant dans ces mêmes objets des intérêts qui nous soient chers, qui y tiennent à la conservation ou à la perfection de notre âme, qui nous fassent sentir agréablement notre propre existence: & c'est le bon. (Batteux, 1746, pp. 87–8)

This type of theory generates disquieting aesthetic demands. Tellingly, Levesque de Pouilly rejects Aristotle's criticism of plots which deal with the unhappiness of virtue, and recommends those where 'notre inquiétude sur le sort d'un homme vertueux, croissant jusqu'à la Catastrophe, fait enfin place à la joie de le voir heureux'. Levesque insists that the pleasure aroused by the spectacle of the unhappiness of a just man is greater than in the case where a tragic fault mitigates the hero's goodness:

Par le pouvoir enchanteur de la Tragédie ces malheurs nous font encore plus de plaisir; ils nous affligent profondément & cette affliction devient délicieuse, quand l'art du Poéte a sû en écarter l'indignation & y faire dominer la Bienveillance, dont le charme secret est assez puissant pour changer la douleur même en plaisir & rendre les larmes plus agréables que le rire. (Levesque de Pouilly, 1747, pp. 60–1)

The pleasure of identification with the good, the self-awareness derived from 'la différente position de l'objet', to use Levesque's phrase, from the fact that the spectator is opposite, cut off and separate, create the sadistic aesthetics of spectacle. Diderot in the *Essai sur le mérite et la vertu*, a translation of Shaftesbury in the main, elaborates and expands Shaftesbury's text to linger on the beauties of unhappy virtue, and the satisfaction it may bring to the spectator:

La vertu ne paroît avec toute sa splendeur que dans la tempête et sous le nuage. Les affections sociales ne montrent toute leur valeur que dans les grandes afflictions. Si ce genre de passions est adroitement remué, comme il arrive à la représentation d'une bonne tragédie, il n'y a aucun plaisir, à égalité de durée, qu'on puisse comparer à ce plaisir d'illusion. (Diderot, *O.C.*, vol. I, p. 175)

The spectator has become the commiserating torturer.

Thus, illusion may be defined as identification with the hero, but a happy freedom from his fate. The pattern of involvement–emotion and pleasure–distance becomes in this context vicarious extension of experience, replication and simulation of it, which then gives ground for complacent self-contemplation. *Amour propre* plays thus a threefold role in such theories: others are involved in suffering, *amour propre* is safe, and pleasure is poss-

ible.[8] Batteux even states: 'Le Goût est la voix de l'amour propre' (Batteux, 1746, p. 77). We increase our *amour propre* by consideration of our sensibility; to which Rousseau rejoins in disgust: 'Tel sanglote à la tragédie, qui n'eut de ses jours pitié d'aucun malheureux. L'invention du théâtre est admirable pour enorgueillir notre amour-propre de toutes les vertus que nous n'avons point' (Rousseau, *Essai sur l'origine des langues*, p. 503, note 1). But *amour propre* adds to pleasure in tragedy in yet another way: by social participation, by communication. According to Shaftesbury–Diderot in the *Essai sur le mérite et la vertu*: 'Le but des affections sociales relativement à l'esprit, c'est de communiquer aux autres les plaisirs qu'on ressent, de partager ceux dont ils jouissent, et de se flatter de leur estime et leur approbation' (Diderot, *O.C.*, vol. I, p. 177).[9] Self-esteem, created by one's own pity, is confirmed by the esteem and approbation of others; the emotion is reflected through the spectacle of others' emotion, and is thus shot through with self-consciousness.

For pleasure in communication of emotion is not so much between actor and audience as among the audience itself. And as such, the aesthetics of this type are based on the theories of natural sociability and the 'société universelle':

Les mêmes spectacles qui nous instruisent du charme secret qui accompagne les mouvements du cœur, nous apprennent aussi qu'on ne peut guère les appercevoir dans les autres sans les partager. C'est à ce commerce établi par la Nature que la société doit ses liens les plus doux et que la Peinture, la Poésie, la Déclamation & l'Eloquence doivent leurs charmes les plus puissants. (Levesque de Pouilly, 1747, pp. 61–2)[10]

Such communication is guaranteed by the constancy man's nature exhibits. This in turn points to a constant value system, available on simple inspection of the order obtaining in the universe, for

Toute pensée qui élève l'âme par la considération de sa propre excellence, ou qui tend à rendre l'homme meilleur, tout ce qui inspire la compassion de l'humanité, a des droits sur son cœur et obtient son suffrage en le ramenant à l'amour de l'ordre & de ses semblables. (Chicaneau de Neuville, 1758, p. 9)

The concepts deployed in such a theory are both moral and aesthetic; the aesthetic has a central role in the foundations of the moral, according to these theorists, since the key notion, *ordre*, belongs to both categories.[11]

The spectacle in the theatre can become the touchstone for our reaction to the spectacle of the world: as the world's order forces our admiration and love, so the theatre shows we are capable of such feelings: 'En questionnant adroitement les spectateurs d'une action tragique sur la nature des sentiments qu'ils éprouvent, on devineroit presque ce qu'ils sont capables de faire' (Madame de Puisieux, 1750, p. 44). Susceptibility to illusion shows, for Madame de Puisieux (and Diderot probably had a hand in her book), that in real circumstances a man might do the same because: 'Connaître toute la valeur des belles actions, c'est presque en être capable. Qui voit bien, agit bien' (Madame de Puisieux, 1750, p. 43).[12] Agent and audience are one, for the theatre shows clearly in miniature the process whereby moral behaviour is assured: 'Mais la vertu en conciliant notre bonheur avec celui des autres hommes fait de notre bien personnel, leur bien commun. Jugeons-en par l'intérêt qu'on prend aux hommes vertueux, que la Tragédie fait revivre sur nos théâtres' (Levesque de Pouilly, 1747, p. 207). The ambiguities of the word 'intérêt' sum up and reflect the interpenetration of moral and aesthetic elements in this theory: 'intérêt' is both our own self-interest, and the delightful concern for others' misfortunes.[13] But if the theatre reflects the functioning of the world's moral order, it also reacts on it: out of illusion springs virtue, in Méhégan's ambivalent formulation: 'Les théâtres ne doivent être élevés que pour inspirer aux citoyens par le charme d'une fiction enchanteresse, tous les devoirs qui font le bonheur de la Société. Heureuse illusion, qui donne les vertus en ne paroissant offrir que des plaisirs' (Méhégan, 1755, p. 224).

Such a theory makes especially acute the problem of the relation between appearance and reality: as Levesque admits: 'Il est vrai que le masque de la vertu produiroit cet effet aussi bien que la vertu même' (Levesque de Pouilly, 1747, p. 207). The theatre is the touchstone of a man's moral behaviour, but any judgement based on this will be based on signs of feeling, on tears, sighs, and other expressions of emotion. There is a queer confluence here between moral and epistemological theories – one's access, other than linguistic, to what people think and feel, is through facial expression and gesture. Tears acquire symptomatic significance: as a sign of feeling they may be enjoyable both to watch flow and to shed: 'C'est l'intérêt qui fait verser ces larmes délicieuses que l'on répand avec un si grand plaisir. Miracle sensible de l'art, le signe ordinaire de la douleur devient celui du plaisir' (Seran de la Tour, 1762, p. 206). Yet such signs can be imitated, so that the sincerity of the communication is not certain; what, moreover, is the value of this vicarious feeling?

J'ai donné le nom de magie à la déclamation, en la voyant nous conduire à nous affliger par de pompeuses chimères quelquefois plus sincèrement que ne feroient plusieurs d'entre nous pour des événements qui intéresseroient leurs parens ou leurs amis. (Rémond de Sainte Albine, 1747, pp. 246–7) Is not such an experience insincere rather than magical? But real discussion of this problem of the relation between sincerity and signs of feeling is transposed from audience to actor. The question of the authenticity of the actor's show of emotion, of whether the appearance he creates coincides with his reality, is discussed ardently in the treatises on acting from Rémond de Sainte Albine to Diderot, rather than in accounts of what happens to the audience. It will here be considered in connection with acting.

Rousseau and Diderot

It is not by accident that the quarrel between Diderot and Rousseau defined itself in public round the theatre. Rousseau takes Constance's 'Il n'y a que le méchant qui soit seul' in the play *Le Fils naturel* to be directed at him: it was to the preface of the *Lettre à d'Alembert*, often called *Lettre à d'Alembert sur les spectacles*, that he added the note which announced their break to the world. For their ideological and personal difference centres round the question of man's sociability, a theme at the basis of contemporary theories of the theatre. If man is social by nature, then society is necessary; then society, and reason, are coeval with man, for reason founds both society and natural law. Rousseau comes to see that such a theory is essentially conservative. But personally, also, Rousseau had reason to distrust the moral importance which Diderot attached to presence in society, and thus to social presence, which could cause the latter to write letters, such as that of 14 March 1757, urging him with such pompous insistence back to Paris. Rousseau had cause to question the value of the self-conscious charity that Diderot enjoined on him.

The *Essai sur le mérite et la vertu* defines both the good and the beautiful in terms of order and proportion; admiration of order is virtue and is necessarily natural and rational. Virtue's reward is not herself, but the esteem of others; self-congratulation made possible by other's flattering contemplation. The theatre is thus the model for the cosmic order; its aesthetic order, which creates admiration in the audience, who share and communicate their enthusiasm, reflects the moral order of the world. The moral effect of the theatre is then identical with apprehension of its aesthetic order.[14]

In this way the wicked man is brought to lament actions he himself would cheerfully commit outside the theatre, and his example is used in turn to demonstrate the fundamental goodness of human nature. The stock example is that of the tyrant (usually Sulla) shedding tears: 'Cruel par intérêt et humain par penchant, il payoit sur le théâtre à des hommes [. . .] de qui il n'avoit rien à craindre le tribut de Bienveillance qui leur étoit dû' (Levesque de Pouilly, 1747, p. 59). Rousseau, in the *Essai sur l'origine des langues,* though sceptical of the value of such incidents, accepts that pity is not unreflective: it is based on identification, which is conscious: 'Nous ne souffrons qu'autant que nous jugeons qu'il souffre' (Rousseau, *Essai,* p. 517). In the *Inégalité* he rejects *bienveillance,* so often equated with pity, because it implies both sociability and submission to others' opinion, and in fact arises from *amour propre*: 'L'homme sociable toujours hors de lui ne sait vivre que dans l'opinion des autres, et c'est pour ainsi dire, de leur seul jugement qu'il tire le sentiment de sa propre existence' (Rousseau, *O.C.,* vol. III, p. 193). Social virtues for Rousseau are not to be equated with pity but may be derived from it. Thus man is not naturally sociable; pity is spontaneous and not conscious, not induced by reflection. However, Jean-Jacques quotes the example of Sulla's weeping in the theatre as proof of such pity: 'Telle est la force de la pitié naturelle, que les mœurs les plus dépravées ont encore peine à détruire' (Rousseau, *O.C.,* vol. III, p. 155).

Diderot, unable to resist paradoxical formulations, sharpens this account in the *Discours sur la poésie dramatique*: 'Le parterre de la comédie est le seul endroit où les larmes de l'homme vertueux et du méchant soient confondues. Là, le méchant s'irrite contre des injustices qu'il aurait commises, compatit à des maux qu'il aurait occasionnés, et s'indigne contre un homme de son propre caractère'; but he concludes none the less that such a man 'sort de sa loge moins disposé à faire le mal' (Diderot, *Discours,* p. 196). The *Lettre à d'Alembert,* published almost at the same time as the *Discours,* reflects Jean-Jacques' growing consciousness of the precise substance of his disagreement with Diderot, and takes an opposed position. Sulla's tears prove this time the worthlessness of such surrogate experience: 'Une émotion passagère et vaine, qui ne dure pas plus que l'illusion qui l'a produite' (Rousseau, *Lettre à d'Alembert,* p. 78), its fragility underlined by the return to older connotations of 'illusion'. In brilliant fashion, Rousseau describes how the factitious life of social man erases the possible moral effect of the theatre, precisely because of the self-congratulation provoked by tragedy:

Au fond, quand un homme est allé admirer de belles actions dans des fables, et pleurer des malheurs imaginaires, qu'a-t-on encore à exiger de lui? N'est-il pas content de lui-même? Ne s'applaudit-il pas de sa belle âme? Ne s'est-il pas acquitté de tout ce qu'il doit à la vertu par l'hommage qu'il vient de lui rendre? Que voudrait-on qu'il fît de plus? qu'il la pratiquât lui-même? Il n'a point de rôle à jouer, il n'est pas comédien. (Rousseau, *Lettre à d'Alembert*, p. 79)

Diderot, in the *Discours sur la poésie dramatique*, no doubt influenced both by discussions with Jean-Jacques, and by the *Inégalité*, admits the escapist value of the theatre, yet affirms it. Edifying plays will allow the good men to escape from the wicked: 'C'est là qu'ils trouveront ceux avec lesquels ils aimeraient à vivre; c'est là qu'ils verront l'espèce humaine comme elle est et qu'ils se reconcilieront avec elle' (*Discours*, pp. 192–3). But the sad truth is accepted in the *Paradoxe sur le comédien*, which owes so much to Rousseau. The theatre does not improve morally: 'Mais l'expérience a bien démontré que cela n'était pas vrai, car nous ne sommes pas devenus meilleurs' (Diderot, *Paradoxe sur le comédien*, p. 354). And though he continues to assert the value of some imaginative adherence to virtue, against Helvétius and Seneca, it goes no farther than this: 'Exposons les tableaux de la vertu, et il se trouvera des copistes' (Diderot, *O.C.*, vol. xiii, *Essai sur les règnes de Claude et de Néron*, p. 503). A work like the *Salon de 1767* is more cynical, quoting La Rochefoucauld's maxim on our pleasure in others' misfortune: 'Nous la [la vertu] suivons jusqu'au pied de l'échaffaud, mais pas plus loin' (*Salon de 1767*, p. 143). He contradicts Helvétius' argument that the tragic hero offends the *amour propre* of the audience (Diderot, *O.C.*, vol. xi, p. 586). On the contrary, Diderot maintains that the *amour propre* is in fact involved in our admiration of the hero, but unlike most of his contemporaries, he brings out the ambiguities in such an account: 'Il [member of the audience] devenoit subitement l'auteur ou l'objet du bienfait; [que] toutes les fois que nous ne nous sentions pas capables d'une grande action, nous prenions le parti de montrer que nous en sentions tout le prix' (Diderot, *Correspondance*, vol. v, p. 76, 1 aoust 1765).

So far the grounds for disagreement appear restricted though not trivial. Was Rousseau guilty of touchiness in applying to himself the words: 'Il n'y a que le méchant qui vit seul'? Not if the whole play is considered. Paul Vernière has compared the Dorval of the *Entretiens* to Rousseau; Blandine McLaughlin has argued that many of the characteristics of the Dorval of the play must have touched Rousseau (including – as a refinement of cruelty – the discussion of children).[15] But in fact the whole play can be seen in relation to Rousseau. For the subtitle is 'les épreuves de la vertu', the theme is in fact that of the justification of the good man who doubts the goodness of the world order. He is saved from solitude and despair precisely by his return under Constance's guidance to an acceptance of man's social nature, symbolised by his children as yet unborn. Rousseau never despaired of the cosmos, but Diderot does not separate world order and social order at any point in his thought before *Le Neveu de Rameau*. Given Rousseau's decision to separate himself from society (or rather Parisian society – the two were the same for Diderot) Constance's plea appears as an overbearing marking out for Rousseau of what his conduct should be. (The play's theme has of course equal though different relevance to Diderot's life.) For she uses the example of the theatre, whose reform proves the improvement of society, and the goodness of the 'système général des êtres sensibles'.

Il y a sans doute encore des barbares; et quand n'y en aurait-il plus? Mais les temps de barbarie sont passés. Le siècle s'est éclairé. La raison s'est épurée. Ses préceptes remplissent les ouvrages de la nation. Ceux où l'on inspire aux hommes la bienveillance générale sont presque les seuls qui soient lus. Voilà les leçons dont nos théâtres retentissent et dont ils ne peuvent retentir trop souvent [. . .]. Non, Dorval, un peuple qui vient s'attendrir tous les jours sur la vertu malheureuse ne peut être ni méchant ni farouche. (Diderot, *O.C.*, vol. III, p. 92)

The world order will justify the good man (and the world order is a precise social one, as the reference to *peuple* shows) just as it justifies the play. And beyond this, in the context of the whole work, Dorval will at last be justified by, and will acquire faith in, the world order. Here there is an analogy with the way arguments are deployed in the accompanying manifesto, in the *Entretiens* which by an irritating *captatio benevolentiae* both claim that the play can be justified aesthetically and demand the reader's assent by postulating that both the play and the events on which it is based are real. Constance's speech thus contains in thematic form the aesthetic and moral structure of the play: it comments on itself, being constructed according to the complex of ideas associated with theories of sociability and taking these as its theme. But the central assumption, that the world and the social order are identical is never accepted by Rousseau: he admits the benevolence of the first in order the better to criticise the second. Rousseau shows up the complaisant intellectual sharp practice in the flattering of the audience by such means as Constance's speech. Indeed, the theatre's morality can differ in no sense from society's, he replies to Diderot in the *Lettre à d'Alembert*, and this identity between social and theatrical morality prevents the theatre having a moral effect. Man's love of morality is innate, not acquired by rational contemplation of the world order. And the rules of morality which are derived rationally from this contemplation, rules of the 'do as you would be done by' school, likewise fail:

Quel traité plus avantageux pourrait-il faire que d'obliger le monde entier d'être juste, excepté lui seul; en sorte que chacun lui rendît fidèlement ce qui lui est dû, et qu'il ne rendît ce qu'il doit à personne? Il aime la vertu, sans doute, mais il l'aime dans les autres. (Rousseau, *Lettre à d'Alembert*, p. 77)

Rousseau had indeed reason to recognise himself in *Le Fils naturel* and to locate the source of his difference from Diderot both philosophically and existentially in the latter's attitude to man's sociability.

In addition to this type of theory, however, Diderot in his works on the theatre uses an analogy which has a different significance for the way in which the psychological process of the audience is conceived. In the *Entretiens*, it is painting which serves as a criterion for 'vérité': 'Il faut que l'action théâtrale soit bien imparfaite encore, puisqu'on ne voit sur la scène presque aucune situation dont on pût faire une composition supportable en peinture. Quoi donc! La vérité y est-elle moins essentielle que sur la toile?' (Diderot, *Entretiens sur le 'Fils naturel'*, p. 89). And such remarks recur throughout Diderot's writings. But the analogy goes further: the audience is outside and opposite a painting. Thus the spectators at the theatre are by analogy situated outside, looking in. The stage should be regarded by the author as a room, the curtain as a fourth wall: 'Ne pensez non plus au spectateur que s'il n'existait pas. Imaginez, sur le bord du théâtre, un grand mur qui vous sépare du parterre; jouez comme si la toile ne se levait pas' (Diderot, *Discours*, p. 231). This is a radical privatisation of the theatre – compare Diderot's account of the success of the *Père de famille* at Marseille: 'A peine la première scène est-elle jouée, qu'on croit être en famille et qu'on oublie qu'on est devant un théâtre. Ce ne sont plus des tréteaux, c'est une maison particulière' (Diderot, *Correspondance*, vol. III, p. 280, 1 décembre 1760). No attention is to be paid by the author or actor to the audience. The audience, like Moi, stowed away in Clairville's salon to watch the *Fils naturel* (for that is how the *Entretiens* begin) are voyeurs: 'Vous n'aurez pas de peine à croire qu'il y a quelques scènes où la présence d'un étranger gênerait beaucoup' says Dorval to Moi as he helps him to hide (Diderot, *O.C.*, vol. III, p. 36). In this respect, painting, in particular Poussin's *Testament d'Eudamidas*, can be used to justify the interest of the proposed play, *La Mort de Socrate* (Diderot, *Discours*, p. 276), but more important, it expresses a constant in Diderot's way of working: 'C'est de saisir par la pensée les objets, de les transporter de la nature sur la toile, et de les examiner à cette distance où ils ne sont ni trop près, ni trop loin de moi' (Diderot, *Discours*, p. 195). But the meaning of the picture analogy is more composite and complex, and is relevant to the relation of scene and audience. The audience, separated from the action, can voluntarily linger over ideas, treated as sensations, and sensations which because they are 'agréables' can take on aesthetic status: 'Une belle scène contient plus d'idées que tout un drame ne peut offrir d'incidents; et c'est sur les idées qu'on revient, c'est ce qu'on entend sans se lasser, c'est ce qui affecte en tout temps.' Painting is used to clinch judgements of theatrical value:

Prenons deux comédies, l'une dans le genre sérieux, et l'autre dans le genre gai; formons-en, scène à scène, deux galeries de tableaux et voyons *celle où nous nous promènerons le plus longtemps et le plus volontiers*, où nous éprouverons les sensations les plus fortes et les plus agréables et où nous serons le plus pressés de retourner. (Diderot, *Discours*, pp. 200, 195)

Aesthetic experience is used as an analogy to explain the unarbitrary nature of moral judgement; but also, by a reverse process, the moral is recommended for the more powerful aesthetic experience it can provide. (The possible role of Greuze in this is ill understood at present.) The lone walk filled with agreeable sensations is also a theme of Rousseau's (Starobinski, 1978), but the difference from Diderot is absolute. For Diderot, the 'walk' is hypothetical, mental, in front of a picture or in front of a theatrical scene. The loneliness is not existential, but aesthetic, the spectator is alone, locked into his sensations, provoked by what he hears or sees. There is a radically new siting of the spectator in regard to the theatrical action. This is followed in practice by the Lauraguais reform, when the spectators were banished from the stage to the auditorium. Henceforward, the spectators are not, during the performance, themselves part of the spectacle, but are radically separate from the action – they overhear or overlook it: 'Le spectateur verra Ptolémée, Mithridate, Sertorius, et Mahomet, retirés dans le fond de leur palais pour y décider seuls du destin des empires et [. . .] ce même spectateur sera seul le témoin de leurs résolutions' (Lekain, 1825, p. 142).

Yet Diderot and other writers clearly hanker after violent and communal feeling in the audience:

Ce ne sont pas des mots que je veux remporter du théâtre, mais des impressions [. . .]. O poètes dramatiques, l'applaudissement vrai que vous devez vous proposer d'obtenir, ce n'est pas ce battement de mains qui se fait entendre subitement après un vers éclatant, mais ce soupir profond qui part de l'âme après la contrainte d'un long silence, et qui la soulage. Il est une impression plus violente encore [. . .] c'est de mettre un peuple comme à la gêne. (Diderot, *Discours*, p. 197)

The effect of the Ancient theatre, which was one of public emotion and expression of emotion (Diderot, *Entretiens*, p. 115),[16] must be attained. Such an effect of communal feeling is often connected with illusion: 'A Rome on vit plus d'une fois la multitude entraînée par l'illusion suivre machinalement les différens mouvemens du tableau dont elle était frappée, pousser des cris, répandre des pleurs, partager les fureurs d'Ajax ou les tendres douleurs d'Hécube' (Cahusac, 1754, vol. II, pp. 61–2). But how then can Diderot reconcile the siting of the spectator as a 'voyeur', and this communal drunkenness? 'Celui qui ne sent pas augmenter sa sensation par le grand nombre de ceux qui la partagent, a quelque vice secret' (Diderot, *Entretiens*, p. 122). Here the individual experience is increased by participation. Rousseau specifically contradicts this contemporary received opinion: 'L'on croit s'assembler au spectacle, et c'est là que chacun s'isole' (Rousseau, *Lettre à d'Alembert*, p. 66).[17] Diderot in fact does not discern the incompatibility of the spectator as 'voyeur' and the audience as taken up with communal emotions, just as he does not properly separate the drawing room drama of his own plays and the civic theatre he also wishes for; just as he wishes not to have to distinguish the use of the everyday and the eternal relations expressed by the themes of the 'mother', the 'judge' and the 'father of the family'. And both situations ascribed to the spectator, the private and the public, though free of the kind of consciousness which sabotages illusion, are yet suffused with another awareness. On the one hand the pleasure of the 'voyeur' arises not only from what he sees, but from his hidden position. On the other, feeling must be publicly manifest if it is to be perceived by others, but this in turn mediates self-awareness. Diderot believes that unalloyed illusion is obtained in these two cases, yet, in fact, in neither does the spectator lose his self-awareness.

7

ACTORS

Illusions and the actor-artist

Diderot wishes the spectator both to be a kind of *voyeur* and to participate in communal emotions. Marmontel rephrases this problem, and locates it in the spectator's relation with the actors:

> Mais pour un Poëme qui veut produire l'effet de la vérité même, ce n'est pas assez d'obtenir une croyance raisonnée, il faut que par le prestige de l'imitation, il rende son action présente, que l'intervalle des lieus & des tems disparoisse, & que les spectateurs ne fassent plus qu'un même peuple avec les Acteurs. (Marmontel, 1763, vol. I, p. 369)

Here, communal feeling is created in the audience by virtue of a communion between actors and spectators. The audience identifies with the actor as stage character, with his experiences, and feelings. But if the audience's feeling is to be that of the character, with no mediation or modulation, then the actor too must identify with what he plays. The safeguarding of communal feeling leads to the insistence that the actor feels, or should feel; the attempt to reject awareness from the audience's experience leads to an insistence that the actor is also in a state of illusion. On the other hand, the theory of audience participation which implicitly or explicitly held that it was shot through with self-consciousness can be related to an insistence on the part of certain theoreticians that the actor incorporates into his performance distance from the character he is portraying.

The quarrel of the actor, for quarrel it is, bears a curious relation to the Lauraguais reform. The Comte du Lauraguais indemnified the Comédie française for the loss of audience seats on the stage and in 1759 they were removed. These seats on stage had necessarily provided a constant reminder that what was seen was appearance, and this was excised, or at least vastly diminished, by their removal. In general terms, the Lauraguais reform is yet another example of the abolition of the mediating intersubjective area be-

tween art and consumer; it shows once again that the work of art is
being constituted into an object-replica which can be true or false
to a model. Correspondingly, if the spectator is to react in
immediate fashion to the work then he must react in unselfconsci-
ous directness of feeling: he must believe in the truth of what he
sees. The actor's technique, which would mediate between audience and spectator, must be annulled by becoming belief in what he
represents: 'Il ne peut bien [. . .] représenter [son rôle] qu'autant
qu'il se croit lui-même celui qu'il représente' (Maillet Duclairon,
1751, p. 14). Or, to push this towards paradox, the actor's belief
may itself become technique.

Actor's illusion and sensibility

The history of the discussion extends far back in the eighteenth
century, as Xavier de Courville has shown in his biography of Louis
Riccoboni (Courville, 1943). Dubos, although denying that the
audience at a play are involved to the point of making a mistake,
yet attributes illusion to the actor (Dubos, 1719, vol. I, pp. 37–8,
395). Grimarest, in his *Traité du récitatif dans la lecture* (1707),
insists on the contrary that the actor must retain self-control; he
implicitly contradicts Horace, for the actor must beware of tears,
which may prevent his being heard. And in the anonymous poem
L'Art du théâtre (1744) it is said of the characteristics of a role:

> Ne vous y trompez pas, l'art est de le paroître
> Et pour réussir mal, il suffiroit de l'être.
>
> (*L'Art du théâtre*, 1744, p. 10)

The discussion becomes controversy with Rémond de Sainte
Albine's *Le Comédien* (1747), overtly contradicted by Louis Riccoboni's son, François, in 1750. Rémond de Sainte Albine's ideas
take a curiously circuitous route to be paraphrased by Sticotti in
Garrick ou les acteurs anglois (1769). It was of course out of
Diderot's review of Sticotti's book that the *Paradoxe sur le
comédien* developed.[1] The argument for the actor's sensibility
develops out of rhetorical tradition. Sainte Albine makes the
actor's and the audience's processes parallel, and reinterprets
Horace in terms of illusion:

Horace a dit, *Pleurez si vous voulez que je pleure*. Il adressoit cette maxime
aux Poëtes. On peut adresser la même maxime aux Comédiens. Les
Acteurs Tragiques veulent-ils nous faire illusion? Ils doivent se la faire à
eux-mêmes. Il faut qu'ils s'imaginent être, qu'ils soient effectivement ce
qu'ils représentent & qu'un heureux délire leur persuade que ce sont eux
qui sont trahis, persécutés. Il faut que cette erreur passe de leur esprit à leur

cœur, & qu'en plusieurs occasions un malheur feint leur arrache des larmes véritables. (Rémond de Sainte Albine, 1747, pp. 91–2)

The actor's 'heureux délire' induces illusion in the spectator: it consists of 'Ces écarts, cette fougue impétueuse, & cet involontaire oubli de soi-même [. . .] qui enlève au Spectateur le temps de l'Examen' (Dorat, 1766, p. 21). What is 'feint' produces 'véritable' tears, yet the play Sainte Albine makes between them seems close to an illusion which contains consciousness. The use of a term like 'écart' which implies a return to the position from which the actor's 'heureux délire' has been a deviation, likewise includes awareness. And in that such accounts make the actor's feeling into a technique – only the natural can succeed as art[2] – the 'natural feeling' will inevitably become questionable and ambivalent. (This point will be developed later: below, pp. 203–4ff.).

But in general, where a parallel between actor's and audience's activity at a play is drawn, 'illusion' serves as an account of the mode of communication between them, and is defined as a transmission of states of soul from identifying actor to identifying audience:

Ils [danseurs et comédiens] doivent également enchaîner le public par la force de l'illusion & lui faire éprouver tous les mouvements dont ils sont animés. Cette vérité, cet enthousiasme qui caractérisent le grand Acteur & qui est [*sic*] l'âme des Beaux-arts, est si j'ose m'exprimer ainsi, l'image du coup électrique: c'est un feu qui se communique avec rapidité, qui embrase dans un instant l'imagination des Spectateurs, qui ébranle leur âme, & qui force leur cœur à la sensibilité. (Noverre, 1760, pp. 285–6).[3]

This goes well beyond an account of illusion which holds that the audience are in the same emotional state as they would be, if the play were real. Instead, illusion has become a flash of intense communication between actor and spectator. The strength of it is measured by its involuntariness, at least on the part of the audience. An effect, the involuntariness, that is, the fact that the emotion is elicited by force ('ébranle leur âme & [. . .] force leur cœur'), becomes a mark of the spontaneity of the feeling. As a result, the emotion is held to be more easily communicated by spontaneous and involuntary signs than by language. If the actor-dancer identifies himself strongly enough with his subject, gestures expressive of his emotion will automatically result (Nougaret, 1769, vol. I, p. 350). Such gestures do not even have to be interpreted: 'L'action en matière de Danse est l'Art de faire passer par l'expression vraie de nos mouvements, de nos gestes & de la physio-

Actors

nomie, nos sentiments & nos passions dans l'âme des Spectateurs' (Noverre, 1760, p. 262). Gestures are natural signs, which 'par eux-mêmes, et indépendamment du choix que nous en avons fait [font connaître] l'impression que nous éprouvons, en occasionnant quelque chose de semblable chez les autres' (Condillac, 1947, vol. I, p. 19). Gesture was the first, the 'natural' language. The first steps of dance were invented after the Creation as an expression of thanks to God. David danced in front of the ark as a thank-offering (Cahusac, 1754, vol. I, p. 17). This is the source of critics' concern with ballet and pantomime (for example, Diderot in the *Entretiens sur le 'Fils naturel'*, Cahusac, Noverre and, earlier, Dubos and Bonnet) for they offer a mode of communication more immediate than the spoken word.

Sensibility and awareness

But what is meant by the term 'feeling' when it is asserted of the actor that he 'really' feels? The controversy is far from being as simple as has been maintained – by Diderot among others. When the social context is considered – actors were excommunicate although accepted at great mens' tables – when the quarrel over the morality of the theatre, going back through the exchanges between Caffaro and Bossuet to the early Fathers of the Church, is borne in mind, the insistence on the actor's intelligence and sensibility appears as a defence, a concealed wish to improve his status.[4] If the player's performance is a result of intelligent intention, than it is valuable. And if he really feels the emotions he shows, he is not false, but sincere. Thus, writers who appear to recommend 'sensibility' as the most important quality all insist on intelligence as well. However, what is meant by sensibility is far from straightforward.

Sensibility may be equivalent to inspiration extended from author to actor: 'On ne réussit dans les compositions théâtrales qu'autant que le cœur est agité; que l'âme est vivement éprise; que l'imagination est embrasée, que les passions tonnent et que le génie éclaire' (Noverre, 1760, p. 59). In that case, enthusiasm must almost by definition transgress bounds to be itself, to prove itself as enthusiasm: 'On aime à voir la nature triompher des règles de l'art' (Sticotti, 1769, p. 68).[5] But if nature vanquishes art and the actor is overcome by his emotion, he may be inaudible. Difficulties begin to appear in this kind of account of sensibility. The actor needs to change the very scale of his feeling in order to project himself in a large auditorium, and this is impossible if the expression of emotion is unreflective (L. Riccoboni, 1738b, pp. 20, 29–30). As a consequence, even those who wish nature and art to be one may be forced to recognise their lack of coincidence. Diderot in the *Entretiens sur le 'Fils naturel'*, for instance, claims as a general thesis that the actor 'réfléchit peu', that he is at one with his feeling. Yet Diderot finds 'exagération', that is, separation between nature and art, even in the Ancient theatre, and traces it, tellingly, to the poetic form, which, he suggests, is perhaps used in order to ensure that the actor's words are heard. It may even be, he surmises, that the exaggeration results from poetic declamation, from an *original* lack of coincidence between nature and art:

Quoi qu'il en soit: que la poésie ait fait naître la déclamation théâtrale; que la nécessité de cette déclamation ait introduit, ait soutenu sur la scène la poésie et son emphase; ou, que ce système, formé peu à peu, ait duré par la convenance de ses parties, il est certain que tout ce que l'action dramatique a d'énorme se produit et disparaît en même temps. L'acteur laisse et reprend l'exagération sur la scène. (Diderot, *Entretiens sur le 'Fils naturel'*, p. 123)

That the notion of sensibility has to be unconsciously revised under pressure from such problems can be shown from d'Aigueberre's account of the great actress Lecouvreur. He insists on the need for feeling, but adds: 'Au surplus, elle disposoit à son gré de son cœur et de ses sentimens' (d'Aigueberre, 1870, p. 34). Another example of this revision is provided by Rémond de Sainte Albine, who insists that faults in acting come about because 'On n'est pas véritablement irrité ou attendri selon que l'exige la situation du personnage'; and – seeking to better the actor's status without exploring, as do Rousseau and Diderot, the contradiction between the actor's marginal social status and his heroic roles – he writes: 'Quiconque n'a point l'âme élevée, représente mal un Héros' (Rémond de Sainte Albine, 1747, pp. 149, 85).[6] But much of Rémond de Sainte Albine's detailed discussion of the actor's technique, in spite of the triviality of its context, runs counter to this crude account: 'Les mouvemens d'un Acteur n'étant qu'empruntés, il ne devroit pas être dans le même cas qu'une personne chez qui ces mouvemens sont naturels; cependant il fait sur nous la même impression' (Rémond de Sainte Albine, 1747, p. 63). He shows that the actor works on the poet's text, where very different passions are juxtaposed, by consciously modulating one passion into another (Rémond de Sainte Albine, 1747, pp. 24–5). He declares outright that 'esprit' should be the actor's pilot, for 'Il ne suffit pas qu'il soit capable de se passionner, on veut qu'il ne se passionne qu'à propos' (Rémond de Sainte Albine, 1747, p. 21). All this is so much proof of consciousness and intelligence. But Sainte Albine's inconsistencies cannot be excised by assuming that intelligence is assigned the role merely of elaboration of the part.[7] Indeed, at one point he seems rightly to be undermining the very opposition between intelligence and 'sensibilité', for feeling is said to be the actor's medium, and his intelligence is shown through his use of it: 'L'esprit dans la Tragédie doit chez l'Acteur ainsi que chez l'Auteur ne se montrer pour l'ordinaire que sous la forme du sentiment' (Rémond de Sainte Albine, 1747, pp. 29–30). He in fact radically redefines 'sentiment':

Il désigne dans les Comédiens la facilité de faire succéder dans leur âme les diverses passions, dont l'homme est susceptible. Comme une cire molle, qui sous les doigts d'un savant Artiste devient alternativement une Medée ou une Sappho, il faut que l'esprit & le cœur d'une personne de Théâtre soient propre à recevoir toutes les modifications que l'Auteur veut leur donner. (Rémond de Sainte Albine, 1747, p. 32)

Thus the actor is both active and passive, like wax moulded to the author's intentions, but these must be embodied by actions of his own, by causing his soul to take on the succession of feelings which constitutes the part.

The problems in Sticotti's work are naturally very similar, given the genesis of his text (a reworking of an English reworking of Sainte Albine's book), and cause a similar redefinition of sensibility. The actor 'doit sentir fortement les passions qu'il veut nous inspirer' (Sticotti, 1769, p. 62). And he appears to accept some of the consequences of the thesis: 'Ses talens dépendent des dispositions momentanées de son âme & de ses organes [. . .]. L'Acteur le plus consommé ne peut répondre, en se présentant au public, des moindres traits qu'il va rendre' (Sticotti, 1769, p. 40, note g). He pours scorn on the idea that acting consists in imitation: 'Emprunter la manière de rire & de pleurer de quelqu'un dans l'intention de passer pour sincère aux yeux du public, est une idée extravagante, digne d'Arlequin' (Sticotti, 1769, pp. 30–1, note c). But if the actor is not to imitate, then his soul must be capable of the whole universe of emotion with all its degrees; and more clearly than Sainte Albine, Sticotti draws the consequences: 'On sent que le caractère propre du grand Acteur est de n'en avoir aucun' (Sticotti, 1769, p. 71). This capacity is named by him 'sensibilité universelle'. Earl Wassermann has shown how close this theory is to the English Romantics' conception of the poet, in particular to Keats' idea of the chameleon poet (Wassermann, 1947). (Out of this developed, too, the idea of the artist as feelingless in his actual life (Sticotti, 1769, p. 71),[8] the great twentieth-century working of which is Mann's *Doktor Faustus*.)

François Riccoboni explicitly answers Sainte Albine and contradicts his own father, yet works out an account of the actor's identification with his part which is less removed from theirs than he appears to think. Far more closely argued than Sainte Albine, his dismissal of the notion that the actor 'really' feels foreshadows Diderot – as do both Marmontel and Charpentier.[9] The actor does feel, but feels an emotion generated by acting, and not that of the role he is playing (F. Riccoboni, 1750, p. 41).[10] He rephrases the account of the actor's identification in a way parallel to that in which many theorists rephrase the spectator's identification: 'Un homme qui serait vraiment en pareille situation ne s'exprimeroit pas d'une autre manière, & c'est jusqu'à ce point qu'il faut porter l'illusion pour bien jouer' (F. Riccoboni, 1750, p. 36). The actor is not, then, in a state of illusion while acting, though the spectator may be: 'Lorsqu'un Acteur rend avec la force nécessaire les sentimens de son rôle, le Spectateur voit en lui la plus parfaite image de la vérité' (F. Riccoboni, 1750, p. 36). Like Sainte Albine and Sticotti, he takes as the central fact of the actor's existence the variety of his roles: 'Se métamorphoser [. . .] changer de contenance, de voix & de phisionomie toutes les fois qu'on change d'habit' (F. Riccoboni, 1750, p. 64). But for Sainte Albine, the metamorphosis is inner and the actors have a 'facilité de faire succéder dans leur âme les diverses passions dont l'homme est susceptible', which interior change necessarily results in a changed exterior; for Riccoboni, on the contrary, though there may be a relation between the actor's character and the role he is playing (Riccoboni, 1750, p. 57), the concept of imitation is to be taken seriously.[11] The actor's imitation and his attention are outward, directed towards the imaginary projection, the role he places before the audience. Whereas for Sainte Albine and Sticotti the actor is at one with that projection, they never dissociate the actor's physical metamorphosis from his sensibility: 'La sensibilité est la base de toutes ces imitations. Celui qui ne sent pas plusieurs passions à la fois ne sauroit passer à propos d'une passion à une autre passion. Les imitations si diverses & si fréquentes dans la comédie rendent la sensibilité universelle indispensable au Comédien' (Sticotti, 1769, pp. 83–4). And it is this that Diderot criticises in the *Paradoxe*: 'Ce serait un singulier abus des mots que d'appeler sensibilité cette facilité de rendre toutes les natures, même les natures féroces' (Diderot, *Paradoxe*, p. 343).

Actors

Diderot is right: the argument has misdirected itself by centring on a word.[12] The actual question is on a different axis, as Clairon's commentary on the actor shows: 'Quelle étude ne faut-il pas faire d'abord pour cesser d'être soi?' is not, as it may appear, a denial that the actor feels (Clairon, an vii, pp. 249–50). Two different conceptions of the actor are involved: one in which what the actor creates is an exterior construction, an imitation in an exact sense: 'Il semble que le Comédien ne puisse atteindre la perfection de son art, qu'en s'oubliant entièrement soi-même; qu'en ne mettant rien du sien dans son jeu, qu'en ne montrant dans tous ses mouvements qu'une copie continuelle' (Charpentier, 1768, vol. ii, p. 61). Such is the conception shared by Charpentier, Diderot, Préville, Molé, and François Riccoboni. And the alternative conception, in which the actor 's'affecte, se pénètre de tous les caractères qu'il doit imiter' (article *Déclamation théâtrale*, in the *Encyclopédie*), is that of Marmontel, Sticotti, and Sainte Albine.[13] In the former conception, the actor is the epitome of social man:

Si l'on se métamorphose journellement & sans le moindre effort, dans les divers rôles que l'homme joue sur la terre, pourquoi le Comédien n'emprunteroit-il pas dans le sien la même facilité, un ton de grandeur & des affections que la nature lui auroit refusés? (Charpentier, 1768, vol. ii, pp. 55–6)

Diderot in particular develops images to describe him: the marionette, the courtier, the nothingness, who according to exterior demands takes on different stances and different expressions:

Un grand courtisan, accoutumé, depuis qu'il respire, au rôle d'un pantin merveilleux, prend toutes sortes de formes, au gré de la ficelle qui est entre les mains de son maître. Un grand comédien est un autre pantin merveilleux dont le poète tient la ficelle, et auquel il indique à chaque ligne la véritable forme qu'il doit prendre. (Diderot, *Paradoxe*, p. 348)

Whereas in the second conception, that of Sainte Albine, the actor, like the poet in Romantic theory, is an aeolian harp. Says Talma, 'Il s'ébranle aux inspirations du poète aussi facilement que la harpe eolienne résonne au moindre souffle de l'air qui la touche' (Talma in Lekain, 1825, p. xxxii).[14]

But the indeterminate area between these two conceptions is explored by other writers in other metaphors. For Dazincourt, Préville – 'vrai Protée, [qui] prend toutes les formes indistinctement' (Dazincourt, in Préville, 1823, p. 377) – takes on others' feelings by imitating their gestures and expressions:

L'art du véritable comédien, consiste à connaître parfaitement quels sont les mouvements de la nature dans les autres, et à demeurer toujours assez maître de son âme pour la faire à son gré ressembler à celle d'autrui. (Préville, 1823, p. 177)

Garrick, 'Vrai Chaméléon [. . .] prendra toutes sortes de formes indistinctement' (Servandoni d'Hannetaire, 1774, p. 140). There are signs that these conceptions of the actor crystallise round an opposition between 'acteur' and 'comédien', and that specific actors come to symbolise this: Molé is 'acteur sublime' but Préville is 'véritable comédien' (Dazincourt, in Préville, 1823, p. 377; cf. Diderot, *Paradoxe*, p. 336); 'M. Le Kain est un grand Acteur, Mlle. Clairon est une grande Actrice & M. Garrick un grand Comédien' (Servandoni d'Hannetaire, 1778, p. 140). However, the actresses Clairon et Dumesnil are contrasted on a different axis, that of an opposition between art and nature, a contrast used by Diderot in the *Paradoxe*, and prompted perhaps in part by la Dumesnil's appearing in Palissot's *Les Philosophes* (Myers, 1962, p. 264). Dumesnil acts her own nature, whereas of Clairon opinion tends to say: 'Tout est forcé dans ses rôles; & le Spectateur trouve à peine à respirer tant il souffre de la contrainte où il la voit' (Maillet Duclairon, 1751, pp. 83–4).[15] Diderot's adoption of Clairon in the *Paradoxe* as the symbol of the technical element in the actor's performance springs thus from his contemporaries' estimation of her.[16] Yet Clairon's technique is valued differently both within his own work – *Le Neveu de Rameau*[17] – and by his contemporaries.[18] This double attitude to Clairon reflects Diderot's ambiguity towards the artist's technique that I have explored elsewhere (Hobson, 1973). Yet the other bearer of the *Paradoxe*'s argument, Garrick, is not the subject of a similar ambiguity of judgement. For Diderot, as for his contemporaries, Garrick is always the Protean actor *par excellence*. But the explanation of his transformations does undergo a change. In the *Salon de 1765*, Garrick is Roscius, 'commandant à ses yeux, à son front, à ses joues, à sa bouche, à tous les muscles de son visage, ou *plutôt à son âme, qui prend la passion qu'il veut*, qui dispose ensuite de toute sa personne' *(Salon de 1765*, p. 213)[19] – an account not far removed from those of the writers who believe that the actor must feel. But everything changes with the *Paradoxe*. There, Garrick does not feel, yet his importance to the text does not consist merely in the fact that he does not use his own feelings in the elaboration of his roles. What he projects to the audience is not just a carefully calculated imitation; it is a work of the imagination, a 'fantôme imaginaire de la poésie' (*Paradoxe*, p. 315). Just as Chardin's work and talk may have forced Diderot to recognise the role of technique in creation, so it is round the figure of Garrick that the recognition that the art object is imaginary crystallises.

Diderot and the paradox of technique

In the two types of theory of acting discussed above, the actor could either feel everything or nothing. In feeling everything, his nature is exceptional – in feeling nothing, he performs a trick on the audience: 'pure imitation, leçon recordée d'avance, grimace pathétique, singerie sublime [. . .] l'illusion n'est que pour vous; il le sait bien lui, qu'il ne l'est pas' (*Paradoxe*, pp. 312–13). He is the ancestor of Felix Krull, the confidence trickster. The classical theories of the power of the orator, which were the ancestors of the theories of the actor, take a dubious form: 'Ce n'est pas l'homme violent qui est hors de lui-même qui dispose de nous; c'est un avantage reservé à l'homme qui se possède' (*Paradoxe*, p. 309; cf. p. 381). Diderot sharpens the paradox glossed over by Sainte Albine, that of the 'malheur feint [qui] arrache des larmes véritables'. The audience may be in a state of illusion; they are as if unconscious. But the actor deliberately provokes this illusion, by using his body, even the outward signs of feeling, as a technique to elicit this unconsciousness.

Actor and audience thus complement each other:

C'est qu'il s'est démené sans rien sentir, et que vous avez senti sans vous démener [. . .]. Les larmes du comédien descendent de son cerveau, celles de l'homme sensible montent de son cœur: ce sont les entrailles qui troublent sans mesure la tête de l'homme sensible; c'est la tête du comédien qui porte quelquefois un trouble passager dans ses entrailles. (*Paradoxe*, p. 313)

As a result, a relation of mutual dependence is created. The audience, which cannot do without them, despises the actors (*Paradoxe*, p. 356). And Diderot's anecdotes show sufficiently how in turn actors despise the public on whose approbation they yet depend. The actor turns his attention outwards to watch the audience: 'Spectateur froid et tranquille' (*Paradoxe*, p. 306); his task is 'regarder [. . .] reconnaître, [. . .] imiter' (*Paradoxe*, p. 310). Yet his observation is doubled with critical self-awareness: 'S'entendre, se voir, se juger, et juger les impressions qu' [il] excitera. Dans ce moment [il] est double' (*Paradoxe*, pp. 308–9). The actor is not then himself, but copies himself: 'Copiste rigoureux de lui-même ou de ses études, et observateur continu de nos sensations' (*Paradoxe*, pp. 306–7).[20] Unlike other artists he himself embodies his own creation, which is only made possible by 'cette incompréhensible distraction de soi d'avec soi' (*Paradoxe,* p. 318). The *Salon de 1767* describes the *audience's* reaction as double, using the actress Lecouvreur as bearer of the analogy: 'Je suis Lecouvreur et je reste moi' (*Salon de 1767*, p. 144). How much more complex in the *Paradoxe* is the actor's alienation: he is constantly watching the audience, and his own movements and expressions. Yet his performance does not quite coincide with what is the third object of his attention: the *modèle idéal*, the internal model, the imaginary construction he is copying (see the *Salon de 1767*, p. 308). The actor completes and thus reverses the process of alienation; instead of being conscious of watching eyes on him, and responding to their projection, he watches the audience to appraise their reaction to his projection on to them. The actor, like the Hegelian phenomenal consciousness, 'se manifeste au dehors et à l'extérieur de soi pour se poser et se réfléchir en soi-même dans son être-autre' (Hyppolite, 1946, p. 109).

This third object of his attention, the *modèle idéal*, is created by a relaying system of imitation. The epistemology underlying this account of acting is quite different from that on which the concept of the *transmission* of feeling is based. There is an unbridgeable gap here between what is felt and the gesture which expresses it. The 'real' feeling is translated into signs, which we must scrutinise to interpret. The fact that these signs mediate, are separated from what they signify, gives the actor his chance. He imitates the signs which are consonant with his internal model, the *modèle idéal*, and the signs are interpreted by the audience as referring to a heroic being: 'Qu'est-ce donc que le vrai talent? Celui de bien connaître les symptômes extérieurs de l'âme d'emprunt, de s'adresser à la sensation de ceux qui nous entendent, qui nous voient et de les tromper [. . .] par une imitation qui agrandisse tout dans leurs têtes' (*Paradoxe*, p. 358). 'L'acteur s'est longtemps écouté lui-même; c'est qu'il s'écoute au moment où il vous trouble, et que tout son talent consiste, non pas à sentir comme vous le supposez, mais à *rendre si scrupuleusement les signes extérieurs du sentiment*, que vous vous y trompiez' (*Paradoxe*, p. 312). This is a relay from appearance (the manifestation of emotion), to what appears (the signs of emotion) which is in turn appearance (in that the signs are imitated). This is in fact what I have called *aletheia*.

It is noteworthy that the kind of behaviourism which subtends Diderot's account of the actor has brought with it a kind of atomism. Signs are curiously discrete, and can be organised into a scale of transitions. Thus Diderot twice gives the example of Gar-

rick passing through a range of emotions, and calls this a 'gamme', a
scale (*Paradoxe,* p. 328). The study of discrete signs is recommended by actors in their memoirs: Clairon describes how she
studied anatomy, and the works of Buffon, in order to characterise
the emotions clearly – a notion clearly related to painting theory
and to Le Brun's categorisation of passion: 'Tous les mouvemens
de l'âme doivent se lire sur la physionomie: des muscles qui se
tendent, des veines qui se gonflent, une peau qui rougit, prouvent
une émotion intérieure, sans laquelle il n'est jamais de grand
talent' (Clairon, an vii, pp. 283, 280–1). Préville in his memoirs
minutely classifies gesture (Préville, 1823, p. 105) and emotion too
must be categorised in order that each may be indicated by a
different sign: 'Que d'étude ne faut-il pas pour parvenir à distinguer la différence de l'ironie au dédain? du dédain au mépris?'
(Clairon, an vii, pp. 280–1).[21]

Diderot, in the *Paradoxe* as in *Le Neveu de Rameau*, pushes the
relay of appearance even further. He considers the case of
Tartuffe, where the actor must act an actor; and Rameau's nephew
acts out the acting out of social position. But in both cases, that of
the actor and that of Rameau's nephew, the relay of appearance is
inserted into a closed, determined system. The theatre is an elaborate construction of gazes which focus on the imaginary object, on
the actor's phantom, the projection of the *modèle idéal*. The actor,
who from an extreme corner watches the phantom and the audience, can by his alienation influence the structure of these gazes.
Rameau, by his playing out of the 'grand branle de la terre', has
secured, by his alienation, a kind of foothold in the universe of
jerking marionettes, the universe of 'positions'. In that both make
themselves something they are not, both are able to watch those
who watch. The actor is in a position of power – an absolute power,
but one resulting from the internal scission, the alienation he provokes in himself, which, while making him the pasture of people's
gaze, also enables him to remove himself from that gaze, to watch
them and to work on what they watch, to alter the 'fantôme
imaginaire' in order to affect them. Once again, as in the *Vernet*
article for the *Salon de 1767* (see above, pp. 58ff.), Diderot
locates both necessity and freedom in the situation of the artist, a
position at once of power and of dependency.

The audience and the actor-artist

For Diderot, what the artist creates – the *fantôme* – is at once
objective and imaginary, the projection from and on to his own

body of a fictitious personality. The actor becomes the paradigm for the poet, and the *Paradoxe* explicitly broadens the controversy over the actor's intelligence and sensitivity into a discussion of the artist: 'Et pourquoi l'acteur différerait-il du poète, du peintre, de l'orateur, du musicien?' (*Paradoxe*, p. 309). The artist's 'incompréhensible distraction de soi avec soi' is the example of the artist's abnegation: abnegation towards his vision but also towards his technique, for an artist does not just create but must structure what he imagines by the technical means at his disposal.

Author, actor, and spectator are in analogous relations to one another, for the actor has the same process of production as the author–poet, and must be able to intuit the state of mind of the spectator, if only to be able to work on it. This extension, from actor to artist in general, of the actor's process is not exclusive to Diderot. The proponents of sensibility frequently and explicitly describe the actor's process of identification in the same terms as the poet's. This tendency also appears negatively from those who, like Charpentier, deny intelligence or sensibility to the actor, in order the better to emphasise the poet's creative faculty. It appears positively from Sainte Albine's and Sticotti's claim that the actor is creative: 'Ce n'est donc pas assez d'entendre parfaitement une pièce; l'acteur doit être, pour ainsi dire, Auteur lui-même' (Sticotti, 1769, p. 40). 'Il faut qu'il [l'acteur] devienne Auteur lui-même; qu'il sache non seulement exprimer toutes les finesses d'un rôle mais encore en ajouter de nouvelles; non seulement exécuter mais créer' (Rémond de Sainte Albine, 1747, p. 22).

Acting theory discussed in fact a certain aspect of the poet's relation to his material far more successfully than the poetics of the time. Those writers who are concerned to emphasise the reality of the actor's feelings disengage themselves from the concept of 'imitation' (in the one art where it has obvious meaning) and move towards a view of the actor which clearly anticipates the Romantic idea of art as the expression of personal experience. But as has been shown, from the force of the facts, where 'sensibilité' is seriously ascribed to the actor, it becomes so profoundly modified as to make the term inapposite. The problem of the artistic process and the artist's sincerity is explored through a figure, the actor, which forces the discussion towards a nuanced and complex view of the artist's creativity.

Correspondingly, the audience's participation in the actor's role becomes, in the view of critics, an interiorisation of the experience, a kind of inner theatre:

Un seul trait passionné rendu d'après nature nous enlève, nous met à la place du Poète, de l'Acteur & du Personnage; *ce n'est plus l'imagination, c'est notre âme toute entière qui représente ce qu'elle applaudit*; le héros est en nous-mêmes, nous soupirons nos douleurs, nos plaisirs, nous croyons être tout ce que nous admirons. (Sticotti, 1769, p. 97)

The spectacle has become inner, the subjectivity is in play. Illusion now is internal, and the self-consciousness involved in the experience of art becomes a deeper self-awareness. This movement in aesthetics is illustrated even more clearly in the poetics of the period, to which the next part of this book is devoted.

The development of theories of the actor can be summarised by a comparison of Diderot and Rousseau. What was an account of the author in Rousseau's notes for the *Lettre à d'Alembert* (based on Plato's *Republic*, and known as *De l'imitation théâtrale* (Rousseau, 1764, vol. IV, p. 15)), is developed by him into an account of the actor:

Mais un comédien sur la scène, étalant d'autres sentiments que les siens, ne disant que ce qu'on lui fait dire, représentant souvent un être chimérique, s'anéantit, pour ainsi dire, s'annule avec son héros; et dans cet oubli de l'homme, s'il en reste quelque chose, c'est pour être le jouet des spectateurs. (Rousseau, *Lettre à d'Alembert*; p. 165)

But for Rousseau, the actor's existence comes only from the audience's attention. And this is close to the situation of social man in the *Inégalité* who 'ne sait vivre que dans l'opinion des autres' (Rousseau, *O.C.*, vol. III, p. 193). Rousseau thus confirms, by his criticism, the relation between theories of sociability and theories of acting I have established earlier. For Rousseau, whereas social man moves outwards to make himself at one with others' opinion of him, here the audience's gaze concentrates inwards on to the actor to shape his nothingness. Jean-Jacques rejects the awareness of self which is based on others' opinion, which is built out of a process of reflection in both intellectual and visual senses, in favour of the spontaneously flowing 'sentiment de sa propre existence'. The analysis in the *Lettre à d'Alembert* certainly influenced Diderot's *Paradoxe*. But Diderot takes self-consciousness, awareness of self as seen by others, as something to be exploited, something making possible a movement between successive moral engagement and disengagement. Whereas Rousseau experiences this awareness as an infringement of autonomy, to escape which the self must turn back upon itself, for Diderot the awareness creates the possibility of a kind of escape from necessity through alienation, through being one jump ahead, through the actor's not being present where the audience expects to find him. Diderot's analysis of the alienation which the artist must undergo, taking up Rousseau's discussion of the actor and of social man, suggests perhaps that the art object, or at least the actor's art object, is the same kind of imaginary construction as the social projection of the self on to others, or of others on to the self. In the eddies of the relation of watching, social man creates his image of himself, and the artist creates the object.

Yet Diderot in the *Paradoxe*, true to his dislike of such *papillotage*, such movement away from and back to self, also *denounces* the actor and his *fantôme*. In that the actor is not himself, he is not natural; his technique, by which his art creates the appearance of nature, is all the more scandalous for being the manipulation not of brush and paint but the use of his own corporeal and vocal signs.

For Diderot and for Rousseau, then, what the actor creates is in some sense an object even though it is imaginary, a projection of something he is not. In this they disagree with the common run of their contemporaries, for whom the actor does not create an object, but simulates a model. For the latter half of the century, and for Rousseau, though not for the later Diderot, the art medium must be transparent, there must be no awareness of illusion. As a result, the simulation of the model, allowed in preparation of the role, must be effaced in the actual performance. The actor must in acting become transparent, he must not constitute part of a relay of imitation. Actor and audience must thus 'identify' with the role (the word is first in current usage in the eighteenth century); further, the actor is not a relay for the artist, he *is* the artist. This total transparency can only be maintained by an interiorisation of the feelings the actor 'really' feels.

Part Four

ILLUSION AND THEORIES OF POETRY: FROM FICTIONS TO FORGERIES

'Illusion' during the early eighteenth century designates an inter-subjective game, in which different levels of fiction can succeed each other, precisely because, no doubt, there is a socially under-stood, practical separation of art and reality (compare Bouhours, above, pp. 37–8). But the theories of painting, novel and drama already discussed show that during the century the junction of true and false is broken: 'illusion' is applied sometimes to the work of art conceived as a public object which can be true or false, and sometimes to the consumer's or artist's state of mind, which may be a fantasy or an authentic experience, but in either case internal and private. With this sundering of inner and outer comes the constitu-tion of the concept of representation as replica. For those arts which can hardly be considered to create a public object – one that can be true or false in the replication of its model – the replica must be internal. This is the case for poetry and music. From this point of view, drama acts as a bridge, having both internal and external replicas. It creates an external object which can be passed off as real; and the actor creates a state of mind which is adequate to that of the character he portrays and which produces a replica of itself within the spectator.

Poetry's status is more doubtful. As a result, its theorists derive from the drama two implicit questions which they strive to answer: 'Who is speaking and on what authority does he say what he says?', and 'Why does the poet use the language he does?' These questions force their way into the common run of accounts of poetry, and constantly underlie the discussions of verse forms, of the nature of the epic, and so forth. They are particularly obtrusive because poetry is being interpreted in terms of illusion, both as a state of mind in the poet and as a state induced by his language in the reader or listener. It is in fact the status of subjectivity which is in doubt – with whose voice does the poet speak? (The relation to the

209

problems of the novel is evident.) One type of solution, I have suggested, was given by the discussion of the actor. It is, however, the answer to the second question, as to the nature of poetic language, which finally renders the first irrelevant, for language comes to take on a validity of its own which endorses and justifies the poems, be they ancient lays, modern musings, or even forgeries.

8
ILLUSION AND THE POET'S VOICE

'La logique de la fureur'

There is at the end of the seventeenth century a general disquiet about truth in literature. What is the status of a novel? How does the novelist come to know what he is recounting? – such are the tacit questions which the false memoirs, the prefaces recounting the discovery of letters in secret drawers and old castles, and, on a theoretical level, 'illusion' are designed to answer. The disquiet can undoubtedly be related to the great advances in textual criticism, in particular of the Bible, made in the period. Now such questions cannot be sensibly posed of the drama, for each character speaks in his own voice (and the century is sensitive to the choric aspect of ancient drama and expends effort in discussing whom the chorus represents). But they can be asked of poetry. The question of poetic voice becomes problematic, as a comparison of Boileau's and Marmontel's commentaries on the fable and *conte* illustrates. Boileau, who was writing almost a hundred years earlier than Marmontel, and for whom a sophisticated attitude to literary genre is still possible, defends La Fontaine's *Joconde* against its source, Ariosto, thus: 'Le secret donc en contant une chose absurde, est de s'énoncer d'une telle manière que vous fassiés concevoir au Lecteur que vous ne croiés pas vous même la chose que vous lui contés. Car alors il aide lui-même à se décevoir & ne songe qu'à rire de la plaisanterie agréable' (Boileau, 1966, p. 312). 'Se décevoir' is part of the vocabulary of that illusion which hides and reveals, and which here asserts and negates the movements of an ironic attitude. Marmontel, writing in the *Encyclopédie*, eliminates this irony and treats the fable as a private communication: 'Quelle est donc l'espèce d'illusion qui rend la *fable* si séduisante? On croit entendre un homme assez simple et assez crédule, pour répéter sérieusement les contes puérils qu'on lui a faits' (*Encyclopédie*, article *Fable*).

211

The poet must persuade his readers that he really believes that foxes and donkeys talk.[1]

This loss of theoretical sophistication, this concern for *adequatio* between what is said and what is intended, is by no means due merely to the opportunistic simple-mindedness typical of Marmontel. It is probably a response to the attacks on poetry made at the turn of the century and associated with the *Querelle des Anciens et des Modernes*. Such attacks are characterised by their disdain of poetry. Bayle, relentless critic of the authority of texts, writes: 'C'est une chose qui ne se comprend pas, que parmi les créatures qui se glorifient d'être raisonnables, comme de leur caractère de distinction, il y ait un métier public dont les principales propriétés sont de nous repaître de fables et de mensonges' (Bayle, quoted Gillot, 1914, p. 537).[2] Tannegui Lefèvre, son of the classicist and brother of Anne Dacier, the most important translator of Homer of the century, publishes *De futilitate poetices* in 1697.[3] Poetry is the art of fiction, Perrault perfidiously makes his old-fashioned President say in its defence. The consequence that he intends to be drawn is that it is the art of untruth (Perrault, 1693, vol. II, p. 5). One of the possible answers to these attacks is given by the supporter of poetry in Perrault's dialogue: poetry's essence consists of 'fictions' – here applied to mythological characters, the appurtenances of the *merveilleux* – and 'fictions' suggests powerfully in this context that the supernatural and the incredible are coinciding. The plural form itself insinuates frivolity, a decoration of the void, a *dissimulatio*.[4] Indeed, in the earlier part of the century, certain poems appear much like the practice of a poetics of *dissimulatio*: the fabulous beings which people them divert attention from their emptiness. Thus Louis Racine denounces the opinion of those who claim that poetry cannot be divorced from untruth: 'Assurant que la Poësie est inséparable des fables [ils] ne placent que parmi les Versificateurs ceux dont les ouvrages ne sont point animés de la présence de quelques personnages feints, ou de quelques Divinités allégoriques' (Louis Racine, 1731, p. 389). Such a view of poetry is at once, for Racine, a development and a lamentable derogation from religion. 'Fables', myths, were used in modern poetry precisely because of this origin, but, having lost their religious significance, are justified, according to Louis Racine, by a different but equally fallacious argument:

Un poète, disent-ils, doit toujours créer; son nom même ne signifie autre chose que *Créateur*, ainsi, pour répondre à sa profession & pour créer toujours, il doit abandonner les préceptes aux Philosophes, les faits véri-

tables aux Historiens, & ne débiter que des mensonges agréables, sous
l'écorce desquels il peut seulement enfermer quelque vérité utile. (Louis
Racine, 1731, p. 390)

Indeed Baillet, an *Ancien*, uses this argument, which allots verity
itself to history, for the benefit of classical poetry: it is because the
Christian concept of truth has limited the art of fiction that Latin
and Greek poetry is greater than contemporary (Baillet, quoted
Gillot, 1914, p. 380). The semantic slips which allow such attacks
are well analysed by the abbé de La Barre, who attacks Vatry's
reworking of Le Bossu on the epic, by attempting to dissociate
'fable' as a properly aesthetic term, meaning plot, from 'fable'
meaning allegory, or hidden moral truth, and from 'fable' meaning
'fiction'.[5]
Louis Racine's own reply to these dilemmas and attacks is to
insist on the contrary of *dissimulatio*, on *aletheia*: it is given in
La Religion, a poem moving in its awkwardness:

> Je sais bien que féconde en agrémens divers
> La riche fiction est le charme des vers.
> Nous vivons du mensonge, & le fruit de nos veilles
> N'est que l'art d'amuser par de fausses merveilles;
> Mais à des faits divins mon écrit consacré
> Par ces vains ornements seroit déshonoré. [. . .]
> L'âme de mon récit est la simplicité
> Ici tout est merveille, & tout est vérité.
>
> (Louis Racine, 1742, p. 82)

It is in religious poetry that art and truth, the marvellous and
reality, can coincide – the fiction is made truth, or rather points to
truth. Moses is thus the first poet, but is truly inspired. 'Moïse, le
premier & le plus sublime des Poètes' (Louis Racine, 1731, p. 404)
cannot be said to proffer fiction but to glorify God. The Daciers in
their defence of classical poetry make similar observations – Bibli-
cal poetry is *revelation* of truth immediately perceived (A. Dacier,
1701; cf. Fénelon, 1718, p. 191). And it is because Batteux in 1746
wishes to retain truth as a property of religious texts that he insists
that art is imitation.

Etoit-ce l'Homme qui chantoit dans Moïse, n'étoit-ce point l'esprit de
Dieu qui dictoit? Il est le maître: il n'a pas besoin d'imiter, il crée. Au lieu
que nos Poëtes dans leur yvresse prétendue n'ont d'autre secours que celui
de leur Génie naturel [. . .]. Qu'ils ayent eu un sentiment réel de joie: c'est
de quoi chanter, mais un couplet ou deux seulement. Si on veut plus
d'étendue, c'est à l'art à coudre à la pièce de nouveaux sentimens qui

213

ressemblent aux premiers. Que la Nature allume le feu, il faut au moins
que l'art le nourrisse & l'entretienne. (Batteux, 1746, pp. 238–9)

And no doubt it is this religious concern (though this is never made
explicit) which causes Batteux to make it the heart, rather than the
reason, which recognises the unreality of art (Batteaux, 1746, pp.
93–4). Such a tradition allows immediate, continuous expressivity
only to God, but later in the century, when a notion of personal
subjectivity is fully constituted, the individual will replace his
creator. However, the time of the rivalry between poet and God as
bearers of truth, the time of Shelley's *Prometheus*, is not yet, and
Chant V of *La Religion* relates poet's and God's word only in the
silence of the poet:

> Faible & fière Raison, dépouille ton audace
> Le vent souffle: qui peut en découvrir la trace?
> Etonnés de son bruit, nous sentons son pouvoir.
>
> (Louis Racine, 1742, p. 107)

This type of relation between truth and poetry constitutes an
answer to attacks on poetic fictions, but easily accompanies a view
of modern poetry as ephemeral falsehood, as decadence; in mid-
century, the Marquis Le Franc de Pompignan writes religious
poetry and his brother the bishop attacks contemporary literature
for triviality – both continue the *Ancien* position in the *Querelle
des Anciens et des Modernes*.

For Louis Racine, poetry referred outwards, but to higher truth.
The *Moderne* party, on the contrary, assumes poetry's frivolity.
For them poetry plays with its own emptiness (an evident relation
to the *papillotage* of the fine arts). Writers such as Fontenelle and
La Motte use 'illusion' as a relay of 'fictions', in the sense of 'illusions'. They write eclogues or idylls, and justify as follows their
deliberate choice of the conventionally natural:

> Souvent par des fantômes vains
> Notre raison séduite avec plaisir s'égare
> Elle-même jouit des objets qu'elle a feints
> Et cette illusion pour quelque tems répare
> Le défaut de vrais biens que la Nature avare
> N'a pas accordés aux Humains.
>
> (Fontenelle, 1688, p. 5)[6]

The idyll is presented as a deliberate giving up of self to the obviously imaginary: 'Je me doute bien que les Bergers ne sont pas tels
qu'on me les y représente, & je saurois bien, si je voulois, que ceux
qu'on me peind sont imaginaires; mais je ne veux pas le savoir & je

me livre au plaisir qu'ils me font par le plaisir que j'ai à m'y livrer' (Rémond de Saint Mard, 1734, p. 48; 1749, vol. IV, pp. 76–7).[7] Curiously, the *Moderne* party will not extend this imaginative tolerance to include the *merveilleux*, that is, the supernatural, as it appears in Homer for instance, though it is often defended by his admirers in terms of 'illusion'.[8] This provokes the defenders of Homer into examining more closely the type of adhesion that can be given to poems written at a time radically different from the present, and into insisting on a degree of historical imagination in the reader.[9] La Motte and Fontenelle, the *Modernes*, accept highly localised conventions because they are local, and thus evident. The movement of referring comes back to rest where it began: the 'illusions' are merely illusions and are seen to be such. Whereas, with Homer, as in Louis Racine's interpretation of religious poetry (the *Anciens*' defence of the bard was often in terms of religion), the conventions were obviously not merely conventions but layers of possible interpretation behind which a truth could be glimpsed without being fully understood.[10]

The ode: an apparent solution to poetry's lack of truth

For the eighteenth century, if a kind of poetry is to be sought which is not 'illusion' in that it is not imitation at all, it must be looked for among the ancients, among the Greeks and, above all, the Hebrews:

Il y a longtemps qu'on ne fait plus d'odes. Les Hébreux en ont fait, et ce sont les plus fougueuses; les Grecs en ont fait, mais déjà avec moins d'enthousiasme que les Hébreux [. . .]. Les Romains ont imité les Grecs dans le poëme dont il s'agit, mais leur délire n'est presque qu'une singerie. (Diderot, *Salon de 1767*, p. 154)

The connection between religious poetry and the ode is apparent here; and it is the ode which is the counter-example given in answer to accusations of triviality, to definitions of poetry as a *jeu d'esprit*, and is cited as such by, for instance, Perrault's abbé (in Perrault, 1693, vol. II, p. 14). The ode is in fact the supreme form of poetry, that in which the poetic language is farthest removed from common speech: 'Mais les Poëtes lyriques, j'entends les Auteurs d'Odes, peuvent & doivent même étaler toutes les richesses de la Poësie. Ils peuvent, sans nuire néanmoins à la clarté, parler autrement que le commun des hommes.'[11] The ode is the poem of the poet inspired, and it is his enthusiasm which justifies the richness of his language. La Motte, Jean-Baptiste Rousseau – known to his contemporaries as 'le grand Rousseau' – and 'Pindare' Le Brun, all proclaim in verse their vaticination:

> Qu'aux accens de ma voix la terre se réveille:
> Rois, soyez attentifs: Peuples, ouvrez l'oreille:
> Que l'Univers se taise & m'écoute parler,
> Mes chants vont seconder les accords de ma Lire
> (J.-B. Rousseau, *Ode sur l'aveuglement des*
> *hommes du siècle*, in Bonafous, 1739, p. 101)

The odes use a formal device known as 'désordre' – abrupt transitions from subject to subject. Boileau, earlier, speaks merely of 'sages transports' in the *Art poétique*, but the eighteenth century goes much further: '*Aucun genre de poésie n'échappe plus au compas géométrique*, aucun n'est plus exposé à ces caprices heureux que l'art ne sauroit prévoir, à ces fougues du génie qui souvent arrive à son but sans trop connoître lui-même les sentiers qu'il a pris' (Le Brun, 1811, vol. IV, p. 294).[12] The movement of inspiration which engenders the ode appears to escape from regularity: 'On appelle cela aujourd'huy des Ecarts' (Rémond de Saint Mard, 1734, p. 241; 1749, vol. V, p. 72). But the very term, 'écarts', used in the plural, and applied to this movement shows that the ode is believed to return to its subject, that is, to oscillate – it completes that return to rest typical of early eighteenth-century aesthetics, having gone through what is a pre-planned trajectory. The movement out and return to rest, as I have already suggested in the discussions of Rococo art, is only a variety of *papillotage*, not an escape from it. For a series of quick jumps, 'écarts', are imposed on the attention by objects, but this occurs within a movement to and fro; the apparently necessitated movement out which returns to its starting point is a kind of imbrication of *papillotage* within itself. The ode's apparent freedom is in fact a variation in a heavier key of a Marivaudian type of 'esthétique du hasard':

Pleine du beau feu qui l'agite, forcée d'obëir aux différens mouvemens qui la transportent, l'ame se porte avec une espèce de complaisance, jusqu'à ce que le premier et le dominant objet, venant tout de nouveau la frapper, la ramène tout-à-fait à lui. De là, ces écarts, tant vantés dans l'Ode. (Rémond de Saint Mard, 1734, p. 223; 1749, vol. V, pp. 50–1)[13]

Typically for the eighteenth century, spontaneity is seen in terms of compulsion, of what can no longer be retained or avoided. The *écart* is forced on the poet by his own excitement. It is thus the compelled sign, that is, the symptom of inspiration: 'Le poète, pour marquer un esprit entièrement hors de soi, rompt la suite de son discours' (Le Brun, 1811, vol. IV, p. 296). But such symptoms are discrete, they can be classified and, worse, simulated, for they are exterior manifestations. Diderot actually classifies poetry by the gestural attitude of the poet, and unwittingly shows the relation between a behaviourist explanation of action (whereby interior states can be diagnosed only through gesture or expression) and the inflated posturing of much eighteenth-century poetry:

Est-ce un poète qui compose? Compose-t-il une satire ou un hymne? Si c'est une satire, il aura l'œil farouche, la tête renfoncée entre les épaules, la bouche fermée, les dents serrées, la respiration contrainte et étouffée: c'est un furieux. Est-ce un hymne? Il aura la tête élevée, la bouche entr'ouverte, les yeux tournés vers le ciel, l'air du transport et de l'extase, la respiration haletante: c'est un enthousiaste. (Diderot, *Discours sur la poésie dramatique*, pp. 286–7)

Diderot's symptoms are visual: as transpositions of inspiration from verb to eye, they proclaim their own inauthenticity. But the ode in particular and poetry in general had early been attacked on such grounds (Le Clerc, 1699, p. 1). The poet emits inflated signs of inspiration, but he is not truly inspired. This brings back the question which had been crucial for the early part of the century: on what authority does the poet speak? Is it his own, self-attributed? The concept of the sublime provides one answer to this question.

It is the sublime that is held to characterise the ode: 'L'Ode tend particulièrement au Sublime' (La Motte, *Discours sur l'ode*, 1754, vol. I, part 1, p. 34). The term evolves from a moral concept to a quality characterising literature, and finally describes the emotion evoked in the reader.[14] In the seventeenth century, the sublime was a fashionable if vague critical term, as La Bruyère's commentary in his chapter 'Des ouvrages de l'esprit' testifies (La Bruyère, 1962, p. 90), although Boileau's translation of Longinus' treatise had given the term more substance and provided critics with a point of reference. Boileau had in fact justified the sublime because it provides an answer to the problem about the status of what the poet is saying:

Il n'y a point de Figure plus excellente que celle qui est tout à fait cachée, et lorsqu'on ne reconnoît point que c'est une Figure. Or il n'y a point de secours ni de remède plus merveilleux pour l'empêcher de paroître que le Sublime et le Pathétique, par ce que l'Art ainsi renfermé au milieu de quelque chose de grand et d'éclatant à tout ce qui luy manquoit et *n'est plus suspect d'aucune tromperie.* (Boileau, 1966, p. 370)

The relation with illusion is clear: there is 'tromperie', and the poet does deceive, but his deception can be masked if he can deceive enough. The sublime is an extension of, not a departure from, contemporary aesthetics, and this is confirmed by the critics' reductive definitions as they discuss and re-discuss Boileau's examples; La Motte, for instance, writes: 'Le sublime *n'est autre chose que* le vrai & le nouveau réunis dans une grande idée, exprimée avec élégance et précision' (La Motte, 1754, vol. i, part 1, p. 35; cf. Rémond de Saint Mard, 1734, p. 205). Yet in the manner of the ode, its vehicle, so the sublime shows its force by its compulsion: it is so powerful that it leaves no time for reflexion. Rollin speaks of the effects of one of Cicero's speeches thus: 'Ces cris, & ces applaudissements [. . .] ne furent point libres & volontaires, ni la suite des réflexions, mais l'effet subit d'une espèce de ravissement & d'enthousiasme, qui les enleva hors d'eux-mêmes, sans leur laisser le tems de songer ni à ce qu'ils faisoient, ni au lieu où ils étoient' (Rollin, 1726–8, vol. ii, p. 103).[15] Mere persuasion, on the other hand, 'n'a sur nous qu'autant de puissance que nous voulons. Il n'en est pas ainsi du sublime. Il donne au discours une vigueur noble, une force invincible qui enlève l'âme de quiconque nous écoute' (Rollin, 1726–8, vol. ii, p. 102). But with most writers, up to the mid-century, the effect of the sublime is described as an oscillation between inspiration and implicit awareness (even with Boileau there had been awareness, albeit one admitted negatively: 'n'est suspect d'aucune tromperie'). Condillac suggests that the sublime involves the rapid experience of contradictory feelings – that is, oscillation.[16] Rémond de Saint Mard places the contradiction between the greatness of the thing expressed, and the simplicity of the expression. The effect of this contradiction is astonishment: '[Le sublime] nous étonne, nous saisit, nous enlève & fait sur nous cette impression vive & piquante [. . .]' (Rémond de Saint Mard, 1749, vol. v, p. 20). He actually uses the verb 'frémir' of the reader's reaction.

Not only does the effect of the sublime – oscillation between involvement and awareness – relay that attributed to illusion; other concepts, notably the *merveilleux*, do so too, by their effects.[17] Rémond de Saint Mard emends the 1734 edition of the *Réflexions sur la poésie* where the sublime is defined in terms of admiration, by adding the underlined phrase: 'Tout ce qui excède nos forces, tout ce qui passe notre pouvoir, *tout ce qui tient par quelque coin au merveilleux la* [admiration] *réveille*' (Rémond de Saint Mard, 1734, p. 198; 1749, vol. v, p.7).[18] Another concept which relays the sublime and the *merveilleux* is *enthousiasme*. As a word applicable to religious as well as poetic inspiration, it underwent attack from critics who were defending the Christian notion of truth and who were insisting on the pagan quality of such definitions.[19] But unlike the *écart* in the ode, it can never be a *symptom* of inspiration – on the contrary it *is* inspiration itself, compelled and uncontrolled. As a result, the rationalist *Modernes* have little faith in it. The feebleness of La Motte's enthusiastic odes is defended thus by Fontenelle: 'Ce n'étoit point un *enthousiasme involontaire* qui le saisît, une fureur divine qui l'agitât; c'était seulement une volonté de faire des vers, qu'il exécutoit, parce qu'il avoit beaucoup d'esprit' (Fontenelle, in La Motte, 1754, vol. I, part 1, pp. xlvii–xlviii). The involuntariness of enthusiasm in the usual conception meant that it is no better than animal instinct (La Motte, 1754, vol. I, part 1, p. 29). On the contrary, the enthusiasm of La Motte is self-provoked – 'une chaleur d'imagination qu'on excite en soi & à laquelle on s'abandonne'. For his enthusiasm, like his definition of the sublime, has a reflexive element: 'Une certaine grandeur d'âme [qui augmente] en nous l'idée de notre propre excellence' (La Motte, 1754, vol. I, part 1, pp. xxxv, 1).[20] This was the aspect of the sublime, and of enthusiasm, which attracted criticism (see p. 182). For these notions embody a gap – between thought and what is – which corresponds on the level of sensibility to the *écart* in the trajectory of the ode. Marivaux, typically, seizes on this discrepancy. He divides the sublime into 'sublime de sentiment' and 'sublime de pensée' (and is radically different in this from Rémond de Saint Mard, for example, who distinguishes between the 'sublime des tours' and the 'sublime en trait'). The 'sublime de pensée' is in fact a mere ladder to success: 'C'est l'image des efforts de l'esprit auteur: ce sublime nous peint ce qu'un auteur se fait devenir' (Marivaux, 1969, p. 59).[21] The 'sublime de sentiment' is, on the contrary, radically twisted into a Marivaudian aesthetic: 'L'auteur nous peint ce qu'il devient; il est l'effet des impressions qu'il reçoit et qui le surprennent.'

Later, however, both sublime and enthusiasm are said to provoke a state of inspired excitement in the poet and thus in the audience (*Encyclopédie*, article *Image*). This theory assumes a mechanical identification of audience and poet: 'Nous sommes machinalement disposés à recevoir l'impression des sentimens dont les autres sont affectés' (Trublet, 1754–60, vol. II, p. 269; cf. Rémond de Saint Mard, 1734, pp. 202–3). 'On a cru qu'un homme devoit être tout à fait hors de lui-même pour pouvoir produire des choses qui mettoient réellement hors d'eux-mêmes ceux qui les voyoient ou les entendoient' (Cahusac, who goes on to insist against this that enthusiasm is 'le chef d'œuvre de la raison', in his article *Enthousiasme* for the *Encyclopédie*).

But in general the sublime and enthusiasm are states of excitement which can only be analysed after their abatement, though they may be self-consciously enjoyed for their duration.[22]

The sublime and genius

In classical and traditional eighteenth-century rhetoric, orator and poet are held to have a common aim – that of affecting the audience/reader, and text-books of rhetoric or of poetics inevitably concentrate on the classification and transmission of techniques of persuasion. The tears of the orator are merely part of the armoury of techniques. In post-Revolutionary theory this changes completely. It is now the artist's state which is central, and not its communication. Indeed, the expression of the artist's experience becomes, in modern theory, part of the experience to be expressed. The sublime acts as a conceptual hinge in this 'radical shift to the artist in the alignment of aesthetic thinking' (Abrams, 1958, p. 3). For, particularly in connection with the ode, the idea of the rule-breaking disordered genius becomes for the first time something more than a topos, and is freed from *papillotage*:

Le génie est ce feu, cette conception vive, originale et presque surnaturelle qui s'élève dans notre âme et la transporte hors d'elle-même, définition que je ne puis mieux achever que par l'ingénieuse allégorie de Prométhée dérobant le feu du ciel. Cet enthousiasme qui en est comme l'essence [. . .] concentre les idées et force l'imagination à ne voir qu'un seul objet; il enfante par besoin, toujours avec chaleur, et, pour l'ordinaire, avec un certain désordre. (Caylus, 1910, pp. 130–1)[23]

It is 'enthusiasm' which, for many critics, balances the defects of the notion of imagination, which for the century is fundamentally associative. 'L'imagination est la faculté de se rappeler des images' (Diderot, *Discours*, p. 218).[24] Marmontel for this reason, in a passage where the assimilation of poetry to the theatre is apparent, distinguishes imagination and identification: 'Je ne confonds pas avec l'imagination un don plus précieux encore, celui de s'oublier soi-même, de se mettre à la place du personnage que l'on veut peindre' (Marmontel, 1763, vol. I, p. 69). Enthusiasm takes over from the sublime, and 'identification' moves from a windy imitation of an exterior model to a notion of creativity springing from inner depths of energy: 'Dans le feu de l'enthousiasme il [le génie ennemi de la contrainte] ne voit que le grand, il n'aime qu'à créer' (Charpentier, 1768, vol. I, p. 10).[25]

The extent to which the religious tradition helped to keep the notion of creativity available is suggested by the work of the abbé Pluche, who denies that the artist is like the painter Zeuxis, merely piecing together various pre-existing beauties to form a whole. Beauty, he asserts, can be created out of ugliness. Beauty is in no sense imitation; it is creation: '[Elle n'a] rien qui la devance & qui l'annonce. C'est une création neuve [. . .] Elle provient du raisonnement & de l'intention de l'homme qui a mis entre ces matières détachées & désordonnées une union & une harmonie' (Pluche, 1751, pp. 237, 241).[26] Art acquires thus a metaphysical and not merely social function: 'Les arts sont une imitation de la conduite du Créateur' (Pluche, 1751, p. 258).[27]

In the common run of mid-century theory this creativity is not restricted to the artist. The sublime allows the reader to participate in the transports of poetic creation, just as, in theories of acting, the audience partook of the sweep of the heroic emotions in a kind of communion with the actor's and the author's genius: 'Pour sentir bien vivement les grandes beautés, il faut un peu du génie qui les a enfantées.'[28] In this passage it seems clear that the intersubjective space between audience and artist is being eliminated: the audience, which is now more isolated, more unknown, must feed on and appropriate the poet's emotions.

'La fureur de la logique'

The opening up of emotional possibilities for the reader through such concepts as 'illusion', the sublime and enthusiasm is counterbalanced if not contradicted by the most persistent explanation of pleasure in poetry to be found in the first half of the century, that of 'difficulté vaincue'. The enjoyment of poetry, according to this theory, lay in appreciating each poem as an answer to a technical problem and in admiring the elegance of the poet's solution. The enjoyment offered by this account is thus of a kind opposite to that allowed by the term 'illusion'. To be aware of difficulty is to be all awareness, uniquely attached to poetic form. The reader in fact recreates the poet's technical process, just as in theories of identification he participates in the poet's emotional process. As a result, the theory of 'difficulté vaincue' repeats *à propos* of form the structure of one of the theories of illusion.

In that the reader admires technical prowess, astonishment is part of the pleasure of 'difficulté vaincue' just as it was of 'illusion'. To understand technical perfection is to be capable of it, and La Motte can maintain: 'Les Poëtes ne peuvent être bien goûtés que par ceux qui ont comme eux le génie poëtique' (La Motte, letter to Fénelon, 15 février 1714, in La Motte, 1715, p. 64). Moreover, 'difficulté vaincue', like the sublime, contains an oscillation: 'On est touché de la difficulté qu'il y avoit à une pareille entreprise, & charmé qu'on ait sû en triompher' (Rémond de Saint Mard, 1749, vol. v, p. 102; 1734, p. 263).[29] The effect is one of being halted at the difficulty, and of delight at being able to move on once the difficulty has been vanquished. In order, then, to perform a function complementary to that of 'illusion', 'difficulté vaincue' has been endowed with a very similar structure. It is clearly a *papillotage*, in that technical brilliance displays itself at the expense of meaning – indeed the gap between intention and execution is exhibited rather than closed. This process, whereby enjoyment is seen to reside not in meaning itself but in the overcoming of difficulty, is comparable to the relation established much later, by the Rousseau of the *Dialogues*, between the primitive passions and their civilised replacements: 'Détournées de leur objet par des obstacles, elles s'occupent plus de l'obstacle pour l'écarter que de l'objet pour l'atteindre' (Rousseau, *O.C.*, vol. i, p. 669).

'Difficulté vaincue' is clearly related to the crisis about poetic form which arises with the *Querelle des Anciens et des Modernes* at the turn of the seventeenth century, but continues throughout the eighteenth. French prosody is of such strictness that to surmount its difficulties rather than to express something becomes the aim. 'Difficulté vaincue' supplies an answer to the question which, as we saw earlier in this section, most critics pose: why does the poet use the language he does? For Fontenelle the extreme difficulty of French prosody can alone justify the poet's abuse of language.[30] For Perrault, on the contrary, the difficulty consists precisely in eliminating the apparent abuse: 'Il est constant qu'une des grandes beautés de la Poësie consiste à dire les choses aussi naturellement & aussi clairement, malgré le nombre infini de difficultés qui s'y trouvent, que si l'on écrivoit en prose' (Perrault, 1693, vol. ii, p. 79). The opposition is however only apparent, for in both cases poetic form is held to be conventional, though the underlying ideas of convention are different. For Fontenelle, poetic form uselessly embroiders a basic meaning; for Perrault, poetic form is a set of conventional restrictions on expression. In both cases, there is no reductive notion of meaning present; poetry disguises nothing and there is no illusion. However, for La Motte and for his group poetic form is an illusion: 'Il m'arrive souvent d'aimer en vers ce que je ne ferois qu'approuver en prose'; and the illusion is derived from the

surprise provoked by the overcoming of the difficulty: 'La surprise
agréable [. . .] naît de la difficulté vaincue' (La Motte, 1754, vol. I,
part 2, p. 554). On the other hand, Rémond de Saint Mard defends
thus the conventional nature of poetic form, and dismisses free
verse as lacking in illusion: 'Comme la Poësie y est extrêmement
naturelle, rien n'y fait illusion, rien ne jette de la poudre aux yeux.
Ce plaisir de convention qui fait tant d'effet quand l'oreille y est
façonnée, la rime, n'y relève presque point l'éclat de ce qu'on a à
dire' (Rémond de Saint Mard, 1734, p. 291).[31] Where attack and
defence of poetry are in such close agreement, the defence can only
be ambivalent, and the whole business may collapse into 'a matter
of taste', into a discussion of whether the rules of poetry are to be
accepted or rejected (this is one of the antinomies that Kant
resolves in the *Critique of Judgement*).[32] If taste was arbitrary on an
individual level, convention was felt to be so on a social level.
Convention founds form in the theories of social contract, but in
poetics it is felt to trivialise form.

Fontenelle and La Motte, both of the *Modernes* party, reduce
poetic form to convention and then criticise it for being merely
conventional, as contrary to the truth which only exact expression
can engender.[33] La Motte's poetics was certainly interpreted at the
time as implying that awareness of form breaks the reader's involvement – in other words, that illusion and 'difficulté vaincue'
are incompatible. Of this commentary on *Télémaque*, a hostile
critic says: 'Le vrai sens de ces paroles rouloit sur ce que le *Télémaque* étant en vers auroit passé pour une fiction Poétique, au lieu
qu'étant en prose on le pouvoit prendre pour une véritable Histoire'
(Gacon, 1715, p. 367, an interpretation amply justified by other
passages in La Motte's writings). La Motte indeed makes the same
objection to a tragic heroine's speaking in verse as opponents of
opera do to song instead of speech: it is less credible (La Motte,
1754, vol. I, part 2, p. 556). The analogy with music is revealing: the
century is to experience closely related difficulties in assigning
meaning to poetic language and to musical form. Because verse is a
less 'credible' form than prose, because its convention breaks the
illusion, it inevitably trivialises what is expressed. In a similar way,
Prévost attacks Bouhier's comparison of poetic form to the dance:
if this were true, poets would be mere acrobats, and the only experience obtainable from their work would be that of pleasure in
'difficulté vaincue' (Prévost, *Pour et contre*, 1736, vol. 10, article
cxlvi). In critics of Prévost's persuasion, rhyme rather than rhythm
is held to be the defining element of poetry, and a whole series of

critics suggests a liberalising of French prosody by the use of poetic prose.[34]

But 'difficulté vaincue' is actually used by both sides, both to attack and to defend poetry, as Trublet makes clear.[35] Although the notion is apparently opposed to 'illusion', it is compatible with 'illusions', for La Motte's and Fontenelle's poetic practice is held by contemporaries to consist in self-conscious exploitation of conventions in a new 'preciosity'. It is a critical commonplace that by constantly bidding higher for novelty – a movement which has, significantly, the same structure as that associated with the sublime – La Motte and Fontenelle have sought novelty, 'le piquant', at any price in order to surpass their literary predecessors.[36] Yet their poetry is a manipulation of conventions in which they have no faith.[37] Their poetic practice and concept of poetry are thus intimately entwined: the difficulty of French poetry is overcome by a series of tricks which provoke in the reader momentary surprises followed by appreciation of the cleverness which had sparked off their astonishment.

The contemporary explanation for this self-consciousness is based on an opposition between creative and analytic process, held to have been generated by the 'esprit philosophique': 'M. de La Motte ne s'aperçoit point que l'esprit philosophique est absolument opposé à la poësie: que ce phlegme est bon pour juger mais inutile pour faire des Vers' (Fourmont, 1716, vol. II, p. 27). The opposition is not trivial: critics of the *Modernes* were right to relate their account of contemporary poetry to the concept of poetry which was in vogue. The 'esprit critique' they say, has created a climate intolerant of poetry; Diderot declared:

Partout décadence de la verve et de la poésie [. . .]. L'esprit philosophique veut des comparaisons plus resserrées, plus strictes, plus rigoureuses, sa marche circonspecte est ennemie du mouvement et des figures. Le règne des images passe à mesure que celui des choses s'étend. Il s'introduit par la raison une exactitude, une précision, une méthode, pardonnez-moi le mot, une sorte de pédanterie qui tue tout. (Diderot, *Salon de 1767*, p. 153)

Similarly, 'Et que voulez-vous que des arts qui ont tous pour base l'exagération et le mensonge deviennent parmi des hommes sans cesse occupés de réalités et ennemis par état des fantômes de l'imagination, que leur souffle fait disparaître' (Diderot, *Salon de 1769*, pp. 111–12). In the quotations above, however, it is clear that while the 'esprit philosophique' is attacked, nothing is offered to replace its concept of language and meaning; 'exagération', 'mensonge' have the same role as 'illusion' had in La

The poet's voice

Motte's poetics: Diderot remains within the aesthetic even while attacking it.

One of the prolongations of the *Querelle des Anciens et des Modernes* in mid-century takes the form of the literary survey: some enquirers struggle to prove that artistic progress has been made in the century (Bricaire de la Dixmérie, Méhégan); others contradict this, and lament poetry's fate, 'le sort de la poésie dans ce siècle philosophique' (Chabanon, 1764b). The politics of the quarrel are complex: those who are politically conservative act as the defenders of poetry, yet Diderot and Rousseau, for example, agree with them to a large extent. How far then do Diderot and Rousseau distinguish 'philosophie' from 'esprit philosophique' in the relation to poetry? That they both reject the intellectual *papillotage* of the 'esprit philosophique' is evident. But the Platonic temptation, to denounce all imitation, even poetic, is also present. Rousseau bases his *De l'imitation théâtrale*, and Diderot his *Preface* to the *Salon de 1767*, on the *Republic*. From this tension there stems the ambivalent attitude to the novel in the *Préfaces* to *La Nouvelle Héloïse* as well as the constant interplay between art as lie and art as truth in Diderot's aesthetics.

The politics of the quarrel need to be related to the larger issue of the contemporary view of cultural history, and of the eighteenth century's place in it. The 'esprit philosophique' is set by hostile critics within a cyclic view of cultures: they grow, blossom and die.[38] The 'esprit philosophique' is not merely a state of the cycle: it is both a product and an acceleration of decadence. But as symptom or cause of these cycles, critics propose economic factors. Fénelon had protested against affluence, 'luxe', and Mandeville in *The Fable of the Bees* had satirised the view that the manufacture of luxury goods is favourable to art and literature in that it provides necessary conditions for their development. Mandeville's work, however, was not always seen by contemporaries to be a satire. Voltaire and Cartaud, in the 1730s, still seek to relate 'luxe' and the fine arts. Affluence is associated by them with politeness, with civilised manners, with badinage, and hence with *papillotage*. But 'luxe' is increasingly also related to decadence, to the enervation of force and energy. Diderot, for example, blames artistic decadence on economic circumstance, both directly (*Le Neveu de Rameau*) and indirectly, through the intellectual climate which he says is created by an obsession with financial activity (*Le Salon de 1769*). The poetic ideal in fact moves from one of politeness to one of force: the sharpening historical sense behind the concept of

225

decadence generates a less muddy idea of energy than the sublime was able to convey. For the sublime was never really in opposition to 'esprit philosophique', but was merely its opposite in the same system; it was already neutralised: its écarts' were in fact 'retours'. It was a 'logique de la fureur' whose counterweight was merely the 'fureur de la logique' denounced by Saint Mard.[39] These are interdependent concepts, complements operating within the same aesthetic space. Later critics can dismiss, rightly, pleasure in 'difficulté vaincue' as too conscious, as 'gothic', in other words, arbitrarily elaborate, offering mere 'plaisir de réflexion'. 'Difficulté vaincue' in its *papillotage* between obstacle and overcoming of obstacle merely repeated on a technical level the structure of the sublime which, in its elaborate system of permitted *écarts*, endorsed and controlled the poetic voice.

9

WHY DOES THE POET USE THE LANGUAGE HE USES?

'Illusion' and poetic voice

Poetic theory in the early part of the century is cast largely in terms of structure. As has already been pointed out, many critics discuss, for instance, whether poetry can be written without strict rhythm and without rhyme (a problem given acuity by Fénelon's *Télémaque*: the French epic existed at last, but in prose). The partisans of rhyme compare poetic form to the dance, but with none of the depth found in contemporary theories of language, where the ritual origins of poetry and dance are taken into account (Voltaire, Kehl, vol. I, p. 342; d'Olivet, 1738, p. 153). Indeed, for Voltaire and d'Olivet, French poetry has been reduced to such utter simplicity that rhyme and transpositions are necessary to demarcate poetry from prose (Voltaire, Kehl, vol. I, p. 341; d'Olivet, 1738, p. 76). Another school of critics, whether writing for or against poetic prose, insists that it is the actual type of language which is distinctive: 'Ce sont des mots anciens, des mots détournez de leur signification naturelle, plus figurez, plus énergiques, plus doux ou plus rudes que les termes qui s'employent dans l'usage ordinaire pour signifier la même chose' (Fraguier, 1731, pp. 425–6).[1] Ramsay's defence of *Télémaque* proclaims: 'Ce qui fait la Poësie n'est pas le nombre fixe et la cadence réglée des syllabes mais la fiction vive, les figures hardies, la beauté, la variété des images' (Ramsay in Fénelon, 1719, p. xxvii). In the course of the century, the distinguishing feature of a poem in critics' minds moves from the formal structure (rhythm, rhyme) to the metaphor (a transition parallel to that in the associated linguistic theory, where interest moves from order to word) and then to the sound of the word. It is this transition which will in the next century grant autonomy to poetic language, and remove the problem of the poetic voice.

In the *Grammaire* (1660) and *Logique* (1662) of Port-Royal, syntax is the main bearer of meaning and ensures an 'adequation' between language, thought and reality – Arnauld and Nicole are thus able to refute Hobbes' contention that both vocabulary and syntax are a product of human discourse, and that truth is a property of a relation between propositions rather than a product of a relation between propositions and reality (Arnauld and Nicole, 1965, p. 43). For Port-Royal, translation is not a problem, since the deep structure which generates meaning can be mapped on to any particular surface structure (Chomsky, 1966, pp. 33ff.). The liveliness commonly attributed to the 'stile figuré' is taken to derive from the fact that it conveys affect as well as meaning: 'Les expressions figurées signifient, outre la chose principale, le mouvement & la passion de celui qui parle, & impriment ainsi l'une & l'autre idée dans l'esprit, au lieu que l'expression simple ne marque la vérité toute nue' (Arnauld and Nicole, 1965, p. 96). But in the second half of the eighteenth century, the word will be held to derive its power from its sound and from its etymology, independently to some degree of the man who uses it. In discussions of poetry, this view will eliminate the question of who is speaking, of the poet's voice.

It is the concern for word order as the bearer of meaning which lies behind the passionate eighteenth-century debates on whether Latin or French represents the 'natural' order.[2] The most famous, which awaits further investigation, centres upon Diderot's *Lettre sur les sourds et muets* of 1751, which is part of his complex reply to Batteux. Batteux had in 1748 written the *Lettre à M. d'Olivet* which replied to Dumarsais' theories on word order (Ricken, 1978, pp. 131ff.). Beauzée, the grammarian of the *Encyclopédie*, had replied, and in turn Batteux answers him and Diderot. For Port-Royal, for Dumarsais and for Beauzée, French was the 'natural' order, the order which corresponds most closely with the true, logical relation between ideas.[3] However other critics' considerations are more directly aesthetic. Batteux struggles to show that Latin is the 'natural' order because he believes that the phonic poverty of a language can be compensated for by word arrangement, which in his theory is thus not so much a factor in the creation of meaning as an element in the creation of aesthetic effect.[4] (Fénelon, whose reflexions on the problems facing French poetry are incomparably more profound than those of other writers of his time, maintains that the attempt to avoid inversions impoverishes both the sound value and the expressive matter of poetry.)[5] Diderot's *Lettre sur les sourds et muets*, answering Batteux, picks up the question of inversions. But Diderot tackles the question in such a way that the force of individual words becomes the main issue, and he is led to deal both with the poet's mind and with the effect of words on the hearer (cf. Todorov, 1977, pp. 165–6).

Metaphor

If many *grammairien-philosophes* tended to assume, in the earlier part of the century, that an inverted word order would have to be decoded by the hearer/reader, the attitude to metaphor was similar. La Motte presents this view, not as his own but all too plausibly:

Pourquoi ne pas dire à la lettre ce qu'on veut dire, au lieu de ne présenter une chose, que pour servir d'occasion à en faire penser une autre? Pour les Figures, ceux qui ne cherchent que la vérité ne leur sont pas favorables, & ils les regardent comme des pièges que l'on tend à l'esprit pour le séduire. (La Motte, 1754, vol. I, part 1, p. 15)

But such attitudes are often placed in a historical context: 'L'Excès choquant de Ronsard nous a un peu jettés dans l'extrémité opposée. On a appauvri, desséché & gêné notre Langue. Elle n'ose jamais procéder que suivant la méthode la plus scrupuleuse & la plus uniforme de la Grammaire' (Fénelon, 1718, pp. 317–18).[6] Moreover, contact with oriental literatures, and in particular the placing of the Bible in a historical and geographical context, leads later to historical understanding of the impatience with metaphor. Arnaud, in a note to Turgot's commentary on Ossian, suggests that had the Bible influenced the constitution of the French language (as the Koran did that of Arabic, and, one may add, as did Luther and the Authorised Version that of modern German and English), then perhaps the 'stile figuré' would not have been so separated from the tone and form of common speech.[7] To most seventeenth- and early eighteenth-century critics, the oriental style seemed unanalytic, even illogical: 'Leur esprit tout de feu ne peut se contenter d'un seul sens dans un discours [. . .]. Les esprits du pays où nous sommes [. . .] ne veulent ou ne peuvent comprendre qu'une seule chose à la fois, encore faut-il qu'elle soit exprimée bien nettement et avec une grande précision' (Perrault, 1693, vol. II, p. 44). This near-boasting of the logical simplicity of French – the positive version of the 'esprit philosophique' to be criticised a few decades later – might appear silly, were it not for the epistemological concern over fifty years later with the problem of whether one can think of more than one thing at a time – a problem Diderot approaches in the *Lettre sur les sourds et muets*

Illusion and theories of poetry

(cf. also Hobson, 1977b). Condillac, writing later than Fénelon, relates the poetic impoverishment of French to a later stage than does Fénelon, and sees it as a result not of rationalist use of language, but of preciosity (one and the same thing, in fact, in the works of La Motte and Fontenelle). The impoverishment is, says Condillac, a result of excessive refinement, where the search for new methods of expression – 'le principe de vie' – becomes destructive (Condillac, 1947, p. 102). And indeed, the *arts poétiques* of the end of the eighteenth century take the form not of rhetorics but of considerations on the decadence of poetry, and on the reasons for linguistic and poetic poverty in particular. (An interesting example of this genre is Chénier's unfinished *Essai sur les causes et les effets de la perfection et de la décadence des lettres et des arts*.)

Although Fénelon's diagnosis was essentially accurate, it did not effect a cure. For at least the earlier part of the century, metaphor was held to be a complicated way of saying something essentially more simple, and expressible more simply. Voltaire's comparison of Racine's *Phèdre* with Pradon's assumes this: 'C'est pourtant dans les deux le même fonds de sentiment et de pensées' (Voltaire, Kehl, vol. I, pp. 228–9), as does Pope's 'What oft was thought, but ne'er so well expressed' (Pope, *An Essay on Criticism*, l.298). A way out of this concept of the relation of language to thought is suggested by the work of Dumarsais: tropes are a transference, a twisting of words away from their original significance. In the context of his general grammatical theory, which is concerned with transformation of syntactic relations, this is a much more profound view than his reliance on 'original significance' might lead one to suppose. But Dumarsais died leaving his work incomplete.

If there is a basic meaning or thought which is dressed up or expressed by metaphor, translation poses no problem. One of the focal points of the *Querelle des Anciens et des Modernes* is Madame Dacier's translation of Homer and La Motte's adaptation of it. Madame Dacier insists that there are nuances in the Greek which cannot be expressed in French: La Motte replies to the criticism that he undertook the adaptation without knowing Greek, by saying that he had supposed every elegance in the original. The arbitrariness of the association between word and idea, with the accompanying assumption that there is a common stock of ideas (as distinct from relations, as in the Port-Royal theory), is the commonplace of modernist defences of French and of attacks on the *Anciens'* notion that Greek is in the last resort untranslatable. It is an arbitrator of the Homer quarrel, Fourmont, who puts the problem most forcibly, in a critique of La Motte. The latter had maintained that his criticism of Homer was in fact addressed to Homer's thought, not his expression (which he could not read). Fourmont replied: 'La question seroit donc de savoir si le fond des choses dont il prétend juger, n'est point tellement lié aux expressions, qu'il en dépende totalement ou pour la plus grande partie' (Fourmont, 1716, vol. i, p. 43).

Marivaux's whole creation was an answer to this problem, as the attacks made on him show. He is attacked both for preciosity – by which his contemporaries mean his attempt to forge variations in syntax which will convey his precise meaning (Marivaux, 1969, p. 385) – and for his neologisms – a refusal to accept meaning pre-solidified. The account of the child learning a language becomes a model for him:

Que cet enfant retienne tous les mots qu'il entend dire, on le comprend; mais que de chaque mot qui ne va jamais seul, et que nous mettons toujours avec d'autres il parvienne à en saisir le sens que nous ne lui disons jamais, il entre dans cette opération-là plus de façons qu'on ne se l'imagine: c'est presque deviner et non pas apprendre, c'est un secret entre la nature et lui qui n'est guère explicable. Un cerveau tendre, une âme neuve, vide d'idées, plus étonnée qu'elle ne le sera jamais des sons que nous articulons et qui la frappent, par conséquent plus attentive qu'on ne peut le dire à l'air et à la manière dont nous prononçons les mots, cherchant à savoir à quoi ils aboutissent et ce qu'ils signifient et le cherchant avec une curiosité dont l'exactitude, la finesse et l'activité ne se retrouvent plus, et ne sont jamais attachées qu'aux premiers étonnements que l'âme éprouve, voilà vraisemblablement ce qui met encore un enfant en état de s'éclairer sur les mots de sa langue. (Marivaux, 1969, p. 479)

The model for the relation between language and meaning is that between the hazards of existence and the awakening mind. The mind construes the world just as the expressions and the gestures of the women envious of Marianne's beauty in the novel *La Vie de Marianne* are translated into actual phrases. His contemporaries' suspicion of originality, says Marivaux, has meant that it is possible to express only what they know already, a point made in reported speech. This typical twisting or translation of words into other words, or of gestures into words, reflects, in the very texture of Marivaux's writing, the self-commentary which is one part of his weaving of the relation between language and meaning.

Metaphor and illusion

In 1726 Rollin actually gives the reader he is instructing in rhetoric a series of classical figures and their translations: 'Pour dire *il n'y avait point eu encore de guerre*: on n'avoit point encore entendu le son effrayant des trompettes ni le bruit pétillant des épées qu'on forge sur les enclumes' (Rollin, 1726–8, vol. I, p. 290). In fact he answers a possible objection to metaphor for its lack of truth by insisting on the meaning behind the metaphor: 'En effet, loin que toutes ces figures, quand elles sont emploiées sagement, fassent aucune illusion à l'esprit; ce sont toutes manières de parler vives & majestueuses qui expriment sensiblement & en peu de mots ce qu'on ne pouvoit dire que froidement par un plus long circuit de paroles' (Rollin, 1726–8, vol. I, p. 261). There are signs that by mid-century this conception of metaphor as a decoding and recoding is thought of as forcing on the reader a movement between code and message, and as such it is connected with *papillotage*. Some writers now tend to insist that metaphor should provoke illusion. Marmontel, whose whole aesthetic is based on illusion, denies that there is any transference or displacement of meaning in metaphor and insists instead on the adequation of language to reality: 'Cet équivalent universel des signes des Arts, la parole, fait au commun des hommes assez d'illusion pour les émouvoir au même degré que le souvenir le plus fidèle, & pour reproduire aux yeux de l'âme l'univers physique & moral' (Marmontel, 1763, vol. I, p. 43). The adequation between poetry and reality is ensured here for Marmontel by the essentially visual means poetry is held to use. The term 'peinture' suggests this in the early poetics of the century. In the poetics of mid-century the implications of the term are made sharper (as in the Marmontel passage just quoted) and as a result rejected by the most original critics. But this will take some time. For vision is the model for mental processes (even for Diderot, 'notre âme est un tableau mouvant': *Lettre sur les sourds et muets*, p. 543). 'Penser, à parler en général, c'est former en soi la peinture d'un objet ou spirituel ou sensible' (Rollin, 1726–8, vol. II, p. 174). Most writers limit tropes to images, following Dubos:

Tout ce qui n'est pas sentiment veut autant que la nature du poème & la vraisemblance le permettent nous être représenté sous des images qui forment des tableaux dans notre imagination. Il faut donc que nous croyions voir pour ainsi dire en écoutant des vers. Ut Pictura Poesis, dit Horace. (Dubos, 1719, vol. I, p. 265)[8]

And for the images to be possible, to be adequate to an actual situation, we have to be inspired, in a state of illusion: 'Les images sont des discours que nous prononçons, lorsque par une espèce

232

d'enthousiasme ou émotion extraordinaire de l'âme, nous croyons voir les choses dont nous parlons & que nous tâchons de les peindre aux yeux de ceux qui nous écoutent' (*Encyclopédie*, article *Image*). The tropes that take on the greatest force are two: one visual – hypotyposis – and one of speech – prosopopœia: '*L'Hypotypose* est une figure qui peint l'image des choses dont on parle avec des couleurs si vives qu'on s'imagine les voir de ses propres yeux, et non simplement en entendre le récit' (Rollin, 1726–8, vol. i, p. 282). 'La règle constante et invariable, pour l'emploi de ce qu'on appelle l'hypotypose, et la prosopopée, est donc l'*apparence du délire*: hors de là plus de vraisemblance; & la preuve que celui qui emploie ces mouvemens du style est dans l'illusion, c'est le geste & le ton qu'il y met' (Marmontel, 1763, vol. i, p. 158). In these circumstances the poet can be taken literally, and illusion has become adequation.[9]

But metaphor works both ways round, so to speak: '[elle] donne tout à la fois, & de l'âme aux choses matérielles [prosopopée] & du corps aux pensées métaphysiques [hypotypose]' (d'Olivet, 1738, p. 155; cf. Chicaneau de Neuville, 1758, p. 6). 'La prosopopée consiste à faire parler un mort, une personne absente, ou même les choses inanimées' (Dumarsais, 1775, p. 8). For Marmontel, it derives its effect from benevolent self-interest, as did the audience's identification with the suffering hero, in the acting theory of the time: 'Cet intérêt universel répandu dans la Poésie, le plaisir de nous trouver partout avec nos semblables, de voir que tout sent, que tout pense, que tout agit comme nous.' But this pleasure can be obtained only by the poet's illusion (Marmontel, 1763, vol. i, p. 155).[10]

A quarrel about the 'récit de Théramène', in the last act of Racine's *Phèdre*, and in particular, about the line:

Le flot qui l'apporta recule épouvanté

runs from La Motte to at least Diderot and the *Lettre sur les sourds et muets*. The quarrel centres on whether the speech and the line should be justified as an example of hypotyposis, as vivid imagery, or as an example of personification – a variety of prosopopœia. Dumarsais treats the whole speech as an example of hypotyposis, but he is doubtful whether to include the figure among tropes at all, precisely because its words retain their normal meaning and do not have to be decoded (Dumarsais, 1775, p. 151). For Marmontel, personification could be justified only if the poet appeared to be inspired beyond the normal bounds of language, so that he could in some sense be taken literally. Thus d'Olivet had defended Théramène's speech in *Phèdre* against rationalist attack by main-

taining that it was literal, an expression of ancient science: 'Ainsi
le langage de la Poësie fut originairement le langage de la
Physique, ou du moins ne fut qu'une conséquence & une extension
des idées généralement reçues par les plus célèbres Physiciens'
(d'Olivet, 1738, p. 100). The commonplace that the literal meanings of words are dead metaphors has been inverted: metaphors
are dead literal meanings. But d'Olivet's defence exposes Racine
to attack on different grounds: he has chosen a 'system' of imagery
which is outside the beliefs of his century.[11] And Desfontaines in
his reply to d'Olivet, *Racine vengé*, describes the implication that
the poet believes nature to be anthropomorphic as nonsense: 'La
figure, renfermée dans le vers de Théramène, est toute naturelle.
C'est l'expression de la passion & l'écoulement, pour ainsi dire,
d'une imagination émuë' (Desfontaines, 1739, p. 116). (It was
Rousseau, and not Desfontaines, who developed and deepened
the age-old relation indicated here between metaphor and passion;
Jean-Jacques will interpret it as the weaving of an individual
subjectivity.) But against accounts of this type, Marmontel represents, as we have seen, the tendency to cut out from the idea of
metaphor any concept of transference of meaning. He contrasts
images unfavourably with description: 'La Poësie elle-même perd
souvent à préférer le coloris de l'image au coloris de l'objet. La
ceinture de Vénus, cette allégorie si ingénieuse est encore bien
inférieure à la peinture naïve et simple de la beauté dont elle est le
symbole' (Marmontel, 1763, p. 193). The radical restriction of the
power of language, this insistence on transparency through description rather than tropes, can be related to the tendency in
other arts to negate the medium, to present the model as immediate. Illusion in Marmontel thus at once justifies metaphor and
negates it, for it denies that it displaces meaning. However, I shall
show that, taken as a mistake on the consumer's part, and given
extreme subjective force, it mediates a crucial change in the
century's idea of poetic language.

Illusion, enargeia, energeia

Description and image are, then, contrasted by Marmontel, the
former giving a transparency the latter does not have: 'L'image,
comme je l'ai définie est le voile matériel d'une idée au lieu que la
description et le tableau ne sont le plus souvent que le miroir de
l'objet même' (Marmontel, 1763, vol. I, p. 169).[12] The image must
be more than a mere description of the object; it must be more
striking, or it can be dispensed with: 'Sans quoi l'imagination écar-

The poet's language

terait ce voile insolite' (Marmontel, 1763, vol. I, p. 188). As already suggested, the visual bias in this theory is evident: meaning is given, like an object, not expressed, still less created; its transmission is the same process through whichever medium, just as, in the common-or-garden sensualist epistemology of the time, the different senses give the same information. *Adequatio* is required rather than *aletheia*; Marmontel wants a reciprocal mirror relation rather than a movement out from the metaphor, the 'voile matériel', towards the 'idée'. Marmontel, then, distinguishes image and description in terms of their effect. Caylus, the antiquarian and art critic, rolls them together into the notion of 'peinture', a word which treats indifferently of internal or external image, and which handles both as discrete units. Caylus uses the resulting countability in laying down a standard for poetry:

Plus un poème fournissait d'images et d'actions plus il avait de supériorité en poésie. Cette réflexion m'avait conduit à penser que le calcul des différents tableaux qu'offrent les poèmes pouvoit servir à comparer le mérite respectif des poèmes et des poètes. (Caylus, quoted Lessing, *Laokoon*, 1967, p. 110)

The more 'pictures' a poem supplies, the better it is – a view which takes no account of the medium, but assumes immediate transparency of meaning. This simplistic account of a painting's effect is in fact based on a complex code of references, which are ignored the better to be exploited, as Lessing points out in his attack on Caylus in the *Laokoon* (in many respects analogous to his attack on Voltaire: see above, pp. 172ff.). Grimm criticises the ineptitude of the French opera in making visible the invisible. Lessing criticises Caylus for taking literally the cloud in which Homer wrapped the gods and making it into painting's means of representation of the invisible – a hieroglyph which signals to the onlooker 'you must imagine the invisible', a reference out beyond what the picture represents, a *papillotage*. He goes on to distinguish a specifically poetic picture: 'A poetic picture is not necessarily that which can be transmuted into a material painting; but every feature, every combination of features by means of which the poet makes his subject so perceptible that we are more clearly conscious of this subject than of his words is called pictorial, is styled a picture, because it brings us nearer to the degree of illusion (*Illusion*) of which the material painting is specially capable and which can most readily and most easily be drawn from the material painting' (Lessing, *Laokoon*, 1970, p. 53). Although Lessing is insisting on the difference between poetry and painting, his use of 'illusion' shows

235

that, like Grimm and Diderot, he is concerned to efface awareness of the medium, words. This is confirmed by a later passage: '[The poet] desires rather to make the ideas awakened by him within us living things, so that for the moment we realise the true sensuous impressions of the objects he describes, and cease in this moment of illusion (*Taüschung*) to be conscious of the means – namely, his words – which he employs for his purpose' (Lessing, *Laokoon*, 1970, pp. 60–1). The transparency is a result of the clarity of sensuous effect. Lessing here apparently remains within the tradition of *evidentia*, in which illusion and image are related to visual clarity. This tradition is not, bizarrely, so far removed from the assimilation of poetry and painting through their effect which Caylus makes with his use of the term 'peinture'. But Lessing's own work in fact begins to undermine this aesthetic – he uses the word *lebhaft*, 'living'; moreover, in a note, he links 'peinture' and 'illusion' to concepts of classical rhetoric, to *phantasia* and *enargeia*. 'What we call poetic pictures, the Ancients called Fantasy, as will be clear to the reader from Longinus. And what we call illusion or deceptiveness in these pictures, was called by them Enargeia' (Lessing, *Laokoon*, 1967, p. 111, my translation). Classically, both *phantasia* and *enargeia* are concerned with visualisation, with *evidentia*, but also with power, with fantasy in the modern sense, and with *energeia*, energy; traditionally (a tradition going back to Quintilian), *enargeia* and *energeia* are close enough to be confused in the transmission of texts,[13] and this is no doubt the reason for Lessing's use of *lebhaft*, a word which introduces the notion of force. This shift, unwitting in Lessing, will become conscious in Herder's attack on him.

The transmutation of 'peinture' into phantasy, and 'illusion' into *energeia*, is more easily seen in these German critics, because their discussion turns on these very points. Later, however, I shall discuss a sensualist and atomistic version of the same shift which takes place round Condillac's concept of 'signe naturel'. In that respect, it is interesting that Herder in the *Erstes Wäldchen* (1769) attacks Lessing's account of language as atomistic, that is, as implying the treatment of sensations and words as so many separate, discrete particles. Just as Kant was to attack Hume's associative concept of time as a succession of sensations (and Herder attended many of Kant's lectures) so Herder criticised Lessing's account of poetry: 'A melodic chain of tones can never be called a chain of actions' (Herder, 1878, vol. III, p. 139). On the contrary, it is not succession but force, energy, which constitutes the effect of poetry:

'Power which is concomitant with the word, power which does indeed enter through the ear, but which works directly on the soul. It is this power which is the essence of poetry, not coexistence or successiveness' (Herder, 1878, vol. III, p. 137). This power is not associative, not a stringing together of separate impressions. By using the ancient confusion of *enargeia* with *energeia*, Herder replaces *evidentia* (the Latin translation of *enargeia*), clarity of depiction, by energy of depiction. Visualisation in illusion has shifted from static to dynamic. Herder binds together in this way the sensuous representation of the spatial arts and an energy which is the soul's translation of impressions into power. As a result, the blurring of outer and inner, inherent in Caylus' term 'peinture', residual in Lessing, is abolished – the poet works directly on the reader's soul, *enargeia* becomes *energeia*, *phantasia*, *Phantasie*: 'I learn from Homer that the effect of poetry does not work on the ear through tones, not on the memory, for the length of time I can retain a particular trait out of the succession of traits, but on my fantasy [. . .]. I regret that Herr Lessing did not take this focal point of the essence of poetry, "Effect on the soul, energy" for the object of his sight' (Herder, 1878, vol. III, p. 157). *Phantasie* has taken on the modern sense of 'imagination'. And the type of illusion provoked in the reader must change accordingly, for the notion of subjectivity is constituted in reaction to the sensationist concept of the self as a bundle of sensations (just as the word is a bundle of arbitrary meanings, and the external object is a bundle of attributes). This offers a richer notion of 'illusion', and one which moves outside the word's earlier semantic field. For poetry deceives the *Phantasie*:

Painting intends to deceive the eye, but poetry to deceive the fantasy; not in a literal fashion, so that I recognise the thing by its description, but so that each representation works to the purpose for which the poet puts it before me. The work of art and the poet's energy must be measured by this purpose. The artist works through forms for the duration of one's looking at the work, to achieve illusion for the eye; but the poet works through the spiritual power of words in successive moments to achieve the fullest illusion in the soul. (Herder, 1878, vol. III, pp. 158–9)

'Illusion' here designates less a deception than a subjectivity, less a mistake than the internal nature of imaginative experience.[14]

Condillac

In Herder's reaction to Lessing, that part of the theory of illusion which insisted on the clarity of the transmission of state of mind was uppermost, so that the notion of 'Illusion' (*Taüschung*) was becoming internal. The notion of 'deception' is being transformed into the idea of a subjectivity, which does not perhaps correspond to the world, but is nevertheless individual and justified (not a bundle of impressions, but organically organised). In France, Rousseau's account of the development of metaphor shows the same change in the notion of 'illusion': 'Le langage figuré', he writes in the *Essai sur l'origine des langues*, 'fut le premier à naître, le sens propre fut trouvé le dernier' (Rousseau, *Essai*, p. 505). 'Sens propre' is not chronologically prior. Rousseau imagines primitive man encountering others of whom he was frightened; he would, says Rousseau, first call them 'giants' and only later men: 'L'image illusoire offerte par la passion se montrant la première, le langage qui lui répondait fut aussi le premier inventé; il devint ensuite métaphorique quand l'esprit éclairé, reconnaissant sa première erreur, n'en employa les expressions que dans les mêmes passions qui l'avaient produite' (*Essai*, p. 506). 'Illusion' in language is thus here true in relation to subjective experience: the 'langage figuré' was in fact literal, but becomes metaphorical by development in usage. This contradiction of received eighteenth-century opinion, this paradox, makes of metaphor not a decoding but a transference of meaning: 'Pour m'entendre, il faut substituer l'idée que la passion nous présente au mot que nous transposons; car on ne transpose les mots que parce qu'on transpose aussi les idées: autrement le langage figuré ne signifierait rien' (*Essai*, p. 506).

Condillac was close to Rousseau in the 1740s. Like Rousseau, he was interested in the force of poetic language, as the second part of his first work, *Essai sur l'origine des connaissances humaines* (1746), makes plain: prosody, gesture, 'l'art des pantomimes', music, inversions and metaphors are discussed in relation to their non-discursive, expressive value. All this lies at the surface of the text, and has been much studied, especially in relation to Warburton's *Divine Legation of Moses* (see Derrida, 1977). Condillac's relation of language to illusion, although less explicit than Rousseau's, is none the less present in the *Essai*. Indeed, as as I hope to show, the structure of the contemporary theory of illusion underlies Condillac's description, in the *Essai*, of the whole evolution of the mental faculties in general. In the first part there is a constant recourse to aesthetic examples, which is not accidental, but points to a more deeply imbedded feature of the work. It is as if the work were proposing a subjacent model for the mind's grappling with experience, a model which is closely related to theories of 'illusion'.

The central mental power in the account Condillac gives of the genesis of the faculties is *attention* (cf. Tort, 1976, p. 493). It is worth seeing why this is so. Condillac insists that all perceptions are conscious (though we may forget them).[15] As a result he has to introduce consciousness a second time, so to say, to explain why we can exclude awareness of certain objects to concentrate almost exclusively on others. This power he names attention, and to explain its mode of operation, he introduces a version of his contemporaries' theory of illusion:

L'Illusion qui se fait au théâtre en est la preuve. Il y a des momens où la conscience ne paroît pas se partager entre l'action qui se passe et le reste du spectacle. Il sembleroit d'abord que l'illusion devroit être d'autant plus vive, qu'il y auroit moins d'objets capables de distraire. Cependant chacun a pu remarquer qu'on n'est jamais plus porté à se croire le seul témoin d'une scène intéressante, que quand le spectacle est bien rempli. C'est peut-être que le nombre, la variété et la magnificence des objets remuent les sens, échauffent, élèvent l'imagination et par là nous rendent plus propres aux impressions que le poète veut faire naître. (Condillac, 1947, p. 11)

Consistently with his theory of perception, he denies that consciousness interrupts involvement. On the contrary, a dim awareness of the audience reinforces the movement out of the self: 'Il s'y livrera [. . .] plus volontiers.' As in contemporary theatre theory, consciousness of the reactions of other members of the audience is permanent and increases involvement (cf. above, p. 186). Condillac has embedded this account in his very theory of attention. He then introduces a power which *suspends* (rather than which interrupts, as in much aesthetic theory), which is a kind of consciousness to the second degree, and which he denotes *attention*. Attention is claimed by what has affinity with us (what *interests* us, as the contemporary aestheticians say): 'Les choses attirent notre attention par le côté où elles ont le plus de rapport avec notre tempérament, nos passions et notre état' (*Essai*, p. 13). From attention derives *réminiscence*, an awareness that the perceptions have been ours before; we know this from their relation with 'le sentiment de notre être', and this awareness is common to animals and men. But also from attention derive three 'operations' of the mind – imagination, contemplation, and memory – which are not found in animals. They are peculiar to man in that they depend largely on signs which are accidentally connected with the incident which will be imagined, contemplated or remembered.[16] With the development of institutional signs as opposed to accidental signs, *réflexion* becomes possible. Reflexion has the same relation to the materials supplied by imagination, contemplation and memory as, at a more primary level, attention had to perception. As if to mark this, Condillac illustrates once again with an example taken from aesthetics:

Aussitôt que la mémoire est formée et que l'exercice de l'imagination est à notre pouvoir, les signes que celle-là rappelle et les idées que celle-ci réveille, commencent à retirer l'âme de la dépendance où elle étoit de tous les objets qui agissoient sur elle [. . .]. A la vue d'un tableau, par exemple, nous nous rappelons les connoissances que nous avons de la nature, et des règles qui apprennent à l'imiter; et nous portons notre attention successivement de ce tableau à ces connoissances, et de ces connoissances à ce tableau, ou tour à tour à ses différentes parties. (Condillac, 1947, pp. 21–2)

The ability to pull a perception into full clarity of consciousness, to compare it with knowledge (memory) or with what could have been (imagination), to leave other perceptions only in a 'ticking over' state and then to turn attention away – this is what gives freedom of reflexion to man: a freedom to produce and annihilate our own perceptions. If *réflexion* is structurally analogous to *attention* it is similarly analogous in structure to theories of illusion.

The aesthetic example has suggested this analogy to Condillac: it is confirmed by the close relation which his account of the development of reflexion bears to that language in which voluntary aesthetic illusion is discussed by critics:

L'effet de cette opération [réflexion] est d'autant plus grand que par elle nous disposons de nos perceptions, à peu près comme si nous avions le pouvoir de les produire & de les anéantir. Que, parmi celles que j'éprouve actuellement, j'en choisisse une, aussitôt la conscience en est si vive et celle des autres si foible, qu'*il me paroîtra qu'elle est la seule dont j'aie pris connoissance* [. . .] *on diroit que la réflexion suspend à son gré les impressions qui se font dans l'âme*, pour n'en conserver qu'une seule. (Condillac, 1947, pp. 22–3)

The structure of reflexion here relates to that of voluntary involvement: it is a preoccupation with one impression against a background of awareness. Like Condillac's account of *attention*, *réflexion* suspends awareness of other impressions rather than interrupts them.

Perhaps the most striking illustration of the way in which the model of aesthetic illusion pervades Condillac's thinking in the *Essai* occurs in his discussion of *abstractions*. This starts out in a way reminiscent of conventional post-Lockean criticisms of the mind's (particularly the philosophic mind's) hypostatisation of ideas through the mistaking of words for essences. But as Condillac explicitly admits, the process is a necessary one for any intellectual activity. This process resembles that of attention and reflexion in Condillac's account but it goes yet further towards the underlying aesthetic model. The mind, in order to examine and reflect on its modifications, must first distinguish them, and this it does by contrasting the flux of psychic modifications against a background sensation of permanent being. But how is this possible, when for Condillac, this being itself consists precisely in a flux of modifications: 'Il est certain que ces modifications, distinguées de la sorte de l'être qui en est le sujet, n'ont plus aucune réalité. Cependant l'esprit ne peut pas réfléchir sur rien; car ce serait proprement ne pas réfléchir'? The problem is solved by the mind's contradicting itself:

[Il] continue de les regarder comme des êtres. Accoûtumé, toutes les fois qu'il les considère comme étant à lui, à les apercevoir avec la réalité de son être, dont pour lors elles ne sont pas distinctes, il leur conserve autant qu'il peut cette même réalité dans le temps même qu'il les en distingue. Il se contredit: d'un côté il envisage ses modifications sans aucun rapport à son être, et elles ne sont plus rien; d'un autre côté, parce que le néant ne peut se saisir, il les regarde comme quelque chose, et continue de leur attribuer cette même réalité avec laquelle il les a d'abord aperçues, quoiqu'elle ne puisse plus leur convenir. (Condillac, 1947, p. 50).

There is a kind of identification here: 'Or toutes ces idées présentent une vraie réalité, puisqu'elles ne sont proprement que notre être différemment modifié, car nous ne saurions rien apercevoir en nous que nous ne le regardions comme à nous, comme appartenant à notre être, ou comme étant notre être de telle ou de telle façon' (Condillac, 1947, p. 50). But the identification is simultaneously contradicted by the awareness that the modifications are not real. The pattern of involvement followed by awareness that involvement is illusory is surely a profound version of contemporary theories of aesthetic illusion. This remarkable passage shows how Condillac uses 'illusion' both as involvement *and* as distance in order to structure man's intellectual life and, *ipso facto*, his use of signs.

One can indeed wonder if Condillac's whole account of natural signs (the first language) and of the source of their power does not take illusion as its model. The force of the first human modes of expression lies in the fact that they are both symptom and sign. As symptoms, these gestures or noises are a part of the experience itself; as signs, they refer to that emotion. Likewise in relation to the hearer, as a symptom gesture has immediate instinctual effect (see the account of pity in the preceding chapter); as a sign it is mediate, and can be used on other occasions: it *imitates* the original symptom (*Essai*, p. 61). As a series of signs, the first language of gesture and cries ensures both repeatability (a condition of language), and distance from experience. As a symptom it guarantees meaning in that it is caused by that experience, is part of it. This combination of significatory and causal function in Condillac's account of the effect of the first language (cries, gesture and music) is obvious in his account of Ancient music: 'Aussi vit-on ceux qui étoient moins difficiles à émouvoir, passer successivement par la force des sons, de la joie à la tristesse, ou même à la fureur. *A cette vue*, d'autres qui n'auraient point été remués, le furent presque également' (*Essai*, p. 74). Here the rapid succession of contradictory emotions is engendered by the *observation* of the same succession in others: the symptom becomes sign for others and generates symptoms in them. As so often in eighteenth-century theories, art's power of 'ravissement', 'illusion', is exemplified by the extremes of feeling through which it makes the consumer pass. The mind does not confer reality on the signified through the sign, but is trapped by the contagious symptom, by the movement through a scale of emotions, that is, by *papillotage*.

For the emitter, then, natural language is what it expresses: it is thus also, paradoxically, a *sign of itself*. For the hearer the language of cries and signs is both a replica of the experience and an immediate cause of that experience which is provoked in himself – hence the analogy with theories of 'hard' illusion. It is here that the theories of illusion mediate a deeper notion of subjectivity, and that, when applied to poetry, as I have repeatedly suggested, they make of art something private and intimate. With Condillac, as with Rousseau's discussion of metaphor, the notion of *adequatio* has been stripped of its substitutive quality. The adequate art object could substitute itself for the piece of reality it imitated. Here, as with Rousseau's notion of metaphor, the 'signe naturel' is not *adequate* to the model, it *is* the model in some sense.[17] But the *Essai*'s epistemological development of the structure associated with aesthetic illusion is more far-reaching in its implication, and makes possible a more complex, multi-layered notion of self-awareness. For Condillac, while apparently conducting a sensualist version of faculty psychology in the *Essai sur l'origine des connaissances humaines*, is in fact developing a far more powerful account of the mind. He had set out with the overt intention of demolishing the active power allowed to the mind by

Locke, and which Leibniz saw as the intellectual master key which invalidated Lockean epistemology. But from an intention which is merely associationist, which wishes to reduce mental faculties to the result of a series of impressions, there derives a much deeper notion of subjectivity. Such a bizarre reversal of his philosophic intention is possible because of the interference in his work between the object and the analytic process. That is, the process discerned in the object of analysis, here the mind, and the descriptive or explicatory process, here of the philosopher, coincide, but not totally. (There is a similar pattern in Marivaux.) The philosopher traces out the genesis of self-awareness, but introduces a contradiction – that involvement and distance should be simultaneous where at an object level there is the primal uncontradictory complexity of an intellectual act.[18]

The word and subjectivity

Condillac's account of the development of language is in fact an account of the development of *words*. The word develops from the primal cry or gesture, which is symptom *and* sign. The derivation of the word is in fact a process, the process of acquiring meaning: this is one of the most important intellectual changes in mid-century, but it is one that has been well prepared.

Locke had, indeed, against Cartesian interest in structure and thus in syntax, emphasised the word as a vehicle of meaning. But for him a word's relation to its meaning was arbitrary. The word is a haphazard bundle of associations, historically determined. We have no guarantee that what we call 'gold' is in fact a properly constituted object for scientific investigation (but see Leibniz's reply, 1966, p. 269). Language has already classified reality before we can examine it; what for later writers is a historical or geographical problem was for him an epistemological one.[19] Locke's taking of the word as the unit of language is obviously founded on a discontinuous and atomistic conception of reality. Such a conception is exemplified in the itemisation of sensation inherent in the notion of 'idea' (or Hume's 'impression') as the constituent element of experiential reality, and in the central problem in contemporary mathematics, the nature of the mathematical point. In fact, the word and, more generally, the sign, offer in this perspective a convenient intellectual model for the discontinuous, the merely juxtaposed. This is, in essence, Herder's critique of Lessing's *Laocoon*: that Lessing sees words as individual successive units, instead of considering their composition into meaning and thus into spiritual effect. Both theoretically and practically, Leibniz shows, in opposition to Locke, that the sign's function cannot be reduced to naming, that the laws of its use are not 'conventional' in the Hobbesian sense, but that it has an active, heuristic function within any intellectual system. But this conception applied to language comes up against the objection that the sign is arbitrary. It is for this reason that Leibniz, in his *Nouveaux essais sur l'entendement humain* (written in 1703, but published only in 1765), uses etymology to prove that the phonemic network of a language is related to a conceptual network.

The subtlety of this view is lacking in most of the writers who in the later part of the eighteenth century deny that the relation between sound and meaning is arbitrary. They use Condillac's account, where cries constitute meaning as well as sound and thereby perhaps return to an old religious tradition of wordless praise of God (see Rousseau's article *Neaume* in the *Dictionnaire de musique*). Lamy, for example, had attributed the universal correlation between sound and internal state to act of God (Lamy, 1679, p. 193). Condillac's work shows clearly the type of theory of art that results from this. In a long process, he explains, expression develops from inarticulate cry through gesture to prosody and poetry, music and ballet. Music and pantomime are the social versions of the primitive language[20] which was onomatopœic – non-arbitrarily related to actual events – and tonal (Condillac, 1947, p. 63), so that even up to classical times speech and song were not separated (Condillac, 1947, p. 68). Gradually these were displaced by discursive language which had flatter sounds and analytic structure instead of powerful intonation. Poetry and music represent thus the keeping alive of potentialities which have disappeared from everyday language, and which, through their relation with mankind's past, are storehouses of potential energy and expressive value.

Poetry may try to recover the force of the natural cry by a process of compensation: 'Si dans l'origine des langues, la prosodie approcha du chant, le style, afin de copier les images sensibles du langage d'action adopta toutes sortes de figures et de métaphores et fut une vraie peinture' (Condillac, 1947, p. 79). But for Condillac all conventional language is a slipping away from the energy of the sign-symptom. Warburton, in his work on hieroglyphics, had suggested a possible model for a poetic unit which was more than 'une peinture', which was non-linear, in spite of the successiveness of speech, and like a palimpsest in spite of analytic tendencies of language. Warburton's model is used in this way by both Condillac and Diderot. Diderot adopts Condillac's account of the draining away of energy as language developed, but suggests a mode of compensation which, unlike Condillac's, is not imitative. In the *Lettre sur les sourds et muets*, he insists that a superimposition of expressive functions, as in the hieroglyph, is possible, and that what he calls the 'emblême poétique' is no mere collection of juxtaposed sign–symptoms, but a result of the continuous spontaneity necessary to paint the soul. Herder, as has been shown, takes up Lessing's notion of poetry's successiveness, but, referring also to the simultaneous unity created by the mind, he insists that there must be organic laws of development governing that successiveness, since poetry works on the soul: 'The poet works through the spiritual power of words in successive moments, to achieve the fullest illusion in the soul' (Herder, 1878, vol. III, p. 159). Critics such as Diderot and Herder, in spite of their differences, insist, then, on the simultaneous effect on the mind of the successive words of a poem. It is in this way that the mutation takes place, whereby the sign becomes part of a generative process in the mind, and illusion becomes truly subjective.

As has been said, French linguisticians after 1750 deny that there is an arbitrary relation between word and meaning; on the contrary, there exists a primal, organic, necessary language, common to the whole human race (de Brosses, 1765, vol. I, p. xv). Etymology serves to rediscover this language (de Brosses, vol. I, p. ix); its first words signified an interior state and were accents without articulation. The basic function of language is thus affective (de Brosses, vol. I, p. 230), [21] and external objects were named onomatopoeically (de Brosses, vol. I, p. 217).[22] As in Diderot's theory of the theatre, it is cries and interjections which give direct access to emotional states; sound, rather than the system of intellectual relations, as proposed by Port-Royal, is the bearer of meaning. The work of Court de Gebelin is a vast synthesis of these theories. In the *Monde primitif analysé et comparé avec le monde moderne* (1773) the analysis of sensation is automatically assured, given that he assumes that sound is discrete: 'Chaque son fut destiné à exprimer une sensation différente' (Court de Gebelin, 1773, vol. I, p. 10); and the written sign, too, refers immediately to discrete particles of experience: 'L'Alphabet primitif avait été pris dans la nature; chacun de ses élémens peignoit un objet particulier' (vol. I, p. 12). (The combination of discrete particles and immediate meaning is typical of the *sensualistes* Condillac and Diderot.) Sensations are represented almost exclusively by vowels, ideas by consonants, and he repeats with approval Lamy's postulation of a congruence between object, thought and idea (vol. III, p. 282).[23] Language is no longer in any sense an illusion, a veil, but ensures direct contact between internal states and the exterior world: 'Les rapports des mots avec la Nature sont la source de l'énergie du Discours, le fondement de la Poésie, de l'Eloquence, de l'Harmonie' (vol. III, p. 26).

Within this framework, what sounds like a theory of illusion takes on a different meaning. 'Exprimer les objets absens par des gestes qui les rendent présens, en les figurant tant bien que mal à l'oreille, ou à la vue, pour exciter une sensation pareille à celles qu'ils ont *eux-même excitées par leur présence*' (de Brosses, 1765, vol. II, p. 232):[24] such an aim represents a development which is most fully expressed in contemporary music theory. Illusion does not recreate an absent object, but calls forth sensation. The *adequatio* is to an internal experience, not to an external one. Moreover, it can recreate or reactivate the experience within the bearer of the experience; the adequation is thus not to an internal snapshot, or model, but to a process: '[Les signes] sont en quelque sorte l'anneau intermédiaire par lequel les besoins de l'âme s'unissent aux conceptions de la pensée' (Degérando, an viii, vol. III, p. 259).

This adequation is possible because of the analogical structure of the senses (*geste* is the common factor between the visual and the oral sign in the de Brosses passage just quoted). Whereas Condillac in the *Traité des sensations* (1754) had used the example of the statue to show that all the senses give essentially the same information, the term *geste* makes quite clear that for later writers it is not the information which is common to sensory output, but the process. Copineau, for instance, writes:

Un autre moyen encore proviendra de l'Analogie des sensations: quelque soit l'organe qu'elles affectent, elles agissent toujours par *quelque ébranlement, quelques vibrations dans les nerfs*, comparables à celles que les sons, à raison de leur différent caractère, produisent sur l'oreille. Ainsi, quoique ces sensations ne soient point perceptibles par l'ouïe, elles pourront être exprimées par des sons qui opèrent sur l'oreille à peu-près le même effet qu'elles opèrent sur leurs organes propres et respectifs.

There follows the canonical example of the colour red and how it is to be rendered (Copineau, 1774, p. 34). A vocabulary of sensuous comparisons may thus be built up: 'Il y a des sons qui semblent obscurs comme la nuit [. . .]. Il y a des sons qui paroissent imiter la douceur des parfums' (Degérando, an viii, vol. ii, p. 352). This analogy of process which makes possible the adequation to internal state is *ipso facto* not a copying but a transformation of experience. The problem of poetry's truth has no relevance in this way of looking at language. It is all the more interesting, therefore, to note that, only slightly earlier than Copineau, Diderot uses the same analogy, of the vibrating string, in the *Rêve de d'Alembert*, but with it he plays on the notion of poetry as *falsity*, and he makes d'Alembert say:

Mais son récit exagère, omet des circonstances, en ajoute, défigure le fait ou l'embellit, et les instruments sensibles adjacents conçoivent des impressions qui sont bien celles de l'instrument qui résonne, mais non celles de la chose qui s'est passée.

Bordeu: Il est vrai: le récit est historique ou poétique. (Diderot, *Rêve de d'Alembert,* p. 368)

Diderot, who had in any case always denied the interchangeability of the senses, both in the *Lettre sur les aveugles* (1749) and in *Lettre sur les sourds et muets* (1751), insists here on art's derogation from truth: once again, as in the *Salon de 1767* and the *Paradoxe sur le comédien*, poetry plays between the 'defiguration' and the 'embellishment'.

Metaphor and the nature of poetry

The 'illusion' called forth by poetry implies that the analogy between the senses is one of process and not of the information they supply. The linguistic expression will be metaphor. That tropes were invented to supplement the inadequacy of language is a commonplace (Lamy, 1679, *préface*). For some writers, the investigation into the historical and psychogenetic origins of language has suggested that this 'supplement' is not confined to metaphors but affects all language, that it is an essential principle in the creation of language. The *verb*, the concept of moving, becomes the origin of meaning. The cliché which holds that present words are dead metaphors is radically changed in this perspective. The metaphoricity of language is general, for even the creation of names was a metaphorical act, and a kernel of this energy, transference and movement is present in every word.

The religious origins of such a theory are obvious. They are also clear in a different type of account, which, while insisting on language's energy, claims the immediacy of the cry-symptom. In this type of theory the illusion of poetry, its effect, is guaranteed by its immediate source in human experience. Following Condillac, the theorists make words or sounds into both symptoms and signs. The symptomatic value is used to guarantee the immediacy necessary to any theory of *adequatio*, and here the religious origins of art will supply the symptoms. Rollin had said in the 1720s that poetry had been the cry of admiration made by man at the sight of his Creator: '[la poésie a été] d'abord comme le cri & l'expression du cœur de l'homme ravi, extasié, transporté hors de lui-même à la vûe de l'objet seul digne d'être aimé et seul capable de le rendre heureux' (Rollin, 1726–8, vol. I, pp. 214–15).[25] The energy is here derived from the Origin, God. At the other end of the century, God's delegate, the poet-magus, founder of societies, validates inversions, ellipses, the *copia* of language as closer not to modern thought but to the supposed primal correlation to language and object: 'Les langues durent d'abord être faites pour les poètes qui furent les premiers à en user. Aussi les langues originales sont-elles plus inversives, plus elliptiques, plus propres à peindre les objets' (Degérando, an viii, vol. II, p. 451). Such a view, as I have already pointed out, disposes of the problem of poetry's truth and the poet's function. Concern with the origins of poetry also disposes of the view that poetic form is arbitrary: rhythm and rhyme derive from the oral tradition of poetry and were a mnemonic necessity (Turgot, 1808, p. 68). The concern with the sources of poetry occasions an important revaluation of metaphor.

There was an eighteenth-century *idée reçue* that oriental poetry was particularly full of metaphor – Voltaire had both mocked and admired the language of the Bible. Now however, in this latter half of the century, this *idée reçue* is replaced by another: historical replaces geographical distance, and metaphor is seen not as a peculiarity of exotic, dissimilar peoples, but on the contrary, as a quality inherent in all primitive thought and expression. Even Turgot, who considers present taste to be a real improvement and primitive metaphors to be emphatic and imperfect like the thought they were expressing, yet allows a creative exploratory function to metaphor (Turgot, 1808, pp. 67, 76). He even takes up the *Ancien* position on the superiority of the Greek language. And for some French critics the Greek language comes to represent a moment of linguistic perfection located at the origin of culture, a language of unique richness and exactitude in the transcription of sense-impressions and states of soul:

On diroit que la nature à laquelle il semble qu'ils tenoient de plus près s'étoit offerte à eux par ses côtés les plus riches; qu'avant d'avoir rien nommé ils avoient parcouru l'universalité des choses & saisi les rapports, les différences; l'enchaînement, en un mot, toutes les propriétés des êtres: tant cette langue est l'image fidelle de l'action des objets sur les sens, & de l'action de l'âme sur elle-même. Des mots qui par le mélange heureux de leurs élémens, forment ou plutôt deviennent des tableaux; qui s'étendent, se nuancent et se ramifient conformément à la nature des sensations ou des idées dont ils sont, je ne dis pas l'instrument mais la plus vive image; [. . .] tel est le caractère de cette langue qui [. . .] est aux sciences et aux arts ce que la lumière est aux couleurs, & paroît avoir été formée moins par le besoin & par la convention, que par la nature même. (Arnaud, 1804, vol. I, pp. 4–6)

Arnaud here insists that the Greek language is a replica of internal process: its adequation is guaranteed by its antiquity and this is seen not as tradition but as freshness. The qualities Arnaud attributes to ancient Greek are attributed by him and by others to poetry, which is the natural language both by its adequation and its energy: 'La poésie, qui n'est pour nous qu'un langage artificiel, étoit le langage simple & naturel des hommes, lors de la formation des langues & des sociétés' (Arnaud, 1804, vol. I, p. 209).

Metaphor in this perspective is not, then, a complicated signifier of something which could be more simply signified. It mirrors a directness, a pristine energy in the relations between object and mind. But curiously it was the Ossian forgeries which in France finally set up this notion of metaphor in common currency. The forgeries were assimilated to oriental poetry:

Le caractère de ces Poësies paroît être le même en général que celui de la Poësie des Peuples Orientaux; c'est la même fougue d'enthousiasme, la même incohérence d'idées, la même accumulation d'images, souvent sublimes, aussi souvent gigantesques, toutes prises des plus grands, des premiers objets par lesquels la nature frappe les sens, la même fréquence dans les répétitions, la même irrégularité dans la marche. (*Journal des sçavans*, 1762, novembre, p. 724)

The reviewer points out the resemblances to Isaiah and Vergil, yet he is not merely turning Ossian into an exemplar of all 'early' poetry. On the contrary, there is a definite suggestion that the poems are a forgery (*Journal des sçavans*, 1762, novembre, p. 729). In other words, the journalist, while speculating on the authenticity of the fragments, does not deny the poetic value of Ossian. By his comparisons with the Bible and with Vergil, he is implicitly developing a concept of poetry as necessarily inserted into a tradition; but if the poems are a forgery, they do not really need to deserve the label 'primitive' to justify their use of metaphor. 'Fougue', 'incohérences' can then convert from a negative to a positive evaluation. For the forgery eliminates the oscillation in the permitted *délire* of, for example, a Jean-Baptiste Rousseau. There is no question of granting a licence to the poet to be enthusiastic. By his counterfeit, Macpherson–Ossian has taken that licence without asking. Only a 'forged' poetic voice could finally free poetry from the question: who is speaking? (In the same way, the question is without application in the theatre, where the actor speaks for the role.) It is as if an 'illusion' in the sense of a counterfeit, one perpetrated in all seriousness, was necessary to liberate enthusiasm, inspiration and metaphor from the system of elaborately granted permissions within which poets had operated.

The result is a radical revaluation of 'style oriental', a new function for metaphor.[26] An article on the 'style oriental' in the *Journal des sçavans* of 1765 makes this clear:

> Je n'entends pas par ce mot un style rempli d'invraisemblances et de comparaisons outrées; j'entends un style fécond en images propres à rendre la vérité sensible, qui porte l'empreinte d'une âme qui sent vivement [. . .]. Je crois qu'il seroit à souhaiter qu'il devînt plus général. Notre Littérature en seroit plus intéressante; en prenant un ton de force, elle deviendroit analogue à la sublime vertu dont le propre est d'inspirer toujours des sentimens énergiques. Ce style seroit même *plus naturel* [. . .]. Le bonheur consiste à sentir beaucoup [. . .]. Or, Monsieur, un style rempli d'images qui exprime & fait naître le sentiment, porte le mouvement & la vie dans l'âme du Lecteur [. . .]. Il *multiplie en lui l'avantage d'exister*, en lui faisant éprouver *presque sans intervalle* de nouvelles manières d'être. (*Journal des sçavans*, février 1765, pp. 551–3, 'lettre à M. Fréron sur le style oriental'.)

Illusion or identification here is an importing of feeling and life into the reader's soul, not, as in previous theory, a movement by the consumer *outwards*. Energy and force of expression in the poet produce a richer subjectivity in the reader. And a new criterion for that subjectivity is introduced, one which implants the protean diversity of the actor-chameleon in the reader. The capacity to experience a wide range of feeling is a source of happiness. The oscillation associated with *aletheia*, with 'soft' illusion, has gone – instead, emotions are felt 'presque sans intervalle'. But the more far-reaching notion of illusion as *mensonge* is explicitly rejected: 'Pourquoi un style qui donne un corps aux Etres purement intellectuels ne seroit-il pas propre à les faire connoître [. . .]? Le style oriental n'exclut donc point la justesse des pensées; il est au contraire plus propre à la faire sortir' (*Journal des sçavans*, 1765,

p. 551). Illusion, in the sense of oscillation of vicarious emotion as well as in the sense of the untruth of poetry, has been finally set aside. Poetry is energy, an energy of active creation in the poet, and of subjective creation of experience by the reader.[27]

Metaphor becomes, then, not superficial decoration, but essential to poetry, since the poet's emotion is transmitted like heat in a chemical reaction: 'Les passions vives sont comme la flamme [. . .]. Il lui sera donc possible de transformer ses manières d'être en objets matériels et en employant alors les signes de ceux-ci, il réussira, au moyen d'une double analogie, à faire naître dans l'esprit de son compagnon les mêmes pensées qui l'occupent' (Degérando, an viii, vol. I, pp. 120–1).[28] For Degérando, the 'double analogie' of metaphor transmits states of soul: 'illusion' has become entirely subjective and has lost all trace of pejorative meaning.

Yet the same consciousness of the religious tradition may lead to weight being given to the sounds of poetry, derived from the wordless cry of praise (see p. 244 above). Metaphor creates a replica adequate to internal states in that it causes the same state in the reader in the manner of the Condillacian sign. But sound can have a more immediate effect in that it is caused by the internal state, in the manner of the Condillacian symptom. Arnaud, in the *Variétés littéraires*, says: ' Le langage figuré et métaphorique n'est pas ce qui constitue le langage poétique: le caractère poétique des langues est particulièrement attaché au mélange agréable des sons dans les mots & à l'ordre harmonieux & varié des mots dans les discours'; this is justified by the necessary origin of language: 'Dans la formation des langues, les mots n'étant faits que pour l'oreille, devoient s'adresser directement & plus sensiblement à l'organe & réveiller dans l'âme l'image physique de la chose qu'ils désignoient.' (Arnaud, 1804, vol. I, p. 212). Totally imaginary experiences can thus be recreated: poetry can provide them (Pluche, 1751, p. 249). With this awareness of the importance of sound, music becomes the model for poetry, and the reversal of seventeenth-century values is complete. Boileau, for instance, had said that music was not as expressive as poetry (Boileau, 1966, p. 277). Now, however, poetry and music create an inner state which has no need of objective support from the material world: '[La poésie et la musique] cherchent à mettre en œuvre tout le pouvoir de l'imagination pour nous créer en nous-mêmes comme une seconde existence indépendante des objets extérieurs' (Degérando, an viii, vol. II, p. 372). This reduction of external stimulus goes even further: music is wordless, language becomes almost a hindrance to the poet, and Madame de Staël writes: 'Le véritable poète conçoit, pour ainsi dire, tout son poème à la fois au fond de son âme: sans les difficultés du langage il improviseroit comme la sibylle' (Staël, 1968, p. 208). She shows clearly – because negatively – what is adumbrated in earlier writers, what both Lessing and Diderot seem at times to demand: the medium is to become transparent. Poetry is to be an adequation to an internal experience and awareness of the mediation is to be effaced. The common origin of both 'romanticism' and 'realism', their mutual implication, lies in that effacement. And it is thus that music, representing the elimination of the word, becomes the art *par excellence* of the inner self.

Part Five

ILLUSION AS SUBJECTIVITY: THEORIES OF MUSIC

For the French theorists of mid-century, music was first and foremost the music of the opera. Like theorists of the theatre, their treatment of the opera is based on a reaction against contemporary music, and a striving towards replica, towards an external and identifiable model. But the wished-for transparency of the model is thwarted by the inevitable opacity of the musical medium. Theorists busy themselves trying to erase this conceptual tension by imposing more and more restrictions on opera's matter and mode of presentation; but this tightening is paradoxically merely a reinforcement of the conventions which are the source of the opacity in the first place. In theories of operatic music, as in theories of painting, there is the same contrast in the mid-century between *papillotage* (identified with Rameau) and a new style (identified with *opera buffa*) which should be adequate to its model. But what *is* its model? Music poses with great force the problem of imitation in general. Chapter 9 has suggested the way that theorists take to extricate themselves from this dilemma. I showed there how music and poetry have a common origin for Condillac in 'le cri naturel', which is at the same time symptom, and symptom's illusory replica, the first sign. Sound in particular combines the passive immediacy of an impression with its active transmission: meaning is no longer the product of grammatical articulations but consists in primary units of feeling whose force has gradually been intellectualised and lost during the evolution of culture. Music, and poetry, in that they express reactions, can restore some of that force, and words become for some theorists a transparent medium which gives on to internal experience. If even words are felt to hinder this transparency, to make it opaque, wordless music will, at the end of the century, be held to constitute more fully a replica of that experience. But wordless music, in doing without words, has lost purely intellectual articulations, and its continuity is related by theorists to the continuous rhythms of

253

subjectivity; it becomes part of an experience itself rather than a model of it. Adequation is now internal to the self: but the distance which always exists between model and copy has also been internalised. It is perhaps thus that consciousness is inserted even into spontaneity, a mixing which is characteristic of Rousseau's *sentiment de l'existence* and indeed of modern feeling in general.

10

MUSIC AND ILLUSION

Illusion and opera as theatre

French opera was spectacular, and I discussed the aesthetics of spectacle in my third part. The marvellous was excluded from the theatre – Hippolyte in Racine's *Phèdre* is killed by a monster, but off-stage – and, as if to compensate, the opera traditionally represented the mythical, the unnatural, and, to its critics, the downright improbable. Saint Evremond, it will be remembered, had early rejected bimodal experience of art, in his attack on opera's foolishness; the intelligence, he said, resisted the blandishments of sense impressions, 'les illusions des sens', and remained dissatisfied (above, p. 33). Doubtless La Bruyère was answering such attacks when he insisted on the power of illusion and defined the role of stage machinery thus: 'Elle augmente et embellit la fiction, soutient dans les spectateurs cette douce illusion qui est tout le plaisir du théâtre, où elle jette encore le merveilleux [. . .]. Le propre de ce spectacle est de tenir les esprits, les yeux & les oreilles dans un égal enchantement' (La Bruyère, 1962, p. 84, quoted above, p. 36). 'Illusion', with its magical heritage and with its related terms 'prestige' and 'enchantement', was applied to the effect of *fiction*, of unreality, that such operas intended to create.

The spectacular nature of French opera comes under particular attack in what is known as the *Guerre des Bouffons* (1752–3). This is in fact but one campaign in a running battle between the supporters of French opera and the adherents of Italian opera, the main stages of which are: the quarrel between Raguenet (1702) and Le Cerf de la Viéville (1704); the quarrel occasioned by the arrival in Paris in 1752 of an Italian company with an *opera buffa* repertoire; and finally the quarrel between the Gluckistes and the Piccinistes (1777). In each episode it is a different style of Italian opera which is in question. It is the Bouffonistes, however, who raise in acute form the question of subject matter and who attack the *merveilleux*. In the flurry of pamphlets on music and opera brought about by the *Bouffons* in August 1752, and given new impetus by Rousseau's *Lettre sur la musique française* of November 1753, it may seem at first sight curious that both sides claim illusion. But the fact that radically opposed theatrical practices should both pretend to illusion has already been discussed *à propos* of the theatre. French classical opera jettisoned *vraisemblance*, which was traditionally connected with the unities: gods and goddesses 'flew' or descended in chariots; scenes changed and magical effects were simulated. But this ancestor of the pantomime is constantly defended in terms of illusion:

Avouons de bonne foi que cette douce illusion, qui place le Spectateur à côté du Personnage, qui le met de moitié dans ses projets; que cette Erreur profonde dans laquelle le Spectateur se plonge, s'oublie & se perd, qu'il est si content d'éprouver & dont à son reveil il sait tant de gré aux arts qui l'ont fait naître, est une beauté qui n'appartient qu'à l'Opéra François. Osons dire que ce grand effet n'est jamais produit que par l'imitation simple & parfaitement vraie de la nature, que cette espèce particulière de beauté qu'on seroit peut-être en droit de regarder comme l'unique perfection théâtrale, est une production naturelle à notre terroir. (Rochemont, 1754, pp. 129–30)

(This is very like the defence of opera by La Bruyère, see p. 255 above.) On the other hand, Dorval, in Diderot's *Entretiens sur le 'Fils naturel'*, criticising French opera, argues that illusion in the arts is quite hard enough to obtain without choosing a plot full of 'métamorphoses' and 'sortilèges'. Clearly, what is meant by 'illusion' is changing. Diderot, Grimm and Rousseau all insist on an 'illusion' which is not accompanied by an awareness of unreality, of 'fiction'. Nor could they agree that French opera was 'une imitation simple & parfaitement vraie de la nature', to use Rochemont's phrase. As with the theatre, the concept of what is representable is changing, together with the concept of what ought to be represented, defined tendentiously and legislatively throughout the centuries as 'reality' or 'nature'. This becomes clear when we remember that the *Guerre des Bouffons* in fact set against one another two different genres of opera, and not merely different nationalities or musical traditions. Italian *opera buffa* was contrasted with French *opera seria*. For the quarrel was not only about what could be represented (Rousseau's Saint-Preux writes amusingly of the attempt by French opera to represent the unrepresentable, *O.C.*, vol. II, pp. 281ff.). It was also about subject matter. The subjects of the *opera buffa* were comic, not mythological. Out of it was to grow the *opéra comique*, the only genre, until late in the century, where low subjects could be treated. The *opéra comique* fused with the popular art of the fairs; it took over subjects from the novel, following the work of the Favarts (Garcin, in his *Traité du mélodrame* (1772), constantly applies criteria taken from the novel to the opera); it took subjects like *Tom Jones*, *Le Maréchal ferrant*; playwrights like Sedaine, known for their work in the *comédie sérieuse*, wrote for it. I have already shown *à propos* of the theatre that there is a link in critics' minds between 'low subjects' and anti-spectacular aesthetics based on illusion. Nougaret (*L'Art du théâtre en général*, 1769) exemplifies this link (see above, pp. 157ff.), parodying the assumption that low subjects, being closer to everyday experience, produce uninterrupted illusion. He shows, on the contrary, that 'the everyday' is as much a choice of what should be represented as any other subject. He also shows that in treating low subjects the *opéra comique* raises the problem of the conventional as urgently as does French grand opera, since both types of opera are, by definition, sung.

The defenders of French opera are in fact driven to elaborate a concept of convention in the face of the increasingly rigorous demands of 'illusion'. Denying the possibility of the transparent relation between model and copy that their opponents desire, they maintain that a 'beau arbitraire et de convention' is possible, and that 'ce qui est tout ce qu'il doit être est bon dans son genre' (Chassiron, s.d., p. 479). One defender actually uses the term 'illusion' to mean convention: 'Enfin lorsque je vais à l'Opéra, je ne vais ni à un sermon ni à un plaidoyer; je vais entendre les effets de la nature rendus musicalement. Voilà l'illusion, c'est à moi de m'y prêter ou de ne pas y aller' (Blainville, 1754, p. 51). But this type of argument poses a problem, one already met in theatre theory: if all art is based on convention, does this entail that no work of art can be more natural, nearer nature, than another?

Rousseau, with his incomparably clear perception of subjacent problems, attempts to solve the question of convention in opera. In his article *Opéra* in the *Dictionnaire de musique* he gives a conjectural history of the development of spectacular opera. Poetry, music and language were originally one, but split apart in the development of culture; men were then trapped in the new implausibility brought about by the union of poetry and music, in the opera, and as a result alternately tried to correct and to compensate for it. The use of the *merveilleux* arose from an attempt to escape from this dilemma: men wished to 'éluder ce qu'avoit de peu naturel l'union de la musique & du discours dans l'imitation de la vie humaine

257

[. . .]. Pour soutenir une si forte illusion il fallait éprouver tout ce que l'art humain pouvait imaginer de plus séduisant'; in other words, opera had to *simulate the marvellous*, in order to prevent the judgement from functioning. The resistance created by the implausibility must be overcome by more of the same, by a *supplément* (cf. Derrida, 1967b, pp. 208ff.): 'Car les sens se prêtent mal à l'illusion quand le cœur ne s'en mêle pas.' Like Grimm, Rousseau accuses opera of misunderstanding the conditions of the theatre, and attempting to produce the epic; like Grimm, he speaks of 'une langue hypothétique'. Gradually a less conventional opera evolved, according to Rousseau, for 'commençant à se dégouter de tout le clinquant de la féerie, du puéril fracas des machines, et de la fantastique image des choses qu'on n'a jamais vues, on chercha dans l'imitation de la nature des tableaux plus intéressants et plus vrais'. The elimination of evident convention results in a transparency which will abolish the awareness of the medium itself, seen as one more interposition between hearer and model:

Cette forme plus sage & plus reguliere se trouva encore la plus propre à l'illusion; l'on sentit que le *chef d'œuvre de la musique était de se faire oublier elle-même*, qu'en jetant le désordre et le trouble dans l'âme du spectateur, elle *l'empêchait de distinguer les chants tendres et pathétiques d'une heroïne des vrais accens de la douleur.*[1]

By accounting for the development of French opera in this dialectical fashion, Rousseau intended to dissolve 'convention': but he comes perilously close to dissolving *art*. The article *Opéra* is an account, not only of the 'overbidding' which he sees as the pattern of development in French opera, but also of the ambiguity inherent in the logic of imitation: to be perfect, an imitation must cease to exist, or at least the adequation between model and copy must be so perfect that awareness of their separation, like a screen between them, must be effaced. One can wonder whether the restrictions Rousseau constantly imposes on opera in the *Dictionnaire de musique*, the harassing insistence on *vraisemblance* and on the *bienséances*, are an attempt to force operatic conventions down to a minimum (in a movement like that of Diderot in the *Entretiens sur le 'Fils naturel'*, who strives to reduce conventions to conditions necessary for any representation), or whether, by tightening more firmly the conditions for adequation, by a kind of overbidding, these restrictions are not in fact a reinforcement of convention. For is not any imitation, even the most adequate, less than reality and thus inevitably conventional? The licensed enjoyment of supernatural and improbable happenings is no more nor less arbitrary than any pleasure in the stage. It is thus that defenders of French opera argue: 'Il ne me seroit pas difficile de démontrer qu'il y a autant de convention dans les plaisirs que donnent les Opéras Italiens que dans celui que les nôtres nous occasionnent' (Cazotte, 1753, p. 9). Why, for instance, does Rousseau reject the conventional matter of French opera and not the convention of song? The mythological, it is argued, validates not merely the plot, but the use of music: 'Ces êtres chimériques dont le spectateur n'a pas d'idée bien précise laissent la liberté au musicien de leur donner un langage plus musical' (Mably, 1741, p. 49). Marmontel actually attacks Italian opera because it has retained song while removing the *merveilleux*, an illogical excision of one convention and retention of another: 'Que l'austère vérité s'empare de ce théâtre, elle en change tout le système; & si du prestige qu'elle détruit on veut conserver quelque trace, l'accord, l'illusion n'y est plus' (Marmontel, 1763, vol. ii, p. 329). This argument is extended to criticise the typically *buffa* mixture of speech and song:

> C'est un peuple chantant que la scène propose
> L'illusion nous charme alors qu'on la suppose.
> (Caux de Cappeval, 1755; cf. *Nouvelliste du Parnasse*, 1731, vol. i, p. 317)

As a consequence, *récitatif* must be musical, or else the effect will be interrupted (and even *Bouffonistes* are largely in agreement with this): 'Il faut donc qu'il [le musicien] mette du chant partout, sans cela l'illusion cesseroit' (Yzo, 1753, p. 16); 'La Musique est une langue. Imaginons un peuple d'inspirés & d'enthousiastes, dont la tête seroit toujours exaltée, dont l'âme seroit toujours dans l'ivresse & dans l'extase [. . .] un tel peuple chanteroit au lieu de parler, sa langue naturelle seroit la musique' (Grimm, *Encyclopédie*, article *Poème lyrique*). Such an attitude is at the basis of d'Alembert's ambiguous reaction to Italian opera. He backhandedly attacks it by deliberately assuming that more convention is better than less. Apparently defending the *Bouffons*, he attacks the mixture of speech and song: 'Il est plus facile de se prêter à la supposition d'un peuple qui dit tout en musique qu'à celle d'un peuple dont la langue est mêlée de chant et de discours' (d'Alembert, 1821, p. 531). He pretends to propose a greater degree of 'vérité' (though the excesses of the English theatre are refused) and seems to imply that spoken tragedy is superior to sung tragedy. But this in turn enables him to reverse the position from which he started and to maintain that since opera is in its essence conventional ('les défauts de l'opéra sont essentiellement attachés à sa nature'), there is no possibility of relative closeness to what is defined, within a convention, as reality. This in fact opens the door to all and every convention, and this attitude provokes the answer from Rousseau: 'Il y a une sorte de vraisemblance qu'il faut conserver *même à l'opéra*, en rendant le discours tellement uniforme que le tout puisse être pris au moins pour une langue hypothétique' (Rousseau, *Lettre sur la musique française*, p. 433). Convention cannot be excised from imitation. But, as I said above, for Rousseau it is by its unity and severity that convention becomes transparent, effacing itself in front of the model. Whereas Grimm, no doubt influenced by Diderot's aesthetic of playing truth against falsehood, claims:

Tout art d'imitation est fondé sur un mensonge: ce mensonge est une espèce d'hypothèse établie & admise en vertu d'une convention tacite entre l'artiste & ses juges. Passez-moi ce premier mensonge, a dit l'artiste, & je vous mentirai avec tant de vérité que vous y serez trompé, malgré que vous en ayez. Le poète dramatique, le peintre, le statuaire, le danseur en pantomime, le comédien, tous ont une hypothèse particulière sous laquelle ils s'engagent de mentir & qu'ils ne peuvent perdre de vûe un seul instant sans nous ôter de cette illusion qui rend notre imagination complice de leurs supercheries, car ce n'est point la vérité, mais l'image de la vérité qu'ils nous promettent. (Grimm, *Encyclopédie*, article *Poème lyrique*)

The hypothesis is a lie; it is the necessary basis of all art, promising us the representation of truth which dissimulates art's lack of truth. The gulf between the aesthetics of Diderot and Rousseau, in spite of all their similarities, appears typically in their conception of convention. One uses the relay of representation ('Ce n'est point la vérité mais l'image de la vérité') the other strives to efface that relay, for the perfection of music lies in its causing itself to be forgotten: illusion is transparency of imitation.

Illusion and musical style

Rousseau's account is typical of the *Bouffonistes'* reaction not merely to opera but, incredibly, to music. As in the theory of rhetoric, enthusiasm is to obliterate the awareness of the medium:

[Les Italiens] ont [. . .] des morceaux si supérieurs *qu'on oublie que ce sont des beautés musicales*; l'illusion est forte au point qu'on croit que c'est la chose même que l'on voit, que c'est là qu'on existe. Un feu se répand dans les veines, on se sent soulever l'imagination en désordre, le cœur ému, on est transporté comme dans un autre hémisphère. (Blainville, 1754, p. 31, on the Italian 'accompagnemens de caractère')

The process repeats that of the musician.[2] For such illusion to be

obtained the audience must be 'immersed' in music, and the con-
clusions are pedantically drawn – a continuous flow of impressions
must fill the restlessness of man's senses; over-long rests are to be
avoided, because they allow time for the mind to return to consciousness, to judge and to weaken its impressions (Estève, 1753a,
vol. I, p. 229). Music and voice must move together or else an oscillation will be established: 'Une espèce de flux et de reflux contre
lequel l'attention se brise & où l'illusion fait naufrage' (Garcin,
1772, p. 290).[3] Such an oscillation is to be avoided at all costs, for it
is *papillotage*, reference away from the musical theme.[4] Such an
oscillation was also held to be typical of the musical texture of
Rameau's operas. Just as in the reformist theatrical aesthetics of
the mid-century, any reference to the theatrical nature of the happenings was considered to disturb adequation, so features of
Rameau's musical style are criticised as extraneous to the core of
the opera, as bringing the music to our notice rather than suppres-
sing our awareness of it.

The *Bouffonistes'* attacks on Rameau were not new, and to
understand them one must understand their sources. The poor man
was attacked in two separate phases – at the beginning of his career
for being too Italian, and in the *Guerre des Bouffons* for not being
Italian enough. These attacks in fact constitute a replay and development of the quarrel earlier in the century, where Raguenet defended, and Le Cerf de la Viéville criticised Italian music.

For Raguenet, Italian music is exciting: daring dissonances
create an oscillation between suspense and relief. The French fear
the abrupt transitions and full harmony: 'Les Italiens plus hardis
changent brusquement de ton & de mode, font des cadences
doublées & redoublées de sept ou de huit mesures sur des tons que
nous ne croions pas capables de porter le moindre tremblement'
(Raguenet, 1702, p. 33). The French use slower measures and
minimal accompaniment. (The difference can be well appreciated
from Couperin's work *Les Goûts réunis, ou l'Apothéose de Lulli et
de Corelli*, where he pastiches the two styles.)

Up to the time of the *Bouffons*, Italian music, in particular the
work of Corelli and Vivaldi, is stigmatised by its opponents as
papillotage; the objections made by Bourdelot (1715), for instance, are analogous to those to be made slightly later against
Rococo painting. He complains that the listener must move quickly
between opposed impressions, just as the *papillotage* of painters
seemed to encourage rapid eye movements in the observer. The
music is described as 'Un cahos de sons tricottez et pétillans', and,

he maintains: 'on n'entend plus le sujet'. The continuo which doubles the melody on several instruments drowns the main voice; the virtuoso use of the violin 'qui frise et qui prétintaille', leads merely to a disparate piece, a 'ragoût' (Bourdelot, 1715, vol. ɪ, p. 434). The criticisms pick up the characteristics of Couperin's harpsichord pieces, for instance, and their 'style brisé', which derives from the lute. According to Bukofzer:

> The quickly fading sound of the lute did not lend itself to polyphonic voice leading and called for specific techniques to compensate for the technical limitations of the instrument [. . .]. [The 'style brisé'] is characterised by rapidly alternating notes in different registers that supply in turn melody and harmony. Seemingly distributed in arbitrary fashion over various registers, the notes produced in composite rhythm a continuing strand of sound [creating a free-voiced texture]. (Bukofzer, 1948, p. 165)

The continuous interruption of key, the virtuosity, the complaints about the lack of serious subjects (which must be understood within the French tradition of representative music)[5] – all are close to the definition of *papillotage* previously discussed in painting, and all suppose an oscillation in the listener prompted both by the texture of the music and by the impossibility of totally oblivious consumption. Oscillation however implies movement within bounds. This is brought out clearly in an account of harmony by the anti-Newtonian, Castel. He wrongly thinks of the vibration of the sound wave as discrete, but then the very significance of this passage lies in its mistaken physics:

> Géométriquement, métaphysiquement parlant, l'harmonie est un *nombre* comme les anciens l'ont définie d'après Pythagore. Mais physiquement parlant, elle consiste dans un *nombre de vibrations*, c'est-à-dire, de mouvemens bornés, alternatifs, interrompus. Nous sommes bornés, nos sentimens & nos plaisirs le sont comme nous. Un mouvement ni un repos infinis, c'est-à-dire, continus, ou même trop continués ne sont pas faits pour cette vie; & nous y sommes sans cesse dans l'alternative du mouvement qui nous entraîne sans jamais arriver & d'un repos qui nous attire sans jamais nous fixer. Je me borne au sujet présent: c'est cette interruption intercalaire, mais vive et fréquente, sans être trop forte, ni impétueuse, de mouvement & de repos alternatifs, qui font le nombre & l'harmonie; car le nombre est la grandeur discrète, c'est cette interruption, cette noncontinuité qui rompt la grandeur & la rend discrette. (Castel, *Journal de Trévoux*, 1735, pp. 2026–7)

This text reads like a metaphysics of '*papillotage*'.[6]

More important perhaps, such a conception, though not typical of the texture of French music before Rameau, was fundamental to the type of plot commonly used in French opera. The operas were built linearly, and proceeded from *entr'acte* to *entr'acte* – for the plot was constantly broken by the *fête*, or by a balletic interlude. This form was held to provoke an emotional oscillation: 'Rien n'est plus capable d'émouvoir et d'amuser que le contraste de la danse avec la pitié' (Mably, 1741, p. 4). Dancers would appear and interrupt, with dances of triumph or celebration, the flow of the story: 'L'Excellence du plan français paraît consister dans cette division du poème en dialogue et en fête. Le dialogue doit occuper fortement le spectateur [. . .]. La fête est un repos, un passage à des plaisirs d'un nouveau genre' (Rochemont, quoted Girdlestone, 1972, p. 43). Mably, too, claims that this change of mood is an advantage: 'Mais est-il bien vrai que la Danse interrompe l'impression que doit faire une action intéressante? dans toutes les Tragédies il y a des passages d'une passion à l'autre – C'est *ce flux et reflux* d'espérance et de crainte, les changemens et les contrastes de situations qui produisent un des plus grands plaisirs du Théâtre' (Mably, 1741, p. 119).

The basis of such *papillotage* is more than mere contrast: it is an awareness of the artificiality of the spectacle, which is often embodied in the operatic personage. In Lulli's *Atys*, the hero sings: 'Que de Phantômes vains sont sortis des Enfers.' The *présence d'esprit* implied by the latinism, and its subversion of the ghosts, even as it evokes them, reflects the spectator's oscillation, and is criticised for doing so by Mably (1741, p. 84). The consciousness oscillates between contrasting emotions, which are bounded (as the arc of a pendulum is bounded); it is equally held at a distance. The effect is felt to entrap the mind in mirror-like fragmentary triviality, just as the *esprit philosophique* was accused of doing, and the relation between *papillotage* and *esprit philosophique* is explicit in the critics.[7] Fontenelle and La Motte are the poets to whom the critics compare such music. Though late Vivaldi and Corelli are incomparably greater, the basis of the comparison with La Motte, explicitly made by critics, or expressed in such terms as *papillotage*, *pétillant*, *prétintaille*, is real enough.

On such grounds, and in similar language, Rameau is attacked, once as Italian (by the *Lullistes*), once as anti-Italian (by the *Bouffonistes*). His first operas astounded by their difficulty. The enharmonics of the 'trio des Parques' in *Hippolyte et Aricie* were unsingable at first, and he was accused of being 'singulier, brillant, composé, savant, trop savant quelquefois' (Diderot, *O.C.*, vol. i, p. 534). He was said to destroy illusion with his accompaniments, 'ces Accompagnemens tumultueux qui détruisent l'illusion sur le Théâtre & que malgré leur harmonie on ne devrait pas même souffrir dans nos Concerts' (Mably, 1741, p. 52; cf. Rousseau, *Dictionnaire de musique*, article *Dessein*). His varied, complex harmony was called 'prétintaille', his varied rhythms 'musique [. . .] inégale, cahotante, furieuse' (Grandval, 1732, p. 19). His style is linked with literary preciosity – 'L'inintelligibilité, le galimatias, le néologisme veulent donc passer du discours dans la musique' (*Observations sur les écrits modernes*, 1735, vol. II, p. 238) – or with that familiar bone of contention, the 'récit de Théramène' in Racine's *Phèdre*.[8] Again and again, in the eighteenth century and up to Charles Burney (1771), if Rameau's symphonies are admired he is accused of making the human voice imitate instruments in speed and intonation, just as the Rococo *ornemanistes* were accused of using materials unsuitable to what they represent (Bollioud, 1746, p. 40). 'Enfin parut M. Rameau, et c'est à lui que nous devons un genre bâtard qui passe à présent en France pour la musique italienne: véritable papillotage, nul accord du chant avec les paroles, avec la situation des personnages' (d'Argenson, quoted Girdlestone, 1962, p. 76).[9]

The criticisms made of Rameau in the *Guerre des Bouffons* were, then, not new. For in so far as Rameau is close to Corelli and Vivaldi, he is in opposition to the Neapolitan *opera buffa*, which had its sources in popular or folk song, its singers' lack of virtuosity being turned to account by the writing of simple, theatrically effective music (Robinson, 1961–2).

The musical questions at stake between the two sides crystallise round an opposition between harmony and melody: Rameau's music was one of complex harmony, and this is associated by the *Bouffonistes* with a failure to 'represent' – it is not by accident that his vigorous champion in the 1760s, Chabanon, denies music's power to imitate at all. For the *Bouffonistes*, Rameau represented not merely stage but also musical convention; his was a music which pursued its own development in a genre hopelessly removed from life, the music of the *fermiers généraux*, as Boucher was their painter (Lovinsky, 1965).

For the oscillations which contemporaries discerned in the musical texture of Rameau and Couperin were connected with their daring use of dissonance within harmonic structure – dissonance which was unprepared, repeated, left without resolution, or whose resolution appeared in another voice (see Girdlestone, 1962; Bücken, 1927). Moreover, the burden of Rameau's important theoretical work was on dissonance. Now at an earlier period, in Kepler's *Harmonices Mundi* of 1619 for instance, music is that by which 'the human mind, forming a judgement of what it hears, imitates its Creator by a natural instinct' (Kepler, 1619, p. 2; translation mine). The proportions of consonance, or the 'rational' proportions, are those constructible with a ruler and compass – algebraic, not transcendental. Musical proportions correspond to the construction of the universe. Mersenne in 1636 actually divides music between 'des étoiles', 'humaine' and 'instrumentale'. But during the late seventeenth century and the eighteenth century, with the work of Taylor, the Bernouillis and Euler on the vibrating string, the concept of consonance changes (Truesdell, 1960). Music is now the result of the vibration of sound waves, and continuous, even if imperceptible or even if perceived as discrete; it is subject to the process of the calculation of limits, the finite mind's approximation to the infinite. This change is well brought out when the attitude of Félibien, who proposes music as the model for painting, because of the absolute nature of its division into modes,[10] is compared with that of writers who, developing Newton's work, conceive of sound, like colour, as vibrating along an axis. To this evolution in the conception of consonance and of the nature of sound corresponds a change in the attitude to dissonance. In the Renaissance, where harmony was conceived as a conjunction of intervals, dissonance, an altered proportion, was held in check. But in Baroque chordal harmony, dissonance could be inserted anywhere, the continuo marking the harmonic support against which great freedom could be allowed to the melody (see Bukofzer, 1948, ch. 1). The gradual development of tonality, a system of relations based on a tonal centre, posed anew the problem of harmony and, crucially, of dissonance. Rameau's work on musical theory made what were *ad hoc* rules of composition into laws based on the physical nature of sound, removing the use of dissonance from musical tradition to the domain of accoustics in general. Developing the relation made by Mersenne between a note's overtones and harmony, Rameau was led to postulate that the twelfth and seventeenth overtones vibrate but do not sound. Though harmony was no longer the representation of proportion within the universe, Rameau wished the whole of subjective sound, consonance and dissonance, to be rational and measurable; in his old age, sound was to be the foundation of all science. Daniel Bernouilli and Euler seemed to thrust music back into a particular musical tradition, even if it was one with a scientific basis, for they pointed out against Rameau that the overtones of a sounding body are not all harmonious, and that the materials chosen for musical instruments are precisely ones whose audible overtones are harmonious (Truesdell, 1960). Rameau has radically internalised the intellectualist tradition of music. Music is no longer cosmic harmony, it is mental structure. Consonance and dissonance in music refer to a 'basse fondamentale', an abstract structure which may not be, indeed generally is not, the actually heard bass, but is the inaudible order which pervades a composition. As a structure existent but not necessarily perceived, Rameau's *basse fondamentale* is the counterpart of the *philosophes-grammairiens'* notion of *ordre naturel*, the order regulating, though often not exemplified in, the actual order of discourse (see above, p. 228).

Rousseau's rejection of such theories is inevitable: he denies the scientific basis for the generation of dissonance ('La proportion [. . .] sert [à M. Rameau] pour introduire la dissonance et le défaut de proportion pour la faire sentir': *Dictionnaire de musique*, article *Dissonance*). There must be no divorce between real and abstract structure (and it is significant that he never uses the notion of natural order in language). All intellectual and abstract representation is denied, or equated, by a dialectical reversal, with mere sensuous representation (Derrida, 1967b, p. 300). The music must be what is heard, not what is proportionate to what is heard: for how can there be relation between quantity and sensation, how can there be 'quelque identité entre les propriétés de la quantité abstraite et les sensations de l'âme' (*Dictionnaire de musique*, article *Dissonance*). Rousseau denies that harmony can represent the system of acoustical relationships, *le corps sonore*: 'Le musicien ne considère pas le corps sonore en lui-même, il ne le considère qu'en action. Or qu'est-ce que le corps sonore en action? C'est le son: l'harmonie représente donc le son. Mais l'harmonie accompagne le son: le son n'a donc pas besoin qu'on le représente puisqu'il est là' (Rousseau, *Examen de deux principes avancés par M. Rameau*, p. 454). In the same way, the *Encyclopédistes* reject Rococo theatre or painting, because it refers away from what the play or painting is. Rameau, like the Rococo painter or playwright, tries to empty a sensuous reality of presence, so that it stands as a sign system referring to something outside the actual art object.

An attitude such as Rousseau's must of course imply in music a considerable simplification of texture. Rousseau rejects Rameau's enharmonics: the sudden switches are too fast for the ear to reconstruct the liaison; they no longer have a 'rapport sensible'.

And it should be noted that Rousseau's own theoretical evolution – from weariness with the artifice and over-simplicity of Lulli through dislike, first masked, then open, of Rameau, into advocacy of the Neapolitan school of music, which offered a top line of lilting melody with trommelbass (Robinson, 1961–2) – is matched by the actual evolution of music in the eighteenth century. One thinks, for instance, of how the tensely knit relation between the whole and even the smallest parts in Bach is matched by the flowing phrases of Handel, who still gives the full harmony; and then of how Pergolesi gives the mere melodic line, accompanied by an Alberti bass (Lovinsky, 1965). Rousseau's attitude to both the theory and the practice of Rameau, his preference for octaval accompaniment, has an epistemological basis, and one that has been mentioned before: 'Il est impossible à l'oreille de se prêter au même instant à plusieurs mélodies' (Rousseau, *Lettre sur la musique française*, p. 423). Like Diderot, he thinks that the mind can only attend ('se prêter') to one idea or one sensation at a time, and that the multiplicity of actual experience can be present to the consciousness only in successive units (see below, p. 345 n.17).

Diderot and Rousseau

The *Encyclopédistes* gradually came to oppose Rameau and all his works. The first shot in the *Guerre des Bouffons* was fired by Grimm in his pamphlet *Le Petit Prophète de Böhmischbroda*. It is cast in the form of a satirical dream made by 'le petit prophète' which ridicules French opera and music and praises Italian. The 'petit prophète' has been identified with the musician Stamitz, who had visited Paris in 1751.[11] Now the foremost living French musician, Rameau, had been criticised for musical *papillotage* – extreme harmonic contrasts, even dissonance. But as the theories associated with the opposite, pro-Italian, side of the quarrel developed, Rameau's enemies criticise musical *papillotage* and endorse what might be called emotional *papillotage*. They recommend a simplification of the harmony, that is an elimination of musical *papillotage*, to enable an oscillation between extremes of feeling to take place. For them, music is structured less by tonal form than by the internal dynamics of feeling. Continuous surges in the expression of an emotion are set up, but are also bound by the expression of the opposite feeling, so that the sense of inner compulsion is made even stronger. It seems highly likely that Grimm's knowledge of the Mannheim orchestra, of which Stamitz was for some time director, and in particular, of its technique of playing with what were, for the time, extreme variations in tonal force, may have contributed to this conception of music.[12]

This theoretical and practical use of strong mood-contrast in music is encapsulated in Diderot's *Le Neveu de Rameau*. Again and again (as in his other writings), Diderot presents the oscillation between extremes of passion as a sign of emotion's force and art's power (as Condillac had presented it as one of the effects of Ancient music). Of Rameau's nephew, and of his imitation of the orchestra, it is said: 'Sa voix alloit comme le vent [. . .]. Les passions se succédoient sur son visage. On y distinguoit la tendresse, la colère, le plaisir, la douleur, on sentoit les piano, les forte' (Diderot, *Le Neveu de Rameau*, p. 28).[13] The nephew plays out a succession of opposed passions, just as he plays in mime a whole orchestra of instruments. He does not merely play, however: he *suffers*. As so often with Diderot, the spontaneous is that which is forced out: expression and passion coincide. The suffering of a violent emotion is also the spontaneous bursting through, not so much of expressed emotions as of atomistic signs: 'Ce qui émeut toujours, ce sont des cris, des mots inarticulés, des voix rompues, quelques monosyllabes qui échappent par intervalle, je ne sais quel murmure dans la gorge, entre les dents. La violence du sentiment coupant la respiration et portant le trouble dans l'esprit [. . .]' (Diderot, *Entretiens sur 'Le Fils naturel'*, pp. 101–2). For the swings in feeling to be apparent, each emotion must be differentiated by its opposite, and the atom-sign serves as the differentiating limit: 'Des signes extérieurs qui annoncent un sentiment deviennent froids et languissants s'ils ne sont subitement suivis d'autres signes indicatifs de quelques nouvelles passions qui lui succèdent' (Noverre, 1760, p. 429). But in fact these signs, these accents of passions and expressions of the face, delimit and thus characterise uniquely;[14] they lead to *diagnosis*, they are *symptoms*. As with Condillac's natural language, the accents, gestures and cries are symptoms and signs at one and the same time. With the nephew it is the actual oscillation, the structure of the emission of the cries, which is the symptom-sign. For it is the oscillations, the successive differentiations in his voice, which imitate the sounds of different instruments, and these in turn imitate the 'cri naturel'. So that his movement between opposing passions is a symptom both of his alienation from what he is and of the compulsion which seeks to correct that alienation, which pushes him to find himself in these imitations. As signs they are recognisable: as symptoms they 'escape' from him and need diagnosis – hence the peculiar obscure clarity of Rameau's pantomime: 'Et je suis sûr qu'un plus habile que moi auroit reconnu le morceau, au mouvement, au caractère, à ses mines et à quelques traits de chant qui lui échappoient par intervalles' (Diderot, *Le Neveu de Rameau*, p. 28). The oscillation between extremes, doubled by an awareness of alienation provoked by that movement, is not merely attributed to the nephew, but, tellingly, it is also described by Diderot as part of his own experience, *à propos* of the instrument the *pantaléon*, which is supposed to recreate the effects of Ancient music: 'Je me suis senti frémir et changer de visage et [. . .] j'ai vu les visages des autres changer comme le mien' (Diderot, *Correspondance*, vol. v, p. 177, novembre 1765).[15] The passivity, the alienation both from self and from others, is mitigated only by the activity of interpreting his own sensations and the visual expressions of others. The physiological 'frémissement' repeats the mind's oscillation: 'Au milieu de ses agitations et de ses cris, s'il se présentoit une tenue, un de ces endroits harmonieux où l'archet se meut lentement sur plusieurs cordes à la fois, son visage prenoit l'air de l'extase; sa voix s'adoucissoit, il s'écoutoit avec ravissement' (Diderot, *Le Neveu de Rameau*, p. 27). The symptom is then of a complex psychological movement – of exit from self ('avec ravissement') and contact with self ('s'écoutoit'). By a chiasmatic figure (the term is J. Starobinski's) these opposites reverse into each other – self-consciousness, awareness of self, becomes alienation, but exterior contemplation of the self 'ravishes' back to the self. The movement is similar to the nun's relation to self in *La Religieuse* (see above, pp. 101–2): as in the manuscript variations in the text of that novel, so in the nephew's definition of music, a diametrically opposed choice is given: 'Le chant est une imitation par les sons d'une échelle inventée par l'art ou inspirée par la nature *comme il vous plaira* [. . .] des bruits physiques ou des accents de la passion' (Diderot, *Le Neveu de Rameau*, p. 78). The expressive or gestural signs betray alienation both because they are symptoms and because they are violently differentiated, even opposed extremes.

Yet the alienation of the nephew is illusion created by music, which in turn creates illusion in the spectator who *hears*: 'Son visage prenoit l'air de l'extase. Sa voix s'adoucissoit, il s'écoutoit avec ravissement. *Il est sûr que les accords résonnoient dans ses oreilles et dans les miennes*' (Diderot, *Le Neveu de Rameau*, p. 27). The expressive signs which betray the alienation, and thus the illusion, are also all that a verbal text can show of an interior state – the illusion of an illusion. Diderot 'imitates' in words the pantomime

which imitates instruments which imitate the 'cri naturel'. This is
the typical relay structure, what I have called *aletheia*, in which we
have not the stable model–replica relation, *adequatio*, but an appearance which both is and refers beyond. *Le Neveu de Rameau*
brings out clearly the aesthetics of relay, which underly Diderot's
practice, if not his entire theory.[16] But such a structure is only possible if there is an implied viewer, since a necessary part of it is that
appearance is conceived of as external to what appears; or, at the
very least, there must be a scission between the appearance and
what it is an appearance of. In this way, music is necessarily conceived of as a set of symptoms which must be described in visual
terms. For the viewer or the diagnoser of the symptoms must
remain outside even if he is engaged by what he sees: he will be led
from appearance to appearance.[17] In Diderot, the viewer stands
looking on – his awareness is that what is seen is merely appearance of something beyond. From this follows the relay structure
given to imitation, the structure of *aletheia*. A true listener, on the
contrary, is incorporated by the sound into a circle of transmission
between hearer and speaker-singer. This is Rousseau's aesthetics of
music, as we shall see.

Yet Rousseau's aesthetics is multi-layered. The *Essai sur l'origine des langues*, where the circle of transmission described above is
created, is flanked by the earlier *Encyclopédie* articles and the later
Dictionnaire de musique. In both of these he often sharpens and
tightens what are conventional views of imitation and illusion.
Thus in the 'experiment' recounted in the *Lettre sur la musique
française*, as in so many pamphlets of the time, a stranger, in this
case an Armenian, is taken to the opera and his reactions are
observed. It is precisely his visual expression which is interpreted as
a symptom of feeling, and as a touchstone of the superiority of
Italian music:[18] 'Ces chants divins déchirent ou ravissent l'âme,
mettent le spectateur hors de lui-même, et lui arrachent, dans ces
transports, des cris dont jamais nos tranquilles opéras ne furent
honorés' (Rousseau, *Lettre sur la musique française*, p. 422).
Music's illusion engenders symptoms – involuntary ones torn out
of the spectator's or the listener's passivity. Rousseau, like
Diderot, conceives of music as the passage between extremes:

C'est par elle [la hardiesse des modulations] que le musicien, passant
brusquement d'un ton ou d'un mode à un autre, et supprimant quand il le
faut les transitions intermédiaires et scolastiques, sait exprimer les réticences, les interruptions, les discours entrecoupés, qui sont le langage des
passions impétueuses. (Rousseau, *Lettre sur la musique française*, p. 421)

By his use of the terms 'réticences', 'interruptions', 'discours entrecoupés', Rousseau implies that the silence is not complete, but points to something hidden; like Diderot he implies that the silence must be overcome by a superior force.

Yet if imitation is a relay structure, as in Diderot, then the appearance, in that it refers out to something else, is unreal: 'Les acteurs *semblant* s'oublier eux-mêmes, portent leur égarement dans l'âme de tout spectateur sensible' (Rousseau, *Lettre sur la musique française*, p. 427). There is a kind of taint of unreality in the logic of imitation with which Diderot plays, but which Rousseau expels in the *Lettre à d'Alembert* (1759). The *Dictionnaire de musique* (1765), by its very sharpening of the *Encyclopédie* articles, brings out the final impossibility of 'imitation' (much as Diderot, probably influenced by the *Lettre à d'Alembert*, does in his *Préface* to the *Salon de 1767*). For instance, in his statement 'Les duos sont hors de la nature *dans la musique imitative*', Rousseau adds the underlined phrase to the *Encyclopédie* article when he revises it for the *Dictionnaire de musique*, and in doing so flouts the traditional nature–imitation distinction. The highest art is not to equal nature: 'le chef d'œuvre de la musique est de se faire oublier elle-même'. The awareness can only be forgotten – it has always been there. In speaking of 'forgetting', Rousseau admits that a separation once existed between art and nature, even while he describes that separation as overcome. And that which overcomes, goes beyond nature and so falls short of nature.[19] But these two factors, resistance to imitation, and a kind of overbidding designed to overcome that resistance, create a dynamic version of the movement between involvement and awareness. Even extreme emotion is thus not oscillation but movement; even the passivity of abandonment to emotion is an itinerary, a diapason:

Il [le musicien] [procédait] dans le bas par de petits intervalles pour exprimer les langueurs de la tristesse et de l'abattement, lui arrachant dans le haut les sons aigus de l'emportement et de la douleur, et l'entraînait rapidement, par tous les intervalles de son diapason, dans l'agitation du désespoir, ou l'égarement des passions contrastées. (*Dictionnaire de musique*, article *Expression*)

This transition through extremes is only superficially similar to Diderot's. The very different consequences are underlined by his use of the term 'diapason' which the *O.E.D.* defines as 'in concord through all the notes of the scale'. The extremes are united in a compass, a circle, just as, we shall find in the *Essai sur l'origine des langues*, hearer and speaker are united in a circle of transmission. Even in the passage above, where Rousseau seems closest to Diderot, with 'diapason' we find the completion of a circuit of sound, whereas with Diderot, we find only infinite relay.

11
MUSIC AND IMITATION

In the discussions of operatic representation, the *Bouffonistes* preferred Italian opera to Rameau because it was held to be adequate to a representable model. This preference can be related to the mid-century movement in the theatre associated with Diderot, and, in Germany, with Lessing – a movement away from *papillotage* and towards *adequatio*. In the discussions of musical texture, the *Bouffonistes* preferred Italian to French, Pergolesi to Rameau. They held Pergolesi's music to be of a less formal structure and more melodic. Yet in the case of the two prominent *Bouffonistes*, Diderot and Rousseau, I have suggested that these simple attitudes to operatic representation and musical texture are complicated by concerns working at a deeper level, which oppose their aesthetics as those of 'deux frères ennemis' (the phrase is Jean Fabre's). Most critics until the 1770s concur with this preference. In France it is in fact the eighteenth century which insists most strongly that music 'imitates'. I shall show that in music, as in other art forms, 'imitation' comes to mean reference. Yet music is barely referential, so that as a result either music must be declared 'vague' or the imitation model must be denied or revised beyond recognition. In England it was music, according to M. H. Abrams, that mediated the change from the concept of art as imitation to that of art as expression (Abrams, 1958, p. 50). In France, something more complex occurs. The notion of what is representable shrinks, and comes to apply, in the main, only to objects which can be referred to precisely. The notion of what should be represented changes, and as a result 'illusion' is radically internalised, becoming a mistake obtained through an objective adequation between model and replica, which excludes the consumer, or a subjective experience in which the consumer is both subject and object – in which, so to speak, he includes himself.

The imitation model
The specificity of the French insistence on imitation is perhaps most

273

clearly seen in comparison with German music. In spite of the similarity of vocabulary, the notion of 'imitation' is wider in German theory and practice. Where Lulli had merely repetitive majesty (relying on the excellence of the twenty-four violinists in the royal orchestra, doubling all parts so as to make supplementary harmony unnecessary), the 'strenger Satz' of Buxtehude and Bach balances polyphonic writing and harmony to give unparalleled richness of tone without loss of melodic line. This music was built on a notion of imitation which could be said to be cosmic (for the cosmos is harmonious), on a theory of the emotions and a vocabulary of motifs which the hearer could and was prepared to interpret symbolically. So that 'imitation' in German has meaning in a much wider and more powerful context, closer to the Aristotelian application of mimesis to music.[1] What was known as *'expressio verborum'* was not emotionally expressive music in the modern sense: 'The means of verbal representation in baroque music were not then direct psychological and emotional but indirect, that is intellectual and pictorial' (Bukofzer, 1948, p. 5).[2] Against this the *style galant* develops – C. P. E. Bach breaks up his father's techniques of continuous expansion of a theme and terraced dynamics, in the same way that Couperin earlier had dislocated the sweeping rhythm of Lulli and his followers. And in this reaction against the elder Bach, Quantz, the flute tutor of Frederick the Great, and prominent aesthetician of the *style galant* (Schäfke, 1924), criticises him in terms which in a French context are applied to Rameau – in particular, 'difficulté vaincue' is applied to his virtuosity.

The fact remains that French music is held to imitate and, from Lulli on, to do so in a far more restricted sense of the term than German music. French music had a strong programmatic tradition (Cudworth, 1956–7). Couperin and Rameau in their concertos presented musical portraits of their friends, and Marin Marais wrote a description of a gallstone operation in a solo sonata for gamba and continuo. (The analogy with Rococo *ornemanistes* and their silver tureen in the shape of a lobster seems evident; the effect is deliberately strange, that of an imitation of the bizarre, in a medium which seems unrelated.) Such a use is close to a *reductio ad absurdum* of imitation applied to music. Yet this programmatic use of music is not restricted to Rameau: the *Bouffonistes* were criticised for preferring the imitation of a ticking clock to the evocation of old age – that is, for preferring the *Bouffons* to Mondonville's *Titon et l'Aurore*.[3] The successor of the *Bouffons*, the *opéra comique*, seems to specialise in pieces which imitate sounds: the 'duo du jeu de tric-trac', for instance, in Philidor's opera *Le Soldat musicien* is described thus: 'On peut dire qu'il n'y a pas un coup de dés dans le cornet, sous la main & dessus la table qui ne soit rendu' (Garcin, 1772, pp. 10–11).[4]

The result of the theoretical insistence on imitation and the practice of programmatic composition is that all kinds of music are defended in terms of imitation,[5] or at least of representation. But music is a pathological version of a problem already present for the eighteenth century in metaphor. Fontenelle's question 'Sonate, que me veux-tu?', is quoted approvingly by d'Alembert, Rousseau, and later, with the significant change to 'Musique, que me veux-tu?', by Boyer:[6] if imitation comes to mean replication, what can music replicate? The rationalising answers to the rationalising question 'Sonate, que me veux-tu?' are attempts to find a reference for music, to combat the two accusations: that music has a rational form, but no reference, and is thus arbitrary; and that music merely pleases the senses, and is equally arbitrary.

Now the question whether taste might not be conventional, whether *all* art might not be arbitrary, a question almost tinged with fear, beset much of eighteenth-century speculation on art. Hume's *Essay on Taste* examines it, and it provides one of the antinomies resolved by Kant in the *Critique of Judgement*. But the problem was even more pressing for music than for taste in general. A writer such as Cartaud de la Vilate says in 1736: 'Peut-être en effet, les tons de la musique seroient-ils reconnus pour des assortimens arbitraires si une oreille philosophique et non prévenue en démêloit les rapports' (Cartaud de la Vilate, 1736, p. 301). This is of course a variant of the critique of formal arbitrariness levelled against poetry by the *Modernes* (see above, pp. 222–3). The same writer sketches an interpretation of Castel's colour piano, as a satire on music for being an arbitrary assembling of tone: 'Bien des gens qui ne connaîtront point la sincérité du Père Castel, croiront que le clavecin oculaire est une parodie ingénieuse de la musique.' For although he claimed to have found a scale for colour, so that musical harmony played on the keyboard would result in visual harmony of colour movement in front of the eyes, it is true that Castel appears to equate freedom with what is arbitrary. Like Réaumur, Castel believes that the scientist can only classify the enormous variety of the created world, and that the artist can only exhibit; he thus with one blow enters into conflict with the *philosophes-grammairiens'* natural order, which they presented as the structure of thought, and with Newton's optics, the structure of

275

light. If structure is human classification, then it is conventional, subject to choice, arbitrary.

The standard reply is to assert the unity of musical and rational structure:

Pendant que tous vos concertants lisaient sur le papier chacun sa tablature, vous lisiez aussi la vôtre écrite en notes éternelles et ineffaçables dans le grand livre de la raison qui est ouvert à tous les esprits attentifs. (Le père André, 1843, p. 79)[7]

In this type of rationalist aesthetic, production and consumption are the same process (in the same way that the *ordre naturel* for the *philosophes-grammairiens* underlies both the emission and the reception of speech). If Diderot in the *Lettre sur les aveugles* suggests that even pleasure in symmetry may be conventional, elsewhere in his work the symmetry is founded on a perception of relationships, internal but not subjective: 'Le goût en général consiste dans la perception des rapports. Un beau tableau, un poème, une belle musique ne nous plaisent que par les rapports que nous y remarquons. Il en est même d'une belle vie comme d'un beau concert' (Diderot, *O.C.*, vol. II, p. 578, cf. Bongie, 1977). In neither of these views is music emitted by the spheres with which the mind is supposed, literally, to be in tune. The cosmos is excluded, and the structure of music, one might almost say, is only a rational twist of the mind: 'La Musique, dit M. Leibniz, n'est à bien des égards qu'un calcul obscur & secret que l'âme fait sans s'en appercevoir [. . .] Un tissu de sons amis & proportionnés qui s'entre-exigent les uns les autres, & subsistent en quelque sorte par eux-mêmes' (Arnaud, 1754, pp. 16, 22–3).

Such an intellectualist view of perception of and pleasure in music is related, in musical practice, to highly organised and abstract forms. These are felt by many to be arbitrary, 'gothic', without content, complexities associated with 'difficulté vaincue': 'Fugues, imitations, doubles dessins, et autre beautés arbitraires et de pure convention, qui n'ont presque de mérite que la difficulté vaincue, et qui toutes ont été inventées dans la naissance de l'art' (Rousseau, *Lettre sur la musique française*, p. 425).[8] These rationalist theories of music were opposed:

Je sais qu'il y a dans le monde une espèce de philosophes qui [. . .] prétendent que le sentiment est le seul juge de l'Harmonie; que le plaisir de l'oreille est le seul beau qu'on y doive chercher et que le plaisir même dépend trop de l'opinion, du préjugé des coûtumes reçues, des habitudes acquises pour pouvoir être assujetti à des règies certaines. (Le père André, 1843, p. 77)

Certain of these anti-intellectualist philosophers tried to postulate a kind of structure in pleasurable sensation: the 'theory of agreeable sentiments' of Levesque de Pouilly postulated an equally arbitrary 'goût naturel pour l'ordre qui est la cause physique du plaisir' (d'Olivet, 1738, pp. 7–8).[9] The rationalising sensualism of the day gives a decidedly materialist twist to such theories. Estève, for instance, declares: 'On est encore à soupçonner qu'il pourroit y avoir une force de raison qui développât les principes essentiels du goût & qui par l'action mécanique des sens pût fixer les préceptes de ce qui ne doit point être tout à fait arbitraire' (Estève, 1753, vol. II, p. 204).[10] This type of theory calls 'sensations matérielles' both what is to be imitated and the result in the consumer (Estève, 1753, vol. II, pp. 16–17).

Kant shows the vicious circle in such arguments, based on a double use of the word 'sensation' as pleasure or pain on the one hand, and as sense-data on the other. He brings out clearly and acutely the reflexive element in this form of eighteenth-century thought. For the pleasure is in the sensation of one's state. As a result it is undifferentiated, and is indifferently provoked by a variety of stimuli which cannot be qualitatively distinguished.[11] Rousseau had rejected this sensualism earlier, as he had rejected mere rationalism, and for reasons similar to Kant's.[12] As will be shown, what is a reflexive element in the aesthetics of the minor sensualists – a mere awareness that the hearer is attending to sound – becomes in Rousseau's thought self-awareness at the deepest level, that of relation to self.

Illusion, imitation, reference

The basis of sensualist theories of music was a 'natural pleasure' in sound: 'Tous les sons harmoniques affectent d'une façon agréable, indépendamment des images qu'ils peuvent présenter à l'esprit ou des idées qu'ils sont capables de réveiller' (*Réflexions sur la musique*, 1754, p. 22). Birdsong, for instance, proves that there is a pleasure in sensation without 'images' and without that proportion between harmony and the human mind, which rational thought postulates as the 'natural order'. But materialist tendencies in sensualism and the eighteenth-century conception of music as rational and intellectual are both merely formal accounts of the art, as Rousseau points out clearly in the *Essai sur l'origine des langues:* they leave music without determinate content.

For music arouses in critics what could almost be called a fear of abstract art. 'Sonate, que me veux-tu?', as I have pointed out, is

quoted with approval; the *clavecin oculaire* of le père Castel arouses fascinated scorn:

Partout où il n'y a point d'imitation, il n'y a point de Musique. Croire que cet Art puisse consister dans une suite de sons qui ne représentent rien, c'est croire que la Peinture peut consister dans un assemblage de couleurs sans dessein & le langage dans une suite de mots sans idées. (Garcin, 1772, pp. 60–1)[13]

Likewise, ballet must become pantomime: 'Celui qui ne rouleroit que sur quelques pas communs & combinés seulement de deux ou trois façons ne signifieroit jamais que de la Danse & ne présenteroit nulle autre idée' (Bridard de La Garde, 1740, p. 53), and what is needed in a ballet is a determinate plot, that is, 'Un Ballet qui peint à l'esprit une action suivie & raisonnée en même temps qu'il offre aux yeux un choix agréable & varié des attitudes les plus propres à fixer l'attention.'

'Toute Musique et toute Danse doit avoir une signification, un sens' (Batteux, 1746, p. 260).[14] For instrumental music is 'vague', there is no necessary relation between sounds and ideas.[15] To counterbalance this, d'Alembert demands a detailed sense even for symphonies; the dance airs must be 'caractérisés' – which means that their reference must be capable of being objectively isolated.[16] Everything must be translatable into language:

Il seroit donc à souhaiter qu'il n'y eût dans nos opéras que des symphonies expressives, c'est à dire dont le sens et l'esprit fussent toujours indiqués en détail [. . .] que les airs de danse [. . .] fussent dessinés par le musicien de manière qu'il fût en état d'en donner pour ainsi dire la traduction d'un bout à l'autre. (d'Alembert, 1821, p. 544)

If music is more than a collection of sensations, runs the argument, then it must be able to be reinterpreted linguistically. Against this, certain critics make of this supposed weakness a strength: 'Ce vague même, qui l'empêche de donner à ses accens la précision du discours, en confiant à notre imagination le soin de l'interpréta-tion, lui fait éprouver un empire qu'aucune langue ne sauroit exer-cer sur elle', says a critic of Rousseau. He admits: 'Les images de la Musique ne peuvent avoir la réalité de celles de la Poésie & de la Peinture', yet suggests that, for this very reason, the mind can the more freely enjoy its own creative power (Bonneval, 1753, p. 9). But a defence such as this indicates the problem: that of 'reality'. 'Images' must have 'reality' to refer to. The insistence on language as a guarantor of meaning does not stop at excluding instrumental music,[17] though it reinforces the traditional French preoccupation with opera. Meaning conceived of as 'images' needs to point at reality, and this is a view which inevitably makes of reference a backstop to 'reality'. A suitable subject is a precise reference to an external object, or to an internal state, reified and distinct. This amounts to a severe restriction placed upon what is understood by 'imitation' (comparable to contemporary movements in painting theory).[18] And in this way the insistence on reference becomes more than a Rococo joke, the clash of incompatible medium and subject (as in Marin Marais' sonata, mentioned above). For if 'illusion' is also insisted on, if 'illusion' is to be a mistake based on adequation between model and replica, then it is not an appearance pointing beyond itself to something of which it is the appearance, but, on the contrary, a set of sense-data quasi-identical to normal sense-data. But these sense-data will be divorced from a set of expectations or perceptual context.[19] And that divorce can only be effected if the object about which the illusion is to be created is isolatable, if, in other words, it is an object of reference out of which a replica can be made.

But how can music refer? 'La Peinture, la Poésie, la Musique ont les mêmes fondemens, une même fin. Le Peintre forme des images par le pinceau. Le Musicien réveille celles du cerveau par la voix' (Duval, 1725, vol. II, p. 270). This type of account erases any mediation between model and replica by way of the artist's materials or technique. There is a mechanism of nature, not of the artist. In one such theory, the painter is the model; the brain fibres are so pliant that they receive any impression: they direct quite mechanically the painter's fingers, and thus his brush. As to the musician:

Les cris de joie, d'admiration, de crainte, de douleur, d'accablement, ont frappé son cerveau. Le langage de l'amour, de la haine, de l'indifférence [. . .] a fléchi ses fibres, son âme émue selon les loix de l'union avec le corps, fait prendre aux esprits, en conséquence de ces émotions, de nouveaux mouvemens, & par les trémoussemens qu'ils reçoivent dans les organes de la voix, ils y forment les différents tons de la musique. Le Musicien n'a qu'à mettre dans ces tons les rapports que l'expérience lui a appris, dans les autres les émotions qu'il éprouve en lui-même. (Duval, 1725, vol. II, p. 271)

Music here is merely a writing down of sound, of what is heard, a solution of breath-taking simplicity.

Where a critic goes beyond such a solution, he may appear to be suggesting general expressivity:

Il y a dans ce morceau un sublime que l'on sent mieux qu'on ne peut l'exprimer: L'Harmonie est si belle et la distribution des accords qui accompagnent la voix est si heureusement faite dans toutes les parties que l'*illusion fait croire qu'on entend réellement* les bienheureux célébrer la stabilité du Fils de Dieu assis à la droite de son père. (*Sentiment d'un harmonophile*, 1756, p. 8).

But the replies provoked by such a claim indicate however something radically different. The critical replies statements of this sort receive show that contemporaries interpret such descriptions, and in particular the language of illusion, as implying that the sound of music *replicated* experience. The idea that illusion as a mistake is related by contemporaries to precise reference is thus confirmed:

> On trouve tous les jours des gens qui distinguent dans nos Motets des tableaux, des images, que notre Musique est hors d'état de peindre; ils y voient la grandeur du Tout-puissant, sa bonté, les respects que lui rendent les créatures etc. Je voudrois bien que les gens qui ont les organes assez délicats pour saisir ces images me disent quels rapports ils trouvent entre ces idées purement métaphysiques & des sons, ou en vertu de quelle convention tel ou tel son a acquis le pouvoir de les réveiller. (*Réflexions*, 1754, p. 26)

The extent to which imitation has retracted into reference can be illustrated by the late writer La Cépède's use of 'hieroglyph'. Whereas for Diderot the hieroglyph was the means whereby things are said and represented at one and the same time (Diderot, *Lettre sur les sourds et muets*, *O.C.*, vol. II, p. 549), for La Cépède the term denotes only a set of 'real' sounds inserted in a tissue of musical sound: a replica, not a representation. The logic of this is made clear by another critic: to be expressive, one must refer, one must paint something: 'Il faut [. . .] proposer toujours un modèle à copier; il n'y a pas d'expression sans peinture' (Lacombe, 1758, p. 257).

How does music present 'real' sounds? 'Tout ce qui peut être entendu, la musique le peint en le faisant entendre' (La Cépède, 1785, vol. I, p. 79). Few critics distinguish sounds of definite pitch from noise. Dubos and Batteux both divide music into two types, according to its 'objects of imitation' – one type of music which imitates 'Les sons et les bruits non-passionnés; elle répond au paysage dans la Peinture'; the other which 'exprime les sons animés & qui tiennent aux sentiments; c'est le tableau à personnages' (Batteux, 1746, p. 266).[20] Some such division is common currency: 'La Peinture physique et la Peinture d'expression et de caractère' is a further instance. But, music being hopelessly resistant to reference, the critic has immediately to make a further distinction: 'La Peinture physique' is divided into 'real' and 'artificial'. The 'real' occurs where 'Les choses [. . .] nous sont rendues exactement comme elles existent dans la nature' (the example given is the overture in Rameau's *Acante et Céphise*, where the *vive le roi* is imitated). The artificial, on the other hand, 'renferme les choses que la Musique nous rend *par les dispositions & des progressions de sons analogues à la nature*, & par l'imitation de la mesure des tons & des mouvemens de ces choses' (the standard example is the storm, to be repeated *ad nauseam* both in the theory and the music of the time) (*Sentiment d'un harmonophile*, 1756, p. 68). Music, being unable merely to 'lift' sounds from nature, must work by analogy and this analogy, though not further analysed, is said to produce illusion. This division of the scope of music to allow for 'analogy' is repeated in other types of music theory; it is not merely a result of the non-referential nature of music. The need to have recourse to the concept of analogy is a consequence of the fact that 'reference' is not the same as 'meaning': it is a far more limited concept. But the effect of the allowing of analogy is to free music from the demand that it should replicate. 'Illusion' as a result changes sides. From meaning a replica of sense impressions in the 'peinture physique', 'illusion' moves on to mean something radically different; in such a phrase as 'la peinture d'expression & de caractère qui est tout artificielle et illusoire' it clearly does duty for 'subjective' (*Sentiment d'un harmonophile*, 1756, p. 72). The two late meanings of 'illusion' are here illustrated: either the result of *adequatio*, a transparent relation between model and replica, or, radically internalised, the designation of a private, subjective state of mind.

Music, imitation, emotion

Music's power of reference is limited to those objects which emit noise or sounds of definite pitch. Yet the great classical tradition, going back to Aristotle, for which music was the most 'imitative' of the arts, linked music and the soul's affections: music could create different moods in the hearer according to its mode. However, by mid-eighteenth century, 'imitation' is contracting into 'public act of reference'. But emotions are private, and only their clearly discernible outward manifestations can be imitated in this sense. As a result, music is held to imitate the vocal symptoms of passion, the exterior signs: 'Elle offre les signes des sentiments pour peindre les sentiments eux-mêmes, qui se dérobent à ses pinceaux; & comme toutes les passions ont des signes extérieurs plus ou moins forts qui les caractérisent, elle peut les représenter toutes' (La Cépède, 1785, vol. I, p. 80). The double nature of this 'cri naturel' which is both sign *and* symptom, communication and involuntary cry, has been discussed earlier in connection with *Le Neveu de Rameau* and Condillac's essay.

Yet it was not only the classical tradition of commentary on music, but also the rhetorical tradition in poetry, which tended to bring together the imitation of feeling and the arousal of feeling – as is shown by definitions of music as 'l'art de peindre et d'émouvoir par le moyen des sons' (Laugier, 1754, p. 4). If the listener's reaction is to be more than symptomatic grunt in reply to symptomatic cry, the relation of music to emotion must be modified. Once more, as in the account of the imitation of sound, this is done in terms of analogy:

Puisque notre âme est susceptible de saisir toutes les modifications de la Musique, il s'ensuit que ces modifications ont des caractères relatifs aux objets qui peuvent l'affecter, & ces caractères sont les moyens dont la Musique se sert pour peindre les affections de l'âme en choisissant ceux dont l'expression est analogue aux mouvements que ces affections font naître en elle. (*Sentiment d'un harmonophile*, 1756, p. 72)

The modification is very substantial: arguing from our subjective comprehension of music, the anonymous critic moves to the conclusion that sounds must *therefore* have a relation to 'objects' that affect us. The effect of music is due to that relation, a highly tenuous one, mediated by a series of subjective relays – 'modifications', 'caractères relatifs aux objets', 'affections de l'âme' – which are created by an analogical expression. This is not an unwittingly reflexive sensualist account of pleasure as sensation and sensation as pleasurable, of the kind that Kant criticised in his discussion of the 'sentiments agréables' type of theory. Instead of 'illusion' related to the conditions of its production, we have a mediation which creates a circle between affects expressed and affects experienced. 'Illusion', or rather its satellite terms, moves from designation of a replica to a radical subjectivity, one in which the affects experienced circulate by nourishing themselves from the subjectivity: 'Ce prestige seul nourrit les passions qu'il fait naître' (Séran de La Tour, 1747, p. 45). Illusion is here subjective, self-procreating. As a result, passion is no longer in this type of theory a succession of sharply contrasted moments: it is thought of as flowing feeling.

Direct imitation of emotion by music can only result in a series of cries and grunts. Music and emotions as a result have to be related by a regressive process – the insertions of a mediating analogy – and this theory is characteristic of some of the *Bouffonistes* or those associated with them; for example, the anonymous author of the *Sentiment d'un harmonophile*, or of the *Réflexions sur la musique*, which is sometimes attributed to d'Alembert.[21] It is d'Alembert, in the *Discours préliminaire de l'Encyclopédie*, who, to my knowledge, first makes the suggestion that sounds may be analogous to affects: 'Les sons harmoniques ne peuvent pas peindre le sentiment, mais ils peuvent en réveiller l'idée & mettre l'âme dans l'état où l'on suppose qu'est celle du personnage qu'on fait agir'; and it is d'Alembert who suggests where the analogy might reside. He takes the reflexive element in the sensualist account of art, but changes its level; for the pleasure or pain produced by the sensation is what enables the comparison between sensations to be made:

Quoique les perceptions que nous recevons par divers organes diffèrent entr'elles autant que leurs objets, on peut néanmoins les comparer sous un autre point de vue qui leur est commun, c'est-à-dire, par la situation de plaisir ou de trouble où elles mettent notre âme. Un objet effrayant, un bruit terrible produisent chacun en nous une émotion par laquelle nous pouvons jusqu'à un certain point les rapprocher, & que nous désignons souvent dans l'un & dans l'autre cas ou par le même nom, ou par des noms synonymes. Je ne vois donc point pourquoi un Musicien qui auroit à peindre un objet effrayant, ne pourroit pas y réussir en cherchant dans la Nature l'espèce de bruit qui peut produire en nous l'émotion la plus semblable à celle que cet objet y excite. (d'Alembert, 1751, p. xii)

It is interesting that, at this point, d'Alembert considers that he is extending the field of imitation in music from passions to sensations. But he brings out the fact that the common ground which makes possible the analogy, or the comparison of passions, is our relation to emotion through self-reflexion in pleasure or pain. As a result, the mediation through analogy allows the integration of the hearer into the reaction. It is this that Rousseau in his letter to d'Alembert of 26 June 1751 picks up: '[. . .] à un très-petit nombre de choses près, l'art du musicien ne consiste point à peindre immédiatement les objets, mais à mettre l'âme dans une disposition semblable à celle où la mettoit leur présence' (Rousseau, *Correspondance complète*, vol. II, p. 160). It is in such phrases that one sees how the reflexive element in the sensualist account of art is refined: the pleasure is not automatic but mediating, and as a result, as will be seen, creates a relation to the self which becomes a shadowy component of every emotion.

Music, imitation, and language

One method by which music could imitate emotion was, as I have

shown, to imitate the sounds of emotion – the grunts and cries. Since, through an eighteenth-century confusion, emotion is what cannot be suppressed, it is thought of as spontaneous, as common to all mankind throughout history. Its sounds are 'cris naturels'.

I have also shown how the 'cri naturel' in Condillac's theory yokes together expression and imitation, symptom and sign, spontaneity and established comprehension. Condillac apparently wishes to make the 'signes naturels et accidentels' continuous with the 'signes de convention'. Yet to make the first develop smoothly into the second proves to be impossible. The symptom is involuntary sign, transmitting a sensation or perception; this is automatic in both emitter and receiver: 'Des signes naturels, dont le caractère est de faire connoître par eux-mêmes et indépendamment du choix que nous en avons fait, l'impression que nous éprouvons, en occasionnant quelque chose de semblable chez les autres' (Condillac, 1947, p. 19). What is least voluntary, the symptom, is the closest to the raw moment of experience; the cries that fear or pain extract are those which reveal emotion almost against one's will, and instantaneously, with no temporal or spiritual distance to allow of distortion. By this token, they are not the transmission of information. However, when the symptom is considered as effect by the onlooker, when it is traced back to its cause, when it is diagnosed, then a flow of information occurs. Condillac treats this change as an accident, as a matter of habit (Condillac, 1947, p. 61), and thus tries to smooth the passage into conventional signs. But the hiatus lodges itself within the 'cri naturel' itself. It serves as a basis for the development of language: it is imitated. The 'cri naturel' as sign imitates the 'cri naturel' as expression, as symptom. The imitation, the repetition at one remove, guarantees the meaning of the sign by reference to an origin: but in the imitation the origin is *not there*. The hiatus between convention and natural language cannot be overcome; it is contained within the notions of 'cri naturel', which is authentic when it is original, involuntary sign, but imitated and inauthentic when it is a voluntary sign, that is language.

This ambiguity in the notion of 'cri naturel' is inevitably carried over into music theory, and theorists struggle with it. Condillac tries to neutralise it by making the two elements of the 'cri naturel' into historically separate moments. At first, music and language were one, both developing out of expressive gesture. They imitated, through tonality, those gestures which accompanied the 'cri naturel'. But the tonality gradually became less inflected; language and music became separate. Pantomime and music are, then, in

different ways reinventions of the original language: 'C'est ainsi, que, par un long circuit, on parvint à imaginer, comme une invention nouvelle, un langage qui avoit été le premier que les hommes eussent parlé, ou qui du moins n'en différoit que parce qu'il étoit propre à exprimer un plus grand nombre de pensées' (Condillac, 1947, p. 71). The symptomatic nature of music and its freshness recreated the effect of the 'cri naturel'. Diderot, on the other hand, retains the ambiguity. For if music imitates the 'cri naturel', it both expresses and *is* at the same moment, like Diderot's hieroglyph. In that respect, music can be held to be superior to language, where words, inevitably, are not their meaning. But the very superiority is based on a following *after*, where the image which imitates gains its power from what is imitated, from its reference to a supposed origin which is not present. The imitation of the 'cri naturel' is in fact infinite relay.

But languages have altered since the first days of humanity. The implausibility of opera derives, for Rousseau, from the historical separation of music and speech. As a result, his frontal attack on French opera in the *Lettre sur la musique française* has two prongs: the first is that the French use of recitative fails to make of it the proper equivalent to speech: 'Il est évident [. . .] que le meilleur récitatif dans quelque Langue que ce soit [. . .] est celui qui approche le plus de la parole' (Rousseau, *Lettre sur la musique française*, p. 433). And it was this statement which aroused the ire of those who complained that Rousseau was overlooking convention: 'Il en est de la Musique comme de la Danse; celui qui en dansant approcheroit le plus d'un homme qui marche, n'amuseroit pas beaucoup les Spectateurs' (Bonneval, 1753, p. 10). The second prong of the attack is to argue that all music, not just recitative, is closely related to the sounds of a language. Since the sounds of French are nasal and ugly, French music is inherently disadvantaged and will compensate with a musical style which is much too far from speech. Lulli, says Rousseau, is far removed from the sounds of the language. Yet, for the purpose of his recitative, Lulli was supposed to have studied the actress Champeslé's declamation, and, in doing so, could be thought to have fulfilled Rousseau's criterion of closeness to the language. Rousseau is at pains to show, on the contrary – by dint of a typical eighteenth-century hypothetical experiment, that of giving some lines from Lulli's librettist, Quinault, to an actress to read – that Lulli's recitative had no relation to declamation. Yet even if it had proved to have such a relation, French music is still inferior, because the language itself is phonically inferior.[22]

It is interesting that this is a national, specific, version of a structure of argument typical of Rousseau. Music must be *like* speech, yet it must not *be* speech. The substitution of the spoken word for recitative is difficult, he writes, much later, to Gluck. He uses the problem created by the danger of breaking illusion to warn of the difficulty of mixing speech and music:

Il faut [. . .] prendre de grandes précautions pour rendre cette union supportable, et pour la rendre assez naturelle dans la musique imitative pour faire illusion au théâtre; pourtant quand la violence de la passion fait entrecouper les paroles par des propos commencés et interrompus, tant à cause de la force des sentimens qui ne trouvent point de termes suffisans pour s'exprimer, qu'à cause de leur impétuosité qui les fait succéder en tumulte les uns aux autres, avec une rapidité sans suite et sans ordre, je crois que le mélange alternatif de la parole et de la symphonie peut seul exprimer une pareille situation. (Rousseau, *Observations sur Gluck*, pp. 466, 468)

Yet the mixture which can break illusion, which is justified only as the rendering of the most intense passion (that is, as natural) is fully validated when successful (when it creates illusion). Rousseau's aesthetic moves between near-silence and tumult, both of which are signs of extreme passion.

If both Rousseau, in the *Lettre sur la musique française*, and Diderot, in the *Entretiens sur 'Le Fils naturel'*, use declamation to show the unnaturalness of French recitative, they do so because it was widely believed of Greek tragedy that its declamation had been written down in musical notation. The 'harmonophile' suggests that musicians should use 'Une déclamation notée, qui approchant le plus de la parole, ne fût qu'un vrai Récitatif débité, qui remplaceroit le chant informe à qui nous donnons ce nom' (*Sentiment d'un harmonophile*, 1756, p. 74).[23]

But Condillac, in the *Essai sur l'origine des connaissances humaines* had doubted that it was possible to write down declamation in musical notation. The tones are not sustained enough to be appreciated. He interprets differently the relation of music and language in classical tragedy. In a pattern of thought clearly related to Rousseau's, it is the oddity of contemporary opera which shows its decadence. Present opera compensates for the unnaturalness of the joining of poetry and music by extravagance. At first, according to Condillac, declamation was not composed, it was originally sung, since language *was* music. From such an attitude derives, of course, Rousseau's insistence on the superiority of vocal over instrumental music; and melody, assimilated to *chant*, over harmony. 'Toute musique qui ne se chante pas, quelque harmonieuse qu'elle puisse être, n'est point une musique imitative' (*Dictionnaire de musique*, article *Mélodie*).

From this speculation comes a hesitation between affirming (i) that music's sounds are based on, and justified by, the first language; (ii) that music is the original language; and (iii) that music is the sound of present language. Such a hesitation is found, for example, in the work of La Cépède, who writes: 'La musique considérée en elle-même n'est autre chose que le langage ordinaire dont on a ôté toutes les articulations.' Yet music has a natural and not a conventional basis: 'Ils n'ont tous ensemble eu recours à la musique que par une espèce d'instinct [. . .] sans préparation, sans convention, uniquement parce que ce langage en accords était lié avec un plus grand nombre de sensations' (La Cépède, 1785, vol. i, p. 30). Such a language escapes from convention, whether of representation or notation: 'Il n'est pas plus possible en musique de convenir qu'on emploiera de nouveaux signes pour peindre telle ou telle passion qu'on ne peut convenir en peinture de représenter une surface carrée vue de face par une surface triangulaire aperçue de même.' There are thus in music 'des mots inaltérables, indépendans de toute convention & les seuls dont on doive se servir pour rendre les idées qu'ils désignent' (La Cépède, 1785, vol. i, pp. 52, 54).[24] Such 'words' are the 'cri naturel' seen as an instinctual erratic block still present in unnatural civilised man: 'Ce cri si énergique est partout le même; il est de toutes les langues & de toutes les Nations' (Lacombe, 1758, p. 282).[25] But this cry is not merely seen as the revelation of inner feeling: it is an external symptom of it, for the Condillacian ambivalence lasts right down to La Cépède:

Nous suppléerions à la peinture d'une passion qui ne peut tomber sous les sens, par tous les signes extérieurs qui l'accompagnent, & qui réveilleroient si fort son idée dans ceux qui nous entoureroient que tous la reconnoîtroient au point d'en être fortement émus. [. . . La Musique] offre les signes des sentimens pour peindre les sentimens eux-mêmes. (La Cépède, 1785, vol. i, p. 80)

But in general the thesis that music imitates specific sounds of language proves inadequate and is forced back into a kind of regress. Just as d'Alembert had in relation to emotion, the author of the *Réflexions sur la musique en général et sur la musique française en particulier* has recourse to the notion of analogy when considering music in relation to language. The first sounds were non-conventional: 'Les hommes agités de quelque passion, ou dont l'âme étoit dans un état violent, poussoient des cris qui exprimoient leur état, l'idée de ces passions & de ces états a dû se lier naturellement à ces cris.' The need to communicate what was no longer the case caused the development of arbitrary signs, not attached to particular modifications of tone. Thus expression and meaning were gradually divorced, forcing music to model itself on individual and natural language, and not on natural tones (*Réflexions*, 1754, pp. 14–15), except in moments of extreme passion. Hence music 'a été forcée de se régler sur ceux [sons] que la convention des hommes leur a substitués' (*Réflexions*, 1754, p. 17). The author denies in general music's power to depict emotion, although it can arouse emotion by suggesting it:

Il est certain, en effet, qu'on ne sçauroit apercevoir rien de semblable à un sentiment par exemple, dans aucune des combinaisons possibles des sons harmoniques [. . .] Ainsi les sons harmoniques ne peuvent pas peindre le sentiment mais ils peuvent en réveiller l'idée, & mettre l'âme dans l'état où l'on suppose qu'est celle du personnage qu'on fait agir; & c'est même de tous les moyens qu'elle emploie pour émouvoir, celui qui produit le plus sûrement cet effet. (*Réflexions*, 1754, p. 14)

As d'Alembert had suggested – and the *Réflexions* may be by him – music affects by analogy. But the concept of symptom in the 'cri naturel' theory is thus irrevocably modified. Whereas, for Diderot's Neveu de Rameau, music imitated the 'cri naturel' which calls for a kind of diagnosis, here there is mediation – 'où l'on suppose', says the author – and an interpretation which creates a circle of communication of states of soul. This will be developed by Rousseau.

Imitation attacked

It is the application to music of concepts of imitation restricted to reference which provokes a denial that music can be held to imitate at all. Yet many critics do not rule out imitation as an aesthetic principle entirely (especially in connection with the Gluck controversy).[26]

Morellet, for instance, attacks Garcin's *Traité du mélodrame*. Inspired, as his title suggests, by the *opéra comique*, Garcin had proposed the novelist as model to the musician, and says Morellet, had thought that imitation was the aim of the arts: 'Il a cru avec bien d'autres que l'imitation étoit l'objet des beaux-arts, & que c'est d'elle seule qu'ils tiennent l'empire qu'ils exercent sur nos sens, principe que je crois absolument faux' (Morellet, 1772, p. 16).[27]

Taking his pattern of argument from Diderot,[28] he reduces 'nature' to 'decorum' so that art is a consequential development parallel to, but not adjoining, nature: 'Que l'homme passionné disserte, et qu'un homme froid s'exprime avec enthousiasme, tout cela est contre nature, non pas en soi-même [. . .] mais en conséquence de quelques données précédentes' (Morellet, 1772, p. 17). He uses the principle developed by Dubos out of Locke – curiosity or disquiet – to explain man's attention to art, and divides sensation into two types: 'sensations fortes' and 'sensations agréables'. The first is: 'un moyen de sentir, de renouveller pour ainsi dire leur existence'. The second is inherent in nature, which is 'mécanique', not arbitrary, but not explicable either, a kind of psycho-physiological fact:

Il est impossible de dire pourquoi le cristal des eaux, opposé à la tendre verdure des gazons & aux masses plus rembrunies des ombrages produit une sensation agréable: c'est une affaire de mécanisme, & ce mécanisme, ce n'est pas nous qui l'avons inventé. Or si je ne puis connoître que comme un fait le plaisir que je goûte en voyant un beau paysage, comment pourrai-je me rendre compte de celui que j'éprouve lorsque j'entends les sons successifs de la mélodie ou les sons simultanés de l'harmonie?

Such pleasure is 'antérieur à toute imitation' (Morellet, 1772, pp. 17, 19). From this basic and irreducible sensation there developed in the past 'le sentiment réfléchi de la difficulté vaincue'. Morellet's purpose is not in fact so much to deny imitation as a principle as to deny that it is a unique principle: 'Reconnoissons qu'au lieu d'attribuer l'effet des beaux-arts à un seul principe comme on l'a tenté dans un ouvrage très estimable d'ailleurs, on peut en compter six, savoir, la sensation immédiate, le jugement ou le sentiment de la difficulté vaincue, la variété dans les idées réveillées, l'intérêt ou les passions, enfin la surprise & l'imagination' (Morellet, 1772, p. 20).[29] Morellet integrates reflective pleasure into the consumer's reaction, bringing forward the familiar illusion-accompanied-by-awareness but now laboriously spelled out: 'Que sera-ce si tandis que mon âme est trompée par ce prestige, une petite partie de mon intelligence reste pour ainsi dire sentinelle, observe l'artiste et s'écrie de temps en temps "excellent passage du second violon, bravo l'alto, belle modulation". Alors, rien ne manquera à mon plaisir, & certainement je ne le dois pas à la seule imitation' (Morellet, 1772, p. 22).[30] Too perfect an imitation, like a coloured waxwork, loses this integration of awareness with illusion and produces only 'une illusion désagréable'. This is a revision rather than a refusal of imitation. Morellet's very insistence on the irreducibility of sensation (which works against Condillac's homology of the senses by which a signal through one sense code may become a sign either in that code or in a different one) means that illusion, although contemporaneous with awareness, is radically separated from it. Thus Morellet does not suggest that illusion is a subjective set of impressions created by the analogy between music and experience, as earlier critics had done. Instead, he remains well within the domain of contemporary cliché, that music is imitation.

A far more penetrating criticism of the concept comes from a writer who defends Rameau from the century's increasing disdain. He does not deny the power of music to imitate in certain circumstances (the *vive le roi* in *Acanthe et Céphise*); he merely denies its importance, contradicting flatly and deliberately d'Alembert who, in *De la liberté de la musique*, had found such imitations worthy of praise:

Rien de si dangereux [. . .] que ce projet formé de peindre, surtout en symphonie. Cette intention ne sert qu'à gêner l'imagination du Musicien, à la fixer sur quelques petites ressemblances douteuses auxquelles il sacrifie tout & à le distraire des recherches de la belle mélodie qui seule constitue la véritable Musique [. . .]. L'ouverture de *Naïs*, peint, dites-vous, l'attaque des Titans. En ce cas, on doit y entendre les cris séditieux de ces enfans de la Terre; y voir les rochers déracinés par leurs mains [. . .]. Que l'on me fasse entrevoir ces tableaux, non pas tracés, mais indiqués dans un seul passage de l'ouverture citée, & je passe condamnation. Cette ouverture, selon moi, est une mélodie forte, hardie, & dont le caractère tranchant & particulier est renforcé par quelques pratiques harmoniques extraordinaires. (Chabanon, 1764a, pp. 26–7)

In the *Observations sur la musique et principalement sur la métaphysique de l'art* (1779),[31] Chabanon systematically attacks contemporary applications of 'imitation' to music. Music imitates neither speech nor the 'cri inarticulé des passions'; even recitative cannot be considered as imitative of speech. Most music and pleasant sound cannot be related to emotion or meaning; a bird singing in a cage cannot be said to be communicating anything; folk music often sounds sad, although the singer and the 'meaning' may be happy. Indeed, the same melody can be used to express entirely different feelings when set to different words. Yet it would have been perfectly possible for tones in music to have had a fixed meaning: 'Pour que le chant eût exprimé et transmis des idées, il aurait fallu que la convention les y attachât: rien n'était plus facile' (Chabanon, 1779, p. 106).

Chabanon goes further than Morellet, attacking not merely current theories but the general basis of imitation. His contemporaries

restricted meaning to reference, and reference was guaranteed by imitation. But Chabanon points out that 'imitation' implies not merely an object to refer to, but a model whose structure is to be followed. He is led to attack what may well be Diderot's theory of the *modèle idéal*. (The *Salons* had not been published at this date, but they had been distributed in the *Correspondance littéraire*, and Chabanon had contact with Diderot.)[32] In fact he goes on to attack the concept of imitation itself. He insists on the 'vagueness' of music and ballet: 'Leur effet est une sensation et par conséquent a quelque chose de vague'. 'Il est certaines parties des Arts qui semblent appartenir entièrement à nos sens; ils en sont juges sans la médiation de l'esprit' (Chabanon, 1779, pp. 170–1). Yet Chabanon, though he admits the importance of sensation, does not give a merely sensualist account of music. Imitation is the product of the mind's projection into music: the case is thus the reverse of what Pliny intended his birds to prove, for a mere sign may affect more than full imitation. In other words, he makes a delicate attempt to bring together sensualist and intellectualist elements in music. This is not done by using 'illusion' as the reproduction of sense-data; for aesthetic pleasure does not become greater the more exact the imitation of sound, and, moreover, the ear cannot convert aural into visual sensations: 'Un sens n'est point juge de ce qu'un autre sens éprouve: ainsi n'est-ce pas à l'oreille proprement que l'on peint en Musique ce qui frappe les yeux, c'est l'esprit qui [est] placé [. . .] entre ces deux sens.' To develop this notion of the mind as mediator, Chabanon uses the metaphor of the spider at the centre of its web (a metaphor no doubt derived from Diderot), and insists that all art produces its effects, even those of synaesthesia, by mediation (Chabanon, 1779, p. 13).[33] Chabanon, then, develops a two-tier account of pleasure in art, as sensation and as comparison. Music acts immediately on our senses, but the human mind mixes itself with this pleasure of the senses, to look for analogies, or imitations. But in this model, where there is imitation, illusion is impossible (Chabanon, 1779, p. 31). Chabanon then allows a back-door entry to illusion, not as the brute reaction to sensation, but as a bridge, a mediation between sensation and its interpretation of sensation in the context of art. 'Illusion' justifies the use of language about music when its intellectual content is undecidable:

L'air que nous appellerions *tendre* ne nous constitue peut-être pas positive-ment dans la même situation de corps & d'esprit où nous serions si nous nous attendrissions effectivement pour une femme, un père, un ami. Mais entre ces deux situations, l'une effective, l'autre musicale [. . .], l'analogie

est telle que l'esprit consent à prendre l'une pour l'autre. (Chabanon, 1779, p. 69)

Illusion is here both stop-gap and stepping-stone: used for want of something better to characterise the mind's consumption of art, but part of a ladder which rises from sensation to the complexity of art's effect. As in the accounts of music previously considered, as imitation of sound, or of emotion, or of language, Chabanon has recourse to the idea of analogy to express the relation between music and projected model – though here the model is reduced merely to a linguistic label: 'l'air que nous appellerions tendre'.

The rejection of *adequatio* is, however, in Chabanon's work in part a return to an older idea, that of the self-conscious framework within which an artist works. If part of the originality of his *Eloge de Rameau* is his separation of the emotions represented in music from those which describe the music, and from those felt by the hearer,[34] it is bounded by this turning back to the notion of the overtly self-conscious audience. Such a notion was found, for example, in the rapturous reception of Voltaire, at a performance of one of his plays (cf. above, p. 173). This is set in a self-conscious framework, describing the effect of *Castor et Pollux*:

Le trouble saisit les Spectateurs; il gagne, il s'insinue, il se communique, il s'étend, il s'augmente, un bruit sourd se répand parmi les Spectateurs, il naît de leur plaisir, & il le gêne; on veut écouter, on ne peut se taire; l'impression redouble, l'émotion croit; elle est entière, universelle [. . .]. En ce moment, que ma voix se fasse entendre & prononce le nom de Rameau, son éloge est achevé. (Chabanon, 1764a, pp. 6–7)

The enthusiasm of the spectator is set against, and increased by, the enthusiasm of the panegyrist, which finishes his work before it has begun by naming Rameau before he has had time to praise him. The text echoes passages from Diderot and from Rousseau's writings on music. Adequation has been rejected, but merely to incorporate awareness of the audience. But much earlier, in Rousseau's *Essai sur l'origine des langues*, which was left unpublished, the awareness of others implicit in such texts had already become awareness of self. This self-awareness, it will be shown, deepens and completes the contemporary internalisation of the experience of music – that process which was connected with the *Querelle des Bouffons* and has already been discussed in the theories of music's relation to sound, emotion, and language.

Rousseau and imitation

I have already shown that Rousseau applies to opera a typical movement of overbidding: it must go one better to stay in place (cf. above, p. 256). No imaginative extension of time or place is to be allowed: 'Le poète ne doit point donner à un acte d'opéra une durée hypothétique plus longue que celle qu'il a réellement parce qu'on ne peut supposer que ce qui se passe sous nos yeux dure plus long-temps que nous ne le voyons durer en effet' (*Dictionnaire de musique*, article *Acte*). The conditions of opera in performance must be tightened up so that illusion is more complete. But this involves inconsistencies, for Rousseau allows to the intervals what he will not allow to the opera: the 'moyens d'abuser le spectateur sur la durée effective de l'entr'acte' apparently do not operate during the opera itself. The very severity makes illusion inaccurate; it becomes the receding limit of art's power: 'Le meilleur récitatif [. . .] est celui qui approche le plus de la parole; s'il y en avoit un qui en approchât tellement, en conservant l'harmonie qui lui convient, que l'oreille ou l'esprit pût s'y tromper [il] auroit atteint toute la perfection dont aucun récitatif puisse être susceptible' (Rousseau, *Lettre sur la musique française*, p. 433). The height of illusion is the paring away of the distinction between art and nature, and thus the abolition of illusion. Similarly, imitation is made problematic. Read in context, the statement: 'L'action de la scène est toujours la représentation d'une autre action et ce qu'on y voit n'est que l'image de ce qu'on y suppose' (*Dictionnaire de musique*, article *Ballet*) is an insistence on 'hard' illusion, a removal of self-reference by the actor or dancer. But the language in which Rousseau thus insists in fact undermines imitation altogether. The two phrases are parallel, one conjunctive ('est') one disjunctive ('n'est que'), one using nouns in discussion of the actual state ('action', 'représentation'), one verbal in description of the mental positing of the actual ('y voit', 'n'est que'). What is actually seen is representation of something beyond, not of reality present, so that, conversely, what is seen is merely a ground on which is projected the mind's imaginings: in each case the reality is twice removed – '*représentation* d'une *autre* action, *image* de ce qu'on y *suppose*'. No illusion, in the contemporary sense of a mistake, is possible here: indeed illusion has become impossible just when it seemed that Rousseau was tightening the machinery precisely to make it easier.

This movement whereby illusion is rendered at the same time more possible and more inaccessible is explicated fully in the notion of 'imitation' developed in the *Essai sur l'origine des langues*. This mysterious work was not published till after

Rousseau's death, but was probably composed around 1753. It throws into relief the multi-layered and perhaps unchronological nature of Rousseau's aesthetics. For the overbidding described above cannot be dismissed as an early phenomenon. The articles in which this feature is in evidence, *Acte* and *Opéra* from the *Dictionnaire de musique*, were written specially for that work, and are not reworkings of Rousseau's much earlier *Encyclopédie* articles. However, certain of the corrections in the *Dictionnaire de musique* (1765) point to the *Essai sur l'origine des langues*. It has already been pointed out that the phrase 'les duos sont hors de la nature', a phrase in the *Encyclopédie* article *Duo*, is corrected in the *Dictionnaire* to 'Les duos sont hors de la nature *dans la musique imitative*', and that this paradoxically effaces the traditional distinction between nature and imitation. It is this distinction which is reworked in the *Essai* and, with it, a series of related oppositions: melody/harmony, accents/consonants, tones/grammar, time/space, line/interval (cf. Derrida, 1967b). 'Musique naturelle' is defined thus:

Bornée au seul physique des Sons, & n'agissant que sur les sens, [elle] ne porte point ces impressions jusqu'au cœur & ne peut donner que des sensations plus ou moins agréables. Telle est la musique des chansons, des hymnes, des cantiques, de tous les chants, qui ne sont que des combinaisons de sons mélodieuses & en général, toute musique qui n'est qu'harmonieuse. (article *Musique*)

'Musique naturelle' is both that of the *sensualistes* – the *sentiments agréables* school – and that of Rameau's intellectual calculus. One restricts pleasure to sensation, the other merely represents sound. For the complexities of harmony are based on the *basse fondamentale*, which is not necessarily actualised in music, although those complexities may thereby refer us back, in a roundabout way, to our sensations. The contrast with 'musique imitative' is articulated round the distinction between sight and sound, which is explored in the *Essai sur l'origine des langues*. For 'les signes visibles rendent l'imitation plus exacte, mais [. . .] l'intérêt s'excite mieux par les sons' (*Essai*, p. 503). Rousseau, almost certainly deliberately, contradicts Diderot's theories: 'La seule pantomime sans discours vous laisse à peu près tranquille; le discours sans geste vous arrachera des pleurs' (Diderot in his dramatic theory had insisted on the expressive and effective value of gesture). Painting is closer to nature, but its immobility and simultaneity make it as if dead. Visual signs, gestural language, were dictated by need: they have an aggressive quality (*Essai*, p. 502, in which all the examples chosen concern threats, orders or mockery). Sound, on the contrary, expressed passions; the earliest languages were highly inflected: 'Les premiers discours furent les premières chansons: les retours périodiques et mesurés du rhythme, les inflexions mélodieuses des accens, firent naître la poésie et la musique avec la langue' (*Essai*, p. 529). The opposition between sight and sound is further specified as an opposition between colour and line. Colour, and harmony considered as simultaneous sound, restrict pleasure to the sensations. On the contrary, line, and melodic line, give life:

C'est le dessin, c'est l'imitation qui donne à ces couleurs de la vie et de l'âme; ce sont les passions qu'elles expriment qui viennent émouvoir les nôtres; ce sont les objets qu'elles représentent qui viennent nous affecter. L'intérêt et le sentiment ne tiennent pas aux couleurs; les traits d'un tableau touchant nous touchent encore dans une estampe; ôtez ces traits dans le tableau, les couleurs ne feront plus rien. La mélodie fait précisément dans la musique ce que fait le dessin dans la peinture; c'est elle qui marque les traits et les figures, dont les accords et les sons ne sont que les couleurs. (*Essai*, pp. 530–1)

The unravelling of this analogy proves difficult. In what is melody imitative? Not through mere reference: 'Si mon chat m'entend imiter un miaulement, à l'instant je le vois attentif, inquiet, agité. S'aperçoit-il que c'est moi qui contrefais la voix de son semblable, il se rassied et reste en repos. Pourquoi cette différence d'impression, puisqu'il n'y en a point dans l'ébranlement des fibres, et que lui-même a été trompé?' (*Essai*, p. 534). Illusion is momentary; sensations, to cause action or emotion, must be knitted up into a moral context. It is human movement which constitutes that context. 'Dessin' is not thought of as a closed circuit, but as movement: 'Mais, dira-t-on, la mélodie n'est qu'une succession de sons: sans doute, mais le dessin n'est aussi qu'un arrangement de couleurs. Un orateur se sert d'encre pour tracer ses écrits: est-ce à dire que l'encre soit une liqueur fort éloquente?' (*Essai*, p. 531). The arrangement is not closed – as becomes apparent when the comment on the supposed first invention of drawing is considered, and where it is the movement inscribed in the drawer's line which conveys emotion: 'Que celle qui traçait avec tant de plaisir l'ombre de son amant lui disait de choses! Quels sons eût-elle employés pour rendre ce mouvement de baguette?' (*Essai*, pp. 501–2).

But this movement which is melody and imitation, is not, as in Diderot, a relay away from the listener. The listener, for Rousseau, is passive (unlike the viewer who can turn his eyes away, it serves him little to turn his ears) but his passivity is also activity, for music creates the passions it expresses. What was expressed in the *Encyclopédie* and will be expressed in the *Dictionnaire de musique* in terms of identification: 'Ceux-ci [spectateurs] n'entendant jamais sortir de l'orchestre que l'expression des sentimens qu'ils éprouvent, s'identifient [. . .] avec ce qu'ils entendent, et leur état est d'autant plus délicieux qu'il règne un accord plus parfait entre ce qui frappe leur sens et ce qui touche leur cœur' (article *Entr'acte*), is radically different in the *Essai sur l'origine des langues*. Here Rousseau interiorises this rhetorical circle: 'Ces accens auxquels on ne peut dérober son organe, pénètrent par lui jusqu'au fond du cœur, y *portent malgré nous* les mouvements qui les arrachent et nous font sentir ce que nous entendons' (*Essai*, p. 503). Self-awareness is not alienating, because not inserted into a movement outside the self. Instead, a circle of communication unites listener and emitter: 'Sitôt que des signes vocaux frappent votre oreille, ils vous annoncent un être semblable à vous; ils sont, pour ainsi dire, les organes de l'âme et s'ils vous peignent aussi la solitude, ils vous disent que vous n'y êtes pas seul' (*Essai*, p. 537). The structure of imitation here is in fact spontaneous reception of spontaneous utterance, the unification, through a circuit, of hearer and speaker.

A similar bending back of what with Diderot had been a relay outwards occurs in Rousseau's treatment of the matter, as well as the structure, of imitation. The analogy between sound and colour is false because it is that of a fixed system of relations: whereas Félibien had held music up as a model to painting because it had discrete, measurable sounds and fixed modes, for Rousseau, sound is completely relative to the situation in which it is emitted:

Les couleurs sont durables, les sons s'évanouissent et l'on n'a jamais de certitude que ceux qui renaissent soient les mêmes que ceux qui sont éteints. De plus, chaque couleur est absolue, indépendante, au lieu que chaque son n'est pour nous que relatif, et ne se distingue que par comparaison. Un son n'a par lui-même aucun caractère absolu qui le fasse reconnaître; il est grave ou aigu, fort ou doux, par rapport à un autre, en lui-même il n'est rien de tout cela. (*Essai*, p. 536)

Music is culturally specific. A Carib is not moved by French music, and this proves the moral element in sensation. Rousseau goes far beyond the contemporary notion that music is closely linked to the sound pattern of a particular language:[35] 'Elle imite les accens des langues & les tons affectés dans chaque idiôme à certains mouvemens de l'âme' (*Essai*, p. 533). But he corrects this:

Elle n'imite pas seulement, elle parle; et son langage inarticulé, mais vif, ardent, passionné, a cent fois plus d'énergie que la parole même [. . .]. Le seul bruit ne dit rien à l'esprit: il faut que les objets parlent pour se faire entendre; il faut toujours dans toute imitation, qu'*une espèce de discours supplée à la voix de la nature. (Essai*, pp. 533–4)

Imitation which guarantees worth is insufficient: there must be a *discourse* which fills up what is not enough. The movement of over-bidding is here reversed: where art, with all the machinery of *vraisemblance* and *bienséance*, was insufficient to make an imitation adequate to nature, here nature itself needs a supplement: Rousseau has created both a circle of communication and a circle of reference.

Rousseau's creation of this circle is vastly simplified by his successors. For them, it is the very vagueness of music which allows communication (not, as with Rousseau himself, an interplay between emotions transmitted and emotions aroused): 'Il y a donc dans le langage des sons quelque chose de plus vague, de moins défini; ils semblent établir entre les âmes une communication plus immédiate; le peu d'attention que nous donnons aux moyens qui servent à produire les sons, donnent à leurs effets quelque chose de plus magique' (Degérando, an viii, vol. II, p. 368). Here the wish for transparency characteristic of the latter part of the century is gained by *effacing* the medium, by 'le peu d'attention que nous donnons aux moyens'. Hegel likewise proclaims music to be the art in which the opposition between consumer and work is abolished and in which the exteriorisation disappears precisely because it is exteriorisation (Hegel, 1975, vol. II, pp. 904–9).

The transformations of 'illusion' in its relation to music at the end of the eighteenth century show with extreme clarity the interiorisation of sensation that takes place: the medium becomes transparent, and since music is not a replica, not adequate to a model, only the internal experience, the relation of pure subjectivity, is left for the music.[36]

CONCLUSION

Each part of this book has been concerned with a specific art. Each (with the exception of the part concerning the novel) has exhibited a tension, indeed a struggle, conducted about the middle of the century, between two styles. The earlier style, often referred to by its detractors as *papillotage* is contrasted with another, newer, one, felt to be less frivolous. In painting, the early style is criticised for constantly reminding the viewer of the surface of the picture: by use of reflections of light for instance, which cause the eye to blink (literally, *papilloter*);[1] or by use of unstable planes which slide into each other, as in Boucher's works; or by use of surprise, created either by unexpected materials, or by the great pains taken with ephemera (there is, for example, a fashion for beautifully made marionnettes in the late 1740s). In the theatre, *papillotage* in one form is a game of political references, under the guise of the *tragédie en règle*, in which there is a constant decoding, that is, a moving between interpretation and coded signal; or, in another form, it is a self-conscious use of surprise and reversal in the plots, which calls attention to the means used to attain it. In poetry, the style is held to provoke a movement of astonishment, followed by the analysis of what created that astonishment. The pleasure in poetic form is explained as 'difficulté vaincue', as a set of hurdles which must be cleared successfully. Likewise, the movement of the poet in creation is seen as a series of 'élans', of inspired movements which are justified by their dropping back to the starting point, by a return to rest. In music, *papillotage* fits the structure of French opera, with its constant use of interruption, and where collective choral pieces or ballets precede and follow dramatic arias or duos; but the term is constantly applied to Rameau – to his use of dissonance, where the resolution after the unexpected note is often long-delayed, and to the complexity and difficulty of his harmony.

In each art this style is attacked in the name of a newer one. In painting, the eye was to be purposefully stabilised, its movements to be more deliberate, the awareness of the canvas was to be effaced so that the matter might have all its effect; and effective matter was to be used. The development of Hubert Robert and Loutherbourg, from stylised or 'ideal' countryside to industrial landscapes, shows something of this. In theatre, the *décor*, the play and the actor are no longer to call attention to themselves. The clearest sign of this is the removal, in 1759, of the benches from the stage of the Comédie française. The great plays of the past are felt to be stylised, and thus to impinge on the spectator's attention. Hence the experiments with new genres, the *comédie sérieuse*, the *drame bourgeois*. Linguistics mediates a change in the conception of poetic form; far from being an arbitrary game, poetry is given a validation, sometimes a religious history, for its roots are said to lie in the earliest languages of man. In music, the *opera buffa* troupe which arrived in Paris in 1752 introduced a more linear form of opera, and their composers' use of melody brought both orchestral and sung components together in one melodic line, creating a unity and dynamism felt to be lacking in French grand opera.

These styles are contrasted, by their defenders as by their attackers, in terms of the relation to art as appearance, or rather, in terms of their attitude to the awareness of art as appearance. The earlier admits this awareness into the very experience of art. This experience is seen as what I have called 'soft', or 'bimodal': the consciousness of appearance is an integral part of the imaginative involvement with the appearance. The second, newer style, on the contrary, insists on the separation of these two moments: the imaginative association is considered to be an illusion, a mistake, often indeed called 'identification' (a term first used in an aesthetic sense in the eighteenth century). The object is to be made transparent, made present; distance between the art work and the consumer must be annulled, consciousness of the object as appearance excised. This notion of the experience of art I have called 'hard' illusion, or 'bipolar'. The term 'bipolar' is intended to suggest that, though distance is a necessary complement of involvement, it is believed to interrupt to destroy it, and must be held off for as long as possible.

I have separated out these two styles in order to exhibit clearly their actual scope and the different ways in which they structure the experience of art. Though they correspond to the eighteenth century's perception of the aesthetic issues, they are not hermetically separated but cross each other, within an individual's work as well as within certain genres. Diderot, for instance, is the most obvious example of their practical intertwining: if his theory and part of his practice insist on the excision of consciousness, and of those features in art which will provoke it, his practice – as novelist, art critic (and perhaps as playwright in the late *Est-il bon, est-il méchant?*) – on the contrary constantly reminds the consumer that what he attends to is a mere relay station in a process of imitation which moves from assumed origin to imitation of that origin to imitation of that imitation. In *Le Neveu de Rameau*, for instance, the natural language of gesture, already imitated and degraded by modern man, is further imitated in society; this imitation is in turn imitated by the nephew, in his role as parasite, and this exploitation – imitation is further exhibited to *Moi*; all this exists in words, apparently imitating the exhibition which imitates. Again, such a form as Nivelle de La Chaussée's *comédie larmoyante*, although it seems to be a precursor if not actually a part of the new style, could be held to be a case of *papillotage*, of oscillation between contradictory emotions provoked by the art work – the comedy you watch with a tear in your eye. But it is not merely the many strands in any stretch of history which make inevitable the actual complex mixing of the two attitudes to consciousness, and not merely the obvious fact that ideas are not mutually heterogeneous elements developing chronologically. It is also, as I shall show, in the very nature of appearance to undo any attempt to cut it off from what appears, to undo the effacement of our awareness of appearance. This is a further reason for the practical interleaving of the two styles, and the two attitudes, that I have presented as separate skeins.

It nevertheless remains the case that the positioning of the consumer in regard to the work of art is different in the two styles, as it is in the two attitudes to illusion, and that this difference is of great importance in the history of recent art. *Papillotage* allows movement to the consumer: eye-movement, and the intellectual movements whereby references are decoded in the theatre; it allows the consumer to follow the 'sublime ravishment' of the poet. It may take the form of an oscillation between opposed structures (as in music) or between opposed emotions (the use of surprise, and the reversal from tension into relief in tragedy, from Crébillon to Voltaire, and beyond); or of a contrast between content and vehicle (the silverware of Meissonnier). Or it may take the form of a movement out and return to rest (the 'écart' of the poet, followed by definition, by a return to the path from which the 'écart' was a deviation). This is perhaps merely a slower version of the oscillation in *papillotage*, as a pendulum, after all, oscillates between extremes, but its trajectory is a segment of a circle. This movement between imaginative participation and distance implies not a radical insulation of art object and perceiving subject, but an interplay.

However, if consciousness is excluded, if the observer is to be unaware of the canvas, to be completely absorbed in contemplation, he will tend to place himself at one point, to become merely a single steady gaze towards the picture from the apex of the visual pyramid. Likewise, if the audience is to be unaware of theatrical appearance, to lose its awareness in illusion, then its members will define themselves as voyeurs – hidden, isolated observers. The consciousness of other spectators will become the consciousness of self through other spectators, and finally the consciousness of the self as spectator. In a sense, the distance which interrupted in *papillotage* has been internalised and has changed nature. Now distance does not allow the appearance of art to appear, but, on the contrary, being inscribed in the very relation of spectator–voyeur, it is what allows a self-congratulation and enjoyment. This subjectivisation of the experience of art, this radical internalisation, is even clearer in theories of music, as I shall explain.

The effacement of *papillotage*, the excision of the awareness of appearance, does not entail merely a different positioning of the consumer in regard to art. It implies, and is implied by, a different attitude to representation and a different concept of what is representable. *Papillotage* plays with appearance, so that the representation refers constantly away from itself to what is represented. This I have called *aletheia*, linking the concept with a long philosophical tradition. But if *papillotage* is banned, appearance is stabilised; it will refer uniformly to a model to which it will or will not be adequate. But this has consequences both for the type of subject chosen (which will now have to be a precise moment, a 'character', an anecdote, a snapshot) and for the mode in which that subject is presented (that is, as previously and materially existing – a historical anecdote or *fait divers*). This I have called *adequatio*.

This double determination of subject is part of a new, or different, concept of reality. It is as if, through their concern for adequation to the identifiable and externally existing, certain art forms helped create that new concept. An obvious and straightforward example is the weight acquired by the portrait in the eighteenth century. More interesting is the effect of a sharpened consciousness of opposing genres in theatre and in painting:[2] comedy is opposed to tragedy, the *outré* in painting to the *bambochade*. The space defined between them – what is not art – is felt to correspond to something 'real', and may be identified as a middling reality, neither high nor low.

But the concept of an exterior model to which the appearance must be adequate (ad-equate, near-equal) may be hard to apply. It is not by any means clear what poetry and music can be said to imitate, especially when imitation is interpreted in terms of referring precisely. In these arts, some kind of internal model, be it mood, emotion, or whatever, has to be postulated if 'appearance' is to be held stable. The result is twofold. Since music is distressingly lacking in determinate referential content, the most outspoken attacks on imitation, as an account of what art does, take place in music theory. Secondly, the postulation of an internal model to which music shall be adequate only pushes the problem of representation in music farther back, since some account has to be found of *how* music can represent mental processes, and some justification has to be given for the relation to sound and emotion. This is done in the mid-century theories of language. The primal cry awakened in other men an immediate response. Music imitates that cry. But in the early stages of man's development, music was language, or rather the two had not separated. As a result, the sounds are the affect they represent, and create that affectivity in the listener. The relation between model and copy is symmetrical to that between copy and effect (an affect imitated in music creates that affect). The passage from sound to reception of sound is in fact part of a wider circle from affect to affect. The derivative nature of the involvement (the negative suggestion in the term 'illusion') is abolished. 'Illusion' designates less a mistake than an individual, and hence justifiable, subjectivity.

Though for poetry external reference seems secured by language, this only defers the problem of what its model is. Why does the poet use the language he does, when it corresponds to no external model? Why does he make us aware of poetic form? It is the change in conceptions of language and its relation to mental process which causes poetic form to cease to be a problem. This change causes poetry, and in particular metaphor, to be thought of as original to language; a vivid depiction in language makes what is represented come alive in the reader, and furthermore, it transmits flashes of that energy hidden in words which is needed to

Conclusion

conceive the depiction. Poetry, like music, bears with it energy and meaning. Language in a sense is subjectivity authorised. In the theatre, however, a medium, the actor, seems inevitable. If the transparancy on to a model is to be assured, and awareness of the appearance of the actor as medium effaced, then he must be indistinguishable from his role. This could be attained by the height of art: but the insistence of contemporaries on the transparency of technique is such that they choose the other possibility, that the actor really *is*, in some sense, what he acts. It is *à propos* of the actor that the question of the sincerity of the artist is first posed in a modern way. In the three cases, therefore, of music, poetry and acting, the illusion created by art, since it is related to an internal model, comes to mean something resembling its polar opposite – true subjectivity, or sincerity.

In this way, the historical interdependence of nineteenth-century 'Romanticism' and 'Realism' becomes clear. Both aim at a directness, a transparency, both rely on adequation to a model, an adequation which will efface consciousness of the means used by the artist to obtain it. Their common origin is the refusal of an intersubjective area between art object and art consumer. This movement has continued into the twentieth century. It is no accident that the last stages in the development of techniques of illusive spectacle are the diorama, the camera, and finally the cinema, where the spectator is confined in intimate darkness to one point in the room, the apex of his visual pyramid, and where as a result the means are totally effaced (for who is aware of the canvas screen as canvas, and the shadows that constitute the film? Any awareness must be based on techniques over and done with before the showing – the quality of the print, the cutting, and so on). The excision of consciousness from the consumer's attitude to art amounts to the establishment of a different type of consciousness, at a different level, incorporated in the watching self, lonely, self-intimate. It is a relation to the self rather than to the work, and as such does not interrupt involvement. In fact such a consciousness can be based only on a sharpened and restricted notion of the real, as comprising well-defined external objects. As 'hard' illusion, the experience of art is incompatible with a movement of distance from the art object. But the latter can only be delayed – it is necessarily there. One can wonder whether distance does not take a social form here. Perhaps it comes to imply the total alienation of the 'real', in the conception of the world of nineteenth- and twentieth-century capitalism, from what has been set up as art.

In the second half of the eighteenth century, *papillotage* is replaced by a theory of the arts which ignores the communication between appearance and what appears, setting up the work of art as a self-sufficient replica. The work of art thus becomes something other than a piece worthy of the attention of connoisseurs and men of letters. Nineteenth- and twentieth-century experience of art operates in the wake of this replacement. 'Illusion' has lost its sense of mockery entirely, to become the private reaction to art. *Adequatio* has replaced *aletheia*.

The reasons for this change, which is less a succession than a change of emphasis, are complex. There seems no doubt that it corresponds to a radical alteration in the conception of the nature of mental life, a far-reaching shift in the positioning of the self in relation to the world. The importance of the concept of 'belief' in Hume is indicative here. Whether or not it was derived from Dubos' aesthetics,[3] it is certainly related to the mid-century concern with the internal set with which art is approached. Hume, searching for a suitable description of the way the mind positions itself in regard to fiction and in regard to fact, lights on 'belief' as the term to separate the two. But it was in aesthetics that the problem of what Hume calls 'belief' had been most amply discussed and the problem of the mind's relation to its own impressions most thoroughly mooted. While denying that art creates illusion as a mistake, he extends the problem to the whole of experience. Condillac, in his first work, the *Essai sur l'origine des connaissances humaines*, likewise considers the problem of attention, for him the basis of mental life, in terms of a structure which is that of the contemporary analysis of illusion – his constant use of aesthetic examples suggests as much. With both Hume and Condillac the question of belief or attention is sited very deep in the mind. Our experience, for Hume, is a mental construct, the work of belief and of the imagination. For Condillac, the movement of distance does not so much weaken the mind's involvement, as enable it to use its impressions and enable the dynamic process of the construction of experience to take place.

So far the change in emphasis from *aletheia* to *adequatio* has been correlated with two epistemological changes: on the one hand, with a different conception of 'reality'; and on the other, with an interest in the mind's relation to 'reality', conceived in Hume's terms as 'belief' and in Condillac's terms as a development of the fundamental attitude of attention, which has the structure of contemporary aesthetic theory. At this point it is best to be certain of the nature of the change, for it has been strangely misinterpreted. Stierle, for instance, in repeating that the change is from an aesthetics of taste to one of genius, asserts that the reception of literary texts has increased in subtlety. His contention is that illusion as a mistake existed in the eighteenth century as it exists now in the 'naively pragmatic' reader, but had been rejected in general in favour of more complex methods of reading: 'C'est en particulier depuis le passage d'une esthétique du "goût" à celle du "génie" que la production de fiction en a appelé à une réception qui fût à sa mesure, et que des formes de réception beaucoup plus complexes que la réception pragmatique "naïve" sont apparues' (Stierle, 1979, p. 303). This bland assumption that what comes after is more complicated, that prior to around 1800 illusion as a mistake was the common theory and practice of 'reception' is not consonant with the facts – *Tristram Shandy* and *Jacques le fataliste* are proofs enough.[4] On the contrary, the interesting point about the change in the concept of illusion in the eighteenth century is that from a relatively sophisticated concept working between object and subject in an interstitial space, 'illusion' retracts to a more restrictive notion of adequation to a model.

Now the novel in its development does not exhibit this chronology in the same way as the other arts. The two forms of the novel, which correspond to the attitude to appearance of *aletheia* and *adequatio*, are really contemporary one with another. But it is by considering these two forms that new light is thrown on the relation between *aletheia* and *adequatio*. They are based on two attitudes to 'real'. The notion of 'real' is given meaning by being defined against the way in which the novel can be 'unreal': in one case the novel excludes the unreal, in the other case it integrates it, imbricates it within its structure. In the first case, the novel claims to be real by defining the unreal as a novel – it claims authenticity by claiming that it is not a novel. But this very claim brings in, peripherally, what it excludes, and thereby reveals unintentionally the interdependence of definitions of 'real' and 'unreal'. It is this which allows the parodistic novel to operate: while claiming nothing more than unreality, by its use of *à clé* allusions it mentions what it excludes, what is needed to define the other pole of the couple 'unreal/real'. In the second case, the novel contains within it the contrast real/unreal by adopting the form of the tale within the tale. In both forms the relay of appearance is there, but one form attempts to stabilise it, the other plays with it. The two great eighteenth-century French examples of these forms exhibit this clearly.

Rousseau's *La Nouvelle Héloïse* takes the relation of 'illusion' and 'reality' as a theme, and bends the relay of appearance into a circle within the confines of the book: the question of the illusive-or-not nature of Julie's experience does not refer out beyond the book, but casts a complex light on the events contained within it. On the other hand, Diderot's *Jacques le fataliste* imbricates appearance: by playing with the relay of the tale within the tale, it forces us to be aware of the flickering nature of what appears.

The two forms of the novel are responses to a particular historical situation. The novels of the period must navigate between romance and history, seen as mutually defining and mutually excluding poles. But the opposition of these genres is based on a new specification of *truth*. Reference becomes the paradigm for truth and meaning.[5] 'Truth' is an adequate relation between a statement and a situation or object in the material world, one that enables an identification of that object to take place. As such, the concept supplies a backstop to the process of the search for truth. And it is in this context that the novel, like poetry, can be accused of falsehood. A romance fails to refer, history does not. But a novel, even when it is not a romance, is not, by definition, history. Where truth is what God knows, in his eternal present, a romance is not necessarily false. But truth-as-reference-to-something-existing restricts the concept of truth.[6] Revised definitions of 'real', revised definition of truth, as reference to that 'real': it is the very difficulty of the novel's adaptation to these which shows their historical and epistemological specificity. The novel which claims authenticity can only seem to conform to the criterion of truth as reference by bringing back the mention of the unreal, of art as appearance, which is supposed to have been excised.

The neglect of the oscillating nature of what appears, and of the fact that art is appearance, has come about because we still live in the period of experience of art opened by the eighteenth-century passage from *aletheia* to *adequatio*. The art of *papillotage* diverted the energies of consumer and artist towards appearance. This has been rejected, the dialectic between appearance and what appears has been cut down to one of its terms, and the energy invested now in the stabilising of appearance. We tend to conceive of representation in terms of adequation. It is 'illusion' as a transparency of relationship to external object or internal experience which has moulded the very way we think of art, even to the particular form that modern opposition to adequation takes. For the modern aesthetics which base themselves on the free play of the signifier still tend to define themselves as the contrary of adequation, and thus still to remain within its purlieus (see Introduction, pp. 3–8).

Yet the eighteenth-century novel shows that the stabilisation of appearance, which ensures that we only see what appears, is a kind of balancing act. Both forms of the positioning of mind in relation to art (*adequatio* and *aletheia*) exist, and are bound to exist – they can be found within Stierle's article, already quoted, as they were found at the beginning of this book in the work of the critics Philippe Hamon and Roland Barthes. Stierle criticises Wolfgang Iser's concept of the reading of fiction which is, in the terms elaborated in the present book, a variety of *aletheia*, working in waves of imaginative participation. Stierle's reaction is to stabilise this process. His article reveals that he is working in the wake of the eighteenth-century change in attitude to illusion. He allows an infinite series of interpretations; but these are stabilised, one might almost say, isolated by a decontamination chamber. The relation between fiction and 'reality', far from being defined and produced by each particular novel – (as a variant on the modes of reading historically available) is fixed from the outset. 'Par définition, la fiction suppose non pas une identité mais une différence entre la proposition (*Sachlage*) qu'elle constitue et un état de faits donné (*Sachverhalt*) même si cette différence est partielle' (Stierle, 1979, p. 299). Such a statement is only possible with a referential criterion for truth, as the use of *Sachverhalt* gives away. For Stierle, fiction in general is fiction defined against a world which is non-fiction; the novel is closed, which allows for an infinity of interpretations (as there are an infinity of irrational numbers between 0 and 1), but an infinity of *right* and *wrong* interpretations – he actually speaks of 'une falsification de la fiction'. The backstop to fiction is ensured by fiction's closure, the process of appearance is sealed off. The possibility of a constant interchange between 'reality' and fiction, because of their mutual definition, is rejected.

'Illusion' for the eighteenth century was an answer to the problem of representation. But from being an answer, it has restrictively tended to designate and to shape our conception of that problem. To be aware of its history is to be more aware of what it attempts to exclude, and perhaps to be more prepared to understand those artists and critics who have made it their business to break through its restrictions.

NOTES

I Illusion and likeness

1 [My translation] This is exactly the account of pleasure in tragedy given by Freud in a little-known article, 'Psychopathic characters on the stage' (1905?), in *Standard Edition*, vol. 7, left by him unpublished.

2 For an account of this problem in relation to certain philosophical terms, see Derrida, 1967a, pp. 51–97. Derrida is of course making here a much larger point than that the posing of a problem is tainted by the history of the terms used. The question is, in fact, how can one exit from an intellectual system? (Certainly not by opposition, which rather remains within it.)

3 Ricardou, 1973, p. 76: 'La fascination qu'exercent les aventures d'un récit est inversement proportionnelle à l'inhibition des procédures génératrices'; p. 91: 'le récit tire sa crédibilité d'une certaine illusion référentielle'.

4 Moreover, the concept of 'reference' is tendentious and inadequate, defined at second hand through a quotation from Todorov (1977). 'Référent doit s'entendre comme une réalité extra-linguistique' and this is implicitly linked with the ready-made, the preexisting; whereas its opponent, 'littéralité' is to be produced by the work itself, which 'constitue ce qu'il est censé chercher, et enfin de cette manière, porte l'un des caractères majeurs de la modernité' (p. 27). Such a definition should not be possible seventy years after the Fregean distinction between sense and reference. Todorov's 'réalité extra-linguistique' collapses this distinction into one; it treats meaning as reference, as proper names and definite descriptions ('that chair there' said in a certain context); whereas it is quite clear that a sentence need not refer in this way, but may *create its own meaning*, which is ideal, and not an extra-linguistic reality (which cannot, if it is to be extra-linguistic, be *verbal*) – the type of meaning leading Meinong and Russell to postulate entities which had being but not existence. Frege actually gives examples of such sentences as 'Odysseus was set ashore at Ithaca, while sound asleep', which have perfectly good sense but no reference and *thus no truth value* (see Haack, 1974). Dummett, 1973,

would not accept this use of 'sense'. He defines it as the criterion for identification of the referent. Literature in fact seems to play on this *gap* in truth values – an unfortunate failing in natural languages, according to Frege – so that its statements are not interpretable in the mathematical and Ricardolian sense of having a referent.

5 For example, the situation described in the following statement is never explored: 'A chacune de ses variantes, le récit ne peut accéder au réel qu'à la stricte condition d'y contester cet accès ailleurs, là où il a imprudemment intégré d'autres variantes. Ainsi en quelque façon, le *récit devient allergique à lui-même*. Alliance paradoxale de l'inclusion et de l'exclusion. Récit impossible, récit puisqu'une série d'événements se succèdent; impossible, puisque ces événements s'excluent' (Ricardou, 1973, p. 97).

6 It is possible to see Ricardou's gesture against illusion, Kristeva's against *vraisemblance*, in the light of Husserl's attitude to meaning. Husserl, according to Derrida's analysis, divided signs into expression and indication. Expression is only linguistic: it is the transcendental ego's immediate presence in the sign; whereas indication is mediate, contingent, a sign which reveals what is not controlled, what may be involuntary. 'Dans l'indication au contraire, un signe existant, un événement empirique renvoie à un contenu dont l'existence est au moins présumée' (Derrida, 1972b, p. 47). In this light the *nouvelle critique*'s wish to expel reference seems to resemble Husserl's attempt to find a foundation of language free of indication; to create a *texte* which is its own production seems a project related to the reduction to expression, as the ego's own monologue. Husserl excises indication, that is, the passage beyond the subject towards the empirically existing, towards the subjectivity uncontrolled. 'Illusion' and *vraisemblance* in the examples discussed above are related to the constraints, in the one case physical, in the other ideological and social, of the world outside the novel's own production.

7 An identical account is found in Mannoni, 1969, pp. 10ff.

8 See Panofsky, 1975, pp. 174–5.

9 My account of this remarkable book owes a great deal to two reviews by Klein, 1970, pp. 394–402, and Wollheim, 1963.

10 That we learn to interpret an artist's notation; that there is a conventional acquired element in knowing how to look at pictures, and that naturalism in painting can be characterised in terms of the truth of the information it offers about its referent.

11 Husserl in a famous passage discusses the iterability of the imagination, *à propos* of the Dresden Gallery, which contains a Teniers picture of a picture gallery (Husserl, 1967, §100).

12 For the notion of appearance as a critical tool, see Kowalska-Dufour, 1977.

13 'The forms of productive fancy, most of the objects of artistic representation in painting, statues, poems, etc., hallucinatory and illusory

objects, exist only in a phenomenal and intentional manner, i.e. they do not exist in the authentic sense at all, only the relevant *acts of appearing* exist, with their real (reellen) and intentional contents' (Husserl, 1970, vol. II, p. 869, quoted Saraiva, 1970, pp. 165–6, n. 52).

14 It may seem that this confuses an awareness that the work of art is not real with an awareness that it is art, so that a kind of *Kunstreligion*, which Sartre would be very far from accepting openly, is implicit in the theory.

15 See Panofsky, 1968; and for a repertory of the Platonic *loci*, Pfühl, 1910, pp. 12–28.

16 It can be the material which contradicts the image (Gombrich) or a contradiction within the image itself (Sartre) and perhaps Adorno: 'In that works of art exist, they postulate the existence of something non-existent, and thus come into conflict with the latter's real unavailability' (Adorno, 1973, p. 93).

17 Derrida pointed out and first explored this double bind in a long note (Derrida, 1972a, p. 217, n. 8).

18 The term 'relay' (derived from 'relai', as used by Derrida: compare also the fine last lines of Cleaver, 1969: 'A *way station* on a slow route travelled with all deliberate speed') implies both a process of substitution and a stage in that process. The peculiarity of 'appearance' as a concept is precisely that it combines both what appears and what is behind the appearance, what has been substituted for, that is, relayed.

19 'Plato's criticism of art is thus not applicable, because art negates the literal reality of its material content, whereas he counted it as a lie' (Adorno, 1973, p. 129).

20 These meanings are distinct in the German – *Erscheinung* and *Schein*: 'Works of art are semblance (*Schein*) in that they help that which they cannot be to a kind of secondary, modified being; they are appearance (*Erscheinung*) because that element of non-existence, for whose sake they exist, can achieve being, however patchy, through aesthetic realisation' (Adorno, 1973, p. 167).

21 'So far as concerns the unworthiness of the *element* of art in general, namely its pure appearance and deception, this objection would of course have its justification if pure appearance could be claimed as something wrong. But appearance itself is essential to essence. Truth would not be truth if it did not show itself and appear, if it were not truth for someone and for itself, as well as for the spirit in general too' (Hegel, 1975, vol. I, p. 8). 'Appearance' is analysed at length by Heidegger: what I have called 'seeming' is *Schein*, what I call 'appearance', *Erscheinung* – which is further analysed in ways that are not relevant here (Heidegger, 1967, pp. 51–5).

22 'The uncovering of anything new is never done on the basis of having something completely hidden, but takes its departure rather from uncoveredness in the mode of semblance. Entities look as if. . . . That is, they have, in a certain way, been uncovered already, and yet they

are still disguised. Truth (uncoveredness) is something that must always and first be wrested from entities' (Heidegger, 1967, p. 265). The first definition I give (*adequatio*) is one of the standard definitions of truth. The second, as the above quotation suggests, derives from Heidegger (though with significant differences). It is in the work of Derrida (1972a,) that the relation of these theories to aesthetics (through their relation in Heidegger) has been explored.

II Illusion: old wine, new bottles

1 Pliny, Book xxv, 65. The phrase used to describe Parrhasius' picture of a curtain is '*linteum pictum ita veritate representata*'.

2 Forcellini, 1858–60, describes illusion as a variation of *simulatio*, and in Patristic writings the illusions of the Devil are described as *simulatio Dei*.

3 St Augustine condemns the theatre as a sport made by men for the demons, a kind of offering up of imaginary acts of wickedness (Book viii, ch. xiv).

4 Wartburg's history of the word, though no more than an account of dictionary confirmations of usage (with their inevitable lag behind actual usage) suggests the lateness of the aesthetic usage: 'sorte de songes ou de fantômes qui flottent devant l'imagination ca. 1223, fausse apparence matérielle qui semble se jouer de nos sens seit Palsgrave, 1530, erreur de l'esprit et pensée chimérique qui en résulte seit Cotgrave, 1611, artifice dont on trompe quelqu'un Retz, 1660. *Dictionnaire de l'Académie*, 1718, artifice qui fait que l'on attribue une certaine réalité à ce que nous savons n'être pas vrai, Beaux arts: théâtre seit *Encyclopédie*, 1765' (Wartburg, 1962, vol. iv, article *Illusio*).

5 I make no attempt here to distinguish the various doctrines of Origen, Synesius and Porphyry. See Verbeke, 1945; Dodds, 1933; Walker, 1958; and especially Klein, 1970, pp. 65–88, to which essay this chapter is much indebted.

6 The term 'phantasm' was used for the semi-material, semi-corporeal substance so raised; '*Phantasme* se trouve ainsi placé entre la matière et l'esprit à cette limite mystérieuse où l'âme entre en contact avec les choses sans cesser d'être elle-même' (Gilson, 1930, p. 23).

7 Cf. 'Nous dirons maintenant la même chose des phantasmes. S'ils ne sont pas la vérité mais quelque chose d'autre qui ressemble à la réalité [aux étants], ils ne sont pas dans les esprits qui apparaissent d'eux-mêmes, mais se présentent comme aussi vrais qu'eux; ils ont part au mensonge et à la tromperie, comme les formes qui se voient dans les miroirs sont pareilles; et ainsi ils tirent vainement la pensée vers ce qui ne sera aucun des genres supérieurs, mais ils seront, eux aussi, des déviations fallacieuses; l'imitation de la réalité, ce qui est représenté obscurément et devient cause d'erreur ne convient à aucun des genres vrais et clairs; mais les dieux et leurs suivants dévoilent leurs vraies copies, et ils ne proposent en aucune façon des phantasmes d'eux-

mêmes comme seraient les reflets que produisent des eaux ou des miroirs' (Iamblichus, 1966, p. 94). In this distinction between immediate manifestation, epiphany of the divinity, and the derivative action of the *phantasmata* which copy truth to mislead lies the reason for the iconoclastic tendencies of the early Church.

8 Cf. Porphyry, *Pros Markellan*, where the metaphor of *theatrum mundi* is used to express the playing out and offering up of a life to the gods in the face of mockery.

9 St Thomas quotes St Augustine: ' "Man's imagination, which whether thinking or dreaming takes the form of an innumerable number of things, appears to the other man's senses as it were embodied in the semblance of some animal." This is not to be understood as though the imagination itself were identified with that which appears embodied in the senses of another man: but that the demon, who forms an image in a man's imagination, can offer the same picture to another man's sense' (Bundy, 1927, p. 222).

10 'An illusion: fantaisie, false vision; a mockery or gullery', Cotgrave, 1611; Pajot, 1670, defined illusion as *'inane spectrum'*.

11 The quotation from Erastus seems to rework the discussion by Aquinas, cited in n. 9 above.

12 Quoted by Rodis-Lewis, 1956, pp. 468, n. 35, 466, n. 29.

13 Cf. Lawrenson, 1957, ch. 6, and Schöne, 1933. 'His invention was of more than technical importance. He had made possible just that instant of change, of uncertainty and transition, that was to become one of the most attractive attributes of the baroque stage – a moment's suspense while the clarity of the set dissolves, and then the sudden appearance of a new conception. The audience was allowed to share the actual moment of change and experience the transformation as an imaginative stimulus, just because it could not be grasped clearly by the intellect' (Bjurström, 1961, p. 110).

14 Cayrou (1923) implies that such a use did not develop fully in French until the seventeenth century.

15 Cf. Accolti, 1625.

16 Cf. the opposition in the *Dictionnaire de l'Académie*, 1762, article *perspectif*, between 'plan perspectif' and 'plan géométral': 'Celui-ci représente et fixe la place des objets sans égard aux illusions que causent les distances.' This appears to be the basis of the earlier quarrel between the engraver Abraham Bosse and the Académie des Beaux Arts, around 1666.

17 The passage refers to mirrors, but these were widely used in the construction of anamorphoses.

18 A similar swing from doubt to belief is described by Bayle: 'Comme je sens que je suis né libre, je crois que pour faire un bon usage de ma liberté, je dois douter de tout jusqu'à ce qu'une entière évidence m'oblige comme malgré moy à donner mon consentement' (quoted in Gossiaux, 1966, p. 282). This pattern passes straight into accounts of aesthetic belief.

19 Whereas in the young Descartes, consciousness of appearance without a transcendental reality which discloses itself in appearance is the negative of *aletheia, dissimulatio*; cf. below n. 22, the famous 'larvatus prodeo'.

20 Such is for example the worshippers' position in the *théâtres sacrés* placed in churches on Holy Days, which were perspective *décors*, often circular, within which the church-goer took part in a sacred drama of ritual (Bernheimer, 1956).

21 The form had been used prior to Corneille and Rotrou by Baro, in *Célinde*, 1629; in Gougenot's *La Comédie des comédiens,* acted 1631 or 1632, and in Scudéry's play of the same name of 1632. See Lancaster, 1932, part II, vol. I, p. 107.

22 'Like actors who make themselves prepared lest shame appear on their faces, and put on a mask; so I, moving on to this theatre of the world, in which I have till now been a spectator, go forward hidden' (Descartes, 1907, vol. X, p. 213).

23 The rest of the quotation shows the influence of perspective, which Berkeley (1964) was to reject: 'So that from that which is, truly a variety of shadow or colour, collecting the figure, it makes it pass for a mark of figure, and frames to itself the perception of a convex figure, and a uniform colour, when the idea we receive from these is only a plane variously coloured as is evident in painting.'

24 Cf. Merleau-Ponty, 1964b, pp. 63ff., for criticism of this approach from a different point of view from that of Austin.

25 For a remarkable treatment of this type of phenomenon see Gombrich, 1974, pp. 84–94. Illusion was exploited in classical epistemology to cast doubt on perception; in Gibson's thought this is due to a false distinction between appearance and reality. Gombrich goes on to show that in certain circumstances the distinction is not so much false as one that has to be gone beyond: 'Panofsky's belief in the real curvature of straight lines may be a case in point. If I am right, the curvature does not represent what we really perceive, but what we really do not perceive. It marks the transition to the field we scan for orientation' (p. 89).

26 'When the mind, therefore, passes from the idea or impression of one subject to the idea or belief of another, it is not determined by reason, but by certain principles, which associate together the ideas of these objects, and unite them in the imagination' (Hume, 1967, p. 92). The best commentator on Hume, Kemp Smith (1941), admits the 'unfortunate' consequences of Hume's 'double use' of such terms as 'feigning', or 'illusion' but separates rather than takes account of this double use.

27 'Ideas always represent the object of impressions from which they are derived and can never, without a fiction, represent or be apply'd to another' (Hume, 1967, p. 37). 'To form the idea of an object and to form an idea simply is the same thing; the reference of the idea to an

object being an extraneous denomination of which in itself it bears no mark or character' (p. 20). Vividness may be a mark of a perception originating in reality, or, on the contrary, deriving from excitement or illness. It has not previously been pointed out that the distinction between the vividness of a real impression and the paleness of an imaginary one is exactly that made by Dubos in 1719 in regard to art. Dubos postulates that art can never make as strong an effect, nor provoke as strong a belief, as reality (see p. 40). Hume read Dubos' work and made notes on it, though not on this point (cf. Mossner, 1948).

28   Hume's concept of belief appears rooted in contemporary accounts of aesthetic illusion: an origin hinted at in the great many aesthetic examples given – see especially p. 98, and the revealing return to the problem in the Appendix, where he takes up the critical case of poetry.

29   Failure to recognise this distinction – though it is explicitly formulated in Cayrou, 1923 – has misled commentators on d'Aubignac; cf. for example, Neuschläfer edition of d'Aubignac, 1971.

30   Earlier usage shows more uncertainty: Chapelain says for example in the *Discours de la poésie représentative* 'Le nœud se démêle avec vraisemblance par des voies imprévues d'où résulte la merveille' (Chapelain, 1936, p. 131), where *vraisemblance* is associated with the *merveilleux*. Scudéry, on the other hand, defines *vraisemblance* in terms associated with illusion: 'Si cette charmante trompeuse ne déçoit l'esprit dans les Romans, cette espèce de lecture le dégoûte au lieu de le divertir' (Scudéry, 1641, s.p.).

31   Cf. Bray, 1963, pp. 208–9; and 'Enfin tout ce qui est contre les règles du temps, des mœurs, du sentiment, de l'expression, est contraire à la vraisemblance' (Bray, p. 215).

32   Le Bossu maintains that the vulgar are satisfied with the *merveilleux*, a neat reversal of Castelvetro's thesis that the vulgar are so unimaginative that if the play is not totally *vraisemblable*, they will not believe in it. But Auerbach says of *vraisemblance* that it is a 'notion [. . .] typical of cultivated society. It combines the arrogant rationalism that refuses to be taken in by imaginative illusion with contempt for the "indocte et stupide vulgaire" which is perfectly willing to be taken in' (Auerbach, 1959, p. 158). This comment neglects the fact that *vraisemblance* can be used in two ways – that the classical play was highly precise because it was highly abstract.

33   'Il est certain que le Théâtre n'est rien qu'une Image & pourtant comme il est impossible de faire une seule image accomplie de deux originaux différens, il est impossible que deux Actions (j'entens principales) soient représentées raisonnablement par une seule Pièce de Théâtre [. . .] l'on ne pourroit pas discerner quel seroit l'ordre de toutes ces diverses actions, ce qui rendroit l'histoire infiniment obscure et inconnue' (d'Aubignac, 1927, p. 83). Cf. 'The next usual reproach of *Painting* has been the want of *judgement* in *perspective*, &

bringing more into *History*, than is justifiable upon one *Aspect*, without turning the *Eye* to each *Figure* in particular and multiplying the points of *Sight*' (Evelyn, 1668, s.p.).

34 'Leur imagination se laissant tromper à l'art du Poëte, leur plaisir dure toûjours' (d'Aubignac, 1927, p. 139).

35 Félibien, *Entretiens sur les vies et sur les ouvrages des plus excellens peintres anciens et modernes,* 1666; Fréart de Chambray, *Idée de la perfection de la peinture,* 1662.

36 For details of Dubos' influence, see Lombard, 1913; Dieckmann, 1964.

37 Dubos had met and corresponded with Locke, cf. Bonno, 1950: 'Les passions qui leur [les hommes] donnent les joyes les plus vives leur causent aussi des peines durables & douleureuses; mais les hommes craignent encore plus l'ennui qui suit l'inaction, & ils trouvent dans le mouvement des affaires & dans l'yvresse des passions une émotion qui les tient occupés. Les agitations qu'elles excitent se réveillent encore durant la solitude; elles empêchent les hommes de se rencontrer tête à tête, pour ainsi dire, avec eux-mêmes sans être occupez, c'est-à-dire, de se trouver dans l'affliction, ou dans l'ennui' (Dubos, 1719, vol. i, pp. 9–10).

38 His analysis of the effects of poetry in particular displays this.

39 This is not, as has been thought (e.g. by Finch, 1966, pp. 86–7), an exposition of the theory of the sixth sense.

40 Dubos, 1719, vol. ii, p. 316; cf. p. 309.

41 This argument is clinched by a quotation from Quintilian which in the original refers to imitation in the sense of stylistic borrowings (Quintilian, 1963, Book x, ch. ii).

42 It is clear that Dubos is anxious to ward off attacks on art's morality and yet not to be crudely moralistic. Art shows hypothetically the power of passion, the better to warn the audience off. 'Phèdre criminelle malgré elle même est une fable comme celle de la naissance de Bacchus & de Minerve. Qu'on ne me fasse point dire après cela, que les Poëmes Dramatiques sont un remède souverain & universel en morale. Je suis trop éloigné de rien penser d'approchant' (Dubos, 1719, vol. i, p. 629).

43 One could argue that with Dubos the question of the nature of our attention to art is continuous with the nature of our attention to life; this was sharpened with Hume's 'belief', so that an aesthetic concept is applied by him to the whole of experience.

1 Illusion and the Rococo: the idea of 'papillotage'

1 Cf. Piles, 1708, p. 307; Dandré Bardon, 1765, vol. i, p. 324.

2 Cf. Starobinski, 1971a.

3 Significantly, quoted by Jaucourt, as usual without acknowledgement, in the article *Peinture,* in the *Encyclopédie.*

4 Cf. 'L'Enthousiasme [. . .] ravit l'âme, sans lui donner le tems de rien

examiner' (Piles, 1708, p. 124). 'Le Spectateur [. . .] se laisse enlever tout à coup & comme malgré lui' (*ibid.*, p. 115).

5 Of a flower painting by Bachelier; cf. 'La Perdrix est si douillette & si naturelle que j'en aurois volontiers arraché les plumes' (Gautier d'Agoty, 1753, p. 62).

6 Cf. 'L'âme est mille fois tentée de céder à l'aimable illusion d'un art Créateur qui imite & embellit si parfaitement la Nature, qui trahit ses mystères & reproduit en quelque sorte un second Univers. Je vole ici au devant d'un ami dont la ressemblance est si vive [. . .]. Cependant le nuage de l'illusion se dissipe, les sens sont moins étonnés, les objets s'éclaircissent insensiblement à la vue, la raison reprend son empire' (Lacombe, 1753, p. 8).

7 Laugier asks outright: 'Que se propose la peinture? Sinon de nous donner une représentation de la chose assez vraisemblable pour que l'esprit se prenne au piège dans l'illusion et croie voir la réalité même' (Laugier, 1771, p. 84).

8 'Ce qui excite en nous un double plaisir dans le même instant, celui de la vue d'un objet parfait dans toutes ces parties, & celui d'admirer l'art et la magie de l'imitateur qui nous trompe si agréablement' (La Font de Saint Yenne, 1747, p. 91).

9 Cf. Wölfflin, 1964, p. 35: 'The practice of colouring statues ceased at the precise moment when the painterly style began, that is, when the effect of light and shade came to be confidently relied on for the main effect.'

10 Cf. Kimball, 1949, and the comments he quotes from the obituary of Meissonnier (p. 215) and from Briseux (*Les Maisons de campagne*) (p. 211) where the game of passing to extremes is held to be the reason for the use of the asymmetrical.

11 'Une description est toujours froide en comparaison d'une peinture, où tout se présente à la fois, où l'esprit est agréablement occupé d'un certain empressement à deviner l'intention du Peintre, où chaque objet devient plus piquant par la petite gloire qu'on se fait de l'avoir déchiffré' (Rouquet, 1746, pp. 1–2).

12 'On peut pour attirer la vûe en de certains endroits & la forcer à s'y arrêter parmi des couleurs agréablement unies en hasarder une qui en trouble, pour ainsi dire, le repos & qui leur soit directement opposée' (Coypel, 1721, p. 125). This is a positive account of the same movement, the attraction, the submerging force, 'forcer . . . parmi', the oscillation of the painter and spectator – in the one case tentative, in the other emotional – all suggest 'papillotage'.

13 Falconet insists that the spectator must 'se livrer volontiers à l'impression qu'on cherche à faire sur lui' contrasted in his usage with 'se prêter à l'illusion' (Falconet, 1761, p. 12).

14 (Diderot, *Salon de 1765*, p. 81, a remark added by Grimm. Same comparison about the painter Halle, p. 85.) Is the Rococo's prettification, so often denounced by Diderot, connected with an awareness

of the relativity of values, and a consequent toning down of pretensions? Coypel, for instance, writes of 'la grâce': 'Cependant, quoique la grâce en général doive toucher tout le monde, il ne laisse pas d'être vray que pour ce qui regarde les Arts, chacun s'en fait une idée selon son habitude, selon son goût, ou celui de son Pays. Ce qui est gracieux pour une nation, ne l'est pas toujours pour une autre' (Coypel, 1721, p. 76).

15 Cf. Dandré Bardon's definition of the poet (1765, vol. I, p. 130), exactly what La Font de Saint Yenne is attacking.

16 Used by le père André, 1843 [1741], and Coypel, 1721, as well as by Diderot.

17 Cf. Hogarth, 1955, p. 59, on the beauty of certain leaves, the trefoil and the cinquefoil: 'When you would compose an object of a great variety of parts, let several of those parts be distinguished by themselves, by their remarkable difference for the next adjoining so as to make each of them as it were, one well-shaped quality or part [. . .]. (These are like what they call passages in music.)' And, pp. 55–6: 'And that serpentine line, by its waving and winding at the same time different ways, leads the eye in a pleasing manner along the continuity of its variety [. . .] and which by its twisting so many different ways, may be said to enclose (tho' but 'tis a single line) varied content.' He quotes on p. 118 the lines by Dryden:

> Where light to shades descending plays, not strives,
> Dies by degrees, and by degrees revives.

Such concerns are visual versions of the problems in mathematical analysis investigated during the century.

18 The pages are numbered separately in the manuscript and the article was obviously meant to be detachable.

19 'Je vous raconte simplement la chose; dans un moment plus poétique j'aurais déchaîné les vents [. . .]. Le fait est que nous n'éprouvâmes d'autre tempête que celle du premier livre de Virgile, qu'un des élèves de l'abbé nous récita par cœur' (*Salon de 1767*, p. 138).

20 All these themes are anticipations of other works, of *Le Rêve de d'Alembert*, *Madame de la Carlière*, *Essai sur les règnes de Claude et de Néron*, and *Le Neveu du Rameau*.

2 Art and replica: the imitation of truth

1 Cf. 'Les tableaux plaisent sans le secours de cette illusion qui n'est qu'un incident du plaisir qu'ils nous donnent, & même un incident assez rare. Les tableaux plaisent, quoiqu'on ait présent à l'esprit qu'ils ne sont qu'une toile sur laquelle on a placé les couleurs avec art' (Dubos, 1719, vol. I, p. 624).

2 He writes a *Les Misotechnites aux enfers, ou Examen des Observations*

sur les arts par une société d'Amateurs, in Cochin, 1757–71, vol. III, directed against Saint Yves, 1748.

3 Cf. 'Un portrait par Léonard de Vinci qui est d'une vérité à tromper' (Cochin, 1758, vol. I, p. 137); and 'On ne remarque point dans ces tableaux l'illusion qui trompe dans les nôtres: on y découvre même des défauts de perspective assez considérables' (Cochin, 1754, p. 63, of Roman painting).

4 For details of the textual problems associated with Cochin's text, see bibliography. I have been unable to trace *De l'illusion* in the *Mercure*.

5 'Bambochade' means a genre painting, possibly burlesque in style, derived from the Italian *bamboccio*, the nickname given to the genre painter Peter van Laer (Bonnefoy, 1970, p. 157). See also the curious little book *Bambocciaden*, 1797.

6 'Il est plusieurs ouvrages faisant toute l'illusion dont la peinture est susceptible, qui sont néanmoins regardés comme très médiocres' (Cochin, 1757–71, vol. II, p. 45). Cf. 'Le plus grand trompeur en cet Art est le plus grand peintre' (Piles, 1708, p. 347), though the context of 'trompeur' is built up subtly by an account of the spectator's role in constructing the picture.

7 Even still lifes can create illusion only by a combination of effects of light with a motif large enough to force the spectator to remain at a distance. He uses the example of life-size cut-outs: 'On n'ignore pas que cette illusion, qui ne naît que de la surprise & de l'inattention, peut être produite même par les plus mauvais ouvrages, ainsi qu'il arrive souvent au premier aspect de ces peintures découpées qui représentent une balayeuse ou un suisse & personne n'en a jamais conclu qu'elles eussent atteint le vrai but de l'art' (Cochin, 1757–71, vol. II, p. 47).

8 Children, having less suspicion, are more susceptible. Cf. Diderot's reiterated example of savages taking the figurehead of a ship for a real person (*Lettre sur les aveugles*, p. 134 and *Salon de 1767*, p. 241. a more properly aesthetic case because 'cette erreur ne venait certainement pas du peu d'habitude de voir'.)

9 Looking through post-Impressionist eyes, it is impossible to maintain that Oudry's handling of colour is equal to Chardin's.

10 The comparison between Pradon and Racine probably derives from Voltaire: 'C'est lorsque *Racine* et *Pradon* pensent de même qu'ils sont le plus différents [. . .]. Quand il s'agit de faire parler les passions, tous les hommes ont presque les mêmes idées; mais la façon de les exprimer distingue l'homme d'esprit d'avec celui qui n'en a point', *Préface de Mariamne*, 1725, in Voltaire, Kehl, vol. I, pp. 227–9.

11 Falconet dismisses Pliny's birds, p. 217, with the apt example of the scarecrow. (Cf. Richardson, 1728, vol. II, p. 141). Yet elsewhere Falconet is prepared to use 'illusion' of bas-reliefs (Falconet, 1761, p. 47).

12 'Enfin quelques Peintres des plus modernes se sont avisez de placer

dans les compositions destinées à être vues de loin, des parties de figures de ronde bosse qui entrent dans l'ordonnance, & qui sont coloriées comme les autres figures peintes entre lesquelles ils les mettent. On prétend que l'œil qui voit distinctement ces parties de ronde-bosse saillir hors du tableau, en soit plus aisément séduit par les parties peintes, lesquelles sont réellement plates & que ces dernières font ainsi plus facilement illusion à nos yeux. Mais ceux qui ont vû la voûte de l'Annonciade de Gennes & le Dome de Jesus à Rome où l'on a fait entrer des figures en relief dans l'ordonnance, ne trouvent point que l'effet en soit bien merveilleux' (Dubos, 1719, vol. I, pp. 386–7). For a study of Il Gesù, see Pirenne, 1970.

13 Cf. Cochin, 1758, vol. I, p. 226, on the adaptation of the fresco by changing proportions of the figures in relation to where they are to be seen from; vol. II, p. 121, for criticism of the device of a picture within a picture: 'Ces sortes de sujets ont le défaut que ce qui est supposé tableau est aussi vrai que ce qui est supposé realité.' Grimm also uses 'illusion' to criticise opera *décor*.

14 Diderot, *Salon de 1769*, p. 103. Even Dézallier d'Argenville (1745) and more particularly Descamps (1753–6), whose appreciation of Rembrandt is subtle and genuine, still judge Flemish painting, particularly associated with low genres, in terms of the hierarchy. He regrets that Rembrandt had not mixed in higher society: 'Il auroit fait un plus beau choix de sujets, il auroit mis plus de noblesse, il auroit perfectionné le goût naturel, ce génie de Peintre' (Descamps, 1753–6, vol. II, p. 90); cf. André Fontaine (1909, p. 193) and Piles (quoted in Meusnier de Querlon, 1753, p. 84): 'Les Peintres Flamans dont la plupart sçavent imiter la nature pour le moins aussi bien que les Peintres des autres nations, [mais ils] en font un mauvais choix.'

15 This is an interesting rewriting of one of his sources, Hagedorn, who says: 'Lairesse prétend qu' [. . .] il est très permis à l'art qui a l'illusion pour objet, de transporter l'observateur en imagination sur la scène représentée.' Diderot: 'Cela me semblerait d'aussi mauvais goût que le jeu d'un acteur qui s'adresserait au parterre.'

16 Cf. *Correspondance*, vol. V, p. 230, of a young girl's reaction to Greuze's *Paralytique*, and to Sedaine's play, *Le Philosophe sans le savoir*: 'Je voudrais bien que cette petite fille là eût été la mienne.'

17 Cf. Diderot, *Salon de 1767*, p. 284. But see the English critic Richardson's account of even low genres as an extension of experience (1728, vol. I, p. 4). He also suggests that there is a difference of vision: 'Il se peut que Albert Durer suivant l'idée qu'il avoit des choses, ait dessiné aussi correctement que Raphael, & que l'œil Allemand ait vu, dans un sens, aussi bien que l'œil Italien, mais ces deux Maîtres avoient la conception différente, la Nature ne paroissoit pas à tous deux la même' (ibid., vol. I, p. 118).

18 Falconet rightly criticises this in Diderot: 'Tant que vous confondrez la pensée d'un tableau avec son exécution, je vous le répéterai sans

cesse, vous serez à mille lieues de l'objet' (*Diderot et Falconet,* 1958, p. 194).

19   Cf. Saint Yves, 1748, p. 39: a *bambochade* 'ne demande que de la couleur [. . .]. Un Peintre qui ne nous expose que des actions nobles, où les passions nuancées sont rendues avec force, nous fait éprouver des sensations délicieuses que n'occasionnera jamais la représentation d'un marché, d'un cabaret ou d'une noce de Village.'

20   Laugier (1771) suggests such compilations to relieve the painter's imagination; the projected extract from Prévost's *Histoire des voyages* will ensure geographical and bibliographical accuracy (pp. 87, 270). Caylus presents his *Tableaux tirés de l'Iliade* (1757) in this light. It will also serve as convenient proof of the poem's merit, since 'On est toujours convenu que plus un Poëme fournissait d'images et d'actions, plus il avait de supériorité en Poésie', *Avertissement,* p. v.

21   Rousseau, on the other hand, has his joy in a mountain landscape ruined when he discovers in it a little factory (Rousseau, *O.C.,* vol. I, p. 1071).

22   The term 'peinture d'histoire' does not appear in the theory of the earlier part of the century. Coypel employs the phrase 'tableau héroique', for instance.

23   Diderot had early seen the problem posed by technique in that it seems to make mediate the relation between art and nature. He writes to Mme Riccoboni: 'Votre dessein serait-il de faire de l'action théâtrale une chose technique qui s'écartât tantôt plus, tantôt moins de la nature, sans qu'il y eût aucun point fixe en delà et en deça duquel on pût l'accuser d'être faible, outrée, ou fausse ou vraie?' (Diderot, *O.C.,* vol. III, p. 678). That there was an artistic preoccupation about this can be shown, for example, from Tristram Shandy's '*poco meno, poco piu*' (Sterne, 1938, p. 73).

24   Cf. Baillet de Saint Julien, 1749, p. 64: 'Si le Peintre s'est fait une manière, l'illusion n'est plus parfaite; dès lors plus de vérité.' Cf. also Diderot, *Essais sur la peinture,* p. 673.

25   Castel, 1763, p. xx–xxi: 'Et de ce qu'on démontre qu'il y a entre les couleurs des proportions analogues à celle des sons s'ensuit-il que le clavecin oculaire puisse affecter l'organe de la vue, comme le clavecin acoustique affecte l'ouïe en sorte que l'âme éprouve des deux côtés une sensation à peu près égale?' Cf. Hogarth, 1955, p. 176.

26   Cf. Goethe, for whom reddish blue is the colour which generates all others.

27   Cf. the account in Cochin (1757–71, vol. II, p. 25) of the way in which, by movements of the head as well as by long experience, the retinal projection of objects is made unambiguous, whereas on the canvas 'tout tient réellement'.

28   Cf. Oudry (in Jouin, 1883, p. 386) of his own painting: *Le Canard blanc,* which puts this method into practice.

3 The exclusion of the false

1 Abbé de La Porte, *Observations sur la littérature moderne*, 1749, vol. I, p. 14. Cf. Desfontaines, 1757, vol. I, chapter *des Romans*, Frain du Tremblay, 1713, p. 174, and Madame Dacier, 1714, p. 28.

2 There is a real ambiguity of status in some works of the century. L'Abbé de Saint Réal, 1922, is treated by modern and eighteenth-century critics as history, yet his previous work, *Don Carlos*, which uses similar techniques, is defended as a novel (Dulong, 1921, vol. I, p. 156; Bricaire de La Dixmérie, 1769, p. 384).

3 Labriolle, 1965, speaks of theories circulating at the time of the existence of a manuscript: 'Cet Ouvrage me tomba l'automne passé entre les mains, dans un voyage que je fis à l'Abbaye de . . ., où l'Auteur s'est retiré' (Prévost, *Homme de qualité*, 1728–32, *Avis*). Cf. the *Lettre de l'Editeur* to volume III, where the editor relates how the death of Mr le Marquis de . . . had enabled him to publish the last part of the memoirs, which the Marquis had withheld for personal reasons. Cf. also *Cleveland*, 1777, *Préface*, p. iii.

4 Varillas, a seventeenth-century historian, was author of a great number of histories. 'Les premiers ouvrages de Varillas firent grande sensation dans le monde littéraire. Dans ses préfaces, il parlait de nombreux manuscrits de la bibliothèque du Roi qu'il avait compulsés, du trésor des Chartes qui lui avait été ouvert, et chacun le croyait initié à une foule de secrets historiques et d'intrigues de cabinet [. . .]. On découvrit qu'il mêlait le faux au vrai, que ses citations de titres, d'instructions, de lettres, de mémoires, et de relations étaient le plus souvent imaginaires, que sa chronologie était fausse, qu'il cherchait enfin plutôt à amuser qu'à instruire' (*Nouvelle Biographie générale*).

5 This information on Lenglet is derived from an unpublished thesis by Geraldine Sheridan, 'The Life and Works of Lenglet Dufresnoy' (Warwick, 1980), to whose erudition I am much indebted.

6 Desmolets, 1739, p. 199, quotes the example of the ropes seen at the opera, but also, foreshadowing the *Paradoxe sur le comédien*, by Diderot, that of 'Un Tragique qui dans le fort de notre émotion, interromproit son rôle, pour nous faire honte de ce que nous nous attendrissons pour des sentimens exempts de réalité'.

7 Compare the account by Diderot in the *Salon de 1767*, above p. 78, where he shows it to be impossible to paint a portrait, and condemns painting to use a mode of representation which is not a replica and which for Diderot is thus a lie.

8 Cf. Boursault, 1675, *Préface*: 'Quoy qu'il y ait dans cette petite Pièce assez de circonstances de l'Histoire pour faire présumer que tout en est véritable, on veut, s'il est possible, divertir le Lecteur sans l'abuser & prévenir l'erreur où il seroit s'il ajoutoit foy à tous les incidents qu'il y trouvera.'

9 Cf. Bougeant, 1735, pp. 148–9: 'C'est ce qui me fait admirer la

précaution qu'a prise un de nos Modernes annalistes, de mettre à la tête de son Histoire une Préface raisonnée, pour justifier fort sérieusement les fais qu'il y rapporte, comme si on ne sçavoit pas qu'en qualité d'Annaliste Romancier, il a droit de dire les choses les moins vraisemblables, sans qu'on ait celui de s'en formaliser.'

10   Cf. Béliard, *Zelaskim*, quoted Coulet, 1967, vol. II, p. 154: 'Se peut-il qu'il faille être obligé de rappeler à des hommes raisonnables, qu'il seroit absurde à un Auteur de faire un Ouvrage où il n'auroit que des choses ordinaires et unies, telles qu'elles pourroient arriver à tout moment à tout le monde?'

11   Cf. Mylne, pp. 43–4. The point is that Courtilz admits the *invraisemblance*, the novel-like character of what he recounts, and then asserts nevertheless the historical value of the *Mémoires* (three times in the 1687 preface, for example). In other words, he makes the reader move between the suspicions of the whole having been invented, and the assertions of the genuine nature of the story.

12   Theories of first-degree illusion, those of Mylne, 1965, and Stewart, 1969, cannot deal with such remarks. Stewart, for example, can only note of Mouhy's *La Mouche* that he further discredits his text, by admitting he has left out implausible incidents (Stewart, 1969, p. 182, n. 11).

13   Compare the much simpler *Mémoires du Comte de Grammont*, with statements like: 'Voici [. . .] qui sent bien le roman' (Hamilton, 1964, p. 35).

14   This movement of oscillation in illusion is criticised later in the century in the same way as in art or theatre theory. Baculard d'Arnaud says that he has been historically accurate: 'Persuadé que la fiction ne se pardonne qu'autant qu'elle n'est point apperçue. Dès que le mensonge se trahit, il perd de sa séduction, l'intérêt qu'il avoit excité s'évanouit, & la raison rendue à toute la sévérité de son jugement, critique, & prononce, en quelque sorte, contre le plaisir du sentiment; l'illusion détruite, l'Auteur manque entièrement son objet' (Baculard d'Arnaud, 1782, p. v).

15   Castiglione, *Il Cortegiano*, Book II; the second part of *Don Quixote* contains an elaborate account of *burle* played by the Duchess. Cf. the jokes played on Poinsinet 'le mystifié' by the circle round Fréron, Diderot, *Le Neveu de Rameau*, 1950, p. 150.

16   The playing of a trick, followed by its disclosure, is a technique similar to that of the protagonist, Hardouin, in Diderot's play *Est-il bon, est-il méchant?* who performs services using deliberately unpleasant means, and then lets these be known.

17   This *dédoublement* reflects interestingly on the body of the actual novel, as well as on other of Diderot's works, like *Le Paradoxe sur le comédien*.

18   Cf. *Lettres persanes*: 'Tout l'agrément consistoit dans le contraste éternel entre les choses réelles et la manière singulière, neuve ou

bizarre, dont elles étaient aperçues' (Montesquieu, 1949, vol. I, p. 130) where 'choses réelles' are exemplary concrete instances of political reality. The *papillotage* implied by such a remark is evident.

19 In *Bibliothèque choisie et amusante*, 1749, vol. I (cf. Mortier, 1971).

20 Desfontaines in his preface to his continuation of Swift, *Le Nouveau Gulliver* (vol. 15 of *Voyages imaginaires*, 1787–9, first edition 1730), presents a more conventional account of satiric techniques, but one still based on irony, the gap between what is said and how it is interpreted. He attributes to Swift the power of illusion, 'Qui [. . .] a eu l'art de rendre en quelque sorte vraisemblables des choses évidemment impossibles, en trompant l'imagination & en séduisant le jugement de son lecteur par un arrangement de faits finement circonstanciés et suivis' (Desfontaines, 1787–9, vol. 15, pp. 24–5). But Desfontaines claims for himself awareness based on the discrepancy resulting from the contrast between the techniques of narration and what is narrated. 'La lettre du docteur Ferrigine, qu'on trouvera à la fin du chapitre XXIV, contribuera à donner un air de vraisemblance à toutes les choses qui auront paru extraordinaires dans l'ouvrage qu'on y raconte cependant comme véritables. Le profond savoir de ce docteur, qui fouille dans tous les livres anciens et modernes, pour en tirer de quoi appuyer sérieusement les idées badines qui composent ce livre, fera peut-être un contraste agréable' (Desfontaines, 1787–9, vol. 15, pp. 23–4).

21 May, 1963, worked on clues in the earlier articles by F. C. Green, 1928; see also Mattauch, 1968.

22 Le père Porée's brother wrote a novel satirising convents, *Histoire de D. Ranuncio d'Alétès, écrite par lui-même*, Venise, 1736.

23 'Il allait [. . .] dans les cafés, dans les foyers, recueillait tout ce qu'on y disait, et rentré le soir chez lui il écrivait un roman dans lequel il amalgamait les anecdotes qu'il avait entendu raconter. Il tirait très bien parti de ses écrits: ils étaient affichés partout, il en avait les poches pleines; il les colportait lui-même et l'on était forcé de les acheter pour se débarrasser de ses instances' (d'Estrée, 1897, p. 235).

24 I shall develop this argument further in a future article.

25 'C'est un récit métaphorique rempli d'énigmes et d'allégories assez inintelligibles dans lequel le libertinage se mêle à l'impiété' (Drujon, 1888, vol. II, p. 809a).

26 Day, 1959, p. 182, citing a letter from Abbé Le Blanc to the Président Bouhier, 3 janvier 1735. The *Constitution* is the papal bull, *Unigenitus*, of 1713, which caused friction between 'gallicans' and the pro-papal faction in France during much of the first half of the eighteenth century.

27 The whole passage after the prophecy that Crébillon will not finish *Les Egarements* runs: 'Depuis qu'on a mis les Romans sur le pied de la Comédie, qu'on les a rendus le tableau de la vie humaine, qu'on leur a donné pour but de peindre les hommes tels qu'ils sont, ils donnent

plus lieu que jamais à ces ingénieux rapports. Et de fait, puisque les portraits qu'on fait des défauts & des ridicules sont puisés dans le sein de la Nature, il faut bien que ces portraits ressemblent à ceux qui ont ces ridicules & ces défauts; ils seroient manqués s'ils ne ressembloient à personne' (*Bibliothèque françoise*, 1738, vol. xxviii, p. 147).

28 The logic of Crébillon's attitude is expressed in his early story *Le Sylphe*: 'Ces plaisirs que je vous vante tant, ne sont que des songes, mais il en est dont l'illusion est pour nous un bonheur réel, & dont le flatteur souvenir contribue plus à notre félicité que ces plaisirs d'habitude qui reviennent sans cesse' (Crébillon *fils*, 1772, vol. i, p. 8). A woman delighting in illusion is made love to by a sylphe, an ethereal spirit who can mind-read: 'Les femmes [croient] la vertu idéale & le plaisir réel' (Crébillon *fils*, 1772, vol. i, p. 15). This is most delicately brutal in the dialogues, where the men's actions are designed to show that behind the surface of innocence, the physical realities of desire exist. The novel, like the roué, reveals a truth by ogling reference to it. The reader is manoeuvred like the woman who is to be seduced. See the preface to *Le Sopha*, a gigantic double-take. Can the *Sopha* with its voyeurism and sexual allusiveness be useful to society? Only to the society of *petits-maîtres*, by whom it was, precisely, read.

29 The whole passage runs: 'Qu'est-ce que l'on trouve dans l'Histoire, mille faits, mille incertitudes. Le Roman me satisfait sur tout; sur le lieu, le tems & les caractères, les pensées mêmes de ses Personnages. Je ne vois les Hommes dans l'Histoire que tels que la Politique permet de les faire paroître; dans le Roman, je les vois tels qu'ils sont. L'Histoire me présente la vertu presque toujours opprimée, je la vois toûjours triompher dans un Roman; dans l'Histoire, je trouve mille faits faux que l'on me donne comme vrais; je trouve mille faits vrais dans le Roman sous le voile de la Fable' (Gachet d'Artigny, 1739, p. 81).

30 The passage continues 'Les romans ont été les premiers Livres de toutes les nations. Ils renferment les plus fidelles notions de leurs mœurs, de leurs usages, de leurs vices & de leurs vertus. Ils sont comme autant de tableaux allégoriques qui présentent la vérité voilée ou embellie par la fiction'; cf. Baczko, 1978, especially pp. 46ff.

31 I owe this quotation to Cook, 1982. Cf. Béliard, 1765, vol. i, p. xv: 'La plus grande différence que je trouve entre les Histoires et les Romans, c'est que ceux-ci, sous une apparence de fiction, contiennent un grand nombre de vérités, et que celles-là sous un air de vérité, contiennent beaucoup de fictions.' Cf. Dorat, 1882, p. 15: 'Ce genre surtout ne doit pas être négligé, il est conforme à nos mœurs, à notre goût, à notre caractère; la morale y disparoît sous le voile de l'enjouement.'

32 The increasing appreciation of the novel is reflected in the change in its derivation; no longer considered to have developed from history, it is sometimes ascribed to Arab influence. The *Bibliothèque universelle des romans* included in its compass ancient epic, the *Eddas*, for

instance. See Rivet de La Grange, 1742, vol. VI, pp. 12–17; *Mercure de France,* janvier 1779, p. 127. Such a derivation builds into the novel a greater freedom of form.

33 The defects of a naive reading of Marmontel are shown clearly by the following remark by Renwick, concerning Marmontel's attitude in *Belisaire*: 'Marmontel, theologically and morally speaking was in excellent faith, but conversely the Sorbonne, having applied their knowledge of the techniques [. . .] peculiar to philosophical writings, saw a reprehensible theme and refused to credit his sincerity' (Renwick, 1967, p. 186). The point is precisely that Marmontel was using an ambiguous form. That it was deliberate can hardly be doubted, especially since the publication of his *Neuvaine de Cythère*, a licentious poem (see Kaplan, 1973), more or less contemporary with the *Contes*.

4 The inclusion of the false: the novel within the novel

1 'Voyez-vous ces nymphes [. . .] combien sont-elles différentes de ces femmes de l'île de Chypre dont la beauté était choquante à cause de leur immodestie. Ces beautés immortelles montrent une innocence, une modestie, une simplicité qui charme' (Fénelon, 1968, p. 173) becomes 'Voyez [. . .] voyez si ces jolies filles ressemblent à ces vilaines de la ville où il y avait bal? Ces dernières, mon bon précepteur avaient une gorge débraillée, une tête à l'évent, des mouches, de la craie sur le visage, et du sang de bœuf; mais ces beautés-ci, vertubleu, qu'elles sont modestes; leur gorgerette est collée sur leur poitrine, on voit bien qu'elles ont des tettes, mais c'est à travers un bon corset qui vous les cache' (Marivaux, 1972, p. 797).

2 The early *Homère travesti* (1715, published 1717) separates his intention from Scarron in the *Virgile travesti*. La Motte claimed, and Marivaux in his preface endorses the claim, to imitate the thought and not the style of Homer: 'L'expression de M. de La Motte ne laisse pas d'être vive; mais cette vivacité n'est pas dans elle-même, elle est toute dans l'idée qu'elle exprime; de là vient qu'elle frappe bien plus ceux qui pensent d'après l'esprit pur, que ceux qui, pour ainsi dire, sentent d'après l'imagination' (Marivaux, 1972, p. 963). Likewise, Marivaux claims not to have followed Scarron, whose burlesque is verbal – his own burlesque is to be in the thought. Marivaux rewrites as burlesque La Motte's poem, which was already in one sense a criticism of Homer.

Two other *romans de jeunesse* use the earlier tactic of the tale within the tale – this time to examine different sorts of escape into illusion. *Pharsamon* (c.1712, published 1737) *'ou les folies romanesques'* juxtaposes a satire of the hero's behaviour – he has read too many novels – and an incorporation at a serious level of events every bit as *romanesque* as those of the decried novels. It is as if the narrative imitated on occasion Pharsamon's flight into fancy. The incorporated tales are no more 'real' than some of Pharsamon's satirised reading. Whereas in the later *Voiture embourbée*, the flight is from the uncomfortable reality of an overnight stay with a country curé, which was forced on a carriage full of gentlefolk by a broken axle. The delicately 'low' happenings, then, are not burlesque interference, but a contrast with a scale of *romanesque* stories told by the delayed travellers – a scale which runs through oriental magic (with a touch of sadism, until the young girl of the party debunks it all by turning the whole into a dream) to a picture of village cuckoldry, which, it is claimed, has actually occurred. For Marivaux, see Coulet, 1975.

3 *Bibliothèque raisonnée*, 1736, pp. 378–9, on Wettstein and Smitt's edition of Scarron, whose editor, according to Morillot, 1888, was Bruzen de La Martinière.

4 The famous critical dispute on this point between Poulet, 1952, and Spitzer, 1953 was thus unnecessary.

5 The same is true of *Tristram Shandy*. Ian Watt (1963), is obliged to speak of Sterne's 'precocious technical maturity', p. 303. *Tristram Shandy* has been seen as a reconstitution of the 'characters of nature', and 'characters of manners' distinguished by Johnson. The internal and external approach to character are reconciled thus in the mind of the hero. Of course this is true. But what of the paradoxes in the composition of the novel – that of the author's time, for instance? – are they evidence of an attempt at authenticity (nature) but bizarre because of Shandy's eccentricity (manners)? Surely they are parody – the extreme consequences of authenticity in writing are *also* a *reductio ad absurdum*. The similarity of this procedure to Diderot's *reductio ad absurdum* of the portrait and thus of a certain concept of imitation, in the *Préface* to the *Salon de 1767*, is striking.

6 Diderot, *Jacques le fataliste*, pp. 149, 150. The lament for human unfaithfulness is verbally very close to a passage in the *Supplément au voyage de Bougainville*, see *O.C.*, vol. x, p. 216.

7 The structure of *Jacques* has been studied by Mauzi, 1964.

5 Plays

1 It is true that the *Salle de machines* was so long that actors could scarcely be heard; it was thus especially suited for spectacle.

2 See the brochures, *Description du spectacle de Pandore* (1739); *Lettre au sujet des avantures d'Ulisse* (1741); *Léandre et Héro* (1742); *La Forest enchantée* (1754); *Le Triomphe de l'amour conjugal* (1755); *Description du spectacle de la chute des anges rebelles* (1758).

3 'Aimer le changement jusques dans les plaisirs, c'est le goût de la nature . . . On passe d'un plaisir à l'autre; on rit et l'on pleure tour à tour' (La Chaussée, *préface de Melanide*, quoted Chassiron, 1749, pp. 16–17).

4 Leclerc's remark is made of Corneille's *Andromède*, but she says that the same was true of eighteenth-century *décor*.

5 See La Font de Saint Yenne's complaint about Servandoni's archi-

tecture, ruined by his stage design: 'Accoûtumés à prodiguer les embellissemens nécessaires à l'illusion du Spectacle, à l'eclat des
Décorateurs qui les obligent de multiplier les parties qui en font la
richesse et la somptuosité' (La Font de Saint Yenne, 1747, p. 47).

6 'Les habiles artistes Italiens, tels que Bibiena, osoient présenter leurs
objets sous un point de vue sur l'augle [*sic* for angle] ce qui les rend
plus pittoresques, & offre au Spectateur un coup d'œil agréable &
dont la perspective échappe à sa critique, les lignes fuyantes tendant à
des points, qu'il n'est pas à portée de juger; il s'ensuit en même tems
qu'on ne voit plus le défaut de rapport dans les lignes qu'éprouvent
ceux qui ne sont pas placés directement au milieu de la Salle' (Cochin,
1781, pp. 64–5).

7 Cf. Hyatt Major, 1964, p. vi: 'In designing opera scenery, the Bibienas
traded for a century on an innovation of Ferdinando's which opened
even the tiniest stage to hitherto undreamed-of space and loftiness by
painting buildings as seen at about a forty-five degree angle. A ground
plan of these buildings painted on the backdrops would resemble the
V of the angle of a building driving at the audience like the prow of a
ship, or the upside down V of the corner of a room extending its walls
to embrace the audience, or both plans combined in an X of intersec-
ting arcades that spread outwards towards the proscenium and also led
back through fleeing colonnades. These restless flights of architecture
running diagonally off stage towards undetermined distances revolu-
tionised and dominated scenic design for most of the eighteenth
century.'

8 Marmontel pushes the paradox further by maintaining that the opera
is only *vraisemblable* if it contains the 'merveilleux'; cf. Nagler, 1957,
p. 128, and below, p. 259 on the attitude of d'Alembert.

9 Cf. Algarotti, 1773, pp. 71–2: 'Comment on fait paraître des situations
retrécies ou des endroits grands & spacieux, comment enfin on a porté
l'art de tromper l'œil jusqu'au dernier degré de la perfection.'

10 'Le plus grand défaut que j'y crois remarquer est un faux goût de
magnificence, par lequel on a voulu mettre en représentation le merveilleux, qui n'étant fait que pour être imaginé est aussi bien placé
dans un poème épique que ridiculement sur un théâtre' (Rousseau,
O.C., vol. II, p. 288).

11 'Le faste et l'eclat pompeux de nos Opéras produisent aux yeux du
Spectateur une illusion agréable, et qui tient de l'enchantement, mais
ce fracas de machines dont l'aprêt & la dépense sont souvent considérables, ne causent pas un plaisir aussi constant, aussi vif, que celui qui
naît de l'intérêt de sentiment' (Lacombe, 1758, p. 52).

12 Favart in 1761 writes 'Il y a beaucoup à désirer dans l'exécution des
machines' (1803, vol. I, p. 208). Saint-Preux in *La Nouvelle Héloïse*
gives an account of the inadequacies of the opera *décor* (Rousseau,
O.C., vol. II, pp. 282–8); cf. also Nougaret, 1769, vol. I, pp. 325–66.

13 Cf. La Harpe, quoted Nagler, 1957, p. 136: 'L'exécution théâtrale

etait encore bien défectueuse. Les monstres, les vols, les machines, tout ce qui devait faire illusion aux yeux a produit un effet ridicule, soit par la faute du machiniste, soit que tout cet appareil de merveilleux qui n'en impose point assez à la vue, perde son effet sur l'imagination et commence à passer de mode.'

14 Cf. Noverre, 1760, pp. 162, 190; and Bricaire de La Dixmérie, 1765, p. 17.

15 The interplay of reality and art goes one further, to the interplay of art and art. Servandoni designed Saint Sulpice, and painted landscapes with ruins; these were criticised by La Font de Saint Yenne, 1747, p. 47 see notes above and Cochin, 1757–71, vol. ɪ, p. 108.

16 Cf. Lessing, 1785, vol. ɪ, p. 227; Nougaret, 1769, vol. ɪ, p. 357; Lacombe, 1758, p. 109; Brumoy, 1730, vol. ɪ, p. lx; Grimm, in *Correspondance littéraire*, vol. ᴠɪ, p. 172: 'Tout le système de la tragédie moderne est un système de convention et de fantaisie qui n'a point de modèle dans la nature' (janvier 1765).

17 Cf. Brumoy, 1730, vol. ɪ, p. lviii; Levesque de Pouilly, 1747, pp. 47–8; *Encyclopédie*, article *Unité*.

18 In opposition to the tradition: 'le vrai peut quelquefois n'être pas vraisemblable' (Boileau, *Art poétique*, chant ɪɪɪ), represented by the abbé Nadal, 1738, vol. ɪɪ, pp. 193–4; Cailhava de l'Estendoux, 1772, vol. ɪ, p. 433.

19 Cf. Lessing, 1785, vol. ɪ, p. 37–8: 'Car l'Auteur dramatique n'est pas historien; il ne raconte pas ce qu'on a cru jadis être arrivé; il le fait de nouveau arriver devant nos yeux; & cela non à cause de la vérité historique, mais dans un tout autre & plus important dessein. Ce n'est pas à cette vérité qu'il vise; elle est seulement le moyen dont il se sert pour arriver à son but; il veut nous faire illusion & par là nous émouvoir.'

20 'La chaleur du discours, la pompe de l'action, la vérité du caractère, la fiction même des choses nous font oublier la fiction' (Sticotti, 1769, p. 11).

21 There is a great deal of evidence that classical French dramatic art was felt not to correspond with experience, and in purely aesthetic terms this is translated as the need to go beyond the achievements of Racine and Molière. See Lough, 1957, p. 183, for the lack of success of these authors. For a while it was forbidden to act Molière because of small audiences.

22 Cf. Clairon, an vii, p. 250, of the tragic actor: 'C'est dans l'histoire de tous les peuples du monde qu'il doit puiser ses lumières [. . .]. Il doit [. . .] adapter à chaque rôle tout ce que sa nation peut avoir d'originalité.' See also Fréron, quoted Myers, 1962, p. 59: 'Que de mœurs encore nous restent à peindre. Qu'on nous représente réellement les Chinois, et non pas comme dans la médiocre Tragédie de l'*Orphelin de la Chine*, drame sans coloris, sans caractère; qu'on nous fasse voir les Japonnais . . .; que les coûtumes de chaque nation soient employées avec adresse.'

23 Cf. Bergman, 1961, p. 7, on changes in methods of stage decoration.
24 Clairon's comments on the various roles she has played also reveal an interesting concept of what is real: cf. Clairon, an vii.
25 'On vient de donner sur le théâtre de la Comédie-Italienne, un opéra-comique nouveau, intitulé *Le Serrurier*. Si la police n'y met ordre, toutes les professions passeront en revue sur ce théâtre' (*Correspondance littéraire*, vol. VI, p. 175, 1 janvier 1765).
26 The book has been taken as a serious commendation of the *Opéra comique*: cf. Wolf Frank's article on Nougaret in Cabeen, 1951. But Nougaret himself says in the preface: 'Le lecteur se souviendra donc que la plupart des louanges que je donne à l'Opéra Bouffon ne doivent point être prises à la lettre' (1769, vol. I, p. xx).
27 He compares the opera and the epic poem, for example, in both the characters are seen eating and drinking (Nougaret, 1769, vol. II, p. 107). This was a frequent accusation of triviality in discussions of Greek epic during the *Querelle des Anciens et des Modernes*.
28 He is aiming at operas such as *Blaise le savetier* and *Le Maréchal ferrant*. Marmontel (1763, vol. I, p. 84) had argued that the poet did not need to be a naturalist.
29 Cf. Marmontel, 1763, vol. I, pp. 83–4: 'Le Peintre le plus versé dans le dessein & dans l'étude de l'antique ne rendra jamais la Nature avec cette vérité qui fait illusion, s'il n'a sous les yeux ses modèles. Il en est de même du poète', and 'pour des mouvemens du cœur humain, le dirai-je? c'est avec des hommes incultes qu'il doit vivre s'il veut les voir au naturel'.
30 Diderot rejects voluntary illusion and hence insists: 'On ne verra pas la laideur jouer le rôle de la beauté' (*Entretiens sur le 'Fils naturel'*, p. 106.
31 Maillet Duclairon (1751, p. 40) does make the notion of embellishing nature capable of truly aesthetic reference, describing how apparently remote, trivial, or imaginary events can be made meaningful: 'L'art embellit ce que la Nature ne feroit que montrer grossièrement & ce n'est qu'avec beaucoup de peine que l'on découvre les chemins par lesquels on est parvenu à fixer notre attention sur des sujets éloignés & à nous intéresser à des événements qui n'ont peut-être jamais existé que dans l'imagination du Poete.'
32 Though in the case of Batteux, in keeping with a certain tradition (see below, pp. 213–14), it serves to emphasise the artist's plastic power since he works on the artificial.
33 A common criticism, so much so that it is parodied in Marchand's *Le Vidangeur sensible,* 1880, p. 22.
34 A similar criticism was made of Molière. Rapin had already in 1672 criticised Molière, who makes 'tous les objets plus grands qu'ils ne sont & qu'elles [les comédies] ne copient presque point au naturel' (Lough, 1957, p. 102).

35 See the discussion, from a very different point of view, in Szondi, 1979, pp. 91–147.

36 He is in fact replying on many points to Sainte Albine, who had tended to suggest that if the acting were only good enough, the audience could forget bad scenery or that an old actress could convincingly play a young girl.

37 'Après tout, l'illusion du théâtre est volontaire: on sait en y allant qu'on sera trompé' (Marmontel, 1763, vol. II, p. 153). This appears to contradict his statement in the article *Comédie*, in the *Encyclopédie* (and which he repeats in the 1763 *Poétique*): 'Il faut encore que tout ce qui se passe & se dit sur la scène soit une peinture si naïve de la société qu'on oublie qu'on est au spectacle [. . .]. Le prestige de l'art, c'est de le faire disparaître au point que non seulement l'illusion précède la réflexion, mais qu'elle la repousse & l'écarte.'

38 'La représentation d'un Drame est, pour ainsi dire, un songe qui doit redouter le moment du réveil' (Nougaret, 1769, vol. I, p. 188).

39 Voltaire himself used the *London Merchant* for the fourth act of *Mahomet*: see ed. Kehl. vol. III, p. 132.

40 'De M. Lemière, *Barneveldt*, tragédie. Arrêtée à la police par l'événement de la prison & du procès fait à M. de La Chalotais, dont l'histoire avoit beaucoup d'analogie avec celle du grand pensionnaire de Hollande' (Lekain, 9 mai 1770, in Lekain, 1825, p. 232).

41 No one would have minded, he said, had the *Mariage* been a tragedy.

42 Yet this same theatre is described by Voltaire as being of extreme simplicity, and justified by a covert reference to contemporary epistemology which maintained that the mind could only perform one operation at any single moment (Voltaire, ed. Kehl, vol. I, p. 92).

43 But see the *Préface* to the 1772 edition of Crébillon's plays: 'Cette mort trop précipitée ne produit que de l'étonnement & ce sujet, au fond si tragique, n'inspire qu'une pitié momentanée: on en sort moins ému que surpris' (*Oeuvres de Crébillon*, 1772, vol. I, p. 3).

44 Cf. Lessing who says that a story is credible because of interior plausibility, not because it happened.

45 Cf. Lessing on the psychological *invraisemblance* of Crébillon, and on Corneille's 'sentences' in reverse – epigrammatic expressions of evil ('fanfaronnades de vice') by hero-villains (1785, vol. I, pp. 13, 156). See also the curious remark by Lessing, that the Ancients did not need to interrupt the dialogue by stage directions 'par lesquels l'Auteur se mêle en quelque sorte parmi les personnages' (1785, vol. II, p. 97).

46 The complaint against *sentences* is fairly general: cf. Fréron quoted in Myers, 1962, p. 324.

47 *Correspondance littéraire*, quoted Myers, 1962, p. 66, on Lemierre's heroine Idomenée: 'C'est une femme esprit fort [. . .] mais que je ne puis souffrir en Crète, dans ces temps superstitieux où les dieux

répondaient aux arguments des philosophes par des volcans et des maladies pestilentielles.'

48 'Si leur malheur ne concourt pas immédiatement au but de la Tragédie, s'ils sont de simples instrumens dont le Poëte se sert pour atteindre son but avec d'autres Personnages, il est incontestable que la Pièce seroit meilleure, si elle avoit le même effet sans eux' (Lessing, 1785, vol. II, p. 59).

49 Venturi (1939, pp. 126–7) quotes Mercier's account of Crébillon *fils'* attitude to his father's plays: 'Il riait aux larmes de certaines productions théâtrales et du public, qui ne voyait dans tous les rois de la tragédie française que le roi de Versailles. Le rôle du capitaine des gardes, tantôt traître, tantôt fidèle, selon la fantaisie du poète, le faisait surtout pâmer de joie [. . .]. Aujourd'hui janissaire, le lendemain déposant Tarquin le superbe, cheville ouvrière de tous les dénouements, il avait renversé plus de trônes au bout de l'année, qu'il n'avait de gardes à sa suite.' I wish to suggest that something approaching this attitude (not dissimilar to that with which one watches television serials) was the common enjoyment of the highly stylised tragedy.

50 Cf. Collé, 1868, vol. III, p. 22, février 1765, on the Duc d'Ayen's reaction to Belloy's *Siège de Calais*. This is indicative not so much of the aristocracy's dislike of bourgeois heroes, as of their reaction to the polemics of certain writers who deliberately make the villain an aristocrat (cf. Beaumarchais, 1964, p. 151).

51 Fenouillot de Falbaire in his preface to *Le Fabricant de Londres,* claims that our good impulses can hardly be harnessed by tragedy, for we only infrequently see kings we can pity (p. vii).

52 Fenouillot de Falbaire, *préface* to the *Ecole des mœurs*, pp. ix–x; 'C'est parce que l'Ouvrage était honnête & moral, qu'on a voulu qu'il fût mauvais' (Cailhava, *préface* to *L'Egoisme*, 1777).

53 See Myers, 1962, p. 175, for evidence of the connection made by critics between the use of detail and *drame*. According to Fréron, an excess number of details about domestic trivia was the cause of the failure of Fenouillot's play.

54 A related consciousness is found in Rétif's numerous projects for society's improvement: *La Mimographe, ou Idées d'une honnête femme pour la réformation du théâtre national* (1770); *Le Pornographe, ou Idées d'un honnête homme sur son projet de règlement pour les prostituées* (1769).

55 See the Crébillon *fils* passage quoted at n. 49 above.

6 Spectators

1 For Madame de Puisieux, the variety of opera is a necessary result of the fact that it appeals to the senses; moral judgement can then be brought in if the theatre appeals to the soul which voluptuously contemplates its objects (1750, p. 72).

2 'Le public ne s'intéresse à la peine, au plaisir d'un personnage, & à ses

diverses situations qu'autant qu'il se persuade voir le héros véritable d'une action réelle. L'instruire de son erreur, c'est l'exhorter à ne pas s'intéresser à des avantures imaginaires' (Cailhava, 1772, vol. i, p. 427).

3 'Le public une fois assemblé, ne considère les choses qu'au moment qu'elles paroissent & ne leur donne pas plus d'étendue que le poète [. . .]. Il ne prévient pas ce qui doit arriver . . .' (Cailhava, 1772, vol. i, p. 505).

4 Rousseau actually corrects Dubos by name (*Lettre à d'Alembert*, pp. 78–9).

5 Brumoy, like his contemporary Louis Riccoboni in *De la Réformation du théâtre* (1743), pp. 323–4, accepts the need for emotional stimulus, but, unlike Dubos, both make use of the concept of illusion (see also Lacombe, 1758, p. 103).

6 Granet is quoting *Les sentimens de Marianne*. The irony at such heroism seems typical of authors on the *Modernes'* side of the *Querelle des Anciens et des Modernes*. Cartaud points out that the spectator may in life want everyone else to be Polyeucte and himself to be Félix: 'D'ailleurs, tout est si flotant dans ces hautes maximes de l'héroïsme. Deux grands personnages disent des choses également sublimes & qui roulent sur des vûes toutes opposées' (Cartaud, 1736, p. 204).

7 See Clairon, an vii, p. 365: 'Je m'étois persuadée qu'on ne vouloit voir une tragédie que pour s'élever au-dessus de soi-même, que pour recevoir des grands personnages de l'antiquité les exemples les plus imposans de noblesse, de décence, de courage, de grandeur d'âme', and the editors of the Kehl Voltaire, *à propos* of *Rome sauvée*: 'Elles [ses pièces] ont surtout l'avantage précieux de donner à l'âme de l'élévation précieuse et de la force; en sortant de ces pièces, on se trouve plus disposé à une action de courage, plus éloigné de ramper devant un homme accrédité, ou de plier devant le pouvoir injuste et absolu' (Kehl, vol. iv, p. 194).

8 'Sans inquiéter l'amour que nous nous portons à nous-mêmes, ils [les malheurs d'autrui] intéressent celui que nous portons à tous les hommes vertueux' (Levesque de Pouilly, 1747, p. 62). Shaftesbury, Levesque and the early Diderot are all linked by lines of influence and in each the aesthetic theory becomes the model for the moral.

9 Cf. Jacques Proust's remarkable commentary on this passage (Proust, 1962, p. 359–65).

10 'Comment se peut-il donc qu'un Drame comique, fondé ordinairement sur la fiction, nous intéresse autant que si nous contemplions véritablement dans la société les événemens, dont nous ne sommes témoins qu'au Théâtre?' (Nougaret, 1769, vol. ii, p. 114).

11 'Le bon Goût est un amour habituel de l'ordre. Il s'étend comme nous venons de le dire, sur les mœurs aussi bien que sur les ouvrages d'esprit. La Symmétrie des parties entr'elles & avec le tout, est aussi

nécessaire dans la conduite d'une action morale que dans un tableau' (Batteux, 1746, p. 124).

12 'L'homme qui craint de pleurer, celui qui refuse de s'attendrir, a un vice dans le cœur, ou de fortes raisons de n'oser y rentrer pour compter avec lui-même' (Beaumarchais, 1964, p. 12).

13 'Pour répandre de l'intérêt sur ce cinquième acte, après le quatrième, non pas de l'intérêt violent, l'entreprise était impossible, mais de cet intérêt si doux qui reporte l'âme à sa vraie place après des angoisses terribles, et quand le danger est passé' (Beaumarchais, 1964, p. 703).

14 Cf. Constance's account of the success of the moral theatre quoted above, p. 190, in wish-fulfilling contrast to the difficulties Diderot encountered in getting the play staged (Hobson, 1974).

15 Vernière, introduction to the *Entretiens*, in Diderot: Vernière (1); 1959; McLaughlin, 1968.

16 When Diderot further analyses this type of effect, it is found to take the form of a kind of progress through a graduated scale of emotion, coupled with an awareness of the effect of this display of emotion on others. (See Diderot's account of the 'pantaléon', *Correspondance*, vol. v, p. 177, 17 novembre,1965; or of Garrick's 'pantomime', *O.C.*, vol. iii, p. 677.)

17 The singularity of Rousseau's position is shown, e.g., by Beaumarchais (1964, p. 11): 'Celui qui pleure au Spectacle est seul; et plus il le sent, plus il pleure avec délices.'

7 Actors

1 Hedgecock (1911), Wassermann (1947), Chouillet (1970) have shown that Sticotti's book is a paraphrase of Aaron Hill's *The Actor* (1755), a revision of the latter's earlier book, which in turn was a paraphrase of Rémond de Sainte Albine's *Le Comédien*.

2 'Qu'il est avantageux d'être sensible quand on doit inspirer de la sensibilité aux autres' (Maillet Duclairon, 1751, p. 99). 'Or la nature seule a le pouvoir d'agir sur les cœurs, de les ouvrir, de les resserrer, de les attendrir [. . .]. Il n'est point naturel qu'une Princesse nous rende sensible à des peines qu'elle ne ressent point elle-même & dont elle nous fait le récit avec indifférence' (d'Aigueberre, 1870 p. 19).

3 Cf. Garrick's criticism of the actress Mlle Clairon: 'Her heart has none of those instantaneous feelings, that life blood, that keen sensibility that bursts at once from genius and like electric fire, shoots through the veins, marrow bones and all of every spectator' (quoted by Wassermann, 1947, p. 268). It is clear from Hedgecock (1911) that Noverre was influenced by Garrick.

4 'Ce n'est donc pas assez d'entendre parfaitement une pièce, l'Acteur doit être, pour ainsi dire, Auteur lui-même' (Sticotti, 1769, p. 40; see Rémond de Sainte Albine, 1747, pp. 23–4). This is confirmed by Charpentier, whose aim is to denigrate the actor (e.g. 1768, vol. ii, p. 22).

5 See Prince de Ligne, 1774, p. 107: 'Essaiez, jeunes talens. Livrez-vous. Allez trop loin même, cela sera plus aisé donc que de rester au but.'

6 Cf. Clairon's account of her living up to this creed: 'Sans oublier jamais ma place, je me suis fait un devoir de ne rien faire, de ne rien dire qui ne porte le caractère de la noblesse et de l'austérité. Je n'ignore pas les ridicules que cette manière d'être m'a valus' (an vii, pp. 298–9).

7 This is Talma's explanation of the relation between intelligence and sensibility (in Lekain, 1825, p. xxxix).

8 Cf. Marmontel, quoted by Servandoni d'Hannetaire, from the article *Déclamation théâtrale* in the *Encyclopédie*: 'Celui qui n'a que du sentiment ne joue bien que son propre rôle.' It seems possible that Diderot might have known Charpentier's attack on the actor: certain passages of the second volume are close to the *Paradoxe*, for instance: 'Qu'est-ce qui communément fait le Comédien? l'infortune, le libertinage, l'incapacité pour tout autre état' (Charpentier, 1768, vol. ii, p. 22), which may be compared with Diderot (*Paradoxe*, pp. 349, 355).

9 'Ils ont encore besoin d'une égalité d'âme qui ne souffre chez eux d'autres sentimens que ceux qu'ils doivent représenter' (Maillet Duclairon, 1751, p. 18). 'Une personne de théâtre ne sauroit avoir trop d'attention à ne donner sur elle que le moins de prise qu'il est possible aux événemens heureux ou malheureux qui lui arrivent' (Rémond de Sainte Albine, 1747, pp. 40–1).

10 See Diderot on the 'prêtre incrédule qui prêche la passion' (*Paradoxe*, p. 313).

11 His example of the actor playing Orestes who kills a slave is found in the *Paradoxe*, though Diderot says he is playing Atreus, p. 380. F. Riccoboni points out the weakness of the anecdote as evidence that the actor feels by saying that the Greek actor would never have dreamt of killing another actor.

12 Compare Talma's rejection of Diderot's theories, which he associates, rightly, with Diderot's *désinvolture*, and his recommendation of Rousseau's 'sincere feeling' (in Lekain, 1825, p. xxxv).

13 It seems as if these opposing conceptions of the actor may be developed from an opposition traditionally made between tragic and comic poet. Brumoy says that the tragic poet 'n'a guère qu'à se replier sur lui-même, pour y puiser dans son cœur des sentimens qu'il est assuré de faire entrer dans tous les cœurs, il les a trouvés dans le sien. Le second [the comic poet] doit se multiplier & se produire presqu'en autant de personnes qu'il en veut avoir à contenter & à divertir' (Brumoy, 1730, vol. iii, p. lxi). Cf. Diderot, *Discours,* p. 212.

14 Cf. Abrams, 1958, p. 51, for the importance of this metaphor.

15 Cf. Clairon's account of her technique: 'Pour parvenir à mouiller seulement mes paupières, à faire sauter quelquefois une larme de mes yeux, je joignais à des accens continuellement douloureux, une con-

traction dans l'estomac qui faisoit trembler mes nerfs, une espèce d'étranglement dans la gorge qui gênait mes paroles, ma respiration retenue et coupée indiquoit l'agitation de mon âme' (Clairon, an vii, pp. 372–3).

16 There are some striking resemblances between Clairon's memoirs and the *Paradoxe*; these are indicated by Vernière, in Diderot *Paradoxe*. For example, her reply to the reproach that she uses too much art: 'Eh, que vouloit-on que j'eusse? Etais-je, en effet, Roxane, Aménaïde [. . .]? Devois-je prêter à ces rôles mes propres sentimens et ma façon d'être habituelle?' (Clairon, an vii, p. 253; cf. *Paradoxe*, p. 315).

17 'Lui' says of Mr. de Bissy: 'Celui là est en joueur d'échecs ce que Mademoiselle Clairon est en acteur. Ils sçavent de ces jeux l'un et l'autre, tout ce qu'on en peut apprendre' (Diderot, *Le Neveu de Rameau*, p. 7).

18 'Mlle. Clairon, en substituant l'art le plus profond, l'étude la plus heureuse au naturel qu'elle n'avait pas, nous avait insensiblement écartés de cette simplicité qui fait aux yeux d'un homme de goût le charme de la représentation théâtrale [. . .] cette actrice savait tout imiter jusqu'à la simplicité, au naturel même, mais on ne cessait jamais de voir le fruit de l'étude' (*Correspondance littéraire*, vol. vi, p. 317, juillet 1765).

19 'Le grand art de David Garrick consiste dans la facilité de s'aliéner l'esprit & de se mettre dans la situation du personnage qu'il doit représenter, et lorsqu'il en est une fois pénétré, il cesse d'être Garrick, et il devient le personnage dont il est chargé. Ainsi à mesure qu'il change de rôle, il devient si différent de lui-même qu'on dirait qu'il change de traits et de figure [. . .], tous les changemens qui s'opèrent dans ses traits proviennent de la manière dont il s'affecte intérieurement' (*Correspondance littéraire*, vol. vi, pp. 318–19, juillet 1765). Cf. Molé, on Lekain, who speaks of 'L'obéissance fidèle de ses traits aux affections de son âme' (Lekain, 1825, p. 47).

20 The actor has a private as well as an aesthetic weight for Diderot. Through him he explores his own self-consciousness, as is exemplified in the following: 'J'étois plein de la tendresse que vous m'aviez inspirée quand j'ai paru au milieu de nos convives; elle brilloit dans mes yeux, elle échauffoit mes discours; elle disposoit de mes mouvemens; elle se montroit en tout. Je leur semblois extraordinaire, inspiré, divin' (Diderot, *Correspondance*, vol. ii, pp. 269–70, c. 12 octobre 1759).

21 From this too comes the interest in ancient pantomime, and in Nicolini's spectacles praised at second hand by Diderot (Hobson, 1974).

8 Illusion and the poet's voice

1 See Lacombe, 1758, p. 215: 'Ces Fables perdent alors quelque chose

de leurs agrémens parce que l'on exige trop du Lecteur, pour se prêter à l'illusion.'

2 See Frain du Tremblay, 1713, p. 73.

3 Cahusac appears to have written an *Epître sur les dangers de la poësie*, La Haye, 1739; I have not been able to consult this.

4 Cf. Batteux's critical, and accurate, account of certain theories of poetry: 'C'est une espèce de magie: elle fait illusion aux yeux, à l'imagination, à l'esprit même, & vient à bout de procurer aux hommes des plaisirs réels, par des inventions chimériques' (Batteux, 1746, p. 3).

5 Abbé de La Barre, *Dissertation sur le poème épique*, 1741, p. 378, replying to Abbé Vatry, *Discours sur la fable épique*, 1741.

6 Later writers, for example Lacombe and Marmontel, agree in essence with this attitude, but their greater social awareness leads to a heightened consciousness of the pretence of the pastoral; in response to this, in order to make the form more *adequate*, the subject is changed in the second part of the century and becomes the garden, where man works on nature (Jacques Delille, *Les Jardins ou l'art d'embellir les paysages, poëme*, 1782; Gouge de Cessières, *Les Jardins d'ornemens, ou les Géorgiques françoises, nouveau poème en quatre chants*, 1758). This development is analogous to the evolution of the paintings of Hubert Robert, or Loutherbourg (see above, pp. 71–2).

7 That such an outright admission may have been slightly scandalous is suggested by its having been picked out for quotation by Granet, 1742, vol. VI, p. 33, as the most effective answer to a criticism (Cartaud's?) of poetry.

8 For instance, Lacombe, 1758, p. 91.

9 See La Motte, 1754, vol. II, p. 22 (*Discours sur Homère*); Fourmont, 1716, p. 204; article *Merveilleux* in the *Encylopédie*: 'Il faut se transporter en esprit dans les temps où les Poëtes ont écrit, épouser pour un moment les idées, les moeurs, les sentimens des peuples pour lesquels ils ont écrit'; see also Brumoy, 1730, vol. III, p. xxxvi.

10 Marmontel, much later, continues the *Modernes'* rejection of the *merveilleux*, and makes it more complete. But he does this for totally different reasons. He demands *vraisemblance*, and furthermore, wishes the poet to imitate, within limits, 'things as they are'. To that end, he undermines all and every convention by the most radical of all limitations on *vraisemblance*. From its seventeenth-century meaning of social agreement he restricts it to 'notre manière de concevoir', this having severe epistemological and not merely social limitations. He wishes *vraisemblance* to refer not to what is socially agreed on but to *what we are aware of*. This limitation obviates the need for belief, since, in his eyes, it covers the whole of what is epistemologically available to us: 'Tant que le Poète ne fait que nous rappeler ce que nous avons vu au-dehors ou éprouvé au dedans de nous-mêmes, la ressemblance suffit à l'illusion, & comme nous voyons dans la feinte

l'image de la réalité, le Poète n'a aucun besoin de gagner notre confidence' (Marmontel, 1763, vol. I, pp. 374–5). The image, under this limitation, is *automatically* adequate to internal or external experience, and has no logical independence, no mediating power. It is received rather than constituted by the mind, and the last phrase carefully eliminates the reader's subjectivity from any role in the constitution of art's effect. This later view of poetry as illusion has expelled the reader from 'la feinte' and has a clear relation to the theatrical theory developed by Diderot. As we shall see, the other powerful development of illusion in the second half of the century, on the contrary, implants illusion deep in the reader's soul.

11 La Motte goes so far as to say that the controversial Racinian line 'Le flot qui l'apporta recule épouvanté' would have been acceptable in an ode.

12 See La Motte, 1754, vol. I, part 1, pp. 42–3.

13 See Séran de La Tour, who relates this type of movement to a dislike of symmetry: 'L'art de varier les mouvemens de la balance de l'intérêt est le seul moyen de maintenir l'équilibre entre les ressorts qui le coupent et ceux qui l'entretiennent' (Séran de La Tour, 1762, p. 210). The relation between the ode and *papillotage* is neatly demonstrated by Le Brun's account of Jean-Baptiste Rousseau's *Cantates*: 'Le souffle du zéphir est-il plus séduisant? [. . .] Ce sont des nymphes deminues; une draperie discrète, des ornemens ambitieux n'en offusquent pas les beautés mais une gaze légère les rend plus piquantes' (Le Brun, 1811, vol. IV, pp. 312–13).

14 P. H. Meyer writes: 'A partir de la préface que Boileau avait composée pour sa traduction du traité *Du sublime* (1674) on avait tendance à rattacher le concept à la sensation évoquée chez le lecteur plutôt qu'à son expression stylistique' (Meyer, 1965, p. 36).

15 The extent to which the sublime has become the poetic effect is shown by Bouhier's objection to the use of poetic prose: 'La prose a une certaine démarche grave, posée, qui ne sçauroit guères s'élever de terre sans courir risque de tomber. Comment pourroit-elle donc représenter la poésie qui n'est belle qu'autant qu'elle prend un essor impétueux & rapide, & qu'elle nous enlève pour ainsi dire au-dessus de nous-mêmes?' (quoted in the *Journal des sçavans*, 1737, février, p. 96).

16 'Quand les passions nous donnent de violentes secousses, en sorte qu'elles nous enlèvent l'usage de la réflexion, nous éprouvons mille sentiments divers' (Condillac, *Essai*, p. 35).

17 'Il faut donc entendre par Sublime dans Longin, l'Extraordinaire, le Surprenant, et comme je l'ai traduit, le Merveilleux dans le discours' (Boileau, 1966, p. 338).

18 Silvain maintains that the sublime need not be *merveilleux*: 1732, p. 30.

19 See Frain du Tremblay, 1713, *préface,* but also Louis Racine, 1731,

p. 407, who satirises such a conception by comparing the god who inspires to a magnet attracting a chain of filings: 'L'homme qui récite bien les Vers d'un grand Poëte, inspire à ses Auditeurs le feu dont il est saisi: ce feu lui est inspiré par le Poëte dont il récite l'ouvrage, & le Poëte l'avait reçu d'un Dieu.' For such a theory he substitutes a physiological one.

20 Cf. Levesque de Pouilly, 1748, pp. 172, 714; Jaucourt, *Encyclopédie*, article *Sublime*.

21 La Motte's account of the 'beau désordre' associated with the odes and the sublime bears a relation to Marivaux's aesthetics: 'J'entens par ce beau désordre, une suite de pensées liées entr'elles par un rapport commun à la même matière, mais affranchies des liaisons grammaticales & de ces transitions scrupuleuses qui énervent la Poésie lyrique', La Motte, 1754, vol. I, part 1, p. xxxviii.

22 'On ne peut analyser l'enthousiasme quand on l'éprouve, puisqu'alors on n'est pas maître de sa réflexion; mais comment l'analyser quand on ne l'éprouve plus?' (Condillac, *Essai*, p. 35).

23 Cf. 'Je veux qu'un Poëte qui fait une Ode, frappé de la dignité de sa matière, élevé & soûtenu par elle, ne parle plus comme le reste des hommes, je veux qu'il prenne son vol plus haut: que fait pour aller au grand, il franchisse tout ce qui l'en sépare; je veux que tout tienne de l'ardeur qui l'embrase, que tout sente le désordre qui l'agite, que tout peigne l'agitation de son ame, & qu'enfin livré comme il le doit être à l'emportement des Passions, il rejette ces liaisons timides, ces transitions scrupuleuses, dont leur impatience ne sçauroit s'accommoder' (Rémond de Saint Mard, 1749, vol. v, p. 42; 1734, p. 216).

24 Cf. *Encyclopédie*, article *Imagination* by Voltaire, and particularly, Trublet, who while appearing to lay the conventional eighteenth-century emphasis on judgement at the expense of imagination, yet suggests that the latter supplies a network of relations between ideas that ratiocination cannot: 'L'imagination et la nature font mieux les liaisons que l'art & le jugement; elles lient sans peine les choses les plus différentes [. . .]. C'est quand on est méthodique qu'il est plus difficile d'être lié et suivi' (Trublet, 1754–60, vol. III, p. 154).

25 The comparison with a divinity is clear. Cf. Séran de La Tour, 1762, pp. 126–7, who discusses the relation between creating and discovering; and Castel, for whom 'imaginer', though merely mental imaging, is yet equated with invention; Castel, 1763, p. 14. See also: 'Des idées qui présentent des objets sous des rapports cachés ou peu connus, avec ce ton d'énergie qui caractérise l'invention, c'est surtout cet art de créer ces choses ou de leur donner une nouvelle vie, qui est la marque la plus infaillible du génie' (Chicaneau de Neuville, 1758, pp. 84–5). This is a hesitation between creation and reworking.

26 There are striking analogies between these pages and certain ideas in Kant's *Critique of Judgement*, para. 10, for example. It is not clear that Pluche realises the import of what he is saying.

27 Batteux, on the contrary, stresses the artificiality of art, to separate it from divine creation: 'L'Esprit humain ne peut créer qu'improprement: toutes ses productions portent l'empreinte d'un modèle. [Les hommes de génie] qui creusent le plus, ne découvrent que ce qui existoit auparavant. Ils ne sont créateurs que pour avoir observé, & réciproquement, ils ne sont observateurs que pour être en état de créer' (Batteux, 1746, pp. 10–11). But this very emphasis on artificiality leads to the gloss on Horace's *ex noto fictum carmen sequar*: 'Je feindrai, j'imaginerai d'aprés ce qui est connu des hommes. On y sera trompé, on croira voir la nature elle-même, & qu'il n'est rien de si aisé que de la peindre de cette sorte; mais ce sera une fiction, un ouvrage de génie au-dessus des forces de tout esprit médiocre' (Batteux, 1746, p. 20).

28 This is a note by the editor, Formey, who contradicts Bruzen de La Martinière when the latter asserts: 'Lorsqu'il n'est question que d'apprécier les ouvrages que les autres ont composés, le génie n'est plus si nécessaire, à beaucoup près. Il suffit du goût fortifié par la connaissance des règles de l'art' (Bruzen de la Martinière, 1756, p. 273). But Diderot contradicts Helvétius who asserts: 'Concevoir leurs idées, c'est avoir la même aptitude à l'esprit' (*Réfutation d'Helvétius*, in *O.C.*, vol. XI, p. 544), though see his attitude in *Lettre sur les sourds et muets*, *O.C.*, vol. II, p. 549).

29 Cf. Trublet, 1754–60, vol. III, p. 184: 'L'étonnement où le [le lecteur] jettent de grandes difficultés parfaitement surmontées.'

30 'Ne sont-ce pas les difficultés vaincues qui font la gloire des poètes? N'est-ce pas sur cet unique fondement, par cette seule considération qu'on leur a permis une espèce de langage particulier, des tours plus hardis, plus imprévus; enfin, ce qu'ils appellent eux-mêmes en se vantant un beau, un noble, un heureux délire; c'est à dire, en un mot, ce que la droite raison n'adopterait pas?' (Fontenelle, in Gillot, 1914, p. 535).

31 Cf. 'Bien des gens prétendent que le Beau est arbitraire & veulent le prouver par la différence qu'on remarque dans les Ouvrages du même genre; mais tout ce qu'ils prouvent, c'est que l'Auteur a saisi tel objet dans tel point de vue, & cela relativement à sa manière de sentir' (Chicaneau de Neuville, 1758, pp. 19–20, note). Critics like the père André construct a scale ranging from an absolute beauty to conventional beauty. Others, like Levesque de Pouilly, define beauty at the same time as a necessary conformity with the human perceptual system. For Trublet, beauty is teleological, 'convenance aux usages pour lesquels elle [la chose] est faite', and thus, while dependent on contemporary conventions, it is not itself strictly speaking conventional (Trublet, 1754–60, vol. III, p. 217).

32 See Cartaud de la Vilate, 1736, who is typical of this kind of attitude.

33 Levesque attempts to disprove this by postulating a necessary relation between poetic form and the reader's mind, by the *lois du sentiment*.

Séran de La Tour actually claims that versification increases the 'truth' of the imitations: 'Pourquoi la Poésie est-elle contrainte à la mesure par un assujettissement servile? Parce que cette gêne fortifie l'expression des couleurs, la vivacité des images & qu'il en résulte une imitation plus vraie & plus agréable. Sans cela elle n'est au fond qu'un discours plus paré que la Prose' (Séran de La Tour, 1762, pp. 143–4).

34 Cf. Longue, 1737, p. 4; Rémond de Saint Mard, 1734, p. 28; Levesque de Pouilly, 1747, p. 104, who analyses a prose passage from Fénelon's *Télémaque* to show a poetic use of rhythm. Fénelon's own comment is: 'Bien des gens font des vers sans Poésie & beaucoup d'autres sont pleins de Poésie sans faire de vers' (Fénelon, 1718, p. 99). Rémond de Saint Mard suggests a greater use of 'vers marotiques' that is, freer form, with the possibility of *enjambement* (1734, p. 286). La Chaussée's verses in his *Epître à Clio* show that this quarrel is yet another form of the *Querelle des Anciens et des Modernes*:

Mais ce n'est plus la querelle d'Homere [i.e. between La Motte and
    Madame Dacier]
Il donne encor dans une autre chimère:
Il va, dit-on, du faux charme des vers
Désabuser pour jamais l'Univers;
Et pour donner plus d'essor au génie
Anéantir la rime et l'harmonie.
                          (La Chaussée, 1762, vol. v, p. 146)

35 'Ce défaut de vérité & de justesse dans la plûpart des Ouvrages de ce genre les plus estimés [poèmes] en a dégoûté de tout tems plusieurs bons esprits, & c'est le fondement des accusations tant de fois intentées contre la Poésie & l'Eloquence [. . .]. Quelques-uns même sont allés jusqu'à dire qu'il faut compter presque pour rien le fond des choses dans les vers, & considérer seulement la manière dont elles sont exprimées' (Trublet, 1754–60, vol. ii, pp. 145–6).

36 Cf. Chicaneau de Neuville, 1758, p. 158, on the 'ambition de montrer de l'esprit': 'L'origine de ce défaut, qui dépare le plus grand nombre de nos Ecrits, remonte à La Motte & à M. de Fontenelle qui avoient assez de talens pour se passer de tant d'esprit; mais qui, désespérant de surpasser leurs prédécesseurs dans la carrière qu'ils avaient parcourue avec tant de succès, se sont frayé une nouvelle route et ont acquis plus de réputation que de gloire.' See also Rémond de Saint Mard, 1734, p. 303.

37 See La Motte, 1754, vol. iii, p. 11, writing on the poets' practice of praising themselves: 'Si cependant j'ai suivi quelquefois leur exemple, c'est par pure déférence au goût établi, qui fait regarder ces saillies puériles comme un enthousiasme sublime, & comme une noble confiarce inséparable du génie.'

38 Cf. Rollin, 1726–8, vol. ii, pp. 398–9; Cartaud de la Vilate, 1736, p. 5; Rémond de Saint Mard, 1734, p. 348; Batteux, 1746, p. 63.

39 'Il règne depuis peu en France un goût de précision & de méthode qui
va mal avec les fougues & les emportemens de l'Ode, une je ne sçai
quelle fureur de Logique s'est emparée des esprits' (Rémond de
Saint Mard, 1734, p. 225; 1749, vol. v, p. 55).

9 Why does the poet use the language he uses?

1 Cf. *Journal des sçavans*, février 1737, p. 103, a review of Bouhier; and
especially Desfontaines' criticisms of d'Olivet, 1739, pp. 146, 198,
256.

2 See Court de Gebelin, 1773, vol. ii, p. 488 and Ricken, 1978, for an
account of the controversy.

3 'What is assumed is the existence of a uniform set of relations into
which words can enter, in any language, those corresponding to the
exigencies of thought [. . .]. They repeatedly stress that a case system
is only one device for expressing these relations' (Chomsky, 1966,
p. 45).

4 Court de Gebelin's discussion of this controversy is illuminating. He
sums up thus the respective values of Latin and French: 'L'une est plus
relative au sentiment & à l'harmonie, & l'autre à la clarté, à la précision, à la gravité du Discours' (1773, vol. ii, p. 530).

5 'Le latin a une infinité d'inversions et de cadences. Au contraire, le
français n'admet presque aucune inversion de phrase; il procède toujours méthodiquement par un nominatif, par un verbe, et par son
régime' (Fénelon, lettre à La Motte, 26 juin 1714, in La Motte, 1715,
p. 115). It is interesting that Desfontaines accepts that 'La Grammaire
a une liaison immédiate avec la construction des idées, en sorte que
plusieurs questions de Grammaire sont de vraies questions de Logique
et même de Métaphysique. Chaque Langue a sa Grammaire particulière: cependant comme l'esprit n'a qu'une seule marche & que le
bon sens est le même chez toutes les Nations, il n'y a aussi, dans un
sens, pour tous les Peuples, qu'une Grammaire générale, dont les
Grammaires particulières sont, pour ainsi dire, les diverses modifications' (1739, *préface*); he denies, however, that the particular rules
of French grammar can be applied to a poet's work.

6 Cf. Cartaud, 1736, p. 132; Diderot, *O.C.*, vol. ii, p. 564; Condillac,
Essai sur l'origine des connaissances humaines, p. 75: 'La nôtre
[langue] [. . .] est si simple dans sa construction et dans sa prosodie
qu'elle ne demande presque que l'exercice de la mémoire.'

7 Arnaud, 1804, vol. i, p. 225. Arnaud's article is a commentary on
Turgot's translation, and is entitled: 'Fragmens de poésies écrites dans
la Langue Erse ou Gallique, que parlent les Habitans des montagnes
d'Ecosse, traduits de l'original en anglois, & de l'anglois en françois.
Réflexions préliminaires sur l'histoire & le caractère de ces Poèmes.'

8 Poetry must compensate for the arbitrary nature of language: 'Il faut
que [. . .] le stile de la Poësie soit rempli de figures qui peignent si bien
les objets décrits dans les vers que nous ne puissions les entendre sans

que nôtre imagination soit continuellement remplie de tableaux qui s'y succèdent les uns aux autres, à mesure que les périodes du discours se succèdent les unes aux autres' (Dubos, 1719, vol. I, p. 266).

9 This may be compared with the views of the earlier writer Fraguier, who insists on the trick rather than on adequation: 'Faisant passer des images plus vives, plus grandes, que ne comporte la Prose' (1731, p. 420).

10 Cf. 'Il y a un autre moyen d'animer le style; celui-ci est commun à l'Eloquence & à la Poësie pathétique. C'est d'adresser ou d'attribuer la parole aux absens, aux morts, aux choses insensibles; de les voir, de croire les entendre, & en être entendu. Cette sorte d'illusion que l'on se fait à soi-même & aux autres est un délire qui doit aussi avoir sa vraisemblance' (Marmontel, 1763, vol. I, pp. 157–8).

11 Cf. 'S'il adopte un système, comme il est souvent obligé, celui par exemple, de la Théologie, ou celui de la Mythologie, celui d'Epicure, ou celui de Newton, il se borne lui-même dans le choix des images' (Marmontel, 1763, vol. I, p. 187).

12 A rationalist such as Terrassson attempts to make veil and veiled coincide: 'Ce seroit un bien pour les lecteurs et pour les auteurs sujets à pareille séduction que les mots ne fussent qu'un pur signe ou comme un corps aerien de la pensée de sorte qu'elle parût à nous sous ce voile telle qu'elle est en elle-même' (Terrasson, quoted Ranscelot, 1926, p. 511).

13 For the very old confusion of *enargeia* with *energeia* see Aristotle, *Rhetoric*, 1441 b21, and Quintilian, VIII, 3.89. I owe these references to the kindness of John Easterling. See also Hurst, 1977.

14 Herder owns that he derives the central aesthetic concept used in this attack from James Harris, *Three Treatises*, 1744. Harris' distinction between *ergon* and *energeia* was developed by Humboldt in his work on linguistics. It seems as if it was the evolution of theories of language which gave the impetus to poetics; considerations of the poet's medium, language, giving a deeper notion of creation than exploration of the poet's voice.

15 I cannot agree with Tort that for Condillac this implies an original specularity, a mirror implanted in the heart of perception. Tort seeks to prove this by reference to the *Grammaire*, 1775, a later work (Tort, 1976, p. 497). It is precisely Condillac's unawareness of the problems posed by this stance in the *Essai* which provokes some of Diderot's remarks in the *Lettre sur les aveugles*, 1749.

16 'C'est *au moment où* l'objet présent vient à manquer à la perception, où la perception s'absente elle-même que s'ouvre, avec la fonction de l'imagination, l'espace des signes' (Derrida, 1973, p. 64).

17 Unlike Rousseau, Condillac does not place the metaphor at the origin of the sign: the *architrace*, to use Derrida's term, is not acknowledged.

18 Degérando later uses a much simplified account of the imagination and its merely associative power in his account of illusion: 'Quel effet

résultera pour l'esprit de ces associations toutes nouvelles formées par l'imagination? elles lui représenteraient des faits, puisqu'un fait est l'association de certaines circonstances. Les représentations fourniront de nouveaux matériaux à la croyance. Elles surprendront l'esprit comme l'image réfléchie sur une glace surprend l'oeil peu attentif' (an viii, vol. ii, p. 498).

19 'C'est ainsi que, par un long circuit on parvint à imaginer comme une invention nouvelle, un langage qui avoit été le premier que les hommes eussent parlé, ou qui du moins n'en différoit que parce qu'il étoit propre à exprimer un plus grand nombre de pensées' (Condillac, *Essai*, p. 71).

20 See Grimsley (1971) for Maupertuis and Terrasson as examples of later attitudes.

21 The relation between sound and internal state is universal, and is possible because of the nature of interjections: 'Elles [les interjections] expriment des sentimens et non pas des idées externes' (de Brosses, 1765, vol. i, p. 227).

22 For de Brosses at least, a relation between logic and etymology is thus constructed. Round the etymological root agglomerate aspects of thought related to the initial object: the latter are conventional. The etymological root, which is also the first sound, is thus 'Le véritable et premier sens physique du mot [. . .] un rapport réel entre les termes, les choses et les idées' (de Brosses, 1765, vol. i, p. vi).

23 The process of signification is identical with the development of metaphor: 'Chacun [mot primitif] désignoit au sens propre et étroit un objet physique pris dans la Nature. On fera voir en même temps de quelle manière il s'est pris au figuré et comment il a passé du sens physique au sens moral' (de Brosses, 1765, vol. i, p. 21).

24 De Brosses later quotes Cicero: 'verborum translatio instituta est inopia causa'. See Court de Gebelin, 1773, vol. ii, p. 11.

25 'On y peut voir par des raisonnemens fondus dans une suite d'images que l'origine de la Poësie & sa destination étaient consacrées à l'Etre Suprême, à célébrer ses merveilles' (*Année littéraire*, 1762, vol. iii, p. 268, on Garcin's *Odes sacrées*).

26 For the usual seventeenth- or eighteenth-century valuation, see Prévost, *Le Pour et contre*, 1736, vol. x, article cxlvi, p. 254; or Lamy, 1679, pp. 330–1.

27 Later writers, such as Madame de Staël, attack this notion of energy (Madame de Staël, 1959, vol. i, p. 5). Cf. the very curious satire, *Les Cataractes de l'imagination* (1779) by Chassaignon.

28 Degérando still has to add however: 'Il suffira que par un signe indicateur il avertisse qu'il n'entend point parler des objets extérieurs qu'il rappelle, mais bien de ce qu'il éprouve en lui-même et dont les objets sont la peinture' (an viii, vol. i, pp. 120–1).

10 Music and illusion

1   Cf. Lecerf de la Viéville, 1705, p. 31, who says that the singer must sing so naturally that he causes the audience to forget how unnatural it is that everything should be sung.

2   'Un nuage lumineux l'environne, il est transporté dans un espace immense; c'est là qu'il existe, tous les sens lui prêtent un mutuel secours' (Blainville, 1754, p. 14).

3   Chabanon attributes the following reasoning to Gluck: 'La colère est un sentiment qui ne chante pas. Produisons un effet de symphonie imposant, effrayant, s'il est possible. L'Illusion de cet effet sera reversible sur mon héros, & le Spectateur qui entendra le bruit de tout l'Orchestre croira que ces cent voix sont la voix d'Achille' (1779, p. 134).

4   In the eyes of the *Bouffonistes* this *papillotage* is no doubt parallel to plots which are interrupted, or whose meaning points away from the overt meaning, see above, pp. 170ff.

5   'What does not reproduce an object to the eye and to the understanding, remains outside this aesthetics' (Goldschmidt, 1915, p. 34). Though see the pertinent reservations of Schering, 1918, pp. 298–309, a review tainted, to my mind, by anti-semitism. See also Serauky, 1929.

6   For the scientific background see Fellerer, 1966.

7   Cf. 'Je me hâte de mettre au jour plusieurs Piéces de Poésie dont la variété, l'agrément, la tournure ingénieuse et le vernis Philosophique sont peu connus de nos anciens Poètes', *Les Amusemens du cœur et de l'esprit*, 1741, *Avant-propos*.

8   'Peu à peu une équivalence s'établit entre moderne et italophile, d'une part, entre Ancien et Lulliste de l'autre', Girdlestone, 1962, p. 70.

9   Burney, quoted Girdlestone, 1962, p. 214: 'Après des symphonies pleines de promesse, lorsque l'oreille a été disposée à entendre la suite du prélude, il n'est donné à la voix que des accents brisés et des mesures disloquées.'

10   'Je venois de lire à la campagne, il y aura bientôt deux ans, dans M. *Félibien*, que la peinture seroit toûjours fort imparfaite, quant au *Coloris*, & au *clair obscur*, tandis que'elle n'auroit point ses *Tons* & ses *Modes* déterminés, & une espèce de Diapason ou gamme de couleurs, parallèlement aux tons & aux modes', Castel, 1735, p. 1447. Félibien does not appear to say this in so many words, though he speaks of Poussin's comparison between modes and painting (*Entretiens*, 1725, vol. v, p. 324). Cf. also Coypel, 1721, pp. 136–7.

11   The actual musical alignments are complex. Stamitz was taken up in Paris by Rameau's patron, La Riche de La Poplinière. For Stamitz, see Riemann, *Musiklexicon*, 1979. I have been unable to consult Bettl, *Der kleine Prophet von Böhmisch Broda*, Esslingen, 1951, but there seems no doubt that Grimm knew of Stamitz's work.

12   These were certainly factors in the development of the *style galant* the

German equivalent to the reaction against Rameau. Of Stamitz, Riemann says: 'Originality and freshness of melodic invention characterise the style of his compositions; their themes have rhythms which are often syncopated, there is a very varied use of *tempi*, a new kind of exploitation of the *crescendo*, a surprising use of phrasing in rhythmic and dynamic contrast, and a sudden reversal of the emotion in the context not only of the single movement, but also of the rich working of the *motif* of a single theme' (Riemann, Musiklexikon ii, p. 717a).

13 'A chaque représentation un silence profond dans tout le spectacle annonçoit les approches de ce terrible morceau; on voyait les visages pâlir, on se sentoit frissonner, et l'on se regardoit l'un l'autre avec une sorte d'effroi: car ce n'étoit ni des pleurs, ni des plaintes, c'étoit un certain sentiment de rigueur âpre et dédaigneux qui troubloit l'âme, serroit le cœur, et glaçoit le sang' (Rousseau, *Dictionnaire de musique*, article *Récitatif*).

14 'Les éclats des passions ont souvent frappé vos oreilles; mais vous êtes bien loin de connaître tout ce qu'il y a de secret dans leurs accents et dans leurs expressions. Il n'y en a aucune qui n'ait sa physionomie; toutes ces physionomies se succèdent sur un visage sans qu'il cesse d'être le même' (Diderot, *Eloge de Richardson*, p. 35).

15 Cf. Diderot quoted above p. 269. The *Pantaléon* may be that described by Schubart, 1806, p. 289: 'A midget pianoforte [. . .] The *vibrato* can be perfectly expressed on it.'

16 See Part i of this book.

17 Diderot develops the *corde vibrante* as a metaphor for the physiology of mind. But it is the structure of resonance rather than the actual oscillations that he is interested in. The mind is a 'clavecin sensible': self-awareness, memory and, finally, reasoning are compared to resonance in the *Rêve de d'Alembert*. Taking over an idea floated in the *Lettre sur les sourds et muets*, he suggests how, contrary to received sensualist theory, the mind might think of more than one thing at a time: 'La corde vibrante sensible oscille, résonne, longtemps encore après qu'on l'a pincée. C'est cette oscillation, cette espèce de résonnance nécessaire qui tient l'objet présent tandis que l'entendement s'occupe de la qualité qui lui convient' (Diderot, *Rêve*, p. 272). Creativity in poet or philosopher is described by the same principle: analogy is the search for 'une quatrième corde harmonique et proportionnelle à trois autres dont l'animal entend la résonnance qui se fait toujours en lui-même mais ne se fait pas toujours en nature' (Diderot, *Rêve*, p. 280). In this analogy, a sound represents phenomena, the overtones the mental apprehension of these. The binding factor in intellectual life is resonance of overtones, beyond what is actually taking place; whereas for Rousseau it is the ebb and flow of the 'sentiment de l'existence' which is central to being.

18 'Je remarquai dans l'Arménien durant tout le chant françois, plus de surprise que de plaisir; mais tout le monde observa, dès les premières

345

mesures de l'air italien, que son visage et ses yeux s'adoucissoient: il étoit enchanté, il prêtoit son âme aux impressions de la musique, et quoiqu'il entendît peu la langue, les simples sons lui causoient un ravissement sensible' (Rousseau, *Lettre sur la musique française*, pp. 420–1).

19 'Il faut par une musique douce et affectueuse avoir déjà disposé l'oreille et le cœur à l'émotion pour que l'une et l'autre se prêtent à ces ébranlements violens; et il faut qu'ils passent avec la rapidité qui convient à notre faiblesse, car quand l'agitation est trop forte, elle ne peut durer, et tout ce qui est au-delà de la nature ne touche plus' (Rousseau, *Dictionnaire de musique*, article *Duo*).

11 Music and imitation

1 Musical harmony reflects cosmic harmony. It has been pointed out by his biographers that Bach belonged to a Wolffian circle at Leipzig, though his may have been a passive membership.

2 Bach illustrates 'I tremble' by quivering sounds, literally *tremolo*, and symbolises the lack of firm ground beneath the sinner's feet by a lack of continuo. In general, what is known as the *Affektenlehre* classified feelings into a set of affections (derived from classical times via the *Passions de l'âme* attributed to Descartes) and associated them with musical modes.

3 Richelière, 1752, pp. 7–8. The ticking of a clock must have been imitated in one of the *Bouffons*' operas, as it is frequently mentioned by the pamphleteers in the controversy. The evocation of old age may refer to Mondonville's opera, *Titon et l'Aurore*, first produced in January, 1753 (see Reichenburg, 1937, p. 51, n. 3), though the gap in the dates requires explanation.

4 Cf. 'Dans le duo du tric-trac, il se plaît à évoquer le bruit des dés, par des doubles croches et des batteries', Cucuel, 1914, p. 155.

5 Cf. 'Cette imitation est celle de la nature & reçoit souvent d'autres dénominations telles que celles de *Peinture*, d'*Expression*, & etc. Plus l'imitation est parfaite, plus l'Art aussi approche de la perfection' (Garcin, 1772, p. 60). This vagueness in vocabulary seems general. The *Encyclopédie*, for instance, says of the ballet *De l'empire de l'amour*, performed in 1733: 'MM. Rebel & Francœur qui en ont fait la musique, ont répandu dans le chant une expression aimable & dans la plupart des symphonies un ton d'enchantement qui fait illusion: c'est presque partout une musique qui peint & il n'y a que celle-là qui prouve le talent & qui mérite des éloges' (*Encyclopédie*, article *Ballet*, signed B, i.e. Cahusac). The writer would seem to be commenting on a kind of sensuous and expressive grace, rather than programmatism.

6 D'Alembert, 1821, p. 544; Rousseau, *Dictionnaire de musique*, article *Sonate*; Pascal Boyer, 1776, p. 20.

7 Cf. the discussion in Perrault, 1693, vol. ι, p. 93: 'C'est indépendamment de la convention des hommes & de l'accoutumance de l'oreille,

qu'une octáve ou une quinte doivent estre précisément composées d'une certaine distance de tons.'

8 Cf. Laugier's reply, typical of an architect: 'Prétendre que ce sont là des beautés arbitraires & de pure convention, qu'il n'y a pas moyen d'en tirer avantage pour embellir & fortifier l'expression, c'est raisonner contre une expérience certaine' (1754, p. 55).

9 Cf. 'Le plaisir que cause la Poésie n'est pas chimérique & arbitraire. Si cela étoit, on ne se seroit point accordé dans tout l'Univers à goûter la cadence' (Prévost, *Pour et contre*, 1736, vol. x, p. 245, quoting Bouhier). Also Diderot, *Entretiens sur 'Le Fils naturel'*, where beauty and virtue are both forms of an 'amour de l'ordre'. Cf also: 'En considérant donc le son comme sensation, on peut donner la raison du plaisir que font les sons harmoniques; il consiste dans la proportion du son fondamental aux autres sons [. . .]. On pourroit me dire qu'on ne conçoit pas trop comment une proportion peut causer du plaisir, & qu'on ne voit pas pourquoi tel rapport, parce qu'il est exact, est plus agréable [. . .]. Je répondrai que c'est cependant dans cette justesse de proportion que consiste la cause du plaisir, puisque toutes les fois que nos sens sont ébranlés de cette façon, il en résulte un sentiment agréable' (Buffon, *De l'homme*, in 1833, vol. ix, pp. 136–7).

10 Cf. 'Nous avons encore voulu détromper d'une erreur généralement reçue, qui fait consister le beau dans des rapports ou plutôt dans des opérations de l'esprit, tandis qu'on ne doit chercher la pureté des goûts que dans celle des émotions des sens' (Estève, 1753a, vol. ii, p. 230, possibly an attack on the article *Beau* in the *Encyclopédie*).

11 *Critique of Judgement*, §3. Cf. Hegel, vol. i, p. 24.

12 'Selon le cercle, l'ellipse ou la figure irreprésentable du mouvement historique, la rationalité abstraite et la froide convention rejoignent la nature morte, le règne physique, un certain rationalisme se confond avec le matérialisme ou le sensualisme' (Derrida, 1967b, p. 300).

13 Garcin criticises 'Hayden' (=Franz Joseph Haydn?) for dealing with 'pure music'. Cf. also Batteux, 1746, pp. 14, 269, a criticism of Castel.

14 'Un sens net, sans obscurité, sans équivoque' (Batteux, 1746, p. 264).

15 Cf. Grimm, *Encyclopédie*, article *Poème lyrique*, and Garcin, 1772, p. 88. Beaumarchais, in a decidedly outdated account of his opera *Tarare*, considers that music, like poetry, is merely 'Un nouvel art d'embellir la parole dont il ne faut point abuser' (1964, p. 371).

16 See Part i for the relation of this conception to painting, and in particular the treatment by the theorists of the characteristic expressions of face and body.

17 Schering, in the review referred to in n. 5, p. 344, has criticised Goldschmidt's interpretation of imitation, which the former argues may mean not a desire to refer, but *'techniques* of reference to which we have lost the key'. It is true that merely to carp at such theories is unwise; it is also true that music poses a considerable problem to eighteenth-century French theorists. Rousseau expresses this with his

characteristic trenchancy in the article *Sonate* for the *Dictionnaire de musique*: 'La musique purement harmonique est peu de chose, pour plaire constamment & prévenir l'ennui, elle doit s'élever au rang des arts d'imitation, mais son imitation n'est pas toujours immédiate comme celle de la poésie et de la peinture, la parole est le moyen par lequel la musique détermine le plus souvent l'objet dont elle nous offre l'image, et c'est par les sons touchans de la voix humaine que cette image éveille au fond du cœur le sentiment qu'elle doit y produire.'

18 One guarantee of reference may be the state of mind of the musician: 'Toute cette musique purement instrumentale, sans dessein et sans objet, ne porte ni à l'esprit ni à l'âme, et mérite qu'on lui demande avec Fontenelle, "Sonate, que me veux-tu?".' Les auteurs qui composent de la musique instrumentale ne feront qu'un vain bruit, tant qu'ils n'auront pas dans la tête, à l'exemple dit-on du célèbre Tartini, une action ou une expérience à peindre' (d'Alembert, 1821, p. 544).

19 This is apparent from the work of, for example, Garcin, a hard-core imitationist writing in 1772. He criticises d'Alembert's suggestion that music could use analogy with language for its expression precisely because it introduces a comparative element which will destroy the identification of meaning and reference: 'Il paroît que l'âme aperçoit les rapports de la nature avant ceux du langage, & qu'ainsi cette façon de parler "feu qui s'élève avec rapidité" ne nous aide suffisamment à entendre cette autre, "tons qui s'élèvent avec rapidité" qu'autant que l'analogie de ces phrases est fondée sur une autre analogie entre le mouvement du feu et celui du son' (Garcin, 1772, p. 193, quoting d'Alembert's *Mélanges*).

20 Dubos makes the division between human sound and non-human noise along the axis of a distinction between instrumental and vocal music, whereas Batteux expressly states that instrumental music can imitate feelings (thus moving away from a literal-minded idea of imitation) and expressly denies illusion (Dubos, 1719, vol. I, pp. 637–8; Batteux, 1746, p. 39).

21 The authorship of this important pamphlet is uncertain. The Bibliothèque Nationale catalogue attributes it both to Rousse (following Barbier, who states that he was 'gouverneur des fils de Monsieur d'Héricourt') and to d'Alembert. Reichenburg states 'Thoinan et Durey de Noinville désignent Arnaud comme l'auteur' (1937, p. 80). I think the Arnaud suggestion has dubious value: he wrote a pamphlet in the same year, 1754, the *Lettre sur la musique à M. le Comte de Caylus*, which puts forward a very different conception of music, and which is on the side of French music, unlike the *Réflexions*. I am not happy about the d'Alembert attribution either, though Robert Wokler states that it resembles an unpublished MS of d'Alembert's, without being identical (personal communication). My doubt is shared by Barthélemy, 1966, who states that the pamphlet

appreciates Mondonville's *Titon et l'Aurore,* whereas d'Alembert did not. The arguments given for d'Alembert's authorship by Pappas, 1965, are far from conclusive – most critics of the time recommend imitation, and several recognise music's inability to imitate, which they may get round by giving an inappropriate content to the word 'imitation'. Pappas does, however, quote an unpublished letter to the président Hénault in which d'Alembert admits writing a piece on music, perhaps the MS referred to by Wokler.

22   Rousseau's theories on recitative are part of a long historical tradition. At the end of the sixteenth century, the Florentine Camerata had reacted against Renaissance counterpoint treatment of the word, claiming that the poetry was torn to pieces, for individual voices often sang different words as part of the same chord. (Their attitude signified, no doubt, a radically different idea of meaning, a much more verbal one, than that embodied by the music they attacked.) Here was developed *stile rappresentativo,* an affective style of recitative in free rhythm, and with free use of dissonance, no doubt closely related to theatrical styles. Later in Italy, with the gradual centring of tonality came the *bel canto* style of the mid-seventeenth century and the distinction between aria and recitative; and finally Italian opera developed an instrumental style which dominated the vocal. 'Ce sont à tort & à travers des passages, des tenues, des roulemens, des diminutions, des tremblemens, & tous ces ornemens du Chant qui font sentir à l'oreille tout ce qu'une belle voix peut produire de plus délicat & de plus brillan' (Mably, 1741, p. 135). Mably is here protesting against the Italian tradition which Rameau represented, and his criticism is analogous to that levelled against polyphony by the Camerata.

Likewise, the relation between an interest in ancient music and simple voice style has a long history. The Camerata had concerned itself with Ancient music, and Vicenzo Galileo, who had used monody in his setting of the lamentations of Ugolino from the *Divine Comedy,* had written a *Dialogo della musica antiqua e moderna* in 1581. He had also published songs attributed to Mesomedes, the Emperor Hadrian's court musician. Much of the work of the *Académie des Inscriptions et des Belles-Lettres,*of Burette, Dacier and Dubos had been concentrated on the understanding of Ancient music. It was Dubos, unable to accept an account of Greek tragedy which appeared to bring it close to seventeenth-century French opera, who had suggested that the Greeks had written down their declamation (Dubos, 1719, vol. I, pp. 415ff.).

23   For the German version of this attitude, see Fellerer, 1962.

24   La Cépède nevertheless develops a contradictory notion, that of the uniqueness of sensation. In an elaborate, deliberately pathetic example – a man whose wife has died hears later a sound first heard in his time of mourning – he suggests that sounds have a different

meaning for each of us, that they bring with them a reference to an individual past: 'Si l'on pouvoit savoir l'histoire des différentes impressions qu'elle [une personne] auroit reçues, on pourroit composer pour elle une musique dont tous les chants seroient des mots aussi précis que ceux de la langue la plus exacte' (La Cépède, 1785, vol. I, p. 95). Thus a sound can become a 'mot magique' not merely expressive of feelings but bringing back past feelings: 'Non seulement il aura été uni avec l'idée de ces sentiments, ainsi que les mots qui composent les langues ordinaires, mais encore il aura été joint avec les mouvements que les passions font naître: & il leur donnera l'être, il les produira' (La Cépède, 1785, vol. I, p. 92). Rousseau, in his famous account of the effect of the *Ranz des vaches* on Swiss soldiers, had shown how music can be a 'signe mémoratif' (*Dictionnaire de musique*, article *Musique*).

25 Cf. 'Le chant proprement dit est le premier cri de la nature, c'est la souche de tout l'art musical' (Blainville, 1754, p. 12).

26 It seems as if critics writing in the 1770s (Boyer, Morellet, Chabanon) insist on the part played by the senses in musical pleasure. Boyer insists so much that he denies the possibility of the experience of feeling, critices Fontenelle's search for meaning, and asserts: 'L'Objet principal de la Musique est de nous plaire physiquement sans que l'esprit se mette en peine de lui chercher d'inutiles comparaisons. On doit la regarder absolument comme un plaisir des sens & non de l'intelligence' (1776, p. 33).

27 Morellet in his title gives the date of Garcin's treatise as 1771, although I have found none earlier than 1772. It is likely that Garcin's treatise was postdated.

28 Diderot in the *Lettre sur les sourds et muets* had attacked Batteux's principle of the imitation of beautiful nature.

29 The example of the tempest familiar in art criticism comes back in a definition of illusion (Morellet, 1772, p. 22): 'Un compositeur habile [. . .] sait par des sons analogiques, par des impressions détournées & fugitives me retracer le bruit des flots agités, ou l'incertitude du pilote effrayé, mon esprit se réveille, mon imagination s'échauffe, je me transporte au loin sur un promontoire, d'où je considère le vaisseau battu par les vents, je vois briller l'éclair, j'entends les cris des matelots, & déjà le tableau animé n'est plus l'ouvrage du musicien, c'est celui de mon imagination.'

30 This passage is very close (*mutatis mutandis*) to Marmontel's definition of illusion at the theatre in the article *Illusion, Supplément à l'Encyclopédie*, 1777.

31 Besides the *Eloge de Rameau*, Chabanon wrote two books on music: *Observations sur la musique et principalement sur la métaphysique de l'art* (1779) and *De la musique considérée en elle-même et dans ses rapports avec la parole, les langues, la poésie et le théâtre* (1785), the first part of which is a development of the ideas of the earlier book.

32 'Mais de quoi la nature nous servira-t-elle pour juger d'un Ouvrage

d'Architecture? où a-t-elle placé le modèle que je dois confronter avec l'œuvre de l'Art? Direz-vous que ce modèle existe en nous, que le type idéal du beau est dans notre tête? Cette idée toute platonique me paroît creuse et vuide' (Chabanon, 1779, p. 167).

33 It seems highly likely that he was influenced by Diderot here (see Diderot, *Rêve de d'Alembert*, and *Salon de 1767*). Chabanon is mentioned in Diderot's *Correspondance*, vol. ii, p. 359, in a letter dated by Roth as 'hiver 1762'. Diderot seems to have been present at a reading of Chabanon's play *Eponine*.

34 'Que des personnes peu musiciennes ne cherchent point dans ce Chœur à trouver un rapport entre la descente diatonique du chant & la *chûte des frimats*. Ce n'est là qu'une circonstance accidentelle de ce morceau de musique & qui comme peinture y seroit inutile, étrangère même. Le musicien ne doit point peindre les frimats lorsqu'on bénit le Soleil de ce qu'il les dissipe; s'il y avait dans ce cas quelque chose à peindre ce seroit plutôt la sérénité que les frimats. De plus un ordre diatonique de notes qui descendent ne peint pas plus la chûte des frimats que la chûte de toute autre chose. Mais une mélodie noble, simple, parcourant sans gêne les modulations dépendantes & qui comme autant de branches parties du même tronc, s'épanouissent autour de lui & le couronnent, voilà ce qui parle aux sens & à l'âme, voilà ce qui doit être senti principalement dans ce Chœur, *Brillant Soleil*. Que s'il y faut chercher quelqu'un de ces rapports que l'on nomme peinture, il suffit de celui-ci: ce Chœur inspire un sentiment d'élévation, une sorte d'enthousiasme qui convient à ceux qui adorent le Soleil' (Chabanon, 1764a, pp. 16–17).

35 A movement continued in the article *Sonate* in the *Dictionnaire de musique*, which omits the underlined words from the parallel article in the *Encyclopédie*: 'Et c'est par les sons touchants de la voix humaine *jointe aux paroles* que ce même objet porte dans les cœurs le sentiment qu'il doit y produire.'

36 'The use of painting to illuminate the essential character of poetry – *ut pictura poesis* – so widespread in the eighteenth century, almost disappears in the major criticism of the Romantic period: the comparisons between poetry and painting that survive are casual or, as in the case of the mirror, show the canvas reversed in order to imagine the inner substance of the poet. In place of painting, music becomes the art frequently pointed to as having a profound affinity with poetry. For if a picture seems the nearest thing to a mirror image of the external world, music, of all the arts, is the most remote: except in the trivial echoism of programmatic passages, it does not duplicate aspects of sensible nature, nor can it be said, in any obvious sense, to refer to any state of affairs outside itself. As a result music was the first of the arts generally regarded as non-mimetic in nature; in the theory of the German writers of the 1790s, music came to be the art most immediately expressive of spirit and emotion' (Abrams, 1958, p. 50).

Conclusion

1 'Se dit des yeux lorsqu'un mouvement incertain et involontaire les empêche de se fixer sur les objets' (*Dictionnaire de Trévoux*, quoted by Robert, *Dictionnaire*).
2 For a history of this division in poetics see Genette, 1979, pp. 19ff.
3 See above, p. 32.
4 Much more in the article is not borne out by the facts. The accounts of *Don Quixote* and of Sartre's *Les Mots* over-simplify the attitudes to fiction in these texts, treating them as examples of illusion in what Stierle calls the 'naïve sense', when both are shot through with awareness.
5 This is still apparent in Stierle's definition of truth.
6 Whereas the logicians' concern with tenses, and with modal logic, makes possible a very different notion of truth. See Dummett, 1978, and Prior and Fine, 1977.

BIBLIOGRAPHY

Only works mentioned in the text are cited in this bibliography.

Sources

Accolti, Pietro, 1625. *Lo Inganno degl'occhi, prospettiva practica*, Firenze, P. Cecconcelli.

d'Aigueberre, Jean Du Mas, 1870. *Seconde lettre du souffleur de la Comédie de Rouen au garçon de café, ou Entretien sur les défauts de la déclamation*, in d'Allainval (*q.v.*), Abbé Léonor-Jean-Christine Soulas, *Lettre à Mylord *** sur Baron et la Dlle. Lecouvreur*, ed. Jules Bonnassies, Paris, Wille [1730].

d'Alembert, Jean Lerond, 1751. *Discours préliminaire*, in *Encyclopédie ou Dictionnaire raisonné des sciences, des arts et des métiers, par une société de gens de lettres . . .*, Paris, Briasson.
1821–2. *De la liberté de la musique*, in *Œuvres complètes de d'Alembert*, Paris, Belin, 5 vols.; vol. I, pp. 515–46 [1759].

Algarotti, Francesco, Comte, 1773. *Essai sur l'opéra, traduit de l'italien du comte Algarotti par M*** [le marquis Fr. Jean de Chastellux]*, à Pise, et se trouve à Paris, Rualt.

d'Allainval, 1822. *Lettre à Mylord *** sur Baron et la Dlle. Lecouvreur*, par Georges Wink, in *Collection des Mémoires sur l'art dramatique, Mémoires sur Molière et sur Mme. Guérin, sa Veuve*, Paris, Ponthieu, Jean-Baptiste-Denis Després, pp. 215–61 (*see also* d'Aigueberre).

Les Amusemens du cœur et de l'esprit. Ouvrage périodique. Nouvelle édition, corrigée et augmentée, Amsterdam, Henri du Sauzé, 1741–5, 15 vols.

André, le père Yves, 1843. *Essai sur le beau*, in *Œuvres philosophiques du Père André de la Compagnie de Jésus, avec une introduction sur sa vie et ses ouvrages tirée de sa correspondance inédite par Victor Cousin*, Paris, Charpentier [1741].

Année littéraire, ou Suite des lettres sur quelques écrits de ce temps, 1754–90, Amsterdam, Paris, different publishers, 292 vols.

Aquinas, St Thomas, 1962. *Summa theologiae*, cura et studio Isac. Petri Caramelo, Turin, Marietti, 3 vols.

Arnaud, Abbé François, 1754. *Lettre sur la musique à Monsieur le Comte*

Bibliography

de Caylus, *Académicien honoraire de l'Académie royale des inscriptions et des belles lettres, et de celle de peinture.*

1804. *Variétés littéraires ou Recueil de pièces tant originales que traduites, concernant la philosophie, la littérature et les arts*, Paris, Deterville. With J-B-A Suard [1768].

d'Arnaud, François Baculard, *see* Baculard d'Arnaud.

Arnauld, Antoine, et Nicole, Pierre, 1965. *La Logique ou l'art de penser, contenant, outre les règles communes, plusieurs observations nouvelles, propres à former le jugement.* Edition critique par Pierre Clair et François Girbal, Paris, P.U.F. [1662].

L'Art du théâtre ou le parfait comédien, Poème en deux chants, Approbation dated 7 mai 1744.

d'Aubignac, Abbé François Hedelin, 1927. *La Pratique du théâtre*, éd. Pierre Martino, Paris–Alger, Champion/Carbonel [1657].

1971. *La Pratique du théâtre und andere Schriften zur Doctrine classique*, ed. Hans-Jorg Neuschläfer, Munich, Fink.

Augustine, St, 1973. *City of God*, in *A Select Library of the Nicene and Post-Nicene Fathers of the Christian Church*, edited by Philip Schaff, Grand Rapids, Michigan, Wm B. Erdmann, 14 vols., vol. ix.

Baculard d'Arnaud, François-Thomas-Marie de, 1746. *Les Epoux malheureux, ou Histoire de Monsieur et Madame de La Bedoyère*, Avignon.

1782. *Nouvelles historiques*, Maestricht, Jean-Edmé Dufour et Phil. Roux, 2 vols.

Baillet de Saint Julien, Baron Louis-Guillaume, 1749. *Lettre sur la peinture, la sculpture, et l'architecture, à M.***, Seconde édition, revue et augmentée de nouvelles notes et de réflexions sur les tableaux de M. de Troy*, Amsterdam. Reprinted Minkoff, Geneva, 1972.

1753. *Lettre à Mr. Ch. sur les caractères en peinture*, Genève. Reprinted Minkoff, Geneva, 1972.

Balzac, Jean-Louis Guez de, 1665. *Response à deux questions ou du caractère & de l'instruction de la comédie*, in *Les Oeuvres de M. de Balzac*, Paris, Billaine, 2 vols.; vol. ii, pp. 509–19.

Bambocciaden, 1797. Pictoribus atque poetis. Quid libet audendi semper fuit aequa potestas, Berlin, Friedrich Maurer.

Baro, Balthasar, 1629. *Célinde, poème héroïque du Sr. Baro.* Paris, F. Pomeray.

Batteux, Charles, 1746. *Les Beaux Arts réduits à un même principe*, Paris, Durand.

Beaumarchais, Pierre-Augustin Caron de, 1964. *Théâtre complet; lettres relatives à son théâtre*, éd. Maurice Allem et Paul Courant, Paris, Bibliothèque de la Pléiade.

Béliard, François, 1751. *Rézéda: ouvrage orné d'une postface par M. B****, Amsterdam, pour la Compagnie.

1765. *Zelaskim, histoire amériquaine ou les avantures de la Marquise de P*** avec un discours pour la défence des romans, Paris, Mérigot père, 4 vols.

Bibliography

Bérard de la Bérardière de Battant, 1776. *Essai sur le récit ou entretien sur la manière de raconter*, Paris, Bertin.

Berkeley, George, 1964. *An Essay Towards a New Theory of Vision*, in *The Works of George Berkeley, Bishop of Cloyne*, ed. A. A. Luce and T. E. Jessop, London, Nelson, 9 vols.; vol. i [1704].

Bibliothèque choisie et amusante, Amsterdam, aux dépens de la compagnie, 1745, 6 vols. in 3 tomes.

Bibliothèque françoise ou histoire littéraire de la France, Amsterdam, J-F Bernard, then H. du Sauzet, 1723–46, 42 vols.

Bibliothèque raisonnée des ouvrages des savans de l'Europe, Amsterdam, Wetstein & Smith, 1728–53, 52 vols.

Bibliothèque universelle des romans, ouvrage périodique dans lequel on donne l'analyse raisonnée des romans anciens et modernes, françois ou traduits dans notre langue; avec des anecdotes et des notices historiques et critiques concernant les auteurs ou leurs ouvrages; ainsi que les mœurs, les usages du temps etc., Paris, Lacombe, au Bureau & chez Demonville, 1775–89.

Blainville, Charles Henri, 1754. *L'Esprit de l'art musical ou réflexions sur la musique et ses différentes parties*, Genève.

Blondel, Jacques-François, 1774. *L'Homme du monde éclairé par les arts*, par M. Blondel, Architecte du Roi, Professeur Royal au Louvre, Membre de l'Académie d'architecture, publié par M. de Bastide, Amsterdam, et se trouve à Paris chez Monory. Reprinted Minkoff, Geneva, 1972.

Boileau-Despréaux, Nicolas, 1966. *Œuvres complètes*. Introduction par Antoine Adam. Textes établis et annotés par Françoise Escal, Paris, Bibliothèque de la Pléiade.

Bollioud de Mermet, Louis, 1746. *De la corruption du goût dans la musique françoise*, par M. Bollioud de Mermet de l'Académie des sciences et des belles lettres de Lyon, et de celle des beaux arts de la même ville, Lyon, Imprimerie Aimé Delaroche.

Bonafous, 1739. *Nouveau parterre du parnasse françois ou Recueil des pièces les plus rares & les plus curieuses, caractères, allusions, pensées morales, ingénieuses & galantes des plus célèbres Poètes françois*, par Monsieur D. B. B., La Haye, B. Gibert.

Bonaventure, St, 1885. *Commentaria in quatuor libres sententiarum magistri Petri Lombardi*, in *Opera omnia*, edita studio et cura pp. collegii a S. Bonaventura, Florence, 1882–1902, 11 vols; vols. i-iv.

Bonneval, René de, 1753. *Apologie de la musique françoise et des musiciens françois, contre les assertions peu mélodieuses, peu mesurées & mal fondées du Sieur Jean-Jacques Rousseau, ci-devant Citoyen de Genève*, signed Chevalier d'Oginville.

Bougeant, le père Guillaume-Hyacinthe, 1735. *Voyage merveilleux du prince Fan Fédérin dans la Romancie; contenant plusieurs observations historiques, géographiques, physiques, critiques et morales*, Paris, Le Mercier.

355

Bibliography

Bouhours, le père Dominique, 1971. *La Manière de bien penser dans les ouvrages d'esprit, nouvelle édition, Paris, 1715*, Brighton, Sussex Reprints, French Series no. 3 [1687].

Bourdelot, Abbé Pierre Michon, 1715. *Histoire de la musique et de ses effets depuis ses origines jusqu'à présent, et en quoi consiste sa beauté*, Paris, C. Cochart. (With P. Bonnet-Bourdelot and J. Bonnet.)

Boursault, Edmé, 1675. *Le Prince de Condé*, Paris, Claude Barbin.

Boyer, Pascal, 1776. *La Soirée perdue à l'opéra*, Paris, Esprit.

(?) 1779. *L'Expression musicale mise au rang des chimères*, par M. Boyé, Amsterdam et se trouve à Paris.

Bricaire de La Dixmérie, see La Dixmérie.

Bridard de La Garde, *see* La Garde.

Brijon, 1763. *Réflexions sur la musique et sur la vraie manière de l'exécuter sur le violon*, par M. Brijon, Paris, chez l'auteur et M. Vandemont.

Brosses, le Président Charles de, 1765. *Traité de la formation méchanique des langues et des principes physiques de l'étymologie*, Paris, Saillant, 2 vols.

Brumoy, le père Pierre, 1730. *Le Théâtre des Grecs*, par le R. P. Brumoy, de la Compagnie de Jésus, Paris, Rollin père, Jean-Baptiste Coignard, Rollin fils, 3 vols.

Bruzen de La Martinière, Antoine-Auguste, 1756. *Introduction générale à l'étude des sciences et des belles-lettres*, in Formey, Jean-Louis-Samuel, *Conseils pour former une bibliothèque peu nombreuse mais choisie. Nouvelle édition, corrigée et augmentée. Suivie de l'Introduction générale à l'étude des sciences et des belles-lettres, par M. de La Martinière*, Berlin, Haude et Spener [1731].

Buffon, Georges Louis Leclerc, Comte de, 1833. *Œuvres complètes de Buffon*, mises en ordre et précédées d'une notice historique par M. A. Richard, Professeur à la Faculté de Médecine de Paris, Paris, Pourrat frères, 20 vols.; vol. IX.

Burney, Charles, Mus. D., 1771. *The Present State of Music in France and Italy, or the Journal of a Tour through those Countries, undertaken to collect Materials for a General History of Music*, London, T. Becket & Co.

Bussy Rabutin, Comte Roger de, 1857. *Histoire amoureuse des Gaules*, édition nouvelle avec des notes et une introduction par Auguste Poitevin, Paris, Delahaye, 2 vols. [1665?].

Cahusac, Louis de, 1739. *Epître sur les dangers de la poésie*, par Monsieur le Comte de C***, La Haye. (I have not been able to consult this.)

1754. *La Danse ancienne et moderne, ou Traité historique de la danse*, par M. de Cahusac, La Haye, J. Neaulme, 3 vols.

Cailhava de l'Estendoux, Jean-François, 1772. *De l'art de la comédie, ou Détail raisonné des diverses parties de la comédie et de ses différents genres, suivis d'un traité de l'imitation, où l'on compare à leurs originaux les imitations de Molière et celles des modernes . . ., terminé par l'exposition des causes de la décadence du théâtre et des moyens de la faire refleurir*, par M. de Cailhava, Paris, Didot, 4 vols.

Bibliography

1777. *L'Egoïsme, comédie en cinq actes et en vers*, Paris.

Cartaud de la Vilate, Abbé François, 1736. *Essai historique et philosophique sur le goust*, Amsterdam.

Castel, le père Louis-Bertrand, 1735. *Nouvelles expériences d'optique et d'acoustique, adressées à M. Le Président de Montesquieu*, par le P. Castel, Jésuite, in *Journal de Trévoux*, i.e. *Mémoires pour l'histoire des sciences et des beaux-arts, commencés d'être imprimés l'an 1701 à Trévoux et dédiés à Son Altesse Sérénissime, Monseigneur le Duc Du Maine*, vol. 139, article LXXIX, LXXXV, août 1735; vol. 140, article XCIII, septembre 1735; article CIII, octobre 1735; article CXIII, novembre 1735; vol. 141, article CXXIX, décembre 1735.

1741. *Dissertation philosophique et littéraire, où, par les vrais principes de la physique et de la géométrie, on recherche si les règles des arts, soit méchaniques, soit libéraux, sont fixes ou arbitraires, et si le bon goût est unique et immuable ou susceptible de variété et de changement*, in *Amusemens du cœur et de l'esprit* (*q.v.*), vol. II [1738].

1763. *Esprit, saillies et singularités du P. Castel*, Amsterdam et Paris, Vincent. Attributed to Abbé Joseph de La Porte.

Caux de Cappeval, N. de, 1755. *Apologie du goût françois relativement à l'opéra; poème, avec un discours apologétique et des adieux aux Bouffons*, Paris.

Caylus, Anne-Claude-Philippe de Tubières Grimoard de Pestels de Levis, Comte de, 1757. *Tableaux tirés de l'Iliade, de l'Odyssée d'Homère, et de l'Enéide de Virgile avec des observations générales sur le costume*, Paris, Tilliard.

1910. *Vies d'artistes du dix-huitième siècle. Discours sur la peinture et la sculpture. Salons de 1751 et de 1753. Lettre à La Grenée*, publiés avec une introduction et des notes par André Fontaine, Paris, Renouard.

Cazotte, Jacques, 1753. *Observations sur la lettre de J. J. Rousseau au sujet de la musique françoise*.

Chabanon, Michel-Paul-Gui, 1764a. *Eloge de Rameau*, par M. Chabanon, de l'Académie royale des inscriptions et des belles lettres, Paris, Imprimerie de M. Lambert.

1764b. *Sur le sort de la poésie en ce siècle philosophique*, par M. Chabanon, de l'Académie royale des inscriptions et des belles lettres, Paris, Imprimerie de S. Jorry.

1779. *Observations sur la musique et principalement sur la métaphysique de l'art*, Paris, Pissot père et fils.

1785. *De la musique considérée en elle-même et dans ses rapports avec la parole, les langues, la poésie et le théâtre*, Paris, Pissot père et fils.

Chapelain, Jean, 1936. *Opuscules critiques*, introduction par Alfred C. Hunter, Paris, Société des textes français modernes.

Charpentier, Louis, 1768. *Des causes de la décadence du goût sur le théâtre, où l'on traite des droits, des talens, et des fautes des Auteurs; des devoirs des Comédiens, et de ce que la Société leur doit, et de leurs usurpations funestes à l'Art Dramatique*, Paris, Dufour, 2 vols.

357

Bibliography

Chassaignon, Jean-Marie, 1779. *Les Cataractes de l'imagination, déluge de la scribomanie, vomissement littéraire, hémorrhagie encyclopédique, monstre des monstres, par Epiménide l'inspiré, dans l'Antre de Trophonius au pays des Visions*, 4 vols.

Chassiron, Pierre-Mathieu-Martin de, 1749. *Réflexions sur le comique larmoyant* par Mr. M. D. C., Trésorier de France et Conseiller au Présidial, de l'Académie de la Rochelle [. . .], Paris, Durand, Pissot. *Réflexions sur les tragédies en musique, lues dans une séance de l'Académie de La Rochelle*, par M. de Chassiron.

Chicaneau de Neuville, Dider-Pierre, 1758. *Considérations sur les ouvrages d'esprit*, Amsterdam.

Choderlos de Laclos, Pierre Ambroise François, 1782. *Les Liaisons dangereuses, ou Lettres recueillies dans une société et publiées pour l'instruction de quelques autres*, par M. C. . . . de L. . . ., Amsterdam et Paris, Durand, 4 vols.

Clairon, an vii. *Mémoires d'Hyppolite Clairon et réflexions sur la déclamation théâtrale*; publiées par elle-même. Seconde édition, revue, corrigée et augmentée, Paris, F. Buisson.

Cochin, Charles-Nicolas, and Bellicard, Jerôme-Charles, 1754. *Observations sur les antiquités de la ville d'Herculaneum, avec quelques réflexions sur la peinture et la sculpture des anciens; et une courte description de quelques antiquités des environs de Naples*, par Messieurs Cochin le fils et Bellicard, Paris.

1757–71. *Recueil de quelques pièces concernant les arts, extraites de plusieurs Mercure de France*, Paris, C-A Jombert, 2 vols. (B. N. copy.)

1771. *Œuvres diverses de M. Cochin, Secrétaire de l'Académie royale de peinture et sculpture, ou Recueil de quelques pièces concernant les arts*, Paris, C-A Jombert, 3 vols. (British Museum copy.) The first volume of these two copies appears identical, and was probably issued in 1757. The second volume of the British Museum copy contains works not by Cochin on the *Salons*. The third volume of the British Museum copy appears to correspond to the second volume of the B. N. copy .It is the first volume in both copies that reprints some (?) of Cochin's articles for the *Mercure*. The article *De l'illusion* appears in the second volume of the B.N. copy and in the third volume of the British Museum copy, and in spite of my efforts I have not been able to trace it in the *Mercure*. I doubt indeed whether it appeared there.

1758. *Voyage d'Italie, ou Recueil de notes sur les ouvrages de peinture et de sculpture, qu'on voit dans les principales villes d'Italie*, Paris, C-A Jombert, 3 vols.

1771. éd. *Manière de bien juger les ouvrages de peinture, par feu M. l'Abbé Laugier* [. . .], Paris, C-A Jombert.

1781. *Lettres sur l'opéra*, Paris, L. Cellot.

Collé, Charles, 1868. *Journal et mémoires de Charles Collé sur les hommes de lettres, les ouvrages dramatiques et les événements les plus mémorables du règne de Louis XV (1748–1772)*, nouvelle édition augmentée de fragments inédits recueillis dans le manuscrit de la Bibliothèque impériale du Louvre [. . .] avec une introduction et des notes, par Honoré Bonhomme, Paris, Firmin-Didot frères et fils et Cie, 3 vols.

Condillac, Abbé Etienne Bonnot de, 1947. *Essai sur l'origine des connaissances humaines*, in *Œuvres philosophiques*, ed. Georges Le Roy, Paris, P.U.F., 3 vols.; vol. I.

Copineau, l'abbé, 1774. *Essai synthétique sur l'origine et la formation des langues*, Paris, Ruault.

La Coquette punie ou le triomphe de l'innocence sur la perfidie, 1740. La Haye, au dépens de la Compagnie.

Corneille, Pierre, *L'Illusion comique* [1636].

1862. *Œuvres de Pierre Corneille, nouvelle édition* [. . .], *par M. Ch. Marty-Laveaux*, Paris, Les Grands Ecrivains de France, 7 vols. Renaudot's review of Corneille's *Andromède* is in vol. V, pp. 274–90.

1965. *Writings on the Theatre*, ed. H.T. Barnwell, Oxford, Blackwell.

Correspondance littéraire, philosophique et critique, par Grimm, Diderot, Raynal, Meister etc. Revue sur les textes originaux comprenant, outre ce qui a été publié à diverses époques, les fragments supprimés en 1813 par la censure, les parties inédites conservées à la bibliothèque ducale de Gotha et à l'Arsénal à Paris. Notices, notes, table générale par Maurice Tourneux, 1877–82. Paris, Garnier frères, 16 vols.

Cotgrave, Randle, 1611. *A French and English Dictionary*, London, printed by A. Islip.

Court de Gebelin, Antoine, 1773–82. *Le monde primitif analysé et comparé avec le monde moderne; considéré dans son génie allégorique et dans les allégories auxquelles conduit ce génie*, Paris, chez l'auteur, 9 vols.

Courtilz de Sandras, Gatien de, 1687. *Mémoires de Mr. L.C.D.R. [le Comte de Rochefort], contenant ce qui s'est passé de plus particulier sous le ministère du Cardinal de Richelieu, et du Cardinal Mazarin, avec plusieurs particularités remarquables du règne de Louis le Grand*, Cologne, Pierre Marteau.

1700. *Mémoires de Mr. d'Artagnan, capitaine lieutenant de la première Compagnie des Mousquetaires du Roi, contenant quantité de choses particulières et secrettes qui se sont passées sous le règne de Louis le Grand*, Cologne, Pierre Marteau.

1701. *Mémoires de Monsieur le Marquis de Montbrun, enrichis de figures*, Amsterdam, Nicolas Chevalier et Jacques Tirel.

Coypel, Antoine, 1721. *20 Discours sur la peinture, Discours prononcez dans les conférences de l'Académie royale de peinture et de sculpture*, Paris, Collombat. (Also in Jouin, *q.v.*)

Crébillon, Prosper Jolyot de, 1772. *Œuvres de Crébillon*, nouvelle édition, corrigée, revue et augmentée de la vie de l'auteur, Paris, Compagnie des libraires associés, 3 vols.

Crébillon, Claude-Prosper Jolyot de (Crébillon fils), 1772. *Collection complète des œuvres de M. de Crébillon le fils*, London, 7 vols.

Dacier, André, 1701. *Les Œuvres de Platon, avec des remarques et la vie de ce philosophe avec l'exposition des principaux dogmes de sa philosophie*, Paris, 2 vols.

Dacier, Mme Anne Lefebvre, 1714. *Des causes de la corruption du goût*, Paris, Rigaud.

Dandré Bardon, Michel-François, 1765. *Traité de la peinture, suivi d'un essai sur la sculpture, Pour servir d'introduction à une histoire universelle, relative à ces beaux arts*, par M. Dandré Bardon [. . .], Paris, Desaint, 2 vols.

Degérando, Baron Joseph-Marie, an viii [1799]. *Des signes et de l'art de penser considérés dans leurs rapports mutuels*, par Jh. M. Degérando, Paris, Goujon fils, 4 vols.

Delille, Jacques, 1782. *Les Jardins, ou l'Art d'embellir les paysages*, poème par M. l'abbé de Lille, Paris, Imprimerie de F-A Didot l'ainé.

Della Porta, Giambattista, 1558. *Magia naturalis sive de miraculis rerum naturalium*, Antwerp, ex officina C. Plantini.

Descamps, Jean-Baptiste, 1753. *La Vie des peintres flamands, allemands et hollandois, avec des portraits gravés en taille-douce, une indication de leurs principaux ouvrages et des réflexions sur leurs différentes manières*, par M. J-B Descamps, Peintre [. . .], Paris, C-A Jombert, 4 vols.

Descartes, René, 1897–1908. *Œuvres de Descartes*, publiées par Charles Adam et Paul Tannery sous les auspices du Ministère de l'instruction publique, Paris, Le Cerf, 10 vols.

1963. *Oeuvres*, ed. F. Alquié, Paris, Garnier, 3 vols.

Desfontaines, Abbé Pierre-François Guyot, 1739. *Racine vengé, ou Examen des remarques grammaticales de Mr. l'Abbé d'Olivet sur les œvres de Racine*, Avignon, 1739. (This edition contains *Remarques sur l'usage des inversions ou transpositions dans la prose et les vers*, at the end of the main text.)

1757. *L'Esprit de l'Abbé Desfontaines, ou Réflexions sur différens genres de science et de littérature, avec des jugemens sur quelques auteurs et sur quelques ouvrages tant anciens que modernes*, [publié par l'abbé de La Porte, avec une préface par Giraud] Londres, Clement, 4 vols.

1787–9. *Le Nouveau Gulliver, ou Voyages de Jean Gulliver, fils du Capitaine Lemuel Gulliver, traduit d'un manuscrit anglois par M.L.D.F.*, in *Voyages imaginaires, songes, visions et romans cabalistiques* ornés de Figures, Amsterdam, Paris, rue Serpente, 36 vols.; vol. xv [1730].

Desmolets, le père, 1739. 'Lettre à Mme. D*** sur les romans', in *Continuation des mémoires de littérature et d'histoire*, Paris, Simart, 11 vols.; vol. v, pp. 191–213. (This is also found in the *Bibliothèque françoise* (*q.v.*), 1728, vol. xii, pp. 46–61.)

Dézallier D'Argenville, Antoine-Joseph, 1745. *Discours sur la connoissance des tableaux*, in *L'Abrégé de la vie des peintres*, Paris, chez de Bure l'ainé, 2 vols.

Diderot, Denis. *O.C.* = *Œuvres complètes*, édition chronologique, introductions de Roger Lewinter, Paris, Club français du livre, 1969–73, 15 vols.

Correspondance = *Correspondance 1713–juillet 1784*, publiée par

Bibliography

Georges Roth et Jean Varloot, Paris, Editions de minuit, 1955–70, 16 vols.

Contes = *Contes*, edited by Herbert Dieckmann, London, Athlone Press, 1963.

Diderot et Falconet, 1958 = *Diderot et Falconet: Le Pour et le contre, correspondance polémique sur le respect de la postérité, Pline, et les anciens auteurs qui ont parlé de peinture et de sculpture*, introduction et notes de Yves Benot, Paris, Les Editeurs français réunis.

Diderot, 1963 = *La Religieuse*, nouvelle édition établie et présentée par Robert Mauzi, Paris, Editions de Cluny, 1963.

Diderot–Parrish, 1963 = *Denis Diderot: La Religieuse*, édition critique par Jean Parrish, in *Studies on Voltaire and the Eighteenth Century*, vol. xxii, Geneva, Droz, 1963.

Discours = *Discours sur la poésie dramatique*, 1758. See below, Vernière (1).

Eloge de Richardson, 1762, see below, Verniére (1).

Entretiens sur le 'Fils naturel', 1757, see below, Vernière (1).

Essais sur la peinture, 1766, see below, Vernière (1).

Jacques le fataliste = *Jacques le fataliste et son maître*. Edition critique par Simone Lecointre et Jean Le Galliot. Droz, Geneva, 1976 [1778–80].

Lettre sur les aveugles, 1749, see below, Vernière (2).

Lettre sur les sourds et muets, 1751, in *O.C.* ii, pp. 519–602.

Le Neveu de Rameau, éd. Jean Fabre, Geneva, Droz, 1950.

Pensées détachées sur la peinture, 1775, see below, Vernière (1).

Paradoxe sur le comédien, 1770, see below, Vernière (1).

Rêve de d'Alembert, see below, Vernière (2).

Salons = *Les Salons de Diderot*, texte établi et présenté par Jean Seznec et Jean Adhémar, Oxford, Clarendon Press, 1957–63, 3 vols. (vol. i, *Salons de 1759, 1761, 1763*; vol. ii, *Salon de 1765*; vol. iii, *Salon de 1767*). vol. iv, éd. Jean Seznec, Oxford, Clarendon Press, 1967 (*Salons de 1769, 1771, 1775, 1781*).

Vernière (1) = *Diderot: Œuvres esthétiques*, textes établis avec introductions, bibliographies, notes et relevés de variantes, par Paul Vernière, Paris, Garnier, 1959.

Vernière (2) = *Diderot: Œuvres philosophiques*, textes établis avec introductions, bibliographies et notes par Paul Vernière, Paris, Garnier, 1956.

Discours à Cliton, 1898, in *La Querelle du Cid, pièces et pamphlets publiés d'après les originaux*, par Armand Gasté, Paris, H. Welter.

Doppet, le Général François-Amédée, 1786. *Mémoires de Madame de Warens, suivis de ceux de Claude Anet, publiés par M. C.D.M.D.P. pour servir d'apologie aux Confessions de J-J. Rousseau*, Chambéry.

1789. *Vintzenried ou les Mémoires du Chevalier de Courtille, pour servir de suite aux Mémoires de Madame de Warens, à ceux de Claude Anet, & aux Confessions de J-J. Rousseau*, Paris.

Bibliography

Dorat, Claude-Joseph, 1766. *La Déclamation théâtrale*, Poème didactique en trois chants, précédé d'un discours, Paris, Imprimerie de S. Jorry.

1772. *Les Sacrifices de l'amour, ou Lettres de la Vicomtesse de Senanges et du Chevalier de Versenai*, Paris, Delalain.

1882. *Contes et nouvelles, précédés des Réflexions sur le conte*, Paris, L. Lefilleul [1765].

Dubos, Abbé Jean-Baptiste, 1719. *Réflexions critiques sur la poésie et sur la peinture*, Paris, Jean Mariette, 2 vols.

Duclos, Charles Pinot, 1741. *Les Confessions du comte de **** écrites par lui-même à un ami, Amsterdam.

Dumarsais, Charles Chesneau, 1775. *Des tropes, ou des différens sens dans lesquels on peut prendre un même mot dans une même langue*, Paris, Prault [1757].

Du Perron, 1758. *Discours sur la peinture et sur l'architecture, dédié à Mme. de Pompadour*, Paris, Prault père.

Du Rosoi, Barnabé-Farmian, 1773. *Dissertation sur Corneille et Racine, suivie d'une épître en vers*, Londres, Paris, Lacombe.

Duval, François, 1725. *Lettres curieuses sur divers sujets*, Paris, N. Pepie, 2 vols.

Encyclopédie ou Dictionnaire raisonné des sciences, des arts, & des métiers, par une société de gens de lettres. Mis en ordre et publié par M. Diderot, et quant à la partie mathématique, par M. d'Alembert, Paris, Briasson, 1751–65. 17 vols.

Ballet, vol. II, signed B (Cahusac).

Comédie, vol. III, attributed to Marmontel.

Déclamation des anciens, vol. IV, attributed to Duclos.

Déclamation théâtrale, vol. IV, attributed to Marmontel.

Décoration (Opéra), vol. IV, signed B (Cahusac).

Décoration théâtrale, vol. IV, attributed to Marmontel.

Décoration des théâtres, vol. IV, signed P (Blondel).

Dénouement, vol. IV, attributed to Marmontel.

Didactique, vol. IV, addition by Marmontel to an article by Mallet.

Elocution, vol. V, signed O (d'Alembert).

Eloquence, vol. V, attributed to Voltaire.

Enthousiasme, vol. V, signed B (Cahusac).

Expression (Peinture), vol. VI, attributed to Watelet.

Fable, apologue (Belles lettres), vol. VI, attributed to Marmontel.

Féerie, vol. VI, signed B (Cahusac).

Figure, vol. VI, signed F (Dumarsais).

Goût, vol. VII, attributed to Voltaire.

Image (Belles lettres), vol VIII, unsigned.

Imagination, vol. VIII, attributed to Voltaire.

Merveilleux, vol. X, unsigned.

Narration (Belles lettres), vol. XI, signed G (Mallet).

Opéra (Belles lettres), vol, XI, signed D.J. (Jaucourt).

362

Bibliography

Peintre, vol. xii, signed le Chevalier de Jaucourt.

Poème lyrique, vol. vii, attributed to Grimm.

Sublime, vol. xv, signed Jaucourt.

Unité (Belles lettres), vol. xvii, unsigned.

Epinay, Mme d', 1951. *Histoire de Madame de Montbrillant*. Les pseudo-mémoires de Madame d'Epinay, texte intégral, publié pour la première fois avec une introduction, des variantes, des notes et des compléments, par Georges Roth, Paris, Gallimard, 3 vols.

Estève, Pierre, 1753a. *L'Esprit des beaux arts*, Paris, C. J. Baptiste Bauche fils, 2 vols.

1753b. *Lettre à un ami sur l'exposition des tableaux faite dans le grand Sallon du Louvre, le 25 Aout 1753*.

Evelyn, John, 1668. Translation of Roland Fréart de Chambray, *An Idea of the Perfection of Painting Demonstrated*, by J. E., Esquire, Fellow of the Royal Society, London, In the Savoy, H. Herringman.

Falconet, Etienne, 1761. *Réflexions sur la sculpture, lues à l'Académie royale de peinture et de sculpture le 7 juin 1760*, par Etienne Falconet, Amsterdam, Paris, Prault fils.

Favart, Charles-Simon, 1808. *Mémoires et correspondances littéraires, dramatiques et anecdotiques de C. S. Favart, publiés par A. P. C. Favart, son petit fils, et précédés d'une notice historique redigée sur pièces authentiques et originales*, par H. F. Dumolard, Paris, L. Collin, 3 vols.

Félibien, André, 1725. *Entretiens sur les vies et sur les ouvrages des plus excellens peintres anciens et modernes* [. . .], Trévoux, de l'Imprimerie de S.A.S., 6 vols. [1666–88].

Fénelon, François de Salignac de la Mothe, 1718. *Dialogues sur l'éloquence en général et sur celle de la chaire en particulier avec une lettre écrite à l'Académie françoise par feu Messire François de Salignac de la Motte Fénelon, Précepteur de Messeigneurs les Enfans de France et depuis Archevêque Duc de Cambray, Prince du Saint Empire*, Paris, Jacques Estienne.

1719. *Les Avantures de Télémaque fils d'Ulysse par feu Messire François de Salignac de la Motte Fénelon* [. . .], which contains le Chevalier Ramsay's *Discours de la poésie épique et de l'excellence du poème de Télémaque* [1717], Londres, J. Tonson et J. Watts.

1968. *Les Avantures de Télémaque*, chronologie et introduction par Jeanne-Lydie Gore [. . .], Paris, Garnier–Flammarion [probably written 1694–6].

Fenouillot de Falbaire de Quingey, Charles-Georges, 1771. *Le Fabricant de Londres*, drame en cinq actes et en prose, représenté à la Comédie françoise le 12 janvier 1771, Paris.

1776. *L'Ecole des mœurs, ou les suites du libertinage*, drame en cinq actes et en vers, représenté à la Comédie françoise le 12 mai 1776, Paris.

Foigny, Gabriel, 1693. *Les Avantures de Jacques Sadeur, dans la découverte et le voyage de la Terre Australe, contenant les coutumes et les mœurs des Australiens, leur religion, leurs exercices, leurs études, leurs guerres, les animaux particuliers à ce pays et toutes les raretés curieuses qui s'y trouvent*, Paris, Claude Barbin.

Fontenelle, Bernard Le Bouyer de, 1688. *Poèsies pastorales de M.D.F. avec un traité sur la nature de l'églogue et une digression sur les Anciens et les Modernes*, Paris, M. Guérout.

Fourmont, Etienne, 1716. *Examen pacifique de la querelle de Madame Dacier et de Monsieur de La Motte sur Homère. Avec un traité sur le poème épique et la critique des deux Iliades et de plusieurs autres poèmes*, par Monsieur Fourmont, Professeur en Langue arabique au Collège royal de France, et associé de l'Académie royale des inscriptions, Paris, Jacques Rollin, 2 vols.

Fraguier, Abbé Claude-François, 1731. *Qu'il ne peut y avoir de poèmes en prose*, in *Mémoires de l'Académie des inscriptions et des belles lettres*, Amsterdam, François Changuion, vol. VIII.

Frain du Tremblay, Jean, 1713. *Discours sur l'origine de la poésie, sur son usage et sur le bon goût*, par le Sieur Frain du Tremblay, de l'Académie royale d'Angers, Paris, François Fournier.

Fréart de Chambray, Roland, 1662. *Idée de la perfection de la peinture, démontrée par les principes de l'art, et par des exemples conformes aux observations que Pline et Quintilien ont faites sur les plus célèbres tableaux des anciens peintres, mis en parallèle à quelques ouvrages de nos meilleurs peintres modernes, Léonard de Vinci, Raphael, Jules Romain et le Poussin*, par Roland Fréart, Sieur de Chambray, Au Mans, Imprimerie de J. Ysambart.

Gachet d'Artigny, Abbé Antoine, 1739. *Relation de ce qui s'est passé dans une assemblée tenue au bas du Parnasse, pour la réforme des belles lettres, ouvrage curieux et composé de pièces rapportées selon la méthode des beaux esprits de ce tems* . . . La Haye, P. Paupie.

Gacon, François, 1715. *Homère vengé, ou réponse à M. de La Motte sur l'Iliade*, par L.P.S.F. [le poète sans fard], Paris, E. Ganeau.

Garcin, Laurent, 1772. *Traité du mélodrame, Réflexions sur la musique dramatique*, Paris, Vallat-la-Chapelle.

Gautier d'Agoty, Jacques, 1753. *Observations sur la peinture et sur les tableaux anciens et modernes dédiées à M. de Vandière*, Année 1753, tome I, Paris, Jorry.

Goethe, Johann Wolfgang von, 1971. *Goethes Farbenlehre*, ausgewählt und erläutert von Rupprecht Matthaei, Ravensburg, O. Maier.

Gouge de Cessières, François-Etienne, 1758. *Les Jardins d'ornemens, ou les Géorgiques françoises*, nouveau poème en quatre chants par M. Gouge de Cessières, Paris, Guillyn.

Gougenot, —, 1633. *La Comédie des comédiens*, tragi-comédie par le Sr. Gougenot, Paris, P. David.

Grandval, Nicolas Ragot de, 1732. *Essai sur le bon goust en musique*, Paris, Pierre Prault.

Bibliography

Granet, Abbé François, 1738–9. *Réflexions sur les ouvrages de littérature*, Paris, Briasson, 10 vols.

Grimarest, Jean-Léonor le Gallois, Sieur de, 1707. *Traité du récitatif dans la lecture, dans l'action publique, dans la déclamation et dans le chant, avec un traité des accens, de la quantité, et de la ponctuation*, Paris, J. Le Fèvre.

Grimm, Friedrich-Melchior, Baron von, 1753. *Le Petit Prophète de Boemischbroda*.

Hamilton, Anthony, 1964. *Mémoires du Comte de Grammont*, édition établie, préfacée, et annotée par Gilbert Sigaux, Lausanne [1713].

Harris, James, 1744. *Three Treatises. The first concerning Art. The second concerning Music, Painting and Poetry. The third concerning Happiness*, London, J. Nourse.

Herder, Johann Gottfried, 1877–1913. *Sämtliche Werke*, herausgegeben von Bernhard Suphan, Berlin, Weidmannsche Buchhandlung, 33 vols. (The translations are mine.)

Hogarth, William, 1955. *The Analysis of Beauty*, with the rejected passages from the manuscript drafts and autobiographical notes, edited with an introduction by Joseph Burke, Oxford, Clarendon Press [1753]. (The subtitle to Hogarth's first edition is: *Written with a view of fixing the fluctuating ideas of taste*.)

Hume, David, 1967. *A Treatise of Human Nature*, ed. L. A. Selby-Bigge, M.A., Oxford, Clarendon Press (1888) [1739].

Iamblichus, *Les Mystères d'Egypte*, texte établi et traduit par Edouard des Places, S.J., Paris, Les Belles Lettres, 1966.

Isidore of Seville, *Sententiarum Liber IV, Appendix IX*, in Migne (*q.v.*), vol. LXXXIII, p. 1163.

Jouin, Henry, 1883. *Conférences de l'Académie royale de peinture et de sculpture*, recueillies, annotées et précédées d'une étude sur les artistes écrivains par M. Henry Jouin, Paris, A. Quantin.

Journal étranger, ou Notice exacte et détaillée des ouvrages de toutes les nations étrangères, en fait d'arts, de sciences, de littérature etc., 1754–62, Paris, Michel Lambert, 45 vols.

Journal des sçavans, 1665–1797, Paris, different publishers, 142 vols.

Journal de Trévoux, i.e. *Mémoires pour l'Histoire des Sciences et des Beaux Arts*, 1701–58, Amsterdam, Trévoux, Paris.

Journal de Verdun, i.e., *La Suite de la clef, ou Journal historique sur les matières du tems*, 1717–76, Paris, E. Ganeau, 120 vols., see Passe.

Kant, Immanuel, *Kant's Critique of Judgement*, translated with introduction and notes by J. H. Bernard, New York and London, Hafner, 1966 (1892).

Kepler, Johannes, 1619. *Joannis Kepleri Harmonices mundi libri V* [. . .] Linz, G. Tampachii.

La Barre, Abbé Louis-François-Joseph, 1741, *Dissertation sur le poème épique*, in *Mémoires de littérature . . .* (*q.v.*), vol. XIII, 1741 [1731].

La Bruyère, Jean de, 1962. *Les Caractères*, edited by Robert Garapon, Paris, Garnier [1688].

Bibliography

La Cépède, Bernard-Germain-Etienne de La Ville sur Illon, Comte de, 1785. *La Poétique de la musique*, par M. le Comte de La Cépède [. . .], Paris, de l'Imprimerie de Monsieur, 2 vols.

La Chaussée, Pierre-Claude Nivelle de, 1762. *Oeuvres de Monsieur Nivelle de La Chaussée, de l'Académie françoise*. Nouvelle édition, corrigée, et augmentée de plusieurs pièces qui n'avoient point encore paru, Paris, Prault, 5 vols.

Lacombe, Jacques, 1753. *Le Salon*.

1758. *Le Spectacle des beaux-arts, ou considérations touchant leur nature, leur objet, leurs effets et leurs règles principales, avec des observations sur la manière de les envisager, sur les disposition nécessaires pour les cultiver et sur les moyens propres pour les étudier et les perfectionner*, par Monsieur Lacombe, Avocat, Paris, Hardy.

La Dixmérie, Nicolas Bricaire de, 1759. *L'Isle taciturne et l'isle enjouée, ou Voyage du génie Alaciel dans ces deux isles*, Amsterdam.

1765. *Lettres sur l'état présent de nos spectacles avec des vues nouvelles sur chacun d'eux, particulièrement sur la Comédie françoise et l'Opéra*, Amsterdam, Paris, Duchesne.

1769. *Les Deux ages du goût et du génie français, sous Louis XIV et sous Louis XV*, par M. de La Dixmérie, La Haye, Paris, Lacombe.

1779. *La Sibyle gauloise ou La France telle qu'elle fut, telle qu'elle est, et telle, à peu près, qu'elle pourra être*, ouvrage traduit du Celte et suivi d'un Commentaire par M. de La Dixmérie, Londres, Paris, Valleyre l'aîné.

La Fayette, Marie-Madeleine Pioche de La Vergne, Comtesse de, 1674. *La Princesse de Montpensier*, Paris, Charles Osmont.

La Font de Saint Yenne, 1747. *Réflexions sur quelques causes de l'état présent de la peinture en France avec un examen des principaux ouvrages exposés au Louvre le mois d'Août 1746*, La Haye, Jean Neaulme.

1754. *Sentimens sur quelques ouvrages de peinture, sculpture, et gravure. Ecrits à un particulier en province*.

La Garde, Abbé Philippe Bridard de, 1740. *L'Echo du public sur les ouvrages nouveaux, sur les spectacles et sur les talens, relation d'un François à Mylord**, Duc de - -, Paris, Didot, La Veuve Pissot, Prault fils.

Lambert, Abbé Claude-François, 1741. *Mémoires et avantures d'une dame de qualité qui s'est retirée du monde*, La Haye, aux dépens de la Compagnie, 3 vols.

La Motte, Antoine Houdar de, 1715. *Réflexions sur la critique*, par Monsieur de La Motte, de l'Académie françoise, avec plusieurs lettres de M. l'Archevêque de Cambray et de l'auteur, La Haye, Henri du Sauzet.

1754. *Œuvres de Monsieur Houdar de La Motte*, l'un des Quarante de l'Académie françoise, dédiées à S.A.S.M. le Duc d'Orléans, Premier Prince du Sang, Paris, Prault l'aîné, 10 vols.

Lamy, le père Bernard, 1679. *De l'art de parler*, suivant la copie imprimée, Paris, André Pralard.

Bibliography

1701. *Traité de perspective, où sont contenus les fondemens de peinture*, par le R. P. Bernard Lamy, Paris, Annisson, directeur de l'Imprimerie royale.

Landois, Paul, 1742. *Silvie, tragédie en prose en un acte*, Paris, Prault.

La Place, Pierre-Antoine de, 1746. *Le Théâtre anglois*, Londres, 8 vols.

La Porte, Abbé Joseph de, *see* Castel, and Desfontaines, 1757.

La Solle, Henri-François, 1740. *Bok et Zulba, histoire allégorique*, traduite du portuguais de Dom Anrel Enime.

La Tour, Abbé Séran de, 1747. *Amusement de la raison*, Paris, Durand.
1762. *L'Art de sentir et de juger en matière de goût*, Paris, Pissot.

Laugier, Abbé Marc-Antoine, 1754. *Apologie de la musique françoise contre M. Rousseau*, Paris.
1771. *Manière de bien juger les ouvrages de Peinture, par feu M. l'Abbé Laugier, mise au jour et augmentée de plusieurs notes intéressantes par M*** [Cochin]*, Paris, C. A. Jombert.

Le Blanc, Abbé Jean-Bernard, 1747. *Lettre sur l'exposition des ouvrages de peinture, sculpture, de l'année 1747. Et en général sur l'utilité de ces sortes d'Expositions*.
1753. *Observations sur les ouvrages de M.M. de l'Académie de peinture et de sculpture, exposés au Sallon du Louvre en l'année 1753, et sur quelques écrits qui ont rapport à la peinture*.

Le Bossu, le père René, 1675. *Traité du poème épique*, par le R. P. Le Bossu, Chanoine régulier de Sainte Geneviève, Paris, Michel Le Petit.

Le Brun, Ponce-Denis Ecouchard, dit, 1811. *Œuvres de Le Brun* [. . .], Mises en ordre et publiées par P. L. Ginguené [. . .], Paris, G. Warée, 4 vols.

Le Camus de Mézières, 1780. *Le Génie de l'architecture, ou l'analogie de cet art avec nos sensations*, par M. Le Camus de Mézières, architecte, Paris, l'Auteur. Reprinted Minkoff, Geneva, 1972.

Le Cerf de la Viéville de Freneuse, Jean-Laurent, 1705. *Comparaison de la musique italienne et de la musique françoise*, Bruxelles, François Foppen, seconde édition [1704].

Le Clerc, Jean, 1699. *Parrhasiana ou Pensées diverses sur des matières de critique, d'histoire, de morale et de politique. Avec la défense de divers ouvrages de Mr. L. C.*, par Théodore Parrhase, Amsterdam, chez les héritiers d'Antoine Schelle.

Lefèvre, Tannegui, 1697. *De futilitate poetices*, auctore Tanaquillo Fabro, Tanaquilli filio, Amsterdam, Desbordes.

Leibniz, Gottfried Wilhelm, 1966. *Nouveaux essais sur l'entendement humain*, chronologie et introduction par Jacques Brunschwig, Paris, Garnier-Flammarion. [Written 1703, first published 1765.]

Lekain, Henri Louis Kaïn, dit, 1825. *Mémoires de Lekain, précédés de réflexions sur cet acteur et sur l'art théâtral par M. Talma*, Paris, Etienne Ledoux.

Lenglet Dufresnoy, Abbé Nicolas, 1734. *De l'usage des romans, où l'on fait voir leur utilité et leurs différens caractères: Avec une Bibliothèque des Romans, accompagnée de remarques critiques sur leur choix, et leurs éditions*, Amsterdam, chez La Veuve de Poilras, à la Vérité sans fard (written under the pseudonym M. le C. Gordon de Percel), 2 vols.

1735. *L'Histoire justifiée contre les romans*, par Mr. l'Abbé Lenglet du Fresnoy, Amsterdam, aux dépens de la Compagnie.

Le Noble de Tennelière, Eustache, Baron de Saint Georges, 1694. *Ildegerte, reine de Danemark et de Norwège, ou l'amour magnanime*, Paris, de Luyne.

Lessing, Gotthold Ephraïm, 1785. *Dramaturgie, ou observations critiques sur plusieurs pièces de théâtre, tant anciennes que modernes*, ouvrage intéressant, traduit de l'allemand de feu M. Lessing, par un François, revu, corrigé et publié par M. Junker [. . .], Paris, M. Junker, Durand, Couturier, 2 vols.

1967. *Laokoon oder über die Grenzen der Malerei und Poesie*, mit beilaüfigen Erlaüterungen verschiedener Punkte der alten Kunstgeschichte, ed. Ingrid Kreuzer, Stuttgart, Reklam [1766].

1970. *Laocoon*, translated and edited by William A. Steel, London, Dent, Everyman's Library. (The notes are omitted from this translation.)

Lettres portugaises, 1962. [Par Gabriel de Lavergne de Guilleragues], introduction, notes, glossaire et tables d'après de nouveaux documents par F. Deloffre et J. Rougeot, Paris, Garnier [1669].

Levesque de Pouilly, Louis-Jean, 1747. *Théorie des sentimens agréables, où après avoir indiqué les règles que la Nature suit dans la distribution du plaisir, on établit les principes de la Théologie naturelle et ceux de la Philosophie morale*, Genève, Barillot et fils.

Ligne, Charles-Joseph, Prince de, 1774. *Lettres à Eugénie sur les spectacles*, Bruxelles, Paris, Valade.

Longue, Louis-Pierre de, 1737. *Raisonnements hasardés sur la poésie françoise*, Paris, Didot.

Louvet de Couvray, Jean-Baptiste, 1966. *Les Amours du Chevalier de Faublas*, introduction de Michel Crouzet, Paris, Editions 10/18 [1787].

Mably, Gabriel Bonnot, Abbé de, 1741. *Lettres à Madame la marquise de P . . . sur l'opéra*, Paris, Didot.

Maillet Duclairon, Antoine, 1751. *Essai sur la connoissance des théâtres françois*, Paris, Prault père.

Malebranche, le père Nicolas, 1965-7. *De la recherche de la vérité, où l'on traite de la nature de l'esprit de l'homme et de l'usage qu'il en doit faire pour éviter l'erreur dans les sciences*, ed. Geneviève Rodis-Lewis, Paris, Vrin, 2 vols. [1674].

Mandeville, Bernard de, 1714. *The Fable of the Bees; or, private vices publick benefits*.

Marchand, Jean-Henri, 1880. *Le Vidangeur sensible*, drame en trois actes et en prose par Jean-Henri Marchand, réimprimé sur l'exemplaire de la collection Ménétrier, avec une notice par Lucien Faucou, Paris, Le Moniteur du bibliophile [1777].

Marivaux, Pierre Carlet de Chamblain de, 1957. *La vie de Marianne, ou Aventures de Madame la Comtesse de* ***, éd. Frédéric Deloffre, Paris, Garnier [1731–8].

1969. *Journaux et œuvres diverses* [. . .], éd. Frédéric Deloffre et Michel Gilot, Paris, Garnier.

1972. *Œuvres de jeunesse*, éd. Frédéric Deloffre, avec le concours de Claude Rigaut, Paris, Bibliothèque de la Pléiade.

Marmontel, Jean-François, 1763. *Poétique françoise*, Paris, Lesclapart, 2 vols.

1819–20. *Œuvres de Marmontel*, Paris, Belin, 7 vols.; the *Essai sur les romans, considérés du côté moral* is in vol. III, p. 558–96. (I have been unable to date this. It appears, for example, in vol. XII of *Œuvres complettes de M. Marmontel*, Historiographe de France et Secrétaire perpétuel de l'Académie française, Edition revue & corrigée par l'Auteur, à Paris, Chez Née de La Rochelle, Libraire, rue de Hurepoix près du Pont Saint Michel no. 13, M D CC LXXXVIII. Avec approbation et privilège du Roi. There is no mention of a possible date in the chronology in Ehrard, 1970.)

Méhégan, Guillaume-Alexandre, Chevalier de, 1755. *Considérations sur les révolutions des arts, dédiées à Monseigneur le Duc d'Orléans, premier Prince du sang*, Paris, Brocas.

Mémoires de littérature tirez des registres de l'Académie royale des inscriptions et belles lettres, Amsterdam, François Changuion, 54 vols.

Mercier, Louis-Sébastien, 1771. *L'An deux mille quatre cent quarante, Rêve s'il en fût jamais*, Amsterdam.

1775. *La Brouette du vinaigrier*, drame, Londres.

1784. *Mon Bonnet de nuit*, Neuchâtel, de l'Imprimerie de la Société typographique, 4 vols.

Mercure de France, 1724–91. Paris, 974 vols.

Mersenne, le père Marin, 1636. *Harmonie universelle, contenant la théorie et la pratique de la musique*, par F. Marin Mersenne, Paris, S. Cramoisy.

Meusnier de Querlon, Anne-Gabriel, 1753. *L'Ecole d'Uranie, ou l'Art de la peinture, traduit du latin d'Alph. Dufresnoy [par Roger de Piles] et M. l'abbé de Marsy [par Meusnier de Querlon]*, édition revue et corrigée par le sieur M. D. Qu., Paris, Imprimerie de P-G. Le Mercier.

Migne, J-P, 1844–64. *Patrologiae Cursus Completus*, Paris, excudebat Migne, 221 vols.

Molé, François-René, 1825. *Mémoires de Molé*, précédés d'une notice sur cet acteur par M. Etienne, Paris, Collection de mémoires sur l'art dramatique.

Montesquieu, Charles-Louis de Secondat, Baron de, 1949. *Œuvres complètes*, éd. Roger Caillois, Paris, Bibliothèque de la Pléiade, 2 vols.

Morellet, Abbé André, 1772? *Observations sur un ouvrage nouveau, intitulé Traité du mélodrame, ou réflexions sur la musique dramatique,* à Paris, chez Vallat-la-Chapelle, 1771.

Mouhy, Charles de Fieux, Chevalier de, 1736. *La Mouche ou les Avantures de M. Bigand,* traduites de l'italien par le chevalier de Mouhy, Paris, L. Dupuis.

    1739. *Mémoires d'Anne-Marie de Moras, comtesse de Courbon, écrits par elle-même,* La Haye, P. de Hondt.

    1746–51. *Le Papillon ou Lettres parisiennes, ouvrage qui contiendra tout ce qui se passera d'intéressant, de plus agréable et de plus nouveau . . .,* La Haye, Antoine van Pole, 4 vols.

Nadal, Abbé Augustin, 1738. *Oeuvres meslées,* Paris, Briasson, 2 vols.

Néel, Louis-Balthasar, 1745. *Le Voyage de Saint Cloud, par mer et par terre,* in *Bibliothèque choisie et amusante* (*q.v.*), vol. I.

Newton, Sir Isaac, 1704. *Opticks, or a treatise of the reflexions, refractions, inflexions and colours of light; also two treatises of the species and magnitude of curvilinear figures,* London, S. Smith.

Niceron, le père Jean-François, 1652. *La Perspective curieuse, avec l'optique et la catoptrique de R. P. Mersenne,* Paris, P. Billaine [1638].

Nougaret, Pierre-Jean-Baptiste, 1769. *De l'art du théâtre en général, où il est parlé des différens genres de spectacles et de la musique adaptée au théâtre,* Paris, Cailleau, 2 vols.

Le Nouvelliste du Parnasse, ou, Réflexions sur les ouvrages nouveaux, 1731–2, Paris, Chaubert, 4 vols.

Noverre, Jean-Georges, 1760, *Lettres sur la danse et sur les ballets,* Stuttgart et Lyon, Delaroche.

Observations sur les écrits modernes, 1735–43, Paris, Chaubert, 33 vols.

Observations sur la littérature moderne [par Joseph de La Porte], 1749–52, La Haye, 9 vols.

d'Olivet, Abbé Pierre-Joseph Thorellier, 1736. *Traité de la prosodie,* Paris, Gandouin.

    1738. *Remarques de grammaire sur Racine,* par M. l'abbé d'Olivet, Paris, Gandouin.

Pajot, le père Charles, 1670. *Dictionnaire nouveau françois–latin,* La Flèche, Griveau.

Pascal, Blaise, 1904. *Opuscules et pensées,* publiées avec une introduction, des notices et des notes, par M. Léon Brunschvieg, Paris, Hachette, 3 vols.

Passe, 1749. 'Lettre de M. de Passe à Madame D*** sur les romans', in *Journal de Verdun* (*q.v.*), Paris, vol. LXVI, p. 102–12.

Patte, Pierre, 1782. *Essai sur l'architecture théâtrale, ou de l'ordonnance la plus avantageuse à une salle de spectacle, relativement aux principes de l'optique et de l'acoustique, avec un examen des principaux théâtres de l'Europe et une analyse des écrits les plus importans sur cette matière,* Paris, Moutard.

Perrault, Charles, 1693. *Parallele des Anciens et des Modernes en ce qui regarde les arts et les sciences*, nouvelle édition, augmentée de quelques dialogues, par M. Perrault, de l'Académie françoise, Amsterdam, Georges Gallet, 2 vols.

Piles, Roger de, 1699. *Dialogue sur le coloris*, Paris, N. Langlois [1673].

1707. *L'Idée du peintre parfait, pour servir de règle aux jugemens que l'on doit porter sur les ouvrages des peintres*, Londres, David Mortier.

1708. *Cours de peinture par principes*, composé par M. de Piles, Paris, Jacques Estienne.

Plato, 1961. *The Republic*, translated by H. D. P. Lee, Harmondsworth, Penguin.

1956–70. *The Sophist*, in *Œuvres complètes*, Paris, Les Belles Lettres, 27 vols.

Pliny, 1958. *Naturalis Historiae*, Loeb Library, London/Cambridge Mass., Heinemann/Harvard University Press, 4 vols.

Pluche, Abbé Antoine, 1751. *La Mécanique des langues et l'art de les enseigner*, par M. Pluche, Paris, Vve. Estienne et fils.

Poinsinet le jeune, Antoine-Alexandre-Henri, 1765. *Le Cercle ou la soirée à la mode*, comédie épisodique en un acte et en prose, jouée le 7 septembre 1764.

Pope, Alexander, 1711, *An Essay on Criticism*.

Porée, Abbé Charles-Gabriel, 1736. *Histoire de D. Ranuncio d'Alétès, écrite par lui-même*, Venise [Rouen], F. Pasquinetti.

Préville, Pierre Louis Dubus, dit, 1823. *Mémoires de Préville et de Dazincourt*, revus, corrigés et augmentés d'une notice sur ces deux comédiens, par M. Ourry, Paris, Baudoin frères, libraires.

Prévost, Abbé Antoine-François, 1731. *Mémoires et avantures d'un homme de qualité qui s'est retiré du monde*, Paris, Amsterdam, 7 vols. [1728–32].

Le Pour et contre, ouvrage périodique d'un goût nouveau [. . .], par l'auteur des *Mémoires d'un homme de qualité*, Paris, Didot, 1733–40, 20 vols.

1734. Ed. *Histoire universelle de Jacques-Auguste de Thou depuis 1543 jusqu'en 1607*, traduite sur l'édition latine de Londres, Londres, 15 vols.

1740. *Histoire de Marguerite d'Anjou, Reine d'Angleterre*, par M. l'Abbé Prévost, Aumonier de son Altesse Sérénissime Monseigneur le Prince de Conty, Amsterdam, François Desbordes.

1742. *Histoire de Guillaume le Conquérant, duc de Normandie et roi d'Angleterre*, par M. l'Abbé P***, Paris, Prault, 2 vols.

1742. *Le Doyen de Killerine, histoire morale. Composée sur les mémoires d'une illustre famille d'Irlande, et ornée de tout ce qui peut rendre une lecture utile et agréable*, par l'Auteur des *Mémoires d'un homme de qualité*, Amsterdam, François Changuion, 6 vols. [1735–9].

1777. *Le Philosophe anglois, ou Histoire de Monsieur Cleveland, fils naturel de Cromwell*, écrite par lui-même et traduite de l'anglois, nouvelle édition, Londres, Paul Vaillant, 6 vols. [1731–9].

1965. *Histoire d'une Grecque moderne*, introduction par Robert Mauzi, Paris, Editions 10/18.

Les Princesses malabares, ou le célibat philosophique [par Louis Pierre de Longue?], A Andrinople, chez T. Franco [1734].

Puisieux, Madeleine d'Arsant, Madame de, 1750. *Les Caractères*, par Madame de P***, Londres.

Quesnel, Abbé Pierre?, 1737. *Almanach du diable, contenant des prédictions très curieuses et absolument infaillibles pour l'année 1737*, Aux Enfers.

Quintilian, 1963. *Institutio oratoria*, Loeb Library, London/Cambridge Mass., Heinemann/Harvard University Press, 4 vols.

Racine, Louis, 1731. 'Dissertation sur l'utilité de l'imitation et sur la manière dont on doit imiter', and 'Sur l'essence de la poèsie', in *Mémoires de littérature* (*q.v.*), vol. VIII [British Museum copy].

1742. *La Religion*, poème, Paris, Coignard, Desaint.

Raguenet, Abbé François, 1702. *Parallèle des Italiens et des François en ce qui regarde la musique et les opéra*, Paris, Jean Moreau.

Rameau, Jean-Philippe, 1722–6. *Traité de l'harmonie réduite à ses principes naturels, suivi du nouveau système de musique théorique*, Paris, Ballard, 2 t. in 1 vol.

Rapin, le père René, 1674. *Réflexions sur la poétique d'Aristote et sur les ouvrages des poètes anciens et modernes*, Paris, F. Muguet.

Réflexions sur la musique en général et sur la musique françoise en particulier, 1754.

Rémond de Sainte Albine, 1747. *Le Comédien*, ouvrage divisé en deux parties, par M. Rémond de Sainte Albine, Paris, Desaint, Saillant, Vincent fils.

Rémond de Saint Mard, Toussaint, 1734. *Réflexions sur la poésie en général, sur l'églogue, sur la fable, sur l'élégie, sur la satire, sur l'ode et sur les autres petits poèmes comme sonnet, rondeau, madrigal etc. suivies de trois lettres sur la décadence du goût en France*, par M.R.D.S.M., La Haye, C. de Rogissart.

1741. *Réflexions sur l'opéra*, La Haye, Jean Neaulme.

1749. *Œuvres de Monsieur de Saint Mard*, Amsterdam, Pierre Mortier, 5 vols.

Rétif de la Bretonne, Nicolas Edmé, 1769. *Le Pornographe, ou Idées d'un honnête homme sur un projet de règlement pour les prostituées propre à prévenir les malheurs qu'occasionne le publicisme des femmes, avec des notes historiques et justificatives*, Londres, J. Nourse, La Haye, Gosse junior et Pinet.

1770. *La Mimographe, ou Idées d'une honnête femme pour la réformation du Théâtre national*, Amsterdam, Changuion.

Reynolds, Sir Joshua, 1887. *Discourses*, edited with an introduction by Helen Zimmerman, London, W. Scott.

Riccoboni, François, 1750. *L'Art du théâtre, à Madame ****, Paris, C-F Simon, Giffart fils.

Bibliography

Riccoboni, Louis, 1728. *Dell'Arte rappresentativa*, Londra.

1731. *Histoire du théâtre italien, depuis la décadence de la comédie latine; avec un catalogue des tragédies et comédies italiennes imprimées depuis l'an 1500 jusqu'en l'an 1660, Et une dissertation sur la tragédie moderne*, Paris, Cailleau, 2 vols.

1736. *Observations sur la comédie et sur le génie de Molière*, Paris, Vve. Pissot.

1738a. *Pensées sur la déclamation*, Paris, Briasson.

1738b. *Réflexions historiques et critiques sur les différens théâtres de l'Europe, avec les pensées sur la déclamation*, Paris, Imprimerie de Jacques Guérin.

Lettre à Muratori, in La Chaussée (*q.v.*), vol. v [1737].

1743. *De la réformation du théâtre*.

Richardson, Jonathan, 1728. *Traité de la peinture par Mrs. Richardson père et fils, divisé en trois tomes*, Amsterdam, Herman Uytwerf, Paris, Briasson, 3 t. in 2 vols. [translation of *An Essay on the Theory of Painting*, 1715].

Richelière, Claude de, 1752. *Jugement de l'orchestre de l'opéra*.

Rivet de la Grange, Dom, *et al.*, 1742. *Histoire littéraire de la France*, par des religieux bénédictins de la Congrégation de Saint-Maur, Paris, Osmont, vol. vi, pp. 12–17.

Rochemont, – de, 1754. *Réflexions d'un patriote sur l'opéra françois et sur l'opéra italien qui présentent le parallèle du goût des deux nations dans les beaux arts*, Lausanne.

Rollin, Charles, 1726–8. *De la manière d'enseigner et d'étudier les belles lettres par rapport à l'esprit et au cœur*, Par M. Rollin, ancien Recteur de l'Université, Professeur de l'Eloquence au Collège Roial, et associé à l'Académie roiale des inscriptions et des belles lettres, Paris, J. Estienne, 4 vols.

Rotrou, Jean, 1954. *Le Véritable Saint Genest*, edited with an essay on Rotrou's life and work by R. W. Ladborough, Cambridge, University Press [1647].

Rouquet, Jean-André, 1746. *Lettres de Monsieur ** à un des ses amis à Paris, pour lui expliquer les estampes de Monsieur Hogarth*, Londres, R. Dodsley.

1775. *L'Etat des arts en Angleterre*, par M. Rouquet, de l'Académie royale de peinture et de sculpture, Paris, C-A Jombert. Reprinted Minkoff, Geneva, 1972.

Rousseau, Jean-Baptiste, *see* Bonafous.

Rousseau, Jean-Jacques. *O.C.* = *Œuvres complètes*, édition publiée sous la direction de Bernard Gagnebin et Marcel Raymond, Paris, Bibliothèque de la Pléiade, 3 vols.

Correspondance = *Correspondance complète de Jean-Jacques Rousseau*, édition critique établie et annotée par R. A. Leigh, Geneva–Banbury, 1965– .

De l'imitation théâtrale, in *Œuvres de Monsieur Rousseau de Genève*,

nouvelle édition revue, corrigée et augmentée de plusieurs morceaux qui n'avoient point encore paru, Neuchâtel, 1764, 5 vols., 8°; vol. v.
Lettre sur la musique françoise, Dictionnaire de musique, Observations sur l'Alceste de M. Gluck, Examen de deux principes avancés par M. Rameau, in *Oeuvres complètes de J-J. Rousseau*, édition de Ch. Lahure et Cie, Paris, Hachette, 1863, vols. IV and V.
Essai sur l'origine des langues, où il est parlé de la mélodie et de l'imitation musicale, Belin, 1817, reproduced in Paris, Bibliothèque du Graphe, 1967.
Lettre à M. d'Alembert sur son article 'Genève', ed. Michel Launay, Paris, Garnier Flammarion, 1967.
La Nouvelle Héloïse, nouvelle édition publiée d'après les manuscrits et les éditions originales avec des variantes, une introduction, des notices et des notes, par Daniel Mornet, Paris, Hachette, 1925, 4 vols.

Sade, Donatien-Alphonse-François, Marquis de, 1966–7. *Oeuvres complètes*, édition définitive par Gilbert Lély, Paris, Cercle du Livre précieux, 16 vols.

Saint Evremond, Charles de Marguetel de Saint Denis, Seigneur de, 1709. *Sur les opéra, à M. le Duc de Buckingham*, in *Oeuvres meslées de Saint Evremond, publiées sur les manuscrits de l'auteur*, seconde édition, revue, corrigée et augmentée, Londres, Jacob Tonson, 3 vols.; vol. II, pp. 214–22 [before 1687].

Saint Réal, César Vichard, Abbé de, 1922. *Conjuration des Espagnols contre la république de Venise, en l'année MDCXVIII*, éd. par Alfred Lombard, Paris, Collection des chefs-d'œuvre méconnus [1674].
  1977. *Don Carlos*, introduction et notes par Andrée Mansau, Geneva, Droz [1672].

Saint Yves, 1748. *Observations sur les arts et sur quelques morceaux de peinture et de sculpture exposés au Louvre en 1748, où il est parlé de l'utilité des embellissemens dans les villes*, par une société d'amateurs, Leyden, 1748.

Scarron, Paul, 1951. *Le Roman comique*, texte établi et présenté par Henri Bénac, Paris, Société Les Belles Lettres, 2 vols. [1651, 1657].

Schubart, Christian Friedrich Daniel, 1806. *Ideen zur einer Aesthetik der Tonkunst*, herausgegeben von Ludwig Schubart, Wien, J. V. Degen.

Scudéry, Georges de, 1641. *Ibrahim ou l'illustre bassa*, Paris, chez Antoine de Sommaville, 4 vols.

Sentiment d'un Harmonophile sur différens ouvrages de musique, 1756. Amsterdam, Paris, Jombert. (The date is derived from the *Année littéraire*.)

Seran de La Tour, *see* La Tour.

Servandoni, Jean-Jerôme, 1739. *Description du spectacle de Pandore*. Inventé et exécuté par le Chevalier Servandoni, Peintre et Architecte du Roi, de l'Académie roiale de peinture [. . .], Paris.
  1740. *La Descente d'Enée aux enfers*. Représentation donnée sur le

Bibliography

théâtre des Thuilleries par le Sieur Servandoni le 5e avril 1740, Paris, Vve. Pissot.

1741. *Lettre au sujet du spectacle des avantures d'Ulisse. A son retour du siège de Troye jusqu'à son arrivée en Itaque, tiré de l'Odissée d'Homère.* Ouvert au Palais des Thuilleries, dans la Salle des Machines, au mois de mars 1741, Inventé par le Chevalier Servandoni [. . .], Paris, Prault fils.

1742. *Léandre et Héro*, qui doit estre représenté sur le grand théâtre du Palais des Thuilleries, au mois de mars 1742 par le Chevalier Servandoni, Paris, Vve. Pissot.

1754. *La Forest enchantée.* Représentation tirée du poème italien de la Jérusalem délivrée. Spectacle orné de machines, animé d'acteurs pantomimes accompagné d'une musique (de la composition de M. Geminiani) qui en exprime less différentes actions, exécuté sur le grand théâtre du Palais des Thuilleries pour la première fois le dimanche 31 mars 1754, Paris, Imprimerie de Ballard.

1755. *Le Triomphe de l'amour conjugal*, spectacle orné de machines, animé d'acteurs pantomimes et accompagné d'une musique qui en exprime les différentes actions. Exécuté pour la première fois sur le grand théâtre du Palais des Thuilleries le dimanche 16 mars 1755. Par le Sieur Servandony [. . .], Paris, Imprimerie de Ballard.

1758. *Description du spectacle de la chute des anges rebelles*, sujet tiré du poème du Paradis perdu de Milton. Exécuté pour la première fois sur le grand théâtre de la Salle des Machines, aux Thuilleries, le dimanche 12 mars 1758. Par le Sieur Servandoni [. . .], Paris, Imprimerie de S. Jorry.

Servandoni d'Hannetaire, Jean-Nicolas (son of the preceding, actor), 1774. *Observations sur l'art du comédien. Et sur autres objets concernant cette profession en général. Avec quelques extraits de différens auteurs et des remarques analogues au même sujet, ouvrage destiné à de jeunes acteurs et actrices*, par le sieur D***, ancien comédien, seconde édition, corrigée et augmentée de beaucoup d'anecdotes théâtrales et de plusieurs observations nouvelles, Aux dépens d'une société typographique.

Silvain, 1732. *Traité du sublime, à Mr. Despréaux, où l'on fait voir ce que c'est que le sublime et ses différentes espèces; quel en doit être le stile; s'il y a un art du sublime, et les raisons pourquoi il est si rare*; par M. Silvain, Paris, P. Prault.

Staël, Germaine Necker, Madame de, 1959. *De la littérature considérée dans ses rapports avec les institutions sociales*, éd. Paul Van Tieghem, Geneva–Paris, Droz, 2 vols. [1800].

1968. *De l'Allemagne*, éd. Simone Balayé, Paris, Garnier–Flammarion, 2 vols. [1813].

Sterne, Lawrence, 1938. *Tristram Shandy*, London, Dent [1759–67].

Sticotti, Antonio Fabio, 1769. *Garrick ou les acteurs anglois, ouvrage contenant des réflexions sur l'art dramatique, sur l'art de la représentation, et le jeu des acteurs*, traduit de l'anglois, Paris, Lacombe.

Bibliography

Supplément à l'Encylopédie, ou Nouveau Dictionnaire pour servir de supplément au Dictionnaire des Sciences des Arts et des Métiers [. . .], Amsterdam, M. M. Rey, 1777, 4 vols.

Terrasson, Abbé Jean, 1754. *La philosophie applicable à tous les objets de l'esprit et de la raison*, ouvrage en réflexions détachées par feu M. l'Abbé Terrasson de l'Académie françois [. . .], précédé des réflexions de M. D'Alembert de l'Académie des Sciences, d'une lettre de M. de Moncrif, de l'Académie françoise, et d'une autre lettre de M*** sur la personne et les ouvrages de l'auteur, Paris, Prault et fils.

Trublet, Abbé Nicolas-Charles-Joseph, 1754–60. *Essais sur divers sujets de littérature et de morale*, par M. l'Abbé Trublet, de l'Académie royale des sciences, des belles lettres, Archidiacre et Chanoine de Saint Malo, cinquième édition, corrigée et augmentée, Paris, Briasson, 4 vols.

Turgot, Anne-Robert-Jacques, Baron de l'Aulne, 1808–11. *Discours aux Sorboniques, Tableau philosophique des progrès successifs de l'esprit humain*, in *Œuvres*, Paris, Imprimerie A. Belin, 9 vols., vol. II [1750].

Vairasse d'Alais, Denis, 1702. *Histoire des Sevarambes, peuples qui habitent une partie du troisième continent communément appellé la Terre australe, contenant une relation du gouvernement, des mœurs, de la religion et du langage de cette nation, inconnue jusqu'à présent aux peuples de l'Europe*, Amsterdam, Estienne Roger.

Vasari, Giorgio, 1885–90. *Lives of the most eminent painters, sculptors and architects.* Translated from the Italian with notes by Mrs Jonathan Foster, London, G. Bell, 6 vols.

Vatry, Abbé, 1741. *Discours sur la fable épique*, in *Mémoires de littérature (q.v.)*, vol. XIII [1731].

Voltaire, François-Marie Arouet de, *Œuvres complètes* [duodecimo Kehl], de l'Imprimerie de la société littéraire typographique, 1785, 92 vols.

Wier, Johannes, 1579. *Histoires, disputes et discours des illusions et impostures des diables*, Geneva, J. Chouet [Latin, 1563].

Winckelmann, Johann Joachim, 1756. Compte rendu of his *Gedancken über die Nachahmung der Griechischen Wercke in der Mahlerey und Bildhauerkunst*, in *Journal étranger*, Paris, janvier 1756, pp. 104–63.

Yzo, 1753. *Lettre sur celle de Jean-Jacques Rousseau sur la musique.*

Critics

Abrams, M. H., 1958. *The Mirror and the Lamp. Romantic Theory and the Critical Tradition*, New York, The Norton Library [1953].

Adorno, Theodor W., 1973. *Aesthetische Theorie*, Frankfurt, Suhrkamp [1970].

Auerbach, Erich, 1953. *Mimesis, the Representation of Reality in Western Literature.* Translated from the German by Willard K. Trask, Princeton, University Press.

Bibliography

1959. 'La Cour et la ville', in *Scenes from the Drama of European Literature*, New York, Meridian Books.

Austin, J. L., 1961. 'Pretending', in *Philosophical Papers*, Oxford, Clarendon Press, pp. 200–19.

1964. *Sense and Sensibilia*, Oxford, Clarendon Press.

Baczko, Bronisław, 1978. *Lumières de l'utopie*, Paris, Payot.

Baltrušaitis, Jurgis, 1969. *Anamorphoses, ou magie artificielle des effets merveilleux*, Paris, O. Perrin.

Bapst, Germain, 1893. *Essai sur l'histoire du théâtre, la mise en scène, le décor, le costume, l'architecture, l'éclairage, l'hygiène*, Paris, Imprimerie de Lahure.

Barthélemy, Maurice, 1956. 'L'Opéra français et la querelle des Anciens et des Modernes', in *Lettres romanes*, vol. x, pp. 379–91.

1966. 'Essai sur la position de d'Alembert dans la *Querelle des Bouffons*', in *Recherches sur la musique française classique*, vol. vi.

Barthes, Roland, 1973. *Le Plaisir du texte*, Paris, Le Seuil.

Bergman, G. M., 1961. 'Le décorateur Brunetti', in *Recherches théâtrales*, vol. iv, pp. 6–28.

Bernheimer, Richard, 1956. 'Theatrum Mundi', in *The Art Bulletin*, vol. xxxviii, pp. 225–47.

Bjurström, Per, 1951. 'Servandoni, décorateur de théâtre', in *Revue d'histoire du théâtre*, vol. iii, pp. 150–9.

1956. 'Les mises en scène de *Sémiramis* de Voltaire en 1748 et 1759', in *Revue d'histoire du théâtre*, vol. iii, pp. 299–320.

1959. 'Servandoni et la Salle des Machines', in *Revue d'histoire du théâtre*, vol. xi, pp. 222–4.

1961. *Giacomo Torelli and Baroque Stage Design*, Stockholm, Almquist and Wiksell (Acta universitatis Upsaliensis, nova series, 11).

Blanchot, Maurice, 1967. *Lautréamont et Sade*, Paris, Editions 10/18.

Bongie, Laurence L., 1977. *Diderot's 'femme savante'*, in *Studies on Voltaire and the Eighteenth Century*, vol. clxvi.

Bonnefoy, Yves, 1970. *Rome 1630. L'Horizon du premier baroque*, Milan and Paris, Flammarion.

Bonno, Gabriel, 1950. 'Une amitié franco-anglaise du XVIIᵉ siècle: John Locke et l'Abbé du Bos', in *Revue de littérature comparée*, vol. xxiv, pp. 481–520.

Bray, René, 1963. *La Formation de la doctrine classique en France*, Paris, Nizet [1927].

Brecht, Berthold, 1966. *Nachträge zum kleinen Organon für das Theater*, in *Über Theater*, Leipzig, Reklam [1952–4].

Bruyne, Edgar de, 1946. *Etudes d'esthétique médiévale*, Brugge, 'De Tempel', 3 vols.

Bücken, Ernst, 1927. *Die Musik des Rokoko und der Klassik*, Potsdam, Akademische Verlagsgesellschaft Athenaion.

Bukofzer, Manfred F., 1948. *Music in the Baroque Era, from Monteverdi to Bach*, London, J. M. Dent and Sons [1947].

Bibliography

Bundy, Murray Wright, 1927. *The Theory of Imagination in Classical and Mediaeval Thought*, Urbana, University of Illinois Studies in Language and Literature, vol. 12,2/3.

Cabeen, D. C., 1951. *A Critical Bibliography of French Literature*, vol. IV, *The Eighteenth Century*, edited by George R. Havens and Donald F. Bond, Syracuse, University Press.

Caillois, Roger, 1960. *Méduse et compagnie*, Paris, Gallimard.

Cassirer, Ernst, 1906. *Das Erkenntnisproblem in der Philosophie und Wissenschaft der neueren Zeit*, Berlin, Verlag von Barno, 3 vols.

Cayrou, Gaston, 1923. *Le Français classique, lexique de la langue du dix-septième siècle* [. . .], Paris, H. Didier.

Chomsky, Noam, 1966. *Cartesian Linguistics. A Chapter in the History of Rationalist Thought*, New York and London, Harper and Row.

Chouillet, Jacques, 1970. 'Une Source anglaise du *Paradoxe*', in *Dix-huitième siècle*, vol. II, pp. 207–26.

—— 1973. *La Formation des idées esthétiques de Diderot*, Paris, Colin.

—— 1974. *L'Esthétique des Lumières*, Paris, P.U.F.

Christout, Marie-Françoise, 1967. *Le Ballet de Cour de Louis XIV 1643–1672*, Paris, A. et J. Picard.

Cleaver, Eldridge, 1969. *Soul on Ice, Selected Essays*, London, Cape Editions.

Cook, Malcolm, 1982. *Politics in the Fiction of the French Revolution*, in *Studies on Voltaire and the Eighteenth Century*, vol. CCI.

Coulet, Henri, 1967. *Le Roman jusqu'à la Révolution*, Paris, Colin, 2 vols.

—— 1975. *Marivaux romancier, Essai sur l'esprit et le cœur dans les romans de Marivaux*, Paris, Colin.

Courville, Xavier de, 1943. *Un Apôtre de l'art du théâtre au XVIIIᵉ siècle, Luigi Riccoboni, dit Lélio*, Paris–Geneva, Droz, 3 vols.

Cucuel, Georges, 1914. *Les Créateurs de l'opéra comique français*, Paris, Alcan.

Cudworth, C. L., 1956–7. '"Baptist's Vein"—French orchestral music and its influence from 1650 to 1750', in *Proceedings of the Royal Musical Association*, vol. LXXXIII, pp. 29–47.

Day, Douglas A. 1959. 'Crébillon fils, ses exils et ses rapports avec l'Angleterre' in *Revue de littérature comparée*, vol. XXXIII, pp. 180–91.

Derrida, Jacques, 1967a. 'Cogito et histoire de la folie', in *L'Ecriture et la différence*, Paris, Le Seuil, pp. 51–97.

—— 1967b. *De la grammatologie*, Paris, Le Seuil.

—— 1972a. *La Dissémination*, Paris, Le Seuil.

—— 1972b. *La Voix et le phénomène*, Paris, P.U.F. [1967].

—— 1973. 'L'archéologie du frivole', in Condillac, *Essai sur l'origine des connaissances humaines*, Paris, Editions Galilée.

—— 1977. 'Scribble (pouvoir/écrire)', in Warburton, *Essai sur les hiéroglyphes des Egyptiens* [. . .], Paris, Aubier–Flammarion.

Dieckmann, Herbert, 1952. 'The Préface-annexe of *La Religieuse*', in *Diderot Studies*, vol. II, pp. 21–141.

Bibliography

1964. 'Die Wandlung des Nachahmungsbegriff in der französischen Asthetik des 18 Jahrhunderts', in *Nachahmung und Illusion*, ed. H. R. Jauss, München, Fink Verlag, pp. 28–59.

Dodds, E. R., 1933. ed. Proclus, *Elements of Theology*, Oxford, Clarendon Press.

Drujon, Fernand, 1885–8. *Les Livres à clef, étude de bibliographie*, Paris, E. Rouveyre, 2 vols.

Dulong, Gustave, 1921. *L'Abbé de Saint Réal. Etude sur les rapports de l'histoire et du roman au XVIIᵉ siècle*, Paris, H. Champion, 2 vols.

Dummett, Michael, 1973. *Frege: Philosophy of Language*, London, Duckworth.

1978. *Truth and Other Enigmas*, London, Duckworth.

Ehrard, Jean, 1970. *De l'encyclopédie à la Contre-Révolution: Jean-François Marmontel (1723–1799)*. Etudes réunies et présentées par J. Ehrard, postface de J. Fabre, Collection Ecrivains d'Auvergne, G. de Brissac, Clermont-Ferrand.

Ellrich, Robert J., 1961. 'The rhetoric of *La Religieuse* and eighteenth century forensic rhetoric', in *Diderot Studies*, vol. III, pp. 129–54.

d'Estrée, Paul, 1897. 'Un journaliste policier: le Chevalier de Mouhy', in *Revue d'histoire littéraire*, pp. 195–238.

Fabre, Jean, 1958. 'Le Théâtre au XVIIIᵉ siècle', in *Histoire des littératures*, éd. Raymond Queneau, Paris, Encyclopédie de la Pléiade, vol. III, pp. 793–813.

1961. 'Deux frères ennemis: Diderot et Jean-Jacques', in *Diderot Studies*, vol. III, pp. 155–214.

Fellerer, Karl Gustav, 1962, 'Zur Melodielehre im 18ten. Jahrhundert', in *Festschrift Zoltan Kodaly zum 80ten. Geburtstag*, Budapest, Studia Musicologica, vol. III, pp. 109–15.

1966. 'Zur musikalischen Akustik im 18 ten. Jahrhundert', in *Festschrift Josef Maria Müller-Blattau*, Saarbrücken (*Saarbrückische Studien zur Musikwissenschaft*, vol. I), pp. 80–90.

Finch, Robert, 1966. *The Sixth Sense, Individualism in French Poetry, 1686–1760*, Toronto, University Press (University of Toronto, romance series 11).

Fontaine, André, 1909. *Les Doctrines d'art en France. Peintres, amateurs, critiques, de Poussin à Diderot*, Paris, H. Laurens.

Forcellini, 1858–60. *Totius Latinitatis Lexicon opera et studio Aegidii Forcellinii* [. . .], Prato, Albergettus & Co., 6 vols.

Freud, Sigmund, 1953. *Psychopathic Characters on the Stage*, in *Standard Edition of the Complete Works of Sigmund Freud*, London, Hogarth Press, vol. VII, pp. 303 [1905?].

Gaiffe, Félix Alexandre, 1910. *Le Drame en France au XVIIIᵉ siècle*, Paris, Colin.

Genette, Gérard, 1979. *Introduction à l'architexte*, Paris, Le Seuil.

Gillot, Hubert, 1914. *La Querelle des Anciens et Modernes en France*, Nancy, Crépin–Leblond.

Bibliography

Gilson, Etienne, 1930. *Etudes sur le rôle de la pensée médiévale dans la formation du système cartésien*, Paris, Vrin.

Girdlestone, Cuthbert, 1962. *Jean-Philippe Rameau, sa vie, son œuvre* [Bruxelles], Desclée de Brouwer.

1972. *La Tragédie en musique*, Geneva, Droz.

Goldschmidt, Hugo, 1915. *Die Musikästhetik des 18. Jahrhunderts und ihre Beziehungen zu seinem Kunstchaffen*, Zurich, Leipzig, Rascher u. Co.

Gombrich, E. H., 1962. *Art and Illusion: a study in the psychology of pictorial representation*, London, Phaidon [1960].

1974. 'The sky is the limit: the vault of heaven and pictorial vision', in *Perception, essays in honor of James J. Gibson*, ed. Robert B. Macleod and Herbert L. Pick Jr, Ithaca–London, Cornell University Press.

Gossiaux, Ph., 1966. 'Aspects de la critique littéraire des nouveaux modernes: La Motte et son temps', in *Revue des langues vivantes*, vol. XXXII, pp. 278–308, 349–64.

Green, F. C., 1928. 'The eighteenth-century critic and the contemporary novel', in *Modern Language Review*, vol. XXIII, pp. 174–87.

Gregory, R. H., 1966. *Eye and Brain, The Psychology of Seeing*, London, Weidenfeld and Nicolson.

Grimsley, Ronald, 1971. *Maupertuis, Turgot et Maine de Biran sur l'origine du langage. Etude de Ronald Grimsley, suivie de trois textes* (Langues et Cultures 2), Geneva, Droz.

Haack, Susan, 1974. *Deviant Logic*, Cambridge, University Press.

Hamon, Philippe, 1973. 'Un discours contraint', in *Poétique*, vol. IV, pp. 411–45.

Hazard, Paul, 1935–9. *La Crise de la conscience européenne, 1680–1715*, Paris, Boivin, 3 vols.

Hedgecock, F. A., 1911. *David Garrick et ses amis français*, Paris, Hachette.

Hegel, G. W. F., 1975. *Aesthetics: Lectures on fine art*, translated by T. M. Knox, Oxford, Clarendon Press, 2 vols.

Heidegger, Martin, 1962. *Kant and the Problem of Metaphysics*, translated by James S. Churchill, foreword by Thomas Langan, Bloomington, London, Indiana University Press.

1967, *Being and Time*, translated by John Macquarrie and Edmund Robinson, Oxford, Blackwell.

Hobson, Marian, 1969. 'The concept of illusion in France in the eighteenth century', unpublished Ph.D. dissertation, Cambridge University.

1973. '*Le Paradoxe sur le comédien* est un paradoxe', in *Poétique*, vol. IV, pp. 320–39.

1974. 'Notes pour les *Entretiens sur le "Fils naturel"*', in *Revue d'histoire litteraire de la France*, vol. LXXIV, pp. 203–13.

1976. 'La *Lettre sur les sourds et muets* de Diderot: Labyrinthe et langage', in *Semiotica*, vol. XVI, pp. 291–327.

1977a. 'Du theatrum mundi au theatrum mentis', in *Revue des sciences humaines*, vol. CLXVII, pp. 379–94.

Bibliography

1977b. 'Sensibilité et spectacle: le contexte médical du *Paradoxe sur le comédien* de Diderot' in *Revue de métaphysique et de morale*, vol. LXXXII, pp. 145–64.

1980. 'Kant, Rousseau et la musique', in *Reappraisals of Rousseau, studies in honour of R. A. Leigh*, Manchester, University Press, pp. 290–307.

Hurst, André, 1977. 'La Rhétorique et l'énergie', in *Cahiers Ferdinand de Saussure*, Geneva, vol. XXXI, pp. 109–16.

Husserl, Edmund, 1967. *Ideas, a general introduction to pure phenomenology*, translated by W. R. Boyce Gibson, London, New York, Allen and Unwin.

1970. *Logical Investigations*, translated by J. N. Findlay, London, Routledge and Kegan Paul, 2 vols.

Hyatt Major, A., 1964. *Architectural and Perspective Designs by Giuseppe Galli Bibiena*, New York, Dover [1740].

Hyppolite, Jean, 1946. *Genèse et structure de la 'Phénoménologie de l'esprit' de Hegel*, Paris, Aubier–Montaigne.

Jones, Silas Paul, 1939. *A List of French Prose from 1700–1750*, with a brief introduction, New York, the H. W. Wilson Company.

Kaplan, James Maurice, 1973. *La Neuvaine de Cythère: une démarmontélisation de Marmontel*, in *Studies on Voltaire and the Eighteenth Century*, vol. CXIII.

Kaufmann, Emil, 1968. *Architecture in the Age of Reason. Baroque and post-Baroque in England, Italy and France*, New York, Dover [1955].

Kemp Smith, Norman, 1941. *The Philosophy of David Hume, a critical study of its origins and central doctrines*, London, Macmillan.

Kimball, Fiske, 1949. *Le Style Louis XV, origine et évolution du rococo*, traduit par Mlle Jeanne Maris, Paris, A. et J. Picard.

Klein, Robert, 1970. *La Forme et l'intelligible*, Paris, Gallimard.

Kowalska-Dufour, Gabrielle, 1977. 'L'Imagination maîtresse de vérité', in *Penser dans le temps, mélanges offerts à Jeanne Hersch*, Lausanne, Age d'homme, pp. 111–28.

Kristeva, Julia, 1969. 'La Productivité dite texte', in *Semiotikè: recherches pour une sémanalyse*, Paris, Le Seuil, pp. 208–44.

Labriolle, Marie-Rose de, 1965. *Le 'Pour et contre' et son temps, Studies on Voltaire and the Eighteenth Century*, vol. XXXIV.

Lacan, Jacques, 1973. *Le Séminaire XI*, Paris, Le Seuil.

Lancaster, H. C., 1932. *French Dramatic Literature in the Seventeenth Century*, Baltimore, Johns Hopkins Press, 9 vols.

Lanson, Gustave, 1920. *Esquisse d'une histoire de la tragédie française*, New York, Columbia University Press.

Lawrenson, T. E., 1957. *The French Stage in the XVIIth Century, A Study in the Advent of the Italian Order*, Manchester, University Press.

1965–6. 'The shape of the eighteenth-century French theatre and the drawing board renaissance', in *Recherches théâtrales*, vol. VII, pp. 7–27, 99–109.

Bibliography

Leclerc, Hélène, 1946. *Les Origines italiennes de l'architecture théâtrale moderne*, Paris, Bibliothèque de la société des historiens du théâtre, no. 22.

1953. 'Les Indes galantes 1745', in *Revue d'histoire du théâtre*, vol. v, pp. 259–85.

1959. 'Le Théatre et la danse en France aux 17e et 18e siècles', in *Revue d'histoire du théâtre*, vol. xi, pp. 327–31.

Lewinter, Roger, 1976. *Diderot ou les mots de l'absence: essai sur la forme de l'œuvre*, Paris, Champ libre.

Locquin, Jean, 1912. *La Peinture d'histoire en France de 1747 à 1785. Etude sur l'évolution des idées artistiques dans la seconde moitié du XVIIIe siècle*, Paris, H. Laurens.

Lombard, Alfred, 1913. *L'Abbé du Bos: un initiateur de la pensée moderne (1670–1742)*, Paris, Hachette.

Lovinsky, E., 1965. 'Taste, style and ideology in eighteenth-century music', in *Aspects of the Eighteenth Century*, ed. E. R. Wassermann, Baltimore, Johns Hopkins Press, pp. 163–205.

Lough, John, 1957. *Paris Theatre Audiences in the Seventeenth and Eighteenth Centuries*, London, O.U.P.

McLaughlin, Blandine, 1968. 'A New Look at Diderot's *"Fils naturel"*', in *Diderot Studies*, vol. x, pp. 109–19.

Mannoni, O., 1969. *Clés pour l'imaginaire*, Paris, Le Seuil.

Martin, Angus, Mylne, Vivienne G., Frautschi, Richard, 1977. *Bibliographie du genre romanesque français*, 1751–1800, London/Paris, Mansell/France Expansion.

Mattauch, Hans, 1968. 'Sur la proscription des romans en 1737–8', in *Revue d'histoire littéraire*, vol. lxviii, pp. 610–17.

Mauzi, Robert, 1964. 'La Parodie romanesque dans *Jacques le fataliste*', in *Diderot Studies*, vol. v, pp. 89–132.

'Humeur et colère dans *La Religieuse*', in Diderot, *Œuvres complètes*, éd. Lewinter, vol. iv.

May, Georges, 1954. *Diderot et 'La Religieuse', étude historique et littéraire*, New Haven, Yale University Press.

1955. 'L'Histoire a-t-elle engendré le roman?', in *Revue d'histoire littéraire*, vol. lv, pp. 155–76.

1963. *Le Dilemme du roman au XVIIIe siècle*, New Haven/Paris, Yale University Press/P.U.F.

Merleau-Ponty, Maurice, 1964a. *L'Oeil et l'esprit*, Paris, Gallimard.

1964b. *Le Visible et l'invisible*, Paris, Gallimard.

1972. *La Phénoménologie de la perception*, Paris, Gallimard [1945].

Meyer, P. H., 1965. Ed. *Lettre sur les sourds et muets, Diderot Studies*, vol. vi.

Monselet, Charles, 1860. *Les Originaux du siècle dernier, les oubliés et les dédaignés*, Paris.

Morillot, Paul, 1888. *Scarron, étude biographique et littéraire*, Paris, H. Lecène and H. Oudin.

Mornet, Daniel, 1925. Ed. *La Nouvelle Héloise, see* Rousseau, Jean-Jacques.

Bibliography

Mortier, Roland, 1971. 'Pour une histoire du pastiche littéraire au XVIIIe siècle', in *Beiträge zur französischen Aufklärung und zur spanischen Literatur, Festgabe für Werner Krauss, zum 70sten. Geburtstag*, Berlin, Akademie Verlag, pp. 203–19.

Mossner, E. C., 1948. 'Hume's early Memoranda', in *Journal of the History of Ideas*, New York, vol. IX, pp. 492–518.

Myers, Robert Lancelot, 1962. *The Dramatic Theories of E. C. Fréron*, Geneva, Droz.

Mylne, Vivienne, 1962. 'Truth and Illusion in the "Préface-Annexe" to Diderot's *La Religieuse*', in *Modern Language Review*, vol. LVII, pp. 350–6.

—— 1965. *The Eighteenth-Century French Novel, Techniques of Illusion*, Manchester, University Press.

Nagler, A. M., 1957. 'Maschinen und Maschinisten der Rameau Ära', in *Maske und Kothurn*, vol. III, pp. 128–40.

Naves, Raymond, 1938. *Le Goût de Voltaire*, Paris, Garnier.

Panofsky, Erwin, 1919. 'Die Scala Regia im Vatikan und die Kunstanschauungen Berninis', in *Jahrbuch der preussischen Kunstsammlungen*, Heft IV, pp. 241–78.

—— 1968. *Idea: a concept in art theory*, translated by Joseph Peake, New York, Harper and Row [1924].

—— 1975. *La Perspective comme forme symbolique, et autres essais*, traduction dirigée par Guy Ballangé, introduction de Marisa Dalai Emiliani, Paris, Editions de minuit.

Pappas, J. N., 1965. 'D'Alembert et la Querelle des Bouffons', in *Revue d'histoire littéraire*, vol. LXV, pp. 479–84.

Parret, Hermann, 1976. Ed. *History of Linguistic Thought, and Contemporary Linguistics*, Berlin, W. de Gruyter.

Pastore, Nicholas, 1971. *A Selective History of Theories of Visual Perception, 1650–1950*, New York, O.U.P.

Pfühl, E., 1910. 'Apollodorus o skiagraphos', in *Jahrbuch des kaiserlichen deutschen archäologischen Instituts*, vol. XXV, pp. 12–28.

Pirenne, M. H., 1970. *Optics, Painting, and Photography*, Cambridge, University Press.

Pirro, André, 1907. *L'Esthétique de J. S. Bach*, Paris, Fischbacher.

Poulet, Georges, 1952. 'Marivaux', in *La Distance intérieure*, Paris, Plon, pp. 1–34.

Prior, A. N. and Fine, Kit, 1977. *Worlds, Times and Selves*, London, Duckworth.

Proust, Jacques, 1962. *Diderot et l'Encyclopédie*, Paris, Colin.

Ranscelot, Jean, 1926. 'Les manifestations du déclin poétique au début du XVIIIe siècle', in *Revue d'histoire littéraire*, vol. XXXIII, pp. 497–520.

Reichenburg, Louisette, 1937. *Contribution à l'histoire de la 'Querelle des bouffons', guerre de brochures suscitées par le 'Petit prophète' de Grimm et par la 'Lettre sur la musique françoise' de Rousseau*, Philadelphia.

383

Bibliography

Renwick, John, 1967. 'Reconstruction and interpretation of the *Bélisaire* affair with an unpublished letter from Marmontel to Voltaire', in *Studies on Voltaire and the Eighteenth Century*, vol. LIII, pp. 171–222.

Ricardou, Jean, 1973. *Le Nouveau Roman*, Paris, Le Seuil.

Ricken, Ulrich, 1978. *Grammaire et philosophie au siècle des Lumières: controverses sur l'ordre naturel et la clarté du français*, Lille, Publications de l'Université de Lille III.

Riemann, Hugo, 1979. *Musiklexikon*, Wiesbaden and Mainz, Brockhaus and B. Schott's Söhne, 2 vols.

Robinson M. F., 1961–2. 'The aria in Opera seria 1725–1780', in *Proceedings of the Royal Musical Association*, vol. LXXXVIII, pp. 21–43.

Rodis-Lewis, Geneviève, 1956. 'Machines et perspectives curieuses dans leur rapport avec le cartésianisme', in *Bulletin de la Société d'Etudes du XVIIᵉ siècle*, pp. 462–74.

Saraiva, Maria Manuela, 1970. *L'Imagination selon Husserl*, La Haye, M. Nijhoff.

Sartre, Jean-Paul, 1940. *L'Imaginaire: psychologie phénoménologique de l'imagination*, Paris, Gallimard.

Schäfke, Rudolf, 1924. 'Quantz als Ästhetiker: eine Einführung in die Musikästhetik des galanten Stils', in *Archiv für Musikwissenschaft*, vol. VI, pp. 213–42.

Schering, Arnold, 1918–19. Review of Goldschmidt (*q.v.*), in *Zeitschrift fur Musikwissenschaft*, vol. I, pp. 298–309.

Schöne, Günter, 1933. *Die Entwicklung der Perspektivbühne, von Serlio bis Galli Bibiena nach den Perspektivbüchern*, Leipzig, Theatergeschichtliche Forschungen, Heft 43.

Serauky, Walter, 1929. *Die musikalische Nachahmungsästhetik im Zeitraum von 1700 bis 1850*, Münster, Universitas Achiv no. 17.

Sgard, J. and Oudart, J., 1978. 'La Critique du roman', in *Presse et histoire au XVIIIᵉ siècle, l'année 1734*, sous la direction de Pierre Rétat et de Jean Sgard, Paris, Editions du C.R.N.S.

Sheridan, Geraldine, 1980. 'The life and works of the Abbé Lenglet-Dufresnoy', unpublished Ph.D. Dissertation, Warwick University.

Spitzer, Leo, 1953. 'A propos de la *Vie de Marianne*', in *Romanic Review*, vol. XLIV, pp. 102–26.

Starobinski, Jean, 1964. *L'Invention de la liberté 1700–1789*, Geneva, Skira.

1971a. 'Sur la flatterie', in *Nouvelle Revue de Psychanalyse*, vol. IV, pp. 131–51.

1971b. 'L'Ecart romanesque', in *Jean-Jacques Rousseau, la transparence et l'obstacle*, Paris, Gallimard, pp. 393–414.

1978. 'Espace du jour, espace du bonheur', in *Annali–Studii Filosofici*, vol. I, pp. 1–12.

Stewart, Ph.R., 1969. *Imitation and Illusion in the French Memoir-Novel 1700–1750: The Art of Make Believe*, London, Yale University Press (Yale Romance Studies, Series 2, no. 20).

Stierle, Karlheinz, 1979. 'Réception et fiction', in *Poétique*, vol. X, pp. 299–320.

Bibliography

Svoboda, K., 1927. *La Démonologie de Michel Psellos*, Brno.

Szondi, Peter, 1979. *Die Theorie des burgerlichen Trauerspiels im 18. Jahrhundert*, Frankfurt, Suhrkamp, Taschenbuch Verlag.

Tieje, A. J., 1912. 'The expressed aims of long prose fiction', in *Journal of English and Germanic Philology*, vol. XI, pp. 402–32.

1913. 'A peculiar phase of the theory of realism in pre-Richardsonian fiction', in *Publications of the Modern Languages Association of America*, vol. XXVIII, pp. 213–52.

1916. *The Theory of Characterization in Prose Fiction prior to 1740*, Minneapolis, University of Minnesota, Studies in Language and Literature no. 5.

Tocqueville, Alexis de, 1951. *De la Democratie en Amérique*, in *Œuvres, papiers et correspondances*, éd. définitive publiée sous la direction de J. P. Mayer, Paris, Gallimard, 13 vols., vol. I, ii [1835].

Todorov, Tzvetan, 1977. *Théories du symbole*, Paris, Le Seuil.

Tort, Patrick, 1976. 'Dialectique des signes chez Condillac', in Parret (*q.v.*), 1976, pp. 488–502.

Truesdell, C., 1960. 'The rational mechanics of flexible or elastic bodies, 1638–1788', Introduction to *Leonhardi Euleri Opera Omnia*, vol. X and XI, seriei secundae, Swiss Society for Natural Sciences, Zurich, Orell Fussli.

Venturi, Franco, 1939. *La Jeunesse de Diderot 1713–1753*, trad. par Juliette Bertrand, Paris, A. Skira.

Verbeke, Gérard, 1945. *L'Evolution de la doctrine du pneuma, du stoïcisme à Saint Augustin*, Paris, Louvain, Desclée de Brouwer.

Walker, D. P., 1958. *Spiritual and Demonic Magic from Ficino to Campanella*, London, Studies of the Warburg Institute, no. 22.

Wartburg, Walther von, 1962. *Französisches etymologisches Wörterbuch*, Basel, Zbinden Druck und Verlag.

Wassermann, Earl R., 1947. 'The sympathetic imagination in eighteenth-century theories of acting', in *Journal of English and Germanic Philology*, vol. XLVI, pp. 265–272.

Watt, Ian, 1963. *The Rise of the Novel*, Harmondsworth, Penguin [1957].

Wilson, A. M., 1972. *Diderot*, New York, O.U.P.

Winnicott, D. W., 1974. 'Transitional Objects and Transitional Phenomena', in *Playing and Reality*, Harmondsworth, Penguin.

Wittgenstein, Ludwig, 1968. *Philosophical Investigations*, Oxford, Blackwell.

Wölfflin, Heinrich, 1964. *Renaissance and Baroque*, translated by Kathrin Simon, with an introduction by Peter Murray, London, Fontana.

Wollheim, Richard, 1963. 'Reflections on *Art and Illusion*', in *British Journal of Aesthetics*, London, vol. III, pp. 15–37.

Yates, Frances A., 1975. *The Rosicrucian Enlightenment*, London.

INDEX OF NAMES

Index of names

Dandré Bardon, 53, 56, 76, 315 n.1, 317 n.15
Da Ponte, 179
David, 70
Day, 323 n.26
Dazincourt, 201, 202
Degérando, 246, 247, 248, 251, 297, 342 n.18, 343 n.28
Delille, 336 n.6
Della Porta, 22
Delmas, 103
Derrida, 4, 16, 238, 258, 266, 294, 308 n.2, 309 n.6, 310 nn.17–18, 311 n.22, 342 nn.16–17, 347 n.12
Descamps, 319 n.14
Descartes, 23, 26–7, 29, 30–2, 76, 313 nn.19, 22, 346 n.2
Desfontaines, 85, 92, 106, 234, 321 n.1, 323 n.20, 341 nn.1, 5
Desmolets, 85, 91, 109, 321 n.6
Desportes. 71
Dézallier d'Argenville, 48, 49, 74, 319 n.14
Dictionnaire de l'Académie, 311 n.4, 312 n.16
Dictionnaire de Trévoux, 352 n.1
Diderot, x, 52, 53, 57, 62, 66–7, 69, 73, 97–9, 133, 139, 140, 144, 165–6, 189, 197, 198, 225, 236, 245, 252, 260, 272, 273, 285, 289, 291, 292, 295, 296, 317 nn.14, 16, 319 nn.15–16, 18, 320 n.23, 332 nn.8, 14, 333 n.16, 335 nn.20–1, 336 n.10, 341 n.6, 345 nn.15–17
Essai sur le mérite et la vertu, 184, 185, 187
Les Bijoux indiscrets, 110, 132, 150, 169–70, 172–3, 178, 263
Lettre sur les aveugles, 247, 276, 318 n.8, 342 n.15
Lettre sur les sourds et muets, 228, 229, 232, 233, 247, 276, 280, 339 n.28, 345 n.17, 350 n.28
Entretiens sur 'Le Fils naturel', 152, 160–3, 174, 183, 190, 191–3, 197, 198, 236, 258, 268, 286, 329 n.30, 347 n.9
Le Fils naturel, 174, 187, 190, 191
Discours sur la poésie dramatique, 150–1, 153–4, 162–3, 164, 166, 188, 192–3, 217, 220, 334 n.13
Le Père de famille, 191
La Religieuse, 57, 58, 98–105, 117, 118, 132, 178, 269
Eloge de Richardson, 85, 111–12, 345 n.14

Salon de 1759, 77
Salon de 1761, 54, 57, 68
Salon de 1763, 54, 57, 69, 71, 77, 78, 79
Salon de 1765, 53, 61, 70, 77, 78, 202, 316 n.14
Salon de 1767, 54, 57–61, 71, 73, 74, 78–9, 99, 102, 117, 132, 189, 204, 205, 215, 224, 225, 247, 271, 317 nn.18–19, 318 n.8, 319 n.17, 321 n.7, 326 n.5, 351 n.33
Salon de 1769, 79, 224, 225, 319 n.14
Salon de 1771, 68
Salon de 1781, 74
Essais sur la peinture, 53, 71, 75, 78, 164, 320 n.24
Pensées détachées sur la peinture, 69, 70, 78
Le Rêve de d'Alembert, 247, 317 n.20, 345 n.17, 351 n.33
Le Paradoxe sur le comédien, 73, 79, 164, 170, 173, 189, 195, 200–1, 202, 203–5, 207–8, 247, 321 n.6, 322 n.17, 334 nn.8, 10–11, 335 n.16
Jacques le fataliste, 57, 81, 94, 127–36, 305, 306, 326 nn.6–7
Les Deux Amis de Bourbonne, 98
Madame de La Carlière, 132–3, 317 n.20
Le Neveu de Rameau, 190, 202, 205, 225, 268–9, 282, 288, 300, 317 n.20, 322 n.15, 335 n.17
Réfutation d'Helvétius, 189, 339 n.28
Essai sur les règnes de Claude et de Néron, 189, 317 n.20
Est-il bon, est-il méchant?, 300, 322 n.16
Supplément au Voyage de Bougainville, 326 n.6
Mémoires de Madame de Montbrillant, 62–3
Discours à Cliton, 35
Dieckmann, 99, 100, 315 n.36
Dodds, 20, 311 n.5
Doppet, 94, 97–8
Dorat, 111, 146, 196, 324 n.31
Drujon, 107, 323 n.25
Dryden, 317 n.17
Dubos, 38–42, 67, 68, 72, 174, 181, 182, 195, 197, 232, 280, 289, 304, 314 n.27, 315 nn.36–40, 42–3, 317 n.1, 318 n.12, 332 nn.4–5, 342 n.8, 348 n.20, 349 n.22
Duclos, 105
Dulong, G., 321 n.2
Dumarsais, 228, 230, 233

Index of names

Dumesnil, 202
Dummett, 308 n.4, 352 n.6
Du Perron, 48, 50, 67
Durer, A., 319 n.17
Durey de Noinville, 348 n.21
Duval, 279

Easterling, J., 342 n.13
Ellrich, R., 100, 101
Encyclopédie, 228, 311 n.4
  Ballet, 346 n.5
  Beau, 347 n.10
  Comédie, 330 n.37
  Déclamation théâtrale, 149, 201, 334 n.8
  Décoration, 141, 142
  Décoration théâtrale, 147
  Dénouement, 169, 180
  Enthousiasme, 220
  Fable, 211
  Image, 219, 233
  Imagination, 338 n.24
  Merveilleux, 336 n.9
  Peinture, 315 n.3
  Poème lyrique, 259, 260, 347 n.15
  Sublime, 338 n.20
  Unité, 328 n.17
Epinay, Madame d', 62–3, 97, 98
Erastus, 22, 312 n.11
Esprit des journaux, L', 111
Estève, 48, 72, 261, 277, 347 n.10
Estrée, 107, 323 n.23
Euler, 265
Evelyn, J., 35, 315 n.33

Fabre, J., 139, 273
Falconet, 53, 66, 316 n.13, 318 n.11, 319 n.18
Favart, 152, 257, 327 n.12
Favart, Madame, 146
Félibien, 37, 45, 47, 265, 315 n.35, 344 n.10
Fellerer, 344 n.6, 349 n.23
Fénelon, 124, 213, 222, 227, 228, 229, 340 n.34, 341 n.5
Fenouillot de Falbaire, 176, 331 nn.51–3
Finch, R., 315 n.39
Fontaine, A., 319 n.14
Fontenelle, 38, 53, 214, 215, 219, 222, 223, 224, 230, 263, 275, 339 n.30, 340 n.36
Forcellini, 311 n.2
Formey, 339 n.28
Fourmont, 224, 230–1, 336 n.9

Fragonard, 55, 61
Fraguier, 227, 342 n.9
Frain du Trembley, 321 n.1, 336 n.2, 337 n.19
Francœur, 346 n.5
Frank, W., 329 n.26
Fréart de Chambray, 37, 45, 47, 315 n.35
Frege, 308 n.4
Fréron, 175, 322 n.15, 328 n.22, 331 n.53
Freud, 7, 308 n.1

Gachet d'Artigny, 110, 324 n.29
Gacon, 223
Gaiffe, F., 171, 173, 175
Galileo, Vicenzo, 349 n.22
Garcin, 257, 261, 275, 278, 288, 343 n.25, 346 n.5, 347 nn.13, 15, 348 n.19, 350 n.27
Garrick, 152, 202, 204, 333 n.163, 335 n.19
Gassendi, 29
Gautier d'Agoty, 50, 316 n.5
Genette, G., 352 n.2
Gillot, H., 212, 213, 339 n.30
Gilson, E., 311 n.6
Girdlestone, 263, 264, 344 nn.8–9
Gluck, 286, 288, 344 n.3
Goethe, 320 n.26
Goldoni, 129
Goldschmidt, H., 344 n.5, 347 n.17
Gombrich, 5, 8–11, 12, 16, 310 n.16, 313 n.25
Gossiaux, 312 n.18
Gouge de Cessières, 336 n.6
Gougenot, 313 n.21
Grandval, 264
Granet, 85, 183, 332 n.6, 336 n.7
Green, F. C., 107, 323 n.21
Gregory, R., 9
Greuze, 57, 68, 70, 192, 319 n.16
Grimarest, 195
Grimm, 53, 57, 97, 98, 100, 144, 155, 156, 161, 173, 174, 235, 236, 256, 258, 259, 260, 267, 316 n.14, 319 n.13, 328 nn.16, 25, 330 n.47, 335 n.19
Grimsley, 343 n.20
Guilleragues, 87
Guimard, la, 146

Haack, 308 n.4
Hadrian, 349 n.22
Hagedorn, 319 n.15
Halle, 316 n.14

Index of names

Le Gros, 53
Leibniz, 243, 244, 276
Lekain, 146, 147, 155, 163, 171, 192, 201, 330 n.40, 334 nn.7, 12, 335 n.19
Lemierre, 330 nn.40, 47
Le Moyne, 33
Lenglet Dufresnoy, 85, 89–90, 106, 110, 321 n.5
Le Noble, 96
Leonardo, 24
Lessing, x, 144, 154, 155, 163–5, 169, 172–4, 178, 235–7, 243, 252, 273, 328 nn.16, 19, 330 nn.44–5, 48
Levesque de Pouilly, 182, 184–6, 188, 277, 328 n.17, 332 n.8, 338 n.20, 339 nn.31, 33, 340 n.34
Lewinter, R., 101
Ligne, Prince de, 334 n.5
Lillo, 171
Liotard, 49
Locke, 29, 30, 31, 33, 39, 86, 240, 243, 244, 289, 315 n.37
Locquin, 63, 68
Lombard, 315 n.36
Longinus, 217, 236, 337 n.17
de Longue, 107, 340 n.34
Lough, J., 328 n.21, 329 n.34
Loutherbourg, 71, 299, 336 n.6
Louvet de Couvray, 126–7
Lovinsky, 264, 267
Lucretius, 48, 181
Lulli, 261, 263, 267, 274, 285

Mably, 259, 263, 349 n.22
McLaughlin, 189, 333 n.15
Macpherson, 250
Maffei, 174
Magritte, 49, 69, 94
Maillet Duclairon, 141, 145, 181, 195, 202, 329 n.31, 333 n.2, 334 n.9
Malebranche, 29, 30, 48, 144
Mandeville, 225
Mann, Thomas, 200, 203
Mannoni, O., 12–13, 309 n.7
Marchand, 162–3, 178, 329 n.33
Marigny, Marquis de, 63
Marin Marais, 274, 279
Marivaux, 109, 110, 123–6, 136, 139, 151, 175, 219, 231, 243, 325 nn.1–2
Marmontel, 85, 111, 112, 113–14, 115, 117, 119, 121, 146, 147, 149, 151, 152, 157, 168–9, 180, 194, 200, 201, 211, 220, 232, 233, 234–5, 259, 325 n.33, 327 n.8, 329 nn.28–9, 330 n.37, 334 n.8, 336 nn.6, 10, 342 n.11, 350 n.30

Mattauch, 323 n.21
Maupertuis, 343 n.20
Mauzi, R., 101, 326 n.7
May, G., 85, 86, 98, 105, 106, 323 n.21
Méhégan, 148, 186, 225
Meinong, 308 n.4
Meissonnier, 51, 300, 316 n.10
Mercier, L.-S., 111, 113, 175, 177, 331 n.49
Mercure de France, 49, 324 n.32
Merleau-Ponty, 29, 30, 313 n.24
Mersenne, 265
Mesomedes, 349 n.22
Meusnier de Querlon, 49, 319 n.14
Meyer, P. H., 337 n.14
Michaelangelo, 64
Migne, 19
Molé, 201, 202, 335 n.19
Molière, 129, 132, 160, 328 n.21, 329 n.34
Molyneux, 30
Mondonville, 274, 346 n.3, 348 n.21
Montaigne, 130, 132
Montesquieu, 103–4, 127, 322 n.18
More, T., 96
Morellet, 288–90, 350 nn.26–7, 29–30
Mornet, 93
Mortier, 323 n.19
Mossner, 314 n.27
Mouhy, 95, 107, 108, 322 n.12, 323 n.23
Mozart, W. A., 179
Myers, R., 171, 172, 202, 328 n.22, 330 nn.47, 53
Mylne, 81, 87, 96, 98, 104, 322 n.11

Nadal, 328 n.18
Nagler, 141, 144, 145, 327 nn.8, 13
Néel, 104
Neuschläfer, 314 n.29
Newton, 76, 262, 265, 275
Niceron, 25–6
Nougaret, 149, 157–8, 165, 166, 168, 178, 196, 257, 327 n.12, 328 nn.16, 26–7, 330 n.38, 332 n.10
Nouvelle Biographie générale, 321 n.4
Nouvelliste du Parnasse, 259
Noverre, 145, 152, 155, 196, 197, 268, 328 n.14, 333 n.3

Observations sur les écrits modernes, 92, 264
d'Olivet, 227, 233, 234, 277, 341 n.1
Oppenord, 51
Origen, 311 n.5
Ossian, 229, 249–50

Index of names

Index of names

Lettre sur la musique française, 256, 260, 267, 270–1, 276, 285–6, 293, 346 n.18

Discours sur l'origine de l'inégalité, 188

Essai sur l'origine des langues, 185, 188, 238, 270–1, 277, 292, 293–5

Lettre à d'Alembert, 140, 154, 161, 181, 187, 188–9, 191, 193, 207, 271, 332 n.4

La Nouvelle Héloïse, 85, 111, 116–20, 121, 128, 154, 173, 225, 256, 306, 327 n.12

Dictionnaire de musique, 244, 257, 264, 266, 270–1, 287, 293–4, 345 n.13, 346 nn.19, 6, 347 n.17, 350 n.24, 351, n.35

Examen de deux principes, 266

Observations sur Gluck, 286

Rubens, 54

Russell, 308 n.4

Sade, Marquis de, 115–16, 118, 121

Saint Evremond, 33, 255

Saint Réal, Abbé de, 89, 321 n.2

Saint Yves, 48, 70, 73, 320 n.19

Saraiva, M.–M., 309 n.13

Sartre, 11–12, 16, 309 n.14, 310 n.16, 352 n.4

Scarron, 52, 122–3, 124, 125, 132, 325 nn.2–3

Schäfke, 274

Schering, A., 344 n.5, 347 n.17

Schiller, 44

Schöne, 312 n.13

Schubart, 345 n.15

Scudéry, G. de, 313 n.21, 314 n.30

Sedaine, 257, 319 n.16

Sentiment d'un harmonophile, 280–1, 282, 283, 286

Seran de La Tour, 183, 186, 282, 337 n.13, 338 n.25, 339 n.33

Serauky, 344 n.5

Servandoni, 142, 143, 144, 147, 326 nn.2, 5, 328 n.15

Servandoni d'Hannetaire, 149, 167, 202, 334 n.8

Sgard and Oudart, 89

Shaftesbury, 332 n.8

Shakespeare, 3, 27, 32

Shelley, 214

Sheridan, G., 321 n.5

Silvain, 337 n.18

Sophocles, 3

Spitzer, 326 n.4

Staël, Madame de, 252, 343 n.27

Stamitz, 267, 344 nn.11–12

Starobinski, 51, 119, 192, 269, 315 n.2

Steele, 87

Stendhal, 105

Sterne, *Tristram Shandy*, 129, 305, 320 n.23, 326 n.5

Stewart, P., 81, 87, 88, 93, 98, 103, 104, 322 n.12

Sticotti, 159, 183, 195, 197, 199, 200, 201, 206, 328 n.20, 333 nn.1, 4

Stierle, 305, 307, 352 nn.4–5

Supplément à l'Encyclopédie, article *Illusion*, 169

Svoboda, 20

Swift, 87, 88, 323 n.19

Synesius, 311 n.5

Szondi, 330 n.35

Talma, 155, 163, 201, 334 nn.7, 12

Tartini, 348 n.18

Taylor, Brook, 265

Teniers, 71, 309 n.11

Terence, 161, 164

Terrail, Marquis du, 171

Terrasson, 342 n.12, 343 n.20

Thoinan, 348 n.21

Thomas Aquinas, St, 21, 312 nn.9, 11

Tieje, 87, 89

Titian, 56

Tocqué, 68

Tocqueville, 148, 154–5, 177

Todorov, 229, 308 n.4

Torelli, 24, 147

Tort, P., 239, 342 n.15

Trublet, Abbé, 219, 224, 338 n.24, 339 nn.29, 31, 340 n.35

Truesdell, 265, 266

Turgot, 229, 248, 341 n.7

Vairesse d'Alais, 96

Varillas, 90, 321 n.4

Vatry, Abbé, 213, 336 n.5

Vaucanson, 146

Venturi, F., 331 n.49

Verbeke, 20, 311 n.5

Vergil, 67, 249

Vernet, J., 48, 58–61, 67, 79, 99, 102, 117, 132, 205

Vernière, 189, 333 n.15, 335 n.16

Vien, 56

Vigarani, 147

Vivaldi, 261, 263, 264

Voltaire, 65, 146, 147, 170–3, 175, 227, 230, 235, 248, 292, 300, 318 n.10, 330 nn.39, 42, 332 n.7, 338 n.24

Index of names

Walker, D. P., 21, 311 n.5
Warburton, 238, 244–5
Wartburg, 311 n.4
Wassermann, E., 199, 333 nn.1, 3
Watt, I., 85
Watteau, 55–6, 71
Wettstein and Smitt, 326 n.3
Wier, J., 21–2
Wilson, A., 139
Wilson, R., 74
Winckelmann, 72

Winnicott, 13
Wittgenstein, 8
Wokler, R., 348 n.21
Wölfflin, 316 n.9
Wollheim, R., 309 n.9

Yates, F., 23
Yzo, 259

Zeuxis, 18, 66, 221

CONCEPTUAL INDEX

CONCEPTUAL INDEX